THE MESSAGE WITHIN

THE MESSAGE WITHIN

The Role of Subjective Experience
in Social Cognition and Behavior

Edited by
**Herbert Bless and
Joseph P. Forgas**

USA	Publishing Office:	PSYCHOLOGY PRESS
		A member of the Taylor & Francis Group
		325 Chestnut Street
		Philadelphia, PA 19106
		Tel: (215) 625-8900
		Fax: (215) 625-2940
	Distribution Center:	PSYCHOLOGY PRESS
		A member of the Taylor & Francis Group
		7625 Empire Drive
		Florence, KY 41042
		Tel: 1-800-634-7064
		Fax: 1-800-248-4724
UK		PSYCHOLOGY PRESS
		A member of the Taylor & Francis Group
		27 Church Road
		Hove
		E. Sussex, BN3 2FA
		Tel: +44 (0) 1273 207411
		Fax: +44 (0) 1273 205612

The Message Within: The Role of Subjective Experience in Social Cognition and Behavior

1 2 3 4 5 6 7 8 9 0

Printed by Edwards Brothers, Lillington, North Carolina, 2000.
Cover design by Claire O'Neill.
Cover art, *The Blank Signature* by René Magritte, supplied by the National Gallery of Art in Washington, DC. Collection of Mr. and Mrs. Paul Mellon.
Edited by Hilary Ward and Jim Reed

A CIP catalog record for this book is available from the British Library.
♾ The paper in this publication meets the requirements of the ANSI Standard Z39.48-1984 (Permanence of Paper).

Library of Congress Cataloging-in-Publication Data
CIP information available from publisher.

ISBN (case) 0-86377-690-6
ISBN (paper) 1-84169-020-1

CONTENTS

About the Editors   ix
Contributors   xi
Preface   xv
Herbert Bless & Joseph P. Forgas

1   Social Psychology—The Science of Human Experience

Daniel M. Wegner and Daniel T. Gilbert   **1**

PART I
SUBJECTIVE EXPERIENCE AND INFORMATION PROCESSING

2   On Mere Considering: The Subjective Experience of Truth

Klaus Fiedler   **13**

3   Of Men and Mackerels: Attention, Subjective Experience, and Automatic Social Behavior

Ap Dijksterhuis, John A. Bargh, and Joost Miedema   **37**

4   Experiential and Nonexperiential Routes of Motor Influence on Affect and Evaluation

Roland Neumann and Fritz Strack   **52**

5   Subjective Experience and the Effect of Sample Size on Likelihood Judgments

C. Miguel Brendl   **69**

6   Availability as Input: The Experience of Cognitive
Effort Can Either Strengthen or Weaken Evaluations

Leonard L. Martin and Daniel Whitaker   **88**

PART II
SUBJECTIVE EXPERIENCE AND MEMORY PHENOMENA

7   Subjective Experience of Familiarity:
Functional Basis in Connectionist Memory

Eliot R. Smith   **109**

8   Subjective Ease of Retrieval and Attitude-Relevant Judgments

Geoffrey Haddock   **125**

9   The Effects of Subjective Ease of Retrieval on Attitudinal
Judgments: The Moderating Role of Processing Motivation

Michaela Wänke and Herbert Bless   **143**

10   Drawing Inferences from Feelings: The Role of Naive Beliefs

Ian Skurnik, Norbert Schwarz, and Piotr Winkielman   **162**

PART III
AFFECT AS A SUBJECTIVE EXPERIENCE
AND SOCIAL COGNITION

11   Subjective Experience and Mood Regulation:
The Role of Information Processing Strategies

Joseph P. Forgas, Joseph Ciarrochi, and Stephanie Moylan   **179**

12   The Rocky Road from Affect to Attentional Focus

Constantine Sedikides and Jeffrey D. Green   **203**

13   Negative Affect and Persuasion:
The Role of Affect Interpretation

Gerd Bohner and Thomas Weinerth   **216**

14 The Positive Feeling of Familiarity: Mood as an Information
Processing Regulation Mechanism

Teresa Garcia-Marques and Diane M. Mackie **240**

15 The Subjective Experience of Surprise

Rainer Reisenzein **262**

PART IV
SUBJECTIVE EXPERIENCE, STEREOTYPING, AND
INTERGROUP BEHAVIOR

16 How Do I Feel About Them? The Role of Affective
Reactions in Intergroup Perception

Galen V. Bodenhausen and Kristen N. Moreno **283**

17 Active Search for Information: The Effects of Subjectively
Experienced Control on Stereotyping

Benoit Dardenne, Vincent Yzerbyt, and Christine Grégoire **304**

18 The Experience of a Positive Mood and Its Impact
on Intergroup Differentiation and Stereotyping

Andrea E. Abele **322**

19 Subjective Experiences and Intergroup Relations:
The Role of Positive Affect

John F. Dovidio, Samuel L. Gaertner, and Stephenie Loux **340**

20 The Message Within: Toward a Social Psychology
of Subjective Experiences

Herbert Bless and Joseph P. Forgas **372**

Author Index **393**
Subject Index **400**

ABOUT THE EDITORS

Herbert Bless received his doctorate from the University of Heidelberg in 1986. After holding positions at the University of Heidelberg and at the University of Trier, he is currently Professor of Microsociology and Social Psychology at the University of Mannheim. His main research interests focus on the affective and cognitive determinants of social judgment.

Joseph P. Forgas received his doctorate from the University of Oxford and is currently Professor of Psychology at the University of New South Wales in Sydney. He is Fellow of the Academy of Social Sciences in Australia, of the American Psychological Society, and of the Society of Personality and Social Psychology. His recent work focuses on the role of affect in cognition and behavior. He has published a dozen books and over 100 articles and chapters.

CONTRIBUTORS

Andrea E. Abele
University of Erlangen, Germany

John A. Bargh
New York University, USA

Galen V. Bodenhausen
Northwestern University, USA

Herbert Bless
University of Mannheim, Germany

Gerd Bohner
University of Kent, UK

C. Miguel Brendl
INSEAD, France

Joseph Ciarrochi
University of Wollongong, Australia

Benoit Dardenne
University of Liège, Belgium

Ap Dijksterhuis
University of Nijmegen, The Netherlands

John F. Dovidio
Colgate University, USA

Klaus Fiedler
University of Heidelberg, Germany

Joseph P. Forgas
University of New South Wales,
Australia

Samuel L. Gaertner
University of Delaware, USA

Teresa Garcia-Marques
University of Lisbon, Portugal

Jeffrey D. Green
University of North Carolina, USA

Christine Grégoire
University of Liège, Belgium

Daniel T. Gilbert
Harvard University, USA

Geoffrey Haddock
University of Bristol, UK

Stephanie Loux
University of Minnesota, USA

Diane M. Mackie
University of California at Santa Barbara,
USA

Leonard L. Martin
University of Georgia, USA

Joost Miedema
University of Leiden, The Netherlands

Kristen N. Moreno
Northwestern University, USA

Stephanie Moylan
University of New South Wales, Australia

Roland Neumann
University of Wüzburg, Germany

Rainer Reisenzein
University of Bielefeld, Germany

Norbert Schwarz
University of Michigan, USA

Constantine Sedikides
University of Southampton, UK

Ian Skurnik
University of Michigan, USA

Eliot R. Smith
Purdue University, USA

Fritz Strack
University of Würzburg, Germany

Michaela Wänke
University of Heidelberg, Germany

Daniel M. Wegner
University of Virginia, USA

Thomas Weinerth
University of Mannheim, Germany

Daniel Whitaker
University of Georgia, USA

Piotr Winkielman
University of Denver, USA

Vincent Yzerbyt
Catholic University of Louvain, Belgium

PREFACE

Subjective experience—what it feels like to be in various social situations, and how such elusive "feelings" influence what we think, say, and do—has been one of the core themes of social psychology ever since its inception. Some of the most clever and ingenious social psychology experiments continue to demand our and our students' attention precisely because they open a small window into that most primeval of secrets—the mysterious subjective world of the "other." During the past several decades, and since the advent of the social cognitive paradigm in particular, interest in subjective experiences has increased exponentially. Yet this development came about almost by stealth. As Daniel Wegner and Daniel Gilbert argue in their stimulating chapter that follows, we continue to employ the language and rhetoric of social and cognitive psychology, while increasingly what we are really examining are internal phenomenological states and their consequences for social thinking and behavior. However, these contemporary explorations of subjective experience differ from traditional, speculative, introspective, and qualitative approaches in one fundamental way. Although our interests are often phenomenological, our methods and techniques are strongly rooted in experimental social and cognitive psychology.

One of the key objectives of this book is to bring together some of the most recent developments in this field where "subjective experience" variables play a key role in investigations of social cognition and behavior. As editors, each of us came to this topic by a rather circuitous route. Herbert Bless has long been interested in how subjective experiences of ease of retrieval influence people's thinking, and Joseph P. Forgas has published extensively on how everyday social interaction episodes are subjectively experienced and cognitively represented by people. Both of us have also done extensive research on that most characteristic of subjective experiences, affect and mood, and we are both interested in how such internal states influence social thinking, judgments, and behavior. We approached these topics from the perspective of experimental social psychology, and we share a firm belief and commitment in the applicability and validity of the scientific method in general, and in experimental techniques in particular to the study of subjective experiences. Surprisingly, despite many years of interest in and doing research on subjective experiences, it would not have occurred to either of us until quite recently that this is in fact what we were doing.

This book is the result of some 2 years of planning and collaboration between us that culminated in an intensive 4-day workshop and symposium held at the small mountain resort of Grasellenbach in the Odenwald, near Heidelberg. The objective of that meeting was to allow us to invite key researchers in this field and to provide an opportunity to present and discuss their most recent work in terms of their joint interest in the study of subjective experiences. The meeting was an outstanding success; we shared a real sense of excitement and discovery, and to a greater or lesser extent, we all came away thinking about our research somewhat differently after the meeting. Subjective experience seemed to us a powerful new unifying concept that can establish bridges between research areas previously seen as having little in common. One of our key objectives with this book is to share that excitement with a wider readership, and to provide a stimulus for psychologists to start explicitly considering subjective experience as a legitimate and respectable object of scientific study.

The book that resulted contains chapters by most of the original contributors to the Grasellenbach symposium, as well as several chapters we invited after the meeting. The book is organized into four distinct parts, each representing one key area of study concerned with subjective experience. We do not wish to claim that we were able to provide a comprehensive and exhaustive treatment of the field. Clearly, the theme of "subjective experiences" is too broad and multifaceted to be fully covered in a single volume. Rather, our objective was to show how subjective experiences have been studied within some key areas of recent social psychological inquiry.

The first part of the book contains chapters that discuss the role that subjective experiences play in *social cognition*. In an intriguing chapter on "mere considering," Klaus Fiedler analyzes the variables that influence the subjective experience of truth and some of the consequences of these experiences. Next, Ap Dijksterhuis and colleagues present interesting experimental evidence illustrating how the subjective experience of behavior by others can spontaneously influence our own actions in social situations. In a somewhat related vein, Roland Neumann and Fritz Strack describe their research, showing how proprioceptive subjective experiences associated with motor behaviors suggesting approach or avoidance can surreptitiously influence other, otherwise unrelated affective and evaluative responses. In the next chapter in this section, Miguel Brendl analyzes how subjective experiences associated with drawing samples from larger populations (a fundamental task in most social judgments) can bias subsequent perceptions and judgments. Finally, Leonard Martin and Daniel Whitaker present an ambitious model that argues that the meaning and consequences of subjective experiences (including both affective and cognitive "feelings") is highly context-dependent and cannot be properly understood without a full consideration of the contextual circumstances in which they occur.

The second part of the book explores the relationship between subjective experiences and memory phenomena. Eliot Smith outlines a connectionist theoretical framework within which subjective experiences of familiarity and their consequences can be understood. Geoffrey Haddock looks at the subjective experience of ease of retrieval and describes empirical data showing how ease-of-retrieval experiences may impact attitude judgments, including attitudes towards political leaders. Michaela Wänke and Herbert Bless discuss how subjective experiences of ease of retrieval may provide a critical influence on evaluative judgments, and not only when processing is in some ways constrained, but also when elaboration likelihood is high and information is processed systematically. In the final chapter in this section, Ian Skurnik, Norbert Schwarz, and Piotr Winkielman present a broad conceptual framework and research evidence demonstrating how the subjectively experienced "fluency" of information processing impacts on memory and cognition.

The third part of the book contains chapters that look at the subjective experience of affect and its role in social cognition and behavior. In the first chapter in this section, Joseph P. Forgas and colleagues argue that subjective experiences of mood are subject to a homeostatic mood management system, where subtle changes in information processing strategies serve the purpose of increasing or reducing the intensity of experienced moods. Constantine Sedikides and Jeffrey Green then review interesting theoretical and empirical evidence suggesting a close relationship between the subjective experience of affect and attentional focus. Gerd Bohner and Thomas Weinerth address how different facets of negative affect in the form of fear and guilt influence the processing of persuasive communications. Teresa Garcia-Marques and Diane Mackie provide a very interesting link between the research on affective influences on information processing and feelings of familiarity, thus linking this third part to the issues discussed in part 2. Finally, Rainer Reisenzein discusses research related to the antecedents and consequences of the subjective affective experience of surprise, an experience that is seemingly the opposite of experiences of familiarity.

In the final section, we turn to the question of how subjective experiences can influence stereotyping and intergroup behaviors. Galen Bodenhausen and Kristen Moreno address the important distinction between incidental and integral affect. They discuss how individuals correct for a potential affect intrusion in intergroup perception. The research presented by Benoit Dardenne and colleagues investigates the subjective experience of control and how this experience moderates the impact of stereotypic versus individuating information in social judgment. Andrea Abele examines how experiences of positive mood influence an individual's disposition to differentiate between groups. Her research suggests that positive mood may have a profound impact on group differentiation, particularly under low relevance conditions. Finally, John Dovidio and colleagues link the consequences of positive affect on information processing to the field of intergroup perception. Embedded in a broad conceptualization of intergroup contact, they demonstrate that positive affect may improve or impair intergroup perception, depending on the nature of the intergroup contact.

Finally, we want to express our appreciation and gratitude to many people and organizations without whom this book would not have been possible. Financial support from the European Association of Experimental Social Psychology to support the Grasellenbach meeting, from the Deutsche Forschungsgemeinschaft to Herbert Bless, and from the Australian Research Council (Special Investigator Award) and the Alexander von Humboldt Foundation (Research Prize) to Joseph P. Forgas are gratefully acknowledged. Many people helped with ideas, suggestions, and organizational support during the past 2 years; we particularly appreciate the contributions of Klaus Fiedler. Alison Mudditt at Psychology Press deserves our special thanks—she has been enthusiastic, supportive, and supremely efficient and helpful throughout this project; we could not have wished for a better home for our book than Psychology Press. Last, but not least we are grateful to our partners and many friends and colleagues for their support, friendship, and understanding throughout the long months of working on this book.

We sometimes hear horror stories about how long-standing friendships come to an abrupt end when people embark on a joint book project like this one. We are pleased to say that collaboration between us as editors has been cordial and efficient at all times. Ultimately, our contributions to the book have been approximately equal. Accordingly, our names on the cover are listed in alphabetical order.

Herbert Bless and Joseph P. Forgas

Daniel M. Wegner
Daniel T. Gilbert

CHAPTER 1

Social Psychology—The Science of Human Experience

Once upon a time, people believed the earth was smack dab in the middle of everything and that all the planets revolved around it. Then came Copernicus, who argued that if this were true, something was deeply wrong with the rest of the universe because the observed motions of all the planets just didn't add up. After considerable head scratching, Copernicus concluded that the earth was not at the center of things and the sun was. Knowing this didn't actually change the universe, of course, but it did allow all of its movements to suddenly make sense.

The field of social psychology also has a center. Those of us who constitute the field know that the social interaction of individuals is its intellectual core, and we can all quote Allport approvingly when explaining this to others. How could it be otherwise? If social psychologists primarily cared about things that were neither social nor psychological, then their journals and departments and learned societies would be seriously mislabeled, and all new T-shirts would have to be printed. As tragic as this would be, many of us have had the sneaking suspicion at one time or another that the motions don't quite add up—that if sociality is indeed the center around which our scientific endeavors turn, then something is wrong with the rest of the universe. In this essay, we will argue that the universe is just fine, thank you, and that the problem is actually this: social psychology's center is not where we think.

Where is it? Astronomy teaches us at least two things about centers. First, it teaches us that centers are not always easy to find. The Milky Way

1

galaxy, for example, seems to have at its center an unobservable black hole that, by virtue of its unobservability, is very hard to see. Second, astronomy teaches us that one way to locate a center (especially an invisible one) is to look for the thing that everything else seems to be drawn toward. We believe that the center around which modern social psychology actually turns is the *understanding of subjective experience*. Sometimes it is concerned with things social and sometimes it is not, but far more than any other field of psychology and far more than any other science, social psychology is intimately concerned with the scientific understanding of what it is like to be a person—why our existence at this moment in time and space *feels* the way it does. We would go so far as to say that social psychology is not the science of sociality, but the science of experience. This claim sounds grandiose only because it is, but it is also simple and (we hope) compelling, once you get the idea. Here's the idea.

☐ Sociality: The Official Story

The phrase *social psychology* is usually understood to circumscribe a subfield of psychology that has its place among a variety of other subfields, such as developmental psychology, personality psychology, cognitive psychology, neuropsychology, and the like. Just as one can look at psychological phenomena in light of their development over time, or in light of the differences between individuals who exemplify the phenomena to different degrees, one can also look at phenomena in light of their sociality. People are not alone in the world, and as Triplett's very first social psychology experiment demonstrated, the fact that we have company makes a difference to almost everything worth studying. Social psychology, the story goes, captures a chunk of the variance in the puzzle of human psychology by considering how social situations emerge, unfold, and affect the thoughts, feelings, and actions of their participants.

This is a very lovely story whose only real weakness is its utter failure to conform to the facts. An hour's browse through social psychology's major journals reveals a jarring discrepancy between the official account of the field and the actual state of affairs. Indeed, as one turns the pages, one begins to get the sense that this thing called social psychology is not a subfield of psychology at all, but rather, a *whole field of psychology*—a kind of parallel universe in which just about every issue of interest to any other kind of psychologist receives its own special treatment and spin. Although this is true to some extent of many of psychology's so-called subfields, social psychology is especially remarkable for the range of its sweep. While claiming as its own all the explicitly social topics—such as interaction, relationships, and groups—social psychology also offers thorough treatments of topics such as emotion, perception, cognition, culture, attitudes, personality, mental disorders, development, motivation, health, law, memory, and more. The official story is about sociality, but even a cursory reading of the field's literature suggests that the official story is woefully incomplete, and that social psychology's reach is far greater than its name would suggest. Social psychology was once the science of the social, but in the last few decades, it has become a science of many, many things that are nonsocial as well.

A curious byproduct of social psychology's expansion has been a kind of urban blight at its official core. Topics such as social interaction, relationships, and groups—which are clearly "downtown" social psychology in the official story of the field—have suffered massive decay over the last few decades, with occasional paving and heroic attempts at urban renewal, but no truly sustained growth. As the field's interests have outgrown the downtown area and spilled into the suburbs, the center of social psychology has become a collection of office buildings in which some work and few live. Chapters in textbooks on these downtown topics are sparse, research publications in our best journals on these topics are rare, books on these topics are vastly outnumbered by books on almost everything else, and the prospect of shiny new futures for these areas seems somewhat dim. Commentators who have noticed this shift in the field's demographics have often issued calls for urban renewal, urging us all to take up residence once again in the official center of the city. We, on the other hand, believe that social psychology's downtown area has lost the bulk of its residents for good, and that clarion calls to return will not bring them back. Why? Because social psychology is no longer a city, but a nation, no longer a subfield, but a complete field—an alternative psychology that lives beside, and not within, the psychology spawned by Wundt. And the theme of this new and whole psychology is not sociality, but the scientific understanding of experience.

☐ Experience: The Real Story

Philosophers are fond of remarking on the abject loneliness of human consciousness. One cannot experience the consciousness of others, the observation goes, and others cannot experience one's consciousness either, so it is perfectly reasonable for all of us to wonder what consciousness is and whether anyone other than ourselves actually has it. The question of whether other minds exist, and what it is like to be them if they do, has proved intellectually intractable, and while modern philosophers occasionally reprise the traditional sport of flinging themselves at the problem, most have left more blood than dents on its surface. The trouble is that knowledge of other minds can never be satisfactory in the same way that knowledge of our own minds can. Cogito is so inarguably true that Descartes derived all other truths from it; but if "I think" is an axiom, then "you think" is merely a hypothesis.

The inscrutability of other minds is particularly acute when we grasp at understanding the experience of creatures different from ourselves—as in Nagel's (1974) celebrated essay on what it is like to be a bat. The question of what it is like to be a human, however, is something with which most of us are far more likely to be occupied, and it is thus all the more profoundly puzzling. We can cast a single vote for answers to this question—our own—but we never know beyond that quite how to understand other minds. Each of us is the only object in existence that we will ever truly know what it is like to be.

Humanistic psychology was, at least in part, a response to this unsatisfying state of affairs. Maslow (1966) suggested that people could be understood in either a scientific or an experiential way. Scientific understanding means considering people as though they were somewhat more complicated versions of the other three-dimensional objects that inhabit the physical world, making careful observations of people's actions, developing detailed descriptions of their attributes, and then using those observations and descriptions to make predictions about what they will do next. Maslow argued that this approach was appropriate for the understanding of the behavior of kites or sofas or lava flows, but that when it came to people, it fell oddly flat, because knowing a person in this way does not satisfy our hunger to know what it is like to *be* that person.

Maslow contrasted scientific understanding with experiential understanding, and he urged humanists to get vicarious—to feel what others were feeling and to think what others were thinking in order to bring themselves closer to others than the privacy of human experience would normally allow. He encouraged humanists to make the other person's experience their own, reverberating with it, reveling in it, suffering it, enjoying it, and most importantly, appreciating it in a way that the detached scientist could not. Alas, when all the touching and feeling was over, humanism proved to be a blind alley in the intellectual history of psychology because it valued the subjective by devaluing the objective. Maslow complained bitterly that scientific understanding was the enemy of experiential understanding, and this antiscientific attitude meant that humanism developed no methodology, accumulated no body of knowledge, made no discoveries, and left no legacy (save for the brief popularity of the name *Rollo*). Without the scientific approach, it seems, our experiential understanding of other minds is as transient and insignificant as the taste of a new pinot grigio. Humanism had lots of mouthfeel but no finish. The humanists were right to argue that the other person's experience was the critical object of psychological inquiry, but they were wrong to suggest that nothing about it could be understood from the objective stance. In pointing out the problem and invalidating the method for solution, humanism left a gaping hole in the center of the scientific world.

Social psychology has filled that hole, perhaps unwittingly, by becoming the science of what it is like to be a human and attempting to provide a scientific answer to the problem of other minds. Disguised as the people who investigate social life, we have been secretly investigating inner life instead, and getting away with it only because the two are so intimately connected. Our secret obsession with experience is revealed by our opinions about what's hot and what's not. The social psychology articles we most appreciate and remember are those that transport us into the mind of the subject as he or she faces some special predicament. Such papers inevitably enable us to imagine *being* the subject and to see just how funny or tense or heartbreaking or dull the view is from there. The classic experiments of Milgram, Asch, Festinger, Schacter, Latane and Darley, and others have little in common, save for their ability to make us grasp the experience of the person in the experimental setting. They are often only vaguely social, and can also seem a bit inelegant and incomplete as science. Yet they make us squirm and sigh and worry, as they very quickly render in our own minds the experience of the poor soul who has been "brought into the lab." The work that we celebrate as a field weaves together the objective and the subjective, providing the outsider's view of the insider's view, and when it does this superbly, its other flaws are generously overlooked.

We do not mean to suggest that social psychologists have no legitimate interest in studies of pure mechanism, or in studies that examine behavior alone. Such studies do appeal to us sometimes, but they do so largely to the extent that they promise to illuminate the individual's experience of the world. A theory providing mathematical functions that relate the size of a dinner party to the size of the waiter's tip tells us little about what it is like to be either. But it does provide a handy way to summarize some complex relations, and it isn't so far removed from the experience of social loafing that we can't make the leap ourselves. Nonetheless, given the choice between a formal model of these relations and an insightful description of that crucial moment in the diner's mental life when he reaches for his wallet, pauses, and thinks, "Ah, somebody else will get it," social psychologists will favor the latter every time. As a rule, we would rather not get too involved with theories that treat human behavior as though it were the motion of billiard balls—not because such theories provide the wrong answers, but because they answer the wrong questions. The mechanisms that are so often the focus of cognitive psychology and brain science are fine in their place, but their place isn't our place, because by themselves they don't tell us what we want to know. We want to know lots of things, of course, but mostly, we want to know what it's like *in there*.

Our secret obsession with experience is revealed in other ways as well. When a reporter calls a university's department of psychology and asks a question about this or that, to whom is the question referred? In most cases, the referrals end up in the lap of the resident social psychologist. We are the people inside psychology who talk to people outside psychology about what the field knows—we're the front end. Why? Because while many fields have evolved toward greater formalism, social psychology's official language remains ordinary language, and its official measure remains the verbal report. Like novelists, we offer theories built of words that have the power to transport our listeners into the experience of the people those theories describe. Unlike novelists, we take an objective approach to the subjective, carefully recording and counting people's responses to our questions, and looking for patterns in their answers. We don't always trust what people tell us, of course, but we always trust that what they tell us tells us something. When they say they are feeling sad because their lives are a hopeless mess, we are skeptical about the accuracy of their causal analyses. But we are not skeptical about the quality of the experience itself. The person may not know *why* she is in pain, but she is the world's foremost and sole authority on *whether* she is in pain. The most advanced neurological measure cannot tell us what the candid subject can, namely, "What does it feel like to be you, here and now?"

☐ Some Objections Anticipated

As Copernicus and his scope man Galileo soon learned, centers have a great deal of symbolic utility, and thus people naturally object to having them relocated without prior approval. We cannot anticipate or defend all reasonable objections to our claim, but let us set aside three obvious ones to start. They are: (a) it leaves things out, (b) it doesn't leave anything out, and (c) it was all said long ago by people with better clothes.

First, doesn't this new description of social psychology leave some of the field's most exciting topics standing in the yard? We all know, for example, that there is great interest among social psychologists these days in topics such as automaticity, unconscious process, and implicit everything. If social psychology is the science of experience, then why is the general category of "unexperienced stuff" among its hottest concerns? The problem here is merely semantic. Unconscious process is the flip side of conscious experience; in fact, only someone who was deeply interested in the nature of experience would bother to develop a theory of unconscious process at all. Behaviorism, for instance, was the one school of psychology that was able to abandon the unconscious successfully, but it was able to do this only because it had abandoned the conscious about 15 minutes earlier. Just as we learn about a phenomenon by studying its boundary conditions, we learn about human experience by discovering where it starts and stops. Indeed, it is hard to imagine how a science of experience could talk about how and when things appear in consciousness without also talking about how and when things do not.

The second objection is the complement of the first. If social psychology is the science of both the experienced and the unexperienced, then isn't it the science of everything? And with no one left in the yard, isn't the living room a bit too crowded? We do not think social psychology is the science of everything. One may study vertebrates and invertebrates and still not study jazz, Twinkies, or internal combustion. The biologist who studies vertebrates and invertebrates is using the concept of *skeleton* to parse and study the animal kingdom. Similarly, social psychologists may ask questions about what is inside or outside of experience, how it comes to be that way, and what effect it has—and they may do all this without ever studying the effects of family size on academic underachievement. What gets ignored is the study of people as objects whose attributes can be described, classified, and used to predict behavior. Research on IQ is a nice example. Isn't it curious that social psychologists have generally not been involved with research on a subject that clearly has both social and psychological components? Not really, because modern research on intelligence generally considers people as objects that contain a specific amount of some attribute (smarts), and then asks how they got that amount (genes and environment) and how having that amount influences their behavior (test taking). This work is invaluable, but it does not attract social psychologists because it does not speak to us about the experience of being the person who is bursting with brainpower or trying unsuccessfully to complete just one good thought. It gives us no *feel* for brightness or dullness. In short, plenty of useful questions and answers lie outside the psychology of human experience. Indeed, one of the things we like best about our claim is that it explains why some things that are nominally outside the field of social psychology seem as though they ought to be in, and why some things that are nominally in seem as though they should not be.

If we accept the argument that that a science of experience can have proper boundaries and that these boundaries look suspiciously like the city limits of modern day social psychology, we might still worry that all this talk of experience is merely another way of saying what was said decades ago—an anachronistic appeal for a cognitive, rather than a behaviorist, psychology. Isn't this just the cognitive revolution warmed over? We think it is much more than that. The cognitive revolution's great achievement was that it inserted a C between S and R. Cognition mediates the link from stimulus to response. Of course, C is a hard thing to study, and the cognitive revolutionaries justified giving everyone such hard homework by arguing that knowledge of C would ultimately help us predict R from S. Cognitive psychology would be better than behaviorist psychology, the pitch went, because it would do what behaviorist psychology had wanted done, but it would do it more effectively.

Which it did. But notice two things. First, C is not E. One can believe that what happens inside the machine that changes Ss into Rs is important without ever investigating how it feels to be that machine. Indeed, having a C between one's S and one's R is just as important when the system is a starfish or a pickle slicer as when it is a person. One can develop a psychology of that which mediates the S to R transition without ever noticing that the mediator is awake and enjoying it immensely. Many well-known cognitive models do just that, and these are the models that put social psychologists to sleep. Social psychology does not merely teach us that we should be concerned with what happens inside the person's head; it teaches us that we should be concerned with how these events seem. Brain events and mind events have or lack qualia—that is, they are felt or not felt—and their feltness is the heart of the matter for social psychologists.

The second thing to notice is this: if C isn't E, then R isn't E either. For all its glorious changes, the cognitive revolution remained faithful to the behaviorist mission of studying psychology as a means to predicting behavior. Meet the new boss, same as the old boss. Social psychologists like to predict behavior too—sometimes. And sometimes not. But because social psychology has the understanding of other minds as its intellectual end, it does not need to justify that understanding by appealing to its utility as a predictor of action. Our colleagues in economics are often perplexed by all our mentalistic chatter, and they wonder why we worry about all the messy mind stuff and brain stuff when a fancy equation often does a perfectly fine job of predicting behavior in the aggregate. The reason is that social psychology is not in the business of saying what people will *do* so much as it is in the business of saying what people *are experiencing*. The equation predicts the motions of bodies in space, but it does not give us the view from inside, and thus we just can't get worked up about it.

We study experience because it is the thing about which we want to know, and for a while that made social psychology a rather lonely place to be. But as it happens, scientists in various allied fields are now heading in our direction. The consciousness train has pulled into the station, heralded by the publication of hundreds of new books in the past dozen years that draw on philosophy, neuroscience, and evolutionary biology in the pursuit of new understandings of the inner life of humans. Nobel-winning biologists now proclaim consciousness as the single most important unanswered question in modern science, and famous physicists argue with famous mathematicians about the role that quantum uncertainty might play in producing it. This explosion of interest across many fields is one indication among many that the social psychological approach is a good one. It may well turn out that the understanding of experience is the fundamental requirement for the understanding of human beings, and that the essential center of social psychology is the essential center of human science. We welcome the company, of course, but we should not let them forget that we were here first.

☐ Conclusion

So here's an experience you may have had. You explain your research to an interested colleague, a curious student, or a lost tourist, and at the end of your speech they seem mildly puzzled. "Its all very nice, of course," they say, "but what's *social* about it?" From where we sit, this question seems about as sensible as asking someone named Smith why he doesn't shoe horses, or complaining because one's floppy disk is pretty darn stiff. Social psychology is the name of the tribe from which we are descended. It is a proud name, a good name, and we like it a whole big bunch. But it isn't particularly descriptive of the enterprise as it is actually happening at the cusp of the twenty-first century. Were the field up for a rechristening, it might consider something like *qualiology* or *experiential psychology* or even *experimental subjectology*. But it is called social psychology, and thus some identity confusion is to be expected. Someone picking up this book, for instance, might think that they were holding an edited volume on an new idea at the periphery of the field without realizing that the idea is old and that the book stands precisely at the field's center. It remains to be seen whether knowing where our center is makes any difference to the way we think and talk and operate. For now, it should at least provide some solace to those of us who have worried that, despite our address, we were really somewhere else.

☐ References

Maslow, A. (1966). *The psychology of science.* South Bend, IN: Gateway.
Nagel, T. (1974). What is it like to be a bat? *Philosophical Review, 83,* 435–450.

SUBJECTIVE EXPERIENCE AND INFORMATION PROCESSING

Klaus Fiedler

On Mere Considering:
The Subjective Experience of Truth

This chapter is concerned with an aspect of subjective experience that is not usually covered by the various approaches to the subjective experience of affective episodes and feeling states addressed in this volume. The term "experience" has several referents. It not only refers to the phenomenology of hedonic and affective stimulation; an equally important and common reference is to epistemology. In ordinary language, "experience" constitutes empirical knowledge that affords the basis for valid judgments and expertise, informed decisions, and rational behavior. After all, in the French language, "experience" means "experiment," which is the prototype of a systematic, scientific approach to problem solving. In emphasizing this epistemic aspect of experience, the present article addresses an important function of metacognitive intelligence, namely, the function of *truth monitoring*.

At any point in social communication and information acquisition, the individual cannot evade the problem of discriminating between true and false information and figuring out the truth implications of communicative acts. This metacognitive or metacommunicative monitoring function is ubiquitous; it is always at work and never set off. We can, by default, set the truth monitor to an uncritical positive value, taking any input for granted as long as no suspicion arises and no critical assessment is called

Address correspondence to: Klaus Fiedler, Psychologisches Institut, Universität Heidelberg, Hauptstr. 47-51, D-69117 Heidelberg, Germany. E-mail: Klaus_Fiedler@psi-sv2.psi.uni-heidelberg.de

for (Gilbert, Pelham, & Krull, 1988). However, such an "economy position" of the truth monitor does not mean that the monitoring function has ceased. It is in the ready mode at any time. In the absence of any deceptive intention, even mundane communications carry the potential of truth inversions. The waiter in the restaurant who is asked if the white wine is dry or whether the asparagus is fresh will usually say "Yes." This answer may be wrong and cause frustration in the gourmand. In this example, truth monitoring may have failed because the waiter's acquiescence with each and any question, because he is instructed to present all food in a desirable way, because he does not really understand what a dry wine is, because he has made the experience that most guests cannot discriminate dry and semi-seco wine, or because of an unintended error in speech production. The reasons for wrong and misleading information are manifold but, in any case, judging the validity of incoming information remains a central aspect of intelligent behavior.

In fact, the monitoring of truth or validity is much more complicated than suggested by the waiter example. This is because the feeling of truth, under high uncertainty, is influenced by so many other sources of experience, aside from the contents of the waiter's utterance. For instance, experimental research has shown that the mere repetition of a piece of information can increase its subjective truth (Gigerenzer, 1984; Hasher, Goldstein, & Toppino, 1977). More refined research (e.g., Arkes, Hacket, & Boehm, 1989) has clarified that the crucial factor is the subjective experience of familiarity, rather than the actual number of repetitions. Thus, when a statement is familiar enough to be deemed a repetition—even when, in fact, it is not repeated—the feeling of truth increases. Apparently, then, the familiarity level of a repeated item provides a cue to validity judgment under uncertainty (Jacoby, Kelley, & Dywan, 1989). Repeated experience rules out a nonreplicable random event and points to an invariant, really existing source. Repetition is therefore a widely used strategy in advertising. Rather than instructing the waiter to *pretend* the asparagus is fresh, the restaurant manager might achieve a similar effect by repeatedly announcing fresh asparagus. The advertisement might not even *assert* that the asparagus in this restaurant is always fresh. Different, logically irrelevant speech acts may have a similar effect, such as the repetition of the phrase "fresh asparagus is divine," the question "Did you ever see such delicious asparagus?" or just a picture demonstrating how delicious asparagus can appear. Communicative acts like truisms, suggestive questions, or uncommented pictures do not add any valid information to the problem at hand (i.e., the actual quality of asparagus in this particular restaurant). But they influence the kind of subjective experience that controls the function of truth monitoring in an uncertain world.

☐ Mere Considering and Illusory Truth

While the above introduction already suggests that the truth monitor may not be particularly sensitive to distinct speech acts (assertions, questions, empty truisms, dementia, even nonsensical statements), an extreme variant of illusory truth originates in mere considering. Just as mere thinking about an attitude object has been shown to strengthen that attitude (Tesser, 1978), merely considering a proposition can strengthen the subjective feeling that the proposition is true. This phenomenon, which is central to the remainder of the chapter, will now be illustrated with reference to several prominent paradigms.

Constructive Memory

A good deal of applied memory research on the accuracy of eyewitness reports demonstrates that merely getting an eyewitness to consider a possible item of information can cause corresponding memory illusions (Loftus, 1979). Merely asking witnesses of a (videotaped) car accident *whether* there was a stop sign where the car entered the intersection can mislead the witness to falsely memorize a stop sign on a subsequent recognition test. Or, only asking for the speed of a car before it *crashed* into another car leads to higher estimates than asking for the speed with which two cars *collided* or *hit each other*. Considering, as an inherent part of language comprehension and question answering, can be sufficient to increase the subjective experience of truth for the propositions in question.

Question-Answering and Linguistic Categories

That these phenomena arise in ordinary language comprehension is highlighted in a question-answering paradigm that was originally developed by Semin, Rubini, and Fiedler (1995) and later refined by Semin and Marsman (1997). Using specific verbs in questions can induce mere-considering processes, resulting in answers that confirm the semantic implications of the verbs used for the questions. It is well known that action verbs imply a cause in the sentence subject, whereas state verbs point to a causal origin in the sentence object. Accordingly, when an action verb is used to formulate a question ("Why do you *choose* political science for a subject matter?"), the focus is on an internal attribute within the target person. In contrast, when the same question is asked with a state verb ("Why do you *like* political science for a subject matter?"), the focus is on something attractive about political science. Accordingly, action-verb questions not only lead the respondent to say more about himself or herself and less about the subject matter than state-verb questions. The question-answer cycle will also make the question content subjectively true. Witnesses of the conversational episode will make more internal attributions and fewer situational attributions when overhearing an action-verb question than a state-verb question. Note that this paradigm suggests a process by which merely considering an internal or external cause in a question instigates an answer that creates subjective experience of truth in an audience.

Imagination and Explanation

One particularly effective means of turning mere possibilities into subjective beliefs is imagination, as evident from Koehler's (1991) literature review. Thus, visual imagination of a hypothetical event or behavior increases the subjective belief that the imagined event or behavior is actually true. Of course, this influence of imagination on subjective truth is also involved in the aforementioned memory intrusions of eyewitnesses who were (mis)led by interrogators to imagine possible details that were actually not present in the original information. The most natural intuitive interpretation that suggests itself for this phenomenon is that imagination means, after all, to mentally simulate the truth of an event for a moment. This transitory, self-generated reality then appears to be somehow confused with the original experience, or the authentical reality of an objective event.

The same confusion seems to hold for the other major determinant of truth illusions emphasized by Koehler, namely, explanation. Getting experimental participants to explain some hypothetical outcome will increase the subjective probability that this outcome will actually occur (Wells & Gavanski, 1989). Again, one might intuitively argue that explanation presupposes for a moment that an event to be explained is true; such a transitory truth experience may then be confused with the actual empirical truth of that outcome. An intriguing corollary of this analysis suggests that an implicit explanation process may contribute to the well-known hindsight bias (Fischhoff, 1975; Hawkins & Hastie, 1990; Hertwig, Gigerenzer, & Hoffrage, 1997), that is, the tendency to recall one's own previous estimates as if they were closer to the subsequently presented correct solution than they have actually been.

Confirmation Bias

Another relevant paradigm that had a great impact on social psychological research originates in Snyder's research program on confirmation biases in social hypothesis testing (Snyder, 1984, Snyder & Swann, 1978; Swann, Giuliano, & Wegner, 1982). The task is to test some hypothesis about a trait of an interaction partner (e.g., that the interaction partner is either extraverted or introverted). A typical outcome is that participants (as well as observers) end up with a more extraverted impression when they are testing the extraversion hypothesis and a more introverted impression when testing the introversion hypothesis (Snyder & Swann, 1978). Closer inspection shows that participants need not really expect the target person to be extraverted or introverted; it is sufficient to *merely consider whether* the person has the attribute in question (Semin & Strack, 1980). As with the preceding paradigms, the self-confirming nature of social hypothesis testing has been commonly explained in terms of inter-mediate processes that actually create to some degree the truth, which is then attributed to the hypothesis. Thus, when the hypothesis to be tested points to extraversion, participants would typically ask questions about extravert topics (parties, friends, cheerful behavior, etc.) that give the target person ample opportunities to actually exhibit the hypothetical extra-verted behavior. The target's behavior, therefore, justifies the confirmation bias. What constitutes a "bias" is only that the behavior was not shown spontaneously but elicited by the participants' own biased questions.

Acquiescence

This principle is still more explicit in the acquiescence effect demonstrated by Zuckerman, Knee, Hodgins, and Miyake (1995). Whatever possibility is being considered in social hypothesis testing (e.g., either extraversion or introversion), the respondent is likely to provide affirmative responses. Most respondents would typically affirm the question of whether they like parties (extraversion), but they would as well affirm to enjoy being alone (introversion). This acquiescience bias is familiar from survey re-search (Jackson, 1979). It suggests that merely considering some possibil-ity in social communication will very likely provide confirmatory evidence.

Self-Fulfilling Prophecy

Confirmation bias and acquiescience bias together constitute a self-fulfill-ing prophecy (Jussim, 1991; Rosenthal & Rubin, 1978). A teacher who starts from the stereotypical belief that boys are smarter than girls in math may lend more attention to boys and treat boys in a way that over time really evokes the expected superiority of boys in math. While some re-searchers have questioned the strength of this phenomenon (cf. Jussim &

Eccles, 1992), there is general agreement on the mechanism: an individual starts with an initial expectation that some belief is true, the target persons are then treated as if the belief were true, and this will finally produce the very behavior that actually renders the belief true, justifying the subjective experience of truth.

☐ Truth-Conserving Processes: A Barrier in Theoretical Thinking

Plausible as the depicted explanations of the above variants of mere-considering effects might appear, they are all restricted by one characteristic barrier of theoretical thinking. This barrier is reminiscent of Heider's (1944) insight that a good cause (explanation) has to resemble the effect (phenomenon) it produces. By analogy, a truth-enhancing bias has to be explained by a process that somehow enhances the truth. This rationalist, truth-conserving restriction is common to all the above accounts. Beliefs in the truth of an event or outcome increase through mere considering because imagining creates transitory truth, explanation presupposes truth, questioning elicits selective truth, interaction confirms the truth, and acquiescence warrants truth-conserving responses in other people.

A more refined, and intriguing, variant of this rationalist, truth-conserving account is advocated by Gilbert and colleagues (Gilbert, 1989; Gilbert, Krull, & Malone, 1990). Drawing on the Dutch philosopher Spinoza, they assume that the default truth value of any proposition is positive; that is, when we are exposed to some new proposition, we cannot represent it as a truthless possibility. In the absence of any evidence, the cognitive representation of a *possible fact* is identical with the subjective experience of a *true fact*. This default truth value is only overridden when the individual engages in a critical assessment stage. Empirically, this means that when participants are briefly exposed to a statement, they initially take it to be true. This truth bias can be conserved by a distracter that prevents them from critical assessment. Only when there is no distracter, critical assessment may reveal that the statement is false. Note that in this approach, the truth-conserving logic is secured by a tricky assumption; even when there is no confirmatory evidence, the truth of an initial proposition is guaranteed by default.

However, while the psycho-logic underlying this reasoning seems appealing, it need not be correct and justified. Indeed, there is strong and regular evidence that truth biases, due to mere considering, need not be subject to the theoretical restriction of truth-conserving propositions.

Moreover, this evidence is not new, but has been well known for a long time. It simply has been ignored when thinking about the explanation of confirmation biases and the other variants of truth bias.

For instance, Wegner, Wenzlaff, Kerker, and Beattie (1981) have been concerned with innuendo effects, showing that newspaper headlines ("Bob Talbert Linked with Mafia") had significant impact on impressions of the target persons. However, notably, this effect persisted even for negative innuendos ("Bob Talbert Not Linked with Mafia"). Theoretically, even negated propositions or negative evidence did not prevent an effect of the negated proposition (i.e., the association with Mafia will nevertheless exert an influence).

One of the strongest pieces of evidence that runs counter to the truth-conserving logic is the well-known perseverance effect (Ross, Lepper, & Hubbard, 1975). Debriefing experimental particpants that some treatment (e.g., negative test feedback) was based on deception would not erase the influence of the original deception. Participants whose self-confidence had been challenged would continue to believe in their own inferiority even when it was clearly explained that all the original treatment was completely faked. Apparently, merely considering an outcome (e.g., one's own bad test result) would continue to exert an influence even when fully transparent evidence does not conserve the truth.

☐ Testing Three Metacognitive Explanations

In the remainder of this chapter, I will report a number of experimental demonstrations from our own research for the contention that mere-considering effects are not contingent on the suggested information being considered true. Some of these demonstrations are even more compelling than those already mentioned, because the subjective truth of the input suggestions to be considered is controlled experimentally, independent of the resulting verification bias. This additional experimental control or methodological scrutiny provides the basis for examining three different metacognitive perspectives, offering explanations of mere considering. These three explanatory conceptions—which all abandon the truth-conserving constraint and permit that even suggestions with a low truth value and in the absence of empirical support can lead to verification—include the notions of source monitoring, mental models, and distributive memory. What are the psychological assumptions underlying these conceptions? And what are the implications by which these conceptions can be tested empirically?

Source Monitoring

M. Johnson's (Johnson, Hashtroudi, & Lindsay, 1993; Johnson & Raye, 1981) source-monitoring approach offers a simple and straightforward account. If an eyewitness is asked to merely consider whether there was a stop sign where the car entered the intersection, the subjective truth value may be rather low (because in fact there was no stop sign) and the witness will (correctly) deny. Thus, the truth value is low and there is little evidence to support the existence of a stop sign. When memory load is high enough—because there are many questions and details to be memorized—the witness may nevertheless report having seen a stop sign on a delayed memory test. Moreover, the rate of such intrusions may be above chance; that is, a higher proportion of participants who have been initially questioned about a stop sign and who have correctly denied may later report a stop sign than control participants who were not asked to consider a stop sign.

Source confusion means, simply, that under uncertainty, when part of the memory traces are lost, the participant will remember fragments of information stemming from (at least) two sources, the originally perceived facts and the information conveyed by the experimenter's questions. Source monitoring requires to discriminate whether memory fragments of a stop sign originate in the original perception or in the experimenter's questioning. However, pragmatic source information of this kind is more likely to be forgotten than the substantial content; the individual's subjective experience may therefore confuse the source and believe, erroneously, that the stop sign was really seen, rather than merely suggested by the experimenter.

Source confusion has at least two testable implications, *loss of source memory* and *similarity*. The first of these implications means that the impact of mere considering should be strongest when the individual forgets the source of information. When the individual remembers, on a source-memory test, the intermediate episode of an experimenter asking a question about a stop sign, the probability should increase that the memory of the stop sign is correctly attributed to the experimenter as an extrinsic source rather than the intrinsic source of the original perception. The second implication, similarity, predicts that a memory bias due to source confusion should be most likely when the information stemming from different sources is similar and therefore easy to confuse within the same global representation. Thus, when the original information contained a similar item as the one coming from another source (e.g., when a yield sign was present, quite similar to a stop sign), source confusion should be facilitated. A related argument pertains to the similarity between the memorized traces and the prompt used for the final memory test. Thus, if the effect is due to the intrusion of an item from an extraneous source, a test item that asks for exactly this item (e.g., a stop sign) should produce a stronger memory bias than a more remote test item (e.g., a red and white symbol). In other words, source confusion effects should be manifested in false reproductions of formerly suggested items, more than in false inferences or mental generations. Any active inference effect would indicate that more is at work than source confusion.

There can be no doubt that source confusion can contribute to memory biases of the mere-considering type, and that they will contribute some of the time to some of the phenomena. However, a series of recent experiments (Fiedler, Walther, Armbruster, Fay, Kuntz, & Naumann, 1996) show that source confusion is not a necessary condition. Participants saw a videotape of the interior of a flat, providing views of several different rooms with rich furniture and utensils: a corridor, living room, kitchen, bathroom, etc. Later on, they were presented with a list of questions about the presence of various objects in the flat. Some questions pertained to actually present objects; these objects and their properties were generally remembered quite well, indicating that participants were motivated and participated seriously. Other questions referred to nonobjects; that is, to items that did not occur in the film. Moreover, the list included both open questions ("Did you see an umbrella stand in the corridor?") or presuppositions ("Was the umbrella stand in the corridor made of brass?") that took the existence of the item for granted. In a subsequent recognition test, all the items that had been used for the questioning appeared once more, along with other objects and nonobjects that had not been the target of questioning. Figure 2.1 displays the likelihood of falsely recognized nonobjects as a function of mere considering and the participants' initial response to the intermediate questions.

The left panel shows that the impact of merely considering the possibility that was present in the flat on subsequent memory reports is considerable. The memory illusion is particularly strong for presupposed nonobjects (black bars), but nonobjects mentioned in open questions were also recognized at a higher rate than completely new items (which did not appear in the question list).

The particularly strong effect of presuppositions would at first sight support the truth-conserving rationale. A leading question like "Was the umbrella stand made of brass?" might convey the message that an umbrella stand is a true item. However, the findings in the right panel indicate that this interpretation cannot be maintained. This analysis is based on conditional data; that is, recognition of items that have been denied in the first place. This bar chart shows the proportion of recognition illusions for nonobjects that have been correctly denied in the preceding questioning (e.g., the proportion of participants reporting an umbrella

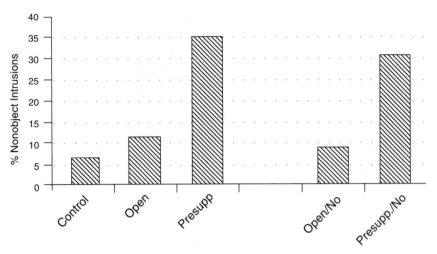

FIGURE 2.1. False recognition of (non)objects not actually presented in a stimulus film, as a function of question type (open vs. presupposition vs. no-question control) and answer (across all items on the left vs. restricted to denied items on the right).

stand, counting only those who have correctly denied the presence of this item initially). Apparently, the rate of the illusion induced by mere considering is approximately as high as in the overall analysis.

Denying the question "Was the umbrella stand made of brass?" need not imply that the presence of an umbrella stand is denied, but may mean that an umbrella stand was there but it was not made of brass. To control for this possibility, another experiment was run in which participants were instructed that there are actually two different films about two different flats. The instruction for the questioning task was altered, asking whether a question pertained to the one flat the participant himself or herself had seen or to the other flat. Thus, a negative answer to an umbrella stand question in this context means that this item belongs to the other flat and was not present in the observed flat. The results were virtually the same, indicating clearly that the impact of mere considering need not be mediated by cognitive inferences that increase the truth value of the considered items. In this study, items were (correctly) denied and there was no other confirming evidence; nevertheless, merely considering an item (especially in a taking-for-granted format, or presupposition) served to markedly increase the subsequent belief that the considered items had been present.

With regard to the source confusion explanation, it is noteworthy that the reported phenomenon was virtually independent of whether the participants remembered having answered a question about the item or not. Thus, source memory did not moderate the effect. Moreover, when the time intervals between the original information (video of the flat), the questioning, and the final recognition test were manipulated, there was no evidence for source confusion either. That is, the rate of memory intrusions was not maximal when the time interval between the questioning (extraneous source) and the recognition test was short relative to the time interval between the original information and the questioning. If participants were simply confusing memory traces stemming from different sources, the impact of the extraneous source should have been strongest when this source is closer to the memory test than the original source.

Let us now look at another empirical investigation that speaks to the similarity implication of a source confusion account. In the findings just reviewed, the influence of mere considering was tested in a recognition test involving exactly the same items that had been suggested by an external source. For example, an umbrella stand was verbally presented in the intermediate questioning, and a copy of the same stimulus, umbrella stand, then appeared in the verbal recognition test. Given this maximal similarity between the extraneous source intrusion and the test format, the confusion of traces stemming from different sources appears to be a plausible account. In the experiment to be reported next (Fiedler, Armbruster, Nickel, Walther, & Asbeck, 1996), the situation was fully different. Merely considering behavioral attributions affected subsequent ascriptions of trait terms that were never mentioned. This demonstration of active trait inferences triggered by mere considering involves more than just the intrusion of memory fragments from an irrelevant source. Beyond the mere confusion of externally provided stimuli, or the failure to encode the source of stimuli, this demonstration means that judges have drawn active inferences and attributions of self-generated traits.

Participants watched a videotaped TV talk show on a motivating topic, so-called "light products" (low-calorie food items that are advertised as health related, which often turns out to be nothing but a marketing trick). Right after the presentation of the group discussion, participants were asked to indicate whether and to what degree they had observed a number of behaviors in a particular target person. Experimental manipulations pertained to the valence and the attributional implications of the verbs that appeared in the set of questions. In one condition, the behaviors to be considered were described by negative *action verbs:* did the target person insult others, provoke others, attack others, etc.? In comparison, in the positive action verb condition, questions referred to whether the target person assisted others, encouraged others, supported others, etc. An important semantic feature of all action verbs is their implicit causality (Brown & Fish, 1983; Fiedler & Semin, 1988); the sentence "A insults B" implies a cause within the sentence subject A, not in the object B. Therefore, all action verb propositions evoke causal schemas that can be expected to induce internal attributions to the target person.

In accordance with these expectations, merely considering positive or negative action verb questions led to increased attributions of positive or negative traits, respectively, on a subsequent impression judgment task. Thus, preceding questions about hurting or attacking increased subsequent attributions of matched traits, brute and aggressive, respectively. As shown in Figure 2.2, when the preceding questions led judges to consider positive as opposed to negative action verbs, judgments of the target person were biased in the positive direction.

In the context of this experiment, the notion of source confusion alone would appear to provide a rather implausible account. The original stimulus behavior was presented audiovisually from the videotape, in a modality rather unlikely to be confused with the paper-and-pencil format of the subsequently presented verbal questions. Moreover, the dependent measure consisted in trait adjectives that were never mentioned in the original stimulus tape. Thus, although the presence of "source confusion" cannot be denied in the most tautological sense of the concept—because information from an extraneous source did finally affect the judgments—the cognitive process is hardly driven by the reproduction of intrusive stimulus traces. As evident from the transfer to trait concepts, the influence of the extraneous source must have been adopted and given rise to genuine constructive memory processes.

It should also be noted that these findings were again independent of truth conservation. When the analysis of trait ratings was restricted to those cases where judges had denied the preceding correspondent behavior (e.g., ratings of *aggressive* when the behavior *to attack* had been de-

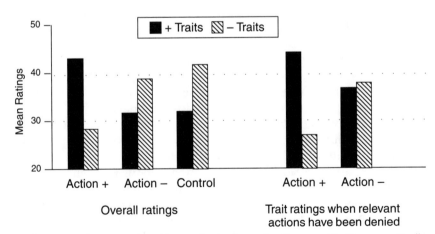

FIGURE 2.2. Judgments of positive and negative traits after considering semantically matched action verbs (+ vs. – valence), pooling over all data (left panel) or restricted to trait judgments when the corresponding action was denied (right panel).

nied), the same effect of mere considering on subjective truth experience was preserved (see right panel in Figure 2.2). Thus, it matters little whether judges found the positive or negative behaviors to be true; it was sufficient to merely consider the target person with reference to these behaviors. Truth inference also did not enter through the back door, in the disguise of conjectural evidence (Swann, Giuliano, & Wegner, 1982) or demand effect. That is, the very fact that participants received a question sheet providing only positive or only negative action verbs could not be regarded as an invitation to bias judgments in this direction, because judges were led to believe that they could themselves draw their own questioning treatment from a fan of question sheets allegedly containing positive as well as negative verbs.

Mental Models

Thus far, I have provided some evidence to demonstrate that neither a truth-conserving process nor a simple source confusion mechanism can provide a sufficient account of the robustness of mere-considering effects. Considering a possibility alone is sufficient—at least under certain conditions—to enhance the belief in that possibility regardless of implicit or explicit evidence for the truth of the introduced possibility and regardless of its similarity or confusibility. This formulation suggests a probabilistic account of the kind offered by Johnson-Laird's (1983) mental model theory. For convenience, the next explanation to be considered is termed a mental model account.

Consider once more the Fiedler, Armburster et al. (1996) study (Figure 2.2). Inspection of the control condition showed that in the absence of any questioning, the impression of target person was also rather negative. Relative to this baseline, considering positive behaviors led to a marked positivity shift, whereas questions about negative behaviors had little effect. The following very simple process might account for this pattern. A negative mental model is spontaneously inferred from the video input. A positive mental model is introduced in the positive question condition as another possibility, thus widening the range of possibilities toward the positive end of an underlying judgment scale. Raising another negative mental model through negative questions has little effect on the range of possibilities (see Figure 2.3). As the final judgments have to be made under high uncertainty, with little direct support for any mental model including the spontaneously inferred model, it is unlikely that the judgment process will exclusively rely on one mental model (e.g., the one elicited by the original video). Rather, the basic uncertainty should be reflected in judgment weights distributed more or less unsystematically

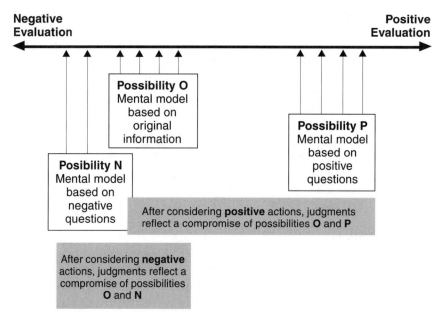

FIGURE 2.3. Graphical illustration of a probabilistic account of mere considering.

over all possibilities. Note that in such a theoretical framework, only the variety of possibilities considered is essential, not their source nor the presence of strong confirming evidence. Note also that such a possibilistic conception is at variance with Gilbert's claim attributed to Spinoza that plain, truthless possibilities cannot be represented cognitively (Gilbert, Krull, & Malone, 1990).

Such an extensional mental model approach would appear to provide an original new perspective on confirmation phenomena. Its theoretical strength arises from its simplicity. However, while the mere inclusion of further possibilities can certainly exert a significant function (if only a prompting function; see Fiedler & Armbruster, 1994; Tversky & Koehler, 1994) this approach cannot explain some essential restrictions of the mere-considering phenomenon. One such restriction is the degree of match between question contents and the epistemic context. For example, in the Fiedler, Armbruster, et al. (1996) investigation, questions about positive versus negative behaviors only influenced the impression of the target person in the videotaped discussion, if questions were applicable to the remaining stimulus information. As the semantic domain of action verbs is to refer to agents who are playing an active part, the influence of action verb questions was constrained to active target persons. In contrast, questions involving state verbs, which refer to passive roles, or patients rather than agents, affected only passive discussion participants who would fit the domain of state verbs.

Thus, for considered questions to affect subsequent judgments, they have to match a knowledge structure, as a vehicle or carrier of a constructive memory process. This rather abstract statement of can be illustrated through recent findings from Walther, Fiedler, and Nickel (1999). In the context of a diagnostic judgment problem, participants in all conditions received the same starting information about some fictitious patient's depression. Then, in a mere questioning treatment, participants were presented with a set of questions revolving around the possibility that the patient was suffering from mania. Only questions were presented, no answers. This treatment was sufficient to increase the belief that the patient was manic-depressive, but only in those participants who were advanced psychology students and already possessed a knowledge structure linking mania and depression. The same questions did not have this effect if they did not match the application condition of an already existing knowledge structure (i.e., in judges without clinical education).

A purely possibilistic account cannot explain this restriction. If merely raising the possibility of manic depression in a set of questions is enough, the effect should not depend on further knowledge. However, the evidence shows that mere considering only works when an existing knowledge structure provides a carrier for the effect. Note that this restriction is not tantamount to a truth requirement. As we have repeatedly demonstrated, it is not necessary that the question leads to affirmative responses. Thus, when judges were asked to answer the open questions about manic depression based on the remaining evidence, they would often deny. What is important, however, is whether the questions are applicable and can be connected to the judge's knowledge structure. Whereas *truth* is a matter of fit between questions and the empirical reality, *applicability* is a matter of fit between questions and other knowledge frames.

Another set of findings that is beyond the simple probabilistic acount comes from experiments in which judgments are based on inductive-statistical evidence. In a recent set of experiments (Fiedler, Walther, & Nickel, 1999), we also used a diagnostic problem setting. In an information search paradigm, judges could ask questions about overt and covert aggression observed in a couple, Heike (female) and Peter (male). The goal was to test the hypothesis that male aggression tends to be overt and female aggression tends to be covert, and that this difference in aggression style is responsible for the problems in Heike and Peter's relationship. Toward this end, judges could select questions about overt or covert aggression from an extended pull-down menu, and the computer would provide feedback on whether that behavior has been observed in the target person or not. In fact, the rate of affirmative feedback was held constant across both persons' aggression types (e.g., 75% in the basic condition). After an extended period of self-determined information search, participants had to estimate the rate of overt and covert aggression observed in

Peter and Heike and to rate both targets in terms of relevant trait attributes.

A typical search strategy in such a task setting is positive testing (Klayman & Ha, 1987). When testing the hypothesis that female aggression is covert and male aggression is overt, they mainly concentrate on the events stated in the focal hypothesis. That is, they tend to draw larger samples of observations on Heike's covert aggression and on Peter's overt aggression, but much smaller samples about the complementary events, Heike's overt aggression and Peter's covert aggression (see Figure 2.4, left panel). Given a constant affirmation rate, the feedback about both kinds of aggression in both targets should be roughly 75%. However, the observation of this constant aggression rate should be based on different sample sizes. As a typical result of positive testing, the samples for female covert aggression and male overt aggression would be twice as large (e.g., 18 confirmed behaviors vs. 6 disconfirmed) as for the nonfocal event (9 vs. 3). Although the ratios are the same in both cases, the subsequent judgments are more pronounced for the larger samples. Frequency estimates as well as trait ratings reflect higher perceived covert aggression in Heike and higher perceived overt aggression in Peter (see right panel of Figure 2.4). Moreover, the degree of this bias is correlated with the degree of positive testing.

Apparently, the effect of merely considering the guiding hypothesis is sensitive to *aggregation*. Given an invariant feedback rate, that is, no difference in truth-related evidence, the actual aggression rate is more readily extracted from larger than from smaller samples. This is a common learn-

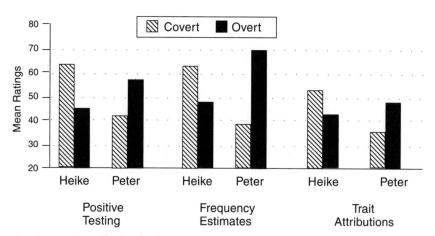

FIGURE 2.4. Considering the hypothesis that female aggression tends to be covert and male aggression tends to be overt leads to positive testing in information search, mediating a corresponding bias in frequency estimates and trait attributions.

ing effect: probability learning increases with numbers of trials. Likewise, doubling the number of stimuli in an impression formation paradigm will lead to accentuated judgments (Shavitt & Sanbonmatsu, 1999). Further, systematic evidence for this principle comes from recent research using a simulated classroom (Fiedler, Walther, Freytag, & Plessner, 1999), in which different participation rates of students with equal ability (i.e., proportion of correct answers) led to different sample sizes, which in turn led to biased judgments (i.e., polarized judgments for large-sample cases).

Once more, the bias in favor of the considered hypothesis was independent of evidence and expectancies of truth. First, the empirical truth evidence was controlled experimentally (i.e., by the constant affirmation rate). Second, the "auto-verification" of the focal hypothesis was largely independent of the participants' preexpectations concerning male and female aggression. And third, the crucial factor was neither the stereotypicality of the hypothesis (testing whether female aggression is covert or overt) nor the focus in the task instruction (the suggestion to look at female covert aggression), but rather the focus of the actually prevailing stimulus samples. Thus, when the sample about female overt aggression was larger, female overt aggression was judged to be high, even though the hypothesis referred to female covert aggression. These findings are not consistent with any account in terms of demand effects or prior expectations.

However, most importantly, the findings are not consistent with a probabilistic account. Note that the same 2 × 2 possibilities (i.e., covert and overt aggression × Heike and Peter) are perfectly evident, although the sample size manipulation only affects the aggregation over repeated trials. Merely considering one particular event more frequently than others produces more subjective verification than considering the same event less frequently. Needless to say, the repetition effect is fully independent of the truth rate. It is at this point that the mere-considering effect resembles the frequency-validity effect (Begg, Armour, & Kerr, 1985; Gigerenzer, 1984); repeated presentations of the same proposition increase the subjective belief in the truth of that proposition.

Distributive Memory as an Explanatory Framework

Thus far, we have seen that the intriguing influence of mere considering is not contingent on truth inferences, and it cannot be reduced to source confusion and the logical possibilities raised in an experimental setting. However, if the basic effect is more robust and at the same time mediated by other factors than suggested in these theories, the open question is which theoretical framework is better suited for explaining mere-considering effects and their restrictions. In my opinion, the empirical evidence on mere considering can be used to make a strong point for a distributive-memory account and for related connectionist models (Fiedler, 1996; McClelland & Rumelhart, 1985). Fully delineating such a model would certainly exceed the scope of the present chapter. However, I will at least try to outline the essential facets of a distributive memory account and how it can naturally deal with all the empirical phenomena reviewed above.

The very notion of distributive memory per se—rather than any particular model with specific parametric assumptions—not only helps to understand the existence of mere-considering effects, but also explains (a) why logical truth implications are not essential, (b) why loss of source memory is not a necessary condition, (c) why the effect is not confined to the reproduction of fragments from extraneous sources, (d) why it is not only a matter of the variety of possibilities but also depends on stimulus frequency and aggregation effects, and (e) why an important condition is that the information to be considered matches the semantic meaning of an existing knowledge structure that is the carrier of the entire process.

A distributive memory approach is essentially constructivist. It does not start from an arbitrary set of assumptions tailored to fit empirical facts. Rather, it builds on basic insights on the nature of social cognition that are rarely questioned but hardly ever employed systematically. The most fundamental insight is that the meaningful concepts that are in the focus of social judgment and decision processes—for example, the concept of *overt aggression* in the experiment just reported—cannot be perceived directly. We have no sense organs to perceive overt aggression as we perceive pitch, color, or brightness. Meaningful entities like overt aggression, risk, attraction, honesty, or danger are not amenable to direct perception but have to be inferred in an active, constructive process from a distribution of stimulus features. For example, the "perception" of overt aggression is based on an inference from a set of features that are not very diagnostic alone but only establish meaning within an entire pattern, or vector of features (see Figure 2.5).

To really understand the essence of a distributive memory model (and not to handicap the approach from the beginning), it is wise to conceive of the features as subsymbolic units that cannot be labeled verbally. However, if such a starting assumption is too abstract to be adopted, one might think of the features mediating the perception of overt aggression as including signs of facial expression, motor cues, voice indicators, linguistic cues, and indicators of the autonomic nervous system. For simplicity, a pattern of binary features (filled and open circles) is used in Figure 2.5 to represent the presence or absence of features, but the model is of course not confined to binary feature values.

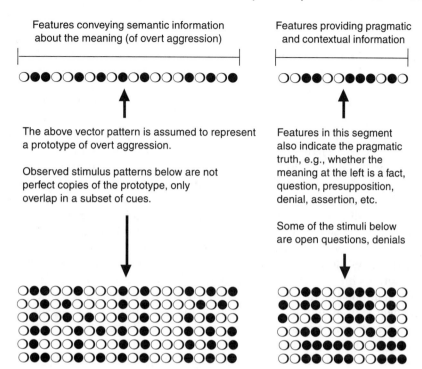

FIGURE 2.5. Graphical illustration of a distributive memory account of mere considering.

It is important to recognize that the "perception" of a distal entity like overt aggression takes place in a distributive, noisy stimulus environment. There is no immediately perceivable, constant stimulus object named "overt aggression," but overt aggression is a construct abstracted from many different feature patterns reflecting behavioral items like "insulting somebody loudly," "throwing objects at somebody," "hitting and kicking at somebody," etc. Virtually all manifestations of overt aggression involve a different specific pattern of features; sometimes vocal cues are most prominent, while on other occasions, the perception is mainly driven by the presence of linguistic or physical motor cues. However, while all stimulus events are different and somehow unique (so that individual cues are weak indicators), all patterns exhibiting overt aggression overlap to some degree; they all resemble a generic vector that can be termed the prototype vector (see the top row vector in Figure 2.5). The prototype can be understood as the ideal pattern in which all potentially relevant features take the value that is most indicative of the distal construct (e.g., overt aggression).

"Perception" of meaningful constructs presupposes a concept. The underlying process of concept learning consists in the induction of commonalities shared by different observations of an entity. One heuristic to understanding this learning process is the Hebbian rule, which says that when any two features are jointly activated, their association is strengthened. Thus, repeated observations of overt aggression will create and gradually strengthen the links between all features that are involved in the prototype of this concept. The result of this associative learning process can be described like a tuning process. Like a radio receiver programmed to be particularly sensitive to certain frequencies, the associative network in the individual's memory is then tuned to perceive the covariation of features resulting from their paired occurrence. As a consequence, newly observed stimulus patterns can be "perceived" as instances of overt aggression even when they contain only part of the stimulus features. A partial match will be sufficient to elicit the entire knowledge structure. However, while this sort of constructive completion of incomplete or ambiguous input is characteristic of distributive memories, it is clear that the likelihood and distinctiveness of the perceived construct increases with the degree of match. If the match is below some minimum, the stimulus vector is simply not applicable to the connected knowledge structure, and no cognitive process will take place.

Crucial to explaining the mere-considering effect in such a distributive framework is the inclusion of two types of features in the same vector. As depicted in Figure 2.5, one subset of features conveys semantic information about the nature of overt aggression (left side), but pragmatic information on the observation context is also included within the same vector (right side). On one hand, this may be information about the situation. Whether overt aggression is observed on the soccer field or in the bedroom can be an essential part of the identification process (Trope, 1986). On the other hand, however, pragmatic information refers to the speech act and the epistemic value of the stimulus. The same reference to overt aggression may appear in an overt question ("Did Peter shout at Heike?"), in a presupposing question ("How loud did Peter shout at Heike?"), in an assertion ("Peter did shout at Heike"), in the imagination of Peter shouting at Heike, etc. Since all these stimuli share the same semantic part, the feature overlap will be considerable, even though a subsegment of features (at the right side in Figure 2.5) reflects the different epistemic status (open question, preupposition, etc.). Even a negated sentence or question ("Peter did not shout at Heike. Did Peter not shout at Heike?") will overlap considerably with the prototype describing a positive experience of overt aggression.

From this sketch of a distributive memory system, it is now evident why the core phenomenon and the boundary conditions of mere-considering effects can be explained. First, the very phenomenon itself follows from the ability of distributive memories to respond to imperfect stimulus patterns—for all perception in such a noisy stimulus world involves only imperfect patterns. Merely considering some behavior can thus produce sufficient overlap with a memorized prototype and mimic an authentic observation of real behavior. Second, this process is not truth conserving because the pragmatic segment of stimulus features (i.e., whether a suggested item is only a question, an assertion, or a factual observation) is only a small and often pallid subset, relative to the vivid and rich segment of features conveying semantic meaning. A negation device (e.g., the word "not" or the suffix "un") may not change the stimulus pattern very much. Even when the pragmatic meaning is noticed by some attentive meta-cognitive device, denied evidence ("Peter did not hit Heike") continues to strengthen the connection between the semantic features and thereby strengthens the associative link between Peter and the semantic field of overt aggression.

Third, it is also clear that frequently repeated observations involving Peter and overt aggression will strengthen the associative connection in comparison with less frequent observations of a similarly aggressive person (e.g., Heike). Moreover, this aggregation or "accrual" effect is not strictly confined to affirmative evidence (valid assertions of overt aggression) but also extends to overlapping suggestions (i.e., mere questions, or even negations). However, a precondition for any stimulus pattern to evoke the overt aggression network is a sufficient match between the stimulus input and an existing knowledge structure. If a stimulus pattern is too far-fetched, or if no structure for the concept of overt aggression is available, there will be little influence.

☐ Concluding Remarks

In this chapter, some old and new evidence was presented for an important function of subjective experience; namely, the everyday monitoring of truth. Merely considering an event will under many circumstances enhance the subjective belief in the truth of that event. While previous explanations of this phenomenon have emphasized direct and indirect truth inferences, recent evidence demonstrates that the mere-considering effect is not confined to situations where truth inferences are encouraged. Rather, even in the absence of confirming evidence or confirming inferences, merely considering an event can enhance its subjective existence. Having discarded the rationalist, truth-conserving account from the beginning, I have then examined three other explanations, in terms of source confusion, range of possibilities raised, and distributive memory.

Only the latter approach appears to be flexible enough to explain the entire pattern of evidence on the partly irrational and ironic consequences of mere considering.

☐ References

Arkes, H. R., Hackett, C., & Boehm, L. (1989). The generality of the relation between repetition and judged validity. *Journal of Behavioral Decision Making, 2,* 81–94.

Begg, I., Armour, V., & Kerr, T. (1985). On believing what we remember. *Canadian Journal of Behavioral Science, 17,* 199–214.

Brown, R., & Fish, D. (1983). The psychological causality implicit in language. *Cognition, 14,* 233–274.

Fiedler, K. (1996). Explaining and simulating judgment biases as an aggregation phenomenon in probabilistic, multiple-cue environments. *Psychological Review, 103,* 193–214.

Fiedler, K., & Armbruster, T. (1994). Two halves may be more than one whole: Category-split effects on frequency illusions. *Journal of Personality and Social Psychology, 66,* 633–645.

Fiedler, K., Armbruster, T., Nickel, S., Walther, E., & Asbeck, J. (1996). Constructive biases in social judgment: Experiments on the self-verification of question contents. *Journal of Personality and Social Psychology, 71,* 861–873.

Fiedler, K., & Semin, G. R. (1988). On the causal information conveyed by different interpersonal verbs. *Social Cognition, 6,* 21–39.

Fiedler, K., Walther, E., Armbruster, T., Fay, D., Kuntz, H., & Naumann, U. (1996). Do you really know what you have seen? Intrusion errors and presupposition effect in constructive memory. *Journal of Experimental Social Psychology, 32,* 484–511.

Fiedler, K., Walther, E., Freytag, P., & Plessner, H. (1999). *Judgment biases and pragmatic confusion in a simulated classroom—A cognitive-environmental approach.* Submitted.

Fiedler, K., Walther, E., & Nickel, S. (1999). The autoverification of social hypotheses: Stereotyping and the power of sample size. *Journal of Personality and Social Psychology, 77,* 5–18.

Fischhoff, B. (1975). Hindsight ≠ foresight: The effect of outcome knowledge on judgment under uncertainty. *Journal of Experimental Psychology: Human Perception and Performance,1,* 288–299.

Gigerenzer, G. (1984). External validity of laboratory experiments: The frequency-validity relationship. *American Journal of Psychology, 97,* 185–195.

Gilbert, D. T. (1989). Thinking lightly about others: Automatic components of the social inference process. In J. S. Uleman & J. A. Bargh (Eds.), *Unintended thought* (pp. 189–211). New York: Guilford Press.

Gilbert, D. T., Krull, D. S., & Malone, P. S. (1990). Unbelieving the unbelievable: Some problems in the rejection of false information. *Journal of Personality and Social Psychology, 59,* 601–613.

Gilbert, D. T., Pelham, B. W., & Krüll, D. S. (1988). When person perceivers meet persons perceived. *Journal of Personality and Social Psychology, 54,* 733–740.

Hasher, L., Goldstein, D., & Toppino, T. (1977). Frequency and the conference of referential validity. *Journal of Verbal Learning and Verbal Behavior, 16,* 107–112.

Hawkins, S. A., & Hastie, R. (1990). Hindsight: Biased judgments of past events after the outcomes are known. *Psychological Bulletin, 107,* 311–327.

Heider, F. (1944). Social perception and phenomenal causality. *Psychological Review, 51,* 358–374.

Hertwig, R., Gigerenzer, G., & Hoffrage, U. (1997). The reiteration effect in hindsight bias. *Psychological Review, 104*, 194–202.

Jackson, J. E. (1979). Bias in closed-ended issue questions. *Political Methodology, 6*, 393–424.

Jacoby, L. L., Kelley, C. M., & Dywan, J. (1989). Memory attributions. In H. L. Roediger & F. I. M. Craig (Eds.), *Varieties of memory and consciousness: Essays in honor of Endel Tulving* (pp. 391–422). Hillsdale, NJ: Erlbaum.

Johnson, M. K., Hashtroudi, S., & Lindsay, D. S. (1993). Source monitoring. *Psychological Bulletin, 114*, 3–28.

Johnson, M. K., & Raye, C. L. (1981). Reality monitoring. *Psychological Review, 88*, 676–685.

Johnson-Laird, P. N. (1983). *Mental models: Towards a cognitive science of language, inference, and consciousness.* Cambridge, MA: Harvard University Press.

Jussim, L. (1991). Social perception and social reality: A reflection-construction model. *Psychological Review, 98*, 54–73.

Jussim, L., & Eccles, J. S. (1992). Teacher expectations: II. Construction and reflection of student achievement. *Journal of Personality and Social Psychology, 63*, 947–961.

Klayman, J., & Ha, Y. (1987). Confirmation, disconfirmation, and information in hypothesis testing. *Psychological Review, 94*, 211–228.

Koehler, D. J. (1991). Explanation, imagination, and confidence in judgment. *Psychological Bulletin, 110*, 499–519.

Loftus, E. F. (1979). *Eyewitness testimony.* Cambridge, MA: Harvard University Press.

McClelland, J. L., & Rumelhart, D. E. (1985). Distributed memory and the representation of general and specific information. *Journal of Experimental Psychology: General, 114*, 159–188.

Rosenthal, R., & Rubin, D. B. (1978). Interpersonal expectancy effects: The first 345 studies. *The Behavioral and Brain Sciences, 3*, 377–386.

Ross, L., Lepper, M. R., & Hubbard, M. (1975). Perseverance in self-perception and social perception: Biased attribution processes in the debriefing paradigm. *Journal of Personality and Social Psychology, 32*, 880–892.

Semin, G. R., & Marsman, G. (1994). On the information mediated by interpersonal verbs: Event precipitation, dispositional inference and implicit causality. *Journal of Personality and Social Psychology, 67*, 836–849.

Semin, G. R., Rubini, M., & Fiedler, K. (1995). The answer is in the question: The effect of verb causality upon locus of explanation. *Personality and Social Psychology Bulletin, 21*, 834–841.

Semin, G. R., & Strack, F. (1980). The plausibility of the implausible: A critique of Snyder and Swann (1978). *European Journal of Social Psychology, 10*, 379–388.

Shavitt, S., & Sanbonmatsu, D. (1999). Broadening the conditions for illusory correlation formation: Implications for judging minority groups. *Basic and Applied Social Psychology.* In press.

Snyder, M. (1984). When belief creates reality. In L. Berkowitz (Ed.), *Advances in experimental social psychology* (Vol. 18, pp. 247–305). New York: Academic Press.

Snyder, M., & Swann, W. B. (1978). Hypothesis-testing strategies in social interaction. *Journal of Personality and Social Psychology, 36*, 1202–1212.

Swann, W. B., Giuliano, T., & Wegner, D. M. (1982). Where leading questions can lead: The power of conjecture in social interaction. *Journal of Personality and Social Psychology, 42*, 1025–1035.

Tesser, A. (1978). Self-generated attitude change. In L. Berkowitz (Ed.), *Advances in experimental social psychology* (Vol. 11, pp. 289–238). New York: Academic Press.

Trope, Y. (1986). Identification and inference processes in dispositional attribution. *Psychological Review, 93*, 239–257.

Tversky, A., & Koehler, D. J. (1994). Support theory: A nonextensional representation of subjective probability. *Psychological Review, 101*, 547–567.

Walther, E., Fiedler, K., & Nickel, S. (1999). *The more we know, the better? Influences of prior knowledge on constructive memeory.* Submitted.

Wegner, D. M., Wenzlaff, R., Kerker, R. M., & Beattie, A. E. (1981). Incrimination through innuendo: Can media questions become public answers? *Journal of Personality and Social Psychology, 40,* 822–832.

Wells, G. L., & Gavanski, I. (1989). Mental simulation of causality. *Journal of Personality and Social Psychology, 56,* 161–169.

Zuckerman, M., Knee, C. R., Hodgins, H. S., & Miyake, K. (1995). Hypothesis confirmation: The joint effect of positive test strategy and acquiescence response set. *Journal of Personality and Social Psychology, 68,* 52–60.

Ap Dijksterhuis
John A. Bargh
Joost Miedema

CHAPTER 3

Of Men and Mackerels: Attention, Subjective Experience, and Automatic Social Behavior

At first sight, it may seem an odd idea to write a chapter about men and mackerels. The differences between men and mackerels are as obvious and as numerous as the differences between a sixteenth century farm-house and the Empire State Building. So why should we bother with a comparison between the two? Do we learn anything about human social behavior by observing a school of fish?

In our opinion, the answer is "Yes." Thinking about the differences between men and fish becomes a less trivial and more interesting affair as soon as we realize that although men and fish differ in many ways, they also have some surprising similarities. When evolution comes up with a new species, it does not throw away old modules or systems so as to make a fresh start. Instead, new parts are simply added to parts that already existed (e.g., the relatively recently added cortical layers of the human brain, wrapped around the "old brain" located at the top of the spine[1]). The fish, in other words, is still in us. If we examine closely some of the basics of human social behavior, signs of this fish can be observed quite

This research was facilitated by a Royal Netherlands Academy of Sciences Fellowship awarded to the first author and Grant SBR-9809000 (NSF) to the second author.

Address correspondence to Ap Dijksterhuis, Dept. of Social Psychology, University of Nijmegen, P.O. Box 9104, 6500 Nijmegen, The Netherlands. E-mail: dijksterhuis@psych.kun.nl

easily. What we see when we sit on a bench in a crowded shopping mall is more similar to what we might see while scuba diving than we might suspect.

☐ The Tendency to Imitate

Many species, including human beings and fish, have a tendency to copy the behavior of others. Pitcher (1983, p. 611) remarked that "parallel swimming in schools is brought about by a form of "social copying" as fish adjust velocity and direction to that of their neighbours." Fish copy the behavior of other fish, and because they do this continuously and fast, schools of fish are typified by an impressive synchronicity. Fish are capable of this synchronic behavior because, for them, perception and behavior are intimately linked. That is, perceiving the movement of another fish cannot be disentangled from the onset of the execution of this same movement.

This perception-behavior link is present in most species, including humans. A century ago, Carpenter (1888), James (1890), and Jastrow (1906) already noted that the subjective experience of perceiving an action (or the thought of an action) results in the tendency to actually engage in this action. Others, including LeBon (1895) and Tarde (1903), have posited that a form of "passive imitation" is the main force eliciting crowd behavior. Recent empirical work on what is called the "common-coding" hypothesis (see Prinz, 1990, for a review) provides a theoretical basis for the existence of perception-behavior link, as it strongly suggests that we use the same mental representations for perception and for our own action. The best evidence in this regard comes from a recent series of studies by Musseler and Hommel (1997). Participants were to press, on a given trial, a specified sequence of left (<) and right (>) arrow keys, such as "> > < >." When they began to type the sequence, a fifth element to the sequence appeared on the monitor screen: they were to add this to the end of the original sequence. The presentation of this symbol (either < or >) was timed, however, to coincide with the typing of the second key of the series. Participants made many more errors in typing the final, added key if it was the same as the one they were typing while that fifth symbol was presented to them, than if it had been the other key.

This is what would be expected if the same mental representation was used in both cases—while being deployed in one way (e.g., action), it is temporarily unavailable for the other (e.g., perception). In other words, we cannot act and perceive the same act at the same time. We do not perceive an action while we are performing this same action, simply because the representation responsible for perception is already "busy" doing the action.

It is no wonder, then, that signs of a direct perception-behavior link—so easily observed among fish—can be found among human beings as well. Chartrand and Bargh (1999; see also Eidelberg, 1929) demonstrated this in a series of experiments. In one such study, they asked a participant to interact for a couple of minutes with a second participant. This second participant was actually a confederate who was instructed to either rub his or her face or to shake his or her foot. The participants imitated this behavior. Under conditions in which the confederate was shaking his or her foot, participants engaged more in foot shaking than in face rubbing, while the opposite was true under conditions where the confederate was instructed to rub his or her face. Postexperiment questioning of the participants revealed no awareness of having engaged in these behaviors. Hence, the natural or automatic tendency to copy the behavior of species conspecifics is also present among humans.

Humans and animals differ, however, as to the sort of perceptions they apply during social interactions. The human social perceptual repertoire is extremely rich in comparison to that of other species. Like many other species, we are able to perceive movements and gestures of others, but we also use abstract cognitive constructs such as personality traits and social stereotypes to characterize others. Just like the more basic perceptions such as representations of movements, these more complex social representations become activated automatically during social interactions (Bargh, 1994; Devine, 1989; Gilbert, 1989; Winter & Uleman, 1984). The activation of trait concepts and stereotypes, in other words, can be conceived of as a basic perceptual process, just like the perception of movements and gestures.

Moreover, as one may expect, the activation of trait concepts and stereotypes in the course of perceiving others has behavioral consequences similar to those of the perception of movements and gestures: such experiences elicit, naturally and effortlessly, corresponding behavior. Empirical demonstrations of this are now abundant. To give just a few examples, experimental manipulations that cause the stereotype of the elderly to become activated also cause participants to walk more slowly leaving the experimental session (Bargh, Chen, & Burrows, 1996, Experiment 2) and to become more forgetful (Dijksterhuis, Aarts, Bargh, & van Knippenberg, in press) compared to the control condition. People react with greater hostility to another person after being perceptually exposed to words related to hostility in an ostensible "language task" (Carver, Ganellen, Froming, & Chambers, 1983) or after activation of the stereotype of African Americans through subliminal presentation of male African American faces (Bargh et al., 1996, Experiment 3; Chen & Bargh, 1997). Similarly, people become more helpful after manipulations that covertly activate the trait concept of helpfulness (Macrae & Johnston, 1998), temporarily smarter (as measured by number of correct answers in a Trivial

Pursuit game) after activation of the stereotype of college professors, and temporarily more stupid after activation of the stereotype of soccer hooligans or supermodels (Dijksterhuis, Spears, et al., 1998; Dijksterhuis & van Knippenberg, 1998). In sum, the activation of mental concepts in the course of perception tends to result in enactment of the corresponding behavior when the perception is of motor movements as well as when the perception involves activation of abstract constructs such as personality traits and stereotypes.

☐ The Difference Between Men and Mackerels

An important difference between humans and fish is that the direct effects of perception on action are (presumably) inescapable for fish and not for humans. The findings discussed in the previous paragraphs may suggest to some that people are simply "victims" of environmental forces, and that our behavior is determined entirely by our social environment. This, of course, is not true. Like many (but not all; see Bargh & Ferguson, 1999; Bargh & Gollwitzer, 1994) automatic processes, the effects of perception on behavior have an important limitation: they are inflexible. Although direct effects of perception on behavior may constitute a "default" behavioral option, there should be room for other mechanisms to override these effects if necessary. Gilbert (1989) used the metaphor of an imaginary garment factory run by inflexible tailors and a smart inspector in order to emphasize the importance of the interplay between automatic processes and the control processes that can override them:

> The primary constraint on the design of this factory is that the little tailors who sew the clothes are simpletons and dullards. They can only be taught to make one size of each garment, and so, when called upon to make a pair of men's trousers, these tailors always make a modal product (e.g., size 34). This is usually not a problem because the modal product will, by definition, fit most customers. But on occasion there will be a Triton among the minnows who requires something in a size 52, and when this happens, the smart inspector must alter the size 34 pants that the stupid tailors have made. (pp. 206–207)

Macrae and Johnston (1998) investigated one of the measures that a smart inspector can take when the perception-behavior link comes up with an inappropriately sized pair of trousers. They covertly "primed" some of their participants with stimuli related to the trait of helpfulness. Subsequently, a confederate passed by and "accidentally" dropped a few things. As expected, helpful-primed participants were more helpful (i.e., they picked up more things) than no-prime control participants. However, under conditions where participants were explicitly given the goal to hurry to the next experimental session, no signs of the prime were apparent. The conscious goal to hurry up overruled the tendency to help, and, hence, effects of the perception-behavior link were successfully eliminated.

Human behavior is not as simply accounted for, of course, in terms of behavioral tendencies automatically suggested via perception, which then are or are not overruled by the demands of conscious goal pursuit. Behavior is guided by a number of different mechanisms integrated in a complex and presumably context-dependent hierarchy (see Bargh, 1997; Koestler, 1967). Therefore, in order to answer the question we posed of when people are, versus are not like fish, we propose a loose hierarchy of experiential systems that can override or moderate the output of various other systems. In such a mental world, there is room for several ways besides a conflicting conscious goal through which the perception-behavior link can be broken.

☐ Focal Attention and Behavioral Time-Outs

Here we would like to explore one such mechanism. As mentioned earlier, the effects of perception on behavior are passive and unintentional. This means that they will occur even though conscious attention is not currently being directed toward one's behavior, toward what one is doing and why, in a "self-focused attention" sense (e.g., Duval & Wicklund, 1972). We would like to propose, however, that it is not just that attention focused on the self is not needed for the execution of these automatized actions; it is that the absence of such self-consciousness—that is, the absence of consciously experiencing such actions—is actually necessary for their execution. We hypothesize that if attention is directed toward one's ongoing behavior, the direct and automatic effects of perception on this behavior (see also Dijksterhuis & van Knippenberg, 1999) are inhibited or eliminated. *That is, if attention is directed elsewhere and for some reason shifts toward one's current behavior, producing a metacognitive awareness of what one is doing, this in itself can be enough to eliminate the influence of activated percepts on that behavior.*

Our hypothesis that self-focused attention can break the perception-behavior link is partly based on evidence demonstrating that the execution of various automatized actions is hampered by devotion of conscious attention to their production (Baumeister, 1984; Baumeister & Showers, 1986; Baumeister & Sommer, 1997; Carver & Scheier, 1981; Dijksterhuis & van Knippenberg, 2000; Hefferline, Keenan, & Harford, 1959; Kimble & Perlmuter, 1970; Langer, 1978; Macrae, Bodenhausen, & Milne, 1998; Martens & Landers, 1972). The available evidence pertains both to studies in which participants were explicitly instructed to focus their attention on their current functioning, as well as to studies in which focal attention was shifted in a less obtrusive manner.

An example of the first set of studies was provided by Baumeister and Sommer (1997) who discussed research by Hefferline, Keenan, and Halford (1959). In these experiments, participants were conditioned to learn a muscle movement. Some participants were explicitly told that they were being conditioned to learn the movement. Other participants were told, but in a much more ambiguous way. Another group of participants received no information about conditioning of the movement. The results showed that when the participants were told about the goal behind the experiment, they learned considerably slower. In other words, consciously experiencing the movement, or consciously focusing on the movement, obstructed performing this movement.

Examples of studies in which focal attention was manipulated in a less overt manner can be found in the research on self-awareness or self-focus (Carver & Scheier, 1981; Duval & Wicklund, 1972; Gibbons, 1990). In this domain, several manipulations have been used to shift focus to the self, the one most often used being the presence of a mirror. Such manipulations direct attention to the self in a more general way, but they also more specifically focus people on their current behavior (Carver, Blaney, & Scheier, 1979; Carver & Scheier, 1981). As would be expected, such manipulations indeed hamper automatic or automatized actions, ranging from well-learned skills to the application of stereotypes (Baumeister, 1984; Macrae, Bodenhausen, & Milne, 1998).

Although many findings demonstrate that focusing attention explicitly on one's behavior inhibits automatic effects on that behavior, it is not entirely clear how this happens. In order to shed more light on the inhibitory effects of focal attention, it is necessary to first take a closer look at behavioral control in general.

Although several mental processes can operate simultaneously, in parallel, behavior is largely serial in nature (Lashley, 1951). The mind is freed from the constraints of space and time, but the physical body is not (Bargh, 1997). The important consequence of this fact is that behavioral control often necessitates a selection process (Lashley, 1951; Macrae & Johnston, 1998; Norman & Shallice, 1986; Powers, 1973; Vallacher & Wegner, 1985). Such a selection process does not have to be active under all circumstances. If there is only one behavioral cue salient at a given point in time, action control can proceed without the need for selection. In our view, social perception provides such cues that often operate without competition. We behave in line with activated percepts (such as traits or stereotypes) as long as no alternative behavioral impulses (such as generated by active goals) compete for action control. In a sense, percepts can be seen as "default" cues, guiding overt behavior in the absence of conscious goals or other potential competitors.

Under many other circumstances, however, a selection process is called for because multiple behavioral cues are competing for action control. Our claim is that attention focused on one's behavior instigates such a behavioral selection process. Carver and Scheier (1981) noted that one of the consequences of self-focus is to make alternative behavioral cues salient. The implication is that focal attention changes the mental landscape from one in which there is only one behavioral cue salient (such as a percept), to one in which a selection process is needed because there are multiple salient possibilities. In other words, attention focused on one's behavior causes a behavioral "time-out."

Now, if attention instigates a process of behavioral selection, the question to be answered is: how does such a selection process work? What criteria are applied to determine which cue will eventually gain control over action and which cues will not? First of all, it is likely that a conscious selection process primarily selects among behavioral options that are very salient and that are available to conscious awareness—especially those options that fit the actor's "theory" as to appropriate behavioral options in that situation (Wilson & Brekke, 1994). This means that when conscious control takes over, it is likely that passive perceptual cues to behavior are no longer among the options, because they are not part of anyone's theory as to appropriate action within a situation (as shown by responses during debriefing by subjects in the Chartrand & Bargh, 1999, studies).

But there is another logical reason why perceptual cues may no longer play a role when conscious selection processes kick in. The purpose of these nonconscious guides to action (such as caused by the perception-behavior link) is to provide a default or "natural" behavioral response in the absence of conscious choice and selection (see Bargh, 1997; Bargh & Chartrand, 1999). It follows that perceptual cues to behavior do not take part in the selection process or are inhibited at a very early stage. They are nonconscious sources of behavior, and there would be little point or reason for us to possess additional conscious control or selection processes if the latter were dominated by the default nonconscious or automatic input (see, e.g., Posner & Snyder, 1975).

The idea that passive, automatic cues are inhibited immediately as soon as behavioral selection is called for was already proposed by James (1890) and is also consistent with more recent treatments of action control. Norman and Shallice (1986), for instance, argue that the outcome of a behavioral selection process is best captured in terms of activation levels. The higher the activation level of a given cue, the higher the probability that this cue wins the battle for dominance and guides action. Importantly, dominant cues actively inhibit cues with a lower activation level (Norman & Shallice, 1986; Shallice, 1988; see also Powers, 1973). So if we are willing to assume that behavioral options that are consciously available (e.g., those generated by important goals) have a higher activation level than percepts that are bypassing consciousness altogether (e.g, stereotypes), one would indeed predict that effects of perception on behavior are eliminated as soon as consciousness takes over.

To summarize, we propose that focusing attention on one's behavior inhibits access of perceptual cues to the behavioral motorium by making alternative behavioral possibilities salient. This enhanced salience of multiple cues instigates a selection process, and such a selection process will eliminate automatic behavioral tendencies through their active inhibition. We can apply this idea to the research on the perception link by using an example. In an earlier experiment, participants were induced to walk slower by the activation of the stereotype of the elderly (Bargh et al., 1996, Experiment 2). In the absence of any competing behavioral cues, people indeed walked more slowly. However, we hypothesize that when people focus their attention on their behavior, alternative behavioral cues become salient ("I have to go to the dentists,'" "I'm thirsty," "Let's go shopping."). This creates the need for a selection process, an active control process that inhibits the access of passive "default" cues to the motorium. The selection process itself, in other words, inhibits the effects of the activated stereotype on people's walking speed. (Note that such an alternative cue does not have to be "competing" in the sense that its behavioral consequences must be the opposite of that of the activated stereotype or trait.)

In the remainder of this chapter, we will report experiments aimed at testing our central hypothesis that a shift of focal attention toward one's current behavior is enough to override the effects of perception on this behavior. The first two experiments are also reported in Dijksterhuis and van Knippenberg (2000). The latter two are discussed here for the first time.

☐ Self-Focus and the Perception-Behavior Link: Two Studies

As pointed our earlier, several relevant studies have shown that heightened self-focus hinders the execution of various automatized actions (see, e.g., Baumeister, 1984; Baumeister & Showers, 1986; Carver & Scheier, 1981). Our more general hypothesis about the consequences of attentional focus is partly based on these findings. For this reason, the first test of our hypothesis was done with a "classic" self-focus manipulation. The question addressed is: are the effects of perception on behavior eliminated under conditions of heightened self-focus?

In the first study, we used as the perceptual manipulation the stereotype of politicians. In an extensive pilot study, we assessed the stereotypes of a large number of social groups, and politicians were shown to be associated with long-windedness. As one of our students reported, "They always talk a lot without saying anything." Based on this observation, we predicted that passive activation of the stereotype of politicians in our participants would lead to their talking or writing longer than would a control group. This prediction was tested by asking participants to write an essay about a political topic (the French nuclear testing program); we subsequently counted the number of words each participant wrote. We compared participants primed with politicians with no-prime control participants to test whether activating the stereotype of politicians would indeed lead to corresponding behavior (i.e., writing longer essays). Priming was accomplished using the standard "scrambled sentence" procedure (Srull & Wyer, 1979, 1980), in which words related to the focal trait concept or stereotype are unobtrusively presented to participants in the form of a sentence comprehension task.

Half of the participants were seated in front of a mirror in order to raise their level of self-focus (cf. Duval & Wicklund, 1972). The remaining participants were not seated in front of a mirror. Based on the hypothesis that heightened self-focus should eliminate effects of social perception on behavior, we expected that participants primed with the stereotype of politicians would write longer essays than no-prime control participants, but only under the absence of self-focus. A 2 (priming: yes vs. no) × 2 (self-focus: high vs. normal) analysis of variance on the length of the essays confirmed our predictions. First of all, in the absence of self-focus, activation of the stereotype of politicians led to longer essays ($M = 123$ words) relative to essays written under no-prime control conditions ($M = 102$). However, no such difference emerged between politician-primed participants ($M = 104$) and no-prime controls ($M = 109$) in the presence of a mirror. Heightened self-focus successfully overruled the effects of the primed stereotype.

In a second study, we made use of the stereotypes of professors and soccer hooligans. In earlier work (Dijksterhuis & van Knippenberg, 1998), we showed that activation of these stereotypes could improve (in the case of professors) or impair (in the case of hooligans) intellectual performance. In these studies, participants were asked to think about either professors or hooligans for a few minutes, after which they were asked to answer 42 multiple choice general knowledge questions (taken from the game Trivial Pursuit). Relative to participants who were not primed, professor-primed participants performed better, whereas hooligan-primed participants performed worse. In the present study, our aim was to replicate this effect with the added feature of a heightened self-focus manipulation.

An advantage of the use of both a positive and a negative stereotype within the same study is that we could rule out an alternative explanation for the findings of the previous experiment. There is a large literature showing that self-focus is related to self-regulation (see Carver & Scheier, 1981; Gibbons, 1990; Higgins, 1996). Under conditions of heightened self-focus, people are generally inclined to bring their behavior in line with their norms and values. Hence, under these conditions, it can be argued that people will be less likely to engage in antinormative behavior. Long-windedness is presumably perceived as undesirable by most people. With the use of both a positive and a negative stereotype, we would be able to show that self-focus overrides behavior in line with perceptually activated constructs in general, for socially valued and "positive" behavior as well as socially negative (undesirable, "antinormative") behavior.

The participants were either asked to think about professors or hooligans for 5 minutes. Afterwards, they were presented with a questionnaire containing 42 general knowledge questions ("Who painted *La Guernica*?" "What is the capital of Bangladesh?"). Importantly, some participants were facing a mirror throughout the experiment, while others were not. The results confirmed the results of the previous study. In the absence of heightened self-focus, participants primed with professor-related stimuli ($M = 56\%$ correct answers) outperformed those primed with hooligan-related material ($M = 42\%$). Under self-focus conditions, however, these effects of stereotype activation on intellectual performance completely disappeared (for hooligan condition, $M = 50\%$; for professor condition, $M = 49\%$). Once again, self-focus eliminated the effects of social perception on social behavior.

These findings demonstrate that a shift in attentional focus toward one's current functioning can inhibit the execution of automatic behavior. Once automatically activated actions become the focal object of attention, a "behavioral time-out" is called for, and the execution of these actions is blocked.

☐ Awareness of Priming and the Perception-Behavior Link: Two Further Studies

Our hypothesis entails that any shift in attention toward one's current functioning has the ability to override automatic behavior. One straightforward way to achieve this attention shift is to make experimental participants aware of the fact that they are primed and that this prime has potential behavioral consequences. Such a manipulation should lead participants to shift their attention to their current behavior, making alternative behavioral cues salient and forcing a behavior selection process that would inhibit the effects of stereotype activation on behavior. Two experiments were conducted to test this assumption.

In the first experiment, participants were seated in a cubicle in which 15 mundane objects happen to be placed (a bag, a poster, a cup, etc.). The experimenter called no attention to the objects; instead, participants were asked to answer some questions presented to them via the computer screen. After about 2 minutes, participants were asked to start a second task and were requested to move to a different cubicle. Here, they were given a blank sheet of paper and were given a surprise free-recall task concerning the previous room. Specifically, they were asked to list as many of the objects they had seen in the previous cubicle as possible.

There were three different experimental conditions. In the no-prime control condition, participants answered questions pertaining to university students. In the prime condition, participants answered questions about the elderly. Our hypothesis was that participants in this condition should show poorer recall of the objects, based on the stereotype of elderly as forgetful and the behavioral effects of its activation. In a third condition, participants were also primed with the stereotype of the elderly, but these participants were also told that they had been primed with elderly related thoughts, and that this procedure is known to change behavior. This information was given prior to the recall task but after participants had left the cubicle containing the objects to be recalled. In this condition, we expected that the effects of the activation of the elderly stereotype on memory performance would be eliminated.

The results confirmed our hypothesis. First of all, participants in the no-prime control condition listed more objects ($M = 2.5$) than did participants who were primed with the elderly stereotype but were unaware of the potential consequences of the priming ($M = 1.5$). This replicates the standard effect of stereotype priming on behavior. However, primed participants who were made aware of the possible consequences of the prime showed the same memory performance ($M = 2.5$) as did no-prime control participants. In sum, the findings confirm the assumption that awareness of the potential behavioral effects of the priming manipulation would focus attention on one's behavior, thus eliminating the effects of the stereotype on behavior.

Of course, it is possible that participants who were made aware of the prime and its consequences became more motivated to do their best. It is very well possible that they were reactant ("I'm not going to let these people mess around with my memory"), which may have caused them to put more effort into retrieving the objects. A second study was therefore designed in order to rule out this alternative explanation.

In this experiment, participants performed a lexical decision task. They were presented with 30 letter strings—15 actual words and 15 nonword random letter strings—and responded to each as to whether it was a word or a nonword. Participants were primed (or not) during the course of this task. All 30 targets were preceded by words presented subliminally for 15 milliseconds each. For half of the participants, these prime words were related to the elderly stereotype (e.g., old, gray, conservative, etc.). For the remaining participants, these words were unrelated to the elderly stereotype. After completion of the lexical decision task, participants were asked to recall as many of the 15 existing words as they could.

Importantly, we added another manipulation to the design. Half of the participants—in both the prime condition and the no-prime control condition—were informed before the recall task that they had been primed with the elderly stereotype during the lexical decision task and that these primes may have effects on their retrieval. In sum, we had four experimental conditions. In one condition, participants were not primed. In a second condition, people were primed with the stereotype of the elderly. In a third condition, people were not primed but they were told that they had been primed with the stereotype of the elderly and that their memory performance may have been affected. And finally, in a fourth condition people were primed and were also told that they had been primed and that their memory performance may have been affected. If it is the case that making people aware of the priming episode leads to more motivation to do well, participants who were told that they were primed should outperform those who were not given this information, both under conditions of actual priming and under conditions of no actual priming. In other words, this explanation would be corroborated if we obtained a main effect of awareness of the prime (in addition to a main effect of the prime itself).

If, however, as we expect, awareness of the prime works to focus attention on one's behavior, and not to increase motivation to do well, the pattern should be different. Primed participants who were made aware of the prime should outperform those who were not made aware, as in the first experiment. But participants who were not primed should show the same results regardless of whether they are told that they were primed or not. According to our hypothesis, then, one would expect a two-way interaction.

And this is what we found. Among those participants who were not told that they had been primed, those who had indeed been primed with the elderly stereotype showed a deterioration in retrieval ($M = 2.8$ words) compared to participants who had not been primed ($M = 5.3$). As in the previous experiment, participants who had been primed and who were told that they were primed showed no signs of any priming influence on their recall ($M = 4.8$). Most critically, participants who had not been primed but who were told that they had been primed did not perform better ($M =$

4.0) than participants who were not primed and who were not told that they were primed. This rules out the motivational alternative explanation for the first experiment, because only for the primed participants did informing them of the potential deleterious effects of the priming improve memory performance.

☐ Mackerels with Moderators

Taken together, these experiments show that activation of a stereotype elicits corresponding behavior, but that as soon as one's behavior becomes the focal object of one's attention, the effects of stereotype activation on behavior are eliminated. To reiterate, we assume that focal attention leads to the salience of alternative behavioral cues. The conscious act of selection forced by having more than one salient behavioral option, in turn, inhibits the behavioral representations associated with the activated stereotype. As a result, the stereotype no longer serves to passively guide behavior. Perception does determine behavior, but not inevitably—at least not for human beings.

So, are people like mackerels? Yes and no. We are similar in the sense that there is a direct and express connection between our perception and our behavior. On the other hand, evolution has provided us with moderators, such as focal attention and motivation, that enable us to override the direct effects of perception on behavior. Of course, it is possible that the behavior of mackerels too is moderated by focal attention, but we believe that this is a red herring.[2]

☐ Notes

[1]Or, as Gilbert (1989) described it, "a reptilian weenie wrapped in a neocortical bun."

[2]It is possible to state the conclusion of this chapter formally: Human = Mackerel + Moderator. The benefit of such an equation is that such simple mathematical tranformations can lead to penetrating new insights. For instance, it follows from our equation that: Mackerel = Human − Moderator. Another transformation can be useful in classes. When an undergraduate asks you to explain what the technical term "moderator" entails, one may present the straightforward equation: Moderator = Human − Mackerel.

☐ References

Bargh, J. A. (1994). The four horsemen of automaticity: Awareness, intention, efficiency and control in social cognition. In R. S. Wyer, Jr. & T. K. Srull (Eds.), *The handbook of social cognition, Vol. 2, Basic Processes* (pp. 1–40). Hillsdale, NJ: Erlbaum.

Bargh, J. A. (1997). The automaticity of everyday life. In R. S. Wyer, Jr. (Ed.), *Advances in Social Cognition, 10,* 1–61. Hillsdale, NJ: Erlbaum.

Bargh, J. A., & Chartrand, T. L. (1999). The unbearable automaticity of being. *American Psychologist, 54,* 462–479.

Bargh, J. A., Chen, M., & Burrows, L. (1996). The automaticity of social behavior: Direct effects of trait concept and stereotype activation on action. *Journal of Personality and Social Psychology, 71,* 230–244.

Bargh, J. A., & Ferguson, M. (in press). The machine in the ghost: The social-cognitive psychology of automatic human behavior. *Psychological Bulletin.*

Bargh, J. A., & Gollwitzer, P. M. (1994). Environmental control over goal-directed action. *Nebraska Symposium on Motivation, 41,* 71–124.

Baumeister, R. F. (1984). Choking under pressure: Self-consciousness and paradoxical effects of incentives on skillful performance. *Journal of Personality and Social Psychology, 46,* 610–620.

Baumeister, R. F., & Showers, C. J. (1986). A review of paradoxical performance effects: Choking under pressure in sports and mental tests. *European Journal of Social Psychology, 16,* 361–383.

Baumeister, R. F., & Sommer, K. L. (1997). Consciousness, free choice, and automaticity. In R. S. Wyer, Jr. (Ed.), *Advances in Social Cognition, 10,* 75–81. Hillsdale, NJ: Erlbaum.

Carpenter, W. B. (1888). *Principles of mental physiology.* New York: D. Appleton.

Carver, C. S., Blaney, P. H., & Scheier, M. F. (1979). Focus of attention, chronic expectancy, and response to a feared stimulus. *Journal of Personality and Social Psychology, 37,* 1186–1195.

Carver, C. S., Ganellen, R. J., Froming, W. J., & Chambers, W. (1983). Modeling: An analysis in terms of category accessibility. *Journal of Experimental Social Psychology, 19,* 403–421.

Carver, C. S., & Scheier, M. F. (1981). *Attention and self-regulation: A control-theory approach to human behavior.* New York: Springer-Verlag.

Chartrand, T. L., & Bargh, J. A. (1999). The chameleon effect: How the perception-behavior link facilitates social interaction. *Journal of Personality and Social Psychology, 76,* 893–910.

Chen, M., & Bargh, J.A. (1997). Nonconscious behavioral confirmation processes: The self-fulfilling nature of automaticity-activated stereotypes. *Journal of Experimental Social Psychology, 33,* 541–560.

Devine, P. G. (1989). Stereotypes and prejudice: Their automatic and controlled components. *Journal of Personality and Social Psychology, 56,* 5–18.

Dijksterhuis, A., Aarts, H., Bargh, J. A., & van Knippenberg, A. (1999). *Direct experience, stereotype strength, and automatic behavior.* Unpublished manuscript, University of Nijmegen.

Dijksterhuis, A., Aarts, H., Bargh, J. A., & Van Knippenberg, A. (in press). On the relation between associative strength and automatic behavior. *Journal of Experimental Social Psychology.*

Dijksterhuis, A., Spears, R., Postmes, T., Stapel, D. A., Koomen, W., van Knippenberg, A., & Scheepers, D. (1998). Seeing one thing and doing another: Contrast effects in automatic behavior. *Journal of Personality and Social Psychology, 75,* 862–871.

Dijksterhuis, A., & van Knippenberg, A. (1998). The relation between perception and behavior, or how to win a game of Trivial Pursuit. *Journal of Personality and Social Psychology, 74,* 865–877.

Dijksterhuis, A., & van Knippenberg, A. (in press). Behavioral indecision: Effects of self-focus on automatic behavior. *Social Cognition.*

Duval, S., & Wicklund, R. A. (1972). *A theory of objective self-awareness.* San Diego: Academic Press.

Eidelberg, L. (1929). Experimenteller Beitrag zum Mechanismus der Imitationsbewegung. *Jahresbücher für Psychiatrie und Neurologie, 46,* 170–173.

Gibbons, F. X. (1990). Self-attention and behavior: A review and theoretical update. In L. Berkowitz (Ed.), *Advances in experimental social psychology* (Vol. *23,* pp. 249–303). New York: Academic Press.

Gilbert, D. T. (1989). Thinking lightly about others: Automatic components of the social inference process. In J. S. Uleman & J. A. Bargh (Eds.), *Unintended thought* (pp. 189–211). New York: Guilford Press.

Hefferline, R. F., Keenan, B., & Harford, R. A. (1959). Escape and avoidance conditioning in human subjects without their observation of the response. *Science, 130,* 1338–1339.

Higgins, E. T. (1996). The "self-digest": Self-knowledge serving self-regulatory functions. *Journal of Personality and Social Psychology, 71,* 1062–1083.

James, W. (1890). *Principles of psychology.* New York: Holt.

Jastrow, J. (1906). *The subconscious.* Boston: Houghton-Mifflin.

Kimble, G., & Perlmuter, L. (1970). The problem of volition. *Psychological Review, 77,* 361–384.

Koestler, A. (1967). *The ghost in the machine.* London: Hutchinson.

Langer, E. (1978). Rethinking the role of thought in social interaction. In J. Harvey, W. Ickes, & R. Kidd (Eds.), *New directions in attribution research* (Vol. 2, pp. 35–58). Hillsdale, NJ: Erlbaum.

Lashley, K. S. (1951). The problem of serial order in behavior. In L. A. Jeffress (Ed.), *Cerebral mechanisms in behavior: The Hixon Symposium* (pp. 112–136). New York: Wiley.

Le Bon, G. (1895). *The crowd: A study of the popular mind.* New York: Viking.

Macrae, C. N., Bodenhausen, G. V., & Milne, A. B. (1998). Saying no to unwanted thoughts: The role of self-awareness in the regulation of mental life. *Journal of Personality and Social Psychology, 74,* 578–589.

Macrae, C. N., & Johnston, L. (1998). Help, I need somebody: Automatic action and inaction. *Social Cognition, 16,* 400–417.

Martens, R., & Landers, D. M. (1972). Evaluation potential as a determinant of coaction effects. *Journal of Experimental Social Psychology, 8,* 347–359.

Müsseler, J., & Hommel, B. (1997). Blindness to response-compatible stimuli. *Journal of Experimental Psychology: Human Perception and Performance, 23,* 861–872.

Norman, D. A., & Shallice, T. (1986). Attention to action: Willed and automatic control of behavior. In R. J. Davidson, G. E. Schwartz, & D. Shapiro (Eds.), *Consciousness and self-regulation: Advances in research and theory* (Vol. 4, pp. 1–18). New York: Plenum Press.

Pitcher, T. J. (1983). Heuristic definitions in fish shoaling behavior. *Animal Behavior, 31,* 611–613.

Posner, M. I., & Snyder, C. R. R. (1975). Attention and cognitive control. In R. L. Solso (Ed.), *Information processing and cognition: The Loyola Symposium* (pp. 55–58). Hillsdale, NJ: Erlbaum.

Powers, W. T. (1973). *Behavior: The control of perception.* Chicago: Aldine.

Prinz, W. (1990). A common coding approach to perception and action. In O. Neumann & W. Prinz (Eds.), *Relationships between perception and action* (pp. 167–201). Berlin: Springer-Verlag.

Shallice, T. (1988). *From neuroscience to mental structure.* New York: Cambridge University Press.

Srull, T. K., & Wyer, R. S., Jr. (1979). The role of category accessibility in the interpretation of information about persons: Some determinants and implications. *Journal of Personality and Social Psychology, 37,* 1660–1672.

Srull, T. K., & Wyer, R. S., Jr. (1980). Category accessibility and social perception: Some implications for the study of person memory and interpersonal judgments. *Journal of Personality and Social Psychology, 38,* 841–856.

Tarde, G. (1903). *The laws of imitation.* New York: Holt.

Vallacher, R. R., & Wegner, D. M. (1985). *A theory of action identification.* Hillsdale, NJ: Erlbaum.

Wilson, T. D., & Brekke, N. (1994). Mental contamination and mental correction: Unwanted influences on judgments and evaluations. *Psychological Bulletin, 116,* 117–142.

Winter, L., & Uleman, J. S. (1984). When are social judgments made? Evidence for the spontaneousness of trait inferences. *Journal of Personality and Social Psychology, 47,* 237–252.

Roland Neumann
Fritz Strack

CHAPTER 4

Experiential and Nonexperiential Routes of Motor Influence on Affect and Evaluation

This chapter focuses on motor influences on affect and evaluation. Previous research has shown that the impact of facial, postural, and behavioral expressions on judgment and evaluation is experientially mediated. This research was inspired by the so-called "facial feedback theory," which holds that feelings are not only a cause but also a consequence of specific motor programs. However, recent research suggests that motor programs can also influence affective processes without a mediating experience. It is therefore necessary to distinguish between two different routes of motor influences that serve different functions: a fast route that triggers either the approach or the avoidance system, and a slow route through which subjective experiences mediate motor influences on evaluative judgments. The following chapter describes the two routes of motor influences and discusses the implications of drawing a distinction between them.

☐ Feeling and Knowing

Phenomenal experiences play an important role in our daily life. Perceptual experiences, for example, constitute the interface between individual

Address correspondence to Roland Neumann and Fritz Strack, Lehrstuhl Psychologie II, Universität Würzburg, Röntgenring 10, 97070 Würzburg, Germany. E-mail: neumann@ psychologie.uni-wuerzburg.de and strack@psychologie.uni-wuerzburg.de

and environment, and an unbiased image of external events guarantees successful interaction. Although we are used to trusting our senses, there are occasions in which we are deluded. For instance, when we come from a bright place outside into a dark room, one might at first gain the impression that the room is darker than it might be after a short while. To the extent that we know that this phenomenon is a result of adaptation of cells in the retina, judgments of the brightness might not be based on this immediate experience. Instead, one might use her or his knowledge about adaptation to correct the judgment. Importantly, however, although one might know that her or his senses are deceived, the experience remains unchanged.

Such illusions illustrate that occasionally one's knowledge and one's experience are in conflict. Because experience can be conceived of as a necessary component of feelings, similar conflicts can arise between what one *knows* and what one *feels*. These conflicts can occur because feelings and knowledge possess different properties. To take these different properties into account, we have suggested that knowledge and feelings hinge on different mental representations (Strack & Gonzales, 1993; Strack & Neumann, 1996). Feelings predominantly rely on experiential representations that may vary in intensity and cannot be "true" or "false." In contrast, knowledge is coded in noetic representations that are activated in an all-or-none fashion and have a definite truth value. Thus, noetic representation can be characterized by using what we know about associative memory. Experiential representations, however, possess perceptual properties in that they are, for example, subject to adaptation (Helson, 1964). Because of these perceptual qualities, one should have conscious access to these representations. Noetic representations, on the other hand, do not necessarily have to possess this property. Similar assumptions about the representation format of feelings and knowledge were advocated by Buck (1980) and Johnson and Multhaup (1992). Note, however, that the assumption that feelings and knowledge are represented differently diverges from conceptualizations that propose a common representation for both mental entities (e.g., Bower, 1981).

☐ Experientially Mediated Motor Influences

As a subset of subjective experiences, feelings are immediately given and refer to perceptual experiences (Strack & Neumann, 1996). Many approaches have proposed that feelings arise from different forms of cognitive processing (for an overview, see Clore, Schwarz, & Conway, 1994). For example, emotions can be conceived of as an end product of the evaluation of the significance of one's circumstances (e.g. Lazarus, 1984;

Roseman, 1984), whereas so-called cognitive or nonaffective feelings—like familiarity or the feeling of knowing—are a byproduct of cognitive processing (Koriat, 1994; Miner & Reder, 1994).

However, cognitive processes are not the only source of feelings. Motor programs such as facial, postural, and behavioral expressions can also elicit feelings. According to William James's (1890) well-known assertion, emotional experience follows, rather than precedes, emotional behavior. Charles Darwin (1872/1965) advanced a somewhat similar view, arguing that bodily expressions might intensify feelings, while their suppression might attenuate them. By now, considerable evidence has accumulated in support of the assumption that facial and postural expressions can exert an influence on subjective feelings (for a review, see Adelman & Zajonc, 1989). Dissenting views, however, exist on how these expressions influence emotional responses. Laird (1974) has advocated the view that a self-perception process mediates the impact of expressions on subjective experience. According to this position, individuals have to infer their subjective experience from their expression when internal cues are weak. One important precondition for such inferences to occur is that people be aware of the meaning of their facial expression.

A number of non-inferential mediating mechanisms have been proposed as an alternative view (Buck, 1980; Ekman, Levenson, & Friesen, 1983; Levenson, 1992). Several studies do, indeed, support this approach, suggesting that expressions are capable of eliciting feelings even in the absence of an inferential process. In one such study, Strack, Martin, and Stepper (1988) manipulated the contraction of the zygomaticus muscle while subjects rated cartoons on their funniness. For this purpose, participants had to hold a pen in their mouth, which either facilitated or inhibited smiling. More specifically, one group held the pen between their teeth (facilitating smiling), whereas the other group held it between their lips (inhibiting smiling). Although participants did not recognize the meaning of their facial expression, they judged cartoons to be funnier when smiling was facilitated than when smiling was inhibited. In a similar vein, Zajonc, Murphy, and Inglehart (1989) demonstrated that pronouncing vowels that required participants to either facilitate smiling (pronouncing the vowel "e") or inhibit smiling (pronouncing the German vowel "ü") exerted a congruent impact on the speakers' affective experiences. In sum, these studies demonstrate that it is not necessary for an individual to recognize the meaning of an activated motor program for it to influence the subjective experience. Hence, inferential processes do not necessarily mediate motor influences on feelings.

Expressions can influence not only affective feelings, but nonaffective feelings as well. For example, furrowing the brow might induce the feeling of mental effort (Larsen, Kasimatis, & Frey, 1992; Stepper & Strack,

1993; Strack & Neumann, in press). Moreover, such proprioceptive influences on subjective feelings are documented not only for facial actions, but also for postures. Stepper and Strack (1993) observed that success in an achievement task resulted in more elevated feelings of pride when the positive feedback was received in an upright as opposed to a slumped position.

Feelings induced by specific motor actions can be the basis for subsequent judgments. The unobtrusive manipulation of the human smile, as developed by Strack et al. (1988), for example, has been shown to influence such diverse judgments as the perceived guilt of a person (Bodenhausen, Kramer, & Süsser, 1994), the evaluation of an ambiguous social situation (Martin, Harlow, & Strack, 1992), and the impression made by a job applicant (Berkowitz, Jaffee, Jo, & Troccolli, 1999). Moreover, the feeling of mental effort induced by furrowing the brow influenced judgments about one's own self-assertiveness (Stepper & Strack, 1993) and judgments of fame (Strack & Neumann, in press).

Taken together, these findings suggest that the influence of motor programs on evaluative and nonevaluative judgments is mediated by feelings. The underlying mechanism apparently operates without a semantic categorization and without syllogistic inferences.

☐ Nonexperientially Mediated Motor Influences

Interestingly, however, recent research suggests that subjective experiences and feelings do not always mediate motor influences on evaluative judgments. Several studies have demonstrated that the isometric flexion and extension of the upper arm influences evaluative processes in the absence of affective experiences (Cacioppo, Priester, & Berntson, 1993; Förster & Strack, 1997; Priester, Cacioppo, & Petty, 1996). In one of these studies, neutral Chinese ideographs presented during arm flexion were subsequently evaluated more favorably than ideographs presented during arm extension (Cacioppo, Priester, & Berntson, 1993). Because arm flexion is usually more closely coupled temporally with the consumption of desired goods, the authors argue that movements toward the body, such as arm flexion, can be interpreted as approach behavior, whereas movements of the hand away from the body can be interpreted as avoidance behavior. Most importantly, participants did not report having any affective experience as an effect of the muscle contraction.

In a similar vein, head movements were shown to exert an influence on evaluative judgments without a mediating affective experience. Wells and Petty (1980) asked participants to move their head either horizontally or vertically while being exposed to a persuasive message. Such head movements are habitually performed in Western cultures to indicate agreement or disagreement. Wells and Petty (1980) found that moving the head horizontally while listening to persuasive messages led to more negative attitude, while nodding the head vertically resulted in a more positive attitude toward the attitude object.

More recently, Förster and Strack (1996) demonstrated that these movements might also exert an influence on recognition performance. They found that participants who were induced to move their head vertically while encoding positive and negative words showed enhanced recognition of positive words. In contrast, participants who moved their head horizontally while encoding were better at recognizing negative words. Further analysis revealed that this effect was due to discrimination whether a word was presented in the learning list, but not to a response bias. This enhanced ability to discriminate words that are compatible with the currently activated motor program was not mediated by a change in the subjective experiences. Förster and Strack (1996) found no evidence that head movements influenced affective experience.

In sum, a variety of movements exerts similar influences on evaluative judgments and memory performance. Although behavior is highly varied, many researchers regard its motivational basis as having a much simpler, two-factor organization (Cacioppo, Gardner, & Berntson, 1997; Davidson, Ekman, Saron, Senulis, & Friesen, 1990; Lang, Bradley, & Cuthbert, 1990; Miller, 1959). According to these models, the motivation to approach pleasant objects and withdraw from unpleasant or hostile objects possesses a central function in the regulation of one's needs. For example, Lang et al. (1990) argue that behavior is driven by two distinct motivational circuits that direct the deployment of primitive approach and withdrawal behavior. In line with this notion, it is reasonable to assume that the cognitive and behavioral components are closely interconnected within each of these two separate motivational systems.

Drawing on these assumptions, it is possible to maintain that the link between affect and motor action might be bidirectional. In fact, there is a considerable amount of evidence that the predisposition for approach or avoidance varies depending on the valence of the processed information. For example, Lang et al. (1990) demonstrated in several studies that defensive reflexes, which can be regarded as a predisposition for overt avoidance responses, are differentially modulated by the valence of currently processed affective information. More specifically, they found that the amplitudes of the blink reflex elicited by startle probes are augmented if affectively negative pictures are the focus of processing. In contrast, if affectively positive information is processed, the blink reflex will show relative inhibition. The two motivational systems are apparently sensitive to the valence of the affective input. Thus, whenever a motivational system is activated by affective information, the individual is prepared to act accordingly.

Such effects, however, are not restricted to automatic reflexes. Although affective information processing should not automatically elicit behavioral intentions (Bargh, Chen, & Burrows, 1996), it is conceivable that affective information processing might influence the execution of overt behavior. Thus, approach or avoidance movements should be initiated faster toward affectively compatible objects than toward incompatible ones. This assumption was examined in an early study in which participants were required to move cards with words that were mounted on a movable stage either toward or away from themselves (Solarz, 1960). Results revealed that movements toward the body were initiated faster with pleasant than with unpleasant words. In contrast, unpleasant words were pushed away faster than pleasant words.

Likewise, in a recent study by Chen and Bargh (1999), participants had to evaluate words on the computer screen as "good" or "bad" in meaning by either pushing or pulling a lever. Consistent with Solarz's (1960) findings, participants were faster at pulling a lever toward them if they were exposed to affectively positive words. Conversely, pushing a lever was executed faster when negative words appeared on the screen. In a further study, Chen and Bargh (1999) demonstrated that this stimulus-response compatibility effect does not depend on the conscious evaluation of the presented words. Although the word evaluation task was replaced by the task of eliminating the word as soon as it appeared on the screen by either pushing or pulling a lever, the same pattern of results appeared. The authors conclude that the automatic evaluation of objects in our environment has the function of preparing the individual to act even in the absence of goal-directed processing.

Taken together, there is evidence that affective processing directly facilitates compatible and inhibits incompatible approach or avoidance behavior. From that point of view, the pervasiveness of the often-observed automatic evaluation of objects in our environment might serve adaptive purposes insofar as this mechanism might prepare the individual to act appropriately (Chen & Bargh, 1999). Moreover, activated motor programs of approach or avoidance influence affective processing. Thus, decreasing (increasing) the distance toward an object might facilitate (inhibit) the processing of positive affective concepts and inhibit (facilitate) the processing of negative affective concepts. Importantly, it is not necessary that an affective experience emerge from this mechanism. Such an assumption provides a parsimonious and conclusive explanation for the observed motor influences on evaluative judgments (Cacioppo et al., 1993; Wells & Petty, 1980) and recognition (Förster & Strack, 1996). However, up to now, the evidence for such a mechanism has been only indirect, because previous findings allow for the alternative explanation that either categorization or storage processes are influenced by the execution of approach or avoidance behavior.

To provide a test that motor programs associated with approach and avoidance exert an impact on the categorization of affective information, we conducted a study in which participants had to categorize adjectives that appeared on the computer screen (Neumann & Strack, 1999). While classifying words as either "positive" or "negative," participants were required to press one palm either on the top or on the bottom of the table. The manipulation of the palm, which was adopted from Cacioppo et al. (1993), was intended to activate either the approach or the avoidance system. Given that the two motivational systems can be activated by isometric contractions of the upper arm, affective processing should be facilitated in a compatible combination of affect and motivational system. Therefore, we expected participants to be faster in classifying evaluatively positive adjectives while contracting their flexor muscle, and to be faster in categorizing negative adjectives while contracting the tensor muscle.

The results show that participants were indeed faster in categorizing positive words while contracting their flexor muscle (see Figure 4.1). They were also faster in classifying negative words while contracting their tensor muscle. This can be taken as a first piece of evidence that motor programs of approach and avoidance exert a direct impact on the categorization of affective information.

If one assumes that head movements exert the same impact on the categorization task, it is likely that the behavioral input has to be categorized in terms of approach or avoidance in order to exert this influence. As an alternative explanation, Zajonc and Markus (1984) presented a "hard interface" approach, which holds that motor movements in themselves possess a representational function that can influence other representations without a cognitive or experiential mediation. From this point of view, contractions of the tensor or flexor muscle in themselves can be regarded as a representation of movements toward or away from an object, which in turn directly influences evaluative processes.

A divergent prediction for these scenarios can be formulated if we take into account that information about approach and avoidance reflects the change in distance toward an object. Given that the change in distance contains the critical cue that triggers the motivational systems, this information is not only provided by proprioceptive cues, but by visual cues as well. Thus, movement toward or away from an object can be monitored by visual as well as by proprioceptive cues. Therefore, assuming that approach and avoidance movements are centrally mediated, we can formulate the prediction that the two motivational systems are also triggered by visual patterns that signal approach or withdrawal. On the other hand, if

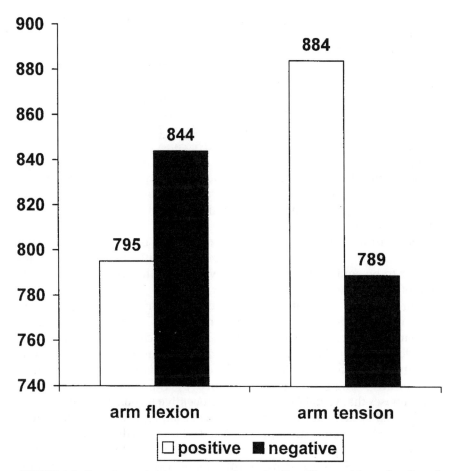

FIGURE 4.1. Experiment 1: Mean response latencies (in milliseconds) as a function of somatic activation and valence of the words.

the information is stored in the muscles themselves, visual cues might be inappropriate to activate the motivational systems.

To test these predictions, the visual impression that one moves either toward or away from the computer screen was induced by a computer simulation. This was achieved through a background of concentric circles, which creates the impression that the observer is moving either forward or backward through a tunnel. The results in a pretest indicated that the impression of movement away from the screen was in fact induced when background circles moved from the center to the edge of the screen, whereas the impression of movement toward the screen was evoked when the background circles moved in the opposite direction. Moreover, participants did not report any reliable changes in their affective experience as an effect of their exposure to the computer simulation.

Because the computer simulation induced the expected impression, we used this procedure to test the assumption that visual cues are equivalent to proprioceptive cues in activating either the approach or avoidance system. We expected that the impression that one is moving toward the computer screen should facilitate the processing of positive concepts, whereas the impression that one is moving away from the computer screen should facilitate the processing of negative concepts.

As Figure 4.2 reveals, positive adjectives were categorized faster than negative adjectives when the background conveys the impression that one is moving toward the computer screen. In contrast, negative adjectives were categorized faster than positive adjectives when the person appeared to be moving away from the computer screen. These findings support our assumption that affective processing is influenced by visual cues that signal approach or avoidance. Apparently, exteroceptive cues appear to be equivalent to interoceptive cues with regard to the elicitation of the two motivational systems.

Moreover, the fact that exteroceptive and proprioceptive cues exerted similar influences on affective processing renders it unlikely that the information about approach and avoidance is exclusively stored in the muscles (Zajonc & Markus, 1984). Rather, it seems that the various sensory inputs of visual and motor cues are projected onto the same dimension of increasing or decreasing distance. Such a conclusion, however, presupposes that visual input and proprioceptive feedback result in internal codes that share at least some aspects of their representational format. In fact, such a claim is strongly supported by findings demonstrating that spatial cues are automatically integrated in the execution of motor programs (Prinz, 1990). Drawing on this line of research, Prinz (1990) suggests that there is a common coding system for action that takes into account the spatial nature of the environment.

In the context of current research, this implies that representations that are sensitive to changes in the distance toward an object trigger motivational systems. The activation of such sensory-motor codes thereby facilitates the processing of compatible affect. However, although the findings presented so far demonstrate the expected congruency effect between motion direction and processed affect, these results are less conclusive about the underlying mechanism. As was previously argued, the activation of either the approach or the avoidance system implies that facilitative and inhibitory influences might be exerted on affective processing. Such an assumption can be derived from the notion that the two motivational systems guide the execution of antagonistic motor programs. That is, one can move toward an object or away from it, but it is impossible to

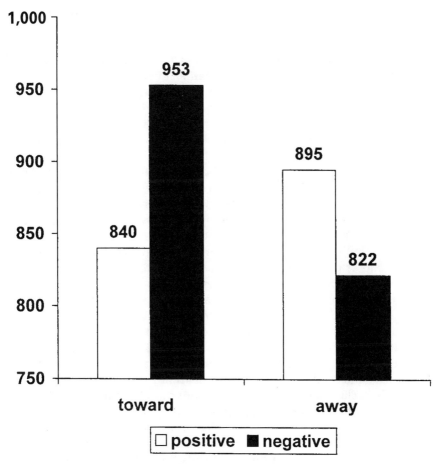

FIGURE 4.2. Experiment 2: Mean response latencies (in milliseconds) as a function of movement direction and valence of the words.

move in both directions simultaneously. Hence, in order to guarantee that movements are executed successfully, it is not enough to activate the intended behavior, but it is also necessary to prevent competing concepts from controlling behavior. This can be achieved by a mechanism that not only activates the dominant action system (Shallice, 1978), but also inhibits the antagonistic response. Lang (1995) speculated whether inhibitory mechanisms might play a role in the context of approach and avoidance behavior. To shed some light on the question of whether both facilitative and inhibitory mechanisms contribute to the obtained effects, a third study was conducted. Here, the same computer simulation was used to induce the impression that one is moving either toward or away from the computer screen. In contrast to the second study, however, a set of neutral target words was included.

Moreover, if the processing of affective information is immediately influenced by the direction of motion, the evaluation task should not play a mediating role. To test whether the obtained effect does not hinge on the intention to evaluate the target words, the evaluation task was replaced by a lexical decision task.

As is evident from Figure 4.3, aside from replicating the basic pattern of our previous findings, we obtained evidence for facilitative and inhibitory effects. That is, subjects responded faster to compatible conditions of affect and motion than to the control condition (neutral words). Incompatible conditions of affect and motion direction, however, drew a slower response than the control condition (neutral words).

In combination, our previous findings clearly suggest that in addition to the experientially mediated influence of motor programs on affective processing, an alternative route of impact seems to exist. Apparently, sensory-motor programs influence affective processing in the absence of any affective feelings. We assume that nonexperiential influences are mediated by two separate motivational systems of approach and avoidance. Supporting evidence comes from the finding that both interoceptive and exteroceptive cues can exert equivalent influences on affective processing. Although the experiments used different kinds of input, apparent movements away from one's own body facilitated the processing of negative information. Conversely, apparent movements toward one's own body facilitated the processing of positive information. Since the only common element between the information provided by interoceptive and exteroceptive cues is the direction of motion, it is likely that a central representation projects the neural information onto the same dimension of increasing or decreasing distance. Thus, in line with Cacioppo et al. (1997), we assume that the motivational systems associated with approach and avoidance operate within the central nervous system.

☐ Implications for Research on Subjective Experience

William James's (1890) claim that emotional experience follows, rather than precedes, emotional behavior has been subject to much criticism (Cannon, 1927). Nevertheless, the basic premise that emotional expressions can influence subjective experience is corroborated by a considerable amount of research. The current chapter has focused on an extension of this view because recent research suggests that aside from specific emotional expressions, broader classes of motor programs exert an influ-

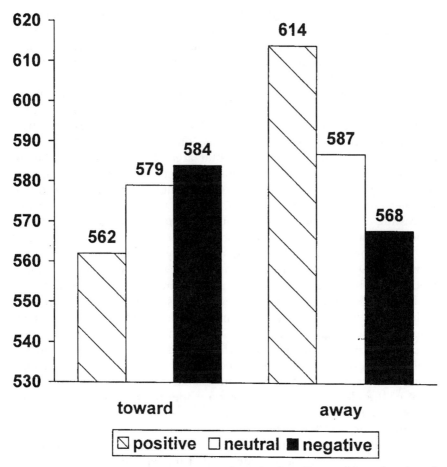

FIGURE 4.3. Experiment 3: Mean response latencies (in milliseconds) as a function of movement direction and valence of the words.

ence on affect and evaluation. In contrast to the traditional view, however, these motor actions influence evaluative judgments and memory performance without a concomitant affective experience. Thus, one might pose the question: what determines whether motor influences on judgments are mediated by a subjective feeling or not? Experiential mediation presupposes that the contributing motor actions are specific to the feeling. Thus, a limited number of expressions are capable to trigger discrete affective and nonaffective feelings (Ekman et al., 1983; Levenson, 1992). In contrast, a nonexperiential mediation might be determined by many different action patterns that map on the approach and avoidance dimension. The fact that approach or avoidance behavior is not specific to a particular feeling state or attitude might explain why this kind of motor action does not evoke subjective experiences. This does mean that unspecific behaviors are not capable of influencing subjective experiences. However, as we will see in the last paragraph of this chapter, in this case different mechanisms trigger the experience.

One important feature of the experiential mediation is that the informational value of feelings can be called into question (Schwarz & Clore, 1996). Relevant research has demonstrated that the influence of affective feelings on evaluative judgments hinges on informational value of the subjective experience for the judgmental target. For example, individuals no longer rely on their subjective mood state to judge their life satisfaction if they recognize that this experience might have been due to the weather (Schwarz & Clore, 1983). Extending this logic to the automatic processing of affect, one might predict that the same discounting effects should be obtained in an affective priming paradigm (Murphy & Zajonc, 1993). This prediction was tested in a study by Winkielman, Zajonc, and Schwarz (1997), in which participants had to evaluate unfamiliar Chinese ideographs that were preceded by a subliminal presentation of either smiling or frowning faces. Furthermore, a misattribution procedure was included in which participants were misinformed about the source of their assumed affective experience to the faces. Consistent with previous findings in affective priming research, they found that the ideographs were evaluated more favorably when preceded by a smiling than a frowning face. However, the misattribution manipulation had no effect on the evaluation of the ideographs. Moreover, no evidence was obtained that the response to the ideographs resulted in an affective experience. One might therefore conclude that a consciously represented experience is a necessary precondition for misattribution effects to occur. Similarly, in none of our studies did we find any evidence that movements toward or away from the body induced affective experiences. Therefore, it is unlikely that motor influences mediated by either the approach or avoidance system could be subject to misattribution.

□ The Mechanisms Underlying Motor Influences

Both routes of motor influences result in phenomenal representations that can be regarded as the outcome of different underlying mechanisms. In this last paragraph, we will describe mechanisms that might mediate motor influences on phenomenal representations. Basically, two different mechanisms can be distinguished: motor actions can either directly trigger phenomenal representations or primarily influence the processing of external stimuli, thereby eliciting a phenomenal representation (see

Figure 4.4). The first mechanism was proposed by James (1890), who assumed that specific expressions might be sufficient to instigate feelings. In support of this assumption, recent research suggests that facial efference can directly evoke feelings (Adelman & Zajonc, 1989). For example, Stepper and Strack (1993) found that the contraction of the corrugator muscle is sufficient to induce the feeling of mental effort. Moreover, there is some evidence that unobtrusively induced smiles might have the potential to induce happy mood in the absence of a humor eliciting stimulus (Bodenhausen et al., 1994; Zajonc, Murphy, & Inglehart, 1989).

The second mechanism, which was first advanced by Darwin (1872/1965), hinges on the combined influence of activated motor actions and external input. Unlike James, Darwin thus argued that motor programs could influence subjective experiences only in combination with an eliciting external event (see Figure 4.4). Support for this assumption comes from the Förster and Strack (1996) study, which demonstrates that the

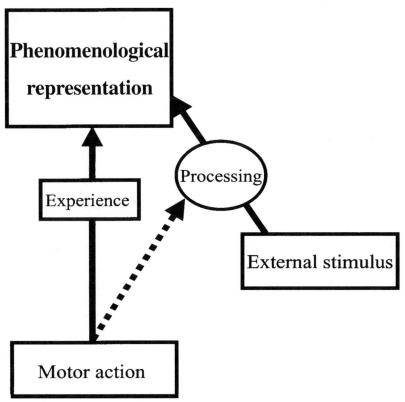

FIGURE 4.4. Two different mechanisms of motor influences on the phenomenological representation.

processing of affective words is influenced by motor actions. Further research reveals that cues signaling approach or avoidance motor actions exert an influence on the categorization of affective information. Therefore, we assumed that the modulating function of motor influences might be due to the activation of either the approach or avoidance system. Moreover, we found that the compatibility mechanism operates automatically (dotted line in Figure 4.4) in that it does not depend on the goal to evaluate the external stimuli (see Figure 4.3) .

Although subjective experiences result from the direct mechanism, this is not necessarily the case for the compatibility mechanism. Whether this mechanism evokes a subjective experience depends on both the activated motor action (see above) and the external input. For example, an upright position alone is not sufficient to elicit the feeling of pride (Stepper & Strack, 1993). Rather, motor actions exert a modulating influence on complex emotions only to the extent that the appropriate information is processed.

This framework provides a parsimonious and conclusive explanation for the observed motor influences in emotion and in attitude research (Adelman & Zajonc, 1989; Cacioppo et al., 1993; Wells & Petty, 1980). Further research has to find out whether the two mediating mechanisms in this framework present complementary rather than conflicted routes of influence. In principle, it might be conceivable that both mechanisms sometimes operate in parallel.

☐ References

Adelmann, P. K., & Zajonc, R. B. (1989). Facial efference and the experience of emotion. *Annual Review of Psychology, 40,* 249–280.

Bargh, J. A., Chen, M., & Burrows, L. (1996). Automaticity of social behavior: Direct effects of trait construct and stereotype activation on action. *Journal of Personality and Social Psychology, 71,* 230–244.

Berkowitz, L., Jaffee, S., Jo, E., & Troccoli, B. T. (1999). On the correction of possible feeling-induced judgmental biases. In J. T. Forgas (Ed.), *Feeling and thinking: The role of affect in social cognition.*

Bodenhausen, G. V., Kramer, G. P., & Süsser, K. (1994). Happiness and stereotypic thinking in social judgment. *Journal of Personality and Social Psychology, 66,* 621–632.

Bower, G. H. (1981). Mood and memory. *Psychology, 36,* 129–148.

Buck, R. (1980). Nonverbal behavior and the theory of emotion: The facial feedback hypotheses. *Journal of Personality and Social Psychology, 38,* 811–824.

Cacioppo, J. T., Gardner, W. L., & Berntson, G. G. (1997). Beyond bipolar conceptualization and measures: The case of attitudes and evaluative space. *Personality and Social Psychology Review, 1,* 3–25.

Cacioppo, J. T., Priester, J. R., & Berntson, G. G. (1993). Rudimentary determinants of attitudes. Arm flexion and extension have differential effects on attitudes. *Journal of Personality and Social Psychology, 65,* 5–17.

Cannon, W. B. (1927). The James-Lange theory of emotions: A critical examination and an alternative theory. *American Journal of Psychology, 39*, 106–112.

Chen, M., & Bargh, J. A. (1999). Consequences of automatic evaluations: Immediate behavioral predispositions to approach or avoid the stimulus. *Personality and Social Psychology Bulletin, 25*, 215–224.

Clore, G., Schwarz, N., & Conway, M. (1994). Affective causes and consequences of social information processing. In R. S. Wyer & T. K. Srull (Eds.), *Handbook of social cognition* (pp. 323–417). Hillsdale, NJ: Erlbaum.

Darwin, C. (1965). *The expression of emotion in man and animals.* Chicago: University of Chicago Press. (Original work published 1872)

Davidson, R. J., Ekman, P., Saron, C. D., Senulis, J. A., & Friesen, W. V. (1990). Approach-withdrawal and cerebral asymmetry: Emotional expression and brain physiology: I. *Journal of Personality and Social Psychology, 58*, 330–341.

Ekman, P., Levenson, R. W., & Friesen, W. V. (1983). Autonomic nervous system activity distinguishes among emotions. *Science, 221*, 1208–1210.

Förster, J., & Strack, F. (1996). Influence of overt head movements on memory for valenced words: A case of conceptual-motor compatibility. *Journal of Personality and Social Psychology, 71*, 421–430.

Förster, J., & Strack, F. (1997). Motor actions in retrieval of valenced information: A motor congruence effect. *Perceptual and Motor Skills, 85*, 1419–1427.

James, W. (1890). *The principles of psychology.* New York: Holt.

Johnson, M. K., & Multhaup, K. S. (1992). Emotion and MEM. In S.-A. Christianson (Ed.), *The handbook of emotion and memory: Research and theory* (pp. 33–66). Hillsdale, NJ: Erlbaum.

Koriat, A. (1994). Memory's knowledge of its own knowledge: The accessibility account of the feeling of knowing. In J. Metcalfe & A. P. Shimamura (Eds.), *Metacognition: Knowing about knowing* (pp. 115–135). Cambridge, MA: MIT Press.

Laird, J. D. (1974). Self-attribution of emotion: The effect of expressive behavior on the quality of the emotional experience. *Journal of Personality and Social Psychology, 22*, 475–486.

Lang, P. J. (1995). The emotion probe: Studies of motivation and attention. *American Psychologist, 50*, 372–385.

Lang, P. J., Bradley, M. M., & Cuthbert, B. N. (1990). Emotion, attention, and the startle reflex. *Psychological Review, 97*, 377–395.

Larsen, R. J., Kasimatis, M., & Frey, K. (1992). Facilitating the furrowed brow: An unobtrusive test of the facial feedback hypothesis applied to unpleasant affect. *Cognition and Emotion, 6*, 321–338.

Lazarus, R. S. (1984). On the primacy of cognition. *American Psychologist, 39*, 124–129.

Levenson, R. W. (1992). Autonomic nervous system differences among emotions. *Psychological Science, 3*, 23–27.

Martin, L. L., Harlow, T. F., & Strack, F. (1992). The role of bodily sensations in the evaluation of social events. *Personality and Social Psychology Bulletin, 18*, 412–419.

Miller, N. E. (1959). Liberalization of basic S-R concepts: Extensions to conflict behavior, motivation, and social learning. In S. Koch (Ed.), *Psychology: A study of science, Study 1* (pp. 198–292). New York: McGraw-Hill.

Miner, A. C., & Reder, L. M. (1994). A new look at feeling of knowing: Its metacognitive role in regulating question answering. In J. Metcalfe & A. P. Shimamura (Eds.), *Metacognition: Knowing about knowing* (pp. 47–70). Cambridge, MA: MIT Press.

Murphy, S. T., & Zajonc, R. B. (1993). Affect, cognition, and awareness: Priming with optimal and suboptimal stimulus exposures. *Journal of Personality and Social Psychology, 64*, 723–739.

Neumann, R., & Strack, F. (1999). *Approach and avoidance: The influence of proprioceptive and exteroceptive cues on encoding of affective information.* Unpublished Manuscript.

Priester, J. R., Cacioppo, J. T., & Petty, R. E. (1996). The influence of motor processes on attitudes toward novel versus familiar semantic stimuli. *Personality and Social Psychology Bulletin, 22,* 442–447.

Prinz, W. (1990). A common coding approach to perception and action. In O. Neumann & W. Prinz (Eds.), *Relationships between perception and action* (pp. 167–201). Berlin: Springer.

Roseman, I. J. (1984). Cognitive determinants of emotion: A structural theory. In P. Shaver (Ed.), *Review of personality and social psychology: Vol. 5. Emotions, relationships, and health* (pp. 11–36). Beverly Hills, CA: Sage.

Schwarz, N., & Clore, G. L. (1983). Mood, misattribution, and judgments of well-being: Informative and directive functions of affective states. *Journal of Personality and Social Psychology, 45,* 513–523.

Schwarz, N., & Clore, G. L. (1996). Feelings and phenomenal experiences. In E. T. Higgins & A. W. Kruglanski (Eds.), *Social psychology: Handbook of basic principles.* (pp. 433–465). New York: Guilford Press.

Shallice, T. (1978). The dominant action system: An information processing approach to consciousness. In K. S. Pope & J. L. Singer (Eds.), *The stream of consciousness* (pp. 117–157). New York: Plenum Press.

Solarz, A. K. (1960). Latency of instrumental responses as a function of compatibility with the meaning of eliciting verbal signs. *Journal of Experimental Psychology, 59,* 239–245.

Stepper, S., & Strack, F. (1993). Proprioceptive determinants of emotional and nonemotional feelings. *Journal of Personality and Social Psychology, 64,* 211–220.

Strack, F., & Gonzales, M. H. (1993). Wissen und fühlen: Noetische und experientielle grundlagen heuristischer urteilsbildung. In W. Hell, K. Fiedler, & G. Gigerenzer (Eds.), *Kognitive täuschungen.* (pp. 291–315). Heidelberg: Spektrum Akademischer Verlag.

Strack, F., Martin, L. L., & Stepper, S. (1988). Inhibiting and facilitating conditions of human smile: A nonobtrusive test of the facial feedback hypothesis. *Journal of Personality and Social Psychology, 54,* 768–777.

Strack, F. & Neumann, R. (1996). "The spirit is willing but the flesh is weak": Beyond mind-body interactions in human decision-making. *Organizational Behavior and Decision Making, 65,* 300–304.

Strack, F., & Neumann, R. (in press). Furrowing the brow may undermine perceived fame: The role of facial feedback in judgments of celebrity. *Personality and Social Psychology Bulletin.*

Wells, G. L., & Petty, R. E. (1980). The effects of overt head movements on persuasion: Compatibility and incompatibility of responses. *Basic and Applied Social Psychology, 1,* 219–230.

Winkielman, P., Zajonc, R. B., & Schwarz, N. (1997). Subliminal affective priming resists attributional interventions. *Cognition and Emotion, 11,* 433-465.

Zajonc, R. B., & Markus, H. (1984). Affect and cognition: The hard interface. In C. E. Izard, J. Kagan, & R. B. Zajonc (Eds.), *Emotions, cognition, and behavior* (pp. 73–102). Cambridge, MA: Cambridge University Press.

Zajonc, R. B., Murphy, S. T., & Inglehart, M. (1989). Feelings and facial efference: Implications of a vascular theory of emotion. *Psychological Review, 96,* 395–416.

CHAPTER 5

C. Miguel Brendl

Subjective Experience and the Effect of Sample Size on Likelihood Judgments

In a manner inconsistent with the laws of probability, the size of a drawn sample affects judgments of probability. For example, people find it more likely to draw a winning ticket out of a bowl with 10 winning and 90 blank tickets than out of a bowl with 1 winning and 9 blank tickets. More generally, holding the objective likelihood of a random event constant, the size of the sample from which a single element (e.g., a lottery ticket) is drawn has been found to affect its subjective likelihood (Denes-Raj & Epstein, 1994; Denes-Raj, Epstein, & Cole, 1995; Kirkpatrick & Epstein, 1992; Miller, Turnbull, & McFarland, 1989; Pelham, Sumarta, & Myaskovsky, 1994). The main question raised in this chapter is whether *subjective experience* is part of the process mediating this sample size effect on subjective likelihood. Consider Miller and colleagues (1989) "cookie jar" paradigm as another example. These investigators asked their participants to imagine the following scenario: their child prefers chocolate chip cookies over oatmeal cookies. Because they keep both cookie types in

The unpublished research was supported by Grant DFG BR1722/1-1 from the German Science Foundation and by a Transcoop grant (with Arthur B. Markman) from the German American Academic Council.

Address correspondence to C. Miguel Brendl, INSEAD, Fontaínebleau, Boulevard de Constance, 77305 Fountainebleau Cedex, France. E-mail: miguel.brendl@insead.fr

one jar, in order to avoid having the oatmeal cookies be left over all the time, they have just implemented the rule that the child draw one cookie at a time from the jar with his or her eyes closed. Upon being told the new rule, the child goes to the kitchen, returning excitedly with a chocolate chip cookie shortly after and claiming he or she drew it according to the new rule. The question to the experimental participants was how suspicious they would be that the child had peeked. Participants were more suspicious when the ratio of chocolate chip cookies to oatmeal cookies in the jar was 1 to 19 rather than 10 to 190. According to these authors, after knowing the outcome, that is, post hoc, a 1 in 19 chance seemed subjectively less likely than a 10 in 190 chance of drawing one chocolate chip cookie.

Miller et al. (1989) have proposed that the sample size effect (in post hoc likelihood judgments) is mediated by the ease with which a mental simulation of an event's occurrence can be carried out. This thesis is grounded in norm theory (Kahneman & Miller, 1986; Miller, Turnbull, & McFarland, 1990) and the availability heuristic (Tversky & Kahneman, 1973): "A person is said to employ the availability heuristic whenever he estimates frequency or probability by the ease with which instances or associations could be brought to mind" (Tversky & Kahneman, p. 208). For example, subjects incorrectly estimated the frequency of words in English starting with the letter *R* as higher than the frequency of words containing the letter *R* in third position. In reality, words which contain the letter *R* in third than first position are more frequent. However, it is experienced as easier to bring a word to mind when the first rather than third letter is used as retrieval cue (Tversky & Kahneman, 1973; Wänke, Schwarz, & Bless, 1995). According to the availability heuristic, people infer likelihood from this subjective experience of bringing to mind or constructing a mental representation. The easier it is for people to bring a class of words to mind, the more frequent that class of words seems. This influence is presumably based on the implicit theory that more frequent events are brought to mind more easily (see chapter 10 by Schwarz & colleagues in this volume). In other words, people are thought to run a mental simulation of bringing to mind a sample of words of each class. The subjective experience of how easily that mental simulation can be carried out is used as information about the frequency of the words of a class. Such inferences from availability (i.e., ways of bringing instances to mind) have been demonstrated in various contexts, even in other judgments that are themselves based on frequency information (see chapter 8 by Haddock in this volume; Raghubir & Menon, 1998; Rothman & Hardin, 1997; Rothman & Schwarz, 1998; Schwarz et al., 1991; Wänke, Bless, & Biller, 1996; Wänke, Bohner, & Jurkowitsch, 1997; for a review, see chapter 9 by Wänke & Bless in this volume). For example, Schwarz et al.'s (1991) participants were asked to recall either few ($N = 6$) or many ($N = 12$) episodes at which they behaved self-assertively. Recalling few episodes was easier than recalling many episodes. Accordingly, in a subsequent task, they judged themselves more self-assertively when they had previously recalled few than many episodes.

Returning to the sample size effect, Miller et al. (1989) hypothesized that the easier it is to imagine that a chocolate chip cookie is drawn, the more likely this event seems. Thus, people are assumed to mentally simulate the occurrence of an event. This proposal seems sensible in the light of a breadth of evidence showing that people use the ease or fluency of mental operations as information for subsequent judgments about or based on frequency and probability (e.g., Jacoby, Kelley, Brown, & Jasechko, 1989; Rothman & Hardin, 1997; Schwarz et al., 1991; Wänke et al., 1995, 1996, 1997).[1] Epstein and colleagues have instead proposed that it is a biased perception of ratios that mediates the sample size effect on subjective likelihood: the ratio of 1:19 is assumed to be mentally represented as a smaller ratio than the ratio of 10:190 (Denes-Raj & Epstein, 1994; Denes-Raj et al., 1995; Kirkpatrick & Epstein, 1992).

I will suggest that these views need not be contradictory if one assumes that a biased ratio perception and a mental simulation are both involved in likelihood estimates. Let me start by reviewing the history of these opposing views before presenting a way to integrate them.

☐ Norm Theory

According to Norm Theory (NT) (Kahneman & Miller, 1986), expectations exisiting before an event occurs *as well as* mental simulations taking place after an event has already occurred will affect the normality of an event. The *normality* of an event corresponds closely to post hoc subjective likelihood; that is, the more normal an event, the more likely it seems subjectively in retrospect (i.e., after one knows that the event actually took place). Although NT acknowledges influences of expectation-based processing, called *precomputation,* it is silent on precomputation. Instead, it seeks to explain processing that is initiated after an event has already taken place, called *postcomputation.* Thus, any precomputational process is compatible with NT. What NT explains is how postcomputation affects the normality of an event that has already taken place at the time of judgment. Such an event is called a *factual.* Events that did not but could have happened are called *counterfactuals* (for a review, see Roese & Olson, 1995). Let me summarize those NT assumptions which are of relevance to this chapter: people infer the normality of the factual from the ease with which they can conduct a mental simulation. Two mental simulations are possible. First, the easier it is to bring to mind the factual event occurring, the more normal this factual event (Miller et al., 1989). Second, the easier it is to bring to mind counterfactual events occurring, the more abnormal the factual event (Kahneman & Miller, 1986). The more normal the factual event, the more likely it seems retrospectively; that is, the less surprising it is.

Although NT usually assumes that people engage in a mental simulation, research on the availability heuristic suggests that people need not always engage in the actual simulation. Rather it might be enough for people to estimate how difficult a mental simulation would be if it were carried out (Tversky & Kahneman, 1973, p. 208). In fact, Wänke et al. (1997) found that thinking about few rather than many reasons to drive a BMW resulted in a more positive attitude toward it, presumably because it is easier to generate few than many reasons. Importantly, this was also true for participants who indicated that they had not thought about specific reasons, suggesting that indeed merely the estimate of how difficult a mental operation would be affects judgments. These considerations suggest that the availability heuristic could affect judgments even when processing resources are fairly low.

As another example for mental simulations, consider the "cookie jar" paradigm mentioned above, in which Miller and colleagues (1989) asked their participants to imagine their child who was "addicted" to chocolate chip cookies having made the lucky chocolate chip draw, *supposedly with eyes closed*. Why were the experimental participants more suspicious that the child had peeked (and were presumably more surprised about the cookie draw) when the child picked a chocolate chip cookie out of a small than large jar (1 desired chocolate chip cookie and 19 less desired oatmeal cookies vs. 10 and 190 such cookies, respectively)? Presumably, the more abnormal the factual of drawing a chocolate chip cookie, the more suspicious (and surprised) participants should be. According to these investigators, it is easier to imagine drawing the one chocolate chip cookie when there are 10 than just 1 of them in the jar. If so, then it is easier to mentally simulate the factual when there are 10 than just 1 "potential factuals" in the jar, and thus the factual is more normal, less surprising, and less suspicion provoking when there are 10 instead of 1 chocolate chip cookies to be drawn from. Miller et al. therefore assumed that in addition to considering the ratio of chocolate chip to oatmeal cookies, participants attended to the absolute number of potential factuals in the jar and inferred the normality of the factual event from the ease with which they could imagine this event occurring. With a larger number of chocolate chip cookies to draw from, it is easier to imagine drawing one. Their explanation of this particular sample size effect, then, presupposed knowledge about the actual outcome and therefore involves postcomputation.

Miller and colleagues also had other participants rate how likely it was that a chocolate chip cookie would be drawn, a precomputational measure because the outcome of the drawing was unknown. In contrast to judgments of suspicion (postcomputation), the number of cookies in the jar did not affect judgments of likelihood. The authors concluded that the effect of absolute numbers of cookies on suspicion (i.e., a sample size effect) must have been due to postcomputation because the precomputational measure of likelihood was not affected by it. In sum, although participants appeared to perceive drawing a chocolate chip cookie from the large and small jars as equally likely, they perceived drawing it from the small jar as more abnormal, or less likely in retrospect. These results were interpreted to support the assumption that people evaluate the normality of the factual by inferring it from how easily they can imagine the factual occurring. In essence, this interpretation includes two assumptions: (a) people mentally simulated (i.e., inferred from ease of imagination), and (b) they did so postcomputationally.

☐ An Alternative Explanation

The conclusion that a postcomputational mental simulation was responsible for this sample size effect is based on Miller et al.'s (1989) observation that sample size affected ratings of suspiciousness (i.e., a retrospective likelihood) but not ratings of prospective likelihood. However, Kirkpatrick and Epstein (1992) theorized that the reason why sample size affected retrospective likelihood ratings but not prospective likelihood ratings was that the prospective likelihood question tapped *objective* likelihood estimates, while the retrospective question tapped *subjective* likelihood estimates. These authors suggested that when participants were asked to judge the prospective likelihood of drawing a chocolate chip cookie (precomputation), they were aware that their objective and subjective likelihood estimates differed. In other words, although people may have an estimate of the objective likelihood of an event, they may concurrently have an estimate of its subjective likelihood that is inconsistent with their estimate of objective likelihood. Because Miller et al.'s precomputational likelihood question explicitly referred to likelihood, presumably their participants wanted to appear rational and thus gave estimates of their objective rather than subjective likelihood. Moreover, the participants who were asked about their suspiciousness were not pressed to appear rational because of the subjective character of the question and thus based their answer on their subjective instead of objective likelihood estimates.

This argument predicts that one should find a sample size effect on prospective likelihood estimates when one takes away from participants the pressure to appear rational in the precomputational question. In a series of experiments, Epstein and colleagues have provided such evidence (Denes-Raj & Epstein, 1994; Denes-Raj et al., 1995; Kirkpatrick & Epstein, 1992). For example, they gave people a choice between picking a jelly bean from one of two bowls each containing 10% jelly beans that could win money. People in this lottery type situation preferred to pick a bean from a bowl with many than from one with few jelly beans, although the objective likelihood was equal in both cases. Consequently, these results question whether in the cookie jar experiment, the sample size effect is due to postcomputation. Similar results were obtained by Pelham et al. (1994). Participants preferred to participate in a lottery where all participants are given 10 rather than 1 lottery ticket. Thus again, holding subjective likelihood constant, increasing the sample of winning tickets appeared to increase the a priori subjective likelihood of winning.

Note, however, that NT's interpretation involved two assumptions, postcomputation and mental simulation. The evidence accumulated by Epstein and colleagues only questions whether in the cookie jar studies, the sample size effect was a result of postcomputation; that is, whether the cookie jar studies are evidence for postcomputation. It does not directly speak to the question of whether mental simulations took place because no evidence for mediational processes was collected. Thus, it is possible that mental simulations did take place in the cookie jar paradigm, but that these simulations were engaged in precomputationally.[2] Before elaborating, let me report Epstein and colleagues' account of the results in the cookie jar paradigm.

☐ Biased Ratio Perception as Explanation for the Sample Size Effect

A low probability of an event might be perceived as lower when it is expressed in terms of a 1 in X proportion than in terms of a larger number proportion (e.g., 10 in 10 $*$ X) because the 1 in X ratio could be perceived as smaller than the 10 in 10 $*$ X ratio (Kirkpatrick & Epstein, 1992; see also Miller et al., 1989, p.587). For example,

$$p_s\left(\frac{1}{9}\right) < p_s\left(\frac{10}{90}\right)$$

(1)

where p_s = subjective probability. In other words, according to inequality (1), the ratio of 1 to 9 is subjectively perceived as smaller than that of 10 to 90. If this is true, people would perceive drawing the chocolate chip cookie as less likely, also in prospective likelihood judgments, when the ratio of chocolate chip cookies to oatmeal cookies is 1 to 9 instead of 10 to 90. The observation that participants in a lottery with a 10% chance of winning prefer (prospectively) to choose from a bowl with the odds described as 1 in 10 versus 10 in 100 (Denes-Raj & Epstein, 1994; Denes-Raj et al., 1995; Kirkpatrick & Epstein, 1992; Pelham et al., 1994) is consistent with the idea of a biased perception of ratios as described in inequality 1. In sum, the data are consistent with the idea that the perceived magnitude of ratios is affected by sample size. Therefore, the sample size effect could be mediated by a biased perception of ratios. However, there is no data available that would directly test biased ratio perception as a *mediating process* for the sample size effect.

Why would there be a biased perception of ratios? In my opinion, there currently are two types of potential explanations. One type of explanation assumes that, to some degree, the absolute frequency of one event affects the perceived ratio of the fequencies of both events. When described algebraically, the focused-on event is placed in the numerator of the ratio. For example, Epstein and colleagues assume that people focus on the less frequent of the two events because the less frequent event is more salient; that is, acts like a figure against the ground. These investigators describe this focus by placing the less frequent event in the numerator of the ratio of the two event frequencies. Further, they assume that people perceive a ratio as larger when its numerator is larger. Their reasoning is that frequencies are more concrete than ratios, and that more concrete numbers have a larger impact on a judgment, so people "factor" absolute frequencies into their ratio perception (Denes-Raj & Epstein, 1994; Denes-Raj et al., 1995; Kirkpatrick & Epstein, 1992). For example, in the lottery with 10% winning and 90% blank tickets, people are assumed to focus on winning tickets presumably because these are less frequent than blank tickets. They prefer to draw a ticket out of a large bowl because there are more winning tickets in the large than small bowl. Note that in order to make clear predictions, this type of explanation needs to explicitly assume which event people focus on. If people focused on blank tickets, then this account would predict that people should prefer drawing from the small bowl, because there are fewer (undesired) blank tickets in the small than large bowl. Thus, the likelihood for an undesired event would seem smaller in the small than large bowl drawing (inequality 2). Thus, predictions reverse depending on which ticket type people focus on. This is immediately apparent by comparing inequalities 1 and 2 because they are not equivalent.

$$p_s\left(\frac{9}{1}\right) < p_s\left(\frac{90}{10}\right)$$

(2)

If one makes an explicit assumption about which one of two events people focus on, the numerosity heuristic would make similar predictions. According to this heuristic, people overinfer actual quantity (or magnitude) from numerosity; that is, from the number of parts into which a stimulus is divided (Pelham et al., 1994). Thus, assuming a focus on the numerator, a 1:9 ratio would seem smaller than a 10:90 ratio (inequality 1). Again, if one makes an explicit assumption which one of two events people focus on, the availability heuristic (Tversky & Kahneman, 1973) would also make similar predictions because drawing a single winning ticket from a sample of 10 tickets than from a sample of 1 ticket is easier to imagine. Note however, that neither of these two heuristics makes an explicit assumption about which event people would focus on. They are silent on this issue.

I shall call the above type of explanation *focus dependent* because all of its variants share the property that a change in the focused-on event changes the perceived magnitude of the ratio. The second possible type of explanation is *focus independent*. Here, the magnitude of small number ratios compared to large number ratios is polarized because the subjective magnitude of large numbers is overproportionally smaller than that of large numbers. As before the ratio's numerator is smaller than its denominator (inequality 1), small number ratios are perceived as smaller than large number ratios (inequality 1). As a novelty however, when the ratio's numerator is larger than its denominator, small number ratios are not perceived as smaller than large number ratios (inequality 2) but as larger than large number ratios (inequality 3).

$$p_s\left(\frac{9}{1}\right) > p_s\left(\frac{90}{10}\right)$$

(3)

One possibility how such a property could result is from certain psychophysical functions of the perceived magnitude of numbers. There is evidence that at least under certain conditions, the subjective perception of numbers is described by a compressed perceptual scale (Banks, Fujii, & Kayra, 1976; Indow & Ida, 1977; Krueger, 1982; Wing, 1971) for limiting conditions (Banks & Coleman, 1981; Holyoak, 1978).[3] In other words, as the subjective distance between two numbers decreases, the larger these numbers become. For example, the difference between the numbers 1 and 2 would be perceived as greater than the distance between the numbers 100 and 101. The shape of this function turns out to be critical. If for this shape one assumes a power function, the bias in the numerator and the denominator cancel each other out, and biased ratio perception cannot be accounted for. But if one assumes a logarithmic function for this shape, a polarization as just described would result (i.e., inequalities 1 and 3 would be predicted). Although the psychophysical literature assumes power rather than logarithmic perceptual functions for most perceptual domains, I am not aware of data that would clearly support one versus the other view in the domain of number perception. Note that number perception is different from other domains typically studied by psychophysicists in that it does not involve physical stimulation of receptors. Thus, one would have to at least consider the possibility of a logarithmic perceptual function and the resulting focus-independant bias in ratio perception.

Kirkpatrick and Epstein made a second proposal to account for biased ratio perception based on the concreteness principle: smaller numbers (being more concrete) are understood better than larger numbers, which may make their perception more extreme. This suggestion might also imply inequality 3 and would, in contrast to their first proposal, be focus independent.[4]

In sum, although the exact mechanisms accounting for biased ratio perception are theoretically not well understood, we can distinguish two competing types of accounts. These two types of accounts would be distinguishable if evidence would allow us to infer whether people's judgments are consistent with inequality 2 or with inequality 3. Before reviewing such evidence, however, let us bring this section back to the main question of this chapter; namely, whether subjective experience in the form of the ease with which a mental simulation can be carried out mediates the effect of sample size on subjective likelihood.

Is there room for a mediational role of mental simulations in light of the existing evidence suggesting that biased ratio perception mediates the effect of sample size on subjective likelihood? Note that the existing evidence does not speak to the question of whether mental simulations might contribute to biased ratio perception, or whether biased ratio perception directly affects likelihood judgments without intervening mental simulations. One possibility is that the perception of the (biased) ratio of, for example, the number of winning to blank tickets feeds a mental simulation of how easy it feels to imagine drawing a winning ticket. This feeling of ease could in turn be a basis for the subsequent likelihood judgment. Thus, I suggest that the biased perception of a ratio may not be sufficient to explain the sample size effect because the perception of a ratio may not be directly translated into a likelihood judgment. Rather, a subjective experience, a feeling of ease, may at least partially translate the ratio perception into a subjective likelihood judgment. The sample size effect on subjective likelihood may therefore be caused by at least two components, biased ratio perception and a mental simulations.

☐ The Mediating Role of Mental Simulations

There is need for an experimental test addressing two questions: (a) Does the ease with which a mental simulation can be carried out mediate the sample size effect on subjective likelihood? and (b) which one of the two lottery tickets do people focus their attention on? To address these questions, it would be useful to experimentally manipulate the feeling of ease with which a mental simulation can be carried out. Previous evidence shows that this feeling affects judgment only when this feeling is diagnostic for the judgment. Recall the previously mentioned study by Schwarz and colleagues (1991), in which participants judged themselves to be more self-assertive when they previously tried to recall few ($N = 6$) instead of many ($N = 12$) episodes of having behaved self-assertively, few episodes being easier to recall than many. When people were made aware of the potential influence of recalled behaviors on self-assertiveness judgments, the feeling of how easily the behaviors could be recalled was rendered undiagnostic for the self-assertiveness judgment. Under this condition, greater ease of recalling one's own self-assertive behavior did not lead to judgments of more self-assertiveness. This manipulation of diagnosticity is akin to previously used misattribution techniques (e.g., Schachter & Singer, 1962) because people misattribute to their personality the ease with which they can bring to mind a representation of themselves as self-assertive, when in fact this feeling of ease was caused by the small number of episodes to be recalled. To address the above questions, I conducted an experiment in which I manipulated the diagnosticity for surprise judgments of the ease with which a mental simulation can be carried out (Brendl, 1999). Participants were asked to judge how surprised a Mrs. Müller would be about drawing a specific lottery ticket out of a bowl. I reasoned that if participants mentally simulate the draw of Mrs. Müller's ticket, and if they use the feeling of ease with which they can conduct this simulation as a basis for their surprise judgment (i.e., their likelihood judgment), then manipulating the diagnosticity of this feeling should alter the sample size effect on surprise judgments. On the other hand, if people do not conduct a mental simulation, then manipulating diagnosticity should not alter the sample size effect on surprise judgments.

Participants were told that Mrs. Müller had drawn either a winning or a blank lottery ticket out of a bowl containing 90% winning tickets. Please note that predictions will reverse compared to the previously reported studies that contained 10% winning conditions. The 90% winning condition is of special interest because it can distinguish inequalities 2 and 3. Participants were either told Mrs. Müller's ticket bowl contained few or many tickets (9 winning and 1 blank vs. 900 winning and 100 blank tickets). Up to this point, the design is a 2 × 2 between-participants factorial of actual outcome (winning vs. blank ticket) by bowl size (small vs. large). Before moving on to the details of the critical diagnosticity manipulation, let me explain how this design can reveal the sample size effect in those conditions where participants are expected to base their surprise judgments on a mental simulation. As do some previously discussed accounts, we need to make an explicit assumption about which ticket type participants would focus their attention on. One possibility is that because participants should be motivated to draw a winning ticket, they would precomputationally evaluate the likelihood of drawing a winning ticket (i.e., they would not evaluate the likelihood of drawing a blank ticket). This assumption is based on findings that goals (e.g., winning) guide attention (Gollwitzer, 1993; Huffman & Houston, 1993; Markman & Brendl, in press). As will be reported below, the data support exactly this possibility; that is, a precomputational focus on winning tickets.[5] It follows that participants will mentally simulate the draw of a winning ticket and that they will represent the odds of drawing a winning ticket either as a 9 to 1 ratio or as a 900 to 100 ratio. (And it follows that they would *not* represent these ratios as 1 to 9 and 100 to 900, because the latter ratios represent the odds of drawing a blank ticket.)

Revealing the sample size effect, a significant interaction of sample size (small vs. large) by actually drawn ticket (winning vs. blank) showed that participants were less surprised about Mrs. Müller drawing a winning ticket from the small than large bowl, but more surprised about Mrs. Müller drawing a blank ticket from the small than large bowl. Presumably then, the chances of drawing a winning ticket appeared higher for the small than large bowl. This result supports the assumption that a subjective probability based on a 9 to 1 ratio is larger than one based on a 900 to 100 ratio (inequality 3) and is inconsistent with inequality 2. However, this conclusion can only be drawn if one additionally assumes a focus on winning tickets. Otherwise the possibility remains that participants reframed the ratios into 1 to 9 and 10 to 90 ratios, focusing on blank tickets (inequality 1). The diagnosticity manipulation addresses this possibility.

If a biased perception of ratios is translated via a mental simulation into surprise judgments, then the 2 × 2 interaction of sample size (small vs. large) and actually drawn ticket (blank vs. winning) should be stronger when the diagnosticity of the ease of conducting the mental simulation for the surprise judgment is high instead of low. On the other hand, if a biased perception of ratios is translated directly (i.e., without an intervening mental simulation) into surprise judgments, then the level of diagnosticity should not have any effect on surprise judgments. The diagnosticity for surprise judgments of the feeling of how easily one could imagine drawing a ticket was manipulated by making the feeling appear more or less normal. How should the normality of a feeling affect its diagnosticity? NT (Kahneman & Miller, 1986) and other models of causal reasoning (Einhorn & Hogarth, 1986; Hilton & Slugoski, 1986) propose that it is abnormality that gives causes their causal relevance. In other words, it is abnormal conditions, not normal conditions, that are perceived as causes of effects. People may have an implicit theory about how a feeling of ease of imagination causes surprise: when it is easy to imagine that an event will take place and it does not take place, one will be surprised, and vice versa. Thus, the more abnormal the feeling of ease of an event taking place, the more that feeling should be viewed as causing a certain level of surprise. In other words, the more abnormal the feeling of ease of imaging a specific ticket draw is, the more relevant it should be as a cause for surprise, and the more a judgment of surprise should be based on this feeling.

How can the normality of a feeling be manipulated? An experimental manipulation developed by Schwarz et al. (1991) was used (see also Rothman & Hardin, 1997). In the experiment just described, when participants read about their ticket bowl, they were asked "to concentrate even if they found it easy (vs. difficult) to imagine the situation" (varied between participants). It is self-evident that it is actually easy to imagine drawing a winning ticket when there are 90% winning tickets in the bowl. Because of this, when participants were exposed to a message implying that it usually feels difficult to imagine drawing a winning ticket, the actual feeling of ease was rendered abnormal because this actual feeling deviated from the usual. On the other hand, because it was in reality easy to imagine drawing a winning ticket, when participants were exposed to a message implying that it usually feels easy to imagine drawing a winning ticket, the actual feeling of ease was rendered normal because this actual feeling matched the usual. In sum, when the message mismatched the actual feeling, the actual feeling was made more abnormal and therefore more diagnostic. In contrast, when the message matched the actual feeling, the actual feeling was made more normal and therefore less diagnostic.

If participants based their surprise judgments on the ease of a mental simulation, the observed sample size effect should increase when the feeling of "ease" is made more diagnostic (message claiming difficulty) and/or decrease when the feeling of "ease" is made less diagnostic (message claiming ease). This is exactly what happened. The sample size effect was present when the feeling of ease of conducting a mental simulation was made more diagnostic (i.e., a significant 2 × 2 interaction of sample size and actually drawn ticket). However, the sample size effect was significantly weaker, even to the point of being absent, when this feeling was made less diagnostic.

In addition, this result suggests that participants mentally simulated drawing a winning ticket; that is, that they focused on winning tickets instead of blank tickets. Note that our definition of diagnosticity assumes that people focus on winning tickets. If we make the assumption that participants focused on the less frequent tickets, that is, the 10% blank tickets, then because of the low likelihood of drawing a blank ticket, it would be difficult to imagine drawing a blank ticket. It would follow from this hypothetical assumption that the message claiming "difficulty" should make the actually felt difficulty more normal and therefore less diagnostic, and/or the message claiming "ease" should make the actually felt difficulty even more abnormal and therefore more diagnostic. Note that these predictions following from the hypothetical assumption of an attentional focus on blank tickets are the exact opposite predictions about diagnosticity than the ones following from the assumption of a focus on winning tickets. The results, however, are consistent with the assumption of a focus on winning tickets, because it would not follow from our knowledge about diagnosticity that the sample size effect is wiped out by high diagnosticity. Instead, it should be wiped out by low diagnosticity. As discussed above, a focus on winning tickets is consistent with explanations of biased ratio perception that predict that a ratio of 9 to 1 is perceived as larger than a ratio of 90 to 10 (inequality 3) that is, with the focus independent type of explanation. It is not consistent with focus dependent explanations.

Is it possible that the high diagnosticity misattribution message caused some kind of demand effect? For example, could the discrepancy between actual and proposed feelings have made people aware of the attempted influence of the message and caused a contrast effect? This is extremely unlikely because diagnosticity, then, should have had foremost some effect on additionally taken ratings of how easily one can imagine drawing a ticket. However, diagnosticity did not affect these ratings.

In sum, this experiment provides evidence that the sample size effect on subjective likelihood is affected by the ease of a mental simulation and that people focus their attention on the winning ticket. The latter finding is consistent with focus independent types of explanations for biased ratio perception and is inconsistent with focus dependent types of explanations. Further, this evidence reveals the properties that biased ratio perception has in representations of large likelihood ratios (e.g., likelihood ratios of 9 to 1 appearing larger and therefore more likely than one of 90 to 10; i.e., inequality 3). These findings suggest that biased ratio perception is at least partially translated into subjective likelihood by means of mental simulations.

☐ When Is the Sample Size Effect Mediated by Pre- Versus Postcomputational Mental Simulations?

The translation process from objective frequencies to subjective likelihood that I proposed so far is carried out precomputationally; that is, it is not influenced by a person's knowledge of whatever lottery ticket was actually drawn. The work by Miller et al. (1989) predicts, however, that knowledge of the actually drawn lottery ticket would additionally affect likelihood judgments. The fascinating implication of this hypothesized postcomputational influence is that it would lead to irrational likelihood judgments. For example, Miller et al. (1989) suggest that people can postcomputationally simulate the occurrence of the event that actually took place, the factual. The easier it is to mentally simulate the factual, the more likely it seems post hoc. Let's assume people drew a winning ticket out of our bowl with 90% winning tickets, and let us ignore all precomputational effects for the moment. If people conducted a postcompuational mental simulation, then they should find it easier to imagine drawing a winning ticket out of the large than small bowl because there are more winning tickets in the large than small bowl. Consequently, they should find it subjectively more likely (i.e., less surprising) to draw a winning ticket from a large than small bowl. Just for exemplification, let us assume a subjective likelihood (p_s) of drawing a winning ticket (w) from the large bowl of $p_{sw}(large\ bowl) = .90$ while the subjective likelihood of drawing a winning ticket from the small bowl $p_{sw}(small\ bowl) = .85$. If people were consistent about their subjective likelihood estimates, then they should judge the subjective likelihood of drawing a blank ticket (b) as $p_{sb} = 1 - p_{sw}$. Thus, for drawing a blank instead of a winning ticket from the large versus small bowls, the relation of the magnitudes of the subjective likelihoods would reverse; that is, the subjective likelihood of drawing a blank ticket would be estimated as $p_{sb}(large\ bowl) = .10$ when it comes from the large bowl but as $p_{sb}(small\ bowl) = .15$ when it comes from the small bowl. In sum, if people's likelihood estimates are not influenced by the actual outcome, then there should be an interaction of sample size and actual outcome:

$$\text{Iff } p_{sw}(large\ bowl) > p_{sw}(small\ bowl),$$
$$\text{then } p_{sb}(large\ bowl) < p_{sb}(small\ bowl) \tag{4}$$

However, for this example, it follows from Miller and colleagues' (1989) assumptions that if people draw a blank ticket and if they simulate this draw postcomputationally, then they should find it again easier to imagine drawing a blank ticket from the large than small bowl because there are more blank tickets in the large than small bowl. Consequently, they should find it subjectively more likely (i.e., less surprising) to draw a blank ticket from a large than small bowl. Hence, if people do postcomputational mental simulations, sample size does not interact with the actual outcome; instead, there should be a main effect of sample size independent of the actual outcome. People always find it more likely that an actually drawn ticket comes from a large than small sample, no matter what the ticket type:

$$p_{sw}(large\ bowl) > p_{sw}(small\ bowl)\ \&\ p_{sb}(large\ bowl) > p_{sb}(small\ bowl) \qquad (5)$$

It is theoretically conceivable that such postcomputational mental simulations are conducted in addition to the precomputational mental simulations, and both effects are detectable at the same time. However, in the previous experiment, we did not find such evidence. One possibility is that at least in the current paradigm in which people do not actually go through a precomputational stage and subsequently through an additional postcomputational stage but go through one stage only, strong precomputation might wipe out postcomputation.

It follows that if we weaken precomputational processes, postcomputational processes might surface in addition to whatever precomputational effects there are left. One way to weaken precomputational processes is to defocus people precomputationally, to take away an event that people can obviously focus their attention on precomputationally. If in a winning versus blank ticket lottery, people do indeed focus on winning tickets, then making both tickets about equally attractive should weaken the precomputational influence and lead to postcomputational sample size effects on likelihood judgments. I attempted to defocus participants in another experiment by describing a draw of tickets from a bowl where (a) none of the tickets could win or lose anything, and (b) the two ticket types had either a triangle or a square printed on them to distinguish them. Triangles and squares were pretested to be about equally "attractive." To diminish any possible effect of biased ratio perception, each ticket type had a frequency of 50%. Again participants were asked how surprised someone would be about drawing one specific ticket (with a triangle vs. a square) from either a small or large bowl (i.e., small vs. large sample). This time, there was a main effect of sample size on surprise judgments.[6] Participants were more surprised when the ticket came from the small than large bowl; that is, there was a postcomputational influence of the knowledge of the actually drawn ticket on surprise (i.e., likelihood) judgments.

In sum, the last two experiments suggest that the sample size effect on subjective likelihood is partly mediated by the ease with which a mental simulation can be carried out. The mental simulation can be carried out pre- or postcomputationally. Additional factors, such as people's goals in a situation, determine which event is mentally simulated. I expect that many factors can guide attention to a specific event precomputationally. At least in a situation as described here, where people learn about an event for the first time after it occurred, a precomputational simulation might undercut further postcomputational simulations. NT currently does not make assumptions about the conditions that cause mental simulations of one versus another event (see also Kirkpatrick & Epstein, 1992). Future development of the theory should include identifying such conditions because, as we have seen, a focus on different events can lead to very different judgments.

☐ Conclusions

The evidence reviewed in this chapter suggests several conclusions. The perception of ratios is biased, and this bias has effects on actual behavior (e.g., Denes-Raj et al., 1995). An explanation for this bias is currently incomplete, but the available evidence puts the following constraints on an explanation. Small number ratios are polarized compared to large number ratios (inequalities 1 and 3). While this phenomenon could be accounted for by perceptual processes, the effect of biased ratio perception on subjective likelihood seems to involve subjective experience, more specifically, the ease with which a mental simulation of an event can be carried out. Possibly, mental simulations translate biased ratio perception into subjective likelihood estimates. Thus, not only is a ratio of 1 to 9 perceived as smaller than that of 10 to 90, it is also easier to imagine that one draws the favored cookie from a bowl with 1 favorite and 9 mediocre ones than from one with 10 favorites and 90 mediocre ones and are affected by this feeling in their likelihood estimates.

The biasing effect of a ratio's sample size may extend well beyond judgments of frequency and probability to judgments that are merely based on frequency and probability. In fact, recent work has extended the availability and numerosity heuristics beyond judgments of frequency and probability to evaluative judgments that are affected by frequency information (e.g., see chapter 8 by Haddock, chapter 10 by Schwarz & colleagues, chapter 9 by Wänke & Bless in this volume; Pelham et al., 1994). Similarly, biased ratio perception should affect judgments of valence when these judgments are based on frequency information. For example, a health food that has 9 out of 10 instead of 90 out of 100 healthy ingredients may be perceived as more positive as a result of biased ratio perception.

☐ Notes

[1]These studies all have in common people who have an implicit theory according to which a frequent occurrence of an event leads to an experience of ease or familiarity when thinking about the event. A related domain of research, "perceptual fluency," also shows effects of subjective experience on judgments, but here the attribution process may be different. The more a stimulus is associated with an experience of fluent processing, the more familiar it may seem and the more it may be liked (see chapter 10 by Schwarz & colleagues in this volume). This process has been suggested as an explanation for the mere exposure effect (Klinger & Greenwald, 1994).

[2]With one exception (Denes-Raj et al., 1995), the experiments conducted by Epstein and colleagues were not intended to evaluate whether postcomputation contributes to the sample size effect. The experiments were instead focused on providing an alternative interpretation (precomputation) for the postcomputational interpretation of the results. This issue is discussed in detail in Brendl (1999). We will see below that under certain conditions, postcomputation does contribute to the sample size effect.

[3]It should be noted that some studies find a linear subjective scale of number and some, although very few, an accelerated relationship. A discussion of these latter results is beyond the scope of this chapter, but in general, some of these studies have been discussed to be methodologically flawed (for such an argument, see Banks & Coleman, 1981), whereas others suggest that some contexts produce a subjective scale of numerosity that is not compressed. In general, however, there seems to be agreement that the size of small numbers (between 1 and 6 to 20) is perceived accurately whereas that of large numbers is underestimated (Kaufman, Lord, Reese, & Volkmann, 1949; Krueger, 1982; Minturn & Reese, 1951). At minimum, the existing evidence suggests that a compressed subjective scale of numerosity exists under certain conditions.

[4]In this case, one proposal derived from CEST would predict inequality 2, and the other one would predict inequality 3. Thus, an empirical test between the two would be called for.

[5]I do not suggest that when there are positive and neutral events, people will always focus on the positive ones. A number of factors may affect focus and could lead to different foci under other conditions.

[6]There was also an interaction effect of bowl size (small vs. large) and actual event (ticket with triangle vs. square drawn), suggesting that a precomputational effect was additionally present. The details of this effect are discussed in Brendl (1999).

☐ References

Banks, W. P., & Coleman, M. J. (1981). Two subjective scales of number. *Perception and Psychophysics, 29*(2), 95–105.

Banks, W. P., Fujii, M., & Kayra, S. F. (1976). Semantic congruity effects in comparative judgments of magnitudes of digits. *Journal of Experimental Psychology: Human Perception and Performance, 2*(3), 435–447.

Brendl, C. M. (1999). *Of mental simulations, biased ratio perception, and subjective probability.* Unpublished paper.

Denes-Raj, V., & Epstein, S. (1994). Conflict between intuitive and rational processing: When people behave against their better judgment. *Journal of Personality and Social Psychology, 66*(5), 819–829.

Denes-Raj, V., Epstein, S., & Cole, J. (1995). The generality of the ratio-bias phenomenon. *Personality and Social Psychology Bulletin, 21*(10), 1083–1092.

Einhorn, H. J., & Hogarth, R. M. (1986). Judging probable cause. *Psychological Bulletin, 99*(1), 3–19.

Gollwitzer, P. M. (1993). Goal achievement: The role of intentions. *European Review of Social Psychology, 4,* 141–185.

Hilton, D. J., & Slugoski, B. R. (1986). Knowledge-based causal attribution: The abnormal conditions focus model. *Psychological Review, 93*(1), 75–88.

Holyoak, K. J. (1978). Comparative judgments with numerical reference points. *Cognitive Psychology, 10*(2), 203–243.

Huffman, C., & Houston, M. J. (1993). Goal-oriented experiences and the development of knowledge. *Journal of Consumer Research, 20*(2), 190–207.

Indow, T., & Ida, M. (1977). Scaling of dot numerosity. *Perception and Psychophysics, 22*(3), 265–276.

Jacoby, L. L., Kelley, C., Brown, J., & Jasechko, J. (1989). Becoming famous overnight: Limits on the ability to avoid unconscious influences of the past. *Journal of Personality and Social Psychology, 56*(3), 326–338.

Kahneman, D., & Miller, D. T. (1986). Norm theory: Comparing reality to its alternatives. *Psychological Review, 93*(2), 136–153.

Kaufman, E. L., Lord, M. W., Reese, T. W., & Volkmann, J. (1949). The discrimination of visual number. *American Journal of Psychology, 62,* 498–525.

Kirkpatrick, L. A., & Epstein, S. (1992). Cognitive-experiential self-theory and subjective probability: Further evidence for two conceptual systems. *Journal of Personality and Social Psychology, 63*(4), 534–544.

Klinger, M. R., & Greenwald, A. G. (1994). Preferences need no inferences? The cognitive basis of unconscious mere exposure effects. In P. M. Niedenthal & S. Kitayama (Eds.), *The heart's eye* (pp. 69–85). San Diego, CA: Academic Press.

Krueger, L. E. (1982). Single judgments of numerosity. *Perception and Psychophysics, 31*(2), 175–182.

Markman, A. B., & Brendl, C. M. (2000). The influence of goals on value and choice. In D. L. Medin (Ed.), *The psychology of learning and motivation* (Vol. 39, pp. 97–128). San Diego: Academic Press.

Miller, D. T., Turnbull, W., & McFarland, C. (1989). When a coincidence is suspicious: The role of mental simulation. *Journal of Personality and Social Psychology, 57*(4), 581–589.

Miller, D. T., Turnbull, W., & McFarland, C. (1990). Counterfactual thinking and social perception: Thinking about what might have been. In M. P. Zanna (Ed.), *Advances in experimental social psychology. Vol. 23* (pp. 305–331). Orlando, FL: Academic Press.

Minturn, A. L., & Reese, T. W. (1951). The effect of differential reinforcement on the discrimination of visual number. *Journal of Psychology, 31,* 201–231.

Pelham, B. W., Sumarta, T. T., & Myaskovsky, L. (1994). The easy path from many to much: The numerosity heuristic. *Cognitive Psychology, 26*(2), 103–133.

Raghubir, P., & Menon, G. (1998). AIDS and me, never the twain shall meet: The effects of information accessibility on judgments of risk and advertising effectiveness. *Journal of Consumer Research* (1), 52–63.

Roese, N. J., & Olson, J. M. (Eds.). (1995). *What might have been: The social psychology of counterfactual thinking.* Mahwah, NJ: Erlbaum.

Rothman, A. J., & Hardin, C. D. (1997). Differential use of the availability heuristic in social judgment. *Personality and Social Psychology Bulletin, 23*(2), 123–138.

Rothman, A. J., & Schwarz, N. (1998). Constructing perceptions of vulnerability: Personal relevance and the use of experiential information in health judgments. *Personality and Social Psychology Bulletin, 24*(10), 1053–1064.

Schachter, S., & Singer, J. E. (1962). Cognitive, social, and physiological determinants of emotional state. *Psychological Review, 69*(5), 379–399.

Schwarz, N., Bless, H., Strack, F., Klumpp, G., Rittenauer-Schatka, H., & Simons, A. (1991). Ease of retrieval as information: Another look at the availability heuristic. *Journal of Personality and Social Psychology, 61*(2), 195–202.

Tversky, A., & Kahneman, D. (1973). Availability: A heuristic for judging frequency and probability. *Cognitive Psychology, 5*(2), 207–232.

Wänke, M., Bless, H., & Biller, B. (1996). Subjective experience versus content of information in the construction of attitude judgments. *Personality and Social Psychology Bulletin, 22*(11), 1105–1113.

Wänke, M., Bohner, G., & Jurkowitsch, A. (1997). There are many reasons to drive a BMW: Does imagined ease of argument generation influence attitudes? *Journal of Consumer Research, 24*(2), 170–177.

Wänke, M., Schwarz, N., & Bless, H. (1995). The availability heuristic revisited: Experienced ease of retrieval in mundane frequency estimates. *Acta Psychologica, 89*(1), 83–90.

Wing, H. (1971). The influence of context and stimulus range on the judgment of numerousness. *Psychonomic Science, 24*(4), 199–200.

Leonard L. Martin
Daniel Whitaker

Availability as Input: The Experience of Cognitive Effort Can Either Strengthen or Weaken Evaluations

Our subjective experiences can be powerful sources of information in the guidance of our thoughts and behaviors. Consider, for example, what you would do if you began to experience boredom while reading this chapter. You might stop reading. Suppose what you experienced was confusion, rather than boredom. Although this experience might cause you to stop reading, it is also possible that it would motivate you to continue reading in the hope of obtaining clarification. Finally, what would happen if you began to experience anger while reading this chapter? Perhaps you were upset by some of the ideas presented here. If your anger were strong enough, then you might decide to confront the authors at a conference and tell them where they got things wrong.

In this chapter, we explore some implications of the mood as input model (Martin, 2000; Martin, Abend, Sedikides, & Green, 1997; Martin, Achee, Ward, & Harlow, 1993; Martin & Davies, 1998; Martin & Stoner, 1996; Martin, Ward, Achee, & Wyer, 1993) for our understanding of the role of subjective experiences other than mood on evaluation. Because we explore the nonmood implications of the mood as input model, we

Address correspondence to Leonard L. Martin, Department of Psychology, University of Georgia, Athens, GA 30602. E-mail: llmartin@arches.uga.edu

refer to the model in this chapter as the *experience as input model*. This model has some assumptions in common with a number of other theoretical models, but it is unique in the role it assigns to contextual factors in moderating the effects of feelings on thought and behavior. According to most models, there are inherent relations between certain subjective experiences and certain cognitive, motivational, and behavioral predispositions, and it is the role of contextual factors to determine whether or not these predispositions are manifested. By comparison, the experience as input model suggests that there are no default or inherent relations between various subjective experiences and various cognitive, motivational, and behavioral predispositions. From this perspective, contextual factors do not override inherent predispositions; they instantiate different evaluative and motivational implications in different contexts.

In this chapter, we discuss these two views of context effects. Then, we discuss a study designed to test implications of each view. Our specific focus is on the way in which contextual factors influence the effect of experienced cognitive effort (i.e., ease of retrieval) on judgment. In brief, most researchers (see chapter 8 by Haddock, chapter 10 by Skurnik et al., and chapter 9 by Wänke & Bless in this volume) assume that effort retrieval lowers evaluations (i.e., the availability heuristic). We explore the possibility that in some contexts, effortful retrieval can strengthen evaluations. We end with a discussion of the general implications of our findings for the way in which psychologists have tended to depict the social perceiver. We suggest that social perceivers use subjective experiences in ways that are much more sophisticated and subtle than most current models of processing suggest.

☐ The Default + Interference Model

Although no theoretical model we know of assumes that individuals who have certain subjective experiences invariably *behave* in certain ways, there are some theoretical models that assume that individuals who have certain subjective experiences are invariably *predisposed* to behave in certain ways. For example, researchers have assumed that negative subjective experiences (i.e., negative moods) induce a predisposition toward negative evaluations (Forgas, in press; Mayer, Gaschke, Braverman, & Evans, 1992; Schwarz, 2000), systematic thinking (Schwarz & Bohner, 1996), bottom-up processing (Bless, 2000; Fiedler, 2000), mood repair (Clark & Isen, 1982), and aggressive behavior (Berkowitz, 1993), whereas positive subjective experiences (i.e., positive moods) induce a predisposition toward positive evaluations (Forgas, 2000; Mayer et al., 1992; Schwarz, 2000), capacity restrictions (Mackie & Worth, 1989), top-down processing (Bless, 2000; Fiedler, 2000), mood maintenance concerns (Clark & Isen, 1982; Wegener & Petty, 2000), and flexible, creative processing (Estrada, Isen, & Young, 1994; Hirt, Melton, McDonald, & Harackiewicz, 1996). These predispositions are assumed to be the natural or default effects of having the negative or positive subjective experiences. Thus, the predispositions will be manifested unless some outside factor interferes. What are these outside factors? They include such things as awareness of the predisposition and its inappropriateness (Berkowitz, 1993), attempts to change one's mood (Clark & Isen, 1982), extra processing time (Mackie & Worth, 1989), and competing goals (Schwarz, in press).

We refer to this general view of context effects as the *Default + Interference view* (see the top of Figure 6.1). According to this view, contextual factors do not influence the causal relations between subjective experiences and evaluative or motivational predispositions because these relations are given. People who have certain subjective experiences are presumably predisposed to act in certain ways. What contextual factors do is determine whether or not these predispositions are manifested. They do this by determining whether individuals use their subjective experiences in their processing (e.g., attribute feelings to a nontarget source), and, if so, whether individuals inhibit the predispositions inherent to these experiences.

One particularly clear instance of the Default + Interference view is the Berkowitz (1993) neoassociationistic model of aggression. According to Berkowitz, "People who are feeling bad, whatever the reason . . . are theoretically apt to feel angry, have hostile thoughts, and be disposed to attack a suitable available target" (p. 10). However, when people become "highly conscious of what they [are] feeling and what they [are] attempting to do, these people presumably [engage] in 'higher order' thinking, so that they [consider] the possible appropriateness of their emotions and urges in the given circumstances and then [decide] to restrain themselves" (p. 35). In short, Berkowitz proposed that when individuals experience negative feelings, they are automatically and inevitably predisposed to display some form of aggression. This predisposition will not be manifested, however, if individuals engage in a conscious, effortful inhibition process.

Another instance of the Default + Interference view is the Mayer et al. (1992) account of mood-congruent judgment. According to Mayer et al., mood-congruent judgment is a general effect that "automatically occurs for every judgment for which there is a class of legitimate responses that can be distinguished according to their mood congruence. The effect would fail to occur only when a second process interferes" (p. 119). The inherent predisposition, in this case, is a mood-congruent judgment. Individuals in positive moods are predisposed to render positive judgments, whereas individuals in negative moods are predisposed to render negative judg-

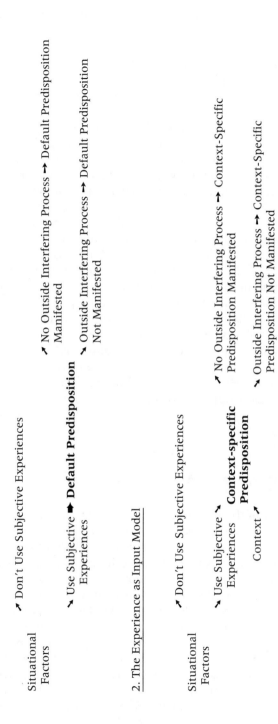

FIGURE 6.1. Two models of the way in which context moderates the effects of subjective experience on evaluations.

ments. These predispositions will be manifested unless some "second process interferes."

The Default + Interference view can also be seen in the work of Schwarz and his colleagues (e.g., Schwarz & Bohner, 1996). Their work on mood and processing, for example, has been based on the assumption that negative moods signal a problematic situation that, in turn, induces individuals to attend to the details of the situation and engage in careful, effortful processing. Positive moods, on the other hand, do not signal a problem, so individuals in positive moods can feel free to engage in less effortful, but more flexible and creative processing. These relations are assumed to be inherent in the sense that they "are most likely to be observed in the absence of instructions or task demands that require a specific processing style" (Schwarz, 2000, p. 11). Of course, the predispositions are not always manifested. As Schwarz (2000) noted, "the impact of moods on the spontaneous adoption of processing styles can be overridden by other variables" (p. 11), such as other currently active goals.

To summarize, the Default + Interference view assumes that contextual factors do not influence the relations between one's subjective experiences and certain evaluative and motivational predispositions. These relations are given. Rather, contextual factors influence whether individuals use their subjective experiences in their processing, and, if so, whether individuals suppress the evaluative and motivational predispositions inherently engendered by these experiences. From this perspective, if individuals use their subjective experiences in their processing and if they do not inhibit the output of this processing, then their behavior will manifest the evaluative and motivational predispositions inherent in their subjective experiences.

☐ A Configural View of Context

An alternate view of the role of context in moderating the effects of subjective experiences is contained within the *experience as input model* (see the bottom of Figure 6.1). According to this model, there are no inherent relations between various subjective experiences and various cognitive, motivational, and behavioral predispositions. Rather, the same experiences can induce different predispositions in different contexts (see Hirt, McDonald, Levine, Melton, & Martin, 1999; Sanna, Turley, & Mark, 1996). This view of context is generally compatible with a connectionist view of processing (Read & Miller, 1994). According to that view, individuals do not process discrete bits of information and then combine these together to generate a response. Rather, individuals respond to the overall configuration of information. In this way, each element of the stimulus configuration can simultaneously constrain the implications of the others.

The word *pool*, for example, could refer to a body of water, a game, or the act of adding money to a communal pot. Similarly, the word *bank* could refer to a financial institution, the side of a body of water, or a turn by an airplane. So, when these two words are used in a sentence, how do we know which of these possible meanings are intended? The answer is that each word in the sentence helps to constrain the meaning of others. This is why it is easy to understand the sentence "Bill added his money to the pool and then took it to the bank." For this combination of words to make sense, pool cannot refer to a body of water nor to a game, nor can bank refer to the side of a body of water nor to the turn of an airplane. It is clear that Bill added his money to a communal pot and then took the entire sum of money to a financial institution. Each word of the sentence constrained the implications of the other, and it did so quickly and easily.

According to the experience as input model, a similar process occurs with subjective experiences. Subjective experiences do not have evaluative and motivational implications independent of the context within which individuals have these experiences. Rather, the context helps to determine the implications of one's subjective experiences at the same time that these experiences help to determine the implications of the context. This is why there are no inherent evaluative or motivational predispositions to override. The predispositions are created within the context (see the bottom of Figure 6.1).

Let's apply these ideas to one of our opening examples. Suppose you start to experience boredom while reading this chapter. Because no one wants to read a boring chapter, this experience might predispose you to stop reading. What would happen, though, if you started to experience boredom while reading a draft of one of your own manuscripts? Because no one wants to *produce* a boring article, experiencing boredom in this context might induce you to read more intently and to think seriously about the changes you could make to increase the manuscript's appeal to readers. In both cases, your boredom informs you that the article you are reading is uninteresting. The motivational implications of this uninterestingness, however, depend on the context. In the context of reading our chapter, your boredom-based lack of interest might predispose you to disengage, whereas in the context of reading your own manuscript, this same uninterestingness might predispose you toward greater engagement.

☐ How Does It Work?

The experience as input model raises the possibility that any subjective experience can give rise to any evaluative or motivational effect, depending on the context. Considering only this possibility, it is easy to get the impression that the experience as input model is one of those models that can "explain" everything, yet predict nothing. A closer look, however, reveals that this is not the case. The experience as input model is as precise in its predictions as any of the Default + Interference models.

To make predictions using experience as input logic, we need to know (1) the criteria relative to which a target is being evaluated, (2) the kinds of subjective experiences that suggest satisfaction of those criteria, and (3) the extent to which the judge is having those experiences. Favorable evaluations arise when individuals' subjective experiences indicate that the target is satisfying desired criteria, whereas unfavorable evaluations arise when individuals' subjective experiences indicate that the target is satisfying undesirable criteria.

To evaluate whether a meal is good, for example, we need to know what it is that constitutes a good meal and how the meal we are eating compares to "a good meal." Presumably, a good meal not only has the appropriate combination of foods and presentation, but also elicits favorable tastes in the diner and leaves him or her feeling satisfied. Thus, a meal that elicits these experiences would be evaluated more favorably than a meal that does not elicit these experiences. This is what we mean by the term "experience as input." Individuals can use their subjective experiences to help determine the extent to which a target has fulfilled the role for which it is being evaluated (e.g., a good meal).

In the meal example, positive experiences were associated with a positive evaluation. Within a role fulfillment system, however, this need not always be the case. A negative subjective experience can lead to a positive evaluation when this experience signals fulfillment of a positive role. The movie *Titanic*, for example, was designed to elicit sadness. So, how would a viewer feel if the movie fulfilled its role (i.e., if it were a good movie)? The viewer would feel sad. In fact, the sadder the viewer felt after watching the movie, the more the movie fulfilled its role. So, from an experience as input perspective, the sadder the viewer felt after watching the movie (presumably within some limit), the more favorably he or she would evaluate the movie. In experience as input terms, the sadness indicates that the movie fulfilled its role of making the viewer experience the poignancy of a lost love, which in the context of a movie is a positive experience. So, a negative subjective experience can give rise to a positive evaluation if that experience indicates that the target satisfied the criteria for a favorable role (e.g., a good heart-wrenching movie). Evidence to this effect was obtained by Martin et al. (1997).

More generally, the experience as input model makes a distinction between the information communicated by subjective experiences and the evaluative and motivational implications of that information. The former may be inherent. The latter is not. Thus, the experience of sadness may inform you of a loss, but this loss does not inherently or invariably predispose you to any particular evaluation or motivation. The evaluative and motivational predisposition you experience depends on the context within which the loss is experienced. In the remainder of the chapter, we show how the assumptions of the experience as input model can help us understand the effect of experienced retrieval effort on attitude ratings.

Experienced Ease of Retrieval as Input

Tversky and Kahneman (1973) proposed that individuals sometimes estimate the frequency or likelihood of an event's occurrence by assessing the ease with which they can retrieve instances or associations of that event. For example, because it is easier to retrieve words beginning with r than words with r as the third letter, individuals may estimate that there are more instances of the former than the latter (Tversky & Kahneman, 1973). The tendency to use the ease or difficulty of retrieval as a cue in estimating frequency has been termed the *availability heuristic.*

Although a number of studies have presented data consistent with the availability heuristic, most of them did not provide direct evidence that individuals were in fact relying upon ease of retrieval. Rather, in these studies, differences in retrieval effort were inferred from the nature of the task (e.g., retrieve words beginning with r or words that have r as the third letter). To move beyond these limitations, Schwarz, Bless, Strack, and Klumpp (1991) examined the availability heuristic in a situation in which they directly manipulated ease of retrieval. Specifically, these investigators had participants recall either 6 or 12 instances in which they had behaved assertively (or nonassertively). Then, they had participants rate how assertive (or nonassertive) they were.

Although participants who retrieved 12 instances had twice as much evidence for their possession of the trait than those who retrieved 6 instances, they also experienced greater difficulty retrieving the instances. So, if participants were relying upon the availability heuristic, then those who retrieved 12 instances should see themselves as possessing less of the trait than those who retrieved six instances. This is in fact the result obtained by Schwarz et al. (see also chapter 8 by Haddock, in this volume; Raghubir & Menon, 1998; Rothman & Schwarz, 1998; chapter 9 by Wänke & Bless, in this volume; Wänke, Bless, & Biller, 1996; Wänke, Bohner, & Jurkowitsch, 1997). Thus, their results provide strong support for the availability heuristic and suggest that individuals really do rely upon the experienced ease with which they can retrieve instances as evidence of the frequency of those instances (i.e., evidence for their possession of the target trait).

☐ Contextual Factors and the Availability Heuristic

We know that the effects of moods can be moderated by contextual factors (e.g., Forgas, 2000; Martin, 2000). Can the effects of experienced ease of retrieval also be moderated by such factors? It appears that they can. If reliance on experienced ease or difficulty of retrieval as information is a heuristic processing strategy (Tversky & Kahneman, 1973), then individuals may be most susceptible to relying upon the availability heuristic when they are not exerting a great deal of cognitive effort while making their judgment. In fact, when they exert effort, then they may switch to a more systematic strategy, such as basing their judgment on the amount of descriptive content to which they have access.

Rothman and Schwarz (1998) explored the moderating effects of cognitive effort on the availability heuristic by having male students generate a list of either three or eight factors that could increase (or decrease) one's risk of developing heart disease. The amount of cognitive effort was operationalized as the self-reported history of heart disease in the participant's family. Presumably, participants with a family history of heart disease would find the risk factors more personally relevant and hence would exert more effort in listing those factors than participants without a family history of heart disease (e.g., Chaiken, Liberman, & Eagly, 1989).

After participants generated their list of risk factors, they answered a series of questions concerning the likelihood that they would develop heart disease at some point in their lives. If individuals use ease of retrieval as information, then those who retrieved three risk factors (easy) would report having a higher likelihood of developing heart disease than individuals who retrieved six risk factors (difficult). These results were obtained, but, as expected, only among participants who presumably did not exert much cognitive effort while making their judgments. Specifically, among participants not reporting a family history of heart disease (low effort), those who recalled six risk factors reported a smaller likelihood of experiencing heart disease than those who recalled three risk factors. Among participants reporting a family history (high effort), those who recalled six risk factors actually reported a greater likelihood that they would experience heart disease than those who recalled three risk factors.

Rothman and Schwarz (1998) summarized their findings by suggesting that "people who are not sufficiently involved with the judgment task should process information heuristically, relying on the ease with which risk-relevant information comes to mind. We assume this to be the default information processing strategy that people use. On the other hand, people who are personally involved with the judgment task should process information systematically, focusing on the content of the accessible information" (p. 1056).

This study is interesting in at least two ways. First, the results demonstrate that contextual factors can determine the extent to which differences in subjective ease of retrieval reflect themselves in the typical availability effect. Second, the explanation offered by Rothman and Schwarz is essentially a two-process account (e.g., Default + Interference). Participants who did not exert effort relied upon ease of retrieval, whereas participants who did exert effort based their risk judgments on the amount of descriptive content they recalled. Although this is a plausible interpretation, from an experience as input perspective, it makes sense to ask whether we need to resort to two different processes to account for a crossover interaction. If the implications of subjective experiences really are defined within the context, then it should be possible to find a context in which the experience of effortful thinking would be interpreted as a sign of even greater evidence for the target behavior, thus reversing the availability heuristic. To produce this result, we would need to find a context in which effortful cognitive processing signaled fulfillment of a positive role (e.g., a greater likelihood of rendering a correct answer).

☐ Ease of Retrieval and Role Fulfillment

If individuals expect retrieval to be relatively easy, then they may interpret their difficulty in retrieving as a sign that they are having trouble. More specifically, they may see the unexpected effort as a sign that they have less of the target information than they thought they did (or at least think they should). It is in this context that we might observe the traditional availability heuristic, because in this context, effortful retrieval signals fulfillment of an undesired role (lack of information).

Suppose, however, individuals are performing a cognitive task they expect to be challenging. In this case, the expenditure of cognitive effort might not only be expected, but it might also be desired. It might be seen as the appropriate way to approach the task. If so, then in a difficult retrieval task, individuals may interpret overly easy retrieval as a sign that they did not process the information sufficiently. Such an inference would give rise to the opposite of the availability heuristic. Those who had difficulty retrieving may actually have more polarized judgments than those who had little difficulty retrieving. From an experience as input perspective, we would say that in the context of a challenging task, effortful processing signals fulfillment of a desirable role (thinking at the level of a challenging task).

Note that with this role fulfillment explanation, we can account for both the availability heuristic and its opposite in terms of the same mechanism. We do not need to hypothesize the operation of an outside, interfering process. We need only assume that in the context of simple problems, the exertion of a small amount of cognitive effort is a good sign (giving rise to the availability heuristic), whereas in the context of challenging problems, the exertion of more effort is a good sign (giving rise to the opposite of the availability heuristic).

☐ Ease of Retrieval as Input: The Evidence

In order to test the role fulfillment extension of the availability heuristic, we needed to have participants experience different degrees of retrieval effort, but we needed to do this in a way that did not confound effort with the amount of information retrieved. If effort covaried with amount retrieved, then any deviations from the availability heuristic could be attributed to participants relying upon accessible content rather than subjective experience (Rothman & Schwarz, 1998). So, we manipulated experienced effort in much the same way as Stepper and Strack (1993). These investigators asked participants to recall six instances in which they had behaved either assertively or nonassertively. Then, they asked participants to rate how assertive or unassertive they were. Stepper and Strack manipulated ease of retrieval by having participants hold one of two facial expressions. Half of the participants retrieved the instances while furrowing their brows, an expression associated with effortful processing (Cacioppo & Petty, 1981), whereas half retrieved the instances while not furrowing their brows. Consistent with the hypothesis that experienced difficulty of retrieval (independent of amount retrieved) is associated with an inference about lack of evidence, Stepper and Strack found that participants who contracted their brows during retrieval rated themselves less extreme in the direction of the retrieved instances (assertive or nonassertive) than those who did not furrow their brows.

Using a variant of the Stepper and Strack procedure, we presented participants with two posters, asked them which of the posters they preferred, and then asked them to list six reasons for their preference. Following this, we had participants rate the extent to which they liked each of the posters. We assumed that the more evidence participants felt they had for their preference (i.e., the greater the availability of their reasons), the greater the difference in their evaluations of the two posters would be.

We manipulated experienced retrieval effort by having participants contract either their brows (difficult retrieval) or their cheeks (easy retrieval) while generating their reasons. Specifically, we placed electrodes on participants' brows or cheeks and told participants to contract the associated muscles as part of a physiological recording task (ostensibly, we needed to establish a baseline for a task to appear later in the experiment). The effectiveness of this technique was revealed in our manipulation check at the end of the experiment. Participants who had contracted their brows rated the generation task as more difficult than did participants who had contracted their cheeks.

According to the role fulfillment hypothesis, the evaluative implications of these differences in experienced retrieval effort should depend on the extent to which the effort signals fulfillment of a desirable or an undesirable role. To manipulate the desirability of the role for which participants' effort was input, we had participants choose between two posters that were either extremely similar to one another (both woodland scenes) or moderately different from one another (one depicted a woodland scene, the other depicted a sailboat on the ocean). If our role fulfillment hypothesis is correct, then when participants experienced difficulty (i.e., brows) generating reasons for what should be an easy choice (the two dissimilar posters), they should report less of a difference between their choices than those who experienced little difficulty (i.e., cheek). After all, when participants experience difficulty generating reasons in a context in which they expect it to be easy, they may infer that they have little evidence for their choice. Such a result would replicate the traditional availability heuristic. The greater the retrieval effort, the smaller the difference in participants' evaluations of the two posters.

When participants generate reasons for a difficult choice (i.e., preferring one of two very similar posters), however, those who experienced difficulty (brows) should report a greater difference between their evaluations of the posters than those who experienced little difficulty (cheek). In this context, participants may interpret their more effortful retrieval as greater systematic thinking on a task that required systematic thinking. This would yield the opposite of the availability heuristic. In this context, effortful thinking fulfills the desired role of adequate cognitive processing. Thus, participants who experienced their retrieval as effortful may infer that they have more evidence for their choice than those who did not experience effort, and this would lead to a greater split between their evaluations.

Our results supported this reasoning (see Figure 6.2). When participants generated reasons for preferring one of the dissimilar posters, those who contracted their brows (difficult) reported less of a difference between their ratings of the two posters than those who contracted their cheek muscles (easy). In contrast, when participants generated reasons for preferring one of the two similar posters, those who contracted their brows (difficult) reported more of a difference between their ratings of the two posters than those who contracted their cheek muscles (easy). The former finding reflects the availability heuristic; the latter finding reflects the opposite.

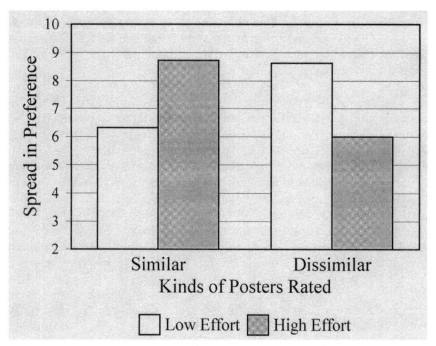

FIGURE 6.2. Spread in poster evaluations as a function of poster similarity and subjective effort.

Taken together, these results suggest that experienced ease of retrieval conveys different evaluative implications in different contexts. Greater differences between participants' evaluation of the posters occurred when participants either (a) experienced little retrieval effort in a context in which little effort was appropriate, or (b) experienced greater effort in a context in which greater effort was appropriate. In other words, polarized evaluations arose when participants experienced the feelings that fulfilled a positive role (efficient processing or systematic processing). Less polarized judgments occurred when there was a mismatch between the experienced effort and the amount of effort considered appropriate. In other words, the availability heuristic occurred only when difficulty of retrieval signaled fulfillment of a negative role (i.e., insufficient information).

The results of this study are not easily interpreted in terms of the dual-process model proposed by Rothman and Schwarz. They interpreted their crossover interaction in terms of participants using different kinds of information in different contexts. Specifically, Rothman and Schwarz proposed that participants relied upon the availability heuristic when they exerted little cognitive effort, but relied upon the amount of descriptive content they recalled when they exerted more effort. In our study, the amount of descriptive content participants retrieved was held constant. So, the Rothman and Schwarz proposal cannot apply. This does not mean, of course, that the Rothman and Schwarz proposal is wrong. It simply means that their proposal does not apply to our results. Our results are best interpreted in terms of the experience of subjective effort being input into a role fulfillment evaluation process and giving rise to different evaluative implications in different contexts.

The possibility that subject effort can have different implications in different contexts was also raised by Waneke and Bless (see Wänke chapter 9 in this volume). These investigators suggested that subjective ease of retrieval might influence the perceived quality (as opposed to amount) of retrieved information. They also suggested that ease of retrieval may be more likely to influence judgments when individuals process systematically than when individuals process heuristically. Both of these suggestions are compatible with the suggestions made in our chapter.

Along with these points of agreement, however, are some differences. First, Wänke and Bless suggested that although difficulty of retrieval might have implications for different kinds of judgments (amount, validity, credibility), these implications are always negative. According to Wänke and Bless, difficult retrieval implies either a paucity of information or that the information is low in validity, diagnosticity, or credibility. Our role fulfillment model, by comparison, allows effortful retrieval to be a sign of high-quality systematic processing as well.

Another difference lies in the mechanism through which context is assumed to moderate the implications of experienced retrieval effort. Wänke and Bless suggested that individuals' attributions can influence the implications of effortful retrieval. Although we do not disagree with this proposal, the experience as input model does not emphasize attributional processing. We assume instead that context can influence the implications of subjective experiences due to the configural nature of the judgmental process. In configural judgments, each piece of the stimulus configuration helps to constrain the implications of the other (Read & Miller, 1994). To put it another way, changes in implications are a natural byproduct of the way our evaluative system works.

Finally, although Wänke and Bless suggested that different contexts can change the implications of subjective effort, they did not provide a coherent theoretical mechanism to account for these changes. We did. Our role fulfillment mechanism specifies what one needs to know to understand and predict how context will moderate the influence of subjective cognitive effort on evaluations.

☐ Applications to Other Social Psychological Phenomena

Our study explored the possibility that experienced cognitive effort in the form of easy or difficult retrieval could convey different evaluative implications in different contexts. Our results may have implications for any number of phenomena to which experienced cognitive effort is a contributor. For example, in our study, participants were asked to give reasons for choosing one poster over another. This kind of activity is a core component of studies on the reasons analysis effect (Wilson, Hodges, & LaFleur, 1995). In those studies, participants have been asked to give reasons for their choice of posters, their preference in jams, and their attitudes toward their relationships. According to Wilson and colleagues, when participants generate reasons for such behaviors, they retrieve plausible theories rather than the actual reasons. To the extent that these theories are accessible as participants subsequently evaluate the target, participants' evaluations may be based on the theories rather than on their real reasons. What this means is that participants' evaluations will change. Some evaluations will become more favorable; some will become less favorable. This dispersal of evaluations following explanation is the reasons analysis effect, and it is attributed to a change in content brought about by attempted explanation.

It seems likely, though, that participants will not only bring different information to mind, but that they will also differ in how effortful they think the explanation task will be and in how effortful they actually find the task to be. If so, then some participants might interpret their effort as a sign that they do not have many reasons for their choice, whereas others might interpret the effort as a sign that they have good, thoughtful reasons for their choice. If so, then these different interpretations could decrease the evaluation of the former but increase the evaluations of the latter. In this way, we could produce a reasons analysis effect even if participants retrieved the real reasons for their behavior.

Consider also how the role fulfillment mechanism might operate in the context of classic cognitive dissonance research. In this research, participants must justify their performance of what is essentially a difficult-to-justify behavior (i.e., a behavior that is freely chosen as well as counter attitudinal). In the postdecision paradigm, for example, participants are asked to choose between either two similar alternatives or two different alternatives (Brehm, 1956). The assumption is that participants should have difficulty justifying a choice between the similar alternatives. So, in an attempt to maintain consistency, participants increase their evaluation of the alternative they had chosen.

In our study, participants chose between two very similar posters, a difficult task. So, when our experimental participants actually experienced effort while generating their reasons, they interpreted this effort as a sign that they had thought systematically about a difficult choice. As a result, their evaluations of the two posters spread apart. Perhaps participants in the dissonance paradigm may do the same. They may have difficulty justifying why they freely choose one stimulus over a very similar alternative. They may realize that the decision was a difficult one, and this realization may increase the likelihood that participants (in the low justification condition) would interpret their effort as a sign that they had engaged in systematic thinking with regard to their decision. This interpretation, in turn, would cause the low justification participants to feel good about their decision, and thus would lead them to more polarized evaluations. In other words, participants' interpretations of their effort may contribute to the spread of alternatives in the dissonance paradigm.

Another possible application of the role fulfillment mechanism involves attitude polarization. Tesser (1978) has shown that thinking about a previously evaluated stimulus can polarize subsequent evaluations of that stimulus. This polarization has been explained in terms of participants retrieving evidence congruent with their initial evaluation. Our work suggests, however, that retrieval of congruent evidence may not be enough. As participants retrieve this evidence, they may also exert different amounts of effort and differ in how they interpret this effort. If two people exert cognitive effort while coming up with six pieces of evidence, for example, one may interpret this effort as a lack of evidence, whereas the other may interpret it as a sign that he or she processed the evidence systematically. These differences in interpretation would lead the latter to a more polarized evaluation than the former, even though both retrieved the same amount of congruent evidence.

The role fulfillment mechanism might also apply to the classic priming paradigm (Higgins, Rholes, & Jones, 1977), the false fame effect (Jacoby, Kelley, Brown, & Jasechko, 1989), and the theory perseverance effect (Anderson, Lepper, & Ross, 1980). Obviously, these applications are speculative. Our results do suggest, however, that the contribution of subjective experience to a number of basic social psychology effects has been underestimated and overlooked. Even when these experiences have been studied, researchers have typically underestimated the extent to which the same experiences can convey different evaluative and motivational implications in different contexts.

It may be time to move away from a primary reliance on semantic structure and context-free feelings in the explanation of human behavior. The subjective experience of thinking may be as important in determining one's evaluations and actions as the content that is thought about. Moreover, the evaluative and motivational implications of one's subjective experiences are context dependent. What this means is that any given experience can have any number of effects on evaluation, depending on how people interpret their experiences as they process information. Fortunately, the role fulfillment hypothesis of the experience as input model gives us a simple way to predict and explain these effects. Favorable evaluations arise when individuals' subjective experiences indicate that the target is satisfying desired criteria, whereas negative evaluations arise when individuals' subjective experiences indicate that the target is satisfying undesirable criteria. Thus, it is not sufficient to know what people are thinking or experiencing. We need to know how an individual's thoughts and subjective experiences simultaneously constrain the implications of the other. More specifically, we need to know (a) the criteria relative to which a target is being evaluated, (b) the kinds of subjective experiences that suggest satisfaction of those criteria, and (c) the extent to which the judge is currently having those experiences.

☐ References

Anderson, C. A., Lepper, M. R., & Ross, L. (1980). Perseverance of social theories: The role of explanation in the persistence of discredited information. *Journal of Personality and Social Psychology, 39*, 1037–1049.

Berkowitz, L. (1993). Toward a general theory of anger and emotional aggression: Implications of the cognitive-neoassociationistic perspective for the analysis of anger and other emotions. In R. S. Wyer & T. K. Srull (Eds.), *Advance in social cognition* (pp. 1–46). Hillsdale, NJ: Erlbaum.

Bless, H. (2000). Mood and the use of general knowledge structures. In L. L. Martin & G. L. Clore (Eds.), *Theories of mood and cognition: A user's guidebook*. Mahwah, NJ: Erlbaum.

Brehm, J. W. (1956). Postdecision changes in the desirability of alternatives. *Journal of Abnormal and Social Psychology, 52*, 384–389.

Cacioppo, J. T., & Petty, R. E. (1981). Electromyograms as measures of extent and affectivity of information processing. *American Psychologist, 36*, 441–456.

Chaiken, S., Liberman, A., & Eagley, A. H. (1989). Heuristic and systematic processing within and beyond the persuasion context. In J. S. Uleman & J. A. Bargh (Eds.), *Unintended thought* (pp. 212–252). New York: Guilford Press.

Clark, M. S., & Isen, A. M. (1982). Toward understanding the relationship between feeling states and social behavior. In A. Hastrof & A. M. Isen (Eds.), *Cognitive social psychology* (pp. 73–108). New York: Elsevier North-Holland.

Estrada, C. A., Isen, A. M., & Young, M. J. (1994). Positive affect improves creative problem solving and influences reported source of practice satisfaction in physicians. *Motivation and Emotion, 18*, 285–299.

Fiedler, K. (2000). Affective states trigger processes of assimilation and accommodation. In L. L. Martin & G. L. Clore (Eds.), *Theories of mood and cognition: A user's guidebook*. Mahwah, NJ: Erlbaum.

Forgas, J. P. (2000). The affect infusion model (AIM): An integrative theory of mood effects on cognition and judgments. In L. L. Martin & G. L. Clore (Eds.), *Theories of mood and cognition: A user's guidebook*. Mahwah, NJ: Erlbaum.

Higgins, E. T., Rholes, W. S., & Jones, C. R. (1977). Category accessibility and impression formation. *Journal of Experimental Social Psychology, 13*, 151–156.

Hirt, E. R., McDonald, H. E., Levine, G. M., Melton, R. J., & Martin, L. L. (1999). One person's enjoyment if another person's boredom: Mood effects on responsiveness to framing. *Personality and Social Psychology Bulletin, 25*, 76–91.

Hirt, E. R., Melton, R. J., McDonald, H. E., & Harackiewicz, J. M. (1996). Processing goals, task interest, and the mood-performance relationship: A mediational analysis. *Journal of Personality and Social Psychology, 71*, 245–261.

Jacoby, L. L., Kelley, C., Brown, J., & Jasechko, J. (1989). Becoming famous overnight: Limits on the ability to avoid unconscious influences of the past. *Journal of Personality and Social Psychology, 56*, 326–338.

Mackie, D. M., & Worth, L. T. (1989). Processing deficits and the mediation of positive affect in persuasion. *Journal of Personality and Social Psychology, 57*, 27–40.

Martin, L. L. (2000). Mood as input: A configural view of mood effects. In L. L. Martin & G. L. Clore (Eds.), *Theories of mood and cognition: A user's guidebook*. Mahwah, NJ: Erlbaum.

Martin, L. L. (2000). Moods don't convey information: Moods in context do. In J. Forgas (Ed.), *Feeling and thinking: The role of affect in social cognition* (pp. 153–177). New York: Cambridge University Press.

Martin, L. L., Abend, T. A., Sedikides, C., & Green, J. (1997). How would I feel if . . . ? Mood as input to a role fulfillment evaluation process. *Journal of Personality and Social Psychology, 73*, 242–253.

Martin, L. L., Achee, J. W., Ward, D. W., & Harlow, T. F. (1993). The role of cognition and effort in the use of emotions to guide behavior. In R. S. Wyer & T. K. Srull (Eds.), *Advances in social cognition* (Vol. 6, pp. 147–157). Hillsdale, NJ: Erlbaum.

Martin, L. L., & Davies, B. (1998). Beyond hedonism and associationism: A configural view of the role of affect in evaluation, processing, and self-regulation. *Motivation and Emotion, 22*, 33–51.

Martin, L. L., & Stoner, P. (1996). Mood as input: What people think about how they feel determines how they think. In L. L. Martin & A Tesser (Eds.), *Striving and feeling: Interactions among goals, affect, and self-regulation* (pp. 279–301). Hillsdale, NJ: Erlbaum.

Martin, L. L., Ward, D. W., Achee, J. W., & Wyer, R. S. (1993). Mood as input: People have to interpret the motivational implications of their moods. *Journal of Personality and Social Psychology, 64*, 317–326.

Mayer, J. D., Gaschke, Y. N., Braverman, D. L., & Evans, T. (1992). Mood-congruent judgment is a general effect. *Journal of Personality and Social Psychology, 63*, 119–132.

Raghubir, P., & Menon, G. (1998). AIDS and me, never the twain shall meet: The effects of information accessibility on judgments of risk and advertising effectiveness. *Journal of Consumer Research, 25*, 52–63.

Read, S. J., & Miller, L. C. (1994). Dissonance and balance in belief systems: The promise of parallel constraint satisfaction and connectionist modeling approaches. In R. C. Schank & E. Langer (Eds.), *Beliefs, reasoning, and decision making: Psycho-logic in honor of Bob Abelson* (pp. 209–235). Hillsdale, NJ: Erlbaum.

Rothman, A. J., & Schwarz, N. (1998). Constructing perceptions of vulnerability: Personal relevance and the use of experiential information in health judgments. *Personality and Social Psychology Bulletin, 24*, 1053–1064.

Sanna, C. J., Turley, K. J., & Mark, M. M. (1996). Expected evaluation, goals, and performance: Mood as input. *Personality and Social Psychology Bulletin, 22*, 323–335.

Schwarz, N. (2000). Feelings as information: Implications for affective influences on information processing. In L. L. Martin & G. L. Clore (Eds.), *Theories of mood and cognition: A user's guidebook*. Mahwah, NJ: Erlbaum.

Schwarz, N., Bless, H., Strack, F., & Klumpp, G. (1991). Ease of retrieval as information: Another look at the availability heuristic. *Journal of Personality and Social Psychology, 61*, 195–202.

Schwarz, N., & Bohner, G. (1996). Feelings and their motivational implications: Moods and the action sequence. In P. M. Gollwitzer & J. A. Bargh (Eds.), *The psychology of action: Linking cognition and motivation to behavior*. New York: Guilford Press.

Stepper, S., & Strack, F. (1993). Proprioceptive determinants of emotional and nonemotional feelings. *Journal of Personality and Social Psychology, 64*, 211–220.

Tesser, A. (1978). Self-generated attitude change. In L. Berkowitz (Ed.), *Advances in experimental social psychology* (Vol. 11, pp. 289–338). New York: Academic Press.

Tversky, A., & Kahneman, D. (1973). Availability: A heuristic for judging frequency and probability. *Cognitive Psychology, 5*, 207–232.

Wänke, M., Bless, H., & Biller, B. (1996). Subjective experience versus content of information in the construction of attitude judgments. *Personality and Social Psychology Bulletin, 22*, 1105–1115.

Wänke, M., Bohner, G., & Jurkowitsch, A. (1997). There are many reasons to drive a BMW: Does ease of argument generation influence brand attitudes? *Journal of Consumer Research, 24*, 170–177.

Wegener, D. T., & Petty, R. E. (2000). How mood affects judgment: Understanding effects of mood through the elaboration likelihood and flexible correction models. In L. L. Martin & G. L. Clore (Eds.), *Theories of mood and cognition: A user's guidebook*. Mahwah, NJ: Erlbaum.

Wilson, T. D., Hodges, S. D., & LaFleur, S. J. (1995). Effects of introspecting about reasons: Inferring attitudes from accessible thoughts. *Journal of Personality and Social Psychology, 69*, 16–28.

II

SUBJECTIVE EXPERIENCE AND MEMORY PHENOMENA

CHAPTER Eliot R. Smith

Subjective Experience of Familiarity: Functional Basis in Connectionist Memory

What is the origin and nature of our subjective experiences? Why do things feel to us the way they do? While these questions may seem too deep and abstract for anyone but the philosophers, some insight can be gained by considering the potential functional role of some types of experiences. An easy example is the experience of pain, which serves an obvious function in discouraging us from damaging our bodies. In this chapter, I will suggest a possible functional role for the subjective experience of familiarity—the feeling that an object or event is usual, typical, or has been seen before. This feeling, I will argue, is rooted in inherent properties of memory systems.

Feelings of familiarity have been studied in several different lines of research within social psychology (Smith & Zárate, 1992). Perhaps most prominent is work showing that people prefer objects that are familiar (due to prior experimental exposure) over equivalent objects that are less familiar, a phenomenon termed the *mere exposure effect* (Zajonc, 1968). This finding has been replicated in both laboratory and nonlaboratory contexts (e.g., Moreland & Beach, 1992). Even subliminal exposures can produce familiarity and liking, although participants are unable to explicitly recognize that they have seen the stimuli before (Bornstein &

An earlier version of this chapter was presented at a conference in Grasellenbach, Germany, July 1998.

Address correspondence to Eliot R. Smith, Dept. of Psych. Sciences, Purdue University, West Lafayette, IN 47907. E-mail: esmith@psych.purdue.edu

D'Agostino, 1994). This latter finding indicates that familiarity detection is an automatic and preconscious process.

Another line of work suggests that validity is attributed to propositional statements that are familiar from prior exposure. Researchers expose participants to plausible general knowledge statements (e.g., "Baby seals sleep with their eyes open"), and then at a later time, the participants judge the statement's truth or validity. Previously exposed statements are rated more likely to be true (Arkes, Boehm, & Xu, 1991), even when they cannot be explicitly recognized as previously seen.

A third area in which familiarity has effects is in "false fame" judgments. Jacoby, Kelley, Brown, and Jasechko (1989) had participants read made-up names of nonfamous people. After a 24-hour delay participants read a list of those names plus new nonfamous and moderately famous names and rated their fame. Some of the previously exposed nonfamous names now were rated as famous, due to the feeling of familiarity from the prior exposure. The prior exposure could not be explicitly recalled; we know this because if participants could recall that the name appeared on the previous list, they could have inferred that it was nonfamous.

Finally, in cognitive psychology, feelings of familiarity appear to play a role in recognition memory. Two-process theories of recognition (Jacoby & Dallas, 1981; Mandler, 1980) hold that people can correctly recognize a previously studied word either by recalling the study context or by judging that the word is relatively familiar and inferring that it must have been studied. Considerable evidence supports this general notion (e.g., Yonelinas, 1997).

☐ Origin of Feeling of Familiarity

With all this evidence suggesting that feelings of familiarity play an important role in diverse areas including liking, perceptions of validity, and recognition memory, what do we know about the origin of this subjective feeling? My argument is that an ability to detect whether a stimulus object or event is familiar or novel is a fundamental and necessary part of any biologically and psychologically realistic memory system. The reason stems from what has been termed the *stability-plasticity dilemma*.

The Stability-Plasticity Dilemma

One of our familiar metaphors for memory involves a recording instrument like a camera or tape recorder, which takes snapshots of stimuli or events and stores them away as individual records in a file cabinet. In this metaphor, storing a new record does not interfere with or alter other stored records. However, this conception of memory is biologically unrealistic, for it requires indefinitely large amounts of "storage space." A real memory system must be capable of storing indefinitely large numbers of memory traces within finite resources, and the stability-plasticity dilemma arises from this requirement. The stability of a memory system, its ability to retain learned information for the long term, is one key property. A memory system that forgot all yesterday's events as it learns about what happens today would be functionally useless. However, plasticity is also important: the memory system must also store information about new events so that the contents of memory remain up to date.

In a realistic memory system where all memory traces are stored in a finite set of resources, stability and plasticity conflict with each other. New information must somehow be stored using the same resources that also maintain previously learned information; in other words, new and old memory representations are superimposed (van Gelder, 1991). Yet this process must not seriously degrade that older information. For example, we must be able to learn new people's faces yet not forget our parents' faces, learned many years ago (Grossberg & Merrill, 1996). One potential solution is simply to assume that everything worth learning is learned early in life, so that the learning rate (the amount by which new experiences are allowed to have an impact on the memory store) can be turned down (perhaps to zero) after a time. However, this solution fails for creatures that need to adapt to a dynamic environment, as humans do. More realistic solutions have been developed under three different connectionist models of memory. Each of these three models has been worked out in relatively complete detail (e.g., theorists have examined fits between the predictions of their memory models and data from psychological experiments). Under each of these models, as I will argue, resolving the stability-plasticity dilemma involves as a byproduct producing a signal that directly translates into a subjective feeling of familiarity.

Grossberg's ART Model

Grossberg's ART model (Carpenter & Grossberg, 1995; Grossberg, 1976) involves several components. Two interconnected sets of nodes, F1 and F2, together constitute an attention and memory system, linked to a separate orienting system (which, as we will see, functions as a familiarity detector). Inputs coded as a vector of perceptual features activate some of the nodes within network F1 (see Figure 7.1). Each F1 node represents a specific combination of features (e.g., wagging tail plus floppy ears). The subset of F1 nodes that are activated by the input send outputs to the F2

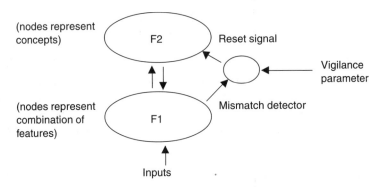

FIGURE 7.1. Conceptual structure of ART memory model (Carpenter & Grossberg, 1995).

network. Each node in F2 represents a category or object (e.g., dog). Several F2 nodes may initially be activated by the inputs from F1, but one will win out in a competition for activation within F2, becoming the network's *hypothesis* about the identity of the input. That node will send activation back over reverse pathways to F1. These pathways activate the F1 nodes that correspond to the *prototype* of the category represented by the F2 node. If the external inputs and the return paths from F2 converge onto the same set of F1 nodes, activation will grow and enter a self-reinforcing or "resonant" state that maintains the patterns of activation in F1 and F2 long enough for learning to take place. The input has been categorized (assimilated) to a specific category represented by the active F2 node.

However, if the external inputs do not match up well enough with the return flow of activation from F2 (which reflects the category prototype), a separate orienting system (shown on the right in the figure) detects this mismatch. When the mismatch exceeds an externally provided "vigilance" parameter, a wave of activation is automatically sent to the F2 network, resetting it and initiating a search for a different hypothesis (different maximally active node in F2). This reset takes place rapidly, before resonance can develop, and therefore blocks learning if the input does not match the selected category prototype. Ultimately, if no F2 node matches the input pattern well enough, a new (previously uncommitted) F2 node is selected to represent this new category.

Thus, the orienting system (mismatch detector) operates to put the attention and memory system (the F1 and F2 networks) into one of two modes. If a good match between bottom-up input and top-down stored categorical knowledge is found, the input is assimilated to the existing category through the resonance process (preserving stability of existing knowledge). If a good match is not found, the input is assigned to a completely new category and the process of learning about the features of that category begins (plasticity). In serving this function, the orienting system produces a signal that reflects the mismatch between the input and the currently selected category, which amounts to an indicator of familiarity versus the novelty of the input.

Metcalfe's CHARM Model

Metcalfe (1994) has discussed the detection of familiarity or novelty within the framework of her CHARM memory model (Metcalfe, 1991). CHARM, or composite holographic associative recall/recognition model, is a model of human episodic memory. Metcalfe notes that this model works better for explicit episodic memory than for implicit memory or for slowly learning very stable representations, such as the meanings of words, with many repetitions over time (see discussion of dual memory systems below). In CHARM, a stimulus item or event is initially represented as a vector of features, which is then transformed by the mathematical operation of convolution. Convolution produces another vector, which is then added into a single composite memory trace that combines all the memory system's individual experiences. The additive superimposition of individual traces into a single composite trace is a key feature of the model, responsible for many of its predictions. However, mathematically, adding a new trace into the composite tends to increase the absolute value of the individual elements of the composite trace vector. In a real neural system, the size of these elements cannot increase without limit, so some sort of "renormalization" process that keeps their magnitude constant must be postulated. Indeed, Metcalfe (1991) has demonstrated that the model cannot work without such a mechanism. This problem is one version of the stability-plasticity dilemma: adding new traces into the composite (to allow plasticity, or learning new information) tends to distort or wipe out the older stored information (weakening the stability of old memory traces).

Within the model, the increase in magnitude of the trace elements is proportional to the similarity of the new incoming information to the information already stored in the composite trace (Metcalfe, 1994). That is, adding in vectors representing relatively familiar stimuli will lead to a larger increase in the size of the elements of the memory trace vector, compared to unfamiliar stimuli. Thus, renormalizing the composite (decreasing the magnitude of its elements by an appropriate proportion) *requires* monitoring the familiarity or novelty of that incoming information. Simply applying a constant decay factor to the composite trace would not work, because different incoming events will differentially affect the magnitude of its elements. But by assessing the increase of the elements of the composite trace as the new event is added to it, the appropriate renormalization can be done. Thus, a rapid assessment of novelty or familiarity, which is necessary in any case to make the memory system work correctly, is available to be subjectively perceived as a feeling of familiarity.

Recurrent Attractor Autoassociative Networks

A third type of connectionist memory is a recurrent autoassociative network, as proposed by McClelland and Rumelhart (1986). In contrast to CHARM, this type of memory is best suited for learning general patterns slowly, through many repetitions; it can be viewed as a "semantic" or "schematic" rather than an episodic memory system. To understand its workings, it is helpful to regard the network as a dynamical system (Churchland & Sejnowski, 1992). An input pattern represented as a vector of activation values is presented to the network and activation flows among the units in response. Because the units in the network are connected recurrently (meaning that flows of activation can make loops or cycles), it takes some time for flows of activation to settle down as the network arrives at a fixed pattern. The flows of activation are described by equations that are analogous to those describing a ball rolling downhill on a landscape formed of many hills and valleys. Thus, one can conveniently visualize the behavior of a recurrent network by thinking of dropping a ball at a certain point (the coordinates of that point corresponding to the input pattern or vector), and then watching the ball roll downhill until it stops at the lowest point that it can reach. Such a point, where no further motion (i.e., no further flow of activation) occurs, is termed an *attractor*.

With this picture in mind, two additional properties of these networks are now easy to grasp. First, the description just given applies to a network that has already learned some patterns from prior exposure. In fact, the valleys and pits on the landscape are created by the learning process. Prior to learning, the landscape is all steep peaks and hillsides, with no flat or smooth areas that make good stopping places for a ball. The network's learning rule creates stopping places—pits in the landscape—at locations corresponding to patterns that have been frequently presented. Think of each ball that is dropped onto the landscape as creating a small crater at its point of impact; if many balls are dropped in the same place a deep pit will eventually be created. Thus, after learning, we can see that a ball dropped *near* the location of a frequently seen pattern will end up at the bottom of that pit; that is, it will be interpreted as an *instance* of the known pattern.

Second, we can now see how familiarity can be rapidly detected. In general, a ball that is dropped at or near the bottom of an existing pit (i.e., a pattern that is familiar) creates minimal flows of activation. The network has to change state only a little before ending up at a stable attractor. In contrast, a ball that is dropped far from its ultimate resting place will generally be on a steep hillside, and will set in motion large-scale flows of activation before an attractor is ultimately reached.

To be useful, an autoassociative memory requires a monitoring process that detects the magnitude of flows of activation. This is because it is necessary to determine when flows of activation have stopped, indicating that the network has reached an attractor and that its current configuration is stable and meaningful for use in further processing. Such a monitor can be readily implemented by simply duplicating each connection between network units, sending a copy of the activation that flows within the network off to an external monitoring unit. Then, strong flows of activation within the network would create strong inputs to the monitoring unit, and weak or no activation flows within the network mean little or no input to the monitoring unit. This monitoring unit is our familiarity detector, for it gives a large signal for inputs that are unfamiliar to the network and a small signal for familiar inputs. The signal is available rapidly—even before the network settles; that is, before the input pattern can be identified or classified.

In a network of this type, the way new information interferes with prior learning (i.e., the stability-plasticity dilemma) has been described with the term *catastrophic interference* (Ratcliff, 1990). Once a network has learned a set A of patterns, if those patterns are no longer encountered but a different set B is encountered instead, the network's ability to remember set A will rapidly decline to zero. Plasticity (the ability to learn new information) conflicts with stability (the ability to retain old information). To solve this problem, McClelland, McNaughton, & O'Reilly (1995) propose that humans and other organisms have two separate memory systems with distinct properties (similar views have been put forward by Alvarez & Squire, 1994; Milner, 1989; Murre, 1995; see Schacter & Tulving, 1994, for additional discussion). The demand for stability means that our memory must record information slowly and incrementally so that the total configuration in memory reflects a large sample of experiences. This is important so that general expectancies and long-term schematic knowledge can be based on the average, typical properties of the environment. The demand for plasticity means that we must also be able to rapidly learn new information so that a novel experience can be remembered after a single occurrence. After all, people can at least sometimes learn things by being told once. The requirements of slow and fast learning appear incompatible.

As a solution to this problem, McClelland et al. (1995) propose that slow and fast learning are handled by separate memory systems. This idea may seem unparsimonious, but many types of psychological and neuro-psychological evidence, summarized in detail in McClelland et al. (1995), point to the existence of two memory systems with properties that corre-spond to slow-learning and fast-learning systems. The slow-learning memory system emphasizes stability. Learning in this system takes place as the system processes each stimulus, and involves only small, incre-mental alterations in synaptic strengths. Slow-learning memory is respon-sible for learning stable, general representations of the typical properties of the environment (e.g., correspondences between word forms and word meanings) over many trials. These representations are then used precon-sciously to process and interpret new information by categorizing, filling in unobserved details, and the like.

The fast-learning memory system is necessary because the effects of a single experience on the slow-learning system will generally not be large enough to allow for full retrieval of the details of that experience on a future occasion. The fast-learning system is responsible for rapidly con-structing new representations (i.e., episodic memories) that bind together information about different aspects of an object or experience in its con-text (Wiles & Humphreys, 1993). This system mediates conscious, ex-plicit recollection. In addition to differences in speed of learning and con-scious accessibility, McClelland et al. (1995) postulate that the slow-learning and fast-learning systems record different types of infor-mation. Slow learning is chiefly concerned with regularities, so it prima-rily records what is typical and expected. In contrast, the fast-learning system records the details of events that are novel, unexpected, and unpredicted. See Smith and DeCoster (1999) for applications of these ideas about dual memory systems to other areas of social psychology.

In this model, the rapid signal of familiarity that arises from monitoring the flows of activation in the slow-learning network when a new stimu-lus is presented is used to "gate" the input information. Information that is relatively unfamiliar or novel (as far as the slow-learning system is concerned) is sent to be recorded in the fast-learning system. In contrast, information that is familiar leaves little trace in the fast-learning system; there is no need to store this information specifically because it corre-sponds with the system's general expectations or schemata.

☐ Effects of Familiarity or Novelty

As we have seen, all three of these memory models propose ways of re-solving the fundamental stability-plasticity dilemma. As part of the resolution, each model generates a signal that can be monitored to indicate the familiarity (or novelty) of an input pattern. In two of these models, the signals are available before the current stimulus is actually recognized or categorized: before resonance occurs in ART, or before the activation pattern settles into an attractor in the recurrent autoassociator. (The time course is less clear in the CHARM model.) This situation contrasts with the seemingly logical notion (stemming from the file cabinet metaphor) that it is impossible to know whether something is new or old before you know what it is. If you are searching through independently stored records in a file cabinet, that *is* impossible. But with connectionist memories that superimpose many traces into a single memory, as we have seen, rapid detection of familiarity is not only possible, but necessary to monitor the memory system and get around the stability-plasticity dilemma.

The signal reflecting the novelty versus familiarity of the current stimulus has many psychological effects. Novelty triggers special processing, so that organisms pay attention to and store a wide range of information about novel stimuli—including not only details of the focal stimulus but also its context (where it occurred in time and place, information that is required for explicit recognition or recall). This basic process of increased attention to and better explicit memory for novel stimuli gives rise to a number of related psychological effects, which can be roughly classified depending on whether novelty is relative to the immediate perceptual context or relative to a long-term baseline of experiences.

Contextual novelty means that in a local set of stimuli, one or more are relatively unusual. A research participant might see 4 photos of male faces and then a female face, or a list of words containing 15 names of fruits and 4 names of items of furniture. In this situation, effects of greater attention and memory for novel stimuli include the following:

- The Von Restorff effect involves one item that comes from a different category or is unusual in some other way, embedded in a list of other types of items. As is well known, the "oddball" item is better recalled than other nearby items from the list (Green, 1956).
- Release from proactive inhibition is demonstrated with a list that shifts from one type of item to another in the middle (e.g., several fruits followed by several vegetables). Each successive item of the first type is recalled successively worse, but then the first item from the new category is recalled very well. Of course, this item is contextually novel at the time it occurs (Gardiner, Craik, & Birtwistle, 1972).
- Cue overload is a term used to describe the pattern of recall performance on a list divided into different categories (e.g., four color words, eight fruits, three types of trees). The fewer the members of a category on the list, the better is recall for those items (Watkins & Watkins, 1975).

- In social cognition, when a target person is described as performing several behaviors of one type (e.g., honest behaviors) and a few behaviors of the opposite type (dishonest behaviors), the latter are recalled better than the former (Srull, Lichtenstein, & Rothbart, 1985). This is true even when the behaviors are randomly ordered rather than blocked into categories. The same effect can be obtained when an initial impression of the individual is provided by a few trait words (e.g., honest, trustworthy) and equal numbers of honest and dishonest behaviors are shown (Hastie & Kumar, 1979).
- An electrophysiological correlate of the contextual novelty of a stimulus is the so-called P300 event-related potential wave (Galambos & Hillyard, 1981). This particular waveform is detectable with scalp electrodes when an oddball or novel stimulus is presented (e.g., as in a Von Restorff paradigm), and it is possible to speculate that it corresponds to the operation of a novelty detection system analogous to those outlined in the connectionist memory theories reviewed earlier. Grossberg's ART model, in fact, explicitly postulates a "wave" of activation being sent to F2 on a mismatch between expectations and current perceptual inputs.

Novelty or familiarity can also be defined in terms of a person's longer-term experience, rather than with respect to the immediate context. Still, the same principle holds: attention and memory tend to be greater for more atypical, unusual, or novel events.

- When people read stories based on familiar behavioral sequences or scripts, such as a visit to a restaurant or a dentist's office, they later effectively show no ability to recognize script-based events that occurred in the story. That is, they may be completely unable to discriminate script events that were presented from events that are part of the script but were not included in the specific story (Graesser, Woll, Kowalski, & Smith, 1980). In contrast, unusual events embedded in the story tend to be well remembered.
- As is well known, low-frequency words give rise to better recall or recognition memory performance than high-frequency or familiar words (Schulman, 1967).
- When people encounter information that is unexpected or inconsistent with their long-term expectations, they are likely to encode the context as well as the focal information itself (e.g., Forster, Higgins, & Strack, 1999).

☐ Why Does Familiarity Feel Good?

As research on mere exposure effects makes clear, the subjective feeling of familiarity is affectively positive (Zajonc, 1968). William James (1892/

1961, p. 155) wrote of recollection as involving a feeling of "warmth and intimacy." Even if familiarity detection is a fundamental part of any realistic memory system, that does not explain the link between familiarity and affective positivity. This link can be understood by considering another important biological function of the ability to rapidly detect familiarity versus novelty: avoidance of danger. For any living creature that can sense its environment and act adaptively, situations or objects that are familiar can be assumed to be (at least relatively) safe. After all, these objects have not killed you yet! Even if they are intrinsically dangerous, at least well-practiced routines for avoiding or combating the dangers may exist. In contrast, novel or strange stimuli signal greater danger. An organism that evolved to use a rapid and automatic novelty detector to become alarmed or at least vigilant toward the potential danger is an organism with a higher likelihood of survival. As many have argued (Schwarz, 1990; Schwarz & Bless, 1991), this function is presumably the reason for our bias to link familiarity with affective positivity and novelty with negativity, and hence the reason for the mere exposure effect.

In fact, a new prediction can be generated from this evolutionary perspective together with Higgins's (1998) promotion/prevention model of motivation. Familiarity should be connected not to all positive and negative emotions equally, but specifically to emotions that are tied to the workings of the prevention system. These are anxiety, fear, and other threat-related emotions on the negative side, and calm, relaxation, and safety-related emotions on the positive side. Emotions (like joy, pride, disappointment, or frustration) that are connected to the promotion system should be only weakly or not at all affected by familiarity. To my knowledge, no data exist that could be used to test this hypothesis.

Other implications of the link between familiarity and affective positivity are also evident in scattered findings throughout the social psychological literature. Bless and Fiedler (1995; see also Fiedler, 1991; Gray, 1971) argued that a positive mood signals not only that the current situation is generally safe and benign, but also that it is reasonable to rely on stable general knowledge (which has ordinarily proven applicable and useful in the past). In contrast, a negative mood warns of danger—of unusual conditions or deviations from normal—and suggests that general rules of thumb may not be adequate; detailed processing of relevant information may be required.

In support of this idea, Bless (in press) reviewed evidence in several areas. Positive mood is associated with increased reliance on judgmental heuristics or stereotypes, which are different types of general knowledge (e.g., Bless, Schwarz, & Wieland, 1996; Worth & Mackie, 1987). Positive mood is also associated with increased creativity (e.g., Isen, Daubman, & Nowicki, 1987), which as Bless argues reflects use of general knowledge structures as a basis for "going beyond the information given" and generating novel ideas. Finally, positive mood is associated with high levels of recall for schema-consistent information from a story, along with higher rates of intrusion of schema-consistent but not presented information (Bless, Clore, Schwarz, Golisano, Rabe, & Wolk, 1996). All of these types of evidence are consistent with the general principle (Bless, in press) that positive mood produces a greater tendency to rely on general knowledge structures (including scripts, schemas, and stereotypes), compared to negative or neutral moods.

In other recent work, Garcia-Marques and Mackie (this volume) have demonstrated links between positive mood and the perception of validity. For example, under a positive mood, people are more likely to report that plausible statements are actually true than when tested under a negative mood. In addition, statements presented repeatedly gave rise to a positive mood as well as to higher ratings of perceived validity. These findings constitute the third leg of a conceptual triangle: they link positive affect and subjective validity, joining the already known relations between familiarity and validity, and familiarity and positive affect.

I have argued that the regulation of memory systems to overcome the stability-plasticity dilemma, as well as the avoidance of novel and potentially dangerous objects, requires some mechanism that can rapidly detect the novelty versus familiarity of a stimulus. But why is that feeling of familiarity subjectively available? It could be part of an automatic, internal regulatory system without our being able to sense it. Yet there are functional reasons for important biological regulatory systems to have subjective counterparts. When our nutritional state is low, we feel hungry. When motivational systems aimed at promoting positive outcomes and avoiding negative outcomes operate, we experience emotions (such as joy, disappointment, relaxation, or anxiety) as subjective counterparts (Higgins, 1996). Similarly, we feel a warm glow of familiarity (James, 1892/1961) if our memory system declares that a stimulus is not too different from what we expect or have seen before. The reason, speculatively, is that the subjective representation of these signals permits rapid and flexible learning and therefore more effective adaptation. An organism that automatically self-regulated (e.g., by seeking to eat when its nutrient levels were low) without any corresponding conscious experience could obviously survive, and worms or molluscs presumably do just that. But the ability to *know* when one is hungry (assuming enough cognitive ability) allows for thinking about that fact, inducing hypotheses or generalizations about situations in which the feeling occurs, and ultimately making, modifying, and carrying out plans based on the actual or anticipated feeling. Flexibility is the hallmark of *conscious* use of information (Eichenbaum, 1997), and information about the operation of self-regulatory systems is important to have available for such flexible use.

☐ Conclusions

In summary, I have suggested that our ability to subjectively sense familiarity is no accident. Indeed, this ability is an inherent and required part of any realistic memory system, as part of a strategy for resolving the stability-plasticity dilemma. We considered above three memory models that all, despite their many differences in detail, generate and use a signal of a stimulus pattern's novelty or familiarity to regulate the processes involved in memory storage and retrieval. The functional role of this signal means, importantly, that it is available early, before the memory system has actually classified a known input pattern. Thus, a sense of familiarity is a rapid and global feeling that can precede actual recognition.

Besides regulating memory systems, a rapid sense of familiarity or novelty has another important function: it can be used to alert an organism to potential danger and trigger appropriate vigilance or escape. I suggest that this function has indeed evolved in higher organisms and that it is the reason for our underlying bias to take familiarity as subjectively positive and novelty as negative. This argument makes self-regulation, rather than affect, fundamental. Feelings of familiarity and other affective experiences are the subjective counterpart of the workings of self-regulatory systems (Higgins, 1996).

In contrast to this view, others have used evidence regarding the rapid emergence of the affectively positive sense of familiarity to argue that in a general sense, affect precedes and is independent of cognition (e.g., Zajonc, 1980). This argument leads to severe conceptual difficulties, including the necessity to postulate ineffable stimulus attributes ("preferenda") and a hypothetical affective processing system that parallels our cognitive perceptual processing system. The self-regulation based model advanced here avoids these difficulties. Our ability to rapidly sense familiarity is an inevitable aspect of self-regulatory processes within cognitive models of the workings of memory (whether ART, CHARM, or a recurrent autoassociative memory). The affectively tinged experiences associated with the sense of familiarity are subjective counterparts of workings of self-regulatory processes, and need not be attributed to a hypothetical separate affective processing system.

☐ References

Alvarez, P., & Squire, L. R. (1994). Memory consolidation and the medial temporal lobe: A simple network model. *Proceedings of the National Academy of Sciences, 91,* 7041–7045.

Arkes, H. R., Boehm, L. E., & Xu, G. (1991). Determinants of judged validity. *Journal of Experimental Social Psychology, 27,* 576–605.

Bless, H. (in press). Mood and the use of general knowledge structures. In L. L. Martin & G. L. Clore (Eds.), *Affective states and cognitive processing*. Mahwah, NJ: Erlbaum.

Bless, H., Clore, G., Schwarz, N., Golisano, V., Rabe, C., & Wolk, M. (1996). Mood and the use of scripts: Does happy mood make people really mindless? *Journal of Personality and Social Psychology, 71,* 665–679.

Bless, H., & Fiedler, K. (1995). Affective states and the influence of activated general knowledge. *Personality and Social Psychology Bulletin, 21,* 766–778.

Bless, H., Schwarz, N., & Wieland, R. (1996). Mood and the impact of category membership and individuating information. *European Journal of Social Psychology, 26,* 935–959.

Bornstein, R. F., & D'Agostino, P. R. (1994). The attribution and discounting of perceptual fluency: Preliminary tests of a perceptual fluency/attributional model of the mere exposure effect. *Social Cognition, 12,* 103–128.

Carpenter, G. A., & Grossberg, S. (1995). Adaptive resonance theory (ART). In M. Arbib (Ed.), *The handbook of brain theory and neural networks* (pp. 79–82). Cambridge, MA: MIT Press.

Churchland, P. S., & Sejnowski, T. J. (1992). *The computational brain*. Cambridge, MA: MIT Press.

Eichenbaum, H. (1997). Declarative memory: Insights from cognitive neurobiology. *Annual Review of Psychology, 48,* 547–572.

Fiedler, K. (1991). On the task, the measures, and the mood in research on affect and cognition. In J. Forgas (Ed.), *Emotion and social judgments* (pp. 83–104). Oxford, England: Pergamon.

Forster, J., Higgins, E. T., & Strack, F. (1999). *Stereotype disconfirmation as personal threat: How prejudice and prevention focus moderates incongruency effects*. Unpublished paper, Universitat Wurzburg, Germany.

Galambos, R., & Hillyard, S. A. (1981). Electrophysiological approaches to human cognitive processing. *Neurosciences Research Program Bulletin, 20,* 141–265.

Gardiner, J. M., Craik, F. I., & Birtwistle, J. (1972). Retrieval cues and release from proactive inhibition. *Journal of Verbal Learning and Verbal Behavior, 11,* 778–783.

Graesser, A. C., Woll, S. B., Kowalski, D. J., & Smith, D. A. (1980). Memory for typical and atypical actions in scripted activities. *Journal of Experimental Psychology: Human Learning and Memory, 6,* 503–515.

Gray, J. A. (1971). *The psychology of fear and stress*. Cambridge, England: Cambridge University Press.

Green, R. T. (1956). Surprise as a factor in the Von Restorff effect. *Journal of Experimental Psychology, 52,* 340–344.

Grossberg, S. (1976). Adaptive pattern classification and universal recoding: I. Parallel development and coding of neural feature detectors. II. Feedback, expectation, olfaction, and illusions. *Biological Cybernetics, 23,* 121–134, 187–202.

Grossberg, S., & Merrill, J. W. L. (1996). The hippocampus and cerebellum in adaptively timed learning, recognition, and movement. *Journal of Cognitive Neuroscience, 8,* 257–277.

Hastie, R., & Kumar, P. A. (1979). Person memory: Personality traits as organizing principles in memory for behaviors. *Journal of Personality and Social Psychology, 37,* 25–38.

Higgins, E. T. (1996). Emotional experiences: The pains and pleasures of distinct regulatory systems. In R. D. Kavanaugh, B. Zimmerberg, & S. Fein (Eds.), *Emotion: Interdisciplinary perspectives* (pp. 203–241). Mahwah, NJ: Erlbaum.

Higgins, E. T. (1998). Promotion and prevention: Regulatory focus as a motivational principle. In M. P. Zanna (Ed.), *Advances in experimental social psychology* (Vol. 30, pp. 1–46). New York: Academic Press.

Isen, A. M., Daubman, K. A., & Nowicki, G. P. (1987). Positive affect facilitates creative problem solving. *Journal of Personality and Social Psychology, 52,* 1122–1131.

Jacoby, L. L., & Dallas, M. (1981). On the relationship between autobiographical memory and perceptual learning. *Journal of Experimental Psychology: General, 3,* 306–340.

Jacoby, L. L., Kelley, C., Brown, J., & Jasechko, J. (1989). Becoming famous overnight: Limits on the ability to avoid unconscious influences of the past. *Journal of Personality and Social Psychology, 56,* 326–338.

James, W. (1961). *Psychology: The briefer course.* New York: Harper & Row. (Original work published 1892)

Mandler, G. (1980). Recognizing: The judgment of previous occurrence. *Psychological Review, 87,* 252–271.

McClelland, J. L., McNaughton, B. L., & O'Reilly, R. C. (1995). Why there are complementary learning systems in the hippocampus and neocortex: Insights from the successes and failures of connectionist models of learning and memory. *Psychological Review, 102,* 419–457.

McClelland, J. L., & Rumelhart, D. E. (1986). A distributed model of human learning and memory. In J. L. McClelland & D. E. Rumelhart (Eds.), *Parallel distributed processing: Explorations in the microstructure of cognition* (Vol. 2, pp. 170–215). Cambridge, MA: MIT Press.

Metcalfe, J. (1991). Recognition failure and the composite memory trace in CHARM. *Psychological Review, 98,* 529–553.

Metcalfe, J. (1994). A computational modeling approach to novelty monitoring, metacognition, and frontal lobe dysfunction. In J. Metcalfe & A. P. Shimamura (Eds.), *Metacognition* (pp. 137–156). Cambridge, MA: MIT Press.

Milner, P. (1989). A cell assembly theory of hippocampal amnesia. *Neuropsychologica, 27,* 23–30.

Moreland, R. L., & Beach, S. R. (1992). Exposure effects in the classroom: The development of affinity among students. *Journal of Experimental Social Psychology, 28,* 255–276.

Murre, J. (1995). Transfer of learning in back-propagation and in related neural network models. In J. P. Levy, D. Bairaktaris, J. A. Bullinaria, & P. Cairns (Eds.), *Connectionist models of memory and language* (pp. 73–94). London: UCL Press.

Ratcliff, R. (1990). Connectionist models of recognition memory: Constraints imposed by learning and forgetting functions. *Psychological Review, 97,* 285–308.

Schacter, D. L., & Tulving, E. (Eds.). (1994). *Memory systems 1994.* Cambridge, MA: MIT Press.

Schulman, A. I. (1967). Word length and rarity in recognition memory. *Psychonomic Science, 9,* 211–212.

Schwarz, N. (1990). Feelings as information: Informational and motivational functions of affective states. In R. M. Sorrentino & E. T. Higgins (Eds.), *Handbook of motivation and cognition* (Vol. 2, pp. 527–561). New York: Guilford Press.

Schwarz, N., & Bless, H. (1991). Happy and mindless, but sad and smart? The impact of affective states on analytic reasoning. In J. Forgas (Ed.), *Emotion and social judgments* (pp. 55–71). Oxford, England: Pergamon.

Smith E. R., & DeCoster, J. (1999). Associative and rule-based processing: A connectionist interpretation of dual process models. In S. Chaiken & Y. Trope (Eds.), *Dual process models in social cognition* (pp. 323–336). New York: Guilford Press.

Smith, E. R., & Zárate, M. A. (1992). Exemplar-based model of social judgment. *Psychological Review, 99,* 3–21.

Srull, T. K., Lichtenstein, M., & Rothbart, M. (1985). Associative storage and retrieval processes in person memory. *Journal of Experimental Psychology: Learning, Memory, and Cognition, 11,* 316–345.

van Gelder, T. (1991). What is the "D" in "PDP"? A survey of the concept of distribution. In W. Ramsey, S. P. Stich, & D. E. Rumelhart (Eds.), *Philosophy and connectionist theory* (pp. 33–60). Hillsdale, NJ: Erlbaum.

Watkins, O. C., & Watkins, M. J. (1975). Buildup of proactive inhibition as a cue-overload effect. *Journal of Experimental Psychology: Human Learning and Memory, 1,* 442–452.

Wiles, J., & Humphreys, M. S. (1993). Using artificial neural nets to model implicit and explicit memory test performance. In P. Graf & M. E. J. Masson (Eds.), *Implicit memory: New directions in cognition, development, and neuropsychology* (pp. 141–165). Hillsdale, NJ: Erlbaum.

Worth, L. T., & Mackie, D. M. (1987). Cognitive mediation of positive affect in persuasion. *Social Cognition, 5,* 76–94.

Yonelinas, A. P. (1997). Recognition memory ROCs for item and associative information: The contribution of recollection and familiarity. *Memory and Cognition, 25,* 747–763.

Zajonc, R. B. (1968). Attitudinal effects of mere exposure. *Journal of Personality and Social Psychology, 9,* 1–27.

Zajonc, R. B. (1980). Feeling and thinking: Preferences need no inferences. *American Psychologist, 35,* 151–175.

Geoffrey Haddock

Subjective Ease of Retrieval and Attitude-Relevant Judgments

How do people decide if they favor a particular politician or social policy issue? Using political attitudes, common sense would dictate that individuals should like politicians about whom they associate positive attributes and dislike politicians about whom they associate negative attributes. Common sense would further dictate that an individual who thinks of eight positive traits about a politician should subsequently report a more favorable attitude than an individual who thinks of only two positive traits. However, is the judgment process always that straightforward? As attested both by other chapters in this volume and research investigating the role of subjective experiences on social judgments (e.g., Haddock, Rothman, Reber, & Schwarz, 1999; Haddock, Rothman, & Schwarz, 1996; Schwarz, 1998; Schwarz et al., 1991; Wänke, Bless, & Biller, 1996), the answer to this question is not as simple as one might expect. Rather than relying upon the *amount* of accessed information in deriving social judgments, research has demonstrated that under many circumstances, individuals rely upon the subjective *ease* with which accessed information is retrieved from memory. Applying this "ease of retrieval" perspective to the example discussed above, a respondent who retrieved eight positive attributes about a politician might subsequently report having a more

---

Address correspondence to Geoffrey Haddock, Department of Experimental Psychology, University of Bristol, 8 Woodland Road, Bristol BS8 1TN, UK. E-mail: G.Haddock@ exeter.ac.uk

negative attitude compared to a respondent who retrieved only two positive attributes—if the former individual had a difficult time retrieving eight positive attributes.

In this chapter, I describe research that my colleagues and I have conducted that investigated the influence of subjective ease of retrieval on attitude-relevant judgments. This research sought to determine both if, and under what conditions, the subjective experiences associated with retrieving different types of information from memory influence subsequent judgments made about the attitude object. These studies demonstrate that individuals' perceptions about the strength of their attitudes, as well as the favorability of their attitudes, are affected by the ease or difficulty experienced when accessing positive or negative information from memory. In addition to describing this research, toward the end of the chapter, the findings will be linked with other relevant research in the attitudes and social judgment literature. I begin, however, with a brief discussion of subjective ease of retrieval.

☐ Subjective Ease of Retrieval and Self-Judgments

A number of studies have investigated the impact of accessibility experiences on social judgments. In one famous study on the availability heuristic, Tversky and Kahneman (1973, Experiment 8) presented participants with two lists of names, one with 19 famous men and 20 less famous women, the second with 19 famous women and 20 less famous men. When subsequently asked to report whether each list contained more male or female names, participants mistakenly reported that there were more men in the first list and more women in the second list. Tversky and Kahneman (1973) interpreted this finding by stating that individuals estimate the frequency of an event by considering "the ease with which instances or associations come to mind" (p. 208). However, Schwarz and colleagues (e.g., Schwarz, 1998; Schwarz et al., 1991) questioned the approach of Tversky and Kahneman's (1973) studies, stating that Tversky and Kahneman's manipulations confounded the ease associated with information retrieval and the amount of information recalled. For example, Schwarz (1998) argued that Tversky and Kahneman's manipulations increased both the subjective ease of recall and amount of recall, leading him to conclude that "this confound renders it difficult to determine whether the obtained estimates of frequency, likelihood or typicality were based on a meta-cognitive strategy that draws on individuals' recall experiences or on a biased sample of recalled information" (p. 88).

In an attempt to disambiguate Tversky and Kahneman's (1973) findings, Schwarz et al. (1991, Experiment 1) asked participants to recall either

6 or 12 instances in which they behaved either assertively or unassertively. Pretesting revealed that recalling 6 examples was easy, whereas retrieving 12 instances was difficult. After completing this behavior recollection task, participants rated their own level of assertiveness. If judgments are influenced by the ease with which information is accessed, one would expect higher judgments of assertiveness among participants who experienced an easy time retrieving instances of assertiveness (i.e., those who recalled 6) or a difficult time retrieving instances of unassertiveness (i.e., those who recalled 12). In contrast, if individuals rely upon the amount of accessed information, one would expect an opposite pattern of findings. Schwarz et al. (1991) found that participants' assertiveness ratings reflected the ease with which behaviors were retrieved from memory— self-ratings of assertiveness were higher after having recalled 6 (rather than 12) assertive behaviors, and 12 (rather than 6) unassertive behaviors. Correlations between self-reported ease and assertiveness provided convergent evidence for the important role played by individuals' subjective experiences. Among participants asked to recall instances of assertive behavior, greater difficulty was associated with lower ratings of assertiveness ($r = -.35$). In contrast, among participants asked to recall instances of unassertive behavior, greater difficulty was associated with higher ratings of assertiveness ($r = .66$).

In a further study, Schwarz et al. (1991, Experiment 3) incorporated a misattribution manipulation in order to provide evidence supporting the role of subjective ease of recall as the mediating variable. In this experiment, Schwarz et al. asked participants to recall 6 (easy) or 12 (difficult) examples of assertive behaviors and informed participants that music played during the recall task would render recall either easy or difficult. As expected, participants relied on their subjective experience only when the alleged side effect of the music contradicted their subjective experience, thus rendering the experience diagnostic.

Schwarz et al.'s (1991) research demonstrated that self-perceptions (i.e., judgments about the degree to which an individual perceives themselves as possessing a particular attribute) are influenced by the subjective ease (or difficulty) associated with recalling attribute-relevant information from memory. However, one can also ask whether individuals' perceptions of their own *attitudes* might also be influenced by accessibility experiences. Previous research in the attitudes literature suggests that other types of subjective experiences, such as mood (see, e.g., Haddock, Zanna, & Esses, 1994) and the quality of integral affective information (see, e.g., Bodenhausen, 1993; chapter 16 by Bodenhausen and Moreno in this volume) influence intergroup attitudes. The research described in the remainder of the chapter consists of studies my colleagues and I have conducted that addressed whether attitude-relevant judgments are influenced by subjective ease of recall experiences. The first study I describe demonstrates that individuals' perceptions about the strength of their attitude toward a social policy issue (doctor-assisted suicide) are affected by the subjective experiences associated with recalling attitude-relevant information from memory. The second set of studies I describe provide both moderating and mediating evidence, suggesting the conditions under which ease of retrieval effects are particularly likely to occur as well as evidence supporting the role of ease of retrieval as the mediator of these effects. The final study I describe demonstrates that the favorability of an individual's attitude toward a political leader can be affected by ease of retrieval experiences, depending upon an individual's level of interest in politics.

Accessibility Experiences and Attitude-Relevant Judgments: An Initial Study

Attitudes differ in the degree to which they are central to an individual. Some attitudes are valued like prized possessions (Abelson & Prentice, 1989), whereas others are less important. The notion that individuals feel more strongly about some topics than others has been conceptualized as attitude strength. Strong attitudes have been described as those attitudes that are persistent over time, more resistant to persuasion, more likely to impact information processing, and more likely to guide behavior (Krosnick & Petty, 1995). Over the years, numerous studies have examined the consequences of possessing strong versus weak attitudes (see Petty & Krosnick, 1995, for a detailed review). However, much less is known about the processes underlying reports of attitude strength (cf. Boninger, Krosnick, & Berent, 1995; Downing, Judd, & Brauer, 1992; see also Festinger, 1957). How do people determine the "strength" of an attitude? Indeed, are perceptions of attitude strength themselves stable over time, or are they sensitive to the context in which they are reported? These questions were addressed in a study by Haddock et al. (1996), who assessed the extent to which reports of attitude certainty, intensity, and importance are affected by the ease associated with retrieving arguments that support or counter one's attitude.

In their study, Haddock et al. (1996) asked participants to recall either three or seven arguments that either supported or opposed their attitude toward doctor-assisted suicide. Pretesting revealed that participants found it easy to recall three arguments, but difficult to recall seven. After completing this task, participants rated the certainty, intensity, and importance of their attitude toward the issue. If participants used their experienced ease (or difficulty) with which they could bring material to mind as a source of information in deriving their judgments of attitude certainty, intensity, and importance, they should report having stronger attitudes after recalling three (rather than seven) supporting arguments, or recalling seven (rather than three) opposing arguments. Haddock et al.'s (1996) results were consistent with this prediction. Participants who retrieved supporting arguments rated their attitude as stronger after having recalled three ($M = 5.0$) rather than seven ($M = 4.7$) arguments.[1] In contrast, participants who recalled counterarguments rated their attitude as stronger after having recalled seven ($M = 4.9$) rather than three ($M = 4.0$) arguments. Convergent evidence was provided by correlational analyses of difficulty ratings and attitude strength reports provided by participants in the supporting and opposing argument conditions. Whereas difficulty ratings were negatively correlated with strength judgments among participants who reported supporting arguments ($r = -.19$), they were positively correlated among participants who reported opposing arguments ($r = .28$). The results of both sets of analyses are consistent with the proposal that participants used their subjective experience as a source of information in deriving their judgments of attitude certainty, importance, and intensity.

Are All Attitude-Relevant Judgments Equally Susceptible to Ease of Retrieval Effects?

Although the study by Haddock et al. (1996) demonstrated that judgments of attitude certainty, importance, and intensity can rest on the ease or difficulty with which arguments come to mind, it presumably is not true that all attitude-relevant judgments are affected by ease of retrieval processes. For instance, attitudes differ in their level of commitment, and it is likely that "involved" and "uninvolved" attitudes are differentially susceptible to ease of retrieval effects. Specifically, judgments concerning stimuli about which an individual is not invested might be especially likely to be affected by subjective experiences. Consistent with this proposal, two lines of reasoning suggest that the impact of subjective ease of retrieval on attitude-relevant judgments should differ as a function of an individual's level of involvement or interest with the attitude object.

A first line of reasoning is derived from recent theorizing in the social psychological literature on attitudes. Traditionally, most social psychologists conceptualized attitudes as stored (i.e., stable) evaluative responses toward an attitude object (see, for example, Allport, 1935; Eagly & Chaiken, 1993, for a comprehensive review). This perspective implies that attitude reports generally should not be affected by the social context in which they are provided. More recently, however, a number of theorists have postulated that attitudes are often constructed on the basis of the information that is temporarily accessible at the time of judgment (see, e.g., Wilson & Hodges, 1992). This perspective implies that many attitude reports should be subject to context effects. Attempts to reconcile these perspectives have considered the concept of attitude strength as a moderating variable, with the suggestion that weak attitudes are more likely to be subject to context effects (e.g., Bassili, 1996a, 1996b; Lavine, Huff, Wagner, & Sweeney, 1998; Wilson & Hodges, 1992). In the past few years, the results of a number of studies are consistent with this moderation hypothesis. For example, research by Wilson and colleagues has demonstrated that thinking about the reasons underlying one's attitude produces attitude change, particularly among individuals with weak attitudes (e.g., Hodges & Wilson, 1993; Wilson, Kraft, & Dunn, 1989). Within the field of political attitudes, Hodges and Wilson (1993) measured attitudes toward Ronald Reagan on two separate occasions, several weeks apart. Before providing their second attitude report, some participants were asked to explain the reasons for their attitude. Hodges and Wilson (1993) found that having participants analyze reasons underlying their attitude led to attitude change, but only among individuals with less accessible attitudes.[2] Similarly, research by Fazio and Williams (1986) demonstrated that the accessibility of an individual's attitude toward a political candidate moderated the attitude-behavior relation in politics, with higher relations among individuals with accessible attitudes. More recently, research by Lavine et al. (1998) tested the moderating influence of attitude strength-related properties on the susceptibility to context effects for social-political policy issues such as defense spending and welfare reform. Their findings demonstrated that context effects were limited to individuals with weak attitudes toward the target issues. One explanation for this effect is that individuals with strong attitudes are more likely to have developed a chronically accessible evaluation of the attitude object (see Bassili, 1996b; Lavine et al., 1998).

As suggested by Haddock et al. (1999), a second line of reasoning consistent with the moderation hypothesis is derived from the differentiation between heuristic and systematic judgmental strategies. Reliance on the relative ease with which information comes to mind can be considered a heuristic judgmental strategy (see Schwarz, 1998), and research suggests that individuals are more likely to rely upon heuristic strategies when the task is less involving and personally relevant (Chaiken, Liberman, & Eagly, 1989; Eagly & Chaiken, 1993; Petty & Cacioppo, 1986; Rothman & Schwarz, 1998). For example, in a study using the ease of retrieval paradigm, Rothman and Schwarz asked men with or without a history of family heart disease to recall few or many behaviors that increase or decrease their personal risk of heart disease before evaluating their own vulnerability to heart problems. Rothman and Schwarz (1998) found that ease of retrieval effects were limited to men without a family history of heart disease. These individuals, for whom the issue was less personally relevant, relied on their recall experiences when they subsequently assessed their own vulnerability. These findings suggest that reliance on subjective accessibility experiences is particularly likely when the issue is not very involving, or, in other words, when an individual most likely possesses a weak attitude about the stimulus object (see Thomsen, Borgida, & Lavine, 1995, for a discussion of involvement or personal relevance as an index of attitude strength).

Taken together, these two lines of reasoning support the notion that subjective ease of retrieval effects on attitude-relevant judgments should be most pronounced among individuals less involved with the target issue. As an initial test of this hypothesis, Haddock et al. (1999, Experiment 1) conducted a study in which participants with an extreme or moderate attitude toward doctor-assisted suicide were asked to provide three or seven arguments that either spoke in favor of or against their attitude toward the issue. They then completed measures assessing the certainty, intensity, and importance of their attitude, before indicating both the difficulty associated with the retrieval task and the quality of their arguments (see Haddock et al., 1999, for a more detailed description of the materials). The results of this study are described in Table 8.1. As can be seen on the left-hand side of Table 8.1, moderate attitude participants who provided arguments that supported their position judged their attitude as stronger after having recalled three ($M = 5.0$) as compared to seven ($M = 4.1$) arguments. Conversely, moderate attitude participants who provided arguments that countered their position judged their attitude as stronger after having recalled seven ($M = 4.6$) as compared to three ($M = 3.8$) arguments. This pattern of means is consistent with the notion that these participants used their subjective experience of ease or difficulty as a source of information in deriving their judgments of attitude certainty, importance, and intensity.

TABLE 8.1. Judgments of attitude strength as a function of argument type, argument number, and attitude extremity (from Haddock et al., 1999, Experiment 1)

| | Attitude extremity | | | |
| | Moderate | | Extreme | |
Argument type	3 Arguments	7 Arguments	3 Arguments	7 Arguments
Supporting	5.0	4.1	5.5	5.4
Counter	3.8	4.6	5.9	5.6

Note. Higher scores represent higher strength ratings.

In comparison, the right-hand side of Table 8.1 presents the mean judgments made by individuals with extreme attitudes. As can be seen, the judgments of these participants did not differ as a function of argument number and argument type.

Two additional sets of analyses from this study warrant discussion. First, an analysis revealed that the last two arguments provided by participants in the seven argument condition were rated as convincing as the last two arguments provided by participants in the three argument condition. Furthermore, there were no significant differences between moderate and extreme attitude participants in the reported quality of their arguments. These findings are important, because the extent to which retrieving many arguments is difficult, those recalled near the end of the task might be less convincing, providing a possible alternative explanation for a shift in certainty, intensity, and importance ratings. Second, an analysis of difficulty ratings revealed that extreme and moderate attitude participants did not differ in the difficulty they experienced retrieving the requisite number of arguments. This finding, which is consistent with other studies (e.g., Haddock, 1998) is important, and implies that the retrieval task was not differentially experienced by participants with extreme versus moderate attitudes.

A second study conducted by Haddock et al. (1999, Experiment 2) incorporated a misattribution manipulation (modeled after that used by Schwarz et al., 1991) to demonstrate that subjective ease of retrieval effects would occur only when the subjective experience was highly diagnostic. In this study, participants with moderate attitudes toward the issue of doctor-assisted suicide were asked to retrieve either three or seven arguments that spoke in favor of or against their attitude toward doctor-assisted suicide before completing reports of attitude certainty, importance, and intensity. However, unlike the previous study, participants completed this task while listening to a selection of music. Some participants were informed that the music would facilitate thought, whereas others were informed that the music would inhibit thought. Learning that the music would facilitate thought should reduce the diagnosticity associated with having an easy time retrieving three arguments. Similarly, learning that the music would inhibit thought should reduce the diagnosticity associated with having a difficult time retrieving seven arguments. The remaining combinations of these variables (learning that the music inhibits thought but having an easy time retrieving three arguments or learning that the music facilitates thought but having a difficult time retrieving seven arguments) should lead participants to conclude that their subjective experience was highly diagnostic. The results of this study supported the prediction: participants drew upon on their ease of recall experience only when it was highly diagnostic.

Taken together, the results of the research by Haddock et al. (1999) provide moderating and mediating evidence regarding the impact of ease of retrieval experiences on attitude strength-relevant judgments. The results of Experiment 1 are consistent with the proposal that individuals with strong attitudes are more likely to have stored evaluations of properties of an attitude object, whereas individuals with weak attitudes are more likely to construct attitudes on the basis of salient information. The results of Experiment 2 are consistent with earlier findings by Schwarz et al. (1991; see also Rothman & Hardin, 1997) demonstrating the mediatory role of accessibility experiences on social judgments.

Subjective Ease of Retrieval and the Favorability of Attitude Reports

The Haddock et al. (1996, 1999) studies that I have described demonstrate that judgments of attitude strength-related properties are affected by accessibility experiences associated with retrieving attitude-relevant information from memory. However, they do not speak to the issue of whether the *favorability* of individuals' attitudes can also be affected by subjective ease of retrieval experiences. Recent research by Wänke and colleagues (e.g., Wänke et al., 1996; Wänke, Bohner, & Jurkowitsch, 1997) suggests that these judgments are also influenced by accessibility experiences, and a brief discussion of this research is warranted.

In one such study, Wänke et al. (1996) asked participants to retrieve either three or seven arguments that were either in favor of or opposed to the issue of public transportation. After completing this task, participants rated their attitude toward the issue. The results of the study revealed that the favorability of participants' attitudes reflected the ease with which arguments could be brought to mind: participants reported more favorable attitudes toward public transportation when they had experienced either an easy time retrieving positive arguments or a difficult time retrieving negative arguments. Furthermore, participants felt more confident about their attitude after having had an easy time retrieving supporting arguments. A subsequent study (Wänke et al., 1997) that investigated attitudes toward different makes of automobiles replicated this effect.

In the final study I wish to describe in this chapter, I was interested in extending these findings by exploring under what conditions evaluative judgments are influenced by the ease with which attitude-relevant information is retrieved from memory. In this study (Haddock, 1999a), participants who were either interested or uninterested in British politics provided either two (easy) or five (difficult) positive or negative attributes about British Prime Minister Tony Blair. After completing this task, they indicated their attitude toward him. Consistent with the findings of Haddock et al. (1999, Experiment 1), it was predicted that the attitudes of those participants uninterested in politics would differ as a function of the ease with which attributes about Tony Blair were brought to mind, whereas individuals interested in politics would be unaffected by the manipulation of attribute type and attribute number.

In this study, participants completed a questionnaire on political issues. On the first page of the questionnaire, participants were asked to indicate their level of interest in British politics, by completing the item "How interested are you in British politics?" (1 = *not at all interested*, 11 = *extremely interested*). On the following page, they were instructed that the researcher was interested in the attributes or characteristics individuals associate with political party leaders. They were then asked to provide two (or five) positive (or negative) characteristics about Tony Blair. These numeric values were obtained from a pilot study that suggested that producing two attributes would be easy, whereas producing five attributes would be difficult. After completing the attribute retrieval task, participants answered two questions assessing their attitude toward Tony Blair: (a) "How much do you like Tony Blair?" and (b) "What is your opinion about Tony Blair?" These questions were answered on seven-point scales, with higher scores representing a more positive attitude. Finally, participants completed a manipulation check, in which they were asked to indicate how easy or difficult they found the attribute retrieval task (1 = *not at all difficult*, 7 = *very difficult*).

The results of the study were consistent with the hypothesis. First, a manipulation check revealed that participants had an easier time retrieving two (as opposed to five) attributes. Furthermore, political interest did not interact with the other manipulated variables to influence difficulty ratings. As for the effects of the experimental manipulations on the favorability of attitudes, a 2 (political interest: high vs. low, based on a median split) × 2 (attribute type: positive vs. negative) × 2 (attribute number: two vs. five) ANOVA revealed a marginally significant three-way interaction. The mean attitude ratings are provided in Table 8.2.[3] As can be seen in the left-hand side of Table 8.2, the attitudes of participants who were uninterested in British politics differed as a function of the ease or difficulty they experienced in producing positive or negative attributes about Tony Blair. Politically uninterested participants who provided positive attributes expressed more favorable attitudes toward Tony Blair after having produced two (*M* = 4.4) as compared to five (*M* = 3.9) attributes. In contrast, politically uninterested participants who provided negative attributes expressed more favorable attitudes toward Tony Blair after having produced five (*M* = 2.8) as compared to two (*M* = 4.1) attributes.

TABLE 8.2. Favorability of attitudes toward Tony Blair as a function of interest in politics, attribute type, and attribute number (from Haddock, 1999a)

| | Interest in politics | | | |
| | Uninterested | | Interested | |
Attribute type	2 Attributes	5 Attributes	2 Attributes	5 Attributes
Positive	4.4	3.9	3.4	3.8
Negative	2.8	4.1	4.3	4.1

Note. Higher scores represent more favorable attitudes.

These differences are reflected by a marginally significant interaction between attribute number and attribute type.

Correlational analyses provide converging evidence that ease of retrieval experiences affected the favorability of judgments made by politically uninterested participants. Among those participants who produced positive attributes about Tony Blair, there was a significant negative correlation between ease and attitude favorability ($r = -.48$), indicating that greater difficulty was associated with a more unfavorable attitude. In contrast, among those participants who produced negative attributes about Tony Blair, there was a significant positive correlation between ease and attitude favorability ($r = .46$), indicating that greater difficulty was associated with a more favorable attitude.

The right-hand side of Table 8.2 presents the mean attitudes of individuals interested in British politics. As can be seen, there were no differences in the favorability of their attitudes as a function of the number and type of attributes produced during the experimental task.

The results of this study converge nicely with those of Haddock et al. (1999, Experiment 1). In both studies, ease of retrieval processes influenced attitude-relevant judgments, but only among those individuals with weak attitudes toward the stimulus object. The results of this study also extend previous research by suggesting that the impact of accessibility experiences on attitude favorability are particularly likely when individuals are less involved with the attitude object.

☐ Summary of the Findings

Following Tversky and Kahneman's (1973) seminal research on the availability heuristic, a large number of studies have illustrated that different types of social judgments are influenced by the subjective ease with which judgment-relevant information can be brought to mind (e.g., Dijksterhuis, Macrae, & Haddock, 1999; Haddock et al., 1996, 1999; Rothman & Hardin, 1997; Rothman & Schwarz, 1998, Schwarz et al., 1991; Wänke et al., 1996, 1997; see Schwarz, 1998, for a review). My colleagues and I became interested in incorporating the ease of retrieval paradigm in an attempt to determine whether subjective experiences influence judgments individuals make about the self-perceived strength of their attitudes and opinions. Our first study asked a simple and straightforward question: Can judgments of attitude-strength–related properties rest on the subjective ease or difficulty associated with recalling attitude-relevant information from memory? Indeed, the results of this study (Haddock et al., 1996) revealed that judgments of attitude certainty, importance, and intensity can rely upon the subjective experience of ease or difficulty associated with recalling attitude-relevant arguments. Not surprisingly, the findings of this initial study provided second-generation research questions, such as: (a) consideration of the circumstances under which ease of retrieval processes are particularly likely to influence attitude-relevant judgments, and (b) whether (and when) subjective ease of retrieval processes influence the favorability of attitudinal judgments. With respect to the first question, it seemed likely to my colleagues and I that one condition that should moderate the presence of ease of retrieval effects is the individual's level of involvement with the stimulus object. A number of theoretical perspectives and research from the attitudes literature suggested that subjective experiences should exert a greater effect among individuals uninvolved with the attitude object (see, e.g., Bassili, 1996a, 1996b; Hodges & Wilson, 1993; Lavine et al., 1998; Petty & Cacioppo, 1986; Rothman & Schwarz, 1998; Schwarz, 1998). Indeed, Schwarz (1998) has stated that processing motivation influences whether individuals rely upon their accessibility experiences when expressing social judgments, with ease of retrieval effects most likely to be obtained among less motivated participants. In a first study designed to test this hypothesis, Haddock et al. (1999, Experiment 1) found, as predicted, that ease of retrieval effects were limited to those individuals with a moderate attitude toward the target issue. A further study (Haddock et al., 1999, Experiment 2) replicated this finding and provided mediating evidence. Yet another study (Haddock, 1999a), assessing the impact of ease of retrieval processes on the favorability of political attitudes, produced a similar set of moderation findings. In this particular study, I found that the subjective ease with which participants could bring to mind positive or negative attributes about British Prime Minister Tony Blair affected a subsequent judgment about him, but only among those participants who were uninterested in British politics. The attitudes of individuals interested in politics were unaffected by the type and number of attributes brought to mind.

Taken together, the results of the studies described in this chapter (see also Rothman & Schwarz, 1998) present a relatively clear picture concerning when subjective ease of retrieval experiences are most likely to influence attitude-relevant judgments. However, it should be noted that other researchers (see chapter 9 by Wänke & Bless in this volume) have reached a different conclusion. In developing their thesis that ease of retrieval effects should be more pronounced under high (rather than low) accuracy motivation, these researchers argue that experienced difficulty might reduce the quality (or convincingness) of the information retrieved, which in turn could lead this information to have less of an impact on subsequent judgments. However, as described earlier in this chapter, data collected by Haddock et al. (1999, Experiment 1; see also Hodges & Wilson, 1993) do not support this explanation. Recall that in their research, Haddock et al. asked participants to evaluate the quality of the arguments they produced. It was found that participants who were asked to generate more arguments rated their last two arguments as convincing as those participants who were asked to produce only three arguments (see also Schwarz et al., 1991). Furthermore, there were no differences in self-reported argument quality or difficulty between moderate and extreme attitude participants. These findings are not consistent with the proposal put forth by Wänke and Bless. Nonetheless, the findings of their research (which used a different experimental procedure from the studies described in this chapter) need to be noted, and additional research would be welcomed that attempts to integrate or reconcile these perspectives.

☐ Implications of the Findings

The findings of the studies described in this chapter have a number of important implications that warrant discussion. For instance, at a general level, the observation that ease of retrieval influences attitude-relevant judgments only among individuals with weak attitudes is relevant to discussions concerning the extent to which attitudinal judgments are stored evaluations of a target that are retrieved from memory, versus judgments that are constructed on the basis of temporarily salient attitude-relevant information. Attempts to reconcile these perspectives (e.g., Lavine et al., 1998; Wilson & Hodges, 1992) have emphasized the concept of attitude strength as a moderating variable, with the proposal that strong attitudes are more likely to be chronically accessible compared to weak attitudes, and, as a consequence, be less susceptible to context effects. Research investigating the impact of attitude strength-related properties on judgmental outcomes such as the favorability of attitudes, the stability of attitude reports over time, and resistance to persuasion have supported this moderation prediction (e.g., Abelson, 1988; Bassili, 1996b; Fazio & Williams, 1986; Hodges & Wilson, 1993; Krosnick, 1988; Lavine et al., 1998). The findings of the present set of studies provide further support for this notion, consistent with the proposal that there are circumstances under which attitudes are more or less likely to be retrieved directly from memory.

The research by Haddock et al. (1996, 1999) also has implications for the study of the construct of attitude strength. The results of these studies are consistent with Bassili's (1996a, 1996b) proposal that individuals do not necessarily have direct access to judgments regarding the strength of their attitudes. What does this imply about the construct of attitude strength? Perhaps most importantly, the results indicate that investigators should be careful when characterizing individuals' attitudes if they are relying solely on subjective dimensions of attitude strength such as certainty, intensity, and importance (cf. Krosnick & Abelson, 1992). Furthermore, the results of the studies described in this chapter are relevant to research that has used attitude strength-related properties as a vehicle to predict outcomes such as attitude change and the attitude-behavior relation. When used as a predictor of outcomes (see Petty & Krosnick, 1995), subjective assessments of attitude certainty, intensity, and importance may themselves be a temporary judgment, and not necessarily a stable feature of an attitude.

The results of the study on political attitudes (Haddock, 1999a) have potential implications for changing political attitudes, particularly among undecided voters. The political views of those individuals who are less interested in politics are likely to be affected by the context in which candidate-relevant information is brought to mind (see Kinder, 1998). As a result, political campaigns might find it beneficial to utilize accessibility experience paradigms in attempts to install public support for their candidate among undecided voters. For instance, if a party was interested in using self-generated arguments as a strategy to gain support, the slogan "All you need is one good reason to vote for our party" would serve as a more effective strategy for gathering support among uncommitted voters than the slogan "I'm sure you can think of seven reasons to vote for our party."

Similarly, it should be noted that the findings of the Haddock (1999a) study are also relevant to other recent findings documenting the extent to which the favorability of political attitudes are influenced by variations in context. For instance, Haddock (1999b), using Schwarz and Bless's (1992) inclusion-exclusion model of assimilation and contrast effects, tested whether attitudes toward the British Labour Party would be differentially affected by whether a previous question asking for their impression of party leader Tony Blair would lead participants to include or exclude him from their mental representation of the group. It was predicted that assimilation and contrast effects would occur (and affect judgments about the party), but only among individuals with ambivalent (i.e., weak) political views. The results supported the hypothesis: overall, and consistent with the inclusion-exclusion model, the correlation between the two responses was higher when Tony Blair could be included in the category. However, this was true only among those participants with ambivalent political attitudes. Furthermore, the favorability of participants' attitudes toward the Labour Party differed depending upon whether their attitude toward Tony Blair was positive or negative, and whether Blair was included in or excluded from the group. Among participants who liked Tony Blair, attitudes toward the Labour Party were more favorable in the inclusion condition. Conversely, among participants who disliked Tony Blair, attitudes toward the Labour Party were more favorable in the exclusion condition. Once again, as with the correlational results, this pattern was true among only those individuals with ambivalent political views. Judgments of the Labour Party made by nonambivalent participants were unaffected by the inclusion-exclusion manipulation. These findings, along with the results of Haddock (1999a) and other studies examining the role of context effects in the favorability of political attitudes (e.g., Haddock & Carrick, 1999; Schwarz & Bless, 1992; Schwarz & Hippler, 1995; Stapel & Schwarz, 1998) suggest that "motivated pollsters" have a number of techniques at their disposal to make their preferred candidate more attractive to voters.

☐ Concluding Thoughts

To conclude, the findings of the research described in this chapter suggest that attitude judgments can be influenced by the subjective experiences associated with recalling attitude-relevant information. Moreover, the studies suggest that these effects are most likely to occur when individuals possess a weak attitude toward the stimulus object. Ongoing research continues to replicate and extend these findings, in an attempt to better comprehend the circumstances under which attitude judgments are affected by subjective experiences. It is hoped that the findings of these studies will continue to increase our knowledge of how and when subjective experiences influence information processing and social judgments.

☐ Notes

[1]Because ratings of attitude certainty, importance, and intensity were highly correlated, they were combined to form a single index. See Haddock et al. (1999) for a more detailed description of separate analyses for each operationalization.

[2]Interestingly, Hodges and Wilson (1993) also found that high and low accessibility participants did not differ in the number of reasons they recalled. This point will become more relevant later in the chapter.

[3]Because responses to the two attitude items were highly correlated, they were combined to form a single score.

☐ References

Abelson, R. P. (1988). Conviction. *American Psychologist, 43,* 267–275.

Abelson, R. P., & Prentice, D. A. (1989). Beliefs as possessions: A functional perspective. In A. R. Pratkanis, S. J. Breckler, & A. G. Greenwald (Eds.), *Attitude structure and function* (pp. 361–381). Hillsdale, NJ: Erlbaum.

Allport, G. (1935). Attitudes. In C. Murchison (Ed.), *Handbook of social psychology* (pp. 798–844). Worcester, MA: Clark University Press.

Bassili, J. N. (1996a). The how and why of response latency measurement in telephone surveys. In N. Schwarz & S. Sudman (Eds.), *Answering questions: Methodology for determining cognitive and communicative processes in survey research* (pp. 319–346). San Francisco: Jossey-Bass.

Bassili, J. N. (1996b). Meta-judgmental versus operative indexes of psychological attributes: The case of measures of attitude strength. *Journal of Personality and Social Psychology, 71,* 637–653.

Bodenhausen, G. V. (1993). Emotions, arousal, and stereotypic judgments: A heuristic model of affect and stereotyping. In D. M. Mackie & D. L. Hamilton (Eds.), *Affect, cognition, and stereotyping: Interactive processes in group perception* (pp. 13–37). San Diego: Academic Press.

Boninger, D. S., Krosnick, J. A., & Berent, M. K. (1995). The causes of attitude importance: Self-interest, social identification, and values. *Journal of Personality and Social Psychology, 68,* 61–80.

Chaiken, S., Liberman, A., & Eagly, A. H. (1989). Heuristic and systematic processing within and beyond the persuasion context. In J. S. Uleman & J. A. Bargh (Eds.), *Unintended thought* (pp. 212–252). New York: Guilford Press.

Dijksterhuis, A., Macrae, C. N., & Haddock, G. (1999). When recollective experiences matter: Subjective ease of retrieval and stereotyping. *Personality and Social Psychology Bulletin, 25,* 760–768.

Downing, J. W., Judd, C. M., & Brauer, M. (1992). Effects of repeated expressions on attitude extremity. *Journal of Personality and Social Psychology, 63,* 17–29.

Eagly, A. H., & Chaiken, S. (1993). *The psychology of attitudes.* Forth Worth, TX: Harcourt Brace Jovanovich.

Fazio, R. H., & Williams, C. J. (1986). Attitude accessibility as a moderator of the attitude-perception and attitude-behavior relations: An investigation of the 1984 presidential election. *Journal of Personality and Social Psychology, 51,* 505–514.

Festinger, L. (1957). *A theory of cognitive dissonance.* Palo Alto, CA: Stanford University Press.

Haddock, G. (1998). *Accessibility experiences and attitudes toward the "Euro."* Unpublished manuscript, University of Exeter.

Haddock, G. (1999a). *Subjective experiences and political attitudes: It's easy to like or dislike Tony Blair.* Unpublished manuscript, University of Exeter.

Haddock, G. (1999b). *The impact of attitude ambivalence on assimilation and contrast effects in political judgments.* Paper presented at the meeting of the European Association of Experimental Social Psychology, Oxford, England.

Haddock, G., & Carrick, R. (1999). How to make a politician more likable and effective: Framing political judgments through the numeric values of a rating scale. *Social Cognition, 17,* 298–311.

Haddock, G., Rothman, A. J., Reber, R., & Schwarz, N. (1999). Forming judgments of attitude certainty, intensity, and importance: The role of subjective experiences. *Personality and Social Psychology Bulletin, 25,* 771–782.

Haddock, G., Rothman, A. J., & Schwarz, N. (1996). Are (some) reports of attitude strength context dependent? *Canadian Journal of Behavioural Science, 28,* 313–316.

Haddock, G., Zanna, M. P., & Esses, V. M. (1994). Mood and the expression of intergroup attitudes: The moderating role of affect intensity. *European Journal of Social Psychology, 24,* 189–205.

Hodges, S. D., & Wilson, T. D. (1993). Effects of analyzing reasons on attitude change: The moderating role of attitude accessibility. *Social Cognition, 11,* 353–366.

Kinder, D. R. (1998). Opinion and action in the realm of politics. In D. T. Gilbert, S. T. Fiske, & G. Lindzey (Eds.), *The handbook of social psychology* (4th ed., Vol. 2, pp. 778–867). Boston: McGraw-Hill.

Krosnick, J. A. (1988). Attitude importance and attitude change. *Journal of Experimental Social Psychology, 24,* 240–255.

Krosnick, J. A., & Abelson, R. P. (1992). The case of measuring attitude strength in surveys. In J. Tanur (Ed.), *Questions about questions: Inquiries into the cognitive bases of surveys* (pp. 177–203). New York: Sage.

Krosnick, J. A., & Petty, R. E. (1995). Attitude strength: An overview. In R. E. Petty & J. A. Krosnick (Eds.), *Attitude strength: Antecedents and consequences* (pp. 1–24). Hillsdale, NJ: Erlbaum.

Lavine, H., Huff, J. W., Wagner, S. H., & Sweeney, D. (1998). The moderating influence of attitude strength on the susceptibility to context effects in attitude surveys. *Journal of Personality and Social Psychology, 75,* 359–373.

Petty, R. E., & Cacioppo, R. E. (1986). The elaboration likelihood model of persuasion. In L. Berkowitz (Ed.), *Advances in experimental social psychology* (Vol. 19, pp. 123–205). San Diego, CA: Academic Press.

Petty, R. E., & Krosnick, J. A. (Eds.). (1995). *Attitude strength: Antecedents and consequences.* Hillsdale, NJ: Erlbaum.

Rothman, A. J., & Hardin, C. (1997). Differential use of the availability heuristic in social judgment. *Personality and Social Psychology Bulletin, 23,* 123–138.

Rothman, A. J., & Schwarz, N. (1998). Constructing perceptions of vulnerability: Personal relevance and the use of experiential information in health judgments. *Personality and Social Psychology Bulletin, 24,* 1053–1064.

Schwarz, N. (1998). Accessible content and accessibility experiences: The interplay of declarative and experiential information in judgment. *Personality and Social Psychology Review, 2,* 87–99.

Schwarz, N., & Bless, H. (1992). Scandals and the public's trust in politicians: Assimilation and contrast effects. *Personality and Social Psychology Bulletin, 18,* 574–579.

Schwarz, N., Bless, H., Strack, F., Klumpp, G., Rittenauer-Schatka, H., & Simons, A. (1991). Ease of retrieval as information: Another look at the availability heuristic. *Journal of Personality and Social Psychology, 61,* 195–202.

Schwarz, N., & Hippler, H.-J. (1995). The numeric values of rating scales: A comparison of their impact in mail surveys and telephone interviews. *International Journal of Public Opinion Research, 7,* 72–74.

Stapel, D. A., & Schwarz, N. (1998). The Republican who did not want to become president: Colin Powell's impact on evaluations of the Republican Party and Bob Dole. *Personality and Social Psychology Bulletin, 24,* 690–698.

Thomsen, C. J., Borgida, E., & Lavine, H. (1995). The causes and consequences of personal involvement. In R. E. Petty & J. A. Krosnick (Eds.), *Attitude strength: Antecedents and consequences* (pp. 191–214). Hillsdale, NJ: Erlbaum.

Tversky, A., & Kahneman, D. (1973). Availability: A heuristic for judging frequency and probability. *Cognitive Psychology, 5,* 207–232.

Wänke, M., Bless, H., & Biller, B. (1996). Subjective experience versus content of information in the construction of attitude judgments. *Personality and Social Psychology Bulletin, 22,* 1105–1113.

Wänke, M., Bohner, G., & Jurkowitsch, A. (1997). There are many reasons to drive a BMW: Does ease of argument generation influence brand attitudes? *Journal of Consumer Research, 24,* 170–177.

Wilson, T. D., & Hodges, S. D. (1992). Attitudes as constructions. In L. L. Martin & A. Tesser (Eds.), *The construction of social judgment* (pp. 37–65). Hillsdale, NJ: Erlbaum.

Wilson, T. D., Kraft, D., & Dunn, D. S. (1989). The disruptive effects of explaining attitudes: The moderating effects of knowledge about the attitude object. *Journal of Experimental Social Psychology, 25,* 379–400.

Michaela Wänke
Herbert Bless

The Effects of Subjective Ease of Retrieval on Attitudinal Judgments: The Moderating Role of Processing Motivation

The central theme of this book is that subjective experience—the subtle phenomenological feelings that accompany the performance of every social task—play a key role in how people think about and respond to their environment. This chapter presents some record and some theorizing about how the phenomenal experience of finding it easy or difficult to retrieve information impacts on subsequent attitudinal judgments based on this information.

As Wegner and Gilbert so eloquently argued in chapter 1, social psychology is the science of experience, and as G. Allport (1935) more or less eloquently argued, attitudes are the most distinctive and indispensable concept in social psychology. From these two positions, it almost seems imperative that linking the two subjects, attitudes and experience, should open up an interesting research area in social psychology. Indeed, some of this area has been explored, namely the relation of attitudes and affective experience. As many chapters in this book testify, psychologists' understanding of how mood influences the construal of attitude judgments has advanced quite a lot in the last 20 or so years (Bless, in press; Forgas, in press; Schwarz & Clore, 1996; and the chapters on affect and cognition

Address correspondence to Michaela Wänke, Institut für Psychologie, PH Erfurt, Postfach 307, 99006 Erfurt, Germany. E-mail: waenke@ipsych.ph-erfurt.de

in this volume). Research on how the subjectively experienced ease of retrieval influences the construal of attitudes has developed only relatively recently. Although information retrieval features quite prominently in social cognition, theoretical accounts focused exclusively on the content of this retrieval and ignored the experiential byproduct of subjectively felt ease or difficulty of this retrieval. This neglect is somewhat surprising, as accessibility, one of the central concepts in social cognition, is often defined as the ease with which information comes to mind. Nowhere however, does this reference to ease entangle a feeling or phenomenal experience as described by Wegner and Gilbert. Rather, in these definitions, ease stands as a synonym for speed or the likelihood that something comes to mind. We focused on the experiential aspect of ease because information retrieval seems such a central process in social judgment, and the subjectively experienced ease of retrieval is an inevitable byproduct. Whenever information is retrieved, some degree of ease or difficulty is experienced and is thus inherently and inseparably linked to the construal of attitudinal judgments. We will first give a short review of previous research in the area (also see chapter 8 by Haddock and chapter 10 by Schwarz & colleagues in this volume) and will then develop our present research question.

☐ State of the Art

Social cognition generally assumes that individuals base their judgments on the information that is accessible at the time of judgment (for reviews, see Higgins, 1989; Wilson & Hodges, 1992; Wyer & Srull, 1989). Accordingly, the resulting judgments reflect the evaluative implications of the temporarily accessible information. For example, one would expect that individuals report more favorable attitudes toward an issue after they have retrieved favorable arguments as compared to unfavorable arguments. Recent research, however, has provided evidence that attitudinal judgments are not only influenced by *what* comes to mind, but also *how* it comes to mind. More precisely, the subjective experience during the retrieval of information may moderate the relationship between the retrieved information and the attitudinal judgment.

The idea that the subjective experience during the retrieval of information influences the subsequent judgments was first introduced by Tversky and Kahneman (1973) for frequency or probability judgments. In their seminal paper on the availability heuristic, they argued that individuals may estimate frequencies or probabilities by using the *ease* with which instances can be brought to mind. For example, individuals find it easier to retrieve words that begin with a particular letter than to retrieve words that have the same letter in the third position, and consequently individuals overestimate the amount of first-letter words as compared to third-letter words (see also Wänke, Schwarz, & Bless, 1995). More recent research has extended this research topic and reported evidence that the ease with which relevant information is retrieved may affect not only frequency judgments, but also a wide variety of other social judgments, such as reported self-assertiveness (Schwarz, Bless, Strack, Klumpp, Rittenauer-Schatka, & Simons, 1991; Stepper & Strack, 1993), attitudinal judgments (Wänke, Bless, & Biller, 1996), brand preferences (Wänke, Bohner, & Jurkowitsch, 1997), estimated health risks (Raghubir & Menon, 1998; Rothman & Schwarz, 1998), political judgments (chapter 8 by Haddock in this volume), and more. In all of these studies, the influence on judgment in the direction of the valence of the retrieved information was stronger when the retrieval was experienced as easy as opposed to difficult. For example, in one study (Wänke et al., 1996), participants recalled arguments either in favor of or against the use of public transportation. Moreover, the subjectively experienced ease with which the arguments were retrieved was varied. In line with Schwarz et al.'s (1991) suggestion that individuals will generally find it easier to recall only a few examples rather than many, participants were either asked to recall three arguments or seven. If judgments merely depended on what comes to mind, one would expect more favorable attitudes toward public transport after the retrieval of pro arguments. Indeed the retrieval of pro arguments led to more favorable attitudes than contra arguments. However, this occurred only when the subjective experience retrieval had been manipulated to feel easy. When the retrieval was made to feel difficult, the impact of the valence of the retrieved information weakened. Attitudes following pro arguments did not differ from those following contra arguments. Other studies even found reversals, insofar as favorable information led to less favorable judgments than unfavorable information when judges were made to subjectively experience the retrieval as difficult. For example, recipients of an ad featuring the slogan "BMW or Mercedes: There are many reasons to choose a BMW. Surely, you know ten" reported less favorable attitudes toward BMW than recipients of the slogan "BMW or Mercedes: There are many reasons not to choose a BMW. Surely, you know ten" (Wänke et al., 1997; see also Schwarz et al., 1991, for reversals). Retrieving 10 reasons for either choice had been judged as extremely difficult, and apparently, experiencing difficulty in information retrieval moderates the impact of the retrieved information on judgment.

☐ Present Research Question

Despite the impressive evidence for what we will refer to as "ease effect," the mediating processes are not entirely understood at this time. Why does the subjectively experienced ease or difficulty of retrieval moderate the impact of retrieved information? In this chapter, we will first address two possible but rather different explanations: one implying that subjective ease operates as a heuristic cue, the other suggesting that subjective ease affects the perceived quality of the retrieved information. According to the former, ease effects are the product of heuristic processing. In contrast, the latter hypothesis assumes that subjective ease effects emerge because the judgment is based on the retrieved information rather than on heuristic cues. These two accounts make different predictions for the emergence of ease effects under processing constraints. Reliance on heuristic cues is particularly likely when processing is constrained due to motivational or cognitive factors. In contrast, information-based judgments are less likely to occur under such processing constraints. We will present two studies that investigate the impact of experienced ease on attitudinal judgments under conditions favoring either heuristic or information-based processing. As we hope to show, our results suggest that ease effects may occur for information-based judgments. In other words, subjective ease of retrieval does not operate solely as a heuristic cue. These findings differ from other research, and we will propose some theoretical ideas about how subjectively experienced ease of retrieval may influence attitude judgments.

☐ Potential Mediators of Ease-of-Retrieval Effects in Attitudinal Judgments

Ease Effects as Results of Processing Constraints

Most research on the ease effect has been rooted in the considerations implied by the availability—or accessibility—heuristic as introduced by Tversky and Kahneman (1973). Although the availability heuristic was originally introduced as a process by which individuals estimate frequencies (or probabilities), it is also applicable to other judgments. By relying on the availability heuristic, individuals may conclude that the relative ease with which relevant thoughts come to mind is an indicator of the amount of respective information actually available about the issue. The potential amount of information in turn may have implications for the attitudinal judgment. For example, individuals may reason like this: "If it is so difficult to generate favorable thoughts, there cannot be many positive aspects, thus I'm against it." Similarly, but still drawing on the availability heuristic, individuals may directly infer their attitudes from their experienced ease of generating attitude-relevant thoughts just as they would from overt behavior (Bem, 1972; Fazio, 1987). They may reason like this, for example: "If I have such difficulty generating favorable thoughts, I seem to oppose this issue." Both accounts are based on the heuristic inference regarding the amount of potentially relevant information. If information retrieval is experienced as difficult, individuals will pay less attention to the information actually retrieved and will base their judgment on the fact that it is difficult to retrieve supportive (or opposing) information. Consequently, they will arrive at a less favorable (or unfavorable) judgment than would be the case if retrieval had been easy.

According to this scenario, individuals simplify the judgment process by relying on the experienced ease of retrieval rather than on the retrieved information. If this is so, ease effects should be more pronounced when the processing is constrained and individuals are forced to process in a more heuristic manner (Chaiken, 1987; Petty & Cacioppo, 1986). Systematic processing, on the other hand, would interfere with ease effects, because in that case individuals would base their judgment on the information actually retrieved rather than on heuristic cues. As Schwarz (1998) noted, "Individuals who rely on a systematic processing strategy are likely to draw on accessible content, whereas individuals who rely on a heuristic processing strategy are likely to draw on subjective accessibility experiences" (p. 97). We would therefore expect stronger ease effects under conditions that favor heuristic processing, and weaker ease effects under conditions that favor systematic processing (see also chapter 8 by Haddock in this volume).

Some support of this hypothesis was offered by a recent study on estimated health risks (Rothman & Schwarz, 1998). This study found ease effects, but only when the personal relevance of the task was assumed to be low. If we assume that high personal relevance is likely to induce systematic processing and low personal relevance to trigger heuristic processing, these results support the assumption that subjective ease of retrieval operates as a heuristic cue. We will discuss these results and those presented by Haddock (chapter 8 in this volume) in more detail below. First, we would like to introduce an alternative approach that does not assume that ease operates as a heuristic cue and does not expect stronger ease effects under heuristic processing.

Ease Effects as Results of Information-Based Judgments

As an alternative to the heuristic scenario, the experienced difficulty of retrieval may also reduce the perceived quality of the information actually retrieved. Because the retrieved information is less compelling, it has less impact on judgment. Note that contrary to the heuristic explanation, this hypothesis allows that the judgment is actually based on the retrieved information, but that the perceived quality of the retrieved information partly depends on the subjective ease of its retrieval. We will elaborate this idea in greater detail below. First, however, we will review some evidence suggesting that the retrieval experience may reduce the perceived quality of the information.

Several lines of evidence suggest that experienced difficulty seems to lower one's confidence in the information and in judgments based on this information. For example, Kelley and Lindsay (1993) found that subjects responding to knowledge questions in a quiz were more confident about their answers when these answers had been made highly accessible using a previous priming procedure. Presumably, the ease with which the answer came to mind heightened individuals' confidence in the diagnosticity of that particular piece of information—even if it was wrong (see also Morris, 1990). Our previous research replicated decreased confidence following difficult retrieval also for attitude judgments (Wänke et al., 1996). Difficulty of recall apparently elicits some reluctance to rely on the retrieved information, possibly because it casts some doubt on the diagnosticity of the information. Other research suggested that the ease of categorizing information may be attributed to the greater diagnosticity this categorization (Sherman, Mackie, & Driscoll, 1990), again suggesting the significance of experienced ease for perceived validity or diagnosticity.

Second, it is generally found that the perceived validity of statements increases with the number of exposures (e.g., Arkes, Boehm, & Xu, 1991; Begg, Armour, & Kerr, 1985; Hasher, Goldstein, & Toppino, 1977; Hawkins & Hoch, 1992; Law & Hawkins, 1997; Mady & Newman, 1987). In some of this work, perceived familiarity with the claims mediated this effect, suggesting that when participants experienced a feeling that "it rings a bell," they judged a claim to be more true. Because repetitions facilitate the retrieval of information, it may also be argued that it is the ease of retrieval or recognition that is driving the "truth effect."

In sum, various lines of evidence point to a possible influence of subjectively experienced ease of information retrieval on subjectively perceived information quality. Information that was retrieved with difficulty may seem less compelling, less true, or less diagnostic than easily retrieved information. When individuals use the retrieved information in forming their judgment, easily retrieved information—because it is more compelling—will have more impact than information retrieved with difficulty. This perspective implies that ease effects are stronger the more individuals base their judgment on the retrieved information. Hence, we would expect stronger ease effects under conditions that favor more systematic processing, and weaker ease effects under conditions that favor more heuristic processing.

Juxtaposing the Alternative Explanations

To sum up, the two explanations, the availability heuristic and the quality hypothesis, differ with regard to the role of the recalled information in judgment. According to the former, individuals use subjective ease of retrieval to infer the potential amount of relevant information and use this as a heuristic cue for their judgment. For example, if the experienced difficulty of retrieval suggests a lack of pro arguments, the judgment will be less favorable. The quality or compellingness of the arguments actually recalled may play a minor role. In contrast, the quality hypothesis holds that the experienced difficulty of retrieval affects the perceived quality of the arguments actually recalled. Information that comes to mind less easily may seem less valid and less compelling, and thus may have less of an impact on judgment.

If ease effects are due to the heuristic use of the inferred amount, conditions that favor heuristic processing should also favor ease effects (see chapter 8 by Haddock in this volume; Rothman & Schwarz, 1998; Schwarz, 1998). If, on the other hand, ease effects are caused by the perceived quality of the information, ease effects should be more pronounced the more individuals base their judgments on the information actually recalled; in other words, conditions that favor systematic processing would also enhance ease effects. We shall now examine how conditions favoring heuristic versus systematic processing actually influence the emergence of ease effects.

☐ Ease Effects for Information-Based Versus Heuristic Judgments

Previous Evidence

As already mentioned, there is some evidence in line with the hypothesis of stronger ease effects under heuristic processing as compared to more systematic processing (for reviews see chapter 8 by Haddock in this volume; Schwarz, 1998). Rothman and Schwarz (1998) had participants with and without a family history of heart disease recall either three or eight instances of their own risk-relevant behavior, that is, either risk-reducing or risk-increasing behavior. Note that retrieving eight instances was experienced as more difficult than retrieving three instances. Risk estimates of participants without a family history were more influenced by three rather than eight instances. Participants who had retrieved three risk-increasing (decreasing) behaviors judged themselves as more (less) vulnerable than participants who had retrieved eight behaviors. This clearly reflects an ease effect. Participants with a family history, on the other hand, were more influenced by eight rather than three retrieved behaviors. The authors concluded that participants without a family history used the experienced ease as a heuristic cue, whereas participants with a family history were more involved in the matter and did not rely on the ease heuristic but used the content of the retrieved information. These participants were more influenced the more information they had retrieved.

The finding that ease effects occur only with a low degree of involvement but not with a high degree of involvement clearly supports the assumption of ease as a heuristic cue. A similar conclusion is suggested by research in the political domain. Haddock (chapter 8 in this volume) found that research participants who reported low interest in politics were more affected in their judgments by retrieving fewer pieces of information rather than many, whereas participants who reported high interest in politics showed no difference.

Note, however, that neither study directly measured or manipulated involvement. It is not clear whether the groups really differed in involvement, and whether they also differed on other variables. For example, as Haddock points out, individuals with an interest in politics will probably already have formed an opinion and simply retrieved that opinion rather than construing it in the situation. Consequently, they are less subject to any situational influences. One may also assume that participants with a family history of heart disease were more knowledgeable about risk-related behaviors. It is quite possible that experts interpret the fact that something comes to mind easily differently from nonexperts. Indeed, research has shown that individuals who were led to believe that they were experts on a topic were less influenced by the ease with which they retrieved information than were individuals not manipulated to believe that they were experts (Biller, 1996). Moreover, basing judgments on the amount of retrieved information does not necessarily indicate that the judgment is information based or the result of systematic processing but may in fact indicate the opposite. Petty and Cacioppo (1984), for example, manipulated the personal relevance of a persuasive message, the number of presented arguments, and the compelling nature of the presented arguments. When personal relevance was high, nine arguments were more persuasive than three, but only when the arguments were strong. When personal relevance was low, however, nine arguments induced more attitude change than three arguments, regardless of the strength of the arguments. As these results indicate, more persuasion following a higher amount of information does not necessarily indicate high involvement or systematic processing.

In general, the ease manipulation of asking participants to retrieve few or many instances does not allow us to distinguish between the availability heuristic or the quality hypothesis. If, as in the present research paradigm, experiencing difficulty is confounded with retrieving more information, the greater amount of information may possibly compensate for the reduced quality. Hence, previous research is inconclusive regarding the quality hypothesis.

Present Research

The present research is a first step in investigating the two alternative explanations of subjective ease of retrieval operating as a heuristic cue versus affecting the perceived quality of the retrieved information. In essence, we tested how conditions favoring heuristic versus systematic processing influenced the emergence of ease effects. If ease effects emerge only under conditions favoring heuristic processing but not when the judgment is information based, the assumption that ease operates as a heuristic cue seems likely. If, on the other hand, ease effects emerge only under systematic but not under heuristic processing, this would offer preliminary support to the quality hypothesis.

Judgments regarding the perceived compellingness of the arguments may also prove illuminating. If ease effects are due to the reduced compellingness of the arguments, this should be evident in the compellingness ratings. If ease effects occur because individuals infer a general lack of respective arguments, compellingness ratings need not be affected. The fact that there may not be that many arguments should not interfere with the perceived quality of the "few" arguments actually found.

A further objective of our research was to develop a novel manipulation of experienced ease. All past studies of which we are aware manipulated ease by asking research participants to recall few versus many relevant instances. In general, individuals will find it easier to recall only a few examples rather than many. While this procedure affects experienced ease reliably, it also confounds experienced ease with recalled content. Inevitably, participants who recalled more instances also recalled different information than those who recalled only a few. Previously, we had disentangled this confounding by a yoked design, in which the arguments recalled by one group were presented to another group (Wänke et al., 1996). Thus, we had two groups who had exactly the same information but differed in their recall experience. This design allowed us to separate the impact of retrieved content and the impact of retrieval experience on the resulting judgments. In the present studies, we aimed for more control over the retrieved content by abandoning the procedure of letting participants self-generate information. Instead, we presented information to them and asked them to recall this information. This allows complete control over the information content and merely varies the recall experience.

☐ Empirical Evidence I: Ease Effects as a Function of Measured Accuracy Motivation

Our goal was to induce *information-based versus heuristic judgments* in order to investigate ease effects under both conditions. Processing style is, among other factors, a function of a person's accuracy motivation (e.g., Chaiken, 1987). We assumed that participants who were highly motivated to give an accurate judgment would rely more on the recalled information and less on heuristic cues in forming their judgment. In a first study, we used measured rather than manipulated accuracy motivation. After they had made their judgment, participants reported how important is was to them to give an accurate judgment. We also measured rather than manipulated the experienced ease of recall of previously presented information.

In addition, we varied the quality of the information that was presented to the participants and that they were later asked to recall. The information was either highly compelling or less compelling. We did this to obtain an indicator for the extent to which participants used the recalled claims for their judgment. Information-based judgments should reflect the differences in the quality of the information (Chaiken, 1987; Petty & Cacioppo, 1986). Heuristically formed judgments should differ less following strong versus weak claims. The crucial question, however, was this: for which of the judgments—information based or heuristic—would we be able to observe ease effects?

Participants were presented with an ad for a coffeemaker embedded in a series of tasks disguised as a memory test. All advertised features and benefits were clearly in favor of the coffeemaker, but varied in quality. One ad presented features and benefits that a pilot study had shown to be strongly compelling, while the other ad described less compelling features. Later, participants were asked to recall the arguments and, subsequently, to evaluate the coffeemaker.

Based on median splits on reported ease of recall and on reported accuracy motivation, participants were divided into conditions of experienced ease of recall versus difficulty of recall, and high versus low accuracy motivation. The number of recalled features was used as a covariate in three-way ANOVA with ease of recall, argument quality, and accuracy motivation as between-subjects factors. The covariate was not significant.

Figure 9.1 shows the pattern of evaluations. Under a situation of high accuracy motivation, participants evaluated the coffeemaker significantly more favorably following strong rather than weak ad claims. This suggests that accuracy-motivated participants draw on the presented claims to evaluate the coffeemaker, as was expected. Nevertheless, these participants were also significantly affected by the experienced ease with which the claims had been recalled. They evaluated the coffeemaker less favorably when they had experienced difficulty in retrieving the advertising claims, as Figure 9.1 shows.

We had expected that participants low in accuracy motivation would rely less on features, and therefore their evaluation would be less affected by the quality of the presented features and benefits. The question was whether ease effects observed for information-based judgments (under high accuracy motivation) also emerged when the judgment was not information based (under low accuracy motivation).

The pattern of means suggests that difficulty of recall decreased the evaluation only for weak ad claims but not for strong ones. In other words, when the retrieval of the ad claims felt difficult, participants differentiated between strong and weak claims even under low accuracy motivation. They did not do so when the retrieval felt easy. One may speculate that experienced difficulty induced more systematic processing. However, this pattern was not significant. If we ignore the provocative but nonsig-

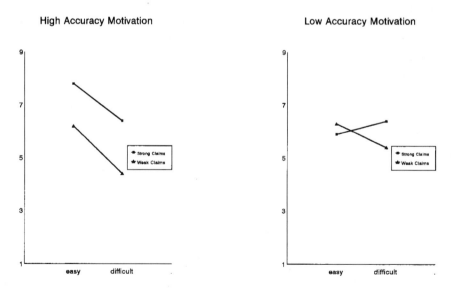

FIGURE 9.1. Mean evaluations as a function of accuracy motivation, ease of retrieval, and strength of the ad claims.

nificant pattern of means for the time being, we find no indication of ease effects under low accuracy motivation.

In sum, Study 1 found ease effects when individuals rely on the information, but no ease effects when participants apparently did not base their judgment on the information but drew on other strategies. These results do not support the assumption that ease effects were mediated by the availability heuristic. They are, however, compatible with the assumption that ease effects occur because difficulty of recall may reduce the compellingness of the retrieved information.

☐ Empirical Evidence II: Ease Effects as a Function of Manipulated Accuracy Motivation

In a subsequent study, experienced ease of recall and accuracy motivation were directly manipulated. As in the previous study, the presented ads differed in the quality of the claims. Note that this is the first study on ease of retrieval effects that experimentally varies processing conditions. All previous research, including the study just described, used other measured variables as proxies (e.g., interest, family history, etc.).

The ad was presented under the cover story that the study dealt with language used in advertising. After the highly compelling or less compelling ad for the coffeemaker had been presented, participants were asked to recall the features of the coffeemaker. In order to manipulate the ease of recall, this task was presented as a word completion task. For each feature, participants were presented with a few letters, and blanks for missing letters. The task was to complete the words by filling in the blanks. In the "easy condition," the presented letters were selected to provide helpful cues; in the "difficult condition," the cues were not particularly helpful. For example, retrieval cues for the feature "temperature-display" would be "t e m _ _ _ _ _ _ _ - d i s _ _ _ _ " in the easy condition, but "_ _ _ _ _ _ _ _ u r e - _ _ _ _ l a y" in the difficult condition. As the manipulation check showed, participants found it easier to recall the claims when helpful cues were provided. After the word completion task, participants were asked to evaluate the coffeemaker and to answer several control questions. Participants were either instructed to answer these questions as accurately as possible, or to use their spontaneous reactions. In the "high accuracy condition," they were told that the task was to test whether they were able to evaluate consumer products accurately and whether they could identify good quality from low quality. In the "low accuracy condition," they were told that we were only interested in their first spontaneous impression. Following these instructions, participants rated the coffeemaker. After manipulation checks for experienced ease of recall and accuracy motivation, mood ratings, and other control questions, participants also rated the compellingness of the advertising claims.

The ratings were analyzed in a three-factorial ANCOVA with amount of correctly recalled features as a covariate. Figure 9.2 reflects the means. The covariate was significant. More importantly, we found a significant triple interaction between experienced ease of recall, accuracy motivation, and argument quality.

Separate analyses for high accuracy motivation revealed a significant effect of the covariate, and, nevertheless, significant main effects of argument quality and ease of recall. Under high accuracy motivation, participants evaluated the coffeemaker more favorably when its features and benefits had been more compelling. Apparently, participants based their evaluation of the coffeemaker on the quality of the retrieved features and benefits. Despite this information-based judgment, experienced difficulty of recall also significantly affected the judgment. When retrieval felt difficult, participants arrived at a more negative evaluation. So far, this replicates the previous results, which also found ease effects for information-based judgments.

For low accuracy motivation, Figure 9.2 shows the same pattern of means as in the study reported earlier. Here, the interaction between ease of recall and quality of the claims was marginally significant. Participants failed to differentiate between strong and weak arguments only when

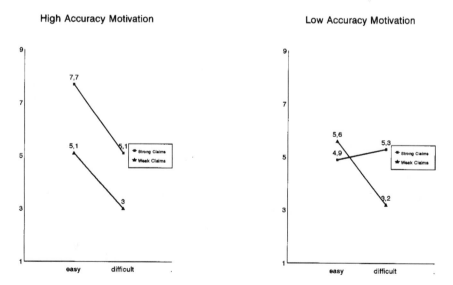

FIGURE 9.2. Mean evaluations as a function of accuracy motivation, ease of retrieval, and strength of the ad claims.

retrieval had been easy. However, when retrieval had been difficult, the same difference between strong and weak arguments emerged as under high accuracy motivation. This suggests that experienced difficulty induced participants to a more systematic processing. No main effects for ease of recall emerged.

As we mentioned above, the perceived compellingness of claims may provide direct insights regarding the quality hypothesis. A priori stronger arguments were rated as more compelling than weaker arguments, indicating a successful quality manipulation. More importantly, the ad claims were also rated as more compelling following easy rather than difficult retrieval. No other effects emerged.

☐ Ease Effects for Information-Based Judgments but Not for Heuristic Judgments

While one study relied on measured ease of recall, ease was manipulated in the other. Although the two studies used different research procedures, the results are remarkably similar. In both studies, accuracy-motivated participants apparently drew on the retrieved information for their judgment, as is reflected by the clear difference between strong and weak ad claims. Nevertheless, in both studies, these content-based judgments were additionally affected by the experienced ease of recall. Accuracy-motivated participants gave lower ratings for the coffeemaker when recall felt difficult rather than easy.

In the absence of an ease effect under low accuracy motivation, these results are not easily compatible with a heuristic processing account. And indeed, we did not find the usual ease effect under low accuracy motivation. What we did find, however, was that in both studies, experienced difficulty of recall decreased the judgment when the arguments were weak, but not when they were strong. Although not significant in either study, this pattern was highly significant when both studies were combined. This observed pattern may suggest that the experienced difficulty may have elicited more systematic processing. As a result, the ratings under difficult recall did not differ between high and low accuracy motivation. The fact that difficulty of recall may induce systematic processing would not come as a complete surprise. As mentioned above, previous studies have found decreased confidence in judgments when they were based on information whose recall felt difficult. In turn, low confidence in the judgment may have elicited more systematic processing in order to arrive at a more confident judgment (Chaiken, 1987). For strong claims, a more systematic processing would produce more favorable judgments. Note, however, that the experienced subjective difficulty of recall would also impair the perceived quality of the claims as discussed above. Thus, while systematic processing leads to a higher impact of perceived argument quality, this very quality may be reduced by the difficult retrieval. For a priori stronger arguments, the two effects may compensate for each other. For a priori weaker arguments, both influences are in the same direction and result in a clearly less favorable judgment. Subjectively experienced ease of recall, similar to the subjectively experienced mood, may influence judgments in two ways: first, by exerting a direct influence on the judgment, and second, by influencing the processing strategy leading to the judgment (for a review on mood effects, see Bless, in press; Forgas, in press; Schwarz & Clore, 1996; also see the chapters on mood and processing in this volume).

We readily acknowledge that the suggestion of the dual effects of experienced ease of recall, or, more specifically, the suggestion that difficulty may trigger systematic processing, needs more support. At present, our interpretation is only preliminary and needs to be scrutinized with care. Only future research will clarify this matter. In contrast, the finding of ease effects under high accuracy motivation when the judgment is information based seems more firmly based, as it was highly significant in both of the two studies. We argue that experiencing difficulty in information retrieval reduces the perceived quality of the retrieved information. This interpretation is also supported by the reduced ratings for the perceived compellingness under difficult retrieval. Because the information seems less compelling, its impact on the judgment is reduced. Accordingly, ease effects will be more pronounced the more the judgment is information based. We found no indication of ease effects operating as a heuristic.

Before we go and try to integrate our present results with the previously available findings research, we would like to address an alternative account of our findings. One may argue that difficulty produced negative affect, which was transferred to the attitudinal target and thus accounted for the more negative evaluation. As this explanation pertains to all studies on ease effects, it should be noted that most previous studies also had conditions in which participants retrieved negative information. Experiencing difficulty in retrieving negative information led to more positive judgments, which is not easily explained by mere affect transfer. Because these effects have been shown numerous times, we used only favorable information in our present studies. With particular regard to our present studies and the role of affect transfer, we may add that in the second study, we assessed participants' mood and found no indication that difficulty of recall led to less positive mood.

☐ Reconciling the Two Accounts

We found no indication of ease effects under heuristic processing but stronger ease effects when the judgment was based on the retrieved information. Other research, as mentioned above, has suggested the opposite (see chapter 8 by Haddock in this volume; Rothman & Schwarz, 1998). How can we reconcile these contradictory findings? While the explanation of a heuristic inference does not seem compatible with our present data, given all the evidence, we cannot rule out that such an inference may mediate ease effects under different circumstances. In the discussion that follows, we will try to account for the various findings.

We start with the assumption that subjectively experienced difficulty of recall elicits attention and instigates a need for explanation. Depending on the situation, individuals may attribute the experience of difficulty to a paucity of relevant instances, their low validity, diagnosticity, credibility, or to other explanations. The chosen inference may in turn influence further judgments. Indeed, Schwarz and Schuman (1997) have shown how experienced difficulty may be accounted for in various ways, depending on accessible interpretations. They replicated a well-known finding that difficulty in a survey question to recall what one´s representative did during his or her term of office leads respondents to report lower interest in politics in a later question. In another condition, a question on the quality of the representative's public relations (PR) work allowed respondents to attribute the experienced difficulty to poor PR, rather than their own lack of interest. Accordingly, their reported interest in politics was less affected. As this study demonstrates, experienced difficulty of recall may be misattributed to many situationally accessible causes.

When individuals self-generate information in order to make a judgment, it seems reasonable that they should take the potential number of supporting or contradicting arguments into consideration. Individuals will rarely undertake an exhaustive search and retrieve all information. If the preliminary search implies that there is a general lack of supportive or contradictory details, this in itself is valid information. In our study, however, participants did not self-generate the information but recalled previously presented information. One would hardly interpret the difficulty in recalling previously presented information as an indicator for a lack of such information. The inference "If it is so hard to remember the ad claims, there cannot have been many" does not make sense intuitively. Besides, participants knew how many claims there had been. More likely, the difficulty will be attributed to some qualitative aspect of the information. Moreover, in our present study, individuals retrieved *arguments*, while some of the other research asked participants to retrieve *behavioral instances*. One may argue that the nature of recalled behavioral instances is quite different from arguments. After all, the most essential characteristic of arguments is how compelling they are. For behavioral instances, in contrast, the quality is less of an issue. For example, while the typicality of instances is certainly not meaningless, their number may be more important. Consequently, quality seems a prime candidate to account for the experienced difficulty when arguments are retrieved, but may be less so when behavioral instances are retrieved.

If the impact of experienced difficulty of retrieval on judgments depends on how this difficulty is attributed, other conditions may either favor or undermine ease effects. If, for example, the difficulty is attributed to the weak quality of the information, conditions that favor an information-based judgment—for example, high accuracy motivation—will also favor ease effects. If difficulty is attributed to the lack of respective information, on the other hand, conditions that favor information-based judgments will impair ease effects. Thus, the question of which conditions favor ease effects may be more complex than previously assumed. Future research will have to identify additional attributions. Moreover, it will be necessary to investigate more closely which conditions favor which attributions in order to predict the impact of experienced ease of retrieval more accurately.

☐ Conclusion

The retrieval of information is a central process in social judgment. Extensive research has provided evidence on how judgments depend on the content of the retrieved information. We have reviewed more recent evidence that social judgment may also depend on whether this retrieval is subjectively experienced as easy or difficult. This evidence further supports Clore's (1992) notion that an "experiential state is not an epiphenomenon, but rather plays a causal role in other cognitive processes" (p. 159). However, despite the considerable evidence for the causal role of subjectively experienced ease of retrieval, the exact nature of this causality has not been sufficiently investigated. While there is sufficient evidence to challenge present content-based models of social judgment, what is lacking is a conceptualization that integrates subjective experience into models of social judgment. At present, subjective experience is simply subsumed under heuristic processes (e.g., Chen & Chaiken, 1999). As our results suggest, this may not be the sole truth—at least not for ease of retrieval effects. But what's more important, how does the notion of experiential influences as heuristic help to understand how they are mediated? In this respect, Clore (1992) has introduced the distinction of whether feelings exert their influence directly at the judgment stage or indirectly by affecting the representation of the target. He interpreted ease-of-retrieval effects—as other experiential influences—as falling into the former category. Our results suggest the latter—at least for ease of retrieval, and at least sometimes. Although at present, we cannot present a unified theory that integrates the influences of ease of retrieval and content of retrieval and specifies the exact processes of their influence, we hope our challenging of previous assumptions stimulates further research that will eventually do so. As we mentioned in the beginning, the link between subjective experience and attitudinal judgments provides a rather novel area of research. At present, it is hard to imagine the size and shape of this area, but we are rather optimistic that it will prove wide and varied.

☐ References

Allport, G. W. (1935). Attitudes. In C. Murchinson (Ed.), *A Handbook of Social Psychology* (pp. 798–844). Worchester, MA: Clark University Press.

Arkes, H. R., Boehm, L. E., & Xu, G. (1991). Determinants of judged validity. *Journal of Experimental Social Psychology, 27*, 576–605.

Begg, I., Armour, V., & Kerr, T. (1985). On believing what we remember. *Canadian Journal of Behavioral Science, 17*, 199–214.

Bem, D. J. (1972). Self-perception theory. In L Berkowitz (Ed.), *Advances in experimental social psychology* (Vol. 6, pp. 1–62). San Diego, CA: Academic Press.

Biller, B. (1996). *Sicherheit und Unsicherheit bei sozialen Urteilen: Die Leichtigkeit der Erinnerung als Information.* [Confidence in social judgments: Ease of retrieval as inforrmation]. Unpublished diploma thesis, Universität Heidelberg.

Bless, H. (in press). The consequences of mood on the processing of social information. In A. Tesser & N. Schwarz (Eds.), *Blackwell handbook in social psychology*, Oxford, England: Blackwell.

Chaiken, S. (1987). The heuristic model of persuasion. In M. P. Zanna, J. M. Olson, & C. P. Herman (Eds.), *Social influence: The Ontario Symposium* (Vol. 5, pp. 3–39). Hillsdale, NJ: Erlbaum.

Chen, S., & Chaiken, S. (1999). The heuristic-systematic model in its broader context. In S. Chaiken & Y. Trope (Eds.), *Dual-process theories in social psychology.* New York: Guilford Press.

Clore, G. L. (1992). Cognitive phenomenology: Feelings and the construction of judgment. In L. L. Martin & A. Tesser (Eds.), *The construction of social judgment* (pp. 133–164). Hillsdale, NJ: Erlbaum.

Fazio, R. H. (1987). Self-perception theory: A current perspective. In M. P. Zanna, J. M. Olson, & C. P. Herman (Eds.), *Social Influence: The Ontario Symposium* (Vol. 5, pp. 129–150). Hillsdale, NJ: Erlbaum.

Forgas, J. P. (Ed.). (in press). *Feeling and thinking: The role of affect in social cognition.* Cambridge, MA: Cambridge University Press.

Hasher, L., Goldstein, D., and Toppino, T. (1977). Frequency and the conference of referential validity. *Journal of Verbal Learning and Verbal Behavior, 16*(1), 107–112.

Hawkins, S. A., & Hoch, S. J. (1992). Low-involvement learning: Memory without evaluation. *Journal of Consumer Research, 19*, 212–225.

Higgins, E. T. (1989). Knowledge accessibility and activation: Subjectivity and suffering from unconscious sources. In J. S. Uleman & J. A. Bargh (Eds.), *Unintended Thought* (pp. 75–123). New York: Guilford Press.

Kelley, C. M., & Lindsay, D. S. (1993). Remembering mistaken for knowing: Ease of retrieval as a basis for confidence in answers to general knowledge questions. *Journal of Memory and Language, 32,* 1–24.

Law, S., & Hawkins, S. A. 1997: Advertising repetition and consumer beliefs: The role of source memory. In W. D. Wells (Ed.), *Measuring advertising effectiveness* (pp. 239–260). Mahwah, NJ: Erlbaum.

Mady, L. A., & Newman, S. E. (1987). Memory for auditorily and visually presented commercials: Effects of repetition and type of claim. *Bulletin of the Psychonomic Society, 25,* 75–76.

Morris, C. (1990). Retrieval processes underlying confidence in comprehension judgments. *Journal of Experimental Psychology: Learning, Memory, and Cognition, 16,* 223–232.

Petty, R. E., & Cacioppo, J. T. (1984). The effects of involvement on responses to argument quantity and quality: Central and peripheral routes to persuasion. *Journal of Personality and Social Psychology, 46,* 69–81.

Petty, R. E., & Cacioppo, J. T. (1986). *Communication and persuasion: Central and peripheral routes to attitude change.* New York: Springer-Verlag.

Raghubir, P., & Menon, G. (1998). AIDS and me, never the twain shall meet: The effects of information accessibility on judgments of risk and advertising effectiveness. *Journal of Consumer Research, 25,* 52–63.

Rothman, A. J., & Schwarz, N. (1998). Constructing perceptions of vulnerability: Personal relevance and the use of experiential information in health judgments. *Personality and Social Psychology Bulletin, 24,* 1053–1064.

Schwarz, N. (1998). Accessible content and accessible experiences. The interplay of declarative and experiential information in judgment. *Personality and Social Psychology Review, 2,* 87–99.

Schwarz, N., Bless, H., Strack, F., Klumpp, G., Rittenauer-Schatka, H., & Simons, A. (1991). Ease of retrieval as information: Another look at the availability heuristic. *Journal of Personality and Social Psychology, 61,* 195–202.

Schwarz, N., & Clore, G. L. (1996). Feelings and phenomenal experiences. In E. T. Higgins & A. Kruglanski (Eds.), *Social psychology: A handbook of basic principles.* New York: Guilford Press.

Schwarz, N., and Schuman, H. (1997). Political knowledge, attribution, and inferred interest in politics: The operation of buffer items. *International Journal of Public Opinion Research, 9,* 191–195.

Sherman, S. J., Mackie, D. M., & Driscoll, D. M. (1990). Priming and the differential use of dimensions in evaluations. *Personality and Social Psychology Bulletin, 16,* 405–418.

Stepper, S., & Strack, F. (1993). Proprioceptive determinants of emotional and nonemotional feelings. *Journal of Personality and Social Psychology, 64,* 211–220.

Tversky, A., & Kahneman, D. (1973). Availability: A heuristic for judging frequency and probability. *Cognitive Psychology, 5,* 207–232.

Wänke, M., Bless, H., & Biller, B. (1996). Subjective experience versus content of information in the construction of attitude judgments. *Personality and Social Psychology Bulletin, 22,* 1105–1115.

Wänke, M., Bohner, G., & Jurkowitsch, A. (1997). There are many reasons to drive a BMW: Does ease of argument generation influence brand attitudes? *Journal of Consumer Research, 24,* 170–177.

Wänke, M., Schwarz, N., & Bless, H. (1995). The availability heuristic revisited: Experienced ease of retrieval in mundane frequency estimates. *Acta Psychologica, 89,* 83–90.

Wilson, T., & Hodges, S. (1992). Attitudes as temporary constructions. In L. Martin & A. Tesser (Eds.), *The construction of social judgments* (pp. 37–67). Hillsdale, NJ: Erlbaum.

Wyer, R. S., & Srull, T. K. (1989). *Memory and cognition in its social context.* Hillsdale, NJ: Erlbaum.

Ian Skurnik
Norbert Schwarz
Piotr Winkielman

10

CHAPTER

Drawing Inferences from Feelings: The Role of Naive Beliefs

Most theories of human judgment assume that we evaluate persons or objects on the basis of declarative or propositional information that bears on the target and that happens to come to mind at the time of judgment (for reviews, see Higgins, 1996; Wyer & Srull, 1989). However, a growing body of research has challenged this assumption by documenting that our subjective experiences and feelings (terms that we propose to use interchangeably) play a crucial role in many judgment processes. The emerging findings can be conceptualized by assuming that our feelings serve informative functions and provide information that we as judges systematically draw on in forming judgments (for a review, see Schwarz & Clore, 1996). Relevant examples include the influence of moods (e.g., Schwarz & Clore, 1983), emotions (e.g., Keltner, Ellsworth, & Edwards, 1993), bodily feelings (e.g., Strack, Martin, & Stepper, 1988), and physical arousal (e.g., Zillman, 1978), as well as cognitive experiences that accompany memory and reasoning, such as the subjective experience of ease or difficulty of recall (e.g., Schwarz, Bless, Strack, Klumpp, Rittenauer-Schatka, & Simons, 1991; Schwarz, 1998) or the experience of perceptual fluency (e.g., Reber, Winkielman, & Schwarz, 1998). When our feelings reflect our actual response to the target, such as when seeing a friend

Address correspondence to Norbert Schwarz, University of Michigan, Institute for Social Research, 426 Thompson St., Rm. 5265, Ann Arbor, MI 48106-1248. E-mail: Nschwarz@umich.edu

elicits a happy mood or makes our heart beat faster, they provide direct and useful information. In these cases, subjective experiences are properly sensitive to the structure of the environment, and are likely to reflect highly adaptive thinking (e.g., Schwarz, 1996; Schooler & Anderson, 1997; Skurnik, Moskowitz, & Johnson, 1999).

In other cases, however, we sometimes mistake feelings from other sources as our response to the target. Thus, we may evaluate our friend more positively for reasons that have little do with him or her, because, for instance, a sunny day has put us in a good mood or because climbing the stairs has increased our heartbeat. When we are aware that our feelings may be due to such irrelevant sources, our feelings' informational value is discredited and we do not draw on our feelings as a source of information. Such discounting effects have been documented for all of the research examples mentioned above, highlighting that we use our feelings as a source of information only when they seem diagnostic for the judgment at hand (for a review, see Schwarz & Clore, 1996).

In the absence of salient conditions that draw attention to an irrelevant source of our feelings, however, we are likely to consider our feelings diagnostic by default. Much as we use the declarative information that happens to come to mind when we think about a target, we use the experiential information that happens to come to mind. In either case, we tend to assume that the information bears on what we think about (or else why would it come to mind?). Higgins (1998) has recently discussed this pervasive tendency as the "aboutness" principle of human inference. Conceptually, the aboutness principle parallels the "relevance" principle of interpersonal communication (Grice, 1975; Sperber & Wilson, 1986), a tacit assumption that holds that every contribution of the speaker is relevant to the aims of the ongoing conversation (or else why would the speaker introduce it?). But much as the relevance of a speaker's contribution can be called into question, so can the relevance of any thoughts or feelings we may experience. When we attribute our mood to an irrelevant source, such as the weather (e.g., Schwarz & Clore, 1983), we are unlikely to rely on it when forming a judgment about an unrelated target. Similarly, when we are aware that some thoughts may only come to mind because they were triggered by an unrelated preceding event (e.g., Martin, 1986; Strack, Schwarz, Bless, Kübler, & Wänke, 1993), we are unlikely to bring these thoughts to bear on the target. In short, we do not rely on the information that comes to mind when its appropriateness to the target is called into question, for example, because we attribute our mood to an irrelevant source (e.g., Schwarz & Clore, 1983) or because we are aware that the declarative information was brought to mind by a preceding irrelevant priming task (e.g., Martin, 1986; Strack et al., 1993). In short, what comes to mind seems relevant by default—or else, why would we have these thoughts or feelings in apparent response to the target? In contrast, assessments that highlight the irrelevance and low diagnosticity of the input need to be triggered by salient features of the situation (cf. Higgins, 1998; Schwarz & Bless, 1992).

But how do people bring an apparently relevant feeling "about" the target to bear on the specific judgment at hand? This is the question we address in the present chapter. We suggest that the inferences that a person may draw from a feeling are constrained by the person's naive beliefs about the working of the mind and the nature of emotions. To take a well-researched example, people believe that it is easier to recall frequent or recent events than to recall rare or distant events. Without this belief, experienced ease of recall would be epiphenomenal and would have no bearing on frequency judgments (e.g., Tversky & Kahneman, 1973) or the dating of events (e.g., Bradburn, Rips, & Shevell, 1987). Conversely, if people believed, for example, that ease of recall was an indication of the recalled event's correspondence with well-formed expectations, rather than an indication of frequency, the expectancy-based illusory correlation effect (Hamilton & Rose, 1980) would not be obtained. Similarly, people believe that desirable events make them feel good, whereas undesirable events make them feel bad (Frijda, 1988, 1999). Without this belief, their apparent affective reaction to a target would not feed into evaluative judgments, and mood effects would not be obtained. Note that these judgment-related beliefs can be employed in an "implicit" manner, in the absence of verbal reports from judges. For instance, in research on semantic priming effects in person perception, people tend to assimilate their judgments of a target person to a primed construct, as if they mistake the high accessibility of the construct as their reaction to the target person (Clore, 1992; Martin, 1986). However, when people are unobtrusively reminded of the priming episode, they seem to realize that the primed construct is accessible for judgment-irrelevant reasons and change their final judgments of the target person in an apparent corrective move. All these effects are found in the absence of any verbal reports about a connection between the priming and judgment tasks (Lombardi, Higgins, & Bargh, 1987; Moskowitz & Skurnik, 1999; Strack et al., 1993; Wegener & Petty, 1997). Tacit beliefs of this type are widely shared and determine the "meaning" of the subjective experience itself for the judgment at hand.

Nevertheless, people may draw different context-dependent inferences from the same subjective experience, as the examples reviewed below illustrate. In the present chapter, we ask: Does this context dependency in judgment imply that our feelings provide *different experiential information* in different contexts? Or does it imply that we draw different, context-dependent conclusions from the *same experiential information*? We address this issue after a review of relevant empirical findings.

☐ How Happy Was Your Childhood? Inferences from Difficulty of Recall

Suppose you are asked, "Are there large parts of your childhood after age 5 that you can't remember?" and are offered the response alternatives "yes," "unsure," and "no" (Ross, 1989). How would you arrive at an answer? How does one evaluate one's own memory for a specified time period? One possibility is that people focus on how much information they can retrieve about the specified time period. The more information retrieved, the better one's memory presumably is. An alternative possibility is based on the notion of the availability heuristic (Tversky & Kahneman, 1973): when judging their memory, individuals may rely on the subjective experience of ease or difficulty of recall. If they do, they may judge their memory as good when recall is experienced as easy, but as poor when recall is experienced as difficult. Supporting the latter prediction, Winkielman, Schwarz, and Belli (1998) observed that judgments of how much one can remember about one's own childhood are based on the ease with which childhood memories can be brought to mind.

Depending on conditions, participants had to recall either 4 or 12 childhood events and were subsequently asked the memory question cited above. If participants base their memory judgments on the total amount of recalled information, they should infer that their memory is better when they had to recall 12 rather than 4 events. Yet, if they base their memory judgments on the subjective recall experience, they should infer that their memory is better when they recall 4 rather than 12 events, reflecting that the former task is easier than the latter. The results supported this ease-of-recall prediction. Whereas 46% of the participants who had to recall 12 memories inferred that they can't remember large parts of their childhood, only 19% of the participants who had to recall 4 events did so. Thus, the former participants inferred poorer memory than the latter, despite the fact that they had just recalled three times as many events. Presumably, they based their judgment on the difficulty they encountered in trying to remember, rather than on the total number of events remembered. Supporting this interpretation, informing participants in another condition that recalling 12 childhood events is a difficult task reduced reports of poor childhood memory to 27%, an estimate that does not reliably differ from the 4-events condition. In this condition, participants (correctly) attributed the experienced difficulty to the nature of the task rather than to the poor quality of their childhood memory, thus eliminating the otherwise observed impact of their phenomenal experience.

These findings bear on a controversial issue at the interface of cognitive and clinical psychology (see Belli, Winkielman, Read, Schwarz, & Lynn,

1998). Some clinical researchers assume that amnesia for childhood events is an indicator of childhood sexual abuse and encourage "memory work" designed to help their clients retrieve presumably repressed childhood memories (e.g., Bass & Davis, 1988; Courtois, 1991; Edwards, 1987). The Winkielman et al. (1998) findings however, suggest, that the more clients attempt to retrieve childhood events, encouraged by their therapist to tell them more, the more likely they are to conclude that they are amnesic for childhood events. This conclusion, in turn, apparently confirms the concern that something bad must have happened, or else, why would they have repressed their childhood memories?

To address this possibility, Winkielman and Schwarz (1999) replicated their earlier study and asked participants to evaluate the quality of their childhood. After completion of the recall task, but prior to rating their childhood happiness, participants were provided with two different theories. Some participants were told that psychologists have found that poor childhood memory indicates an unhappy childhood, with many unpleasant experiences that have been repressed or purged from memory. Others were told that psychologists have found that poor childhood memory indicates a happy childhood: because we ruminate more about unpleasant events than about pleasant ones, pleasant experiences are more likely to be forgotten. For both groups, it was emphasized that these are poorly supported hypotheses and that the relevant evidence is limited to small and unusual clinical samples, making it worthwhile to test these hypotheses with a general college population. As predicted, participants' ratings of their childhood depended on the subjective theory offered to them. Finding it difficult to retrieve 12 childhood events, participants who were told that happy events fade from memory evaluated their childhood as happier than did participants who were told that bad events fade from memory.

These findings have applied as well as theoretical implications. On the applied side, the findings suggest that "memory work" is likely to contribute to the conclusion that one's childhood was problematic. In a therapeutic setting, the attempt to retrieve childhood events is motivated by this problem hypothesis to begin with, and the experienced retrieval difficulties will serve to confirm it (see Belli et al., 1998, for a more detailed discussion). On the theoretical side, these findings illustrate second-order effects in a series of inferences that underlie the judgment. First, the experience that it is difficult to bring childhood memories to mind suggests that few childhood memories are available in memory, unless the informational value of this experience is discredited (Winkielman et al., 1998). At the next step, people have to decide what their perceived memory performance means for the quality of their childhood. Their inferences at this step depend on the naive beliefs about the link between childhood memory and childhood quality that they bring to bear on the task. As a result, they draw different inferences from the *same* experiential information.

Note that these results also indicate that people use theories about the implications of their experience to construct an initial judgment, and not only to correct or revise a judgment that they have already formed. This suggests that recent theorizing about how people use naive beliefs and theories need not cast subjective experience and naive beliefs as altogether different bases for judgment (e.g., Kelley & Jacoby, 1996; Wegener & Petty, 1995, 1997). Instead, the impact of subjective experience on judgments requires beliefs that connect the experience to the judgment task. Without such beliefs, the experiences would simply not bear on the task. In the research on perceptions of childhood memory described above, participants were explicitly informed about the probable meaning of having many versus few childhood memories. Next, we describe research in which participants derive beliefs through more incidental exposure to information. The topic of this research is the "illusion of truth" effect, where familiar information seems true on no basis other than its familiarity.

☐ Illusions of Truth and Falseness: Inferences from Familiarity

In a study of rumor transmission during World War II, Allport and Lepkin (1945) observed that the strongest predictor of belief in wartime rumors was simply repetition of the rumors. Certainly there are circumstances in which repetition is good grounds for belief, especially if the information in question has been heard from a number of independent and credible sources. The curious aspect of Allport and Lepkin's finding was that in some cases, the source of repetition of rumors was a special newspaper column that warned people about false and unfounded rumors. By all indications, people took the column very seriously—but, paradoxically, repeating rumors in order to identify them as false increased later belief in those rumors. Since then, this "illusion of truth" effect (Begg, Anas, & Farinacci, 1992) has been reproduced many times in laboratory studies with information such as trivia statements or words from a foreign language (Arkes, Hackett, & Boehm, 1989; Begg et al., 1992; Brown & Nix, 1996; Gilbert, Krull, & Malone, 1990; Hasher, Goldstein, & Toppino, 1977). Chapter 2 by Fiedler in this volume suggests that merely considering information is enough to make it seem true, an effect that contributes to a wide variety of phenomena, such as belief perseverance and constructive memory errors induced by the use of active versus state verbs.

Begg et al. (1992) argued that the illusion of truth occurs when we make a decision about truth value based only on a feeling of familiarity.

We might prefer to rely on more detailed memory records for information and the context of its acquisition, but clear and accurate memories are not always available. This explanation relies on a general distinction in memory theories between familiarity, which is a vague sense of pastness that arises automatically and lasts for a very long time, and more clear and detailed memories that fade quickly without constant rehearsal (e.g., Jacoby & Dallas, 1981; Mandler, 1980). Begg et al. suggested that the illusion of truth emerges when we judge the truth of information by relying on a sense of familiarity in the absence of recollected details.

The illusion of truth effect depends on a number of crucial inferences. First, information must be judged as familiar. This judgment of familiarity depends on attributing the feeling of ease or fluency of mental processing to prior exposure (e.g., Jacoby & Whitehouse, 1989; Whittlesea, Jacoby, & Girard, 1990). Sometimes familiarity is described as a subjective experience or feeling in its own right (see, e.g., Jacoby & Whitehouse, 1989). Whether it is a feeling or merely a conclusion based on a feeling of fluency is an interesting question, but not material to our argument here: in both cases, a belief about the meaning of familiarity is necessary for it to influence further judgments.

One way of increasing the fluency with which information is processed is by repeating the information. But fluency from other sources can be mistakenly attributed to past exposure and can ultimately contribute to familiarity (Whittlesea, 1993). For example, Reber and Schwarz (in press) influenced truth judgments by manipulating fluency from visual contrast, rather than from repetition. They presented statements like "Osorno is a city in Chile" for one second on a computer screen and asked participants to decide, as fast as possible, whether each statement was true or false. To manipulate ease of processing, the statements were shown in colors that made them easy (e.g., dark blue) or difficult (e.g., light blue) to read against a white background. As expected, the same statement was more likely to be judged "true" when it was easy rather than difficult to read. Thus, the ease of visual processing resulted in an illusion of truth, presumably because the experience of perceptual fluency elicited a feeling of familiarity. Similarly, McGlone and Tofighbakhsh (in press) found that novel but rhyming aphorisms were rated truer than their semantically similar but nonrhyming counterparts.

But why should people assume that an apparently familiar statement is also likely to be a true statement? Recent research addressing this issue (Skurnik, 1998; Skurnik, Moskowitz, & Johnson, 1999) proposes that the connection between familiarity and truth is not unmediated. Instead, people develop a belief that familiarity is diagnostic of truth, and this belief leads people to infer truth from familiarity. Such a belief has been hypothesized to reflect the operation of the tacit assumptions that underlie the conduct of conversation in daily life. As the philosopher Grice (1975) noted, daily communications proceed on the basis of a cooperativeness principle that invites speakers to present information that is truthful, relevant, and clear. Listeners therefore interpret speakers' utterances on the basis of the assumption that they live up to this ideal (for reviews of psychological research bearing on this issue, see Hilton, 1995; Schwarz, 1994, 1996). If information seems familiar, then the most logical inference to draw, in the absence of more detailed memories, is that the information is likely to be true.

If such a "metacognitive" belief about the meaning of familiarity drives the illusion of truth effect, then a change to the belief should change the nature of the illusion effect. For example, if people developed a belief that familiarity is diagnostic of *falseness* rather than of truth, then an "illusion of falseness" effect should result. A series of recent studies has found exactly this sort of reversal (Skurnik, 1998; see also Skurnik, Moskowitz, & Johnson, 1999). In these studies, participants read two different lists of statements on a computer screen; each statement was identified as either true or false as it was presented. Participants were told that the computer selected the first list of statements entirely at random, but the list was actually compiled specifically to be 2/3 true or 2/3 false, depending on condition. Then participants studied a second list of different statements that was always exactly half true and half false. Finally, participants engaged in a standard memory test for the illusion of truth: they saw the second list of statements again, with new statements mixed in, and had to decide whether each statement was true from the second list, false from the second list, or new. All participants were correctly told the only repeated statements they would see would be from the second list (which had equal numbers of true and false statements), and not from the first list (which had unequal numbers of true and false statements).

Results from these studies showed that participants whose initial list was 2/3 true showed the standard illusion of truth effect for their memories of the second list. Specifically, participants in this condition mistakenly called originally false statements "true" more often than they mistakenly called new statements "true" and more often than they mistakenly called originally true statements "false." However, participants whose first list was 2/3 false showed the first-ever demonstration of the illusion of falseness: they called true statements from the second list "false" more often than they called new statements "false" and more often than they called false statements "true." In other words, when the first list of statements was 2/3 false, participants switched their default belief about the meaning of familiarity from "true" to "false," resulting in the illusion of falseness.

In sum, the feeling of familiarity that is elicited by the experience of fluent processing resulted either in an illusion of truth or in an illusion of falseness, depending on the experimental context. However, as in the childhood memory example, what changed in this experiment is not the meaning of the experiential information itself: fluency always indicated familiarity; yet which inference participants drew from familiarity depended on the distribution of true and false items—when most items presented were false (true), the familiar ones are probably false (true) as well.

☐ When Positive Feelings Result in Negative Judgments: Inferences from Affective States

So far, we addressed the informative functions of cognitive experiences that accompany the thought process, like ease of recall or fluency of perception. As noted earlier, the same conceptual logic holds for affective experiences, like moods and emotions (for reviews, see Bless, in press; Forgas, 1995; Schwarz & Clore, 1996). Instead of drawing on declarative information about the target, people may simplify the judgment process by consulting their apparent affective response to the target, essentially asking themselves, "How do I feel about it?" In doing so, people may misread their preexisting mood state as a response to the target, resulting in more positive judgments when they are in a happy rather than sad mood. Consistent with this analysis, mood effects on evaluative judgments are eliminated when people attribute their mood to an unrelated source, such as the weather or side effects of the experimental room, thus undermining its informational value with regard to the target (Schwarz & Clore, 1983; for conceptual replications, see Keltner, Locke, & Audrain, 1993; Savitsky, Medvec, Charlton, & Gilovich, 1998; Schwarz, Servay, & Kumpf, 1985; Siemer & Reisenzein, in press, among others).

Much as we have seen for the case of ease of recall and perceptual fluency, however, it is possible to create conditions under which the default effect is reversed, for example, conditions under which individuals arrive at more negative judgments when they are in a positive mood, as Martin, Abend, Sedikides, and Green (1997) demonstrated. To use an example from their ingenious experiments, suppose that a person is put in a happy mood and asked to read a sad story. Next, the person is asked "how effective the story had been in inducing the intended mood" (i.e., sadness; Martin et al., 1997, p. 244) and how much he or she liked the story. Feeling happy due to the preceding mood induction, the person infers that the story obviously wasn't very effective, or else he or she would now feel sad. Hence, he or she concludes that this story was a poor sad story. Under these conditions, feeling good results in a negative judgment.

As in the preceding examples, this reversal does not indicate a change in the meaning of the experiential information itself. Instead, it reflects that the same experiential information has different implications for different criteria of judgment. Much as a sweet cookie makes for a poor salty snack, a story that apparently leaves us in a happy mood is a poor sad story—but the meaning of the happy feelings themselves changes as little as the sweet taste of the cookie.

☐ Conclusions

As the contributions to the present volume illustrate, a large body of research in social and cognitive psychology has documented that our feelings and subjective experiences can profoundly influence the judgments we make. The specific nature of their influence, however, is context dependent, and it is useful to distinguish different forms of context dependency.

One type of context dependency derives from the perceived diagnosticity of the feeling. As many studies demonstrated, we only draw on our feelings as a source of information when they seem relevant to the judgment at hand. As a default, we tend to assume that our thoughts and feelings pertain to whatever we think about (Higgins, 1998; Schwarz & Clore, 1996), or why else would they come to mind at this point? When we become aware that our feeling may be due to an irrelevant source, its informational value for the judgment at hand is discredited. Conversely, when we perceive influences that seem likely to inhibit the feeling, its informational value is enhanced. As a result, discounting as well as augmentation effects have been observed (for a review, see Schwarz & Clore, 1996). If the informational value of the feeling is discounted, we turn to alternative sources of information to form a judgment. If alternative sources of information are not available, we attempt to correct for any undue influence of our discredited feelings, usually resulting in an overcorrection (for a review, see Strack & Hannover, 1996).

A second type of context dependency derives from the beliefs that connect the subjective experience to the judgment at hand. In the examples we reviewed above, the meaning that people gave to their subjective experience itself did not change: people always took ease of recall as an indication of large amounts of information in memory and fluency of perception as an indication of familiarity. What changed were their belief-based second-order inferences: having a copious childhood memory could mean either a good or bad childhood, and familiarity could be diagnostic of truth or falseness, depending on naive beliefs or theories. Similarly, a good mood indicates a positive response—but whether a positive response leads to judging a target as "good" or "bad" depends on the particular criteria for judgment and the wording of the response request, as Martin et al.'s (1997) studies demonstrated. Context effects of this type indicate that people can draw different inferences from the *same* experiential information.

A third type of context dependency may derive from changes in the meaning of the experiential information itself. This possibility is suggested by Schachter and Singer's (1962) classic demonstration that unexplained arousal may acquire different emotional meaning, depending on the context in which it is experienced. Recent research in psychophysiology and psychological neuroscience indicated, however, that the physiological responses that accompany different emotions are better defined and more specific than had been assumed at the time of Schachter and Singer's research (for a review, see Winkielman, Berntson, & Cacioppo, in press). If so, this type of context effect may be less prevalent than the popularity of Schachter and Singer's (1962) theorizing among social psychologists would suggest.

In sum, the inferences drawn from experiential information are context dependent, as are the inferences drawn from any other information. The available evidence suggests, however, that this context dependency usually does not reflect a high malleability of meaning of the experiential information itself: ease of recall indicates that a large rather than a small amount of information is available in memory, fluency of processing indicates familiarity rather than novelty, and a positive mood indicates a positive rather than negative apparent reaction to the stimulus. Instead, context effects derive either from differences in the perceived diagnosticity of the experiential information or from differences in belief-based second-order inferences of the type reviewed above.

☐ References

Allport, F. H., & Lepkin, M. (1945). Wartime rumors of waste and special privilege: Why some people believe them. *Journal of Abnormal and Social Psychology, 40,* 3–36.

Arkes, H. R., Hackett, C., & Boehm, L. (1989). The generality of the relation between familiarity and judged validity. *Journal of Behavioral Decision Making, 2,* 81–94.

Bass, E., & Davis, L. (1988). *The courage to heal: A guide for women survivors of child sexual abuse.* New York: Harper & Row.

Begg, I. M., Anas, A., & Farinacci, S. (1992). Dissociation of processes in belief: Source recollection, statement familiarity, and the illusion of truth. *Journal of Experimental Psychology: General, 121,* 446–458.

Belli, R. F., Winkielman, P., Read, J. D., Schwarz, N., & Lynn, S.J. (1998). Recalling more childhood events leads to judgments of poorer memory: Implications for the recovered/false memory debate. *Psychonomic Bulletin and Review, 5,* 318–323.

Bless, H. (in press). The consequences of mood on the processing of social information. In A. Tesser & N. Schwarz (Eds.), *Blackwell handbook of social psychology,: Vol. 1. Intraindividual processes.* Oxford, England: Blackwell.

Bradburn, N. M., Rips, L. J., & Shevell, S. K. (1987). Answering autobiographical questions: The impact of memory and inference on surveys. *Science, 236,* 157–161.

Brown, A. S., & Nix, L. A. (1996). Turning lies into truths: Referential validation of falsehoods. *Journal of Experimental Psychology: Learning, Memory, and Cognition, 22,* 1088–1100.

Clore, G. L. (1992). Cognitive phenomenology: Feelings and the construction of judgment. In L. L. Martin & A. Tesser (Eds.), *The construction of social judgments* (pp. 133–164). Hillsdale, NJ: Erlbaum.

Courtois, C. A. (1991). Theory, sequencing, and strategy in treating adult survivors. *New Directions for Mental Health Services, 51,* 47–60.

Edwards, D. J. (1987). The dream as a vehicle for the recovery of childhood trauma. *Clinical Social Work, 15,* 356–360.

Forgas, J. P. (1995). Emotion in social judgments: Review and a new affect infusion model (AIM). *Psychological Bulletin, 117,* 39–66.

Frijda, N. H. (1988). The laws of emotion. *American Psychologist, 43,* 349–358.

Frijda, N. H. (1999). Emotions and hedonic experience. In D. Kahneman, E. Diener, & N. Schwarz (Eds.), *Well-being: Foundations of hedonic psychology* (pp. 190–211). New York: Sage.

Gilbert, D. T., Krull, D. S., & Malone, P. S. (1990). Unbelieving the unbelievable: Some problems in the rejection of false information. *Journal of Personality and Social Psychology, 59,* 601–613.

Grice, H. P. (1975). Logic and conversation. In P. Cole & J. L. Morgan (Eds.), *Syntax and semantics: Vol. 3. Speech acts* (pp. 41–58). New York: Academic Press.

Hamilton, D. L., & Rose, T. L. (1980). Illusory correlation and the maintenance of stereotypic beliefs. *Journal of Personality and Social Psychology, 39,* 832–845.

Hasher, L., Goldstein, D., & Toppino, T. (1977). Frequency and the conference of referential validity. *Journal of Verbal Learning and Verbal Behavior, 16,* 107–112.

Higgins, E. T. (1996). Knowledge activation: Accessibility, applicability, and salience. In E. T. Higgins & A. Kruglanski (Eds.), *Social psychology: Handbook of basic principles* (pp. 133–168). New York: Guilford Press.

Higgins, E. T. (1998). The aboutness principle: A pervasive influence on human inference. *Social Cognition, 16,* 173–198.

Hilton, D. J. (1995). The social context of reasoning: Conversational inference and rational judgment. *Psychological Bulletin, 118,* 248–271.

Jacoby, L. L., & Dallas, M. (1981). On the relationship between autobiographical memory and perceptual learning. *Journal of Experimental Psychology: General, 3,* 30–340.

Jacoby, L. L., & Whitehouse, K. (1989). An illusion of memory: False recognition influenced by unconscious perception. *Journal of Experimental Psychology: General, 118,* 126–135.

Kelley, C. M., & Jacoby, L. L. (1996). Adult egocentrism: Subjective experience versus analytic bases for judgment. *Journal of Memory and Language, 35,* 157–175.

Keltner, D., Ellsworth, P., & Edwards, K. (1993). Beyond simple pessimism: Effects of sadness and anger on social perception. *Journal of Personality and Social Psychology, 64,* 740–752.

Keltner, D., Locke, K. D., & Audrain, P. C. (1993). The influence of attributions on the relevance of negative feelings to satisfaction. *Personality and Social Psychology Bulletin, 19,* 21–30.

Lombardi, W. J., Higgins, E. T., & Bargh, J. A. (1987). The role of consciousness in priming effects on categorization: Assimilation versus contrast as a function of awareness of the priming task. *Personality and Social Psychology Bulletin, 13,* 411–429.

Mandler, G. (1980). Recognizing: The judgment of previous occurrence. *Psychological Review, 87,* 911–271.

Martin, L. L. (1986). Set/reset: Use and disuse of concepts in impression formation. *Journal of Personality and Social Psychology, 51*, 493–504.

Martin, L. L., Abend, T., Sedikides, C., & Green, J. D. (1997). How would it feel if . . . ? Mood as input to a role fulfillment evaluation process. *Journal of Personality and Social Psychology, 73*, 242–253.

McGlone, M. S., & Tofighbakhsh, J. (in press). Birds of a feather flock conjointly (?): Rhyme as reason in aphorisms. *Psychological Science.*

Moskovitz, G. B., & Skurnik, I. (1999). The differing nature of contrast effects in person perception following trait and exemplar primes. *Journal of Personality and Social Psychology, 76*, 911–927.

Reber, R., & Schwarz, N. (in press). Effects of perceptual fluency on judgments of truth. *Consciousness and Cognition.*

Reber, R., Winkielman, P., & Schwarz, N. (1998). Effects of perceptual fluency on affective judgments. *Psychological Science, 9*, 45–48.

Ross, C. A. (1989). *Multiple personality disorder: Diagnosis, clinical features, and treatment.* New York: Wiley.

Savitsky, K., Medvec, V. H., Charlton, A. E., & Gilovich, T. (1998). What, me worry? Arousal, misattribution, and the effect of temporal distance on confidence. *Personality and Social Psychology Bulletin, 24*, 529–536.

Schachter, S., & Singer, J. E. (1962). Cognitive, social, and physiological determinants of emotional state. *Psychological Review, 69*, 379–399.

Schooler, L., & Anderson, J. R. (1997). The role of process in the rational analysis of memory. *Cognitive Psychology, 32*, 219–250.

Schwarz, N. (1994). Judgment in a social context: Biases, shortcomings, and the logic of conversation. *Advances in Experimental Social Psychology, 26*, 123–162.

Schwarz, N. (1996). *Cognition and communication: Judgmental biases, research methods and the logic of conversation.* Hillsdale, NJ: Erlbaum.

Schwarz, N. (1998). Accessible content and accessibility experiences: The interplay of declarative and experiential information in judgment. *Personality and Social Psychology Review, 2*, 87–99.

Schwarz, N., & Bless, H. (1992). Constructing reality and its alternatives: An inclusion/exclusion model of assimilation and contrast effects in social judgment. In L. L. Martin & A. Tesser (Eds.), *The construction of social judgments* (pp. 217–248). Hillsdale, NJ: Erlbaum.

Schwarz, N., Bless, H., Strack, F., Klumpp, G., Rittenauer-Schatka, H., & Simons, A. (1991). Ease of retrieval as information: Another look at the availability heuristic. *Journal of Personality and Social Psychology, 61*, 195–202.

Schwarz, N., & Clore, G. L. (1983). Mood, misattribution, and judgments of well-being: Informative and directive functions of affective states. *Journal of Personality and Social Psychology, 45*, 513–523.

Schwarz, N., & Clore, G. L. (1996). Feelings and phenomenal experiences. In E. T. Higgins, & A. Kruglanski (Eds.), *Social psychology: A handbook of basic principles* (pp. 433–465). New York: Guilford Press.

Schwarz, N., Servay, W., & Kumpf, M. (1985). Attribution of arousal as a mediator of the effectiveness of fear-arousing communications. *Journal of Applied Social Psychology, 15*, 74–78.

Siemer, M., & Reisenzein, R. (in press). Effects of mood on evaluative judgment: Influence of reduced processing capacity and mood salience. *Cognition and Emotion.*

Skurnik, I. (1998). *Metacognition and the illusion of truth.* Unpublished doctoral dissertation, Princeton University.

Skurnik, I., Moskowitz, G., & Johnson, M. K. (1999). *The illusions of truth and falseness: Irrational biases or metacognitive inferences?* Manuscript under review.

Sperber, D., & Wilson, D. (1986). *Relevance: Communication and cognition.* Cambridge, MA: Harvard University Press.

Strack, F., & Hannover, B. (1996). Awareness of influence as a precondition for implementing correctional goals. In P. M. Gollwitzer & J. A. Bargh (Eds.), *The psychology of action: Linking cognition and motivation to behavior.* New York: Guilford Press.

Strack, F., Martin, L. L., & Stepper, S. (1988). Inhibiting and facilitating conditions of the human smile: A non-obtrusive test of the facial feedback hypothesis. *Journal of Personality and Social Psychology, 53,* 768–777.

Strack, F., Schwarz, N., Bless, H., Kübler, A., & Wänke, M. (1993). Awareness of the influence as a determinant of assimilation versus contrast. *European Journal of Social Psychology, 23,* 53–62.

Tversky, A., & Kahneman, D. (1973). Availability: A heuristic for judging frequency and probability. *Cognitive Psychology, 5,* 207–232.

Wegener, D. T., & Petty, R. E. (1995). Flexible correction processes in social judgment: The role of naive theories in corrections for perceived bias. *Journal of Personality and Social Psychology, 68,* 36–51.

Wegener, D. T., & Petty, R. E. (1997). The flexible correction model: The role of naive theories of bias in bias correction. In M. P. Zanna (Ed.), *Advances in experimental social psychology* (Vol. 29, pp. 141–208). Mahwah, NJ: Erlbaum.

Whittlesea, B. W. A. (1993). Illusions of familiarity. *Journal of Experimental Psychology: Learning, Memory, and Cognition, 19,* 1235–1253.

Whittlesea, B. W. A., Jacoby, L. L., & Girard, K. (1990). Illusions of immediate memory: Evidence of an attributional basis for feelings of familiarity and perceptual quality. *Journal of Memory and Language, 29,* 716–732.

Winkielman, P., Berntson, G.G., & Cacioppo, J. T. (in press). The psychophysiological perspective on the social mind. In A. Tesser & N. Schwarz (Eds.), *Blackwell handbook of social psychology: Vol. 1. Intraindividual processes.* Oxford, England: Blackwell.

Winkielman, P., & Schwarz, N. (1999). *Difficulty of recall and childhood happiness.* Manuscript in preparation.

Winkielman, P., Schwarz, N., & Belli, R.F. (1998). The role of ease of retrieval and attribution in memory judgments: Judging your memory as worse despite recalling more events. *Psychological Science, 9,* 124–126.

Wyer, R., & Srull, T. (1989). *Memory and cognition in its social context.* Hillsdale, NJ: Erlbaum.

Zillman, D. (1978). Attribution and misattribution of excitatory reactions. In J. H. Harvey, W. I. Ickes, & R. F. Kidd (Eds.), *New directions in attribution research* (Vol. 2, pp. 335–368). Hillsdale, NJ: Erlbaum.

PART

III

AFFECT AS A SUBJECTIVE EXPERIENCE AND SOCIAL COGNITION

Joseph P. Forgas
Joseph Ciarrochi
Stephanie Moylan

CHAPTER 11

Subjective Experience and Mood Regulation: The Role of Information Processing Strategies

Being in a good or a bad mood is perhaps the most ubiquitous and universally experienced subjective state that accompanies us throughout our daily lives. Most of the time, these underlying mood states are neither intense nor salient enough to command conscious attention. What are the mechanisms that help us to maintain everyday moods within a relatively narrow, nonintrusive range? How do people manage to balance their affective states without experiencing too extreme fluctuations? If social psychology is indeed the science of subjective experience, as Wegner and Gilbert claim in their provocative introductory chapter to this volume, one key question we need to understand is exactly how affective experiences are spontaneously regulated as we pass through our everyday routines.

During the past two decades we have learned much about how affective states influence a person's thoughts, memories, and actions (Forgas, 1995a, 1998b, 1999a, 1999b). Although moods do have a powerful mood-congruent influence on how people think and act, surprisingly there is

Support from the Australian Research Council (Special Investigator Award) and the Alexander von Humboldt Foundation (Research Prize), Germany, is gratefully acknowledged.

Address correspondence to Joseph P. Forgas, School of Psychology, University of New South Wales, Sydney 2052, Australia. E-mail: JP.Forgas@unsw.edu.au; Internet: http://www.psy.unsw.edu.au/staff/jforgas.htm

179

little evidence for affective states becoming self-perpetuating or indeed self-accentuating, except in the case of clinical mood disorders such as depression. Despite powerful evidence for cognitive and behavioral mood congruence, what accounts for the apparent stability of daily moods? It seems that we still know relatively little about the processes that help to calibrate and regulate subjective affective experiences so that extreme and debilitating states are relatively rarely attained.

Popular interest in how to achieve and maintain an optimal affective state has never been higher. Managing affective states—"emotional intelligence"—is now often seen as a panacea, even though the scientific understanding of this concept lags far behind popular expectations (Ciarrochi, Forgas, & Mayer, in press; Mayer, in press). In this chapter, we hope to outline a promising theoretical approach to understanding the mechanisms of spontaneous affect management, and will describe some preliminary empirical findings that seem to support this approach.

We propose here that processes of affect infusion (when affect influences cognition in a mood-congruent direction) and affect control (when targeted cognitive activity is employed to control or change affect), traditionally thought of as distinct, separate processes, should in fact be seen as two sides of a single, integrated mood management system. A prevailing affective state may thus lead to affect infusion (and an accentuation of the affective state itself) or affect control (and an attenuation of the affective state), depending upon subtle contextual differences that may selectively trigger substantive processing (and affect infusion) or motivated processing (and affect control). Based on the recent Affect Infusion Model (Forgas, 1995a), we will argue that substantive processing and motivated processing function as two countervailing cognitive strategies that jointly constitute a dynamic, self-correcting mood management system. In this sense, affect management occurs not only when people employ conscious, effortful cognitive strategies to cope with an intense emotional state. Rather, we see affect management as a continuous, subtle, and frequently subconscious homeostatic process, where people spontaneously switch between information processing strategies in ways that help them to calibrate their prevailing moods. We will use the term *mood management* to describe this ongoing process of dealing with subjective affective experiences (Figure 11.1). We will also present some preliminary evidence demonstrating the operation of mood management strategies in the second half of this chapter.

☐ Background

Our notion of mood management assumes that affect and cognition function as closely interactive psychological systems, a view that is increas-

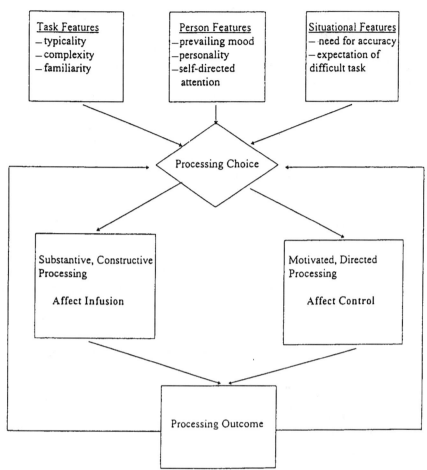

FIGURE 11.1. Outline of the mood management hypothesis: task, person, and situation features jointly influence the kind of information processing strategy adopted to deal with a social cognitive task. Substantive processing produces affect infusion and mood congruity, while motivated processing produces affect control. Information processors automatically switch between these two processing strategies, helping them to maintain a balanced affective state. Thus, substantive processing and motivated processing operate in an interactive fashion, jointly constituting a homeostatic mood management system.

ingly supported by neuroanatomical and neurophysiological evidence (Adolphs & Damasio, in press; Ito & Cacioppo, in press). Although common sense as well as philosophical analyses have long suggested that affect and cognition are indeed interrelated phenomena, most empirical research in psychology continues to assume that these "faculties of the mind" can and should be studied in isolation from each other (Hilgard, 1980). The study of affect was traditionally of little interest either to behaviorists, or within the recently dominant cognitivist paradigm. It is now belatedly recognized that the ideal of affectless or "cold" cognition or behavior is probably a meaningless abstraction (Neisser, 1982). Thinking and behavior are always affectively loaded (Adolphs & Damasio, in press; Damasio, 1994), and affective states in turn are influenced by ongoing changes in cognitive processing strategies and behavior. Subjective experience—what it feels like to be a person—is the product of the continuous, subtle, and self-correcting interaction of thinking, affect, and behavior. Our objective here is to explore a small part of this puzzling process, and to outline some preliminary ideas about how different styles of thinking may impact on affective states.

We are well aware of the many conceptual pitfalls facing such an enterprise. Even the definition of what we mean by terms such as *affect* is highly problematic. Bypassing the usual definitional arguments, we will simply use affect here as a broad, generic label to refer to both moods and emotions (Mayer, 1986; Petty, Gleicher, & Baker, 1991). *Moods*, in turn, will be understood as "low-intensity, diffuse, and relatively enduring affective states without a salient antecedent cause and therefore little cognitive content (e.g., feeling good or feeling bad)," whereas *emotions* "are more intense, short-lived, and usually have a definite cause and clear cognitive content" (e.g., anger or fear; Forgas, 1992a, p. 230). Although emotions have received far more attention in psychology in the past, recent research suggests that moods, even though less intense, may often have a more insidious and enduring influence on people's thinking and behaviors (for a recent overview, see Forgas, in press). Accordingly, most of this discussion will focus on subtle and automatic processes of mood management, rather than the conscious, intentional strategies often used to deal with emotions.

☐ Thinking Influences Feeling?

The psychological literature is replete with terms that refer to cognitive strategies used to control affect, such as information control, decision control, cognitive control, retrospective control, and secondary control (Wegner & Pennebaker, 1993). However, such targeted affect management strategies assume an explicit motivation to change, and are often brought about by experiences of loss of control (Pittman & D'Agostino, 1989) or high control motivation (Burger & Hemans, 1988). Such explicit cognitive attempts at affect control are not always successful, as research on worrying suggests. Paradoxically, worrying—thinking about affect—itself often becomes uncontrollable and a source of anxiety. Thus, as "an example of mental control, worry appears to be in some ways successful, and in other ways not" (Roemer & Borkovec, 1993, p. 226). This conclusion is also supported by studies showing that a ruminative, reflective cognitive style can exacerbate rather than improve affective problems (Nolen-Hoeksema, 1987).

Thus, conscious affect control strategies are not always successful. In fact, it may be preferable to think of affect and cognition as essentially interactive mental faculties. We are thus more interested here in the subtle interplay between cognitive activity and moods that typically does not intrude into consciousness yet can have a significant influence on our thinking and behaviors. We suggest that there are two sides to this interaction. Frequently, existing mood states infuse ongoing thinking in a mood-congruent direction. Such affect infusion occurs when people engage in open, constructive information processing, labeled substantive processing within the Affect Infusion Model ([AIM]; Forgas, 1995a). Evidence for affect infusion will be briefly reviewed later.

The countervailing process, motivated processing, occurs when people engage in controlled processing in the service of an overriding objective, such as mood repair (Clark & Isen, 1982; Forgas, 1998c). In our terms, affect control is not limited to conscious cognitive strategies designed to deal with emotions. Rather, mood management assumes the continuous operation of built-in, automatic regulation mechanisms employed by people to deal with low-intensity affective states in the course of their everyday lives. From this perspective, mood management is not an extraordinary, conscious event, but a routine, automatic and ongoing process. We see mood management as comprising the interaction of two complementary information processing styles: substantive processing leading to affect infusion and the accentuation of the affective state, and motivated processing leading to affect control (Figure 11.1).

☐ Mechanisms of Affect Infusion

The last two decades produced extensive evidence for mood effects on both the content of cognition (what people think), as well as the process of cognition (how people think) (Bower, 1981; Forgas, 1992a, 1995a; Schwarz & Clore, 1988). Such *affect infusion* occurs because affectively loaded information exerts a disproportionate influence on, and becomes incorporated into, a person's cognitive processes, entering into their constructive deliberations and eventually coloring the outcome in a mood-congruent direction (Forgas, 1995a). As processing novel social information often requires high-level inferential cognitive processes (Asch, 1946; Heider, 1958), the prevailing affective state of a person can become part of the constructive informational base used (Fiedler, 1991, 2000). Of course, mood-congruity is rarely an open-ended process: at some stage, it will become necessary for a change in information processing style to occur in order to reverse mood congruence.

The recent Affect Infusion Model (Forgas, 1995a) argues that the nature and extent of affect infusion into cognition critically depends on what kind of cognitive strategy is adopted by a person in response to contextual requirements. The model identifies four distinct processing strategies. Two of these strategies, the *direct access* of preexisting information and *motivated processing* in service of a preexisting goal, represent highly predetermined and directed information search patterns that require little generative, constructive processing, limiting the scope of affect infusion effects. Motivated processing in particular is the key strategy for reversing and controlling a prevailing affective state, and is expected to play a critical role in everyday mood management.

In contrast, when tasks require a degree of open, constructive processing, people may adopt either a *heuristic*, simplified or a *substantive*, elaborate processing strategy to compute a response. These are high-infusion strategies, as they require some degree of constructive thinking (Fiedler, 1990, 1991; Forgas, 1992a), and thus allow affect to infuse outcomes either indirectly (through primed associations; Forgas & Bower, 1988) or directly (through misattribution; Schwarz & Clore, 1988). Considerable evidence now suggests that it is substantive processing, and the incidental use of affectively loaded associations in constructive thinking, that is the main vehicle of affect infusion (Bower & Forgas, in press; Forgas, 1999a, 1999b; Sedikides, 1995). Affect-priming (Bower, 1991; Forgas & Bower, 1988) is more likely when substantive processing is adopted, while affect-as-information (Schwarz & Clore, 1988) should be limited to conditions when heuristic processing is used.

The *affect-as-information* model suggests that "individuals may . . . ask themselves: 'How do I feel about it?' [and] in doing so, they may mistake feelings due to a preexisting state" as informative about the current situation (Schwarz, 1990, p. 529). Supporting evidence comes from studies reporting mood congruence in certain evaluative judgments (Clore & Parrott, 1991). However, this kind of simple, heuristic processing that typically produces misjudgments is most likely when processing resources are limited, prior knowledge and evaluations are not available, and the task is unfamiliar, nonspecific and, most importantly, of little personal relevance. There is so far little evidence that heuristic processing plays any significant role in mood management strategies.

In contrast, the *affect-priming* mechanism suggests that affect infuses cognitive processes by facilitating access to related cognitive categories (Bower, 1981, 1991; Isen, 1984). According to this view, the activation of an emotion node spreads activation throughout the memories to which it is connected, increasing the chance that those memories will be retrieved (Bower & Forgas, in press). Support for the affect-priming model includes extensive evidence for mood-congruent biases in attention, encoding, learning (Bower, 1981; Forgas,1992b; Forgas & Bower, 1987), memory retrieval (Bower, 1991; Forgas & Bower, 1988; Mayer, Gayle, Meehan, & Harman, 1990), and interpretations and judgments (Forgas & Bower, 1987). Evidence for greater affect infusion in conditions that are conducive to substantive processing specifically supports this account (cf. Bower 1991; Forgas, 1991, 1992b, 1993, 1995b, 1998b; Forgas & Bower, 1987, 1988; Mayer, Gaschke, Braverman, & Evans, 1992; Sedikides, 1995).

According to the AIM, choice of processing strategy (and thus, subsequent affect-infusion or affect-control outcomes) is influenced by three sets of contextual factors: features of (1) the *task*, (2) the *person*, and (3) the *situation*, respectively (cf. Forgas, 1992a, 1995a). *Task features* include familiarity, typicality, and complexity; *person features* include subjective relevance, specific motivation, cognitive capacity, motivation to be accurate, affective state, and individual difference variables; *situational factors* include features such as degree of critical scrutiny expected, accuracy expectations, etc. Several testable principles may be derived from this model. For example, cognitive tasks that are familiar should be processed using a direct access strategy, unless further processing is recruited by other variables (Srull, 1983, 1984). A strong prior motivation should also lead to directed and truncated information search strategies and the absence of affect infusion. Such a pattern was found in experiments looking at mood effects on motivated decisions (Forgas, 1991, Forgas & Fiedler, 1996). The model also predicts that all things being equal, personally relevant tasks are more likely to be processed using the motivated strategy (if a prior objective exists), as found in some recent experiments (Forgas, 1989, 1991).

The original Affect Infusion Model included an explicit feedback loop suggesting an interactive relationship between affective states and cognitive processing strategies. According to the AIM, affect itself plays a critical, dual role in regulating processing strategies. This may be due to several factors. In terms of *capacity explanations,* affect may impair attention and cognitive processing capacity both in negative (Ellis & Ashbrook, 1988) and in positive moods (Stroessner & Mackie,1992). In terms of *functionalist* explanations, affective states "exist for the sake of signalling states of the world that have to be responded to" (Frijda, 1988, p. 354). Good moods tell us "everything is ok" and lead to more loose, creative, and heuristic processing strategies (Isen, 1987). Bad moods tell us "something is wrong" and lead to careful, analytic, substantive processing strategies (Forgas, 1992b). Finally, *motivational* explanations argue that affect may be the source of a specific motivation eliciting mood maintenance (in positive moods) or mood repair (in negative moods) (Clark & Isen, 1982; Erber & Erber, 1994; Forgas, 1991). A more recent integrative reformulation of the processing consequences of affect was proposed by Bless (in press) and Fiedler (in press), who argue that positive and negative moods selectively facilitate either a top-down, schema-based, and assimilative information processing style, or a bottom-up, particularistic, and accommodating information processing style, respectively. These processing effects of mood were incorporated within the AIM as a feedback loop from affective states to information processing choices.

☐ The Evidence for Affect Infusion

The first component of our homeostatic mood management model assumes the spontaneous infusion of affect into thoughts and behaviors whenever an open, constructive, and substantive information processing style is adopted. Numerous studies found evidence for affect infusion. Perceptions of observed social interactions (Forgas, Bower, & Krantz, 1984), evaluations of job candidates (Baron, 1987), judgments about health and illness (Croyle & Uretzky, 1987; Salovey & Birnbaum, 1989), and attributions for the causes for various outcomes were all subject to affect infusion (Forgas, Bower, & Moylan, 1990). Affect infusion has been demonstrated not only in the laboratory, but also in many real-life situations (Schwarz & Clore, 1988), including responses to street surveys by people who have just seen a happy or a sad film (Forgas & Moylan, 1987). In a study specifically testing the AIM, Sedikides (1995) found that peripheral self-conceptions that required the most elaborate, substantive processing were in fact most influenced by affect infusion, as predicted by the AIM.

Critical support for affect infusion comes from studies that found that more extensive, substantive processing increases the extent of mood congruence (Forgas & Bower, 1987). In several experiments, the time required for processing was manipulated and recorded through varying the complexity and difficulty of the tasks, using people (Forgas, 1992b), relationships (Forgas, 1993, 1995b; Forgas, Levinger & Moylan, 1994; Forgas & Moylan, 1991) and conflict episodes (Forgas, 1994) as stimuli. We found greater affect infusion when participants had to judge difficult, atypical rather than typical people and situations. Indeed, the size of mood effects was proportional to the length of processing required (Forgas, 1995b). These affect infusion effects also influence complex and personally relevant cognitive tasks, such as perceptions of our intimate partners (Forgas et al., 1994), and explanations for personal conflicts (Forgas, 1994; Figure 11.2). Affect infusion impacts not only on thoughts, memories, and judg-

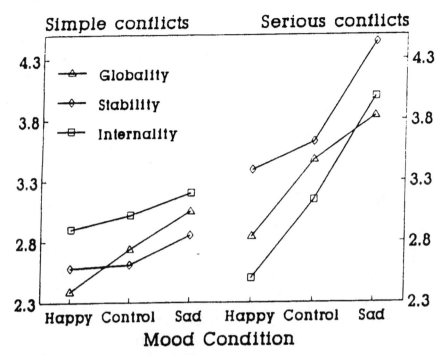

FIGURE 11.2. Demonstration of affect infusion in a realistic judgment: explanations of real-life relationship conflicts show significant mood congruence and affect infusion. Further, mood has a significantly greater impact on judgments about serious, complex conflicts that require longer, more substantive processing (After Forgas, 1994).

ments, but also on actual social behaviors, as long as these require some degree of open, constructive processing. Thus, mood has a congruent influence on planned and actual negotiation strategies, the generation and use of strategic verbal messages, and actual responses to interpersonal communication (Forgas, 1998a, 1998b; 1999a, 1999b; Figure 11.3).

Taken together, these results may have important implications for our understanding of everyday mood management. Low-level, fluctuating moods seem to have a continuous, and often imperceptible influence on how people think about, remember, and evaluate complex social information. It seems that the longer and more constructively we need to think about a task, the more likely that affect infusion will have a mood-congruent impact on the outcome. Why is it that despite these powerful mood-congruent effects, most of the time we manage to maintain a more or less balanced mood state? Affect infusion during substantive processing is only one side of the mood management equation. We shall next consider the complementary process of affect control.

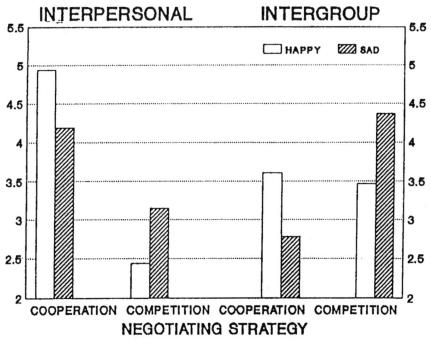

FIGURE 11.3. Demonstration of affect infusion in a strategic interpersonal task: planned and actual negotiating strategies show significant mood congruence. Positive mood produces more cooperation and less competition, and negative mood produces more competition and less cooperation both in interpersonal and in intergroup bargaining encounters (After Forgas, 1998a).

☐ Affect Control Through Motivated Processing

As we have seen, affect can and does impact on our cognitive processes, often in ways that we barely realize. However, the opposite can also occur. Targeted, motivated cognitive activity can influence affective states. Such affect control occurs when a motivated processing strategy is adopted in terms of the Affect Infusion Model. The defining feature of motivated processing is that people engage in highly selective and targeted information search and integration strategies guided by a motivational objective. Motivated processing is the major vehicle for counteracting affect infusion and producing mood incongruence. Intense emotions often directly trigger motivated processing (Wegner & Pennebaker, 1993). In terms of the mood management hypothesis, motivated processing should also be spontaneously adopted when a prevailing affective state reaches threshold intensity due to ongoing affect infusion processes (Sedikides, 1994).

Merely directing a person's attention to their internal states seems sufficient to trigger motivated processing, not only reducing affect infusion, but also producing mood-incongruent outcomes (Berkowitz, 1993; Berkowitz, Jaffee, Jo, & Troccoli, 2000). Simply becoming aware of the correct source of a mood often produces similar effects (Clore & Schwarz, 1988). Increased personal relevance also induces affect control. In several studies, we documented changes in the step-by-step, targeted information search and processing strategies adopted by personally involved subjects as they sought to achieve mood repair through a directed search for rewarding outcomes (Forgas, 1989, 1991). Several other studies have also shown that affect infusion disappears under conditions that are conducive to motivated processing, such as a high self-relevance, when attention is internally focussed, and in tasks requiring deliberate processing (Berkowitz, Jo, Troccoli, & Monteith, 1994; Erber & Erber, 1994, in press; Martin, 1986).

Convergent evidence comes from studies showing that motivated processing is often used to alleviate dysphoria, indicating that "people are active mood regulators who are sensitive to situational demands" (Erber & Erber, 1994, p. 6). Personally relevant social choices, such as preferences for interaction partners, are especially affect sensitive (Locke & Horowitz, 1990). For example, Weary, Marsh, and McCormick (1994) found that depressed subjects selectively and spontaneously preferred others perceived as potentially most useful to them. In another recent study, Erber and Erber (1994) found that "when subjects were motivated to change their sad mood . . . they tended to recall mood incongruent, that is positively valenced material" (p. 86) as part of a motivated affect control strategy. Sometimes a motivated attempt to control negative affect can lead to the more negative evaluations of, and even discrimination against, others. In several studies, Forgas and Fiedler (1996) found that sad subjects, to whom group membership was personally relevant, engaged in significantly more motivated intergroup discrimination than did happy subjects. It seems that in this case, motivated processing in the service of affect control can be an important source of prejudice and discrimination against outgroups (Figure 11.4). In another series of ingenuous experiments, Berkowitz (1993; Berkowitz et al., 1994, 2000) found that judgments were "affectively congruent when the subjects' attention was directed away from themselves, presumably because of the relatively automatic influence of the affective state, but displayed an affective incongruence . . . after the subjects had attended to their feelings" (Berkowitz et al., 1994, p. 2). It appears that self-directed attention alone was sufficient to induce a controlled, motivated affect control strategy here.

Within a multiprocess framework, the spontaneous regulation and fine-tuning of prevailing moods can be understood as due to people routinely

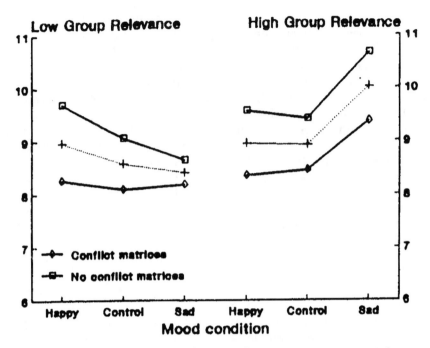

FIGURE 11.4. Personal relevance and motivated processing in intergroup judgments: when membership in a group is of low relevance, positive mood increases intergroup discrimination. When group membership is of high relevance, negative mood produces motivated processing and greater intergroup discrimination (After Forgas & Fiedler, 1996, Experiment 3).

and automatically switching between two complementary information processing strategies: substantive processing, which results in affect infusion, and motivated processing, which results in affect control outcomes. An outline of the mood management hypothesis is shown in Figure 11.1, indicating that the choice of either a substantive (affect infusion) or motivated (affect control) processing strategy is determined by a combination of input variables. Most variables that feed into the mood management system are personal rather than situational. So far, we know that motivated rather than substantive processing is more likely when (a) the task is of direct personal relevance (Forgas, 1991), (b) people experience self-directed attention (Berkowitz, 1993), (c) they score high on individual differences measures that indicate motivated tendencies (Forgas, 1998a), and (d) they experience aversive affect (Weary et al., 1994). Situational variables may also impact on processing choices (Wegner & Erber, 1993). However, by their very nature, motivational goals derived from situations tend to recruit a high level of awareness, and thus fall outside the scope of the kind of automatic, self-correcting mood management system we are primarily interested in here.

A critical feature of the mood management model is that it incorporates a feedback loop between the outcome of the existing processing strategy and subsequent processing choices. This allows for automatic and continuous changes in processing style as a function of the prevailing mood state, a link that is now supported by empirical evidence (Clark & Isen, 1982; Forgas, 1995a; Sedikides, 1994). Such a feedback link was already included in the earlier Affect Infusion Model, but its implications for mood management were not explicitly emphasized. Evidence for just such a pattern has recently been found both in experimental studies (Forgas, 1991; Sedikides, 1994), and in research with mildly depressed persons as well (Weary et al., 1994).

☐ Empirical Evidence for Spontaneous Mood Management

The apparent switch from affect infusion to affect control is particularly nicely illustrated in a recent study by Sedikides (1994). In this experiment, subjects received a guided imagery mood induction; subsequently, they were asked to generate open-ended self descriptions. Consistent with other studies showing affect infusion into such generative tasks, initial responses showed a clear mood congruent pattern. However, in contrast with most other experiments, in these studies, changes in self-description valence over time were also analyzed. Sedikides found that with the passage of time, the self-descriptions produced in the negative mood group became markedly less negative, and tended to become more positive. This suggests the adoption of a motivated affect control strategy to "repair" sad mood, but only after the initially negative mood-congruent effects became sufficiently aversive.

Our mood management model predicts that negative mood initially leads to affect-infusion until a threshold level is reached, at which point people switch to motivated mood control and mood-incongruent associations. Sedikides's (1994) results are certainly consistent with such a hypothesis. More recently, we (Forgas & Ciarrochi, 1999) conducted several additional studies specifically testing the hypothesis that in constructive tasks, induced affect should first lead to spontaneous affect infusion, followed by an automatic shift to a motivated affect control strategy. In the first experiment, positive or negative mood was induced by asking participants to recall and think about positive or negative experiences from their past. Next, in an allegedly unrelated study, we asked them to participate in a "creative" sentence completion task; their job was to generate as many trait adjectives as they could to complete a series of sentence of the type "Bill is . . . ," "John is . . . ," etc. In fact, we were interested in spontaneous changes in the valence of the trait adjectives they came up with. First, in a pilot experiment, we established that subjects are capable of generating a very large number of adjectives in such a task, so that any change in adjective valence over time was not due to subjects running out of suitable words. We found that initially, those in a positive mood generated more positive, and those in a negative mood generated more negative, valenced trait adjectives, as predicted by the affect infusion hypothesis. However, as timed passed, subjects spontaneously switched to generating mood-incongruent adjectives consistent with the adoption of a motivated affect control strategy. This strategy was most marked in those induced initially into a negative mood, who now selectively recalled and reported more positive traits (Figure 11.5).

In the next experiment, a different task requiring substantive processing was used. Participants were now asked to complete single words starting with particular letters rather than sentences, in order to control for the possibility that different names may trigger valenced associations, potentially confounding the results. Thus, to the cue "t.........," participants could

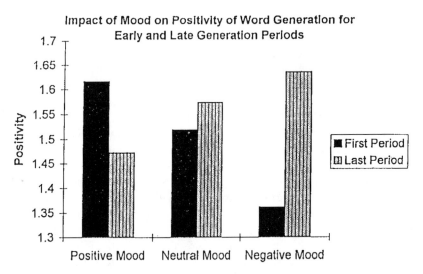

FIGURE 11.5. Evidence for spontaneous mood management: proportion of positive to negative words retrieved for first and second half generation periods. The valence of words generated in the first period, immediately after mood induction, shows significant mood congruence. In contrast, the valence of words spontaneously generated in the second period shows a significant reversal of mood congruence (After Forgas & Ciarrochi, 1999).

respond with trait words that were positively or negatively valenced (e.g., "terrible" or "terrific"). Again, we first established that subjects are unlikely to "run out" of words in such a task. The valence of the list of words generated was independently rated for positivity and negativity by two judges who achieved an interrater reliability of .89. Next, a time-series regression analysis was used to construct a best-fitting line, indicating changes in valence over time for each individual subject. The slope of such a line represents an index of changes in the positivity or negativity of associations over time. A positive value indicates an upward-sloping line and increased positivity over time, while a negative value indicates a downward sloping line and increased negativity over time. These beta values for each subject were then averaged within each induced mood condition and subjected to an analysis of variance.

Results showed a significant mood effect on changes in word valence. Those in the positive mood condition spontaneously became more negative over time, and those in the negative mood condition became more positive. This effect was not simply due to a mood decay process, as initially valenced associations did not simply become more neutral. Rather, there was clear evidence for a switch toward generating opposite-valence words, especially in the negative mood group. It seems than that once a threshold level of affect intensity was reached due to affect infusion, subjects (and sad subjects in particular) spontaneously switched to motivated, incongruent recall, as if seeking to control their mood.

The next experiment introduced several changes. First, a different mood induction procedure was used. As all mood induction procedures are potentially confounded by unintended cognitive and motivational effects, it is important to use a variety of mood induction procedures to ensure that the underlying effects are due to mood and can be reproduced using different induction methods. This time, mood was induced by providing participants with manipulated positive or negative feedback about their performance on a bogus "spatial abilities task." This experiment also explored the role of individual difference variables, such as self-esteem, in the use and efficacy of affect management strategies. Previous work suggests that people low in self-esteem are less likely or less able than others to engage in conscious affect control (Smith & Petty, 1995), and we wanted to test whether this also inhibits the shift toward mood-incongruence in a generative task. After mood induction, participants completed a series of sentences similar to the 20 statements test, asking them to complete a series of sentences like "I am......." The valence of each response was independently rated by two judges, and the slope of a regression line indicating valence changes over time was calculated for each subject. An analysis of variance again confirmed a significant mood effect, showing a clear pattern of "first congruent, then incongruent" responses. Interestingly, the shift toward incongruent responses was significantly stronger for high self-esteem people. Those scoring high on self-esteem were able to rapidly eliminate a mood-congruent bias in their associations, especially in negative mood. In contract, low self-esteem people persevered with mood congruent responses for much longer.

This finding suggest that traits such as self-esteem may be significantly linked to mood management efficacy. The experiments by Sedikides (1994) and our studies (Forgas & Ciarrochi, 1999) show convergent empirical support for a homeostatic mood management mechanism. Of course, support for the mood management hypothesis also requires that we identify not only temporal changes on mood congruence, but also corresponding changes in processing strategies as initially substantive processing (producing mood congruence) gives way to motivated processing (producing incongruence). We are currently working on this question.

These studies show that spontaneous mood management is more marked in negative than positive mood. In some situations, however, people may also be highly motivated to eliminate positive moods, relying on similar homeostatic mood management strategies (Parrott, 1993). For example, when people expect to undertake a complex, demanding task (such as meeting a stranger for the first time), they may prefer to enter this situation in a calm, low-key affective state. In an interesting study illustrating motivated processing to control positive mood, Wegner and Erber (1993) used music to induce mood in subjects who later expected to either interact with a stranger or spend some time alone. When given an opportunity to read depressing, neutral, or cheerful newspaper articles, people who expected to be alone preferred mood-consistent articles. However, subjects who expected a demanding interaction with a stranger preferred articles that were the opposite in affective tone to their own mood; in effect, subjects made to feel euphoric now preferred neutral articles, as if trying to tone down their prevailing mood. These results nicely illustrate how the appraisal of situational factors (Smith & Kirby, 2000) can play a dominant role in selectively triggering affect infusion or affect control strategies.

Overall, these studies suggest that the pattern of fluctuating positive and negative mood states most of us experience in the course of our daily lives may be understood as the product of two complementary information processing strategies. One produces affect control (in the course of motivated processing), the other allows affect infusion (in the course of substantive processing). The mood management hypothesis also assumes that these changes in processing style occur because mood extremity reaches a threshold level as a result of continuous affect infusion. One would need to continuously and nonreactively measure subjects' mood during these tasks in order to obtain direct evidence for this prediction. Unfortunately, we know of no reliable empirical method currently available to accomplish this. The difficulty of getting reliable, valid, and nonreactive measures of fluctuating internal states such as moods remains one of the major obstacles in the way of developing a geniunely scientific approach to the study of subjective states.

Of course, there are important individual differences between people in their tendency and ability to rely on these mechanisms. Self-esteem especially may be closely related to mood management efficacy (Forgas & Ciarrochi, 1999; Smith & Petty, 1995). In the next section, we will briefly consider the role of individual differences in the management of subjectively experienced mood states.

☐ Individual Differences in Mood Management

There are likely to be important individual differences between people in their ability or willingness to successfully engage in effective mood management. The still ill-defined concept of "emotional intelligence" has been advanced to highlight such differences between people (Mayer, in press; Mayer & Salovey, 1988; Salovey & Mayer, 1990). Interestingly, there may well be some gender-based differences in preferred processing strategies that mediate affect infusion effects. It appears that the more ruminative, substantive processing style adopted by women rather than men when in a depressed mood significantly enhances affect infusion and tends to prolong and exacerbate female depression (Nolen-Hoeksema, 1993). Several studies provide suggestive evidence for the role of individual differences in mediating mood management strategies. For example, high affective intensity in people increased the likelihood of affect infusion effects, as "high/affect intensity Ss may have a more elaborate network of information connected to their mood states, thus leading to heightened mood-judgment effects" (p. 203). A link between individual differences in cognitive style and affect infusion was also reported by Wegener, Petty, and Klein (1994). In this study, happy subjects overestimated positive outcomes and had more positive attitudes to a persuasive message, but only if they had high scores on a need for cognition measure—that is, they were most inclined to process information in a constructive, generative way.

On the other hand, affect infusion tends to be reduced or even reversed for people who score high on individual difference measures that would lead them to treat an issue in a motivated, predetermined manner. For example, Rhodewalt, Strube, and Wysocki (1988) found that affect infusion into perceptions of control were greater among people who had a type B personality. In contrast, affect infusion was reduced for people with type A personality, as these individuals may have processed information in a more targeted, motivated manner that eliminated affect infusion effects. Evidence for individual differences in affect control also comes from the studies by Smith and Petty (1995), who found that negative mood led to mood congruence in low-self-esteem (SE) subjects, but resulted in mood incongruence in high-self-esteem individuals, who presumably used more motivated processing strategies in the service of mood regulation. In fact, the sadder high-self-esteem people felt, the more positive were their autobiographical memories.

Individual differences were also important in moderating affect infusion in a recent series of studies (Forgas, 1998a), where we explored the effects of temporary good or bad mood on people's planned and actual bargaining strategies. Results showed that affect infusion effects were weaker for subjects who scored high on measures that predicted a motivated approach to interpersonal tasks, such as social desirability and Machiavellianism. These subjects were less likely to engage in genuine, open, constructive information search strategies, and their bargaining behavior showed reduced affect infusion. These effects suggest that affect infusion is constrained when people are habitually inclined to use targeted, motivated processing rather than open, substantive processing in assessing a situation (Forgas, 1991; Sedikides, 1994).

Subsequently, we (Ciarrochi & Forgas, 1999) also explored the role of trait anxiety in moderating mood management strategies. White undergraduates in an aversive or control mood condition read information about a threatening, radical Black group, and then made judgments and recalled information about the group. We predicted and found a negative mood-congruent bias in judgments and recall but only by more self-confident, low-trait-anxious people. In contrast, aversive mood produced more lenient, positive judgments and less negative recall than high-trait-anxious people, which is consistent with their adoption of a defensive, motivated information processing strategy. This pattern was replicated in a more recent experiment (Moylan & Ciarrochi, 1999). Happy and sad students who scored high or low on neuroticism (a construct closely related to trait anxiety) were asked to make performance appraisal judgments about university professors. Highly neurotic individuals showed a significant mood-incongruent bias. In other words, the more negative their mood, the more positive were the judgments they made. This result suggests that negative affect selectively led highly neurotic people to switch to motivated processing and thus correct their familiar negative tendencies, while low neurotics showed no such effect.

☐ Summary and Conclusions

We argued in this chapter that automatic and often subconscious mood management strategies represent an important, and so far rather neglected aspect of how subjective experiences are spontaneously regulated. We proposed that mood management is composed of two closely linked cognitive processing strategies with opposing outcomes. Affect infusion—the impact of mood on cognition in a mood-congruent direction—predominantly occurs in circumstances that are conducive to the adoption of constructive, substantive processing strategies. Affect control—based on motivated processing that produces mood-incongruent outcomes—is the complementary strategy. We have reviewed past evidence demonstrating the operation of both of these processes, albeit in isolation from each other. Few attempts have been made to combine these essentially complementary processing strategies into something like an automatic, self-correcting mood management model, as proposed here. The key principle underlying the mood management hypothesis is based on the Affect Infusion Model (Forgas, 1995a), and its core assumption is that people may readily shift between alternative processing strategies when performing a cognitive task. Several recent studies suggest the conjoint operation of these mechanisms.

The idea that social thinking encompasses a variety of distinct information processing styles is now increasingly accepted in the recent social cognition theorizing (Fiedler, 1991; Kruglanski, 1989; Petty et al., 1991; Petty, DeSteno, & Ruker, in press). As the AIM suggests, the choice between alternative processing strategies is determined by a combination of judge, target, and situational characteristics, which can ultimately be summarized in the form of a series of testable predictions (Forgas, 1995a). Despite the overall promise of such an integrated mood management model, much work remains to be done in exploring the role of specific situational, personal, and task characteristics in processing choices. What we attempted to do here is to outline the basic features of such an integrated mood management model, and to review a range of empirical studies that illustrate the occurrence of affect infusion in conditions of substantive processing, and affect control in conditions of motivated processing.

Evidence for affect infusion in particular now includes a variety of interesting, if counterintuitive findings. It appears that more extensive and substantive processing recruited by unusual, complex, or otherwise problematic tasks will paradoxically increase rather than decrease affect infusion effects, as such strategies offer greater scope for affectively valenced information to be incorporated into constructive cognitive processes

(Forgas, 1992a, 1993, 1994, Forgas & Bower, 1987). Such affect infusion in the way information is selected, retrieved, and interpreted plays an important role in many real-life decisions and judgments in organizations, consumer choices, clinical practice, and health-related judgments (Baron, 1987; Forgas & Moylan, 1987; Salovey & Birnbaum, 1989).

We may conclude that the management of subjective experiences of mood can be best understood as a function of subtle changes in cognitive information processing strategies. The style of thinking people adopt can sometimes maintain or amplify existing moods, and also influence perceptions, judgments, and behaviors. According to the mood management hypothesis, however, a normally functioning mood management system should be able to automatically detect and correct excessive affect infusion effects by switching from a substantive to a motivated processing strategy (Figure 11.1). Experiments reviewed here demonstrated that with normal subjects at least, excessive negativity in memory, feelings, associations, and judgments can spontaneously lead to a change in processing style toward a more motivated, mood-incongruent strategy.

The role of individual difference variables in mood management in particular is also beginning to receive serious attention (Ciarrocchi et al., in press; Rusting, in press; Salovey & Mayer, 1990). Two basic principles can be discerned here. People scoring high on individual difference measures that are indicative of a motivated, predetermined approach to a particular cognitive task (such as social desirability, Machiavellianism, type A personality, etc.) generally show reduced affect infusion effects. Second, people with high scores on measures of negative affectivity (such as trait anxiety, neuroticism, clinical depression) also tend to be more sensitized to, and aware of, their own negative tendencies, and appear more ready to adopt motivated processing to control and reduce negativity in their judgments (Ciarrochi & Forgas, 1999). We hope that the mood management model outlined here and the supporting evidence reviewed will stimulate further interest in this interesting research domain. We believe that a better understanding of how everyday mood states are managed and regulated is a key task for a social psychology of subjective experiences.

☐ References

Adolphs, R., & Damasio, A. (in press). The interaction of affect and cognition: A neurobiological perspective. In J. P. Forgas (Ed.), *The handbook of affect and social cognition*. Mahwah, NJ: Erlbaum.

Asch, S. E. (1946). Forming impressions of personality. *Journal of Abnormal and Social Psychology, 41*, 258–290.

Baron, R. (1987). Interviewers' moods and reactions to job applicants: The influence of affective states on applied social judgments. *Journal of Applied Social Psychology, 16*, 911–926.

Berkowitz, L. (1993). Towards a general theory of anger and emotional aggression. In T. K. Srull & R. S. Wyer (Eds.), *Advances in social cognition* (Vol. 6, pp. 1–46). Hillsdale, NJ: Erlbaum.

Berkowitz, L., Jaffee, S., Jo, F., & Troccoli, B. T. (2000). On the correction of feeling-induced judgmental biases. In J. P. Forgas (Ed.), *Feeling and thinking: The role of affect in social cognition* (pp. 131–152). New York: Cambridge University Press.

Berkowitz, L., Jo, E., Troccoli, B. T., & Monteith, M. (1994). *Attention-activated regulation of feeling effects.* Unpublished manuscript, University of Wisconsin, Madison.

Bless, H. (2000). The interplay of affect and cognition: The mediating role of general knowledge structures. In J. P. Forgas (Ed.), *Feeling and thinking: The role of affect in social cognition* (pp. 201–222). New York: Cambridge University Press.

Bower, G. H. (1981). Mood and memory. *American Psychologist, 36,* 129–148.

Bower, G. H. (1991). Mood congruity of social judgments. In J. P. Forgas (Ed.), *Emotion and social judgments* (pp. 31–53). Elmsford, NY: Pergamon.

Bower, G. H., & Forgas, J. P. (in press). Affect and social memory. In Forgas, J. P. (Ed.), *The handbook of affect and social cognition.* Mahwah, NJ: Erlbaum.

Burger, J. M., & Hemans, L. T. (1988). Desire for control and the use of attribution processes. *Journal of Personality, 56,* 531–546.

Ciarrochi, J., & Forgas, J. P. (1999). On being tense yet tolerant: The paradoxical effects of aversive mood and trait anxiety on intergroup judgments. *Group Dynamics, Theory, Research and Practice, 3,* 227–238.

Ciarrochi, J. V., Forgas, J. P., & Mayer, J. (Eds.). (in press). *Emotional intelligence: A scientific approach.* Philadelphia: Psychology Press.

Clark M. S., & Isen, A. M. (1982). Towards understanding the relationship between feeling states and social behavior. In A. H. Hastorf & A. M. Isen (Eds.), *Cognitive social psychology* (pp. 73–108). Amsterdam: Elsevier/North-Holland.

Clore, G. L., & Parrott, G. (1991). Moods and their vicissitudes: Thoughts and feelings as information. In J. P. Forgas (Ed.), *Emotion and social judgments* (pp. 109–123). Elmsford, NY: Pergamon.

Croyle, R. T., & Uretzky, M. B. (1987). Effects of mood on self-appraisal of health status. *Health Psychology, 6,* 239–253.

Damasio, A.R. (1994). *Descartes' error.* New York: Grosste/Putnam.

Ellis, H. C., & Ashbrook, T. W. (1988). Resource allocation model of the effects of depressed mood state on memory. In K. Fielder & J. P. Forgas (Eds.), *Affect, cognition, and social behavior* (pp. 25–43). Göttingen, Germany: Hogrefe.

Erber, M. W., & Erber, R. (in press). The role of motivated social cognition in the regulation of affective states. In J. P. Forgas (Ed.), *The handbook of affect and social cognition.* Mahwah, NJ: Erlbaum.

Erber, R., & Erber, M. W. (1994). Beyond mood and social judgment: Mood incongruent recall and mood regulation. *European Journal of Social Psychology, 24,* 79–88.

Fiedler, K. (1990). Mood-dependent selectivity in social cognition. In W. Stroebe & M. Hewstone (Eds.), *European review of social psychology* (Vol. 1, pp. 1–32). New York: Wiley.

Fiedler, K. (1991). On the task, the measures, and the mood in research on affect and social cognition. In J. P. Forgas (Ed.), *Emotion and social judgments* (pp. 83–104). Elmsford, NY: Pergamon.

Fiedler, K. (2000). Toward an integrative account of affect and cognition phenomena using the BIAS computer algorithm. In J. P. Forgas (Ed.), *Feeling and thinking: The role of affect in social cognition* (pp. 223–252). New York: Cambridge University Press.

Forgas, J. P. (1989). Mood effects on decision-making strategies. *Australian Journal of Psychology, 41,* 192–214.

Forgas, J. P. (1991). Mood effects on partner choice: Role of affect in social decisions. *Journal of Personality and Social Psychology, 61,* 708–720.

Forgas, J. P. (1992a). Affect in social judgments and decisions: A multi-process model. In M. Zanna (Ed.), *Advances in experimental social psychology* (Vol. 25, pp. 227–275). San Diego, CA: Academic Press.

Forgas, J. P. (1992b). On bad mood and peculiar people: Affect and person typicality in impression formation. *Journal of Personality and Social Psychology, 62,* 863–875.

Forgas J. P. (1993). On making sense of odd couples: Mood effects on the perception of mismatched relationships. *Personality and Social Psychology Bulletin, 19,* 59–71.

Forgas, J. P. (1994). Sad and guilty? Affective influences on the explanation of conflict episodes. *Journal of Personality and Social Psychology, 66,* 56–68.

Forgas, J. P. (1995a). Mood and judgment: The affect infusion model (AIM). *Psychological Bulletin, 117,* 39–66.

Forgas, J. P. (1995b). Strange couples: Mood effects on judgments and memory about prototypical and atypical targets. *Personality and Social Psychology Bulletin, 21,* 747–765.

Forgas, J. P. (1998a). On feeling good and getting your way: Mood effects on negotiation strategies and outcomes. *Journal of Personality and Social Psychology, 74,* 565–577.

Forgas, J. P. (1998b). Asking nicely? Mood effects on responding to more or less polite requests. *Personality and Social Psychology Bulletin, 24,* 173–185.

Forgas, J. P. (1998c). Happy and mistaken? Mood effects on the fundamental attribution error. *Journal of Personality and Social Psychology, 75,* 318–331.

Forgas, J. P. (1999a). On feeling good and being rude: Affective influences on language use and request formulations. *Journal of Personality and Social Psychology, 76,* 928–939.

Forgas, J. P. (1999b). Feeling and speaking: Mood effects on verbal communication strategies. *Personality and Social Psychology Bulletin, 25,* 850–863.

Forgas, J. P. (Ed.). (2000). *Feeling and thinking: The role of affect in social cognition.* New York: Cambridge University Press.

Forgas, J. P., & Bower, G. H. (1987). Mood efforts on person perception judgments. *Journal of Personality and Social Psychology, 53,* 53–60.

Forgas, J. P., & Bower, G. H. (1988). Affect in social judgments. *Australian Journal of Psychology, 40,* 125–145.

Forgas, J. P., Bower, G. H., & Krantz, S. (1984). The influence of mood on perceptions of social interactions. *Journal of Experimental Social Psychology, 20,* 497–513.

Forgas, J. P. Bower, G. H., & Moylan, S. J. (1990). Praise or blame? Affective influences on attributions for achievement. *Journal of Personality and Social Psychology, 59,* 809–818.

Forgas, J. P., & Ciarrochi, J. (1999). *Evidence for automatic mood management: Mood congruent and incongruent thoughts over time.* Manuscript submitted for publication.

Forgas, J. P., & Fiedler, K. (1996). Us and them: Mood effects on intergroup discrimination. *Journal of Personality and Social Psychology, 70,* 39–70.

Forgas, J. P., Levinger, G., & Moylan, S. J. (1994). Feeling good and feeling close: Affective influences on the perception of intimate relationships. *Personal Relationships, 1,* 165–184.

Forgas, J. P., & Moylan, S. J. (1987). After the movies: The effects of transient mood states on social judgments. *Personality and Social Psychology Bulletin, 13,* 478–489.

Forgas, J. P., & Moylan, S. J. (1991). Affective influences on stereotype judgments. *Cognition and Emotion, 5(5/6),* 379–395.

Frijda, N. (1988). The laws of emotion. *American Psychologist, 43,* 349–358.

Heider, F. (1958). *The psychology of interpersonal relations.* New York: Wiley.

Hilgard, E. R. (1980). The trilogy of mind : Cognition, affection, and conation. *Journal of the History of the Behavioral Sciences, 16,* 107–117.

Isen, A. (1984). Towards understanding the role of affect in cognition. In R. S. Wyer & T. K. Srull (Eds.), *Handbook of social cognition* (Vol. 3, pp. 179–236). Hillsdale, NJ: Erlbaum.

Isen, A. (1987). Positive affect, cognitive processes and social behaviour. In L. Berkowitz

(Ed.), *Advances in experimental social psychology* (Vol. 20, pp. 203–253). San Diego, CA: Academic Press.

Ito, T., & Cacioppo, J. (in press). Affect and attitudes: A social neuroscience approach. In J. P. Forgas (Ed.), *The handbook of affect and social cognition.* Mahwah, NJ: Erlbaum.

Kruglanski, A. W. (1989). *Lay epidemics and human knowledge: Cognitive and motivational bases.* New York: Plenum Press.

Locke, K. D., & Horowitz, L. M. (1990). Satisfaction in interpersonal interactions as a function of similarity in level of dysphoria. *Journal of Personality and Social Psychology, 58,* 823–831.

Martin, L. L. (1986). Set/reset: Use and disuse of concepts in impression formation. *Journal of Personality and Social Psychology, 51,* 493–504.

Mayer, J. D. (1986). How mood influences cognition. In N. E. Sharkey (Ed.), *Advances in cognitive science* (Vol. 1, pp. 290–314). Chichester, England: Horwood.

Mayer, J. D. (in press). Emotion, intelligence, and emotional intelligence. In J. P. Forgas (Ed.), *The handbook of affect and social cognition.* Mahwah, NJ: Erlbaum.

Mayer, J. D., Gaschke, Y. N., Braverman, D. L., & Evans T. W. (1992). Mood congruent judgment is a general effect. *Journal of Personality and Social Psychology, 63,* 119–132.

Mayer, J. D., Gayle, M., Meehan, M. E., & Harman, A. K. (1990). Toward a better specification of the mood-congruency effect in recall. *Journal of Experimental Social Psychology, 26,* 465–480.

Mayer, J. D., & Salovey, P. (1988). Personality moderates the interaction of mood and cognition. In K. Fiedler & J. P. Forgas (Eds.), *Affect, cognition, and social behavior* (pp. 87–99). Göttingen, Germany: Hogrefe.

Moylan, S. & Ciarrochi, J. (1999). *The role of neuroticism in mediating mood effects on appraisal judgments.* Unpublished manuscript, University of New South Wales, Sydney, Australia.

Neisser, U. (1982). Memory: What are the important questions? In U. Neisser (Ed.), *Memory observed* (pp. 3–12). San Francisco: Freeman.

Nolen-Hoeksema, S. (1987). Sex differences in unipolar depression: Evidence and theory. *Psychological Bulletin, 101,* 259–282.

Nolen-Hoeksema, S. (1993). Sex differences in control of depression. In D. M. Wegner & J. W. Pennebaker (Eds.), *Handbook of mental control* (pp. 306–324). Englewood Cliffs, NJ: Prentice-Hall.

Parrott, W. G. (1993). Beyond hedonism: Motives for inhibiting good moods and for maintaining bad moods. In D. M. Wegner & J. W. Pennebaker (Eds.), *Handbook of mental control* (pp. 278–305). Englewood Cliffs, NJ: Prentice-Hall.

Petty, R. E., DeSteno, D., & Rucker, D. (in press). The role of affect in attitude change. In J. P. Forgas, (Ed.), *The handbook of affect and social cognition.* Mahwah, NJ: Erlbaum.

Petty, R. E., Gleicher, F., & Baker, S. (1991). Multiple roles for affect in persuasion. In J. P. Forgas (Ed.), *Emotion and social judgments* (pp. 181–200). Elmsford, NY: Pergamon.

Pittman, T. S., & D'Agostino, P. R. (1989). Motivation and cognition: Control deprivation and the nature of subsequent information processing. *Journal of Experimental Social Psychology, 25,* 465–480.

Rhodewalt, F., Strube, M. J., & Wysocki, J. (1988). The type A behaviour pattern, induced mood, and the illusion of control. *European Journal of Personality, 2,* 231–237.

Roemer, L., & Borkovec, T.D. (1993). Worry: Unwanted cognitive activity that controls unwanted somatic experience. In D. M. Wegner & J. W. Pennebaker (Eds.), *Handbook of mental control* (pp. 220–238). Englewood Cliffs, NJ: Prentice-Hall.

Rusting, C. (in press). Personality as a mediator of affective influences on social cognition. In J. P. Forgas (Ed.), *The handbook of affect and social cognition.* Mahwah, NJ: Erlbaum.

Salovey, P., & Birnbaum, D. (1989). Influence of mood on health-related cognitions. *Journal of Personality and Social Psychology, 57,* 539–551.

Salovey, P., & Mayer, J. D. (1990). Emotional intelligence. *Imagination, Cognition, and Personality, 9*, 185–211.

Schwarz, N. (1990). Feelings as information: Informational and motivational functions of affective states. In E. T. Higgins & R. Sorrentino (Eds.), *Handbook of motivation and cognition: Foundations of social behavior* (Vol. 2, pp. 527–561). New York: Guilford Press.

Schwarz, N., & Clore, G. L. (1988). How do I feel about it? The informative function of affective states. In K. Fiedler & J. P. Forgas (Eds.). *Affect, cognition, and social behavior* (pp. 44–62). Göttingen, Germany: Hogrefe.

Sedikides, C. (1994). Incongruent effects of sad mood on self-conception valence: It's a matter of time. *European Journal of Social Psychology, 4*, 161–172.

Sedikides, C. (1995). Central and peripheral self-conceptions are differentially influenced by mood: Tests of the differential sensitivity hypothesis. *Journal of Personality and Social Psychology, 69*(4), 759–777.

Smith, C., & Kirby, L. (2000). Consequences require antecedents: Towards a process model of emotion elicitation. In J. P. Forgas (Ed.), *Feeling and thinking: The role of affect in social cognition* (pp. 83–108). New York: Cambridge University Press.

Smith, S., & Petty, R. (1995). Personality moderators of mood congruency on cognition: The role of self-esteem and negative mood regulation. *Journal of Personality and Social Psychology, 68*, 1092–1107.

Srull, T. K. (1983). Affect and memory: The impact of affective reactions in advertising on the representation of product information in memory. In R. Bagozzi & A. Tybout (Eds.), *Advances in consumer research* (Vol. 10, pp. 244–263). Ann Arbor, MI: Association for Consumer Research.

Srull, T. K. (1984). The effects of subjective affective states on memory and judgment. In T. Kinnear (Ed.), *Advances in consumer research* (Vol. 11, pp. 530–533). Provo, UT: Association for Consumer Research.

Stroessner, S. J., & Mackie, D. M. (1992). The impact of induced affect on the perception of variability in social groups. *Personality and Social Psychology Bulletin, 18*, 546–554.

Weary, G., Marsh, K. L., & McCormick, L. (1994). Depression and social comparison motives. *European Journal of Social Psychology, 24*, 117–130.

Wegener, D. T, Petty, R. E., & Klein, D. J. (1994). Effect of mood on high elaboration attitude change: The mediating role of likelihood judgements. *European Journal of Social Psychology, 24*, 25–44.

Wegner, D. M., & Erber, R. (1993). Social foundations of mental control. In D. M. Wegner & J. W. Pennebaker (Eds.), *Handbook of mental control* (pp. 36–56). Englewood Cliffs, NJ: Prentice Hall.

Wegner, D. M., & Pennebaker, J. W. (1993). Changing our minds: An introduction to mental control. In D. M. Wegner & J. W. Pennebaker (Eds.), *Handbook of mental control* (pp. 1–12). Englewood Cliffs, NJ: Prentice-Hall.

Constantine Sedikides
Jeffrey D. Green

CHAPTER 12

The Rocky Road from Affect
to Attentional Focus

The subjective state of affect has fascinated thinkers and scholars through-out human intellectual history. Another subjective state, attentional focus, has relatively recently become the target of serious scientific inquiry. In keeping with the theme of this volume, our chapter is concerned with the interplay between these two subjective states.

More specifically, this chapter is the story of our efforts over the last several years to clarify the elusive relation between affective states and attentional focus. This theoretical and empirical journey has turned re-peatedly into an easy stride, a marathon, a short one-way street, and a complex highway structure—not necessarily in that order. The road from affect to attentional focus has indeed been rocky, to paraphrase Ned Jones (1979).

We have been concerned with the causal relation between affective states and attentional focus, and more specifically, with the question "what affective states lead to what kind of attentional focus?" Building on litera-ture tradition (Sedikides, 1992a), we initially narrowed our empirical quest to the subjective experience of the affective states of sadness and happi-ness. Likewise, in congruence with established theory and research (Carver, 1979; Duval & Wicklund, 1972; Gibbons, 1991), we conceptualized attentional focus as falling on a bipolar continuum. One pole of the con-

Address correspondence to Constantine Sedikides, Department of Psychology, University of Southampton, Highfield Campus, SO17 1BJ Southampton, UK. E-mail: C.Sedikides@soton.ac.uk

tinuum represents attentional resources that are directed internally, namely, to the self. The other pole of the continuum represents attentional resources that are directed externally, namely, to other persons or environmental objects.

We have been preoccupied in particular with one pole of the attentional continuum: self-focused attention. We were not alone. Understanding the nature of self-focused attention has been the primary or secondary objective of research on attributions and perspective taking (Gibbons & Wright, 1983; Greenberg, Pyszczynski, Burling, & Tibbs, 1992; Stephenson & Wicklund, 1983), perceptions of control (Mikulincer, Gerber, & Weisenberg, 1990), alcohol consumption (Hull, 1981; Hull, Levenson, Young, & Scher, 1983), belief perseverance (Davies, 1982), group interaction (Mullen, 1991), and communication in close relationships (Trommsdorff & John, 1992), as well as prosocial behavior (Berkowitz, 1987; Gibbons & Wicklund, 1982) and antisocial behavior (i.e., aggression and cheating; Carver, 1975; Diener & Walbom, 1976). Importantly, elevated levels of self-focused attention have been associated with psychological disorders, such as anxiety (Carver & Scheier, 1986) and schizophrenia (Exner, 1973). Most importantly, increased self-focused attention has been linked empirically to depression (Gibbons et al., 1985; Ingram, Lumry, Cruet, & Sieber, 1987; Larsen & Cowan, 1988). Self-focused attention has been hypothesized to maintain and exacerbate depressive episodes (Ingram, 1990; Pyszczynski & Greenberg, 1987).

The discovery of an association between depression and self-focused attention instigated empirical forays into the causal direction of the link between sadness, a key correlate of depression, and self-focus. Does sadness increase self-focus?

☐ Why Sadness Increases Self-Focused Attention

Sadness is typically elicited by such events as a personal setback or the loss of a loved one. Appraisal theories of emotion have emphasized the role of controllability reduction in the experience of sadness. Sadness is accompanied by the perception that the unpleasant event is uncontrollable and inevitable (Smith & Ellsworth, 1985). Inaction is the consequence. Indeed, sadness is associated with a state of resignation (Ekman & Friesen, 1975; Roseman, 1984), passivity, absence of relational activity, and withdrawal (Frijda, 1986).

The retrenchment and barricading of the self from the social environment is an adaptive response in coping with permanent loss (Roseman, 1984). Turning inward avoids reminders of the loss (Frijda, 1986) and enables one to rest, recover, and redirect one's goals (Sedikides, 1992a), perhaps through increased thinking (Forgas, 1998). Indeed, this pattern of increased thinking has been labeled by various theorists as accommodation (Fiedler & Bless, in press), ample mental capacity (Mackie & Worth, 1989) or effort (Schwarz, 1990), and central processing (Wegener, Petty, & Smith, 1995).

The evaluation of one's goals, the examination of why and how these goals have been thwarted, and the adjustment of goals are processes that are well served by an inward orientation (Ortony, Clore, & Collins, 1988). In summary, sadness instigates an inaction tendency and an avoidance orientation in reference to the outside world, as well as an inclination to turn inward and consider the implications of the unpleasant event for the self. It is likely then that sadness elicits self-focused attention.

The Empirical Evidence

The proposition that sadness elicits self-focused attention was taken to laboratory experimentation. In the typical laboratory procedure, the experimenter places participants in a mood state and then measures the degree to which participants' attentional focus is directed inward.

The first question of interest is whether sad mood elicits self-focused attention in comparison to neutral mood. The pioneering research by Wood, Saltzberg, and Goldsamt (1990a) speaks to this question. In Experiment 1, Wood et al. placed participants in a sad or neutral affective state via a 20-minute guided imagery task. As part of this task (Wright & Mischel, 1982), participants imagined hypothetical events and recalled personal events that were either sad or neutral. Wood et al. measured attentional focus through a pronoun choice task (Wegner & Giuliano, 1980). This task involves the selection of one of three pronouns (i.e., I, we, or they) for the ostensible purpose of sentence completion. The number of selected first-person singular pronouns serves as an index of self-focused attention. Participants in a sad mood state indeed self-focused more than did participants in a neutral mood state. Sad mood, in comparison to a neutral affective state, elicits self-focused attention.

A related question, though, remains to be answered. Does sad mood heighten self-focused attention in comparison to happy mood? Wood et al. (1990a) also addressed this question in Experiment 2. They placed participants in a sad, neutral, or happy mood by playing a musical selection for 10 minutes. Wood et al. measured attentional focus through both the Private Self-Consciousness (PSC) subscale of the Self-Consciousness scale (Fenigstein, Scheier, & Buss, 1975) and an open-ended thought-listing task. They coded the thought sample units that referred to internal states, abilities, or characteristics as self-focused. Then, these researchers calculated a self-focus ratio, defined as the number of self-focused thought units divided by the total number of thought units. Sad participants indeed self-focused more than either neutral or happy participants on both the PSC subscale and the thought-listed ratios. Sad mood heightens self-focused attention in comparison to happy mood.

However, the conclusiveness of the Wood et al. (1990a) results remained to be fully established. The results are open to two alternative hypotheses, which Wood et al. identified. The first hypothesis pertains to the affect induction task. This task may have produced affective states of unequal absolute magnitude. That is, sad-condition participants may have felt sadder than happy-condition participants felt happy. There is indeed a glimpse of evidence for this assertion in the manipulation check data of Wood et al.'s Experiment 2. Sedikides (1992b) addressed this alternative hypothesis in three experiments. Participants imagined sad, neutral, or happy events, and then wrote down thoughts and feelings related to the events. The absolute magnitude of sad and happy affective states, as judged by their respective distance from the manipulation check scale mean, was approximately equal in all three experiments. The PSC subscale was modified to reflect momentary, rather than dispositional, self-focus. In all three experiments, sad participants self-focused more than either neutral or happy participants, as assessed by the PSC subscale. In addition, Experiments 2 and 3 included a thought-listing task. In both experiments, sad participants listed more self-focused thoughts than either neutral or happy participants. Thus, the first alternative hypothesis was not deemed viable.

The second alternative hypothesis to Wood et al.'s (1990a) findings also concerns the affect induction task. The argument is that the guided imagery task confounds the induction of affect with the induction of body centeredness (i.e., self-focus). Sad affective states are more likely to lead to body centeredness than are happy affective states. Sedikides (1992b, Experiments 2–3) controlled for this potential confounding. In Experiment 2, participants imagined a friend, rather than the self, as the referent of the affect-inducing event. In Experiment 3, body centeredness was manipulated. Half of the participants imagined events that referred to their physical bodies. These events were disfigurement by fire in the sad condition, mentally reviewing body parts in the neutral condition, and having one's hair done by a skilled hairdresser in the happy condition. The other participants imagined non–body-centered events. These events were a canceled Caribbean cruise in the sad condition, riding a bus in the neutral condition, and winning a free Caribbean cruise in the happy condition. The crucial interaction between affect and body centeredness was not significant. Even when the affect and self-focus inducing aspects of the imagination task are unconfounded, sadness still elicits self-focused attention to a greater extent than either neutral or happy affect. Therefore, the second alternative hypothesis to the findings of Wood et al. was also deemed untenable.

In summary, both Wood et al. (1990a) and Sedikides (1992b) obtained support for the notion that sad affect elicits self-focused attention to a greater extent than either neutral or happy affect. The empirical landscape began to clear.

However, this temporarily serene state was interrupted abruptly by a wave of data reported by Salovey (1992). Participants in Salovey's two experiments were placed into a sad, neutral, or happy affective state by imagining emotional events of personal (i.e., autobiographical) significance. A modified version of Wegner and Giuliano's (1980) pronoun choice task was used to measure self-focus. Consistently with Wood et al. and Sedikides, Salovey found that sadness elicited higher self-focus than neutral affect. However, contrary to Wood et al. and Sedikides, Salovey reported that happiness also elicited higher self-focus than neutral affect. Salovey's second experiment used the same affect induction task, but measured self-focus by means of Linville's (1985) self-complexity procedure, in which participants describe themselves by sorting 33 traits into separate piles. Salovey validated this task as an index of self-focus by demonstrating in a pilot study that one lists a greater number of self-aspects when one's attention is directed to the self. Replicating the results of his first experiment, Salovey found that both sad and happy participants were more self-focused than neutral participants.

How can the partially contradictory findings of Wood et al. (1990a) and Sedikides (1992b), on the one hand, and Salovey (1992), on the other, be reconciled? Green, Sedikides, Saltzberg, Wood, and Forzano (2000) suggested that Salovey's results are not due to (sad or happy) affect per se, but rather to the fact that the affect induction task was confounded with the induction of self-focus. Participants imagined personal events that made them feel sad, neutral, or happy. The sad and happy scenes conjured up by participants implicated the self to a greater extent than the neutral scenes, leading to heightened self-focused attention in both conditions. Parenthetically, the Wood et al. (1990a) Experiment 1 is also subject to the same criticism, as participants imagined hypothetical events *and* recalled personal events. However, in Experiment 2, Wood et al. addressed this problem.

Green et al. controlled for the potential confounding in Salovey's (1992) mood induction task by employing a within-participants design. Participants experienced a neutral affective state and either a happy or sad affective state on two separate occasions by listening to musical selections. Participants listed significantly more self-focused thoughts when placed in the sad-affect condition than when placed in the neutral-affect condition. Using musical selections as the mood induction technique, Carr,

Teasdale, and Broadbent (1991) and Green and Sedikides (1999) also reported that sad mood induced heightened self-focused attention compared to happy mood.

Our intellectual journey seemed to have come to an end: Sad affect, compared to neutral states, induces heightened self-focused attention. However, the conclusion of our journey was seeming rather than real. A new hurdle came in sight. How about happy affect? Does happiness decrease self-focused attention relative to a neutral affective state?

☐ Why Happiness Decreases Self-Focused Attention

Happiness likely evolved from a more primitive approach response (Plutchik, 1970) and is associated with increased action readiness and stimulation seeking (Roseman, 1984). Happiness is thought to facilitate the performance of adaptive approach behaviors, such as exploration, affiliation, and reproduction (Plutchik, 1970), to strengthen social bonds (Frijda, 1986; Izard, 1991) and to sustain efforts for the attainment of valued goals (Lazarus, Kanner, & Folkman, 1980). Indeed, participants in an elated affective state, relative to those in a neutral state, express preferences for social activities such as attending a party or spending time with friends (Cunningham, 1988).

In summary, happiness is associated with an approach, expansive, exploratory, and affiliatory orientation. Given the bipolar nature of attention, an external focus implies reduced internal focus. Hence, we propose that happy, relative to neutral, mood states decrease self-focused attention.

The Empirical Evidence

The conjecture that happy mood decreases self-focused attention relative to neutral mood seemed to be rooted in logic. However, empirical results did not appear equally cooperative. Some investigators (Wood et al., 1990a, Experiment 2) did not obtain a significant difference between happy and neutral mood in the elicitation of self-focus. Additionally, Salovey (1992) found that happy mood increased, rather than decreased, self-focus relative to neutral mood. As a reminder, however, concluding in the case of Wood et al. (1990) that happy and neutral moods do not differentially influence self-focus is unwarranted, because according to manipulation checks, the happy mood induction was not as potent as the sad mood induction. Concluding in the case of Salovey (1992) that happy mood increases self-focus relative to neutral mood is also unwarranted, because the sad and happy scenes that participants visualized were likely more self-involving and thus led to heightened self-focused attention compared to neutral scenes.

Green et al. (2000) tested the proposition that happy mood, relative to neutral mood, decreases self-focused attention by controlling for several of the potential shortcomings of past research. First, they used musical selections in an effort to overcome the likely confound between visualization mood induction procedures (e.g., imagining autobiographical events) and self-focused attention. Second, as mentioned above, they used a within-participants design in order to counter the possibility that happy mood inductions are less powerful than sad mood inductions. Specifically, each participant served as his or her own control by experiencing a neutral mood state on one occasion and either a happy or a sad mood state on another occasion. Green et al. (2000) found that happy mood, as opposed to neutral mood, indeed decreases self-focus attention.

Once again, our intellectual journey seemed to have come to an end: in comparison with neutral affect, happiness decreases self-focused attention. However, as to be expected, unexpected detours emerged. How is the subjective experience of self-focus transformed as a function of other affective states, besides sadness and happiness?

☐ The Dimension of Affect Orientation

All of the relevant research so far has capitalized exclusively on a single affective dimension—that of valence. This is understandable and legitimate, as valence has achieved the status of a classic affective and evaluative dimension in psychological research (Osgood, Suci, & Tannenbaum, 1957; Scherer, Koivumaki, & Rosenthal, 1972). Nevertheless, another critical dimension may have escaped empirical scrutiny. This is the dimension of affect orientation, proposed by Green and Sedikides (1999). We believe that this dimension can enrich the relational contingencies between affect and self-focus.

Some affective states orient individuals spontaneously toward inaction. These states heighten awareness of the self and thus instigate internal-oriented cognitive and behavioral responses. Green and Sedikides (1999) termed such states *reflective*. Examples of reflective affective states are sadness and contentment. Other affective states, however, orient individuals spontaneously toward corrective or affiliative action. These states heighten awareness of the environment and instigate external-oriented cognitive and behavioral responses. Green and Sedikides termed such states *social*. Examples of social affective states are happiness and anger.

As is evident from the above examples, reflective and social affective states can be either positive or negative. Sadness is a negative and reflective state, whereas contentment is a positive and reflective state. In a parallel vein, anger is a negative and social state, whereas happiness is a positive and social state. Hence, the affect orientation dimension can be conceptualized as orthogonal to the affect valence dimension.

Green and Sedikides (1999) proposed that reflective affective states induce higher degrees of self-focused attention than social affective states. Rationale for this proposal follows.

Reflective Affective States

We have already provided a rationale pertaining to why sadness leads to increased self-focused attention. We wish to extend this rationale to contentment.

The state of contentment signals to the organism that obstacles to one's goals are either surmountable or nonexistent (Ellsworth & Smith, 1988; Scherer, 1984). Hence, little further effort is needed, and a careful consideration of environmental contingencies is unnecessary. Contentment has also been conceptualized as a "breather" affective state (Lazarus et al., 1980), because it allows individuals to free themselves, at least temporarily, from the stress of negative life events and to feel safe and comfortable with their accomplishments. The experience of contentment has been described as feeling relaxed, quiet, free of conflict, and in touch with physical sensations (Davitz, 1969). Naturally, contentment is associated with reduced action readiness. This state is adaptive, as the organism can rest, replenish resources, and ponder new courses of action. It follows that contentment is likely to elicit heightened self-focused attention.

Social Affective States

We have already provided a rationale as to why happiness leads to decreased self-focused attention. We will extend this rationale to anger.

According to the cognitive appraisal view of emotions, anger communicates a disapproval of another's behavior and a displeasure with the resulting consequences of this behavior (Clore, Ortony, Dienes, & Fujita, 1993). The cognitive construal of anger involves making attributions about an outside agent; that is, the eliciting conditions of anger are thought to be characteristics of the external environment. Anger, a high action readiness state, directs the organism at intervention that will likely modify these characteristics (Smith & Ellsworth, 1985). In fact, according to the functional view of emotions, anger enables the organism to confront predators and directs the organism toward preparation for fight or flight

(Berkowitz, 1990; Frijda, 1986; Plutchik, 1994). In short, anger is likely to instigate an action tendency, thus directing the organism's attention toward aspects of the environment. By implication, anger is likely to reduce self-focused attention.

The Empirical Evidence

Green and Sedikides (1999) conducted two experiments in which they tested the hypothesis that two reflective and opposite-valenced affective states (i.e., sadness and contentment) heighten self-focused attention compared to two social and opposite-valenced affective states (i.e., happiness and anger). These researchers induced the corresponding affective states either through an imagination task (Experiment 1) or an imagination task coupled with musical selections (Experiment 2). They assessed self-focused attention using the PSC subscale (Experiment 1) or the PSC subscale and a state behavioral measure. The state behavioral measure consisted of 10 statements that assessed the degree to which participants intended to behave in an introverted manner. Examples include the following statements: "Right now, I feel like I would prefer to read a book alone at home," "At this moment, I feel like I would rather spend time alone in my room getting my life organized," and "Right now, I feel I would enjoy taking a solitary walk."

The results were consistent with the hypothesis. Participants who experienced reflective affective states manifested higher degrees of self-focused attention than participants who experienced social affective states. In short, the introduction of the affect orientation dimension broadened the understanding of the causal association between affect and self-focus.

These findings provide another reconciliation to the contradictory reports of Wood et al. (1990a) and Sedikides (1992b), on the one hand, and Salovey (1992) on the other. As a reminder, the former researchers reported that sadness induced higher self-focus than happiness, whereas Salovey reported that sadness and happiness were equally likely to increase self-focus in comparison to neutral mood. This discrepancy may be due to the techniques that these researchers used to induce happiness. Wood et al. (1990a) and Sedikides (1992b) used techniques similar to those of Green and Sedikides (1999): exhilarating music and visualization of strongly positive hypothetical scenaria. However, Salovey used happiness-inducing scenaria that seemed to be milder in positivity and intensity. In fact, Salovey's scenaria may have induced contentment rather than happiness. Stated otherwise, these scenaria may have induced two reflective affective states (e.g., sadness and contentment), a possibility that would explain the lack of difference in the degree to which these states induced self-focus.

☐ Concluding Comments

A few years ago, we ventured into a theoretical and empirical journey whose purpose was to clarify the interplay between two subjective experiences: affective states and attentional focus. More specifically, we examined the unidirectional relation between affective states and self-focused attention. (For work that examines whether self-focused attention induces affective states, see Sedikides, 1992c; Wood, Saltzberg, Neale, Stone, & Rachmiel, 1990b.) We believe we have arrived at a destination. Sadness and contentment increase self-focused attention, whereas happiness and anger decrease self-focused attention.

These findings have theoretical, methodological, and practical implications. From a theoretical standpoint, the relation between affect and self-focus has been shown to be multifaceted. The affect valence dimension is insufficient to account fully for this relation. Indeed, the affect orientation dimension explains findings that otherwise would appear puzzling. From a methodological standpoint, our journey will hopefully sensitize researchers to think somewhat differently about the potential consequences of sad versus happy moods on the dependent measures of their choice. Sadness and happiness instigate spontaneously differential degrees of self-focused attention, which may act as a proximal mediator on the dependent measures of interest. From a practical standpoint, our research improves the understanding of phenomena in which self-focus is a correlate. For example, in comparison to individuals in reflective affective states, individuals in social states will be more likely to make situation rather than person attributions (Keltner, Ellsworth, & Edwards, 1993), consume more alcohol, and engage in antisocial behavior.

Despite progress, additional obstacles remain to be overcome. Are there any other affective determinants of self-focused attention, besides the affect dimensions of valence and orientation? What are the microscopic processes leading from an affective state to the elicitation of self-focused attention? Are there different types of self-focused attention? Although the road from affect to attentional focus has been half paved, the adventures in paving the remaining half promise to be even more unpredictable and exciting.

☐ References

Berkowitz, L. (1987). Mood, self-awareness, and willingness to help. *Journal of Personality and Social Psychology, 52,* 721–729.

Berkowitz, L. (1990). On the formation and regulation of anger and aggression: A cognitive-neoassociationistic analysis. *American Psychologist, 45,* 494–503.

Carr, S. J., Teasdale, J. D., & Broadbent, D. (1991). Effects of induced elated and depressed mood on self-focused attention. *British Journal of Clinical Psychology, 31,* 273–275.

Carver, C. S. (1979). A cybernetic model of self-attention processes. *Journal of Personality and Social Psychology, 37,* 1251–1280.

Carver, C. S., & Scheier, M. F. (1986). Functional and dysfunctional responses to anxiety: The interaction between expectancies and self-focused attention. In R. Schwarzer (Ed.), *Self-related cognitions in anxiety and motivation* (pp. 111–141). Hillsdale, NJ: Erlbaum.

Clore, G. L., Ortony, A., Dienes, G., Fujita, F. (1993). Where does anger dwell? In T. K. Srull & R. S. Wyer (Eds.), *Advances in social cognition* (Vol. 5, pp. 57–87). Hillsdale, NJ: Erlbaum.

Cunningham, M. R. (1988). What do you do when you're happy or blue?: Mood, expectancies, and behavioral interest. *Motivation and Emotion, 12,* 309–331.

Davies, M. F. (1982). Self-focused attention and belief perseverance. *Journal of Experimental Social Psychology, 18,* 585–605.

Davitz, J. R. (1969). *The language of emotion.* New York: Academic Press.

Diener, E., & Walbom, M. (1976). Effects of self-awareness on antinormative behavior. *Journal of Research in Personality, 10,* 107–111.

Duval, S., & Wicklund, R. A. (1972). *A theory of objective self-awareness.* New York: Academic Press.

Ellsworth, P. C., & Smith, C. A. (1988). Shades of joy: Patterns of appraisals differentiating among pleasant emotions. *Cognition and Emotion, 2,* 301–331.

Ekman, P., & Friesen, W. (1975). *Unmasking the face.* Englewood Cliffs, NJ: Prentice-Hall.

Exner, J. E. (1973). The Self-Focus Sentence Completion scale: A study of egocentricity. *Journal of Personality Assessment, 37,* 437–455.

Fenigstein, A., Scheier, M. F., & Buss, A. H. (1975). Public and private self-consciousness: Assessment and theory. *Journal of Consulting and Clinical Psychology, 43,* 522–527.

Fiedler, K., & Bless, H. (in press). The formation of beliefs of the interface of affective and cognitive processes. In N. Frijda, A. Manstead, & S. Bem (Eds.), *The influence of emotions on beliefs.* Cambridge University Press.

Forgas, J. P. (1998). On being happy and mistaken: Mood effects on the fundamental attribution error. *Journal of Personality and Social Psychology, 75,* 318–331.

Frijda, N. H. (1986). *The emotions.* New York: Cambridge University Press.

Gibbons, F. X. (1991). Self-evaluation and self-perception: The role of attention in the experience of anxiety. In R. Schwarzer & R. A. Wicklund (Eds.), *Anxiety and self-focused attention* (pp. 15–25). Chur, Switzerland: Harwood Academic.

Gibbons, F. X., Smith, T. W., Ingram, R. E., Pearce, K., Brehm, S. S., & Schroeder, D. J. (1985). Self-awareness and self-confrontation: Effects of self-focused attention on members of a clinical population. *Journal of Personality and Social Psychology, 48,* 662–675.

Gibbons, F. X., & Wicklund, R. A. (1982). Self-focused attention and helping behavior. *Journal of Personality and Social Psychology, 43,* 462–474.

Gibbons, F. X., & Wright, R. A. (1983). Self-focused attention and reactions to conflicting standards. *Journal of Research in Personality, 17,* 263–273.

Green, J. D., & Sedikides, C. (1999). Affect and self-focused attention revisited: The role of affect orientation. *Personality and Social Psychology Bulletin, 25,* 104–119.

Green, J. D., Sedikides, C., Saltzberg, J. A., & Wood, J. V., & Forzano, L. B. (2000). Happy mood decreases self-focused attention. Unpublished manuscript. University of North Carolina at Chapel Hill, USA.

Greenberg, J., Pyszczynski, T., Burling, J., & Tibbs, K. (1992). Depression, self-focused attention, and the self-serving attributional bias. *Personality and Individual Differences, 13,* 959–965.

Hull, J. G. (1981). A self-awareness model of the causes and effect of alcohol consumption. *Journal of Abnormal Psychology, 90,* 586–600.

Hull, J. G., Levenson, R. W., Young, R. D., & Scher, K. J. (1983). Self-awareness-reducing effects of alcohol consumption. *Journal of Personality and Social Psychology, 44*, 461–473.

Ingram, R. E. (1990). Self-focused attention in clinical disorders: Review and a conceptual model. *Psychological Bulletin, 107*, 156–176.

Ingram, R. E., Lumry, A. E., Cruet, D., & Sieber, W. (1987). Attentional processes in depressive disorders. *Cognitive Therapy and Research, 11*, 351–360.

Izard, C. E. (1991). *The psychology of emotions.* New York: Plenum Press.

Jones, E. E. (1979). The rocky road from acts to dispositions. *American Psychologist, 34*, 107–117.

Keltner, D., Ellsworth, P. C., & Edwards, K. (1993). Beyond simple pessimism: Effects of sadness and anger on social perception. *Journal of Personality and Social Psychology, 64*, 740–752.

Larsen, R. J., & Cowan, G. S. (1988). Internal focus of attention and depression: A study of daily experience. *Motivation and Emotion, 12*, 237–249.

Lazarus, R. S., Kanner, A, D., & Folkman, S. (1980). Emotions: A cognitive-phenomenological analysis. In R. Plutchik & H. Kellerman (Eds.), *Emotion: Theory, research, and experience: Vol. 1. Theories of emotion* (pp. 189–217). New York: Academic Press.

Linville, P. W. (1985). Self-complexity and affective extremity: Don't put all of your eggs in one cognitive basket. *Social Cognition, 3*, 94–120.

Mackie, D. M., & Worth, L. T. (1989). Cognitive deficits and the mediation of positive affect in persuasion. *Journal of Personality and Social Psychology, 57*, 27–40.

Mikulincer, M., Gerber, H., & Weisenberg, M. (1990). Judgment of control and depression: The role of self-esteem threat and self-focused attention. *Cognitive Therapy and Research, 14*, 589–608.

Mullen, B. (1991). Group composition, salience, and cognitive representations: The phenomenology of being in a group. *Journal of Experimental Social Psychology, 27*, 297–323.

Ortony, A., Clore, G. L., & Collins, A. (1988). *The cognitive structure of emotions.* Cambridge, England: Cambridge University Press.

Osgood, C. E., Suci, G. J., & Tannenbaum, P. H. (1957). *The measurement of meaning.* Urbana: University of Illinois Press.

Plutchik, R. (1970). Emotions, evolution, and adaptive processes. In M. Arnold (Ed.), *Feelings and emotion* (pp. 3–24). New York: Academic Press.

Plutchik, R. (1994). *The psychology and biology of emotions.* New York: Harper–Collins.

Pyszczynski, T., & Greenberg, J. (1987). Self-regulatory perseveration and the depressive self-focusing style: A self-awareness theory of the development and maintenance of depression. *Psychological Bulletin, 102*, 122–138.

Roseman, I. (1984). Cognitive determinants of emotion: A structural theory. In P. Shaver (Ed.), *Review of personality and social psychology: Emotions, relationships, and health* (Vol. 1, pp. 11–36). Beverly Hills, CA: Sage.

Salovey, P. (1992). Mood-induced self-focused attention. *Journal of Personality and Social Psychology, 62*, 699–707.

Scherer, K. R. (1984). Emotion as a multicomponent process: A model and some cross-cultural data. In P. Shaver (Ed.), *Review of personality and social psychology: Emotions, relationships, and health* (Vol. 1., pp. 37–63). Beverly Hills, CA: Sage.

Scherer, K. R., Koivumaki, J., & Rosenthal, R. (1972). Minimal cues in the vocal communication of affect: Judging emotions from content masked speech. *Journal of Personality and Social Psychology, 1*, 269–285.

Schwarz, N. (1990). Feelings as information: Informational and motivational functions of affective states. In R. M. Sorrentino & E. T. Higgins (Eds.), *Handbook of motivation and cognition: Foundations of social behavior* (Vol. 2, pp. 527–561). New York: Guilford Press.

Sedikides, C. (1992a). Changes in the valence of the self as a function of mood. *Review of Personality and Social Psychology, 14*, 271–311.

Sedikides, C. (1992b). Mood as a determinant of attentional focus. *Cognition and Emotion, 6,* 129–148.

Sedikides, C. (1992c). Attentional effects on mood are moderated by chronic self-conception valence. *Personality and Social Psychology Bulletin, 18,* 580–584.

Smith, C. A., & Ellsworth, P. C. (1985). Patterns of cognitive appraisal in emotion. *Journal of Personality and Social Psychology, 48,* 813–838.

Stephenson, B., & Wicklund, R. A. (1983). Self-directed attention and taking the other's perspective. *Journal of Experimental Social Psychology, 19,* 58–77.

Trommsdorff, G., & John, H. (1992). Decoding affective communication in intimate relationships. *European Journal of Social Psychology, 22,* 41–54.

Wegener, D. T., Petty, R. E., & Smith, S. M. (1995). Positive mood can increase or decrease message scrutiny: The hedonic contingency view of mood and message processing. *Journal of Personality and Social Psychology, 69,* 5–15.

Wegner, D. M., & Giuliano, T. (1980). Arousal-induced attention to the self. *Journal of Personality and Social Psychology, 38,* 719–726.

Wood, J. V., Saltzberg, J. A., & Goldsamt, L. A. (1990a). Does affect induce self-focused attention? *Journal of Personality and Social Psychology, 58,* 899–908.

Wood, J. V., Saltzberg, J. A., Neale, J. M., Stone, A. A., & Rachmiel, T. B. (1990b). Self-focused attention, coping response, and distressed mood in everyday life. *Journal of Personality and Social Psychology, 58,* 1027–1036.

Wright, J., & Mischel, W. (1982). Influence of affect on cognitive social learning person variables. *Journal of Personality and Social Psychology, 43,* 901–914.

13
CHAPTER

Gerd Bohner
Thomas Weinerth

Negative Affect and Persuasion: The Role of Affect Interpretation

Subjective experiences have always played a central role in work on attitudes and persuasion. Early theorists described the affect experienced in response to an attitude object as an integral part of a person's attitude (e.g., Rosenberg & Hovland, 1960). Later, researchers studied how incidental affect—mood states that are present independent of the attitude object—influence attitudinal processing (see, e.g., Schwarz, Bless, & Bohner, 1991), and in recent years, nonaffective subjective experiences such as perceptual fluency and ease of processing were shown to impact on attitude judgments (e.g., Reber, Winkielman, & Schwarz, 1998; Wänke, Bless, & Biller, 1996). In this chapter, we discuss the mechanisms by which incidental negative affect can influence the processing of persuasive messages. We present experimental evidence for the view that people who experience negative affect may scrutinize message content either more or less thoroughly, depending on how they interpret their negative affect. In doing

The research presented in this chapter was supported by grants from the Deutsche Forschungsgemeinschaft (Bo 1248/1-3 and Er 257/1-5). We gratefully acknowledge stimulating discussions with Hans-Peter Erb, Norbert Schwarz, and Frank Siebler. Herbert Bless and Norbert Schwarz provided insightful comments on previous drafts. Finally, we would like to thank David Reimer, Wolfgang Reiter, and Knut Schmälzle for their assistance in data collection.

Address correspondence to Gerd Bohner, Department of Psychology, University of Kent, Canterbury, Kent CT2 7NP, Great Britain. E-mail: G.Bohner@ukc.ac.uk

so, we mainly draw upon the affect-as-information model (Schwarz, 1990) and its mood-as-input extension (Martin, Ward, Achee, & Wyer, 1993).

☐ Affect as Information

Various studies indicate that affective states influence the processing of persuasive messages. Generally, message recipients who are in a negative mood during message exposure have been found to process more systematically than recipients who are in a positive mood (see Schwarz et al., 1991). An explanation that seems to account most thoroughly for these findings is the mood-as-information model (Schwarz, 1990; Schwarz & Clore, 1988). This model starts from the assumption that "emotions exist for the sake of signaling states of the world that have to be responded to, or that no longer need response and action" (Frijda, 1988, p. 354). Accordingly, people use their affective state as information about the current situation, inferring from negative states that some aspect of the situation is threatening or otherwise problematic, and inferring from positive states that the situation is benign. This in turn leads them to adopt a piecemeal, effortful, systematic processing style (which is functional for analyzing a problematic situation to determine adequate reactions) if they experience negative affect, and a schema-guided, often less effortful, heuristic processing style if they experience positive affect (Schwarz, 1990; cf. Bless, 1997). Importantly, these processing differences should only be observed if the individual perceives the current processing task (e.g., the persuasion setting) as a potential cause of the experienced mood; it should be eliminated if the individual's attention is drawn to an irrelevant cause of their current mood (Schwarz & Clore, 1983, 1988).

In a persuasion context, recipients may interpret their negative mood as indicating that the issue under consideration is problematic, which in turn may lead them to process systematically the persuasive message. Various studies yielded results in line with this reasoning and with dual-process accounts of persuasion (e.g., Bohner, Moskowitz, & Chaiken, 1995; Petty & Cacioppo, 1986). They have demonstrated that the thoughts and judgments of individuals who feel sad while processing a message were influenced more strongly by the quality of message arguments than those of individuals who feel happy while processing (e.g., Bless, Bohner, Schwarz, & Strack, 1990; Bless, Mackie, & Schwarz, 1992; Bohner, Crow, Erb, & Schwarz, 1992, Experiment 2). In addition, Sinclair, Mark, and Clore (1994) observed that the processing difference between positive and negative affect disappeared when participants' attention was drawn to the true, judgment-irrelevant cause of their mood (e.g., the pleasant or unpleasant weather).

Alternative accounts for mood effects on persuasion have also been offered. Some researchers proposed that positive mood may increase the accessibility of positive thought content (e.g., Worth & Mackie, 1987), which is further assumed to be comprehensive and highly interrelated in memory (Isen, Shalker, Clark, & Karp, 1978; Matlin & Stang, 1979). This heightened accessibility of a large number of positive thoughts, mostly being irrelevant to the topic of the persuasive communication, may reduce the cognitive capacity for the processing of this message. This view, however, has difficulty accommodating the finding that mood effects on processing are affected by attributional manipulations (as in Sinclair et al., 1994). Furthermore, findings showing that reduced processing under happy mood can be overridden by instructions to pay attention to message content (Bless et al., 1990, Experiment 1) also seem incompatible with a cognitive capacity account. And finally, some results indicate that the impact of mood on message processing may reverse under certain conditions: if the message can be expected to be especially uplifting, happy recipients tend to process more systematically than do sad recipients (Wegener, Petty, & Smith, 1995).

The latter finding has been explained through the operation of mood management concerns (Wegener et al., 1995). These concerns seem to be able to override processing preferences based on mood-as-information under specific conditions, for example, when positive hedonic consequences of processing are highly salient. In this chapter, we will argue that the mood-as-information principle itself can explain both enhanced and reduced message processing under negative mood, depending on how message recipients interpret their affective state and use the information thus provided.

☐ Proper Problem or Propaganda? The Affect-Interpretation Hypothesis

We propose that whether negative affect increases or decreases message scrutiny depends on the way recipients interpret their affect. This interpretation, in turn, largely depends on more general expectations about the issue, the message, and its source. It seems reasonable to assume that the judged *legitimacy* of the persuasion attempt will influence the inferences people draw from their negative affect. In real life, the persuasive intent of a message is often quite obvious, but can be seen as more or less legitimate. We assume that the recipient's expectations regarding a persuasive message can be ordered along a continuum ranging from "legitimate" to "propagandist." For example, in advertising contexts, information favoring a consumer product may be judged rather propagandist, whereas similar information may be seen to be objective if it is presented by an independent consumer research institute. Other examples for highly propagandist persuasion attempts are politicians' speeches, especially during election campaigns. Messages with similar content may be seen more legitimate if the information is presented by a more trustworthy source, for example, an independent journalist or a close friend. But source and context factors are not the only variables determining propagandist expectations. Recipient factors, such as prior attitudes, value orientations, or vested interests, play an important role as well. This implies that the same message may be perceived as propagandist by one group of recipients but legitimate by another. For example, smokers may perceive anti-smoking campaigns as propaganda, whereas nonsmokers may see them as legitimate.

How do affective states operate within this framework? Let us first discuss the idealized case of a *legitimate* message. A recipient who experiences negative affect when encountering a persuasive message that is expected to be legitimate is likely to interpret his or her affect as indicating a problematic issue. This should result in systematic processing of the persuasive message. In line with Schwarz's (1990) affect-as-information model, this affect-interpretation effect should be moderated by the perceived cause of affect. Negative feelings that are attributed to a cause that is clearly independent of the persuasion setting (such as the current weather) should not be considered informative and therefore be disregarded (Sinclair et al., 1994). If the informational value of the affective state is discounted, the amount of systematic processing should not differ from the baseline processing of recipients who expect a legitimate message, which should be low, assuming that recipients are generally guided by the principle of effort minimization (e.g., Chaiken, Liberman, & Eagly, 1989).

Our predictions differ for the idealized case of a *propagandist* message. People who expect to be subject to a propagandist influence attempt can be assumed to be attentive and to process the persuasive message systematically by default (Cialdini & Petty, 1981; Hass, 1981; Hass & Grady, 1975). When these recipients experience negative affect, however, they are likely to interpret their feeling as a reaction to the illegitimate attempt at influencing their judgment, which should *lower* their motivation to scrutinize the presented arguments. Again, this affect-interpretation effect should be moderated by the salience of a judgment-irrelevant cause of affect. If the informational value of negative affect is discounted, the amount of systematic processing should not differ from the high baseline processing of recipients with propagandist expectation.

In short, the processing consequences of negative affect are assumed to differ according to its perceived cause: is this state caused by a "proper problem," or just a reaction to propaganda (Weinerth & Bohner, 1999)? Our *affect-interpretation hypothesis* states that the same negative affect induces different processing strategies depending on objective versus propagandist expectations: (a) when recipients expect a persuasive message to be legitimate and experience negative affect, they interpret their affect as indicating a genuine problem and process more systematically than the baseline level of processing for legitimate messages, which is low; (b) when recipients expect a persuasive message to be propagandist and experience negative affect, they interpret their affect as a reaction to propaganda and process less systematically compared to the baseline level of processing for propagandist messages, which is high; and (c) each of these effects is attenuated when the negative affect is attributed to a cause irrelevant to the persuasion setting.

The reader will note that these predictions bear some similarity to assumptions made within the mood-as-input approach presented by Martin and his colleagues (1993; Hirt, McDonald, Levine, Melton, & Martin, 1999). These authors proposed that people can draw different inferences from the same affective state. In their studies, participants were instructed to use certain "stop-rules" in deciding when to terminate processing; and participants were assumed to use their current affective state in doing so. For example, participants who had been put in positive or negative moods were asked to read information in order to form an impression about a target person. Half of the participants were instructed *to stop reading when they felt they had read enough* (sufficient information condition); the other half was asked *to stop when they no longer enjoyed the task* (enjoy condition). Results indicated that participants used their affect as information in answering different questions ("Have I done enough?" vs. "Do I still enjoy the task?"): in the sufficient information condition, happy participants stopped sooner than sad participants; in the enjoy condition, the reverse was true (Martin et al., 1993, Experiment 1). These findings suggest that the instructions directed people toward a certain interpretation of their affect, which in turn led to different amounts of processing. Although this procedure is suitable for demonstrating that people can draw different inferences from the same affect, it may not be ecologically meaningful. It thus seemed worthwhile to study spontaneous processes that may bring about different interpretations of affect.

To summarize, our affect-interpretation hypothesis can be characterized as an extension of the affect-as-information and mood-as-input models. In accordance with the affect-as-information model, we assume that people use their affective states as information that bears on subsequent processing strategies, depending on attributions about the cause of affect (Schwarz, 1990). Like proponents of the mood-as-input hypothesis, we assume that the same affective state may have different processing implications, depending on the type of question that it is used to answer (Martin et al., 1993). We go beyond the predictions of these two models by assuming that people's expectations about a situation determine the way in which they spontaneously interpret their affect. In a persuasion setting, an important dimension on which expectancies can differ is the perceived legitimacy versus propagandist nature of the message.

A Note on Specific Emotions

In our discussion so far, we focused on the valence dimension of affect, making predictions for negative (as opposed to neutral or positive) affect regardless of other dimensions of emotional experience. In the two studies to be reported, we induced negative affect by having participants recall events related to two different specific emotions, fear and guilt. Although some studies point to the possibility that negative affect of different emotional quality may have different processing consequences (especially anger vs. sadness; see Bodenhausen, 1993; Bohner, Hauschildt, & Knäuper, 1994), both fear-induced and guilt-induced affect had highly similar effects on processing effort in our studies. This seems to indicate that participants indeed interpreted their affective experience according to their perception of the situation. We will get back to the possibility of differential effects of specific emotions when reporting our experiments, and also in the General Discussion section.

☐ Testing the Affect-Interpretation Hypothesis

We conducted two persuasion studies to test our affect-interpretation hypothesis, using different empirical realizations of affect, expectations, and persuasive messages. We also applied the attribution logic introduced by Schwarz and Clore (1983) by inducing negative affect through tasks that were unrelated to the persuasive message, and by varying the salience of these judgment-irrelevant causes of affect. In the first study, we relied on individual differences in expectations about the legitimate versus propagandist nature of the influence attempt, whereas in the second study, we experimentally manipulated this expectation.

Study 1: Smokers' and Nonsmokers' Processing of an Antismoking Appeal

In our first experiment, we studied smokers and nonsmokers, assuming that these two groups would differ in their expectations regarding the nature of antismoking appeals. In today's society, smokers are exposed to various appeals that plead for them to give up or reduce smoking. They are faced with arguments threatening a cherished behavior, which they may also experience as difficult to give up, and are thus likely to experience these antismoking appeals as propaganda.[1] Experiencing negative affect when encountering such an antismoking message then should be interpreted by smokers as a negative reaction to a propagandist persuasion attempt, which in turn should lower their motivation to scrutinize the message. Nonsmokers, on the other hand, are likely to judge an antismoking message as more objective and legitimate to begin with, and negative affect, for them, would unlikely be experienced as a reaction to propaganda. Instead, they should perceive their negative affect as indicating a problematic issue, which should enhance their processing motivation.

We ran baseline conditions in which smokers and nonsmokers were simply confronted with an antismoking message that contained either strong or weak arguments. In the remaining conditions, negative affect was induced, and the induction task either was or was not made salient as the cause of participants' affect before participants (smokers and nonsmokers) were confronted with the strong or weak antismoking message. We predicted that nonsmokers to whom the affect induction task was not made salient would process *more* systematically than (a) nonsmokers in the baseline condition and (b) nonsmokers to whom the affect induction task was made salient, replicating previous results (e.g., Bless et al., 1990; Sinclair et al., 1994). However, smokers to whom the affect induction task was not made salient were assumed to process *less* systematically, compared to (a) smokers in the baseline condition and (b) smokers to whom the affect induction task was made salient.[2]

The amount of systematic processing was inferred from differences in cognitive responses and attitudes between the strong and weak message conditions. Furthermore, we assumed that smokers who experience negative affect and to whom the affect induction task is not made salient would be particularly likely to refer spontaneously to the propagandist nature of the message in their cognitive responses.

Participants, Procedure, and Independent Variables

Participants were 224 students at the University of Mannheim (102 smokers and 122 nonsmokers), who had been recruited for two unostensibly related studies. In the "first study," negative affect was induced; in the "second study," the persuasive message was presented and the dependent variables were assessed. Participants were randomly assigned to the conditions of a 2 (message quality: strong vs. weak) × 2 (salience of affect induction: high vs. low) design or to one of two baseline conditions (strong vs. weak message) without affect induction. The distinction between smokers and nonsmokers was used as an additional, quasi-experimental, factor.

Affect Induction and Salience of the Affect Induction Task.   Purportedly to help with the construction of a "Life Event Inventory" (see Bless et al., 1990), participants were asked to write within 10 minutes a vivid report of a fearsome life event. Afterwards, students were asked to report how they felt right at that moment. When students had completed this "first study," the salience of the affect induction task was manipulated. In the *high salience* conditions, participants were told that "participating in the first study possibly might have aroused some of you. However, we ask you now to approach the second study in a neutral manner." In the *low salience* conditions, nothing about potential carryover effects of the "first study" was mentioned.

Persuasive Message.   Participants were informed that the "second study" concerned judgments about current issues and that they would receive a text on the topic of "smoking vs. nonsmoking," which would contain arguments for cutting down on smoking. Then they were given 1 minute to read the persuasive message, which contained either five strong or five weak antismoking arguments.[3] Pilot testing had established the intended difference in argument quality, and had further shown that smokers and nonsmokers did not differ in their evaluation of the arguments' validity when instructed to pay close attention to content.

Dependent Variables

To check the effectiveness of the *affect* manipulation, participants were asked to indicate on several adjective scales how they felt at the moment (see Merten & Krause, 1993). An index of negative affect was created by averaging across 15 items (e.g., *downhearted, afraid, sad, discouraged, joyful* [reverse-scored]).

The two central dependent variables were cognitive responses and postmessage attitudes. After reading the persuasive message, participants were given 3 minutes to list all thoughts that had come to mind while they were reading the text. Based on two independent judges' ratings of these thoughts, an index of *valenced cognitive responses* was created by subtracting the proportion of unfavorable from the proportion of favorable thoughts that pertained to the issue of reducing smoking. After the thought listing, the students indicated how much they agreed with seven attitude statements (e.g., *"I favor an increase of the tobacco tax"; "The author's arguments were precisely to the point"*). From these seven items, an index of *attitude toward a reduction of smoking* was formed.

We further directly examined the *processing effort* expended with an explicit measure. Participants indicated the extent to which they had "skimmed the text rather than checking every argument for its validity." Immediately afterwards, they indicated why they processed the way they stated before, on a scale ranging from 1 (*"because I did not feel the topic was problematic"*) to 7 (*"because the text came from a rather propagandist author"*). To gain further insight into the assumed underlying processes, we content analyzed the thought listings with regard to *thoughts addressing the propagandist character* of the persuasion attempt (e.g., "It is always the same," "The text is propagandist").

Results and Discussion

Negative *affect* was successfully induced. Participants who had described a fearsome life event reported experiencing more negative affect ($M = 3.30$) than participants in the baseline conditions ($M = 2.32$).

Means of the *attitude index* are displayed in Figure 13.1. Quite unsurprisingly, main effects of argument strength and of smoking behavior emerged, indicating that strong arguments led to more positive attitudes than weak arguments, and that smokers agreed less than nonsmokers with the proposal to cut down on smoking. More importantly, the interaction pattern of smoking behavior, argument strength, and salience of the affect-inducing event was significant and supported the affect-interpretation hypothesis. Looking at the baseline conditions first (Figure 13.1, top panel), we found a marginally significant interaction between argument quality and smoking behavior: smokers' attitudes tended to be more affected by argument strength than those of nonsmokers. This pattern is in line with our prediction that smokers would process systematically by default, whereas nonsmokers would have a lower baseline level of processing. Turning to the negative-affect conditions (Figure 13.1, bottom panel), we note that the data pattern for nonsmokers replicated previous findings (e.g. Sinclair et al., 1994): as predicted by the affect-interpretation hypothesis, nonsmokers were not affected by argument strength when the affect induction task had been made salient, but agreed more with strong rather than weak arguments when the affect induction task had not been made salient. Also as predicted, the result pattern for the smokers was clearly opposite: smokers agreed more with strong rather than weak arguments when the affect induction task had been made salient, but were less affected by argument strength when it had not been made salient.

A highly similar and even more clear-cut pattern emerged for the valence of participants' *cognitive responses* (see Figure 13.2 for means). Strong arguments generally led to more favorable issue-relevant thoughts than weak arguments, and smokers generated less favorable thoughts than nonsmokers did. More pertinent to our theoretical focus, the interaction

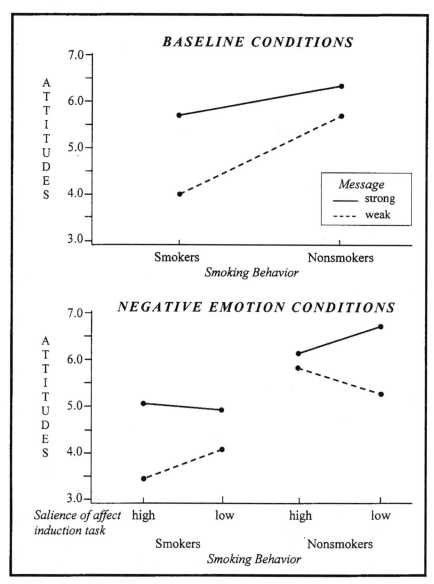

FIGURE 13.1. Attitudes as a function of argument quality, affect, salience of affect induction, and smoking behavior (Study 1). Note: attitude scores can vary between 1 and 9, with higher values indicating more positive attitudes toward the antismoking appeal.

pattern of argument quality, salience, and smoking behavior again supported our hypotheses. In the baseline conditions (Figure 13.2, top panel), as predicted, smokers generated more favorable thoughts in reaction to strong rather than weak arguments, but no such difference emerged for

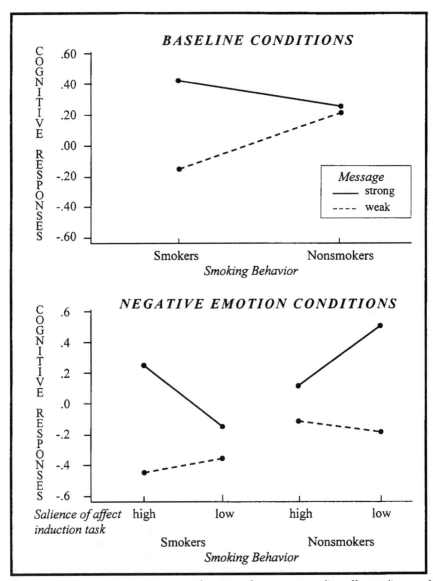

Figure 13.2. Cognitive responses as a function of argument quality, affect, salience of affect induction, and smoking behavior (Study 1). Note: cognitive response scores can vary between −1 and +1, with higher values indicating more positive thoughts about the antismoking appeal.

nonsmokers. This finding again indicates that the baseline level of processing was higher for smokers than for nonsmokers. Within the negative-affect conditions (Figure 13.2, bottom panel), we observed that nonsmokers thought valence was less affected by argument strength under high salience of the affect induction task than under low salience. Conversely, smokers to whom the affect induction task had been made salient generated more favorable thoughts in response to strong rather than weak arguments, but no such difference emerged for smokers to whom the affect induction task had not been made salient.

In sum, the data of both postmessage attitudes and cognitive responses provide strong support for the affect-interpretation hypothesis. Nonsmokers, who did not harbor any propagandist expectation, processed more systematically when they were likely to attribute their negative affect to the persuasion setting than when they were likely to attribute it to the affect induction task. Smokers, however, who were likely to expect being exposed to propaganda, processed less systematically when they were likely to attribute their negative affect to the persuasion setting.

An examination of participants' self-reported *processing effort* corroborates the preceding analysis. As predicted, both smokers to whom the affect induction task had been made salient and nonsmokers to whom it had not been made salient reported to have skimmed the text (rather than having checked every argument for its validity) to a greater extent than both smokers to whom the affect induction task had not been made salient and nonsmokers to whom it had been made salient (see Figure 13.3 for means). The interaction of smoking behavior and salience of the affect induction task was significant. We further compared the two groups who reported to have processed the message at a low level (smokers/low salience and nonsmokers/high salience). This comparison showed that the smokers reported to have done so because they judged the author of the text to be propagandist to a greater extent than the nonsmokers did, although this difference failed to approach significance. An additional analysis within the smokers, however, showed that the degree to which participants perceived a propagandist source as the reason for their low processing effort was highly correlated with the number of cigarettes smoked ($r = .58$). These results provide some evidence for the assumed underlying processes of the affect-interpretation hypothesis. Smokers and nonsmokers seem to have processed at a low level for different reasons—smokers because they judged the communicator as propagandist, nonsmokers because they judged the situation to be unproblematic. Furthermore, it is interesting to note that smokers judged the source to be less propagandist when the salience of the affect induction task was high rather than low. This result supports the assumption that smokers interpreted their negative affect as a reaction to a propagandist communicator only if no other plausible cause for their affect was highly accessible.

Finally, the content analysis of the thought-listing measure revealed that overall, smokers spontaneously listed more thoughts addressing the presumed propagandist nature of the appeal ($M = .25$) than did nonsmokers ($M = .10$).[4] More important, within the negative-affect conditions, a sig-

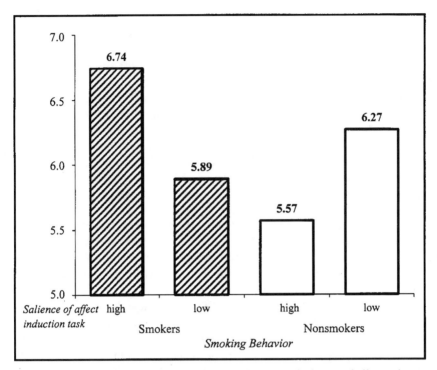

Figure 13.3. Self-reported processing effort as a function of salience of affect induction and smoking behavior (Study 1). Note: effort scores can vary between 1 and 9, with higher values indicating greater subjective processing effort.

nificant interaction of smoking behavior and salience emerged, indicating that smokers to whom the affect induction task was not made salient expressed more propaganda-related thoughts ($M = .36$) than smokers to whom it had been made salient ($M = .21$). This can be taken as further evidence that for smokers, it is the expectation of propaganda that mediates the affect-interpretation effect.

Summary of Study 1

Overall, the data pattern obtained for nonsmokers, who expected the message to be legitimate, replicates previous findings (Bless et al., 1990; Bohner et al., 1992, Experiment 2; Sinclair et al., 1994): negative affect increased systematic processing of message content unless it could be attributed to an irrelevant cause. When an irrelevant cause of affect was salient, the nonsmokers' processing level did not differ from nonsmokers' low processing baseline. Importantly, this result pattern reversed for smokers, who expected the message to be propagandist: when the affect induction task was not salient, smokers processed *less* systematically than did smokers in the baseline conditions. Again, a discounting effect occurred when the mood-induction task had been made salient as the true, irrelevant cause of participants' feelings; now the smokers' processing level did not differ from smokers' high processing baseline. Therefore, Experiment 1 provides initial evidence for the assumption that negative affect is capable of causing a spontaneous increase or decrease in the amount of message processing, based on recipients' more general expectations about the persuasive situation.

Issue-Specific Fear as an Alternative Explanation?

As our affect induction involved the recall of a fearsome life event, we should briefly consider a potential alternative explanation of our findings in terms of smokers' issue-specific fear. A study by Schwarz, Servay, and Kumpf (1985) suggests that attitude and behavior change exhibited by smokers who process an antismoking message may depend on their attributions of experienced fear. In that study, smokers were confronted with a fear-arousing antismoking film. Before watching the film, participants were given a placebo pill that was said to have arousing, tranquilizing, or no side effects. Participants showed less intention to reduce smoking when they could attribute the fear they experienced to the presumably arousing pill, and greater intention to do so when they expected the pill to be tranquilizing, than when they expected no side effects.

Concerning the extent of message processing, two competing interpretations of these results are possible: (a) participants who perceived their fear as a reaction to the pill may have judged the situation as nonproblematic and processed the message less extensively, whereas participants who perceived the pill to have tranquilizing or no side effects may have interpreted their fear as indicating a problematic situation and thus processed the message more thoroughly; or (b) participants who attributed their fear to the message (tranquilizing/no side effect conditions) may have interpreted their affect as a reaction to a propagandist influence attempt, which in turn led to decreased message processing, whereas participants who perceived their fear as a reaction to the pill may have processed systematically by default. As Schwarz and his colleagues (1985) did not vary argument quality, it is impossible to distinguish between the above alternatives (a) and (b). If the arguments presented in the fear-arousing film were convincing, alternative (a) would be more consistent with the results, but if these arguments were unconvincing, alternative (b) would be more likely. This is because more favorable attitudes may be the result of *more* systematic processing when message quality is high, or of *less* systematic processing when message quality is low (see Petty, Wells, & Brock, 1977).

In any case, we believe that a purely attributional explanation based on issue-specific fear is unlikely to account for the results of our own Study 1. Nonsmokers would be unlikely to interpret their feelings as fear aroused by the message, and even if they did, why would this specific interpretation affect their processing effort in an opposite direction than that of the smokers? Nevertheless, it seemed desirable to demonstrate that the results we observed are not dependent on a specific negative emotion, but rather represent a generalized effect of negative affect. Therefore, in the second study we conducted, a different type of emotional content was elicited in the affect induction task.

Furthermore, we addressed another problem of the smoker/nonsmoker paradigm. Smokers and nonsmokers may differ not only in their general expectations concerning an antismoking appeal, but also in a host of other characteristics that are difficult to control. Thus, to provide direct evidence that differences in propagandist expectation triggered the observed effects, it is expedient not to rely solely on differences between existing groups, but to experimentally manipulate propagandist expectation.

Study 2: Processing a Message from a Propagandist Communicator

In our second study, an objective versus propagandist expectation was directly manipulated by providing information about the alleged message source, who was described in generally positive terms, but for half of the participants also as propagandist. Negative affect was induced through the recall of a guilt-related experience, and later, this affect induction task was or was not made salient as the cause of participants' affect. Participants then were confronted with a persuasive message pleading for a fictitious road construction project.

We predicted that participants without propagandist expectation would process more systematically when the affect induction task was not salient than when it was salient, thus replicating the result pattern for nonsmokers in Experiment 1. On the other hand, participants who expect an influence attempt by a propagandist communicator were hypothesized to interpret their negative affect as a reaction to propaganda, which should lower their motivation to process the presented arguments unless the irrelevant cause of their negative affect had been made salient. Accordingly, participants with propagandist expectation were assumed to process more systematically under high salience of the affect induction than under low salience, thus replicating the result pattern for smokers. As in Study 1, the affect-interpretation hypothesis predicts a specific three-way interaction of argument quality, salience of the affect induction task, and propagandist expectation.

Participants, Procedure, and Independent Variables

One hundred fifty-eight male students at the University of Mannheim participated in Study 2. They were randomly assigned to the conditions of a 2 (message quality: strong vs. weak) × 2 (salience of affect induction task: high vs. low) × 2 (expectation: propagandist vs. nonpropagandist) factorial design or to one of two control conditions who only received either the strong or the weak message (without affect induction or expectation manipulation). The cover story this time referred to three independent studies. The "first study" provided the expectation manipulation, the "second study" served as affect induction, and the "third study" featured the persuasive message and assessment of the dependent variables.

The "first study," designed to vary *propagandist expectation*, was introduced as a person perception task. Participants were asked to read a text describing a target person, whom we called "Rüdiger Althaardt," and to form an impression of the target. In the propaganda conditions, Rüdiger was depicted as propagandist, whereas in the nonpropaganda conditions, no such information was contained. To avoid any confounding of propaganda expectation and the target's likability, the information concerning propagandist behavior was presented with a positive touch (e.g., "although some people reproach him of being a mere propagandist, I think that, maybe just because of this trait, he does good work in public relations"). Also, it was embedded in additional information describing the target as generally likable (e.g., "he is a good husband and father"). Pilot testing and manipulation checks confirmed that the variation of propagandist versus nonpropagandist expectations was successful, whereas, as intended, the two conditions did not differ in perceived likeability of the target.

To induce *negative affect*, in the ostensibly independent "second study," participants were asked to write a vivid report of a life event that made them feel guilty. As in Study 1, this was purportedly done to help with the construction of a "Life Event Inventory." Afterwards, they indicated on a series of adjective scales how they felt at the moment. Subsequently, the affect induction task *either was or was not made salient* in the same way as in Study 1.

Participants were then informed that the "third study" was related to the "first." They learned that they would read a text written by Rüdiger Althaardt, containing his arguments in favor of the construction of a new road connecting Germany and the Czech Republic. Participants were given

1 minute to read this message, which was headed "Text by Rüdiger Althaardt" and consisted of six either *strong* or *weak arguments.*[5] Pilot testing had confirmed the intended difference in argument quality.

Dependent Variables

The effectiveness of the *affect* manipulation was checked by the same adjective checklist as in Study 1. The procedure to assess participants' *cognitive responses* also was the same as in Study 1. To assess postmessage *attitudes,* students were asked to indicate their judgments concerning five attitude statements (e.g., *"The road should be built;" "The author's arguments were precisely to the point"*), and the mean of these items was used as an attitude index.

Results and Discussion

The manipulations of *propagandist expectation* and of *affect* were each successful. Participants who read the propagandist description of the target person agreed more ($M = 7.73$) with the statement that he "argued in a rather simplistic and propagandist manner" than did participants who had received nonpropagandist information ($M = 4.54$). Students who had described a life event that had made them feel guilty reported experiencing more negative affect ($M = 3.56$) than participants in the control conditions ($M = 2.43$).

Overall, strong arguments led to more positive *attitudes* than weak arguments. More importantly, the predicted three-way interaction on attitudes was highly significant (see Figure 13.4, top panel, for means). As predicted, a priori comparisons showed that for participants without propagandist expectation, strong arguments elicited more positive attitudes than weak arguments when the affect induction task was not made salient, but attitudes were not affected by argument strength when the affect induction task had been made salient. This pattern reversed for participants with propagandist expectation. Their attitudes were more affected by argument strength under high salience of the affect induction task than under low salience.

A main effect of argument strength also emerged on the index of valenced *cognitive responses,* indicating that strong arguments led to more favorable issue-relevant thoughts than weak arguments. Supporting our central hypothesis, the predicted three-way interaction was highly significant for the cognitive response measure as well. As can be seen in Figure 13.4 (bottom panel), the pattern of means paralleled that of the attitude index. A priori comparisons also showed parallel results, and in terms of effect size provided even stronger support for the affect-interpretation hypothesis.

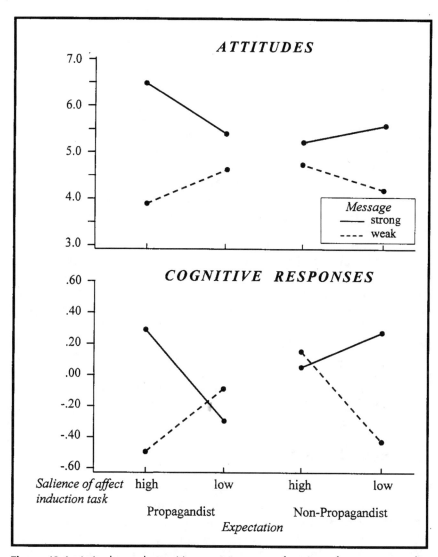

Figure 13.4. Attitudes and cognitive responses as a function of argument quality, salience of affect induction, and expectation (Study 2). Note: attitude scores can vary between 1 and 9, with higher values indicating more positive attitudes toward the proposed road construction project. Cognitive response scores can vary between –1 and +1, with higher values indicating more positive thoughts about the proposed road construction project.

Summary of Study 2

In sum, the attitude and cognitive response data in Study 2 fully support the affect-interpretation hypothesis: participants without propagandist expectation processed more systematically when they were likely to attribute their negative affect to the persuasion setting than when they were likely to attribute it to an irrelevant cause. Participants with propagandist expectation, conversely, processed less systematically when they were likely to attribute their negative affect to the persuasion setting. The results in the no-propaganda conditions replicate the pattern for non-smokers in Study 1 as well as previous findings (e.g., Sinclair et al., 1994). Conversely, the results in the propaganda conditions replicate the pattern for smokers in Study 1. It thus seems reasonable to assume that recipients who expect a legitimate message spontaneously interpret negative affect as an indicator of a problematic issue, which is worthy of systematic thought. However, recipients who expect a propagandist message interpret negative affect as a reaction to propaganda, which lowers systematic processing by indicating that the message is not worthy of further consideration.

The similarity of the two studies' findings suggests that it does not matter whether differences in expectations about the message are based on individual characteristics or on situational features. Furthermore, the affect-interpretation effects we observed seem to require that the affect not be attributed to a cause irrelevant to the persuasive issue. If it is attributed to such an irrelevant cause, the amount of message processing returns to the baseline level of recipients who do not experience negative affect. Finally, the similarity of findings across studies suggests that the affect-interpretation mechanism may be a generalized effect of experiencing negative affect, independent of the specific emotional tone of this affective experience.

☐ General Discussion

Several lines of research indicate that affect influences the way people process persuasive communications (e.g., Baron, Logan, Lilly, Inman, & Brennan, 1994; Bless et al., 1990; Gleicher & Petty, 1992; Schwarz et al., 1991; Sinclair et al., 1994). According to the affect-as-information model (Schwarz, 1990; Schwarz & Clore, 1988), negative feelings have informational value. Negative affect has been shown to inform the perceiver that a situation is problematic (e.g., Sinclair et al., 1994). However, negative affect does not invariably signal a problematic issue and thereby increase the amount of systematic processing. Negative feelings may also inform the perceiver about an annoying influence attempt and thus lead to a decrease in systematic processing. The findings of two experiments suggest that the informational value of negative affect is not stable and support our hypothesis that people's *interpretation* of their negative affect moderates its impact on processing style (see also Martin et al., 1993).

Interestingly, our studies indicate that the specific emotional tone of the negative affect experienced does not seem to affect the results in terms of processing effort, at least as far as guilt and fear are concerned. In Study 1, fear could be seen as an emotion naturally related to the persuasive topic, at least for the smokers, whereas in Study 2, guilt does not seem to have any obvious affinity to the road construction topic. In another persuasion study we recently completed (see Weinerth, 1999), we directly compared these two different negative emotions. We induced negative affect through the recall of either fearsome or guilt-inducing experiences. Participants then read a pro-environmental persuasive message that was designed to contain both guilt-related and fear-related arguments. Propagandist expectation was studied quasi-experimentally by comparing participants with high versus low environmental awareness, assuming that low aware participants would be more likely to perceive an environmental message as propaganda. In terms of *amount* of processing, the results fully replicated Studies 1 and 2, lending further support to the affect-interpretation hypothesis, and the effects of the two specific negative emotions were indistinguishable. At the same time, however, the *content* of participants' message elaborations clearly reflected the emotional tone of the negative affect induced, with guilty participants elaborating more on guilt-related aspects of the topic, and fearful participants elaborating more on fear-related aspects. Thus, future research and theorizing should pay closer attention to the differentiation of amount of processing and the content at which processing is directed.

The "Smell of Propaganda"

In the absence of negative affect, people who expect to be subject to an illegitimate or propagandist influence attempt are likely to process systematically by default (Cialdini & Petty, 1981; Hass, 1981; Hass & Grady, 1975). When people feel negative affect, however, and subjectively interpret this state as a reaction to an influence attempt that has a "smell of propaganda," their motivation to scrutinize the message should be lowered. In our first study, we used a person-situation combination in which a "natural smell of propaganda" was present (see also Weinerth, 1999)— smokers confronted with an antismoking appeal. Under low salience of a judgment-irrelevant cause of affect, smokers who were feeling negative affect processed the antismoking message quite superficially and reported to have done so because of the propagandist communicator. They also expressed more thoughts of being annoyed by the propagandist influence attempt than did smokers to whom the judgment-irrelevant cause of their affect had been made salient.

In our second study, we generated an "artificial smell of propaganda" for some recipients by directly inducing them to expect the communicator to be propagandist. Again, negative affect whose true judgment-irrelevant cause was not salient led to a low extent of systematic message processing, replicating the results of the first experiment for the smokers. In both experiments, the expectation to be subject to a propagandist influence attempt in combination with a negative affective state led to a lower extent of message processing.

Propagandist Expectation as an Inherent Feature of Persuasion

The results of our studies indicate that processing effects of negative feelings are variable: if the persuasion attempt "smelled" propagandist, negative feelings led to decreased message processing compared to high baseline processing levels. On the other hand, if the persuasion situation lacked the "smell of propaganda," negative affect increased the amount of processing compared to low baseline processing levels. However, it could be argued that these findings are of minor importance, because these experiments merely identified one particular condition—propagandist expectation—under which negative affect decreased the extent of systematic processing. Other conditions would cause similar effects, for instance, lowered processing due to fear-based defensive avoidance (Jepson & Chaiken, 1990) or evading cognitive effort because of goal-related satisfaction motives (Gleicher & Petty, 1992). These effects can be seen as relatively situation-specific, depending on a particular emotion or the existence of a particular goal, respectively.

The "propaganda effect" seems to be more general. Persuasion attempts bear a general resemblance to propaganda, but differ in the degree to which they are perceived as propagandist. What makes them "smell of propaganda" may depend on various features of the situation, the communicator, and the perceiver. In Study 1, for example, propagandist expectation was based on characteristics of the arguments (one participant noted "it sounds like propaganda by the Ministry of Health") combined with personal features of the perceiver (smoking behavior). In Study 2, topic-unrelated personal characteristics of the communicator caused a propagandist expectation. Assuming a continuum of "propaganda likeness," the same persuasive appeal may be higher or lower on this continuum depending on who brings forward the arguments, to whom they are addressed, and in what kind of situation they are presented. Concerning day-to-day persuasion attempts, especially through the mass media, propagandist expectation seems not to be the exception, but rather the rule. We are confronted with hundreds of TV commercials every day, endure seemingly endless speeches by politicians, and are faced with hypocrites offering the one and only spiritual welfare. These are but a few examples in which the experience of negative affect should reduce rather than increase the motivation to engage in systematic processing of the presented information. Thus, propagandist expectation seems not to be just another special case in which negative affect lowers the extent of systematic processing, but rather a feature that is inherent in a lot of persuasion situations in daily life. It seems plausible that the expectation of propaganda may typically be low in laboratory experiments on persuasion, which may have contributed to the usual finding of increased message scrutiny under negative affect.

☐ Notes

[1]We made the assumption above that people who expect to be subject to a propagandist influence attempt are rather attentive and process the persuasive message systematically by default (Cialdini & Petty, 1981; Hass, 1981; Hass & Grady, 1975). It is important to note that this should only be true if recipients are not accustomed to such persuasive appeals, for example, due to excessive exposure. If this were the case, they should have low default motivation to scrutinize the presented arguments despite propagadist expectation. However, we did not think that this would be the case for smokers: although they are rather often exposed to antismoking appeals, the amount of such persuasion attempts is not (yet) overwhelming. Nevertheless, this may be different in other countries (e.g., the United States).

[2]Our predictions do not address the objective versus biased nature of processing. One may speculate that smokers who are experiencing negative affect mainly reduce *objective* elaboration and engage in biased counterarguing. Alternatively, they may show biased processing by default, and when reducing processing effort may simply reject the conclusions of the message irrespective of its content. Our results seem more consistent with the latter alternative, but we will not further discuss this aspect in the present chapter.

[3]Weak argument example: "Smokers are physically and psychologically dependent. Smoking reflects a character deficiency that causes smokers to be emotionally less stable than nonsmokers; they more often use 'harder' drugs as well. The cigarette thus serves as a first step towards using illegal drugs." Strong argument example: "Women who smoked during pregnancy have babies with lower weight at birth; premature births and birth defects are more frequent with smoking mothers, and infant mortality is increased. These risks are present even for pregnant women who are passively exposed to cigarette smoke."

[4]This analysis includes participants in the baseline conditions.

[5]Weak argument example: "There will be a facilitation of private contacts between the two countries. Cross-border traffic can be used to visit relatives and friends in the other country and to make new acquaintances. An expected 12% of the residents in the border regions will make use of this opportunity." Strong argument example: "The construction of the new road will lead to a clear reduction of traffic on the existing roads and at border check points. The average volume of traffic at the currently used check points will decrease by 30%; the average waiting time for crossing the border will be reduced by 40%."

☐ References

Baron, R., Logan, H., Lilly, J., Inman, M., & Brennan, M. (1994). Negative emotion and message processing. *Journal of Experimental Social Psychology, 30*, 181–201.

Bless, H. (1997). *Affect and thinking*. Bern, Switzerland: Huber.

Bless, H., Bohner, G., Schwarz, N., & Strack, F. (1990). Mood and persuasion: A cognitive response analysis. *Personality and Social Psychology Bulletin, 16*, 331–345.

Bless, H., Mackie, D. M., & Schwarz, N. (1992). Mood effects on attitude judgments: Independent effects of mood before and after message elaboration. *Journal of Personality and Social Psychology, 63*, 585–595.

Bodenhausen, G. V. (1993). Emotions, arousal, and stereotypic judgments: A heuristic model of affect and stereotyping. In D. M. Mackie & D. L. Hamilton (Eds.), *Affect, cognition, and stereotyping: Interactive processes in group perception* (pp. 13–37). San Diego, CA: Academic Press.

Bohner, G., Crow, K., Erb, H.-P., & Schwarz, N. (1992). Affect and persuasion: Mood effects on the processing of persuasive message content and context cues and on subsequent behaviour. *European Journal of Social Psychology, 22*, 511–530.

Bohner, G., Hauschildt, A., & Knäuper, B. (1994). Impact of happy, sad, and angry mood on the processing of persuasive communication. *The German Journal of Psychology, 18*, 136–138.

Bohner, G., Moskowitz, G. B., & Chaiken, S. (1995). The interplay of heuristic and systematic processing of social information. *European Review of Social Psychology, 6*, 33–68.

Chaiken, S., Liberman, A., & Eagly, A. H. (1989). Heuristic and systematic information processing within and beyond the persuasion context. In J. S. Uleman & J. A. Bargh (Eds.), *Unintended thought* (pp. 212–252). New York: Guilford Press.

Cialdini, R. B., & Petty, R. E. (1981). Anticipatory opinion effects. In R. E. Petty, T. M. Ostrom, & T. C. Brock (Eds.), *Cognitive responses in persuasion* (pp. 217–235). Hillsdale, NJ: Erlbaum.

Frijda, N. H. (1988). The laws of emotion. *American Psychologist, 43*, 349–358.

Gleicher, F., & Petty, R. (1992). Expectations of reassurance influence the nature of fear-stimulated attitude change. *Journal of Experimental Social Psychology, 28*, 86–100.

Hass, R. G. (1981). Effects of source characteristics on cognitive responses and persuasion. In R. E. Petty, T. M. Ostrom, & T. C. Brock (Eds.), *Cognitive responses in persuasion* (pp. 141–172). Hillsdale, NJ: Erlbaum.

Hass, R. G., & Grady, K (1975). Temporal delay, type of forewarning, and resistance to influence. *Journal of Experimental Social Psychology, 11*, 459–469.

Hirt, E. R., McDonald, H. E., Levine, G. M., Melton, & Martin, L. L. (1999). One person's enjoyment is another person's boredom: Mood effects on responsiveness to framing. *Personality and Social Psychology Bulletin, 25*, 76–91.

Isen, A. M., Shalker, T. E., Clark, M., & Karp, L. (1978). Affect, accessibility of material in memory, and behavior: A cognitive loop? *Journal of Personality and Social Psychology, 36*, 1–12.

Jepson, C., & Chaiken, S. (1990). Chronic issue-specific fear inhibits systematic processing of persuasive communications. In M. Booth-Butterfield (Ed.), Communication, cognition, and anxiety [Special issue]. *Journal of Social Behavior and Personality, 5*, 61–84.

Martin, L. L., Ward, D. W., Achee, J. W., & Wyer, R. S., Jr. (1993). Mood as input: People have to interpret the motivational implications of their moods. *Journal of Personality and Social Psychology, 64*, 317–326.

Matlin, M., & Stang, D. (1979). *The pollyanna principle*. Cambridge, MA: Schenkman.

Merten, J., & Krause, R. (1993). DAS—Differentielle Affekt Skala [Differential Affect Scale].

Arbeiten der Fachrichtung Psychologie der Universität des Saarlandes, No. 173. Saarbrücken, Germany.

Petty, R. E., & Cacioppo, J. T. (1986). The elaboration likelihood model of persuasion. *Advances in Experimental Social Psychology, 19,* 124–203.

Petty, R. E., Wells, G. L., & Brock, T. C. (1976). Distraction can enhance or reduce yielding to propaganda: Thought disruption versus effort justification. *Journal of Personality and Social Psychology, 34,* 874–884.

Reber, R., Winkielman, P., & Schwarz, N. (1998). Effects of perceptual fluency on affective judgments. *Psychological Science, 9,* 45–48.

Rosenberg, M. J., & Hovland, C. I. (1960). Cognitive, affective, and behavioral components of attitudes. In M. J. Rosenberg, C. I. Hovland, W. J. McGuire, R. P. Abelson, & J. W. Brehm (Eds.), *Attitude organization and change* (pp. 1–14). New Haven, CT: Yale University Press.

Schwarz, N. (1990). Feelings as information: Informational and motivational functions of affective states. In E. T. Higgins & R. M. Sorrentino (Eds.), *Handbook of motivation and cognition: Foundations of social behavior* (Vol. 2, pp. 527–561). New York: Guilford Press.

Schwarz, N., Bless, H., & Bohner, G. (1991). Mood and persuasion: Affective states influence the processing of persuasive communications. *Advances in Experimental Social Psychology, 24,* 161–199.

Schwarz, N., & Clore, G. L. (1983). Mood, misattribution and judgments of well-being: Informative and directive functions of affective states. *Journal of Personality and Social Psychology, 45,* 513–523.

Schwarz, N., & Clore, G. L. (1988). How do I feel about it? Informative functions of affective states. In K. Fiedler & J. Forgas (Eds.), *Affect, cognition, and social behavior* (pp. 44–62). Toronto, Canada: Hogrefe.

Schwarz, N., Servay, W., & Kumpf, M. (1985). Attribution of arousal as a mediator of the effectiveness of fear-arousing communications. *Journal of Applied Social Psychology, 15,* 178–188.

Sinclair, R.C., Mark, M. M., & Clore, G. L. (1994). Mood-related persuasion depends on misattributions. *Social Cognition, 12,* 309–326.

Wänke, M., Bless, H., & Biller, B. (1996). Subjective experience versus content of information in the construction of attitude judgments. *Personality and Social Psychology Bulletin, 22,* 1105–1113.

Wegener, D. T., Petty, R. E., & Smith, S. M. (1995). Positive mood can increase or decrease message scrutiny: The hedonic contingency view of mood and message processing. *Journal of Personality and Social Psychology, 69,* 5–15.

Weinerth, T. (1999). *Persuasive Kommunikation: Einfluß emotionaler Zustände auf Einstellungen und Gedankeninhalte* [Persuasive communication: The impact of affective states on attitudes and thought content]. Doctoral dissertation, University of Mannheim, Germany.

Weinerth, T., & Bohner, G. (1999). *Proper problem or propaganda? Negative affect can increase or decrease the processing of persuasive messages depending on recipients' affect interpretation.* Manuscript submitted for publication.

Worth, L. T., & Mackie, D. M. (1987). Cognitive mediation of positive affect in persuasion. *Social Cognition, 5,* 76–94.

Teresa Garcia-Marques
Diane M. Mackie

The Positive Feeling of Familiarity: Mood as an Information Processing Regulation Mechanism

People's feelings affect their judgments in multiple ways. Not only do feelings impact judgments directly, but they also influence how information is processed to achieve those judgments (see Forgas, 1994; Mackie & Worth, 1989; Schwarz, 1990). The substantial literature on the impact of mood on information processing provides many confirmations of such influence. Studies in the persuasion field show that individuals in positive moods elaborate persuasive messages less and rely on heuristic processing more (see Mackie, Asuncion, & Rosselli, 1992; Schwarz, Bless, & Bohner, 1991, for reviews). Studies of priming effects (e.g., Bless & Fielder, 1995; Fiedler, Asbeck & Nickel, 1991) of the impact of stereotypes on judgments (e.g., Bodenhousen, 1993; Bodenhausen, Kramer, & Susser, 1994; Stroessner & Mackie, 1992) and of the activation of scripts (Bless, Clore, Schwarz, Golisano, Rabe, & Wolk, 1996) all suggest that happy individuals are more influenced by knowledge structures activated in memory than are others. In the decision-making and problem-solving

This work was supported by a Praxis XXI Grant from the Fundacao para a Ciencia e Tecnologia de Lisboa to Teresa Garcia-Marques, and by National Science Foundation Grant SBR 9209995 to Diane Mackie.

Address correspondence to Teresa Garcia-Marques, Instituto Superior de Psicologia Aplicada, Rua Jardim do Tabaco, 44, 1100 Lisboa, Portugal. E-mail: gmarques@mail.telepac.pt

literature, studies suggest that those who feel good tend to simplify decisions and solve problems quickly (Isen, Daubman, & Nowicki, 1987), use more heuristic strategies (Forgas, 1989), and take more time to solve analytical tasks (Melton, 1995; Palfai & Salovey, 1993). Many of these studies also suggest that, in contrast, individuals who are not happy engage in more careful, analytic processing and rely less on the product of mere memory activation processes.[1] We will refer to the association of positive mood with nonanalytic, top-down processing, and the association of nonpositive mood states with analytic, bottom-up processing,[2] as the *mood information processing effect* (MIPE).

Most theoretical accounts of the MIPE conceptualize it as mediated by one or both of cognitive or motivational factors (see Schwarz & Clore, 1996, for a review). Capacity explanations argue that positive mood primes a highly interconnected and diverse context of information, which reduces the cognitive resources available for processing (Isen, 1987; Mackie & Worth, 1989; Worth & Mackie, 1987). Motivational accounts for the MIPE argue either that individuals in happy moods avoid deep processing to avoid distraction from their positive state (Isen, 1987; for processing that offers hedonic rewards should this occur, see Wegener, Petty, & Smith, 1995) or that positive affect signals a benign environment in which careful analytic processing of information is not necessary (Schwarz, 1990; Schwarz & Clore, 1996).

The mediational roles of capacity and motivational factors claim support from studies that manipulate mood and either capacity or motivation independently (e.g., Schwarz & Clore, 1996, for a review). The finding that happy people with more time to deal with information process as systematically as people in neutral affective states has been claimed as support for the capacity account for the MIPE (Asuncion & Lam, 1995; Mackie & Worth, 1989). Studies that show that happy individuals engage in systematic processing when extra incentives are given (Bless, Bohner, Schwarz, & Strack, 1990; Bodenhausen, Kramer, & Susser, 1994) or when such processing is expected to increase rather than detract from positivity (Wegener, Petty, & Smith, 1995) have been marshaled as support for the motivational account. However, studies that focused specifically on the mediational issue (Bless, Clore, et al., 1996; Bless & Fiedler, 1995; Bless, Schwarz, & Wieland, 1996) have demonstrated that happy individuals show evidence of heuristic processing even while suffering no motivational or cognitive deficits. In Bless and colleagues' (1996) study, for example, happy, neutral, and sad participants listened to a highly script-consistent story about dining out in a restaurant while completing a secondary task. A later recognition test indicated that compared to others, happy participants relied on a general knowledge structure (that is, an "eating out" script) to organize the information in the story. Yet their superior performance on the secondary task also indicated that this nonanalytic response was not caused by a general lack of motivation or capacity. Thus, although motivational and capacity factors may moderate the impact of mood on information processing, mood seems to influence how individuals deal with information without affecting their capacity and motivation to engage in more systematic, analytic processing.

If the MIPE is not mediated by motivation or capacity, then mood must have an intrinsic or inherent effect on the information processing system. "How" and "why" thus become the relevant questions. For Bless and his colleagues (1996), the answer to these questions lies in the informative role that affect exerts (see Schwarz & Clore, 1996). In their view, positive mood's direct effect on processing arises from a combination of the fact that positive mood signals the current situation to be benign and the fact that, in the past, reliance on general knowledge structures has proven adaptive in such benign situations. In fact, some evidence does suggest that happy individuals make more positive evaluations than nonhappy individuals, at least when their mood state is thought to rise from the hedonic valence of the situation (Johnson & Tversky, 1983; Schwarz & Clore, 1983, 1988).

However, no evidence clearly supports the idea that individuals process situations they perceive as benign nonanalytically. On the contrary, some data suggests that happy individuals only engage in such superficial processing if the situation is perceived as mood threatening, with benign situations often processed fully. Moreover, sad individuals engage in deeper processing even when they perceive the situation to be positive (Wegener, Petty, & Smith, 1995). It is thus possible that the role of positive mood in triggering nonanalytic thinking might not arise from mood being informative about how safe or unsafe a situation is. In this chapter, we propose a new explanation for the MIPE by suggesting that mood interacts with the mechanism that regulates whether processing is more conceptual or more data driven. By doing so, we suggest a way of integrating the MIPE into more general conceptualizations of human information processing. We draw this perspective from previous theorizing in social and cognitive psychology about the role of feelings in the information processing system.

☐ Foundational Assumption:
The Feeling of Familiarity as an Information Processing Regulation Mechanism

Consistent with both cognitive and social cognitive views of the mind, we understand the human information processing system to be characterized by two distinct computation modes (see Smith & DeCoster, in press, for an overview).[3] In one mode, which we will refer to as *analytic*, individuals attend to the particulars of a situation and analyze them carefully and systematically. This analytic processing mode can be characterized as involving bottom-up activation, deliberate retrieval and use of information, elaboration of relevant information, and production of new responses. It is thus a consciously controlled, slow, and effortful process. In contrast, the alternate mode, which we term *nonanalytic* processing, is characterized by automatic access to knowledge previously associated with the focal stimuli. It is a reproductive top-down process that is quick, implacable, and not necessary under conscious control.[4]

Such dual process assumptions raise questions about how the processor "knows" which of these modes of processing is appropriate in any given situation (Sherman, 1987). Only some dual process models address this question directly. Some of these models assume the existence of a mechanism that regulates switching between modes.[5] One such regulatory mechanism, developed in the problem-solving domain, is described as a "feeling of knowing" (Reder & Ritter 1992; Schunn, Reder, Nhouyvanisvong, Richards, & Stroffolino, 1997). Reder (1987, 1988) considers this feeling to be part of a process that helps to regulate whether problems are solved by selecting direct retrieval or more analytic strategies. In her studies, for example, participants made rapid judgments about whether they felt they could retrieve the answer to a problem or whether they had to compute it. This judgment was independent of actually knowing the answer but closely dependent on the familiarity of the situation (Reder & Ritter, 1992; Schunn et al., 1997). Familiar situations gave participants a "feeling" that they "knew" the answer, and thus promoted less effortful top-down retrieval strategies. Unfamiliar situations, in contrast, triggered more effortful bottom-up computational strategies. Thus, the "feeling of knowing," viewed as an initial rapid assessment of familiarity, functions to regulate the processing mode selected to solve problems (Nhouyvanisvong & Reder, 1998).

The idea that processing is regulated by implicit awareness of familiarity is common to other approaches as well. One example is *mismatch theory* (Johnston & Hawley, 1994). Although this theory does not discuss a regulation mechanism, it assumes that familiar information activates top-down processing and inhibits bottom-up activity. Detailed processing of well-known, frequently encountered, or familiar situations is assumed to be a waste of limited capacity that should be invested in other, particularly novel, situations. When stimulus situations match memory representations, initial bottom-up processing occurs with an "ease" or "fluency" that results in an (implicit) feeling of "similarity," "recognition," or "familiarity" (Eich, 1982; Fiske, 1982; Gillund & Shiffrim, 1984; Higgins, 1996; Hintzman, 1988; Humphreys, Bain, & Pike, 1989; Jacoby & Dallas, 1981;

Murdock, 1982). Familiar situations are dealt with more efficiently by nonanalytic processing, and are thus associated with reduced bottom-up processing (although specific goals or tasks may induce more elaborative processing; see also Fiske, 1982, 1988; Fiske & Neuberg, 1990; Fiske & Pavelchak, 1986; Neuberg & Fiske, 1987).

In general, these models seem to suggest that what determines or regulates processing mode activation is an implicit feeling of familiarity that varies continuously in intensity (Yonelinas, 1994), depending on the ease or fluency with which the stimulus is processed (Jacoby, 1988; Jacoby & Kelley, 1990). Thus, ease of processing, associated with an implicit feeling of familiarity, triggers nonanalytic processing of incoming information. Evidence supporting this assumption can be found in different fields of research. For example, both the frequency and recency of memory trace activation increases the likelihood of top-down processing (e.g., Fazio, Powell, & Herr, 1983; Higgins, Bargh, & Lombardi, 1985; Sherman, Mackie, & Driscoll, 1990; Smith & Branscombe, 1987; Srull & Wyer, 1979). Top-down priming effects have also been shown to depend on prime-stimulus similarity (Smith & Branscombe, 1987; Smith, Branscombe, & Bormann, 1988; Smith, Stewart, & Buttram, 1992). In addition, the role of general knowledge structures in processing supports this point of view. Natural scenes, scripts, stereotypes, and other "schemas" in memory are automatically activated by focal stimulus information. The match between the two sets of information seems to be a necessary and sometimes sufficient condition for the schema activated in memory to guide further processing (reducing bottom-up processing). Such schemas facilitate apprehension of the gist of the situation but inhibit memory for its details (see, e.g., Grasser, 1981; Schank & Abelson, 1977; von Hippel, Jonides, Hilton, & Sowmya, 1993). Studies in anomaly detection also suggest the inhibition of bottom-up processing in familiar contexts (e.g., Barton & Sanford, 1993; Erickson & Mattson, 1981).

On the other hand, unfamiliar or unexpected inputs seem to enhance bottom-up processing. Evidence for the detail-oriented processing of unexpected information comes from diverse areas of research in the cognitive (see Johnston & Hawley, 1994, for a review) and social cognitive literatures (e.g., Bargh & Thein, 1985; Fiske & Taylor, 1991; Hastie & Kumar, 1979; Higgins & Bargh, 1987; also see Rojahn & Pettigrew, 1992; Stangor & McMillan, 1992, for reviews). For example, incongruent information typically enhances deeper, more systematic, bottom-up processing (Srull, 1981). Research on the costs and benefits of expertise also offers some instructive findings. Experts are by definition people very familiar with a specific, highly related set of information. In the presence of input related to their expertise, they engage in less effortful processing, relying on essentially top-down processing (e.g., Arkes & Freedman, 1984;

Chase & Simon, 1973; Egan & Schwartz, 1979; Schmidt & Boshuizen, 1993). Nonexperts, unfamiliar in the same domain, attend more carefully to all information and engage in bottom-up processing.

In sum, we argue that the assumption of information processing as dualistic implies a need for a regulation mechanism. In line with some suggestions in the cognitive literature, we assume that this regulation mechanism is a feeling that varies continuously in intensity and is associated with the ease or fluency with which the stimulus is processed. Specifically, the fluency that results from a match between initial stimulus processing and stored representations is experienced as a feeling of familiarity. Familiarity signals that the situation can be dealt with on the basis of what is already known, and thus that nonanalytic processing is appropriate (see Figure 14.1).

☐ Explaining the MIPE: Mood as Familiarity

The feeling of familiarity associated with matching has been characterized as being positive in valence (Jacoby & Kelley, 1990; Jacoby, Kelley, & Dywan, 1989; Pittman, 1992). Thus, familiarity seems to be a feeling with a positive affective tone (see Figure 14.1). Familiar situations feel good, whereas unfamiliar situations fail to trigger this subjective experience of positivity.

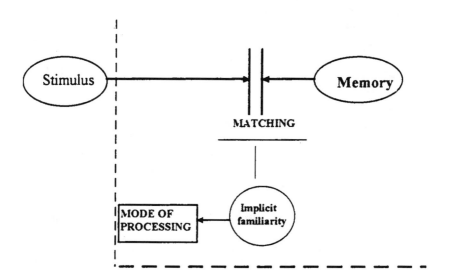

FIGURE 14.1. Information processing regulation mechanism.

Given the diffuse nature of feelings, (mis)interpretations are not only possible but likely (Jacoby & Kelley, 1990). Thus, it is possible that implicit familiarity, with is positive overtones, would be consciously experienced as other feelings with the same valence. More than 200 studies replicate Zajonc's (1968) "mere-exposure effect," suggesting that familiarity increases the *positivity, liking, interest value, attractiveness, pleasingness, appeal, pleasantness,* and *preference* with which a stimulus is rated (see Bornstein, 1989, for a review). Thus, it is possible that the implicit positivity of familiarity is experienced very similarly to what we label positive "mood." That is, it is possible that familiarity is consciously experienced as positive mood.

In addition, it is possible that the positive feelings induced by experimental manipulations or event-related activation of good mood may also be confounded with the feeling of familiarity.[6] The fact that "mood" is experienced as a continuous, low intensity, and diffuse state that changes in a small range from positive to negative valence (e.g., Morris, 1992; Schwarz & Clore, 1988; Sedikides, 1992) makes its operation compatible with that of a regulation mechanism for two reasons. First, these characteristics match those usually associated with the feeling of familiarity. Second, they allow such feelings to function in the background of processing without really disrupting it (Bless & Fiedler, 1995). Given that the implicit feeling of familiarity regulates processing mode activation and that this feeling may be experienced very similarly to what we label a positive mood state, it is possible that mood caused by sources other than familiarity may also be associated with processing mode activation. This hypothesis offers a new explanation for the MIPE: that mood influences processing of information because the information processing system is regulated by a valenced feeling—familiarity.

In summary, the social psychological literature has demonstrated a relation between positive mood and nonanalytic processing (the MIPE). The cognitive literature has demonstrated a similar relation between an implicit feeling of familiarity and nonanalytic processing (the FIPE). We argue that the positive feeling that accompanies this implicit feeling of familiarity is often consciously experienced as positive mood, and that the diffuse nature of feelings allow mood induced by other sources to be confounded with familiarity. It is this confounding that would explain the MIPE.

In this chapter, we report the results of a set of studies that provide initial support for two ideas central to the regulation hypothesis. First, we demonstrate that the implicit feeling of familiarity (as studied in the cognitive literature) is a positive feeling. Second, we provide evidence that familiarity and positive mood have interchangeably identical effects on information processing.

☐ The Close Relation Between Mood and Familiarity

Our hypothesis regarding the MIPE relies on the assumption that positive affect is integral to the implicit feeling of familiarity and thus that familiarity can be subjectively experienced as positive mood. In order to test this assumption, we first manipulated familiarity and then measured participants' feelings within a paradigm introduced to investigate the effects of feelings of familiarity on ratings of validity (Bacon, 1979; Begg & Armour, 1991; Begg, Armour, & Kerr, 1985). The feeling of familiarity is produced in this paradigm by varying the number of presentations or repetition of a stimulus. Statements that are either completely novel (unfamiliar) or to which participants have already (subtly) been exposed (familiar) are usually presented in random order and rated as to their perceived truth. The impact of familiarity on perceived validity is inferred from the fact that familiar statements are repeatedly judged to be truer than novel ones (Bacon, 1979; Begg, Anas, & Farinacci, 1992; Begg & Armour, 1991; Begg et al., 1985). To the usual list of randomly presented familiar and novel items, we added a final block of 10 either novel or familiar items that were also rated on perceived validity on a 7-point scale. As expected, participants' estimations of the truth were higher for the repeated statements than for the novel statements, both for the within subjects comparison of responses to the first part of the list ($M = 5.51 > M = 4.26$, $F(1,154) = 267.75$, $p < .0001$, $MSe = .482$) and for the between subjects comparison of responses to the last 10 items ($M = 5.41 > M = 4.12$, $F(1,155) = 99.10$, $p < .0001$, $MSe = .672$). These findings indicated that repeated sentences had indeed induced an implicit feeling of familiarity that then translated into higher validity ratings (on a parallel with Begg et al., 1985, 1992) and that we had thus successfully induced the "feeling of familiarity." Immediately after making these ratings, participants' mood was assessed using 3 items, each rated on an 11-point scale. Importantly for our hypothesis, participants reported their mood as significantly more positive ($M = 7.10$) after evaluating familiar statements than after evaluating unfamiliar statements ($M = 6.32$, $F(1,151) = 3.89$, $p < .05$, $MSe = 6.18$). The results were thus consistent with our hypothesis that manipulations of the feeling of familiarity would produce parallel variations in self-reported mood, consistent with the idea that positive affect is integral to the feeling of familiarity.

Our explanation of the MIPE also implies that positive mood induced by sources other than familiarity can be misinterpreted as familiarity. If this is so, mood manipulations must be able to produce the same type of effects that feelings of familiarity do. We sought support for this in a study testing the hypothesis that induction of positive moods would affect truth ratings in the same way that manipulations of familiarity do.

Because feelings of familiarity might vary with, and thus affect the judgment of, any actual stimulus sentence (Begg & Armour, 1991), and because such feelings of familiarity might disrupt a manipulation of mood, we created a situation in which participants could use only their affective state in making their judgments. We accomplished this by inducing nonpositive (neutral) or positive mood and then leading participants to believe (falsely) that they had been subliminally exposed to stimulus sentences whose validity they were then forced to judge.

Nonpositive (neutral) or positive mood states were induced by having participants evaluate a manufactured newspaper article adapted from Kuykendall and Keating (1990). The stories had been used successfully as mood inductions in this population before (Queller, Mackie, & Stroessner, 1996; Wegener & Petty, 1994, Experiment 2; Wegener, Petty, & Smith, 1995, Experiment 2). To check the effectiveness of the manipulation, a "post-experimental questionnaire," including two items associated with a 9-point (1 = sad, 9 = happy) scale, was used to assess participants' current mood state. Responses to these items indicated that those participants in the positive mood condition were happier ($M = 6.52$) than those in the neutral condition ($M = 5.70$, $t(58) = 2.10$, $p < .02$, one-tailed, $MSe = 1.49$), indicating the success of the manipulation.

Immediately after this "first" newspaper evaluation study, participants were introduced to what they thought was a separate experiment. In this "study of unconscious processes," participants were led to believe that flashes on the computer screen signaled the very brief presentation of two short sentences. Participants were then led to believe that their unconscious processing of these sentences would influence their subsequent performance on a task asking them to guess some of the sentences' features.

After seeing the flashes participants were asked to press either the T (true) key or the F (false) key, using the first answer that popped into their heads, to complete the following sentence: "*My feeling is that the two sentences were. . . .*" More than 65.6% of the happy participants judged the sentences to be true, whereas more than 63% of the subjects in the neutral mood condition judged them to be false ($\chi^2(1, N = 60) = 4.79$, $p < 0.03$). The proportions of true responses in each mood condition were also compared to those expected if participants were simply guessing using the "one-sample test for the parameter of a binomially distributed variable." The proportion of true responses made by participants in positive moods was significantly higher than 50%, $Z = 1.71$, $p < .05$ (one-way), and the proportion of true responses made by nonpositive mood participants was marginally lower than 50%, $Z = -1.41$, $p < .08$. Given that analytic processing was impossible because no stimuli were actually presented, it appears that participants used their subjectively positive feelings as a cue to decide that the statements were true, just as a feeling of familiarity would typically have been used. Thus, the hypothesis that familiarity and positive mood are similarly experienced received further support. These data are made even more compelling by the fact that positive mood had this impact, even though positive mood was induced prior to the presentation of all sentences.

The two studies presented corroborate the idea that mood is closely related to familiarity. Not only do they show that familiarity can be consciously experienced as positive mood, but they also indicate that mood may be confounded with familiarity, producing similar effects. Together, these two effects make viable the possibility that the MIPE is explained by the confusing of positive mood with implicit familiarity.

Further support for this explanation of the MIPE was obtained in two studies that showed familiarity to be functionally equivalent to mood. From the mood-as-familiarity perspective, and based on the results of the two studies just described, we expected that manipulations of feelings of familiarity would produce the same pattern of results as would manipulations of positive mood. Thus, in replicating a study that clearly demonstrated the MIPE with the key difference that a familiarity manipulation replaced the mood manipulation, we expected to replicate exactly the same pattern of results.

Most investigations of the impact of positive compared to nonpositive moods on information processing have as their theoretical framework dual processing models of persuasion, such as the Heuristic-Systematic Model (Chaiken, 1980, 1987) and the Elaboration Likelihood Model (Petty & Cacioppo, 1981, 1986). In these studies, mood is independently manipulated before participants are presented with a message comprised of either weak and specious or strong and compelling arguments. The manipulation of argument quality provides a means of assessing the participants' message processing mode (Petty & Cacioppo, 1986; Petty, Wells, & Brock, 1976). A differential impact of weak and strong arguments on attitude change (that is, strong arguments produce attitude change and weak arguments do not) is taken to indicate that the persuasive message benefited from extensive elaboration.[7] Assuming that the feeling of familiarity promotes the same information processing effects as positive mood, we expected that participants familiar with a persuasive message would show evidence of superficial processing, just like participants in a positive mood.

To test this hypothesis, we induced different levels of familiarity by aurally presenting participants with a counterattitudinal message zero, one, two, or four times as they made unrelated judgments about superficial message features. Several actions were taken to prevent participants from thoroughly processing message content on these initial exposures. First, the message addressed an issue that was of relatively low interest and involvement for participants. Second, message repetition was interspersed with required judgments and the presentation of a new nonsemantic processing goal rather than being presented in close succession. Third, participants read the message with the explicit goal of forming an opinion toward the issue in a task separate from the one(s) of evaluating its physical qualities.[8] In contrast, every effort was made to allow participants full capacity when they later read the very same message and provided their attitudinal judgments on the issue. Our basic expectation was that the nonrepetition condition would differ from those in which the message was repeated. That is, we expected those in the nonrepetition or unfamiliar condition to systematically process the message and thus differentiate between strong and weak versions of it in their attitudes, whereas we expected those reacting to familiar messages to process more heuristically. However, the choice of four levels of repetition was merely exploratory: we had no a priori expectations regarding how many repetitions would be necessary to induce a feeling of familiarity about the message (especially given that this cut point might vary with context; Yonelinas, 1994).

The results were strongly consistent with our expectations. The feeling that the message was familiar, like a manipulation of a positive mood state, reduced elaboration (see Figure 14.2). Participants for whom the message had been repeated failed to show attitude responses that differentiated strong and weak arguments, whereas participants in the no repetition condition were more persuaded by the strong arguments than by the weak arguments. Our results suggest that in this situation, even a single repetition was sufficient to make the stimulus seem "familiar enough" (that is, the familiarity threshold was very low), since those who received a single repetition of the message showed no differentiation between strong and weak arguments. Of course, a stronger activation of the feeling of familiarity (a higher threshold) might be required to trigger top-down processing in more highly involving or demanding situations.

The results of this study were replicated in another experiment in which the familiarity manipulation was carried out in a different way. We wanted to be sure that the way we manipulated familiarity did not in and of itself prime nonanalytic processing. That is, instead of manipulating only the level of familiarity, the procedure we used in the study just described might have induced differences in the tendency to process information nonanalytically. By asking participants to make superficial judgments as a guise for repeating the message, we may have primed, or made more likely, such superficial processing. Use of a new procedure avoided this problem. Once again, strong and weak versions of the target message were presented aurally during the first repetition phase and in written form when participants later make their attitudinal judgments. During

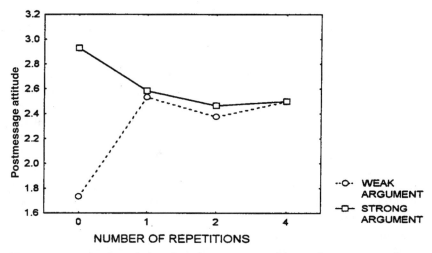

FIGURE 14.2. Attitudes as a function of message repetition and argument quality.

the repetition phase, participants were instructed to listen to the tape-recorded strong or weak versions of the target message "as background noise in the environment" while concentrating on forming an opinion about strong or weak versions of a completely different message on a computer screen. Given the careful distinction made between the main (form an opinion) task and the secondary (just listen) task, we expected participants to differentiate between strong and weak versions of the written message in this phase (Eagly & Chaiken, 1993). In the test phase, all participants read at their own pace either the strong or the weak version of the target message. We had two hypotheses. First, we expected a familiarity information processing effect, or FIPE, on a parallel with the typically studied MIPE. That is, familiarity with the message would be associated with nonanalytical processing. Participants' attitudes were adjusted for initial attitude by introducing this variable as a covariant in the analysis. As expected, familiarity interacted with the quality of message arguments, $F(1,180) = 3.87$, $p < .05$. Participants reading a familiar message showed no attitudinal differentiation between strong and weak versions of the persuasive message ($M_s = 3.49$, $M_w = 3.38$; $t(180) < 1$), whereas participants unfamiliar with the message were more persuaded by strong argument message ($M_s = 3.53$) than by the weak argument message ($M_w = 2.57$; $t(180) = 3.24$, $p < 0.001$). Thus, the results suggest that familiarity, like positive mood, is associated with a more superficial, nonanalytic mode of processing. Given that we assume that repetition produces a warm feeling of familiarity, our second expectation was that participants reading a message they had heard before would report more positive moods than those for whom the message was novel. In fact, when mood was measured immediately after the target message was read, those in the familiarity condition reported feeling happier ($M = 5.51$) than those in the nonfamiliar condition ($M = 4.51$, $t(183) = 3.54$, $p < .0001$).

Together the results of this set of studies support the ideas that (1) familiarity is a feeling with a positive tone that induces positive mood ratings, (2) affect caused by a source other than familiarity can be confounded with familiarity and induce the same type of effects, and (3) familiarity and mood exert parallel effects on how information is processed. The results are thus clearly consistent with our contention that positive affect may signal familiarity, and that this is why positive mood often triggers nonanalytic processing. The kinds of manipulations that have resulted in what has been termed "positive mood" (a term that has been used loosely and with some lack of specificity) in the literature are the kind that induce mild, diffuse, generally positive feelings. Those feelings are just those kinds of feelings that may easily be misinterpreted as the positive feeling that accompanies familiarity. If they are, they are then able to trigger nonanalytic processing (see Figure 14.3).

Of course, induced or naturally arising affect will not always be

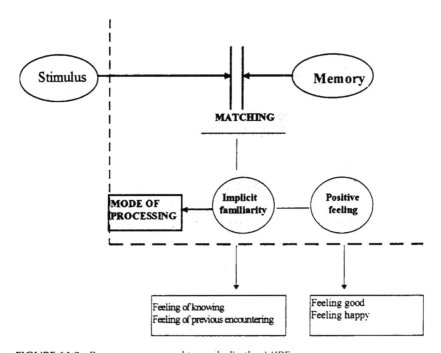

FIGURE 14.3. Processes assumed to underlie the MIPE.

misinterpretated as the affect associated with familiarity. Several circumstances can make such misinterpretations less likely. First, actual familiarity or unfamiliarity with the situation, especially if it is intense, might counteract a mood manipulation, preventing misinterpretations. Second, to the extent that affective states have an external and clearly identifiable cause, they are unlikely to be confounded with or misinterpreted as the positive feeling of familiarity. Emotions, for example, which are often distinguished from mood on the basis of their intensity and clarity of source, may not be amenable to misattribution (although association with causes can decay over time, so that an emotion can degenerate into "mood"; Morris, 1992). Thus we would not expect positive and nonpositive emotions (rather than moods) to influence processing via this mechanism (this is not to say that they may not influence processing via other routes). Similarly, we would not expect abnormal variations of "mood states" to influence processing via this mechanism. More studies with depressive or manic populations that also manipulate mood, emotions, and actual familiarity are needed to clarify these issues.

☐ The Status of the Regulation Explanation of the MIPE

The general assumptions of the regulation explanation are consistent with the predictions made by the majority of previous attempts to explain the MIPE. However, this explanation also has some relatively distinct characteristics that allow it to be contrasted with them. In fact, consistent with all previously suggested explanations, this approach attributes to motivation and capacity a highly important role in processing. However, instead of deeming that role to be mediational, the regulation approach sees the role of motivation and capacity as one of moderation, consistent with the results of Bless et al. (1996). In addition, the regulatory framework suggests two possible ways in which motivation and capacity might interfere with regulation. First, motivation and capacity factors might promote changes in the definition of the focal stimuli, thus influencing the degree of felt familiarity. This in turn would activate more or less analytic processing. In this case motivational and capacity factors, instead of being influenced by how individuals feel (their mood), influence how they feel. Second, motivation might have a direct impact on the level (decision threshold or cut point) of familiarity necessary to induce an analytic processing mode. In fact, since familiarity is a continuous variable and processing mode is a dichotomous variable, it is necessary to assume some level of familiarity that defines the threshold at which information will be processed nonanalytically. Compared to relatively unmotivated individuals, highly motivated individuals may need a higher level of familiarity before they rely on nonanalytic processing.

In contrast to Bless et al.'s (1996) approach, the regulation hypothesis does not consider feelings as informative about the safety of the current situation. If any informational role is to be attributed to mood, it is that positive mood informs the system about how "known" a situation is, whether the situation is one that has been dealt with in the past, and thus whether the system knows how to deal with it now, regardless of whether it is "good" or "bad." From our point of view, even if a situation is negative, we would expect individuals to react to it quickly and without careful thought, as long as it is identified as a known, familiar situation. The regulation explanation may thus be distinguished from such an informational approach by dissociating mood from the hedonic characteristics of the situation.

We hope in the near future to provide empirical evidence demonstrating *that the view of mood as an information processing regulation mechanism is not only a viable and fruitful account of the MIPE,* but also a more inclusive explanation of mood and information processing effects.

☐ Notes

[1]Processing effects associated with negative mood states appear quite variable, with some studies demonstrating increases in analytic processing and others reporting decreases (compare Bless et al., 1990, and Sinclair, 1988, with Ellis & Ashbrook, 1988). Resolution of these apparent inconsistencies awaits specification of the optimal processing requirements of the diverse tasks used in these studies and a systematic concern for variations in intensity and specificity of negative affective states. We are concerned only with the relative state of not feeling positive, and thus chose a neutral control condition.

[2]Not all models of mood posit an association between a particular mood and particular ways of processing information. Some fail to do so because they do not adhere to a dual process view of mind (Isen's Positive Priming Model, 1987, 1993; Ellis & Ashbrook's Resource Allocation Model, 1988). Other models assert the relation between mood and processing mode as completely context dependent (e.g., Wegner & Petty, 1994, 1996).

[3]As Smith and DeCoster (1998) point out, dual process models have been developed in such diverse areas of social cognition research as attitude accessibility (Fazio, 1986), persuasion (Chaiken, Liberman, & Eagly, 1989; Petty & Cacioppo, 1981, 1986), person perception (Brewer, 1988; Fiske & Neuberg, 1990; Neuberg & Fiske, 1987), stereotype activation (Devine, 1989), and attribution (Gilbert & Krull, 1988; Gilbert, Pelham, & Krull, 1988). The same proliferation of dualistic models can be found in cognitive research areas such as automatic processing (Logan, 1988, 1989, 1991), memory (Jacoby & Brooks, 1984; Jacoby & Kelly, 1987, 1990; Kelly & Jacoby, 1996; Mandler, 1979, 1991, 1997), and problem solving and reasoning (Sloman, 1996). Epstein's (1973, 1990, 1994) work is an example of a dual process theory in the personality domain.

[4]Although similar in some ways to the distinction between central and peripheral processing made by Petty and Cacioppo (1986), the two qualitatively distinct modes of processing defined here are not identical to them. Analytic and nonanalytic processing are not distinguished by reference to any particular content of processed information (as are central and peripheral processing), but are instead defined by distinct procedural characteristics.

[5]By assuming independent activation of processing modes, some dual processing models have no need to posit a regulation mechanism (e.g., Kelly & Jacoby, 1996; Logan, 1991; Mandler, 1979, 1997; Sloman, 1996). In these models, individual and/or situational variables determine which process predominates. Brewer's (1988) model differs from all others by assuming that regulation takes the form of a voluntary, intentional decision to engage in one process or the other.

[6]The fact that both feelings have been induced in the laboratory by exactly the same manipulation (contraction of muscles) can be seen as corroborating this hypothesis. Stepper and Strack (1993) manipulated the subjective recall experiences of their participants by asking them to contract either the corrugator muscle or the zygomaticus muscle during the recall task. Contraction of the corrugator muscle (producing a furrowed brow) was assumed to be associated with the experience of effort, and thus to induce a feeling of lack of fluency and a feeling of difficulty in recall. Contraction of the zygomaticus muscle, in contrast, by producing a smile, was understood to be associated with a feeling of ease or fluency in recall. Exactly the same manipulation has been used to manipulate mood: whereas the contraction of the zygomaticus induces positive feelings, contraction of the corrugator muscle induces more negative feelings (Adelmann & Zajonc, 1989; Bodenhausen, Kramer, & Susser, 1994; Laird, 1984; Strack, Martin, & Stepper, 1988).

[7]Bless and Schwarz (1999) call our attention to a logical fallacy (*Affirming the consequence*) associated with the inference of a processing mode on the basis of the differential impact of different quality arguments. They emphasize the importance of distinguishing sufficient and necessary conditions for analytic and non-analytic processing. We agree that this inference is conjectural in nature, but so in fact is all scientific knowledge. We always accept *transiently* a hypothesis that is inductively inferred from verified results that were predicted by it (which is deductively invalid reasoning). In this context, the key word is *transiently*. That is, we should always be ready to abandon this kind of conjectural inference if empirical evidence (rather than pure logic) suggests that is invalid.

[8]All these characteristics of the study differentiate it from studies of repetition conducted by Cacioppo and Petty (e.g., 1989) and no doubt explain differences in obtained results.

☐ References

Adelmann, P. K., & Zajong, R. B. (1989). Facial efference and the experience of emotion. *Annual Review of Psychology, 40,* 249–280.

Arkes, H. R., & Freedman, M. R. (1984). A demonstration of the costs and benefits of expertise in recognition memory. *Memory and Cognition, 12*(1),84–89.

Asuncion, A. G. & Lam, W. F. (1995). Affect and impression formation: Influence of mood on person memory. *Journal of Experimental Social Psychology, 31,* 437–464.

Bacon, F. T. (1979). Credibility of repeated statements: Memory for trivia. *Journal of Experimental Psychology: Human Learning and Memory, 5,* 241–252.

Bargh, J. A., & Thein, R. D. (1985). Individual construct accessibility, person memory, and the recall-judgment link: The case of information overload. *Journal of Personality and Social Psychology, 49,* 1129–1146.

Barton, S. B., & Sanford, A. J. (1993). A case study of anomaly detection: Shallow semantic processing and cohesion establishment. *Memory and Cognition, 2*(4), 477–487.

Begg, I., Anas, A., & Farinacci, S. (1992) Dissociation of processes in belief: Source recollection, statement familiarity, and the illusion of truth. *Journal of Experimental Psychology: General, 121*(4), 446–458.

Begg, I., & Armour, V. (1991). Repetition and the ring of truth: Biasing comments. *Canadian Journal of Behavioural Science, 23,*195–213.

Begg, I., Armour, V., & Kerr, T. (1985). On believing what we remember. *Canadian Journal of Behavioural Science, 17,* 199–214.

Bless, H., Bohner, G., Schwarz, N., & Strack, F. (1990). Mood and persuasion: A cognitive response analysis. *Personality and Social Psychology Bulletin, 16,* 331–345.

Bless, H., Clore, G. L., Schwarz, N., Golisano,V., Rabe, C., & Wolk, M. (1996). Mood and the use of scripts: Does a happy mood really lead to mindlessness? *Journal of Personality and Social Psychology, 71*(4), 665–679.

Bless, H., & Fiedler, K. (1995). Affective states and the influence of activated general knowledge. *Personality and Social Psychology Bulletin, 21*(7), 766–778

Bless, H., & Schwarz, N. (1999). Sufficient and necessary conditions in dual process models: The case of mood and information processing. In S. Chaiken & Y. Trope (Eds.), *Dual-process models in social psychology* (pp. 423–440). New York: Guilford Press.

Bless, H., Schwarz, N., & Wieland, R. (1996). Mood and the impact of categorical membership and individuating information. *European Journal of Social Psychology, 26*(6), 935–960.

Bodenhausen, G. V. (1993). Emotions, arousal, and stereotypic judgments. A heuristic model of affect and stereotyping. In D. M. Mackie & D. L. Hamilton (Eds.), *Affect cognition , and stereotyping. Interactive processes in group perception* (pp. 13–33). New York: Academic Press.

Bodenhausen, G., Kramer, G. P., & Susser, K. (1994). Happiness and stereotypic thinking in social judgments. *Journal of Personality and Social Psychology, 66*(4), 621–632.

Bornstein, R. F. (1989). Exposure and affect: Overview and meta-analysis of research, 1968–1978. *Psychological Bulletin, 106,* 265–289.

Brewer, M. B. (1988). A dual process model of impression formation. In R. S. Wyer & T. K. Srull (Eds.), *Advances in social cognition* (Vol. 1, pp. 1–44). Hillsdale, NJ: Erlbaum.

Cacioppo, J. T., & Petty, R. E. (1989). Effects of message repetition on argument processing, recall, and persuasion. *Basic and Applied Social Psychology, 10*(1), 3–12.

Chaiken, S. (1980). Heuristic versus systematic information processing and the use of source versus messages cues in persuasion. *Journal of Personality and Social Psychology, 39,* 752–766.

Chaiken, S. (1987). The heuristic model of persuasion. In M. P. Zanna, J. M. Olson, & C. P. Herman, *Social influence: The Ontario Symposium* (Vol. 5, pp. 3–39). Hillsdale, NJ: Erlbaum.

Chaiken, S., Liberman, A., & Eagly, A. H. (1989). Heuristic and systematic processing within and beyond the persuasion context. In J. S. Uleman & J. A. Bargh (Eds.), *Unintended thought: Limits of awareness, intention, and control* (pp. 212–252). New York: Guilford Press.

Chase, W. G., & Simon, H. A. (1973). Perception in chess. *Cognitive Psychology, 4,* 55–81.

Devine, P. G. (1989). Stereotypes and prejudice: Their automatic and controlled components. *Journal of Personality and Social Psychology, 56,* 5–18.

Eagly, A. H., & Chaiken, S., (1993). *The psychology of attitudes.* Fort Worth, TX: Harcourt Brace Jovanovich.

Egan, D. E., & Schwartz, B. J. (1979). Chunking in recall of symbolic drawings. *Memory and Cognition, 7*(2), 149–158.

Eich, J. M. (1982). A composite holographic associative recall model. *Psychological Review, 89,* 627–661.

Ellis, H. C., & Ashbrook, P. W. (1988). Resource allocation model of the effects of depressed mood states on memory. In K. Fiedler & J. Forgas (Eds.), *Affect, cognition, and social behavior* (pp. 25–43). Zurich: Hogrefe.

Epstein, S. (1973). The self concept revisited, or, a theory of a theory. *American Psychologist, 28*, 404–416.

Epstein, S. (1990). Cognitive-experiential self-theory. In L. Pervin (Ed.), *Handbook of personality theory and research* (pp. 165–192). New York: Guilford Press.

Epstein, S. (1994). Integration of the cognitive and the psychodynamic unconscious. *American Psychologist, 49*(8), 709–724.

Erickson, T. D., & Mattson, M. E. (1981). From words to meaning: A semantic illusion. *Journal of Verbal Learning and Verbal Behavior, 20*(5), 540–551.

Fazio, R. H. (1986). How do attitudes guide behavior? In R. M. Sorrentiono & E. T. Higgins (Eds.), *Handbook of motivation and cognition: Foundations of social behavior* (pp. 204–243). New York: Guilford Press.

Fazio, R. H., Powell, M. C., & Herr, P. M. (1983). Toward a process model of the attitude-behavior relation: Accessing one's attitude upon mere observation of the attitude object. *Journal of Personality and Social Psychology, 44*(4), 723–735.

Fiedler, K., Asbeck, J., & Nickel, S., (1991). Mood and constructive memory effects on social judgement. Special Issue: Emotion in social life. *Cognition and Emotion, 5*(5–6), 363–378.

Fiske, S. (1982). Schema triggered affect: Applications to social perception. In M. S. Clark & S. T. Fiske (Eds.), *Affect and cognition. The Seventeenth Annual Carnegie Symposium on Cognition.* Hillsdale, NJ: Erlbaum.

Fiske, S. R., & Pavelchak, M. A. (1986). Category-based versus piecemeal-based affective responses: Developments in schema-triggered affect. In R. M. Sorrentino & E. T. Higgins (Eds.), *Handbook of motivation and cognition: Foundations of social behavior* (pp. 167–203). New York: Guilford Press.

Fiske, S. R., & Taylor, S., E. (1991). *Social cognition* (2nd ed.). New York: McGraw-Hill.

Fiske, S. T. (1988). Compare and contrast: Brewer's dual process model and Fiske et al.'s continuum model. In T. K. Srull & R. S. Wyer Jr. (Eds.), *A dual process model of impression formation. Advances in social cognition* (Vol. 1, pp. 65–76). Hillsdale, NJ: Erlbaum.

Fiske, S. T., & Neuberg, S. L. (1990). A continuum of impression formation from category-based to individuating processes: Influences of information and motivation on attention and interpretation. In L. Berkowitz (Ed.), *Advances in experimental social psychology* (Vol. 23, pp. 1– 74). San Diego, CA: Academic Press.

Forgas, J. P. (1989). Mood effects on decision making strategies. *Australian Journal of Psychology, 41,*197–214.

Forgas, J. P. (1994). Sad and guilty? Affective influences on the explanation of conflict in close relationships. *Journal of Personality and Social Psychology, 66*(1), 56–68.

Gilbert, D. T., & Krull, D. S. (1988). Seeing less and knowing more: The benefits of personal ignorance. *Journal of Personality and Social Psychology, 54*, 193–202.

Gilbert, D. T., Krull, D. S., & Pelham, B. W. (1988). On cognitive busyness: When person perceivers meet persons perceived. *Journal of Personality and Social Psychology, 54*, 733–739.

Gillund, G., & Shiffrin, R. M. (1984). A retrieval model for both recognition and recall. *Psychological Review, 91*, 1–67.

Grasser, A. C. (1981). *Prose comprehension beyond the word.* New York: Springer-Verlag.

Hastie, R., & Kumar, A. P. (1979). Person memory: Personality traits as organizing principles in memory for behaviors. *Journal of Personality and Social Psychology, 37*, 25–38.

Higgins, E. T. (1996). Knowledge activation: Accessibility, applicability, and salience. In E. T. Higgins & A. W. Kruglanski, (Eds.), *Social psychology: Handbook of basic principles* (pp. 133–168.). New York: Guilford Press.

Higgins, E. T., & Bargh, J. A. (1987). Social cognition and social perception. *Annual Review of Psychology, 38*, 369–425.

Higgins, E. T., Bargh, J. A., & Lombardi, W. J. (1985). Nature of priming effects on categorization. *Journal of Experimental Psychology: Learning, Memory, and Cognition, 11*(1), 59–69.

Hintzman, D. L. (1988). Judgments of frequency and recognition memory in a multiple-trace memory model. *Psychological Review, 95*, 528–551.

Humphreys, M. S., Bain, J. D., & Pike, R. (1989). Different ways to cue a coherent memory system: A theory for episodic, semantic, and procedural tasks. *Psychological Review, 96*, 208–233.

Isen, A. M. (1987). Positive affect, cognitive processes, and social behavior. In L. Berkowitz (Ed.), *Advances in experimental social psychology* (Vol. 20, pp. 203–253). New York: Academic Press.

Isen, A. M. (1993). Positive affect and decision making. In M. Lewis & J. M. Haviland (Eds.), *Handbook of emotions* (pp. 261–277). New York: Guilford Press.

Isen, A. M., Daubman, K. A., & Nowicki, G. P. (1987). Positive affect facilitates creative problem solving. *Journal of Personality and Social Psychology, 53*, 1112–1131.

Jacoby, L. L. (1988). Memory observed and memory unobserved. In U. Neisser & E. Winograd (Eds.), *Remembering reconsidered: Ecological and traditional approaches to the study of memory* (pp. 145–177). New York: Cambridge University Press.

Jacoby, L. L., & Brooks, L. R. (1984). Nonanalytic cognition: Memory, perception, and concept learning. In G. H. Bower (Ed.), *The Psychology of learning and motivation: Advances in research and theory* (Vol. 18, pp. 1–47). New York: Academic Press.

Jacoby, L. L., & Dallas, M. (1981). On the relation between autobiographical memory and perceptual learning. *Journal of Experimental Psychology: General, 3*, 306–340.

Jacoby, L. L., & Kelley, C. M. (1987). Unconscious influences of memory for a prior event. *Personality and Social Psychology Bulletin, 13*, 314–336.

Jacoby, L. L., & Kelley, C. M. (1990). An episodic view of motivation: Unconscious influences of memory. In E. T. Higgins & R. M. Sorrentino (Eds.), *Handbook of motivation and cognition* (Vol. 2, pp. 201–233). New York: Guilford Press.

Jacoby, L. L., Kelley, C. M., & Dywan, J. (1989). Memory attributions. In H. L. Roediger & F. I. M. Craik (Eds.), *Varieties of memory and consciousness: Essays in honour of Endel Tulving* (pp. 391–422). Hillsdale, NJ: Erlbaum.

Johnson, E., & Tversky, A. (1983). Affect, generalization, and the perception of risk. *Journal of Personality and Social Psychology, 45*, 20–31.

Johnston W. A., & Hawley K. J. (1994). Perceptual inhibition of expected inputs: The key that opens closed minds. *Psychonomic Bulletin and Review, 1*, 56–72.

Kelley, C. M., & Jacoby, L. L. (1996). Memory attributions: Remembering, knowing, and feeling of knowing. In L. M. Reder (Ed.), *Implicit memory and metacognition* (pp. 287–308). Mahwah, NJ: Erlbaum.

Kuykendall, D., & Keating, J. P. (1990). Mood and persuasion: Evidence for the differential influence of positive and negative states. *Psychology and Marketing, 7*(1), 1–9.

Laird, J. D. (1984). Self attribution of emotion: The effect of expressive behavior on the quality of emotional experience. *Journal of Personality and Social Psychology, 29*, 457–486.

Logan, G. D. (1988). Towards an instance theory of automatization. *Psychological Review, 95*, 492–527.

Logan, G. D. (1989). Automaticity and cognitive control. In J. S. Uleman & J. A. Bargh (Eds.), *Unintended thought* (pp. 52–74). New York: Guilford Press.

Logan, G. D. (1991). Automaticity and memory. In W. E. Hockley & S. Lewandowsky (Eds.), *Relating theory and data: Essays on human memory in honor of Bennet B. Murdock* (pp. 347–366). Hillsdale, NJ: Erlbaum.

Mackie, D. M., Asuncion, A. G., & Rosselli, F. (1992). The impact of positive affect on persuasion processes. In M. S. Clark (Ed.), *Emotion and social behavior. Review of personality and social psychology* (Vol. 14 , pp. 247–270). Newbury Park, CA: Sage.

Mackie, D., & Worth, L. T. (1989). Processing deficits and the mediation of positive affect in persuasion. *Journal of Personality and Social Psychology, 57,* 27–40.

Mandler, G. (1979). Organizing and repetition: Organizational principles with special reference to rote learning. In L. G. Nilsson (Ed.), *Perspectives on memory research* (pp. 293–327). Hillsdale, NJ: Erlbaum.

Mandler, G. (1991).Your face looks familiar but I can't remember your name: A review of dual process theory. In W. E. Hockley & S. L. Hockley (Eds.), *Relating theory and data: Essays on human memory in honor of Bennet B. Murdock* (pp. 207–225). Hillsdale, NJ: Erlbaum.

Mandler, G. (1997). Consciousness redux. In J. D. Cohen & J. W. Schooler (Eds.), *Scientific approaches to consciousness* (pp. 469–498). Mahwah, NJ: Erlbaum.

Melton, R. J. (1995). The role of positive affect on in syllogism performance. *Personality and Social Psychological Bulletin, 21,* 788–794.

Morris, W. N. (1992). A functional analysis of the role of mood in affective systems. In M. S. Clark (Ed.), *Review of Personality and Social Psychology* (Vol. 13, pp. 256–293). Beverly Hills, CA: Sage.

Murdock, B. B. (1982). A theory for storage and retrieval of item and associative information. *Psychological Review, 89,* 609–626.

Neuberg, S. L., & Fiske, S. T. (1987). Motivational influences on impression formation: Outcome dependency, accuracy-driven attention, and individuating processes. *Journal of Personality and Social Psychology, 53,* 431–444.

Nhouyvanisvong, A., & Reder, L. M. (1998). Rapid feeling-of-knowing: A strategy selection mechanism. In V. Y. Yzerbyt, G. Lories, & B. Dardenne (Eds.), *Metacognition: Cognitive and social dimension* (pp.35–52). London: Sage.

Palfai, T. P., & Salovey, P. (1993). The influence of depressed and elated mood on deductive and inductive reasoning. *Imagination, Cognition, and Personality, 13,* 517–533.

Petty, R. E., & Cacioppo, J. T. (1981). *Attitudes and persuasion: Classic and contemporary approaches.* Dubuque, IA: Wm. C. Brown.

Petty, R. E., & Cacioppo, J. T. (1986). The elaboration likelihood model of persuasion. In L. Berkowitz (Ed.), *Advances in experimental social psychology* (Vol. 19, pp. 124–203). San Diego, CA: Academic Press, Inc.

Petty, R. E., Wells, G. L., & Brock, T. C. (1976). Distraction can enhance or reduce yielding to propaganda: Thought disruption versus effort justification. *Journal of Personality and Social Psychology, 34*(5), 874–884.

Pittman, T. S. (1992). Perception without awareness in the stream of behavior: Processes that produce and limit nonconscious biasing effects. In R. F. Bornstein & T. S. Pittman (Eds.), *Perception without awareness: Cognitive, clinical, and social perspectives* (pp. 277–296). New York: Guilford Press.

Queller, S., Mackie, D. M., & Stroessner, S. J. (1996). Ameliorating some negative effects of positive mood: Encouraging happy people to perceive intragroup variability. *Journal of Experimental Social Psychology, 32*(4), 361–386.

Reder, L. M. (1987). Strategy selection in question answering. *Cognitive Psychology, 19,* 90–138.

Reder, L. M. (1988). Strategy control of retrieval strategies. *The Psychology of Learning and Motivation, 22,* 227–259.

Reder, L. M., & Ritter, F. E. (1992). What determine initial feeling of knowing? Familiarity with questions terms not with the answer. *Journal of Experimental Social Psychology: Learning, Memory, and Cognition, 18*(3), 435–451.

Rojahn, K., & Pettigrew, T. F. (1992). Memory for schema-relevant information: A meta-analytic resolution. *British Journal of Social Psychology, 31,* 81–110.

Schank, R. L., & Abelson, R. P. (1977). *Scripts, plans, goals, and human understanding: An inquiry into human knowledge structures.* Hillsdale, NJ: Erlbaum.

Schmidt, H. G., & Boshuizen, H. P. (1993). On acquiring expertise in medicine. Special Issue: European educational psychology. *Educational Psychology Review, 5*(3), 205–221.

Schunn, C. D., Reder, L. M., Nhouyvanisvong, A., Richards, D. R., & Stroffolino, P. J. (1997). To calculate or not to calculate: A source activation confusion model of problem familiarity's role in strategy selection. *Journal of Experimental Psychology: Learning, Memory, and Cognition, 23,* 3–29.

Schwarz, N. (1990). Feelings as information: Informational and motivational functions of affective states. In E. T. Higgins & S. Sorrentino (Eds.), *Handbook of motivation and cognition* (pp. 527–559). New York: Guilford Press.

Schwarz, N., Bless, H., & Bohner, G. (1991). Mood and persuasion: Affective states influence the processing of persuasive communications. In M. Zanna (Ed.), *Advances in experimental social psychology* (Vol. 24, pp. 161–199). San Diego, CA: Academic Press.

Schwarz, N., & Clore, G. L. (1983). Mood misattribution, and judgment of well-being: Informative and directive functions of affective states. *Journal of Personality and Social Psychology, 45*(3), 513–523.

Schwarz, N., & Clore, G. L. (1988). How do I feel about it? The informative function of affective states. In K. Fiedler & J. Forgas (Eds.), *Affect, cognition, and social behavior* (pp. 44–62). Zurich: Hogrefe.

Schwarz, N., & Clore, G. L. (1996). Feelings and phenomenal experiences. In E. T. Higgins, & A. W. Kruglanski (Eds.), *Social psychology. Handbook of basic principles* (pp. 433–465). New York: Guilford Press .

Sedikides, C. (1992). Changes in the valence of the self as a function of mood. In M. S. Clark (Ed.), *Review of personality and social psychology* (Vol. 14, pp. 271–311). Newbury Park, CA: Sage.

Sherman, S. J. (1987). Cognitive processes in the formation, change, and expression of attitudes. In M. P. Zanna, J. M. Olson, & C. P. Herman (Eds.), *Social influence: The Ontario Symposium* (Vol. 5, pp. 75–106). Hillsdale, NJ: Erlbaum.

Sherman, S. J., Mackie, D. M., & Driscoll, D. M. (1990). Priming and the differential use of dimensions in evaluation. *Personality and Social Psychological Bulletin, 16,* 405–418.

Sinclair, R. C. (1988). Mood, categorization breadth, and performance appraisal: The effects of order of information acquisition and affective state on halo, accuracy, information retrieval, and evaluations. *Organizational Behavior and Human Decision Processes, 42,* 22–46.

Sloman, S. A. (1996). The empirical case for two systems of reasoning. *Psychological Bulletin, 119,* 3–22.

Smith, E. R., & Branscombe, N. R. (1987). Procedurally mediated social inferences: The case of category accessibility effects. *Journal of Experimental Social Psychology, 23,* 361-382.

Smith, E. R., & Branscombe, N. R. (1988). Category accessibility as implicit memory. *Journal of Experimental Social Psychology, 24,* 490–504.

Smith, E. R., Branscombe, N. R., & Bormann, C. (1988). Generality of effects of practice on social judgments tasks. *Journal of Personality and Social Psychology, 54,* 385–395.

Smith, E. R., & DeCoster, J. (1999). Associative and rule-based processing: A connectionist interpretation of dual-process models. In S. Chaiken & Y. Trope (Eds.), *Dual-process theories in social psychology* (pp. 323–338). New York: Guilford Press.

Smith, E. R., Stewart, T. L., & Buttram, R. T. (1992). Inferring a trait from a behavior has long-term, highly specific effects. *Journal of Personality and Social Psychology, 62,* 753–759.

Srull, T. K. (1981). Person memory: Some tests of associative storage and retrieval models. *Journal of Experimental Psychology: Human Learning and Cognition, 7,* 440–462.

Srull, T. K., & Wyer, R. S., Jr. (1979). The role of category accessibility in the interpretation of information about persons: Some determinants and implications. *Journal of Personality and Social Psychology, 37,* 1660–1672.

Stangor, C., & McMillan, D. (1992). Memory for expectancy-congruent and expectancy-incongruent information: A review of the social and developmental literatures. *Psychological Bulletin, 111,* 42–61.

Stepper, S., & Strak, F. (1993). Proprioceptive determinants of emotional and nonemotional feelings. *Journal of Personality and Social Psychology, 64,* 211–220.

Strack, F., Martin, L. L., & Stepper, S. (1988). Inhibitinig and facilitating conditions of the human smile: A nonobstrusive test of the facial feedback hypothesis. *Journal of Personality and Social Psychology, 54,* 768–777.

Stroessner, S. J., & Mackie, D. M. (1992). The impact of induced affect on the perception of variability in social groups. *Personality and Social Psychological Bulletin, 18,* 546–554.

von Hippel, W., Jonides, J., Hilton, J. L., & Sowmya, N. (1993). The inhibitory effect of schematic processing on perceptual encoding. *Journal of Personality and Social Psychology, 64,* 921–935.

Wegener, D. T., & Petty, R. E. (1994). Mood management across affective states: The hedonic contingency hypothesis. *Journal of Personality and Social Psychology, 66,* 1034–1048.

Wegener, D. T., & Petty, R. E. (1996). Effects of mood on persuasion processes: Enhancing, reducing, and biasing scrunity of attitude-relevant information. In L. L. Martin & A. Tesser (Eds.), *Striving and feeling. Interactions among goals, affect, and self- regulation* (pp. 329–362). Mahway, NJ: Erlbaum.

Wegener, D. T., Petty, R. E., & Smith, S. M. (1995). Positive mood can increase or decrease message scrutiny: The hedonic contingency view of mood and message processing. *Journal of Personality and Social Psychology, 69*(1), 5–15.

Worth, L. T., & Mackie, D. (1987). Cognitive mediation of positive affect in persuasion. *Social Cognition, 5,* 76–94.

Yonelinas, A. P. (1994). Receiver-operating characteristics in recognition memory: Evidence for a dual-process model. *Journal of Experimental Psychology: Learning, Memory, and Cognition, 20,* 1341–1354.

CHAPTER

Rainer Reisenzein

The Subjective Experience of Surprise

Surprise is regarded by many theorists as an emotion that serves important adaptive functions (e.g., Charlesworth, 1969; Darwin, 1965; Ekman & Friesen, 1975; Izard, 1977; Meyer, Reisenzein, & Schützwohl, 1997; Plutchik, 1980; Ribot, 1896; Shand, 1920; Stanley, 1895; Tomkins, 1962). Like all emotions, surprise has a conscious or subjective aspect. This aspect manifests itself in two properties that seem to be central for conscious states generally: phenomenal character and immediate awareness (e.g., Smith, 1989). On the one hand, *it is like something* to be surprised (Nagel, 1974) or, as emotion psychologists usually say, it *feels* in a particular way to be surprised. On the other hand, *one is immediately aware* of one's surprise experience; that is, one is—in a nonfocal, prereflective way— aware of one's experience without, apparently, having to draw any inferences (Smith, 1989; see also Rosenthal, 1986, 1993).[1]

Although people's reactions to surprising events comprise several other components (cf. Meyer & Niepel, 1994), the experiential component of the surprise reaction is most salient to the person, and is viewed as its central component in common sense. Indeed, common sense seems to *identify* surprise with the subjective experience of surprise. These reasons should suffice to justify the scientific investigation of the surprise experi-

I thank Joe Forgas, Wulf-Uwe Meyer, and Michael Niepel for their helpful comments on an earlier version of this chapter.

Address correspondence to Rainer Reisenzein, Department of Psychology, University of Bielefeld, P.O. Box 10 01 31, 33501 Bielefeld, Germany. E-mail: rainer.reisenzein@uni-bielefeld.de

ence (see also chapter 1 by Wegner & Gilbert in this volume). Beyond this, however, it is also likely that the subjective experience of surprise, like most other components of the surprise syndrome, has specific adaptive functions (cf. Meyer, Niepel, & Schützwohl, 1994; Stiensmeier-Pelster, Martini, & Reisenzein, 1995). If so, the experience of surprise *cannot* be ignored in the theory of surprise.

As a matter of fact, the subjective experience of surprise has been paid heed to by most surprise theorists, and has been the main focus for some— particularly during nineteenth century introspectionist psychology, when conscious experience was not just viewed as a legitimate study object of psychology, but as its central subject matter. Most existing theories of the nature and causal generation of the experience of surprise were already developed during this period (e.g., Irons, 1897; Ribot, 1896; Shand, 1920; Stanley, 1895; Wundt, 1911, 1922). However, until recently, no systematic empirical research has been conducted to test these theories.

The present chapter addresses this research lacuna. My focus is on the question of the nature of the subjective experience of surprise, and the closely related question of the causal generation of this experience. I begin with summarizing a recent information processing model of surprise (Meyer, Reisenzein, & Schützwohl, 1995, 1997). Using this model as a background, I then discuss the principal possibilities of explaining the subjective experience of surprise, and briefly describe the major theories. Subsequently, I review the results of recent empirical studies that tested selected aspects of these theories. I conclude with a brief reflection on the possible functional effects of the surprise experience, and the parallels between the feeling of surprise and the experience of other emotions.

However, before proceeding, I would like to submit that the investigation of the nature, causal generation, and function of the subjective experience of surprise is not only of interest in its own right; it may also shed some light on the experience of other emotions. My main reason for believing so is that surprise shares many salient features with prototypical emotions, such as anger or fear. These include a characteristic phenomenal quality that varies in intensity, object-directedness, causation by cognitive appraisals, a characteristic facial expression, old phylogenetic origin, and a plausible biological function. Indeed, these similarities of surprise with prototypical emotions, together with the fact that the investigation of surprise offers several methodological advantages compared to that of other emotions,[2] have led me to propose that the investigation of emotional reactions to surprising events may serve as a paradigm or model of emotion research that allows one to study in a rigorous experimental fashion many controversial issues of general emotion theory (see Reisenzein, Meyer, & Schützwohl, 1996, 1997). At the very least, as will be seen, the theoretical options and methodological issues that arise in formulating and testing theories of emotional experience are essentially the same for surprise as for other emotions.

☐ A Cognitive-Evolutionary Model of Surprise

The core of the cognitive-psychoevolutionary model of surprise proposed by Meyer et al. (1995, 1997; see also Reisenzein, Meyer, & Schützwohl, 1996, 1997) is concerned with the mental processes elicited by surprising events, and is depicted in simplified form in Figure 15.1. (The original model already includes specific assumptions about the subjective experience of surprise; however, because these kinds of assumptions are presently under discussion, they are omitted for now).

Briefly, it is assumed that (ultimately) surprise-eliciting events initiate a series of mental processes that *begin* with the appraisal of a cognized event as exceeding some threshold value of unexpectedness or schema-discrepancy, *continue* with the interruption of ongoing information processing and the reallocation of processing resources to the investigation of the unexpected event, and *culminate* in the analysis and evaluation of this event, plus—if the results of this analysis indicate so—immediate reactions to the event and/or the updating or revision of the schemas that gave rise to the disconfirmed expectation.[3]

The first two steps in this series (detection of a schema-discrepancy and reallocation of processing resources) are assumed to belong to the activity of the surprise mechanism proper. This is taken to be a phylogenetically old mechanism whose main evolutionary functions are to monitor the person's schemas or belief system and to enable quick but nonetheless appropriate schema update in the face of unexpectedness (belief-disconfirmation). The subsequent event analysis (Figure 15.1) consists of the appraisal of the unexpected events along several adaptationally significant dimensions. Meyer et al. (1995, 1997) assume that the event analysis typically comprises at least the following four component processes: the verification of the schema discrepancy, the analysis of the causes of the unexpected event, the evaluation of the unexpected event's significance for well-being, and the assessment of its relevance for ongoing action. However, additional appraisals postulated by cognitive emotion theorists, such as the assessment of the moral significance of another's unexpected action, can also occur in some situations (see Reisenzein & Spielhofer, 1994). The event analysis/evaluation processes serve to optimize (a) the person's immediate reactions to unexpected events (short-term adaptation) and (b) schema-update, which in turn promotes the prediction, control, and effective dealings with future occurrences of the event (long-term adaptation).

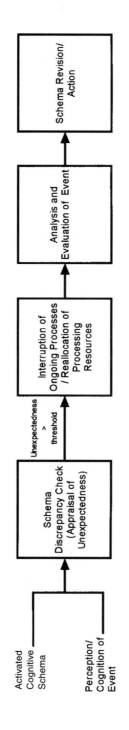

FIGURE 15.1. A cognitive-evolutionary model of the mental processes elicited by surprising events.

An additional important assumption of the model, not included in Figure 15.1, is that the described mental processes are causally responsible, alone or together, for the various observable reactions that have traditionally been associated with surprise, in particular the interruption of ongoing motor action (e.g., Shand, 1920), a characteristic facial expression (e.g., Darwin, 1965; Ekman & Friesen, 1975), and peripheral-physiological activation (for more detail, see Meyer & Niepel, 1994). It is assumed that most of these behaviors, too, occur because they subserve in one way or other—or at least did so in the ancestral environment of humans—the major evolutionary function of the surprise mechanism, namely, to monitor the person's schemas and help update them in the face of unexpectedness (Meyer et al., 1994, 1997).

☐ The Subjective Experience of Surprise in Terms of the Model

When describing the model depicted in Figure 15.1, I made no explicit assumptions about the consciousness versus unconsciousness of the processes that it postulates. However, as noted in the introduction, surprise does have a conscious aspect that probably serves specific adaptive functions, and the theory of surprise must pay heed to this fact. Assuming that the model in Figure 15.1 is correct as far as it goes, this means that the subjective experience of surprise must somehow be fitted into this model, ideally in a way that provides an explanation of this experience.[4] How could this be achieved? In principle, there are two possibilities: (a) the subjective experience of surprise—what people refer to when they (correctly) say that they feel surprised, however vaguely they are aware of the more precise nature of the referent—consists in their being conscious of one or several of the mental processes depicted in Figure 15.1, their outcomes, or of feedback from the bodily reactions that they cause; and (b) the subjective experience of surprise is, or at least includes, an additional mental state not considered in Figure 15.1. What perhaps comes to mind here first is a centrally generated signal that is directly caused by the appraisal of unexpectedness (Figure 15.1), and that, when it exceeds a threshold, is felt as a possibly unique conscious quality (e.g., Stiensmeier-Pelster et al., 1995; see also Oatley & Johnson-Laird, 1987). Note that the same two principal possibilities exist with respect to explanation of the nature and causal generation of other emotional experiences (cf. Reisenzein, 1994).

In the original model by Meyer et al. (1997; see also Stiensmeier et al., 1995), the second path was taken (if somewhat tentatively). Most other surprise theorists, however, have chosen the first path: they have assumed that the experience of surprise is constituted by the person's awareness of one or several of the mental components of the ideal-typical surprise syndrome, of feedback from the behavioral components, or by some combination or fusion of these components (see Reisenzein, 1992, 1994, for more on these matters). The main theories of this second variety are the following: the subjective experience of surprise consists of the awareness of feedback from surprise-related physiological or muscular (especially facial) changes (e.g., Izard, 1977; Tomkins, 1962); of the awareness of a tendency to attend to, or of the actual process of attending to the unexpected event (e.g., Darwin, 1965); of the awareness of the interruption of ongoing mental processes caused by the unexpected event (e.g., Ribot, 1896; Shand, 1920); of the awareness of the cognition of unexpectedness (Ortony, Clore, & Collins, 1988); and finally of a complex or fusion of several or all the mentioned elements, some of which may be nonessential (e.g., Becher, 1916; Irons, 1897; Mandler, 1984). Readers will note that this list includes (suitably adapted variants of) nearly all of the principal theories of the subjective experience of other emotions (see also Reisenzein, 1994).

At second look, the two described, principal theoretical options are not as far apart as they seem. For it is conceivable that the conscious awareness of some of the mental processes depicted in Figure 15.1 essentially involves centrally generated, more or less unique experiential qualities. This concerns in particular the two core surprise processes, the appraisal of unexpectedness and the reallocation of processing resources (Figure 15.1). Reisenzein and Ritter (1999) proposed that the reallocation of processing resources is "sensed" by an internal, centrally located transducer that causes a characteristic, sensation-like experience of mental interruption. According to this hypothesis, the person's primary form[5] of awareness of resource reallocation consists of this interference feeling. Reisenzein (1998, 1999a, 1999b) proposed that the process of unexpectedness appraisal is not, as one may at first think, a propositional inference process that outputs a thought to the effect that something unexpected happened. The "cognition" of unexpectedness produced by the schema-discrepancy check (Figure 15.1) is therefore not a propositional representation. Rather, Reisenzein (1999a, 1999b) proposed, the appraisal of unexpectedness involves a special-purpose, hardwired mechanism that outputs a nonpropositional signal (cf. Oatley & Johnson-Laird, 1987) whose intensity reflects the degree of schema-discrepancy. If one assumes that this signal (if it exceeds a certain threshold) becomes conscious, the person's primary form (see note 5) of awareness of unexpectedness would consist of the sensation-like experience of this schema-mismatch signal.

☐ Empirical Tests of Theories of the Surprise Experience

As part of an ongoing project of our research group at the University of Bielefeld, we have begun to subject the described theories of the surprise experience to empirical test. Our studies are mostly of an experimental nature and investigate surprise in tightly controlled laboratory situations. To date, the effects of three factors on self-reported surprise feelings have been experimentally investigated: degree of unexpectedness, degree of mental interruption caused by the surprising event, and feedback from facial muscles. In the following paragraphs, I summarize the main findings of our studies, as well as the findings of pertinent studies by other researchers.

Surprise Experience and Unexpectedness

Meyer et al. (1995, 1997; see also Stiensmeier-Pelster et al., 1995) assumed that (a) the appraisal of unexpectedness (the disconfirmation of explicitly or implicitly held expectations) is not only the immediate cause of the interruption of cognitive processes (see Figure 15.1), but also of the experience of surprise, and (b) the intensity of felt surprise increases monotonically with the degree of unexpectedness. These assumptions (or the first one at any rate) are in accord with the dominant traditional view of the cognitive appraisal causes of the surprise experience (cf. reviews in Charlesworth, 1969; Desai, 1939; Izard, 1977; Shand, 1920; see also Ortony et al., 1988; Roseman, Antoniou, & Jose, 1996). They also seem to be part of the common-sense, or folk-psychological, theory of mind implicit in ordinary language (e.g., Mees, 1991; Reisenzein & Hofmann, 1990; Ruffman & Keenan, 1996; Smedslund, 1990). For example, Smedslund (1990) suggests that "surprise" is defined in ordinary language as "the state of a person who has experienced something unexpected" (p. 47). This adult concept of surprise seems to be fully mastered by children between the ages of 7 and 9 (Ruffmann & Keenan, 1996). However, the appeal to the implicit assumptions of folk psychology (e.g., Smedslund, 1990) is not convincing to everybody, and a number of divergent opinions concerning the appraisal causes of surprise (including its experiential aspect) have been voiced in the literature (for reviews, see Charlesworth, 1979; Desai, 1939; Meyer & Niepel, 1994; Stiensmeier-Pelster et al., 1995). Therefore, it will be helpful to summarize the experimental evidence that supports the unexpectedness—surprise link (i.e., the evidence from studies in which unexpectedness was experimentally manipulated).[6]

Several of these studies induced surprise by a salient stimulus change after a series of no-change trials. Degree of unexpectedness of the stimulus changes was manipulated in different ways: by varying the number of regular trials preceding the stimulus change (Schützwohl, 1998, Experiment 4), by varying the number of schema-discrepant stimulus elements (Schützwohl, 1999a, Experiment 4), by giving the participants different amounts of information about the upcoming stimulus change (Niepel, 1996; Reisenzein & Ritter, 1999, Experiment 2; Schützwohl & Reisenzein, 1999, Experiment 3), and by repeating the stimulus change (Reisenzein & Bördgen, 1998, Experiment 4; Reisenzein & Ritter, 1999, Experiments 2 & 3). In every case, self-rated surprise intensity increased with the manipulated unexpectedness of the surprise event. Furthermore, no surprise was reported when the stimulus change was fully expected because it had already occurred in the baseline trials (e.g., Meyer, Niepel, Rudolph, & Schützwohl, 1991; Schützwohl, 1998).

These findings were confirmed in two other studies that used rather different methods to induce surprise. Stiensmeier-Pelster et al. (1995, Experiment 3) manipulated success expectancies in a cognitive task (a subtest of the Raven Intelligence Test) by telling participants that the task was normatively easy (on average, seven out of eight students solved it) or difficult (one out of eight students solved it). After the participants had proposed a solution, they received success feedback. Participants who believed that the task was difficult (low success expectancy) were much more surprised, and rated their success as much more unexpected, than those who believed that the task was easy (high success expectancy). Parallel findings were obtained for a second pair of experimental groups whose members were asked to blindly guess the solution: when told that they had guessed correctly, participants who believed that only one of the eight response options was correct were much more surprised than those who believed that seven of the eight alternatives were correct. Reisenzein (2000) studied the relation between degree of unexpectedness and felt surprise on an intraindividual level, using a computerized quiz paradigm. The participants were presented with 45 quiz items, some of which had unexpected solutions. In each trial, they were first shown a quiz question plus several possible answers. They had to choose an answer and rate their confidence that it was correct. Subsequently, the solution was presented, and the participants rated the intensity of felt surprise. The mean intraindividual correlation between degree of unexpectedness of the solution (estimated prospectively from the participants' ratings of certainty about the chosen answer) and self-rated surprise intensity across the 45 quiz items was found to be $r = .78$.

The available experimental evidence is thus consistent with the assumptions that unexpectedness is the proximate cognitive appraisal cause of the surprise experience, and that the degree of unexpectedness determines the intensity of felt surprise. However, the reviewed data say nothing about the nature of the surprise experience: they do not allow one to decide whether, for example, the feeling of surprise is based on feedback from bodily changes or consists of the experience of mental interruption. In fact, the data do not even allow one to rule out the theory that the subjective experience of surprise is simply the person's awareness of unexpectedness (which, as explained earlier, could either be a conscious thought to the effect that something unexpected happened, or the experience of a sensation-like schema-discrepancy signal; cf. Reisenzein, 1998, 1999a, 1999b). For strictly speaking, what the experimental evidence demonstrates with (reasonable) certainty is only that unexpectedness influences people's self-ratings of surprise intensity or—assuming faithful reporting—their beliefs about surprise intensity. This is compatible with the possibility that the surprise experience is simply the person's awareness of unexpectedness, rather than a distinct mental state caused by unexpectedness, and that the self-reports of surprise are thus but an alternative measure of experienced unexpectedness. However, it must be emphasized that the reviewed data do not selectively favor this theory of surprise either, for precisely the same experimental findings would be expected if unexpectedness is the proximal cognitive cause of surprise.

Surprise Experience and Mental Interference

Probably the most popular classical theory of the subjective experience of surprise holds that the feeling of surprise consists, at least in part, of a direct, sensation-like awareness of the mental interruption caused by unexpected events (see Figure 15.1). This *interference theory* of surprise has been proposed, in different variants and with varying degrees of elaborateness, by many theorists, including Adam Smith (1980), Becher (1916), Irons (1897), McDougall (1960), Ribot (1896), Wundt (1911, 1922), and most notably, Shand (1920). The theory was recently revived by Reisenzein and Ritter (1999), who conducted several experiments to test it. The basic idea of these experiments was to vary the degree of interference with ongoing mental activity caused by a surprising event independently of the event's unexpectedness.

To illustrate, in the first study (Reisenzein & Ritter, 1999, Experiment 1), the participants were surprised by a salient stimulus change while they solved addition problems that were presented on the computer screen. To influence the degree of mental interference caused by the stimulus changes, we varied cognitive load: participants were interrupted by the surprising event while they worked on a difficult addition problem (high mental load) or on an easy problem (low mental load). Immediately after the unexpected stimulus changes, they rated the intensity of felt surprise, as well as the degree of mental interruption caused by the event (the latter was measured with the question "How strongly did the change of the stimulus presentation 'throw you off the tracks' of the addition task?"). In line with expectations, mental interference—as indexed by these ratings as well as by objective performance measures—was stronger in the high load condition. Supporting the interference theory of surprise, self-rated surprise was also significantly more intense in the high load condition (effect size, $\eta^2 = .24$). Furthermore, the effect of mental load on surprise was largely eliminated if the presumed mediator, the feeling of interference, was statistically controlled for. This pattern of findings was replicated in three other experiments by Reisenzein and Ritter (1999) and in two experiments by Reisenzein (1999c), as well as in two studies by Schützwohl (1999b, Experiments 1 and 2) that used a different method to manipulate cognitive interference. Furthermore, Schützwohl (1999b, Study 3) found that the intensity of felt surprise in recalled everyday life surprise situations can be well predicted from simultaneous reports about experienced interference and attention capture.

Reisenzein and Ritter (1999, Experiment 4) showed that the mental load—surprise effect occurred even when the participants were engaged in a task (silently reading a text presented on the computer monitor) that had no salient overt motor components and where, as a consequence, mental interruption could not manifest itself in behavioral interference. This finding indicates that the mental load—surprise effect is *not* a behavioral self-perception effect (e.g., Bem, 1992; Laird & Bresler, 1972). Finally, Reisenzein and Ritter (1999, Experiment 2) provided evidence that the effect of unexpectedness on surprise intensity, demonstrated in the studies reviewed in the previous section, is partly mediated by interference.

Taken together, the studies reviewed in this section suggest that the intensity of felt surprise is not only influenced by the unexpectedness of the surprising event, but also by the degree of the event's interference with ongoing mental activity, and that the effect of unexpectedness on surprise is, in fact, partly mediated by mental interference. These findings speak against the hypothesis that the subjective experience of surprise is nothing but the awareness of unexpectedness (however construed). Rather, the findings favor the theory that the feeling of interference is one, although not the only, component of the experience of surprise. At the very least, the findings suggest that people infer the intensity of their felt surprise, in part, from the intensity of their feelings of interference (see Reisenzein & Ritter, 1999).

Surprise Experience and Facial Feedback

Another set of studies (Reisenzein, 1999c) addressed the question of whether feedback from facial expression influences the subjective experience of surprise. The hypothesis that facial feedback has an influence on emotional experience goes back to James (1950; see Reisenzein, Meyer, & Schützwohl, 1995) and has in recent years received some support for other emotions (for reviews, see, e.g., Adelmann & Zajonc, 1989; Laird & Bresler, 1992; Manstead, 1988). However, the facial feedback hypothesis has not so far been experimentally investigated for surprise (although suggestive evidence was obtained in a study by Duclos, Laird, Schneider, Sexter, Stern, & van Lighten, 1989) that manipulated the expression of fear). To fill this research lacuna, Reisenzein (1999c) conducted three studies in which the participants' facial displays were manipulated in unobtrusive ways (cf. Larsen, Kasimatis, & Frey, 1992; Strack, Martin & Stepper, 1988).

In the first facial feedback study (Reisenzein, 1999c, Experiment 1), the participants were asked, under the pretext of a study on the "effects of the size of the visual field on perception," to either "widen the visual field" or to "narrow the visual field" immediately before the appearance of the imperative stimulus in a choice reaction time task. Widening of the visual field was to be accomplished by a rapid, wide opening of the eyes, involving raising the eyebrows and the upper eyelids, whereas narrowing of the visual field was to be achieved by a contraction of the eyebrows (the correct movements, including opening of the mouth in the "widening" group, were demonstrated by the experimenter). The resultant facial expression of the participants in the "widening" group thus corresponded to the ideal-typical surprise display (Ekman & Friesen, 1975, 1978). A control group made no facial movements. In two critical trials, the participants were surprised by a salient change of the mode of stimulus presentation. The participants rated the intensity of felt surprise in both the critical trials and in two baseline trials. The manipulation of facial expression had no significant effect on either kind of ratings, suggesting that feedback from the surprise display (a) does not alone cause an experience of surprise (baseline trials), and (b) has no significant effect on the intensity of a surprise feeling that is induced by other means (critical trials) (see Manstead, 1988, for a discussion of different versions of the facial feedback hypothesis).

In a second study (Reisenzein, 1999c, Experiment 2), a facial expression akin to surprise was induced by an even less obtrusive manipulation. Participants were asked to solve addition problems that were presented in random sequence on either the lower or the upper of two monitors mounted on a rack atop each other. The switch of stimulus presentation from the lower to the upper monitor forced the participants to quickly look up, which induced raising of the eyebrows and upper eyelids (see Blurton Jones & Konner, 1971; Reisenzein & Bördgen, 1998). In addition, the participants were asked to pronounce, as part of their task, the letter *A*, which caused mouth-opening. Taken together, these movements again mimicked the typical facial surprise display. After a series of regular trials, the participants were surprised by a salient change of the stimulus presentation. For half of the participants, the surprising stimulus change occurred on the upper monitor (while they looked up), and for the other half, on the lower monitor (while they looked straight ahead). Analysis of video recordings of the participants' faces showed that this manipulation of facial expression was highly successful, in that nearly all participants in the experimental group showed one or more components of the surprise display, whereas only very few participants in the control group did so. However, the manipulation of facial displays had no significant effect on self-rated surprise. Comparable results were obtained in an improved replication of this study (Reisenzein, 2000, Experiment 3), in which the looking up, and hence the facial expression, was cued by the unexpected event itself, thereby mimicking the timing of naturally occurring surprise displays.

In sum, three experiments, using different nonobtrusive methods to manipulate the facial surprise display and involving altogether some 170 participants, consistently failed to support the facial feedback hypothesis for surprise. This suggests that facial feedback is of little if any practical significance for the subjective experience of surprise. This conclusion is further supported by evidence from other studies that suggests that even when subjective surprise intensity is high, spontaneous surprise displays occur only very rarely in some situations (from 10% to 30% in studies by Reisenzein & Bördgen, 1998; Reisenzein, 2000). If only 10–30% of the people who feel surprised by an event show a facial surprise display, the surprise experience of the remaining 70–90% must be based on other sources. The earlier reviewed evidence suggests that these other sources are centrally generated feelings.

☐ Functions of the Surprise Experience

I conclude with a brief reflection on the possible (evolutionary) functions of the subjective experience of surprise and the parallels between surprise and other emotional experiences. Emotional experience in general is typically ascribed two functions, an informational and a motivational one (e.g., Frijda, 1986; Schwarz & Clore, 1996; see McDougall, 1960). Analogous functions have been proposed for the experience of surprise by Meyer et al. (1994; see also Meyer et al., 1997; Stiensmeier-Pelster et al. 1995). According to these authors, the feeling of surprise serves to inform the conscious self about the occurrence of a schema-discrepancy and to provide an initial motivational impetus for the analysis of the schema-discrepancy by eliciting curiosity about its nature and causes. I believe now that this proposal can be shown to follow plausibly from (a) the previously made assumptions about the overarching function of the surprise mechanism (to monitor the person's schemas and help update them in the face of unexpectedness), plus the assumption that the subjective experience of surprise, like other components of the surprise reaction, subserves this goal; (b) the characteristic functional properties of conscious states in general; and (c) the specific information provided by the surprise feeling.

The most important functional property of conscious states is widely thought to be their system-wide accessibility and their being (thereby) poised for exerting global control (see Baars, 1988; Block, 1995; Chalmers, 1995). The information that the surprise feeling reliably provides (if the previously drawn conclusions are correct) concerns the occurrence and intensity of mental interruption and/or the occurrence and degree of a schema-discrepancy. Note that, on both counts, the formation provided by the surprise feeling can be said to be *metacognitive* in character—that is, it is information about, respectively, the person's cognitive processes or the status of his or her belief system (cf. Nelson, 1996). (Hence, on both counts, surprise can be called a "metacognitive" [Reisenzein & Ritter, 1999; see also Clore, 1992, 1994] or a "metarepresentational" [Reisenzein, 1999a] feeling). Taken together, these points suggest that the function of the surprise experience is to make this information globally available—presumably because this is a precondition for it to exercise global control (specifically, to influence goal-directed actions such as epistemic search). The present analysis suggests, therefore, that the proposed motivational function of the surprise experience rests on its informational function; that is, surprise elicits curiosity *because* it informs the conscious self about the occurrence of schema-discrepancies or of mental interrupts. Preliminary data tend to support both the informational and the motivational hypotheses (Harris, Kruithof, Meerum Terwogt, & Visser, 1981; Reisenzein, 1999d; Stiensmeier-Pelster et al., 1995). However, both hypotheses still await a stringent empirical test.

In the introduction to this chapter, I noted that surprise shares several salient features with prototypical emotions, such as anger or fear. Later, I pointed out that the principal theoretical options available for explaining the nature and causal generation of the surprise experience parallel those available for explaining other emotional experiences, and that most theories of the surprise experience have parallels in theories for other emotional feelings. Finally, I suggested that the experience of surprise serves both informational and motivational functions—functions that have also been proposed for other emotional feelings. All of this supports the suggestion, made in the introduction to this chapter, that the investigation of the subjective experience of surprise may provide insights into the nature, causal generation, and function of emotional feelings generally. However, it may be argued that the subjective experience of surprise nevertheless differs in crucial respects from that of other emotions because, in contrast to the latter, (a) it is hedonically neutral, and (b) the information that it provides is uniquely metarepresentational. Although I do not deny the first of these differences, I have argued (Reisenzein, 1998, 1999a, 1999b) that the feelings of pleasure and displeasure—which are frequently thought to make up the core of the subjective experience of other emotions—can, like the feeling of surprise, be regarded as the subjective experience of nonconceptual outcomes of a metarepresentational monitoring mechanism. That is, both surprise and pleasure-displeasure can be viewed as nonconceptual outcomes of a mechanism that compares newly acquired beliefs with preexisting mental representations. However, in surprise, newly acquired beliefs are compared with preexisting *beliefs*, whereas in pleasure and displeasure, they are related to preexisting *desires*: pleasure is felt if a newly acquired belief is congruent with a preexisting desire; displeasure, if it is incongruent. According to this view, the mechanisms underlying surprise and pleasure/displeasure evolved because they constitute a robust and effective method of monitoring, and (indirectly) of updating, the central action-controlling mental representations of humans—beliefs and desires. Inasmuch as the findings reviewed in this chapter support the character of surprise as a centrally generated, metacognitive feeling, they also lend support to this broader conception, specifically to the assumption that "mental feelings" lie at the heart of other emotions (see also Schwarz & Clore, 1996).

☐ Notes

[1]According to many authors, phenomenality characterizes only a subset of conscious mental states. Furthermore, some authors think that the second property of conscious states is more adequately described as immediate *accessibility* to awareness, rather than immediate occurrent awareness (see Block, 1995, 1997; Davies & Humphreys, 1993). Block (1995) also points out that phenomenal and access consciousness have frequently been confused (perhaps because the two usually occur together), with theories of the latter attempting to explain the former (see also Chalmers, 1995). Having warned of this danger, I will use the terms "conscious," "experiential," and "aware" largely synonymously in this chapter.

[2]Surprise can be easily and reliably induced in the laboratory with excellent control of its temporal onset and intensity; apart from subjective experience assessed by verbal report,

several objective indicators of surprise are available (e.g., interruption or delay of ongoing action, nonverbal expression), and ethical problems can be largely avoided.

[3]The terms "appraisal of [un]expectedness," "disconfirmation of a belief/expectancy," and "detection of a schema-discrepancy" are used synonymously in this chapter.

[4]Note that I do not intend to explain the general fact of consciousness—how it is possible that conscious states emerge in, ultimately, physical systems from their computational or neurophysiological substrates. These are problems for a general theory of consciousness rather than for the theory of the surprise experience. (At present, however, no satisfactory general theory of consciousness exists; see Block, 1995; Chalmers, 1995; Gadenne, 1997). The present explanatory goals are more modest: to explain the nature and causal generation of one specific conscious state, surprise, while taking the existence of conscious mental states in general for granted.

[5]I say the "primary form" of awareness because, as with other sensations, the person may, based on the interference feeling, form a propositional representation (a thought) to the effect that mental interruption occurred.

[6]Additional support stems from nonexperimental studies (Reisenzein & Hofmann, 1990, Study 2; Roseman et al., 1996; Stiensmeier-Pelster et al., 1995, Experiments 2, 4, 5).

☐ References

Adelmann, P. K., & Zajonc, R. B. (1989). Facial efference and the experience of emotion. *Annual Review of Psychology, 40*, 249–280.

Baars, B. J. (1988). *A cognitive theory of consciousness*. Cambridge, MA: Cambridge University Press.

Becher, E. (1916). Gefühlsbegriff and Lust-Unlustelemente [Concept of emotion and hedonic elements]. *Zeitschrift für Psychologie, 74*, 128–154.

Bem, D. J. (1972). Self-perception theory. In L. Berkowitz (Ed.), *Advances in experimental social psychology* (Vol. 6, pp. 2–62). New York: Academic Press.

Block, N. (1995). On a confusion about a function of consciousness. *Behavioral and Brain Sciences, 18*, 227–287.

Block, N. (1997). Biology versus computation in the study of consciousness. *Behavioral and Brain Sciences, 20*, 159–166.

Blurton Jones, N. G., & Konner, M. J. (1971). An experiment on eyebrow-raising and visual searching in children. *Journal of Child Psychology and Psychiatry, 11*, 233–240.

Chalmers, D. J. (1995). Facing up to the problem of consciousness. *Journal of Consciousness Studies, 3*, 200–219.

Charlesworth, W. R. (1969). The role of surprise in cognitive development. In D. Elkind & J. H. Flavell (Eds.), *Studies in cognitive development* (pp. 257–314). Oxford, England: Oxford University Press.

Clore, G. L. (1992). Cognitive phenomenology: Feelings and the construction of judgment. In L. L. Martin & A. Tesser (Eds.), *The construction of social judgments* (pp. 133–163). Hillsdale, NJ: Erlbaum.

Clore, G. L. (1994). Why emotions are felt. In P. Ekman & R. J. Davidson (Eds.), *The nature of emotion* (pp. 103–111). Oxford, England: Oxford University Press.

Darwin, C. (1965). *The expression of the emotions in man and animals*. Chicago, IL: University of Chicago Press. (Original work published 1872)

Davies, M., & Humphreys, G. W. (1993). Introduction. In M. Davies & G. W. Humphreys (Eds.), *Consciousness* (pp. 1–39). Oxford, England: Blackwell.

Desai, M. M. (1939). Surprise: A historical and experimental study. *British Journal of Psychology, Monograph Supplements* (Whole No. 22).

Duclos, S. E., Laird, J. D., Schneider, E., Sexter, M., Stern, L., & Van Lighten, O. (1989). Emotion-specific effects of facial expressions and postures on emotional experience. *Journal of Personality and Social Psychology, 57,* 100–108.

Ekman, P., & Friesen, W. V. (1975). *Unmasking the face.* Englewood Cliffs, NJ: Prentice-Hall.

Ekman, P., & Friesen, W. V. (1978). *Facial action coding system.* Palo Alto, CA: Consulting Psychologists Press.

Frijda, N. H. (1986). *The emotions.* Cambridge, England: Cambridge University Press.

Gadenne, V. (1997). Qualia ohne kausale Wirksamkeit [Causally inert qualia]. *Logos, 4,* 20–39.

Harris, P. L., Kruithof, A., Meerum Terwogt, M., & Visser, T. (1981). Children's detection and awareness of textual anomaly. *Journal of Experimental Child Psychology, 31,* 212–230.

Irons, D. (1897). The primary emotions. *Philosophical Review, 6,* 626–645.

Izard, C. E. (1977). *Human emotions.* New York: Plenum Press.

James, W. (1950). *Principles of psychology* (Volume 2). New York: Dover.

Laird, J. D., & Bresler, C. (1992). The process of emotional experience: A self-perception theory. In Clark, M. S. (Ed.), *Review of personality and social psychology* (Vol. 13, pp. 213–234). Beverly Hills, CA: Sage.

Larsen, R. J., Kasimatis, M., & Frey, K. (1992). Facilitating the furrowed brow: An unobtrusive test of the facial feedback hypothesis applied to unpleasant affect. *Cognition and Emotion, 6,* 321–338.

Mandler, G. (1984). *Mind and body.* New York: Norton.

Manstead, A. S. R. (1988). The role of facial movement in emotion. In H. L. Wagner (Ed.), *Social psychophysiology and emotion: Theory and clinical applications* (Vol. 3, pp. 105–129). Chichester, England: Wiley.

McDougall, W. (1960). *An introduction to social psychology.* London: Methuen. (Original work published 1908)

Mees, U. (1991). *Die Struktur der Emotionen* [The structure of emotions]. Göttingen, Germany: Hogrefe.

Meyer, W.-U., & Niepel, M. (1994). Surprise. In V. S. Ramachandran (Ed.), *Encyclopedia of human behavior* (Vol. 4, pp. 353–358). Orlando, FL: Academic Press.

Meyer, W.-U., Niepel, M., Rudolph, U., & Schützwohl, A. (1991). An experimental analysis of surprise. *Cognition and Emotion, 5,* 295–311.

Meyer, W.-U., Niepel, M., & Schützwohl, A. (1994). Überraschung und Attribution [Surprise and attribution]. In F. Försterling & J. Stiensmeier-Pelster (Eds.), *Attributionstheorie. Grundlagen und Anwendungen* (pp. 105–121). Göttingen, Germany: Hogrefe.

Meyer, W.-U., Reisenzein, R., & Schützwohl, A. (1995). *A model of processes elicited by surprising events.* Unpublished manuscript, University of Bielefeld.

Meyer, W.-U., Reisenzein, R., & Schützwohl, A. (1997). Towards a process analysis of emotions: The case of surprise. *Motivation and Emotion, 21,* 251–274.

Nagel, T. (1974). What is it like to be a bat? *Philosophical Review, 83,* 435–450.

Nelson, T. O. (1996). Consciousness and metacognition. *American Psychologist, 51,* 102–116.

Niepel, M. (1996). *Reaktionen auf unerwartete Ereignisse* [Reactions to unexpected events]. Unpublished dissertation, University of Bielefeld.

Oatley, K., & Johnson-Laird, P. N. (1987). Towards a cognitive theory of emotions. *Cognition and Emotion, 1,* 29–50.

Ortony, A., Clore, G. L., & Collins, A. (1988). *The cognitive structure of emotions.* New York: Cambridge University Press.

Plutchik, R. (1980). *Emotion. A psychoevolutionary synthesis.* New York: Harper & Row.

Reisenzein, R. (1992). A structuralist reconstruction of Wundt's three-dimensional theory of emotions. In H. Westmeyer (Ed.), *The structuralist program in psychology: Foundations and applications* (pp. 141–189). Toronto, Canada: Hogrefe & Huber:

Reisenzein, R. (1994). Kausalattribution und Emotion [Causal attribution and emotion]. In F. Försterling & J. Stiensmeier-Pelster (Eds.), *Attributionstheorie: Grundlagen und Anwendungen* (pp. 123–161). Göttingen, Germany: Hogrefe.

Reisenzein, R. (1998). Outlines of a theory of emotions as metarepresentational states of mind. In A. H. Fischer (Ed.), *ISRE '98. Proceedings of the 10th Conference of the International Society for Research on Emotions, 1998* (pp. 186–191). Amsterdam: Faculty of Psychology.

Reisenzein, R. (1999a). *A theory of emotions as metarepresentational states of mind.* Manuscript under review.

Reisenzein, R. (1999b). Appraisal processes conceptualized from a schema-theoretic perspective: Contributions to a process analysis of emotions. In K. R. Scherer, A. Schorr, & T. Johnstone (Eds.), *Appraisal processes in emotion: Theory, methods, research.* Oxford, England: Oxford University Press.

Reisenzein, R. (1999c). *On the expression and experience of surprise: Evidence for a "reverse" self-perception effect.* Paper presented at the 8th European Conference on Facial Expression—Measurement and Meaning, Saarbrücken, Germany, September 27–30.

Reisenzein, R. (2000). Exploring the strength of association between the components of emotion syndromes: The case of surprise. *Cognition and Emotion, 14,* 1–38.

Reisenzein, R., & Bördgen, S. (1998). *Evidence for strong dissociation between emotion and facial displays: The case of surprise.* Unpublished manuscript, University of Bielefeld.

Reisenzein, R., & Hofmann, T. (1990). An investigation of dimensions of cognitive appraisal in emotion using the repertory grid technique. *Motivation and Emotion, 14,* 1–26.

Reisenzein, R., Meyer, W.-U., & Schützwohl, A. (1995). James and the physical basis of emotion: A comment on Ellsworth. *Psychological Review, 102,* 757–761.

Reisenzein, R., Meyer, W.-U., & Schützwohl, A. (1996). Reactions to surprising events: A paradigm for emotion research. In N. Frijda (Ed.), *Proceedings of the 9th Conference of the International Society for Research on Emotions* (pp. 292–296). Toronto, Canada: ISRE.

Reisenzein, R., Meyer, W.-U., & Schützwohl, A. (1997). Analyse von Reaktionen auf überraschende Ereignisse: Ein Paradigma für die Emotionsforschung [Analysis of reactions to surprising events: A paradigm for emotion research]. In H. Mandl (Hrsg.) *Bericht über den 40. Kongreß der DGPs in München 1996* (pp. 830–836). Göttigen, Germany: Hogrefe.

Reisenzein, R., & Ritter, D. (1999). *Surprise: A "metacognitive feeling."* Manuscript under review.

Reisenzein, R., & Spielhofer, C. (1994). Subjectively salient dimensions of emotional appraisal. *Motivation and Emotion, 18,* 1–47.

Ribot, T. A. (1896). *La psychologie des sentiments* [The psychology of emotions]. Paris: Alcan.

Roseman, I. J., Antoniou, A. A., & Jose, P. E. (1996). Appraisal determinants of emotions: Constructing a more accurate and comprehensive theory. *Cognition and Emotion, 10,* 241–277.

Rosenthal, D. M. (1986). Two concepts of consciousness. *Philosophical Studies, 9,* 329–359.

Rosenthal, D. M. (1993). Thinking that one thinks. In M. Davies & G. W. Humphreys (Eds.), *Consciousness* (pp. 197–223). Oxford, England: Blackwell.

Ruffman, T., & Keenan, T. R. (1996). The belief-based emotion of surprise: The case for a lag in understanding relative to false belief. *Developmental Psychology, 32,* 40–49.

Schützwohl, A. (1998). Surprise and schema strength. *Journal of Experimental Psychology: Learning, Memory, and Cognition, 24,* 1182–1199.

Schützwohl, A. (1999a). *Surprise: A psychoevolutionary paradigm for emotion research.* Unpublished Habilitation, University of Bielefeld.

Schützwohl, A. (1999b). *The structure of the intensity of surprise.* Unpublished manuscript, University of Bielefeld.

Schützwohl, A., & Reisenzein, R. (1999). Children's and adult's reactions to a schema-discrepant event: A developmental analysis of surprise. *International Journal for Behavioral Development, 23,* 37–62.

Schwarz, N., & Clore, G. L. (1996). Feelings and phenomenal experiences. In E. T. Higgins & A. W. Kruglanski (Eds.), *Social Psychology: Handbook of basic principles* (pp. 433–465). New York: Guilford Press.

Shand, A. F. (1920). *The foundations of character.* London: Macmillan. (Original work published 1914)

Smedslund, J. (1990). Psychology and psychologic: Characterization of the difference. In K. J. Gergen & G. R. Semin (Eds.), *Everyday understanding: Social and scientific implications* (Vol. 29, pp. 45–63). London: Sage.

Smith, A. (1980). The principles which lead and direct philosophical enquiries, illustrated by the history of astronomy. In W. P. D. Wightman & J. C. Bryce (Eds.), *The Glasgow edition of the works and correspondence of Adam Smith: Vol. 3. Essays on philosophical subjects* (pp. 33–105). Oxford, England: Clarendon Press. (Original work published 1795)

Smith, D. W. (1989). *The circle of acquaintance. Perception, consciousness, and empathy.* Dordrecht, the Netherlands: Kluwer.

Stanley, H. M. (1895). *Studies in the evolutionary psychology of feeling.* London: Sonnenschein.

Stiensmeier-Pelster, J., Martini, A., & Reisenzein, R. (1995). The role of surprise in the attribution process. *Cognition and Emotion, 9,* 5–31.

Strack, F., Martin, L. L., & Stepper, S. (1988). Inhibiting and facilitating conditions of the human smile: A nonobtrusive test of the facial feedback hypothesis. *Journal of Personality and Social Psychology, 54,* 768–777.

Tomkins, S. S. (1962). *Affect, imagery, consciousness: Vol. I. The positive affects.* (Volumes 1 & 2). New York: Springer.

Wundt, W. (1911). *Grundzüge der physiologischen Psychologie* [Outlines of physiological psychology] (Vol. 3). Leipzig, Germany: Engelmann.

Wundt, W. (1922). *Vorlesungen über die Menschen- und Tierseele* [Lectures on the mind of man and animals]. Leipzig, Germany: Voss.

SUBJECTIVE EXPERIENCE, STEREOTYPING, AND INTERGROUP BEHAVIOR

Galen V. Bodenhausen
Kristen N. Moreno

How Do I Feel About Them?
The Role of Affective Reactions
in Intergroup Perception

When we think about and interact with members of different social groups, we are likely to experience both intellectual and emotional reactions. In recent years, an explosion of research on the topic of stereotyping has examined the cognitive dynamics of our intellectual, belief-based reactions to social groups (for recent reviews, see Fiske, 1998; Macrae & Bodenhausen, in press). In contrast, relatively less attention has been directed at the nature of affective intergroup reactions, or to the interplay between perceivers' cognitive and affective reactions. As the other chapters in this volume attest, it has become increasingly evident in recent years that an understanding of the nature of social judgment and behavior requires us to look beyond consciously articulated intellectual beliefs to the subjective states that form the context for thought and action. Affective reactions constitute perhaps the most pervasive and important class of subjective experiences. As important as stereotypes may be in shaping the nature of intergroup perception and behavior, it is the feeling states that arise in the presence of members of stereotyped groups that provide the background tone for all intergroup interactions. Understanding the role played by these subjective states is no longer an issue that can be

---

Address correspondence to Galen V. Bodenhausen, Department of Psychology, Northwestern University, 2029 Sheridan Road, Evanston, IL 60208-2710. E-mail: galen@nwu.edu

kept on the back burner. No theory can hope to provide a realistic, complete conceptualization of intergroup relations without giving prominent attention to the way we *feel* about the members of other groups.

Of course, the nature of the relationship between feeling and thinking has been a matter of enduring interest to philosophers and psychologists. The issue is complex, and there is good reason to assume that the affect-cognition interface involves flexible interactions between two intimately connected but dissociable systems (see Zajonc, 1998, for a review). For instance, affective reactions may result from cognitive appraisals (e.g., Ortony, Clore, & Collins, 1988) or expectations (e.g., Wilson, Lisle, Kraft, & Wetzel, 1989). Alternatively, affective reactions may give rise to cognitive processes that seek to generate post hoc explanations or rationalizations for these reactions (e.g., Bem, 1972; James, 1884). Of course, it may also be the case that affective and cognitive reactions proceed relatively independently (e.g., Zajonc, Pietromonaco, & Bargh, 1982). Each of these possibilities is interesting in its own right, and consideration of the full range of affect-cognition relationships at play in intergroup contexts would undoubtedly shed considerable light on the nature of intergroup relations. However, in the present chapter, we will focus our attention specifically on the question of how the affective reactions that we experience in the real or imagined presence of outgroup members can come to influence our subsequent intergroup judgments and behaviors.

☐ Affect as Information

Most of the judgments and choices that people face must be made under conditions of some uncertainty or ambiguity. In figuring out how to respond, affective reactions often guide the way. This position has been advocated by Damasio (1994) on the basis of compelling evidence from brain-damaged patients. Looking specifically at patients with perturbations to the neuroanatomical structures responsible for emotional responding (but with intact general intellectual capacities), Damasio found a curious pattern of psychological paralysis. When confronted with a behavioral choice, these individuals were well aware of the various options available to them, yet they seem to be unable to select from among these options. They seem to lack an internal compass that could orient and direct their choice behavior. One of Damasio's cases ("Elliott") epitomizes this rudderless state of being. For medical reasons, a portion of Elliott's brain was surgically removed. As a consequence, he lost the ability to feel emotions, although his IQ, memory, and reasoning skills were unaffected. When shown horrible, grisly pictures, Elliott would describe them as "disgusting," but he would show no physiological evidence of having any emotional reaction. He had an intellectual understanding of emotional states, but he simply no longer had subjective emotional experiences. Despite his high level of intellectual functioning, he became unable to hold a job or function in even a remotely adaptive manner in daily life. The root of his postsurgical problems lies in the fact that he can no longer prioritize or choose among various courses of action, because none of them *feels* better or preferable to the others. On the basis of patients such as Elliott, Damasio (1994) proposed his somatic marker hypothesis, which asserts that subjective feelings play a central role in guiding judgment and choice because they imbue response options with relative value.

The somatic marker hypothesis accords nicely with an extensive program of research conducted by Schwarz, Clore, and colleagues dealing with the informational and directive functions of affective states (e.g., Clore & Parrott, 1991; Schwarz, 1987, 1990; Schwarz & Clore, 1983, 1988). According to this approach, subjective mood states serve as simple judgmental heuristics that can bias evaluative reactions under conditions of uncertainty. Essentially, the affective state serves as a "gut reaction" that informs the person who is experiencing it about his or her evaluative tendencies with respect to an object of judgment. This notion was incorporated into Forgas's (1995) affect infusion model under the rubric of "heuristic strategies." Consistent with the notion of somatic markers, a simple "how-do-I-feel-about-it?" heuristic can be used to inform and direct reactions to external stimuli, but such a heuristic appears to be employed only when perceivers assume that their affective state is indeed a reaction to the to-be-judged stimulus (e.g., Schwarz & Clore, 1983). Much of the research conducted by Schwarz and colleagues has focused on situations in which people mistakenly assume that their affective states actually do represent a reaction to the current object of judgment, when in fact they are based on events from an unrelated prior context. Thus, Schwarz and Clore's affect-as-information model goes beyond the somatic marker hypothesis in postulating the importance of attributional processes in linking feelings to responses. A key insight of their research lies in the recognition that people's ability to monitor the sources of their subjective emotional reactions is far from perfect. Consequently, their use of affective heuristics can result in judgmental biases rather than in simply providing a straightforward, functional prioritization of alternative courses of judgment and action.

When consulting our "gut reactions," it is thus possible that we may accurately detect subjective states that are arising in response to the object of judgment, or we may mistakenly attribute affect arising from unrelated sources to the judgment target. In the context of intergroup relations, Bodenhausen (1993) referred to the former case as "integral affect"—that is, affective reactions to the outgroup itself. Reliance on integral affect would, in principle, represent a legitimate use of the "how-do-I-feel-about-it?" heuristic. In contrast, the term *incidental affect* was proposed to refer to mood carryover effects arising from misattribution (and hence misapplication of the affective heuristic). Whereas a fairly substantial number of studies have examined the effects of incidental affect on intergroup judgments (e.g., chapter 18 by Abele in this volume, plus Abele, Gendolla, & Petzold, 1998; Bless, Schwarz, & Wieland, 1996; Bodenhausen, Kramer, & Süsser, 1994; Bodenhausen, Sheppard, & Kramer, 1994; Forgas & Moylan, 1991; Stroessner, Hamilton, & Mackie, 1992), relatively less work has directly examined the impact of integral affect.[1] In the remainder of this chapter, we will endeavor to review the available literature addressing this question, in particular when integral affective reactions are or are not likely to infuse judgments of outgroups.

For most social outgroups, and certainly for all stigmatized outgroups, the integral affect they most commonly elicit is negative, and we will restrict our attention to such cases. However, the subjective feelings triggered by these groups need not be outright hostility, hatred, irritation, or disgust, but can instead take the form of more subtle feelings, such as discomfort, anxiousness, and vague aversion (see Dijker, 1987; Gaertner & Dovidio, 1986; Stephan & Stephan, 1985). If any of these subjective feelings are used as an affective heuristic, then assimilation biases would be expected. That is, people who experience these feelings will tend to formulate negative evaluations if they indeed attribute their negative "gut feelings" to a particular group member who is being judged. Of course, affective states can sometimes elicit contrast effects, in which stimuli that deviate substantially from the tone of one's prevailing affective state are judged more extremely in the direction opposite of this affect (e.g., Geers & Lassiter, 1999). This kind of contrast effect is not based on the use of a "how-do-I-feel-about-it?" heuristic; instead, it involves very distinct cognitive processes that are beyond the scope of the current discussion (see Schwarz & Bless, 1992, for a comprehensive overview of the determinants and mechanisms involved in such contrast effects). When individual group members do not deviate in a markedly positive manner from a priori expectations about the group, assimilation biases are expected to prevail. Our focus will be on the question of how and when such assimilation biases are likely to be expressed versus controlled by the social perceiver.

☐ The Historical Context of Intergroup Affect and Cognition

Unlike many domains in which the interplay of affect and cognition has been empirically scrutinized, an understanding of this relationship in the domain of intergroup relations clearly requires an understanding of the social and historical context within which contemporary intergroup behavior unfolds. This context has changed dramatically over the twentieth century, and the research evidence clearly reflects this transformation. A number of early investigations examined the extent to which affective and cognitive reactions to outgroups form an internally consistent pattern (i.e., is there evaluative consistency in the way we think and feel about various social groups?). This issue was examined in great depth by Donald Campbell (1947) in his dissertation research. The primary conclusion of his investigation was that the various dimensions or facets of intergroup reactions (including affective and cognitive ones) covary strongly and form the basis for a unified, coherent attitude toward the outgroup. Horowitz (1936) drew similar conclusions, and further found that the degree of coherence across the different response dimensions increased with age. This work indicates that earlier in the century, people tended to develop internally consistent patterns of thoughts, feelings, and behavior with respect to various social groups. As such, one's valenced affective reaction would constitute a rapid and generally valid guide toward responses that are consistent with one's more intellectually articulated beliefs and assessments. In other words, chronic integral affect would indeed serve as reliable information about one's more general reactions to an outgroup.

In more recent research, some evidence suggests that people continue to be likely to rely on affective reactions to a considerable extent in forming their judgments about social groups (Dijker, 1987; Eagly, Mladinic, & Otto, 1994; Haddock, Zanna, & Esses, 1993; Jackson, Hodge, Gerard, Ingram, Ervin, & Sheppard, 1996; Jussim, Nelson, Manis, & Soffin, 1995; Stangor, Sullivan, & Ford, 1991; Verkuyten, 1997). Most of this research suggests that affect plays a larger role in predicting intergroup attitudes and judgments than does cognition. For example, Jussim et al. (1995) found that affective reactions to the category "child abusers" predicted judgments about particular child abusers better than intellectual beliefs or stereotypes about this group did. Haddock et al. (1993) reported evidence suggesting that stereotypes about gays and lesbians did not predict attitudes toward those groups at all, whereas affect consistently did predict intergroup attitudes.[2] Although confirming that integral affect can be an important determinant of intergroup attitudes and judgments, research of this sort suggests that in the latter part of the twentieth century, the different facets of reactions to outgroups have become dissociated. No longer do the beliefs and feelings people have about social groups seem to form a consistent and coherent package. Intellectual and affective reactions seem to have diverged to a substantial extent. Thus, reliance on a simple affective heuristic can potentially lead to reactions that are at odds with one's more intellectually derived stance toward an outgroup.

This state of affairs was presaged by Myrdal (1944), in his classic analysis of race relations in the United States. He noted the fundamental inconsistency between the negative feelings many European Americans have learned to hold toward African Americans and their professed endorsement of egalitarian values (which, in previous generations, tended not to be seen as relevant with respect to many ethnic minority groups). With the rise of the civil rights movement, this tension was thrown into sharp relief in the consciousness of the general public. As documented in extensive detail by Schuman, Steeh, Bobo, and Krysan (1997), endorsement of egalitarian values (specifically with respect to African Americans) among European Americans climbed steeply across recent decades, with pro-egalitarian values being expressed by an overwhelming majority of contemporary respondents. However, there is good reason to doubt that the rise in egalitarianism has been accompanied by a parallel decline in the negative affect elicited by historically stigmatized social groups (e.g., Gaertner & Dovidio, 1986; Katz, Wackenhut, & Hass, 1986). In fact, some theorists have assumed that internalization of negative reactions to stigmatized minority groups such as African Americans and gays are an inevitable consequence of socialization in historically prejudiced cultures. From this perspective, automatic negative reactions in the presence of members of these groups are simply unavoidable (e.g., Bargh, 1999; Devine, 1989).

The tension between these negative reactions and genuinely held egalitarian views has inspired several theoretical models of contemporary intergroup attitudes (e.g., Katz et al., 1986; McConahay, 1983). Gaertner and Dovidio's (1986) theory of aversive racism is especially relevant to the question of how and when negative integral affect will be used to guide reactions to stigmatized groups. In the domain of racial attitudes, the theory posits that culturally conditioned anti-Black affect predisposes people to negative, discriminatory reactions to African Americans. However, the simultaneous existence of egalitarian values (within the same individuals) creates pressures to avoid expressing these negative reactions. Consequently, anti-Black affect tends to find expression in outward behavior only when normative constraints are low and (apparently) nonracial justifications for the negative reaction can be found. Theorizing of this sort makes it clear that the use of affective heuristics in judging outgroup members is anything but straightforward in the contemporary societal climate. "How do I feel about them?" becomes a tricky question to ask oneself, because an accurate assessment of the subjective feelings engendered by a stigmatized outgroup may well yield unpalatable results.

☐ Affect as Inadmissible Information

Although negative affective reactions to minority groups may linger in the modern psyche, there can be no doubt that overt expression of these reactions has become taboo. There are two major sources of motivation to avoid giving voice to negative integral affect: personal and social (e.g., Bodenhausen & Macrae, 1998; Plant & Devine, 1998). The social norms of contemporary society clearly proscribe the overt expression of prejudice, and to the extent that such norms are internalized within the individual, personal standards also act to discourage such expression. Thus, whereas in bygone eras people tended to hold evaluatively coherent attitudes toward social groups and could rely on affective heuristics to provide easily accessible information to guide their responses, in the modern era, thoughts, values, and feelings about outgroups have diverged.

In essence, members of contemporary society are reluctant to express negative reactions to minorities because of the risk of attributions of prejudice. To be labeled a bigot has itself become a stigma of considerable potency. Dutton and Lake (1973) showed that people are likely to feign positive reactions to minority targets, overcompensating to the point of reverse discrimination, in order to ward off the appearance of prejudice (see also Devine, Evett, & Vasquez-Suson, 1996; Ickes, 1984). Moreover, individuals who genuinely endorse egalitarian beliefs and aspire to be free of prejudice are likely to work to avoid the aversive experience of reacting in a negative manner to relevant minority groups (Devine, Monteith, Zuwerink, & Elliot, 1991). For such individuals, negative integral affect will not only tend *not* to be used as a basis for responding to minority group members, it will also elicit further affective reactions of guilt and self-criticism, which in turn will produce motivation to reduce negative reactions to the group in question (Monteith, 1993; Swim & Miller, 1999). Thus, normative and/or personal standards are likely to motivate people to find strategies for avoiding reliance on their socially conditioned negative feelings toward stigmatized and negatively stereotyped social groups. Integral affect, in such cases, has become "inadmissible information."

Strategies for Avoiding Unwanted Affective Influences

There are two principal options available in attempting to mute the influence of negative integral affect on judgments and behavior. Perhaps the most ambitious option is to attempt to avoid being influenced in the first place. By actively suppressing the "inadmissible" group-based feelings that one may have toward minority groups, and instead focusing only on the "admissible" bases for judgment (e.g., concrete, individuating information), it may be possible to formulate overt responses that are free from the taint of unwanted integral affect. Alternatively, if unwanted biases nevertheless creep into one's deliberations, then correction strategies become a second line of defense. Such strategies involve making conscious adjustments to one's reactions in a manner designed to offset the biasing factors that have exerted unwanted influences. In this section, we will summarize the psychological processes that are entailed in these strategies, and in the next section, we will review some of the problems and pitfalls that are likely to arise when these strategies are pursued.

In recent years, there have been major advances in our understanding of the nature of mental control (for reviews, see Wegner & Bargh, 1998; Wegner & Pennebaker, 1993). Much of this work has examined the controllability of unwanted *thoughts*. Our focus here, however, is on the control of unwanted *subjective feelings*. A common view of emotional reactions is that they happen automatically and unavoidably in the presence of evoking stimuli, and to the extent that intentional control enters the picture, it is in the form of trying to turn the emotional reaction off again (e.g., Hansen & Hansen, 1994; Öhman, 1993). As Wegner and Bargh (1998) note, however, this is only part of the story. There is good reason to believe that individuals sometimes seek to intentionally initiate certain types of emotional experiences, rather than simply letting emotions arise spontaneously. Perhaps the most obvious and common form of this activity is trying to be happy (e.g., Goleman, 1995; Klinger, 1982; Thayer, 1996). Of course, the impulse to pursue this kind of controlled evocation of positive affect is likely to arise when one is feeling other, less desirable states (e.g., boredom, anxiety, melancholy) on a more spontaneous basis. An analogous situation arises in the context of unwanted integral affect. If we notice that we are feeling negative reactions (anxiety, discomfort, aversion) in the presence of an outgroup member and we feel that such reactions are inappropriate, we may actively seek to cultivate a positive reaction to replace the original feelings. This kind of situation constitutes *emotional correction*, and it may bear many similarities to other forms of judgmental correction that have been studied in recent years. The nature and prerequisites for such correction activity will be discussed in further detail below, but for the moment, we will turn our attention to the question of controlled stopping of integral affect.

There is good reason to believe that people attempt to stop a range of unwanted negative emotions, including anger, anxiety, and sadness (e.g., Barlow, 1991; Salovey, Hsee, & Mayer, 1993; Tice & Baumeister, 1993). Psychotherapists spend hours with clients attempting to teach them effective strategies for stopping these unwanted feelings, suggesting that it is not a simple matter to "turn off" unpleasant subjective states. Although there may in fact be effective ways to manage these states (for reviews, see Goleman, 1995; Thayer, 1996), the simplest and perhaps most common strategy is *emotion suppression*. In the case of intergroup behavior, this means attempting to turn off integral affect and focus instead on strictly intellectual bases (presumably including egalitarian values) for forming reactions to the outgroup. Unfortunately, there is ample reason to worry about the effectiveness of this strategy. Specifically, even if they are effective in the short term, suppression strategies often provoke subsequent intensification of the unwanted feeling state (e.g., Foa & Kozak, 1986; Wegner, Erber, & Zanakos, 1993). Thus, trying not to feel disgust or discomfort in the presence of an outgroup member may ultimately result in even greater negative integral affect.

Wegner (1994) presented a comprehensive model of mental control that accounts for the psychological processes involved in mental self-regulation. The key components of the model can be described quite concisely. As with any control process, at least two components are necessary for emotional self-regulation (Miller, Galanter, & Pribram, 1960). First, the person must be able to determine whether or not the unwanted mental state exists or is arising. This task requires a monitoring process that scans the consciousness, looking for signs, in the present case, of unwanted integral affect. Second, there must be a process that can get rid of the unwanted state, should it be detected. This operating process most typically attempts to replace an unwanted state with any suitable distractor. For example, the person may attempt to stop feeling aversion in the presence of a member of a stigmatized group, instead seeking to focus on mundane details of the interaction setting or some other nonproblematic stimulus. If both processes are in good working order, emotional control can be accomplished (e.g., Wegner & Gold, 1995).

Should the perceiver be unable to prevent the automatic activation of unwanted integral affect, he or she still has the option of attempting to engage in correction strategies. As previously noted, emotional correction refers to a strategy in which the perceiver attempts to replace negative integral affect with consciously cultivated positive feelings. Alternatively, the person might attempt to make corrections only in the public manifestations of their reactions. Judgmental correction, in this context, occurs when the person attempts to correct responses in order to remove the presumed impact of unwanted integral affect. A good deal of research attention has focused on this sort of correction process recently (Strack, 1992; Wegener & Petty, 1997; Wilson & Brekke, 1994). Correction most commonly involves inferring the direction and extent of the unwanted bias and then adjusting one's judgments in the opposite direction (e.g., Wegener & Petty, 1997). In the present context, this means that the perceiver must gauge how much he or she has been influenced by negative subjective feelings about the target group and make corresponding positive adjustments to judgments and behavioral reactions. When this process is operative, people are quite able to avoid unwanted negative biases. Unfortunately, there is often a calibration problem involved in making corrections, because it is typically difficult to accurately infer exactly how much one has been biased by an unwanted factor. As a result, people often seem to overcorrect for their biases, producing contrast effects in the situation of current focal interest. That is, because people assume that their group-based reactions are negative and will lead to assimilative biases, their corrections often lead to hyperpositive judgments of individual group members (e.g., Dutton & Lake, 1977). Isbell and Wyer (1999) report one example of this phenomenon in the domain of mood influences. Under conditions in which participants were motivated to correct for affective biases in their judgments of a politician, they tended to overcompensate for presumed mood congruency biases, resulting in contrast effects. Although such judgments cannot be said to be free from bias, they are at least free from the specifically unwanted form of bias—in the focal context, negative reactions to minority groups. Thus, both suppression and correction strategies can be effective tools for avoiding the impact of integral affect in intergroup settings. However, they are far from foolproof devices, as we will see in the next section.

Problems in Stifling Integral Affect

To succeed in the suppression or correction of unwanted integral affect, several preconditions must be met (cf. Bodenhausen, Macrae, & Garst, 1998; Strack & Hannover, 1996; Wegener & Petty, 1997; Wegner, 1994; Wilson & Brekke, 1994). First, the perceiver must be aware that the subjective reaction is occurring and may be having an unwanted influence. This requirement may seem trivial, but there is one major impediment to its satisfaction: people often do not want to acknowledge (even to themselves) that they have prejudiced reactions to other groups. Thus, psychological defenses and self-deceptive strategies may be employed to keep negative integral affect out of focal awareness. Second, there must be motivation to do the mental work involved in suppression or correction. Although we have argued that in contemporary society, most people feel some pressure (whether self-imposed or socially imposed) to avoid prejudiced reactions, not everyone feels such pressures consistently, and hence not everyone will be consistently motivated to control negative integral affect. Third, because controlling/stopping and correcting for emotional reactions are effortful processes, they require some free attentional resources (Martin, Seta, & Crelia, 1990; Wegner, 1994). If attention is substantially constrained (e.g., by distraction, mental busyness, time pressure, etc.), then suppression and correction activities may fail. In this section, we will examine the impact of these requirements on successful affective self-regulation in intergroup contexts.

Awareness

Without knowing that one's subjective feelings are intruding on inter-group perceptions and judgments, one would of course never be aware of the need to suppress or correct for their influence (cf. Stapel, Martin, & Schwarz, 1998). Surely, one would think, it would not be hard to notice the subjective feelings that arise in the presence of various minority groups and to gauge whether they are appropriate or instead should be controlled and eliminated. And yet it may be quite threatening to one's self-concept to acknowledge the existence of socially taboo feelings. This idea is at the heart of Gaertner and Dovidio's (1986) theory of aversive racism. As previously noted, the theory posits that due to their socialization in a historically racist society, most people do possess conditioned negative feelings toward African Americans (and, by extension, other culturally stigmatized groups). However, they also genuinely endorse egalitarian standards, and they do not define themselves as prejudiced (an attribution that is highly aversive). As a result, they tend to seek ways of rationalizing their negative feelings away, viewing them as a reaction to strictly nonracial factors. In this way, their negative feelings find expression without threatening their egalitarian self-concepts. Without being aware of prejudiced feelings and their impact, they do not correct for them.

In a series of helping studies, for example, it was found that when there was no ready situational justification for failing to help a person in need, White participants helped African American and European American "victims" to a similar degree. However, when a situational justification was present (e.g., the presence of other bystanders who might intervene), helping rates declined markedly more for Black than for White victims (Gaertner & Dovidio, 1986). These results suggest that anti-Black affect produced a substantial disinclination to help, but only when it was not recognized as negative integral affect because it had been rationalized as arising from some legitimate (i.e., nonracist) factor. When no nonracial justification factor was present, participants clearly corrected (or even overcorrected) for the impact of anti-Black feelings, often helping Black victims to a greater degree than White ones.

Analogous results were reported by Moreno and Bodenhausen (1999) in a quite different domain. In this study, participants were prescreened to determine their level of antigay affect (on the basis of a questionnaire assessing their feelings and emotions with respect to gay men and lesbians). In addition, their commitment to egalitarian principles in the specific context of gay rights was assessed. Although all respondents in the study indicated strong endorsement of egalitarian principles, there was substantial variation in the degree of antigay affect that they expressed. Thus, some participants displayed a consistent pattern of low prejudice (i.e., high egalitarian values and low antigay affect), while others showed the aversive prejudice pattern (i.e., high egalitarian values but also high antigay affect). All participants read an essay advocating gay rights, consistent with their professed egalitarian standards. Of interest was the question of whether antigay feelings might be associated with resistance to this essay, particularly when the resistance could be misattributed to something other than negative integral affect. To manipulate the availability of a misattribution cue, half of the participants read an essay that was written in normal, grammatical English, while the others read the same arguments, peppered with spelling and grammar errors. Reactions to the essay and the essayist were assessed. Consistent with expectations, low prejudice participants were uniformly positive in their reactions, regardless of the presence or absence of spelling errors. Participants who were high in antigay affect had similarly positive reactions to the grammatical version of the essay. However, they derogated the essay and its author significantly when spelling and grammar errors were present. Thus, their negative integral affect was held in check when there was no obvious way of justifying a negative reaction, but when such a justification was introduced, the negative feelings did seem to infuse their judgments in an unchecked manner.

Results such as these suggest that awareness of the existence and influence of negative integral affect is not a given. Sensitivity to the possibility of such bias is likely to vary across persons and across target groups. Even when such sensitivity is present, potent forces of self-deception may lead people not to acknowledge that the bias is occurring in their own reactions. Without awareness and acknowledgment of the problem, no controlled processes will be instigated to correct for it.

Motivation

If the general cultural climate has changed over the century into a milieu in which prejudice is considered a cardinal vice, there is still a range of variation in how the motivation to avoid negative reactions to minority groups is manifested. Plant and Devine (1998) proposed a 2 × 2 typology of such motivational variation. In their model, people can be either high or low in external (normative) motivation to control prejudice, and they can be either high or low in internal (personal) motivation to control prejudice. In their research, they observed each of the four possible combinations of these two motivational orientations. Persons who experience neither significant external nor internal motivation to control prejudice are of course unlikely to attempt to suppress or correct for the influence of negative integral affect. However, to the extent that either (or both) of the orientations is present, then a primary prerequisite for controlled attempts to eliminate the impact of negative intergroup feelings (i.e., motivation) is met. Persons who are high in external motivation but low in internal motivation are likely to be concerned only with overt correction (i.e., adjustment of public responses), but not with the suppression of private, subjective reactions. Persons who are high in internal motivation but low in external motivation are likely to be primarily concerned with changing their private reactions; hence, the strategies of suppression and emotional correction will be more likely to appeal to them. Finally, persons who are high in both types of motivation will likely be quite concerned with both self-criticism and social criticism in response to negative integral affect, so they will seek strategies that prevent both private and public expression of negative intergroup feelings.

Consistency of motivation turns out to be a major factor in the success of attempts at mental control. For example, when the motivation to avoid stereotypic thoughts is only pursued in a transitory manner, rebound effects tend to occur in which the unwanted thoughts become even more prominent in consciousness (Macrae, Bodenhausen, Milne, & Jetten, 1994). This rebound occurs due to an ironic feature of mental control. Specifically, in order to avoid a particular mental state, the perceiver must keep some representation of that state active, even if only at low levels of awareness, so that the monitoring process can know what it is looking for and hence can determine whether the intervention of the operating process is necessary. Thus, the monitoring process itself tends to repeatedly activate the unwanted thought. When motivation for mental control is present, the operating process can successfully counter this activation. However, because the operating process is assumed to be effortful (Wegner, 1994), *consistent* motivation is needed to keep the unwanted reaction out of consciousness; otherwise, the repeated, automatic priming of the unwanted reaction by the monitoring process will result in its "hyperaccessibility" (Wegner & Erber, 1992). Low-prejudice persons who are high in internal motivation to control prejudice may well possess the consistency of motivation that is necessary to avoid the risk of rebound effects (Monteith, Spicer, & Toomen, 1998). However, persons who are low in internal motivation but high in external motivation to control prejudice represent a different case. These persons may be momentarily motivated to suppress or correct for their negative feelings about outgroups, so long as there is some external normative pressure in place, but once the pressure abates, their control motivation is likely to lapse (cf. Kelman, 1958). Such lapses in motivation have been repeatedly tied to rebound effects (Macrae, Bodenhausen, & Milne, 1998; Macrae et al., 1994; see Bodenhausen, Macrae, & Milne, 1998, for a review).

External pressures for the control of one's negative reactions to other groups, in addition to being associated with inconsistency in motivational commitment, give rise to additional sources of concern. First, it is well known that external constraints on the freedom of thought and action are aversive and often give rise to psychological reactance (Brehm, 1966). People experiencing reactance commonly seek to reassert their autonomy by doing (or thinking, or feeling) exactly that which has been forbidden. This kind of dynamic might explain the appeal of "shock jocks" who intentionally invoke taboo prejudices in defiance of prevailing pressures for "political correctness." Without an internalization of the motivation to control prejudice, resentment of external pressures for control may lead people to indulge their negative integral affect (Devine, 1999). Alternatively, they may seek ways to express these feelings while camouflaging their basis in socially unacceptable prejudices. For these reasons, external motivation to control prejudice is likely to be associated with limited, temporary suppression or correction activity (or both), or even with motivation to *express* negative reactions that is stronger than it would have been in the absence of the external, normative constraints.

Motivation to correct for the influence of prejudiced feelings and beliefs may also fluctuate as a function of other, more transitory factors. Lambert, Khan, Lickel, and Fricke (1997), for example, showed that mood can be a factor in the motivation to correct for stereotypic biases. Specifically, they showed that, compared to a neutral mood control group, individuals who had been induced to feel sad were much more likely to correct their social impressions to remove the influence of stereotypes. This pattern was only observed for negative stereotypes, suggesting that the stereotype had to be perceived as inappropriate in order for sad persons to engage in corrective action. Similar processes may operate with respect to correcting for the influence of negative integral affect, and the interplay between chronic integral affect and momentary incidental affect is certainly a question that is worthy of investigation. Situational and dispositional variables such as accountability (Lerner & Tetlock, 1999), need for cognition (Cacioppo, Petty, Feinstein, & Jarvis, 1996), and a host of others may also influence the degree and consistency of motivation to correct for or suppress negative feelings about outgroup members.

Ability/Attentional Resources

Because correction and suppression are assumed to be generally effortful mental processes, they require attentional resources for their successful execution (see Wegner & Bargh, 1998). If the ability to engage in these controlled processes is compromised by distraction, time pressure, or other resource-constraining conditions, then integral affect would be expected to exert its biasing effects on perception and judgment. Research on stereotype suppression certainly supports the notion that even when properly motivated, perceivers must have adequate cognitive resources to suppress or disregard stereotypic ideas. Without sufficient attentional capacity, stereotype suppression not only fails, it tends to produce rebound effects (e.g., Macrae, Bodenhausen, Milne, & Ford, 1997; Wegner, Erber, Bowman, & Shelton, 1996). As Wegner and Bargh (1998) note, however, the act of suppression can become relatively less resource demanding if it is sufficiently practiced. For example, dispelling depressive feelings may be a skill that can be cultivated with consistent effort (see Wegner & Zanakos, 1994). Once automatized, the suppression of unwanted mental states is no longer very cognitively demanding, so factors such as cognitive busyness and distraction no longer interfere with its operation to a noticeable degree (cf. Monteith, Sherman, & Devine, 1998).

Similarly, mental correction processes are typically assumed to require attentional capacity (e.g., Martin, Seta, & Crelia, 1990). In the domain of affective influences, this assumption suggests that mood congruent biases are likely to remain in place, even among perceivers who are motivated to correct for them, if the perceivers lack adequate cognitive resources for determining the likely nature and extent of the bias and then making suitable compensatory adjustments to their overt responses. Only when resources are plentiful will corrections (most commonly, overcorrections leading to contrast effects) occur. Expertise in the domain of judgment reduces the attentional requirements of judgmental correction, making it more likely that initial biases will be successfully removed from final judgments. For example, Ottati and Isbell (1996) induced positive or negative moods and then examined political judgments. Their results indicated that participants with little political expertise showed typical mood congruency effects (i.e., more positive moods were associated with more favorable judgments). However, high expertise participants showed a contrast effect (i.e., more positive moods were associated with less favorable judgments), consistent with a process of overcorrection. The findings were interpreted as reflecting greater efficiency of correction processes among the experts. By extension, these results suggest that individuals who are attempting to correct for biases arising from integral intergroup affect are likely to be more successful in doing so if the judgment domain is one for which they have a substantial degree of familiarity and expertise.

☐ Conclusions and Future Directions

Perceivers may be generally aware of the danger that negative feelings about minority groups can contaminate judgments and behavior. However, being aware of this general possibility and taking steps to prevent it from happening in one's own reactions are two different things. First,

perceivers must become aware of their own culturally conditioned negative feelings, and this can be an uncomfortable thing to acknowledge.
Thus, awareness of bias will often be less than perfect, and the bias will
remain unchecked. Even if awareness of the problem is achieved, the
success of perceivers' efforts to control the influence of negative integral
affect can be limited by problems of inconsistent motivation and insufficient mental resources. Only when the constellation of awareness, motivation, and attentional resources is properly aligned can the perceiver
hope to successfully navigate a path to the control of unwanted, prejudiced feelings.

Of course, much more remains to be learned about the effects of integral affect on intergroup cognition and behavior. The relative dearth of
empirical research that directly investigates the impact of group-based
affective reactions on social perception leaves many important questions
for future research. For example, it seems quite important to determine
whether different types of emotional reactions differ in their consequences
for cognition and in their ability to be successfully controlled. It has long
been recognized that different groups elicit different patterns of affective
response, with some groups eliciting anxiety, some eliciting resentment,
some disgust, and so on (e.g., Bettelheim & Janowitz, 1950; Chein, 1951;
see Smith, 1993, for a theoretical analysis). It has already been shown
that different types of incidental affect (anger vs. sadness vs. anxiety) can
exert specific and distinct effects on social judgment (e.g., Bodenhausen,
Sheppard, & Kramer, 1994; Keltner, Ellsworth, & Edwards, 1993), and
the same may well be true for integral intergroup affect. Some research
has examined intergroup anxiety (e.g., Stephan & Stephan, 1985; Stephan,
Ybarra, Martinez, & Tur-Kaspa, 1998) and guilt (e.g., Swim & Miller, 1999),
but many questions about when and how these (and many other) feeling
states influence social perceptions abound. Ultimately, we have much to
learn about how negative intergroup affect can be controlled, and in particular, about how the process of emotional correction, in which antipa-
thies of the past are traded for positive, cooperative feelings, can be cultivated. As Jones (1997) put it, "Fear, anxiety, and hostility . . . are
responsible for biases in social judgment, perception and behavior. . . . Positive affect is, in the final analysis, the most important means
by which improved intergroup and interpersonal relationships can be
achieved" (p. 529).

☐ Notes

[1]It is important to distinguish between the concepts of prejudice and integral affect. Although some researchers equate prejudice with chronic feelings toward a group, we prefer

to define prejudice as a global evaluative predisposition toward the group, which may be grounded in affect, cognition, past behavior, or some combination of these (cf. Zanna & Rempel, 1988). Although there is a vast literature addressing prejudice, much less work has specifically and directly examined the discrete affective reactions that are experienced in the presence of an outgroup and their impact on processes of social cognition.

[2]Research comparing the relative importance of cognition/stereotypes versus affect in predicting prejudice and discrimination is plagued by many complications, and numerous caveats are necessary. For example, in research designs in which the relative predictive power of the two categories of variables is examined, it is absolutely crucial that both classes of variables be measured with comparable reliability and validity and that both show comparable variability. In many of the published studies, no information relevant to these concerns is presented. Arguments that affect is more important than cognition in dictating intergroup reactions are difficult to support, given the intimate interconnections between the two systems. The importance of stereotypic content in directing discrimina-tory reactions has been developed elsewhere (Bodenhausen, Macrae, & Garst, 1998). For the present purposes, we would emphasize that the important question is not which type of variable is more important, but rather how these variables interact and mutually influ-ence judgment and behavior in the intergroup context.

☐ References

Abele, A., Gendolla, G. H. E., & Petzold, P. (1998). Positive mood and in-group–out-group differentiation in a minimal group setting. *Personality and Social Psychology Bulletin, 24,* 1343–1357.

Bargh, J. A. (1999). The cognitive monster: The case against the controllability of auto-matic stereotype effects. In S. Chaiken & Y. Trope (Eds.), *Dual process theories in social psychology* (pp. 361–382). New York: Guilford Press.

Barlow, D. H. (1991). Disorders of emotion. *Psychological Inquiry, 2,* 58–71.

Bem, D. J. (1972). Self-perception theory. In L. Berkowitz (Ed.), *Advances in experimental social psychology* (Vol. 6, pp. 1–62). New York: Academic Press.

Bettelheim, B., & Janowitz, M. (1950). *Dynamics of prejudice.* New York: Harper.

Bless, H., Schwarz, N., & Wieland, R. (1996). Mood and the impact of category member-ship and individuating information. *European Journal of Social Psychology, 26,* 935–959.

Bodenhausen, G. V. (1993). Emotions, arousal, and stereotypic judgments: A heuristic model of affect and stereotyping. In D. M. Mackie & D. L. Hamilton (Eds.), *Affect, cognition, and stereotyping* (pp. 13–37). San Diego, CA: Academic Press.

Bodenhausen, G. V., Kramer, G. P., & Süsser, K. (1994). Happiness and stereotypic thinking in social judgment. *Journal of Personality and Social Psychology, 66,* 621–632.

Bodenhausen, G. V., & Macrae, C. N. (1998). Stereotype activation and inhibition. In R. S. Wyer, Jr. (Ed.), *Stereotype activation and inhibition: Advances in social cognition* (Vol. 11, pp. 1–52). Mahwah, NJ: Erlbaum.

Bodenhausen, G. V., Macrae, C. N., & Garst, J. (1998). Stereotypes in thought and deed: Social-cognitive origins of intergroup discrimination. In C. Sedikides, J. Schopler, & C. A. Insko (Eds.), *Intergroup cognition and intergroup behavior* (pp. 311–336). Mahwah, NJ: Erlbaum.

Bodenhausen, G. V., Macrae, C. N., & Milne, A. B. (1998). Disregarding social stereotypes: Implications for memory, judgment, and behavior. In J. M. Golding & C. M. MacLeod (Eds.), *Intentional forgetting: Interdisciplinary approaches* (pp. 349–368). Mahwah, NJ: Erlbaum.

Bodenhausen, G. V., Sheppard, L. A., & Kramer, G. P. (1994). Negative affect and social judgment: The differential impact of anger and sadness. *European Journal of Social Psychology, 24*, 45–62.

Brehm, J. (1966). *A theory of psychological reactance*. New York: Academic Press.

Cacioppo, J. T., Petty, R. E., Feinstein, J. A., & Jarvis, B. (1996). Dispositional differences in cognitive motivation: The life and times of individuals varying in need for cognition. *Psychological Bulletin, 119*, 197–253.

Campbell, D. T. (1947). *The generality of a social attitude*. Unpublished doctoral dissertation, University of California.

Chein, I. (1951). Notes on a framework for the measurement of discrimination and prejudice. In M. Jahoda, M. Deutsch, & S. W. Cook (Eds.), *Research methods in social relations* (Vol. 1, pp. 382–390). New York: Dryden.

Clore, G. L., & Parrott, G. (1991). Moods and their vicissitudes: Thoughts and feelings as information. In J. P. Forgas (Ed.), *Emotion and social judgments* (pp. 107–123). Oxford, England: Pergamon.

Damasio, A. R. (1994). *Decartes' error: Emotion, reason, and the human brain*. New York: Putnam.

Devine, P. G. (1989). Stereotypes and prejudice: Their automatic and controlled components. *Journal of Personality and Social Psychology, 56*, 5–18.

Devine, P. G. (1998). *Acceptance of backlash? Response to normative pressure discouraging prejudice*. Paper presented in the 1999 Kendon Smith Lectures, University of North Carolina, Greensboro, November.

Devine, P. G., Evett, S. R., & Vasquez-Suson, K. A. (1996). Exploring the interpersonal dynamics of intergroup contact. In R. M. Sorrentino & E. T. Higgins (Eds.), *Handbook of motivation and cognition* (Vol. 3, pp. 423–464). New York: Guilford Press.

Devine, P. G., Monteith, M. J., Zuwerink, J. R., & Elliot, A. J. (1991). Prejudice with and without compunction. *Journal of Personality and Social Psychology, 60*, 817–830.

Dijker, A. J. (1987). Emotional reactions to ethnic minorities. *European Journal of Social Psychology, 17*, 305–325.

Dutton, D. G., & Lake, R. A. (1973). Threat of own prejudice and reverse discrimination in interracial situations. *Journal of Personality and Social Psychology, 28*, 94–100.

Eagly, A. H., Mladinic, A., & Otto, S. (1994). Cognitive and affective bases of attitudes toward social groups and social policies. *Journal of Experimental Social Psychology, 30*, 113–137.

Fiske, S. T. (1998). Stereotyping, prejudice, and discrimination. In D. T. Gilbert, S. T. Fiske, & G. Lindzey (Eds.), *Handbook of social psychology* (4th ed., Vol. 2, pp. 357–411). Boston: McGraw-Hill.

Foa, E. B., & Kozak, M. J. (1986). Emotional processing of fear: Exposure to corrective information. *Psychological Bulletin, 99*, 20–35.

Forgas, J. P. (1995). Mood and judgment: The Affect Infusion Model (AIM). *Psychological Bulletin, 117*, 39–66.

Forgas, J. P., & Moylan, S. J. (1991). Affective influences on stereotype judgments. *Cognition and Emotion, 5*, 379–395.

Gaertner, S. L., & Dovidio, J. F. (1986). The aversive form of racism. In J. F. Dovidio & S. L. Gaertner (Eds.), *Prejudice, discrimination, and racism* (pp. 91–125). San Diego, CA: Academic Press.

Geers, A. L., & Lassiter, G. D. (1999). Affective expectations and information gain: Evidence for assimilation and contrast effects in affective experience. *Journal of Experimental Social Psychology, 35*, 394–413.

Goleman, D. (1995). *Emotional intelligence*. New York: Bantam Books.

Haddock, G., Zanna, M. P., & Esses, V. M. (1993). Assessing the structure of prejudicial attitudes: The case of attitudes toward homosexuals. *Journal of Personality and Social Psychology, 65*, 1105–1118.

Hansen, C. H., & Hansen, R. D. (1994). Automatic emotion: Attention and facial efference.

In P. M. Niedenthal & S. Kitayama (Eds.), *The heart's eye: Emotional influences in perception and attention* (pp. 217–243). San Diego, CA: Academic Press.

Horowitz, E. L. (1936). The development of attitude toward the Negro. *Archives of Psychology* (No. 194).

Ickes, W. (1984). Compositions in Black and White: Determinants of interaction in interracial dyads. *Journal of Personality and Social Psychology, 47,* 330–341.

Isbell, L. M., & Wyer, R. S., Jr. (1999). Correcting for mood-induced bias in the evaluation of political candidates: The roles of intrinsic and extrinsic motivation. *Personality and Social Psychology Bulletin, 25,* 237–249.

Jackson, L. A., Hodge, C. N., Gerard, D. A., Ingram, J. M., Ervin, K. S., & Sheppard, L. A. (1996). Cognition, affect, and behavior in the prediction of group attitudes. *Personality and Social Psychology Bulletin, 22,* 306–316.

James, W. (1884). What is an emotion? *Mind, 9,* 188–205.

Jones, J. M. (1997). *Prejudice and racism* (2nd ed.). New York: McGraw-Hill.

Jussim, L., Nelson, T. E., Manis, M., & Soffin, S. (1995). Prejudice, stereotypes, and labeling effects: Sources of bias in person perception. *Journal of Personality and Social Psychology, 68,* 228–246.

Katz, I., Wackenhut, J., & Hass, R. G. (1986). Racial ambivalence, value duality, and behavior. In J. F. Dovidio & S. L. Gaertner (Eds.), *Prejudice, discrimination, and racism* (pp. 35–59). San Diego, CA: Academic Press.

Kelman, H. C. (1958). Compliance, identification, and internalization: Three processes of attitude change. *Journal of Conflict Resolution, 2,* 51–60.

Keltner, D., Ellsworth, P. C., & Edwards, K. (1993). Beyond simple pessimism: Effects of sadness and anger on social judgment. *Journal of Personality and Social Psychology, 64,* 740–752.

Klinger, E. (1982). On the self-management of mood, affect, and attention. In P. Karoly & F. H. Kanfer (Eds.), *Self-management and behavior change* (pp. 129–164). New York: Pergamon.

Lambert, A. J., Khan, S. R., Lickel, B. A., & Fricke, K. (1997). Mood and the correction of positive versus negative stereotypes. *Journal of Personality and Social Psychology, 72,* 1002–1016.

Lerner, J. S., & Tetlock, P. E. (1999). Accounting for the effects of accountability. *Psychological Bulletin, 125,* 255–275.

Macrae, C. N., & Bodenhausen, G. V. (in press). Social cognition: Thinking categorically about others. *Annual Review of Psychology.*

Macrae, C. N., Bodenhausen, G. V., & Milne, A. B. (1998). Saying no to unwanted thoughts: Self-focus and the regulation of mental life. *Journal of Personality and Social Psychology, 74,* 578–589.

Macrae, C. N., Bodenhausen, G. V., Milne, A. B., & Ford, R. L. (1997). On the regulation of recollection: The intentional forgetting of stereotypical memories. *Journal of Personality and Social Psychology, 72,* 709–719.

Macrae, C. N., Bodenhausen, G. V., Milne, A. B., & Jetten, J. (1994). Out of mind but back in sight: Stereotypes on the rebound. *Journal of Personality and Social Psychology, 67,* 808–817.

Martin, L. L., Seta, J. J., & Crelia, R. (1990). Assimilation and contrast as a function of people's willingness and ability to expend effort in forming an impression. *Journal of Personality and Social Psychology, 59,* 27–37.

McConahay, J. B. (1983). Modern racism and modern discrimination: The effects of race, racial attitudes, and context on simulated hiring decisions. *Personality and Social Psychology Bulletin, 9,* 551–558.

Miller, G. A., Galanter, E., & Pribram, K. H. (1960). *Plans and the structure of behavior.* New York: Holt, Rinehart & Winston.

Monteith, M. J. (1993). Self-regulation of prejudiced responses: Implications for progress in prejudice-reduction efforts. *Journal of Personality and Social Psychology, 65,* 469–485.

Monteith, M. J., Sherman, J. W., & Devine, P. G. (1998). Suppression as a stereotype control strategy. *Personality and Social Psychology Review, 2,* 63–82.

Monteith, M. J., Spicer, C. V., & Tooman, G. D. (1998). Consequences of stereotype suppression: Stereotypes on and not on the rebound. *Journal of Experimental Social Psychology, 34,* 355–377.

Moreno, K. M., & Bodenhausen, G. V. (1999). *Intergroup affect and social judgment.* Manuscript in preparation.

Myrdal, G. (1944). *An American dilemma.* New York: Random House.

Öhman, A. (1993). Fear and anxiety as emotional phenomena. In M. Lewis & J. M. Haviland (Eds.), *Handbook of emotions* (pp. 511–536). New York: Guilford Press.

Ortony, A., Clore, G. L., & Collins, A. (1988). *The cognitive structure of emotions.* Cambridge, England: Cambridge University Press.

Ottati, V. C., & Isbell, L. M. (1996). Effects of mood during exposure to target information on subsequently reported judgments: An on-line model of misattribution and correction. *Journal of Personality and Social Psychology, 71,* 39–53.

Plant, E. A., & Devine, P. G. (1998). Internal and external motivation to respond without prejudice. *Journal of Personality and Social Psychology, 75,* 811–832.

Salovey, P., Hsee, C. K., & Mayer, J. D. (1993). Emotional intelligence and the self-regulation of affect. In D. M. Wegner & J. W. Pennebaker (Eds.), *Handbook of mental control* (pp. 258–277). Englewood Cliffs, NJ: Prentice-Hall.

Schuman, H., Steeh, C., Bobo, L., & Krysan, M. (1997). *Racial attitudes in America: Trends and interpretations* (Rev. ed.). Cambridge, MA: Harvard University Press.

Schwarz, N. (1987). *Stimmung als Information: Zum Einfluß von Stimmungen auf die Beurteilung des eigenen Lebens.* Heidelberg, Germany: Springer.

Schwarz, N. (1990). Feelings as information: Informational and motivational functions of affective states. In E. T. Higgins & R. M. Sorrentino (Eds.), *Handbook of motivation and cognition: Foundations of social behavior* (Vol. 2, pp. 527–561). New York: Guilford Press.

Schwarz, N., & Bless, H. (1992). Constructing reality and its alternatives: An inclusion/exclusion model of assimilation and contrast effects in social judgment. In L. L. Martin & A. Tesser (Eds.), *The construction of social judgments* (pp. 217–245). Hillsdale, NJ: Erlbaum.

Schwarz, N., & Clore, G. L. (1983). Mood, misattribution, and judgments of well being: Informative and directive functions of affective states. *Journal of Personality and Social Psychology, 45,* 513–523.

Schwarz, N., & Clore, G. L. (1988). How do I feel about it? Informative functions of affective states. In K. Fiedler & J. Forgas (Eds.), *Affect, cognition, and social behavior* (pp. 44–62). Toronto, Canada: Hogrefe.

Smith, E. R. (1993). Social identity and social emotions: Toward new conceptualizations of prejudice. In D. M. Mackie & D. L. Hamilton (Eds.), *Affect, cognition, and stereotyping: Interactive processes in group perception* (pp. 297315). San Diego, CA: Academic Press.

Stangor, C., Sullivan, L. A., & Ford, T. E. (1991). Affective and cognitive determinants of prejudice. *Social Cognition, 9,* 359–380.

Stapel, D., Martin, L. L., & Schwarz, N. (1998). The smell of bias: What instigates correction processes in social judgments? *Personality and Social Psychology Bulletin, 24,* 797–806.

Stephan, W. G., & Stephan, C. W. (1985). Intergroup anxiety. *Journal of Social Issues, 41*(3), 157–175.

Stephan, W. G., Ybarra, O., Martinez, C., Schwarzwald, J., & Tur-Kaspa, M. (1998). Prejudice toward immigrants to Spain and Israel: An integrated threat theory analysis. *Journal of Cross-Cultural Psychology, 29,* 559–576.

Strack, F. (1992). The different routes to social judgments: Experiential versus informational strategies. In L. L. Martin & A. Tesser (Eds.), *The construction of social judgments* (pp. 249–275). Hillsdale, NJ: Erlbaum.

Strack, F., & Hannover, B. (1996). Awareness of influence as a precondition for implementing correctional goals. In P. M. Gollwitzer & J. A. Bargh (Eds.), *The psychology of action* (pp. 579–596). New York: Guilford Press.

Stroessner, S. J., Hamilton, D. L., & Mackie, D. M. (1992). Affect and stereotyping: The effect of induced mood on distinctiveness-based illusory correlation. *Journal of Personality and Social Psychology, 62,* 564–576.

Swim, J. K., & Miller, D. L. (1999). White guilt: Its antecedents and consequences for attitudes toward affirmative action. *Personality and Social Psychology Bulletin, 25,* 500–514.

Thayer, R. E. (1996). *The origin of everyday moods.* Oxford, England: Oxford University Press.

Tice, D. M., & Baumeister, R. F. (1993). Controlling anger: Self-induced emotion change. In D. Wegner & J. Pennebaker (Eds.), *Handbook of mental control* (pp. 393–409). Englewood Cliffs, NJ: Prentice-Hall.

Verkuyten, M. (1997). The structure of ethnic attitudes: The effects of target group, region, gender, and national identity. *Genetic, Social, & General Psychology Monographs, 123,* 261–284.

Wegener, D. T., & Petty, R. E. (1997). The flexible correction model: The role of naive theories of bias in bias correction. In M. P. Zanna (Ed.), *Advances in experimental social psychology* (Vol. 29, pp. 141–208). San Diego, CA: Academic Press.

Wegner, D. M. (1994). Ironic processes of mental control. *Psychological Review, 101,* 34–52.

Wegner, D. M., & Bargh, J. A. (1998). Control and automaticity in social life. In D. T. Gilbert, S. T. Fiske, & G. Lindzey (Eds.), *Handbook of social psychology* (4th ed., Vol. 1, pp. 446–496). Boston, MA: McGraw-Hill.

Wegner, D. M., & Erber, R. (1992). The hyperaccessibility of suppressed thoughts. *Journal of Personality and Social Psychology, 63,* 903–912.

Wegner, D. M., Erber, R., Bowman, R., & Shelton, J. N. (1996). *On trying not to be sexist.* Unpublished manuscript.

Wegner, D. M., Erber, R., & Zanakos, S. (1993). Ironic processes in the mental control of mood and mood-related thought. *Journal of Personality and Social Psychology, 65,* 1093–1104.

Wegner, D. M., & Gold, D. B. (1995). Fanning old flames: Emotional and cognitive effects of suppressing thoughts of a past relationship. *Journal of Personality and Social Psychology, 68,* 782–792.

Wegner, D. M., & Pennebaker, J. W. (1993). *Handbook of mental control.* Englewood Cliffs, NJ: Prentice-Hall.

Wegner, D. M., & Zanakos, S. (1994). Chronic thought suppression. *Journal of Personality, 62,* 615–640.

Wilson, T. D., & Brekke, N. (1994). Mental contamination and mental correction: Unwanted influences on judgments and evaluations. *Psychological Bulletin, 116,* 117–142.

Wilson, T. D., Lisle, D. J., Kraft, D., & Wetzel, C. G. (1989). Preferences as expectation-driven inferences: Effects of affective expectations on affective experience. *Journal of Personality and Social Psychology, 56,* 519–530.

Zajonc, R. B. (1998). Emotions. In D. T. Gilbert, S. T. Fiske, & G. Lindzey (Eds.), *The handbook of social psychology* (4th ed., Vol. 1, pp. 591–632). Boston, MA: McGraw-Hill.

Zajonc, R. B., Pietromonaco, P., & Bargh, J. (1982). Independence and interaction of affect and cognition. In M. S. Clark & S. T. Fiske (Eds.), *Affect and cognition: The Seventeenth Annual Carnegie Symposium on Cognition* (pp. 211–227). Hillsdale, NJ: Erlbaum.

Zanna, M. P., & Rempel, J. K. (1988). Attitudes: A new look at an old concept. In D. Bar-Tal & A. W. Kruglanski (Eds.), *The social psychology of knowledge* (pp. 315–334). Cambridge, England: Cambridge University Press.

17
CHAPTER

Benoit Dardenne
Vincent Yzerbyt
Christine Grégoire

Active Search for Information: The Effects of Subjectively Experienced Control on Stereotyping

As social psychologists, but also as consumers and citizens, we have always been fascinated by Ellen Langer's (1975) work on the illusion of control. Not only does this work wake our students up during our classes (if at all necessary), it also tells us a great deal about the way the human mind operates. Our students are always quite surprised to learn about the impact of manipulations of control on people's willingness to keep lottery tickets (Langer, 1975) or on their health and longevity (Rodin, 1986; Rodin & Langer, 1977). Clearly, Langer's findings help us understand the notion of perceived control.

Perceived control can be defined as the subjectively experienced authority and influence over an event—the availability of directing and regulating it oneself. In the present chapter, we build upon the notion of perceived control and combine two traditions of research. Whereas the first tradition is concerned with the notion of control, the second is dealing with stereotype change. The basic idea is that control over the course of an event could make people more "mindful" (or less "mindless"). As far

We would like to thank our students for carrying out these studies and Nathalie Delacollette and Delphine Lecocq for their valuable comments on earlier drafts of the chapter.

Address correspondence to Benoit Dardenne, University of Liège, Boulevard du Rectorat, 5 (Bat-32), B-4000 Sart-Tilman/Liège, Belgium. E-mail: B.dardenne@ulg.ac.be

as stereotype change is concerned, we propose that an active search for information could lead people to be more watchful about their judgment. They would think more extensively about the evidence, allowing the information to exert a stronger impact on the a priori impression.

In the first section, we briefly review the literature on control. Over the years, numerous studies in different domains have examined people's motivation for gaining or maintaining control. We propose that control might be conceived as a kind of subjective experience, that is, a cognitive assessment that is about the cognitions of the self. Broadly speaking, a subjective state or experience is simply ordinary cognition applied to its own products (see Lories, Dardenne & Yzerbyt, 1998, for a more complete discussion). As the literature reviewed below will suggest, understanding subjective states should be a key concern to social psychologists in that they can have a dramatic impact on people's judgments and behaviors. Moreover, we propose that giving people control over the course of an event could change the perception of the event. In a sense, to control or not to control an object could make the object change. In the second section, we provide a general overview of recent work on stereotype change. We argue that the research on stereotyping has misrepresented the social thinker. Instead of confining the perceiver to the role of a passive observer, we suggest that the perceiver should instead be seen as an active participant who has control of—or at least wants to—control the environment. In the third section, we test the idea that perceived control over the impression formation leads people to assign different weights to the stereotypic information on the one hand and the individuating information on the other. We present recent evidence from our laboratories showing that the mode of information acquisition (active vs. passive; i.e., controlled or not controlled) makes a difference as far as the relative impact of both kinds of data is concerned. In a final section, we examine the mechanisms that could account for the influence of the perceived control over the information-gathering episode.

☐ The Concept of Control as a Subjective Experience

The Concept of Control

There are numerous and possibly very different types of control. Rothbaum, Weisz, and Snyder (1982) distinguished between primary control (e.g., believing that you can influence the course of an event) and secondary control (e.g., accepting or reinterpreting existing realities). Fiske and Taylor (1991; see also Averill, 1973), regarding personal control over stressful or aversive events, distinguished between six types of control:

behavioral, cognitive, information, decision, retrospective, and secondary control. Decision control, which is perhaps the closest kind of control to the one we want to address in this chapter, is the ability to make a decision about the forthcoming event. Decision control may involve the ability to choose among a set of alternatives as well as the ability to regulate the timing or duration of an event. The research about dissonance theory has provided numerous examples of this kind of control (e.g., Zimbardo, 1969). It has been suggested that decision control and the other five types of control could be reduced to two distinct techniques: taking some action (primary control) and thinking differently about the event (secondary control). As we will argue later in this section, taking action over an event also changes the perception of that event.

Perceived primary control has been especially studied in the domain of health psychology, emotional well-being, adjustment to major life events, and performance. For instance, Taylor (e.g., 1989; Taylor, Lichtman, & Wood, 1984) has repeatedly found that women who believe that their breast cancer was controllable were better adjusted psychologically than women who thought that their breast cancer was uncontrollable. As it happens, there is also evidence that people who try to control their cancer live longer than those who do not (Taylor, 1989). Working with elderly people in nursing homes, Langer and Rodin (1976; Rodin & Langer, 1977) showed that giving people control over their lives, or even over tiny events like which night the residents would like to watch a movie, could make them feel happier, more sociable, more self-initiating, and more active. Eighteen months later, 15% of the residents who were in control had died (7 out of 47 participants). In sharp contrast, some 30% of the residents in the no control condition (baseline) had died (13 out of 44 participants). In an even more dramatic replication of this study, Schulz and Hanusa (1978; Heckhausen & Schulz, 1995; Schulz, 1976) had two groups of residents receiving the visit of undergraduate students. One group of residents was allowed to decide when the visits would occur as well as how long they would last. For the other group of residents, the students, not the residents, made all the decisions regarding the visits. Quite normally, the group who was in control lost it all when Schulz and Hanusa's study came to an end. Several months later, the authors found out that 20% of the people in this group had died. In sharp contrast, none of the elderly in the no control condition had died. In sum, giving people control may be detrimental if it is later taken away from them. In order to have long lasting effect, residents should be given an enduring sense of control.

Much of the research has examined the effects of having or not having primary control over the course of an event—most often a stressor or an aversive event. In contrast, Thompson and colleagues (1993) examined secondary control, that is, perceived control over the consequences of an event. In some situations (e.g., when people are dealing with a major negative life stressor like a tumor or HIV positivity), people do not feel like they are having control over the event. However, many of them still believe that they may control the consequences of the event. Thompson et al. (1993) showed that feeling a sense of mastery over the consequences of cancer, that is, the emotional reaction and the daily physical symptoms, is associated with successful psychological adjustment (e.g., less depression and anxiety). In another study, Thompson, Nanni, and Levine (1994) found that psychological adjustment among HIV-positive men was better predicted by their level of secondary rather than primary control.

Up until now, we have considered stressful situations in which people have little if any real control over the course of the events or over their consequences. In some situations, control was exercised over "unimportant" or even trivial aspects of the environment. There are other situations, less or not at all stressful, where people exercise control by doing or not doing an action. Despite these differences, the idea of action/inaction is very close to the primary control discussed earlier. For instance, Fazio, Sherman, and Herr (1982; see also Allison & Messick, 1988) presented participants with different sets of cartoons and asked them to make a yes/no judgment about their "funniness." One group of participants was asked to push a button if they judged the cartoon funny and to do nothing if they judged it unfunny. The other group was told to do the opposite. When asked to rate the cartoons a second time, the participants who had expressed their first opinion actively (by pushing the button when they liked it or disliked it) ended up with a second, more extreme attitudinal judgment than participants who expressed a first judgment by doing nothing (by not pushing the button when they liked it or disliked it). Later, Allison and Messick (1988) also found that active responders displayed a larger false consensus effect (see Ross, Greene, & House, 1977).

Recently, Cioffi and Garner (1996, 1998) conceptually replicated this evaluative asymmetry between action and inaction in the domain of self-persuasion and behavioral intention. They also found that the effect lasted as long as 6 weeks (Cioffi & Garner, 1996, Experiment 1b), and that it had behavioral consequences (Cioffi & Garner, 1996, Experiment 2). Similar action/inaction effects are reported in the literature concerning the regret and blame following a poor outcome. In one of the early studies on that issue, Kahneman and Tversky (1982; Spranca, Minsk, & Baron, 1991; but see Connolly, Ordóñez, & Coughlan, 1997) found that other people's misfortune coming from action leads observers to think that the actor would experience greater regret and blame than other people's misfortune coming from inaction. When the misfortune concerns themselves, however, people tend to regret inaction more than action (see Gilovitch & Medvec,

1994). Other studies, in different domains, have also found action/inaction effect concerning children's memory for location visited (e.g., McComas, Dulberg, & Latter, 1997) and for students' acquisition and memory of academic materials (e.g., Barbetta, Heron, & Heward, 1993). It is important to note that such an effect between action and inaction on future self-perceived skill is found even when the control is totally illusory (cf., for instance, Langer, 1975; Langer & Roth, 1975).

In fact, the distinction between real and perceived control is not very clear. For instance, one may have *actual* control over an event with or without a *perceived* sense of control, or one may *feel* in control without any *actual* control. As suggested by the literature reviewed above, perceived sense of control alone may not need to correspond to reality to have important psychological consequences.

In sum, these and other results seem to indicate that when people have choice (high control), they experience "more intrinsic motivation, greater interest, less pressure and tension, more creativity, more cognitive flexibility, better conceptual learning, a more emotional tone, higher self-esteem, more trust, greater persistence of behavior change, and better physical and psychological health" (Deci & Ryan, 1987, p. 1024) than people who have no choice (low control). This could explain why so many famous psychologists have placed a great emphasis on a human motive to seek out and maintain control (Adler, Bandura, Bruner, Festinger, Jones and Gerard, Kelly, Latane, and Darley, Seligman, White, and others). It should be noted, however, that people may also want to decrease their control on some occasions, for instance, under high uncertainty or very low expertise (see Burger, 1989; Dolinski, 1998).

The Process

But how can we explain the action/inaction effects as well as the effects of having or not having control? Kahneman and Miller (1986, see also chapter 5 by Brendl in this volume), in their Norm Theory, propose a general *"emotional amplification"* effect, which states that the affective response to an event is enhanced if its causes are abnormal. In this theory, which is mainly concerned with counterfactual thinking, action is assumed to be less normal than inaction, so that positive as well as negative consequences of action are felt more strongly that when the same consequences follow inaction. Central to Gilovich and Medvec (1994, 1995) analysis is the idea that *personal responsibility* is at the core of the action/inaction effects on regret and self-blame. Personal responsibility as well as *feeling of choice* are also emphasized in Langer's studies on the elderly nursing home residents (Langer & Rodin, 1976; Rodin & Langer, 1977). In their coin flipping studies, Langer and Roth (1975) speak of a difference in *"involve-*

ment" between the participant who performed the task himself or observed another participant performing the task. In a very interesting set of studies, Cioffi and Garner (1996, 1998) also found that making a volunteer decision by doing something results in more *"commitment," "self-relevance,"* and *"self-implication."* In sum, the action/inaction effect seems to be a question of involvement toward the decision, choice, activity, or event that has been under the volitional control of the individual. In the following section, we will consider the impact of action/inaction on a specific kind of event, that is, the impression formation episode.

What could be said about the underlying process of such a phenomenon? Interestingly, some researchers have emphasized the power of action to alter self-perception. Several mechanisms have been proposed. For instance, it might be that particularly salient behavior (i.e., active or under control) triggers our desire for *consistency* (e.g., Schlenker, Dlugolecki, & Doherty, 1993), promotes its *internalization* (e.g., Bandura, 1986), or induces us to accumulate *justification* and *elaboration* (e.g., Lydon & Zanna, 1990). Action is also usually perceived as being *more informative* than inaction (e.g., Fazio, 1987; cf. also the feature-positive effect, e.g., Kahneman, Slovic, & Tversky, 1982) and thus might be seen as more diagnostic. As expressed by Cioffi and Garner (1996, p. 133), "Behavior can mobilize several cognitive, social, and motivational processes that converge toward a common effect: to justify, solidify, and 'make good' the act."

Control and Subjective Experience

We would like to argue that action/inaction also translates into a subjective experience. A subjective experience could be broadly defined as a metacognitive judgment, that is, a cognitive assessment that is about the cognitions of the self (see chapter 12 by Sedikides & Green in this volume, as well as Jost, Kruglanski, & Nelson, 1998; Lories, Dardenne & Yzerbyt, 1998; Metcalfe & Shimamura, 1994; Nelson, 1992; Nelson, Kruglanski, & Jost, 1998). The literature has usually distinguished between two types of information that provide the basis for such metacognitive judgments. The first kind of information concerns the momentary feelings or impressions like the feeling of familiarity, the feeling of happiness, or the feeling of uncertainty. The second kind of information concerns the more enduring beliefs or theories about, for instance, memorability of information, stability and change of the mind, applicability of stereotypes and inferential rules. The subjective experience, whether coming from a momentary or enduring source, could have a powerful impact on the content of the judgment (for a review, see, for instance, Yzerbyt, Lories, & Dardenne, 1998).

In our view, one of the most powerful and intriguing consequences of subjective experiences on social judgments is that they can modify the object of the judgment itself. In other words, people who feel in control or take action are not judging the same object as people who do not feel in control or do not take action. In order to illustrate our proposition, let us take but one example from the recent literature (see also Darley & Gross, 1983). In their studies on the effects of active versus passive choice on commitment and self-perception, Cioffi and Garner's (1996) participants were asked to volunteer for a university committee or a sex and AIDS awareness education project. Participants indicated their choice either by affirming it (action) or by skipping it (inaction) on two items. Results indicate that active and passive choice leads to a different pattern of self-attribution for the decision. For instance, participants who indicated their choice actively (either to volunteer or not) were less likely to report self-presentation factors as reasons for their decisions than those participants who indicated their choice passively. Active refusers were also more likely than passive refusers to indicate that their decision was more reflective of a usual tendency to refuse such requests. Finally, those participants who had made any decision actively (either to volunteer or not) cited more types of reasons for that decision than those participants who had made the decision passively. According to the authors, active and passive participants "held different construals of themselves and of their decision" (1996, p. 141). Later on, the authors defended the idea that active response apparently made the participants' decision more "tangible and real to them than the non-action response" (1996, p. 144). In our view, this amounts to saying that the object of judgment is not the same for active and passive participants. As exposed in the above lines, the mechanism responsible for this effect could be that the self is more involved and more implicated by action than by inaction (see also Baumeister, Bratslavsky, Muraven, & Tice, 1998).

Before describing the evidence coming from our laboratories showing that active search versus passive reception of the data affects people's impression formation, we briefly review the work done in the stereotype change literature. Interestingly, the work on stereotyping is both characterized by a limited success in changing stereotype and by a perceiver who is not in control. Is giving people control over impression formation able to alter stereotype?

☐ Impression Formation and Stereotype Change

In this section, we would like to sketch the major findings as well as the methodology used in the stereotype formation and change literature, and then move on to propose another way to look at the social perceiver.

Specifically, we propose that social perceivers are best conceived as active information seekers than as passive information receivers.

Judging from the books and papers published each year on stereotype and stereotyping, the study of social categorization is undoubtedly one of the top ten domains in social psychology. Thanks to intensive research efforts, the effects of stereotypes on judgment are now well documented (Bodenhausen & Macrae, 1998; Leyens, Yzerbyt, & Schadron, 1994; Macrae, Stangor, & Hewstone, 1996). As a case in point, the work on stigmatization is replete with illustrations of the negative effects of stereotypes (cf. Eberhardt & Fiske, 1998; Swim & Stangor, 1998). There is thus a widespread agreement about the need for interventions that can bring about stereotype change (cf. Duckitt, 1992; Jones, 1997). Several attempts have been made to reduce stereotyping. The most popular strategies involve cross-categorization (Vanbeselaere, 1991), a reference to common identity (Dovidio & Gardner, 1998; see also chapter 19 by Dovidio and colleagues in this volume), "compunction" (Devine & Vasquez, 1998), increased intergroup contact (Hewstone, 1996), voluntary inhibition (Bodenhausen & Macrae, 1998), "personalization" (Brewer & Miller, 1984), and so on. But although some studies have successfully demonstrated stereotype change in response to disconfirming information, the majority of attempts has met with limited success.

Why are stereotypes so difficult to change ? We see at least two reasons. The first one is that stereotyping, prejudice, and discrimination incorporate a number of automatic aspects. Stereotyping is one example of categorization, a process that has been shown to involve a great many operations that remain outside the conscious control of the perceivers (see Banaji & Greenwald, 1995; Brewer, 1988; Devine, 1989; Fiske, 1998; Tajfel, 1969). The second reason that may explain the difficulty to change stereotypes is that these knowledge structures entail a number of socially pragmatic aspects. In other words, they have some utility for the perceiver (see Dardenne & Leyens, 1995; Fiske, 1992, 1998; Leyens, Yzerbyt, & Schadron, 1994; Yzerbyt, Rocher, & Schadron, 1997).

As noted by Yzerbyt and Leyens (1991), another largely neglected reason for the resistance of stereotypes may be that perceivers are generally actively involved in the construction of social judgment. Interestingly, a standard research practice consists in providing *passive* perceivers with disconfirming instances in order to examine their impact on stereotypes. Admittedly, such a methodology has served extremely well and allowed to uncover a wide range of phenomena. It may be worthwhile, however, to examine alternative means of constructing a judgment. As we mentioned earlier, the very behavior of actively searching for the information may involve more than just a particular selection among the pieces of information. It may give people a sense of control. In sum, the vast majority of studies in the area of stereotyping remain silent about the effect of the active search for information.

Stimulated by Yzerbyt and Leyens' (1991) work on hypothesis testing, Johnston and Macrae (1994; see also Johnston, 1996) gave some of their participants all the available information about a target. The information was either stereotype-confirming, stereotype-disconfirming, or stereotype-irrelevant. Compared to participants who were free to actively request smaller portions of the data, participants who were provided with all the available information expressed fewer stereotypical judgments. In fact, the final impressions of the information seekers did not differ from those of control participants who did not receive any additional information. This result, Johnston and Macrae (1994) concluded, suggests that stereotypes may be more difficult to change in a naturalistic information-seeking setting than in a laboratory setting where participants passively received all the relevant information. Despite the relevance of Johnston and Macrae's (1994) findings, two aspects of their study deserve special attention. First, feedback was always provided in a question-consistent way. Whether the question was expectancy confirming or expectancy disconfirming, all answers given to the participants were positive. This may have been quite puzzling for the participants, as the target may have appeared to have a split personality. A more natural way of responding may be to give feedback that would systematically confirm or disconfirm the stereotype. Second, the appropriate control group may not be the "no additional information" group, but rather a group of participants who passively receive the exact same information as that requested by the information seekers. The use of the passive reception control condition affords the possibility to compare the naturalistic information seeker setting with a more "traditionalist" information receiver setting and to document the mere impact of the active search for information on the final judgment.

In an initial set of studies (Dardenne & Yzerbyt, 1996; 1997, Experiment 1), participants read a short description of a fictitious individual. The description conveyed either a positive or negative expectancy about the person. One third of the participants, the information seekers, could ask for additional information in order to form an impression (they could request 6 traits out of a list of 12 positive and 12 negative traits). For each trait requested, the experimenter successively revealed the proportion of people attributing the trait to the person. Importantly, the feedback was always consistent with the expectancy. Another third of participants, the information receivers, passively received the additional information. It is important to note that passive reception participants were yoked with their active search colleagues in that we gave them exactly the same information. The remaining third of participants served as baseline subjects and neither received nor searched additional information. In line with predictions, we found that those participants who had control over the search for information reported a more extreme and confident final impression than information receivers and baseline participants. Moreover, receivers and baseline participants expressed the same impression and felt equally confident.

In a second study, we wanted to investigate the effect of a disconfirmatory feedback, that is, positively valenced additional information after negative expectancy or negatively valenced additional information after positive expectancy (Dardenne & Yzerbyt, 1996, 1997, Experiment 2). The pattern of results showed that the final impression was very different, depending on the mode of information acquisition. Confronted with entirely disconfirmatory information, searchers in the positive expectancy condition displayed less positive impressions than receivers. The reverse happened with a negative expectancy: searchers displayed more negative impressions than receivers. This pattern of findings bears some similarity with the distinction between a positivity bias and a negativity effect (e.g., Peeters & Czapinski, 1990). As we see it, active control over the information led perceivers to appraise both the old and the new information in a more cautious and responsible manner (i.e., there is more negative judgment for active search, whatever the positive or negative valence of the expectancy). This phenomenon is very close to the interpretation of the action/inaction effect we presented in the first section of the chapter. Elsewhere, we have also proposed that these results plead for an "on-line" influence of metacognitive cues on impression formation (see Dardenne & Yzerbyt, 1999; Yzerbyt, Dardenne, & Leyens, 1998). In the next section, we present some studies dealing more directly with the effects of an active search versus passive reception of disconfirmatory information on stereotyping per se.

☐ Action/Inaction Effects on Stereotyping

However promising, these first investigations leave several questions unanswered. Importantly, the first set of studies used an experimentally induced expectancy about a fictitious individual. It remains to show whether there is a *stereotype* change when searching actively for information rather than receiving passively the exact same information about an individual. Another important question concerns the *process(es)* responsible for the greater impact of disconfirmation under action than inaction. Do the mechanisms have something to do with memory for the disconfirmatory information, differential level of motivation to process the information, a subjective experience, or something else? We investigated some of these questions in a series of experiments.

In a first study (Dardenne & Yzerbyt, 1998, Experiment 1), we presented a brief description of a target (Mr. Henrion, two children, etc.) along with one of two professional labels: the target was either described as a comedian (conveying the idea of extroversion) or as an archivist (conveying the idea of introversion). Again, two modes of information acquisition were proposed. On a list of 12 traits, active participants selected the information they would like to know about the target. They then received feedback by way of yes or no answers. Passive participants simply received the same information accompanied by the feedback. In short, this was again a yoked design. Four kinds of information were available: three positive traits typical of comedians (i.e., positive traits that are thought to be shared by people who are comedians), three negative traits typical of comedians, three positive traits typical of archivists, and three negative traits typical of archivists. For instance, if the target were described as an archivist, meticulous was typical and positive and open-minded was atypical and positive. Two thirds of the feedback answers were stereotype disconfirming. We asked participants to evaluate the target on several stereotypical and counterstereotypical items. Another set of participants was asked to judge a typical archivist or a typical comedian on the same items, without additional disconfirming information (baseline participants). Results showed that for both the archivist and the comedian, judgments differed from the baseline conditions. Specifically, additional disconfirming information lead to a decrease in typicality ratings. However, this trend was significant only in the active search conditions.

We also assessed participants' recall of the feedback answers. More precisely, we were interested in the way participants clustered the recall of the disconfirmatory feedback depending on its mode of acquisition, either actively searched or passively received. Our hypothesis was that information that had been followed by disconfirmatory feedback would be clustered together more in the active than in the passive conditions. Again, the predicted pattern was found. This result is important because it shows that searchers and receivers are processing the information in a different way; that is, searchers have a stronger and more integrated cognitive organization of information than receivers.

In a second experiment (Dardenne & Yzerbyt, 1998, Experiment 2), we tested the idea that elaboration and richness of the impression would be stronger after an active search for disconfirmatory information than after passive reception of the same information. We expected, however, that only active participants who have the necessary cognitive resources to process the information would show this pattern of results. In other words, cognitively busy participants, even if actively searching for information, will not have enough cognitive capacity to process the information and take full advantage of its disconfirmatory status. In line with predictions, we found that only the active and nonbusy participants made a less typical judgment compared to baseline participants. Clearly, though, the advantage of activity in reducing stereotypic judgments requires some cognitive resources. We also found that richness of the impression, as assessed by items like "I feel I have something to say about the target" as well as assessed by external judges on items like "precision," "coherence," and "structuration" of an open portrait of the target written by the participants, was higher in the nonbusy and active condition than in the other three conditions.

We also further reasoned that passive reception of information does not necessarily mean that participants could not take full advantage of the disconfirmatory feedback. Rather, we think that passive participants could be motivated to process the disconfirmatory information in such a manner that their judgment would be as low in typicality as the judgment of active perceivers. To test that idea, we designed a third experiment (Dardenne & Yzerbyt, 1998, Experiment 3) in which we manipulated the need for cognitive closure (see Webster, 1993, for a similar manipulation of cognitive closure). We told both active and passive participants that a second task would have to be done. For half the participants, the second task was introduced as an evaluation of a movie pertaining to the impact of humor on teaching. Presumably, participants in this condition wanted to reach the second task as soon as possible without giving much thought to the initial impression formation task. For the remaining participants, the second task was presented as an evaluation of a movie dealing with the teaching of statistics. Presumably, participants in this condition did not feel any strong pressure or motivation to reach the second task, and therefore took the initial impression formation task more at heart. We predicted, and found, that passive participants in the low need for closure manipulation (i.e., when the second task was about statistics) displayed the same impression of the target as the active participants. Moreover, only passive participants in the high need for closure condition (i.e., when the second task was about humor) ended up with a rating of the target that was significantly higher than the midpoint on the typicality scale. In contrast, the participants in the three other cells ended up with a judgment below the midpoint of the typicality scale.

Some of the data collected in the experiments reported in this chapter also shed some light on the *processes* by which an active search for disconfirmatory feedback could lead to a judgment lower in typicality. For instance, a mediational analysis (see Dardenne & Yzerbyt, 1998, Experiment 2) showed that the effect of action/inaction on the typicality ratings is no longer statistically significant when richness, evaluated by participants' feeling "that they have something to say about the target," is introduced as a mediator. In contrast, diagnosticity of the feedback

(Dardenne & Yzerbyt, 1998, Experiment 2), as well as the mere amount of disconfirmatory feedback recalled (Dardenne & Yzerbyt, 1998, Experiment 1), does not appear to mediate the effect of action/inaction on the typicality rating. As far as "feeling to be able to say something" is a proxy for a subjective experience, this is pretty good evidence that such experience can have an important impact on the impression formation episode.

In the first section, we expressed the idea that the action/inaction effects could be interpreted in terms of a change of the object of the judgment itself. Although there are a number of methodological points that could be worth mentioning, we decided that one way to bypass these problems was to examine the factorial structure of the judgment, and then to compare this structure in one condition to the same structure in another condition. The two conditions of interest here are the following ones: (a) passive participants in the high need for closure condition, and (b) all active participants as well as passive participants in the low need for closure condition. More precisely, we decided to run a factorial analysis on the items from the scale used to assess participants' impression of the target (from Dardenne & Yzerbyt, 1998, Experiment 3). This six-item scale clearly revealed two factors (with latent roots of 2.860 and 1.096), both containing three items. The first factor explains about 38%, and the second about 28%, of the total variance. We then performed a rotated factor analysis and compared the loadings from the first and second factors, respectively, in both conditions. Whereas the Pearson correlation between the loading of the six items on the first factor in the two conditions is positive and highly significant, $r(6) = .905$, $p < .02$, the Pearson correlation between the same six items loading from the second factor is very close to zero and nonsignificant, $r(6) = -.09$, $p > .85$. From our point of view, this is evidence that the object of the judgment is different in the two conditions. In other words, it looks like participants were not judging the same object.

☐ Conclusion and Some Implications

The way people build their judgments has dramatic consequences on the weighing of categorical and individuating information. We focus on one specific factor, namely, the degree of activity of the impression formation process. The present chapter started with an examination of the literature on control and stereotype change. We then presented some data relevant to the distinction between active search versus passive reception of information. When encountering confirmatory feedback, active participants ended up with a more extreme and confident impression than passive participants. When encountering disconfirmatory feedback, however, active participants ended up with a more negative impression than passive participants. We then presented data from several additional experiments that support the idea that an active search for information leads perceivers to give more weight to information that disconfirms the stereotype.

Several important questions remain unanswered and deserve further examination. For instance, although it does not seem that action/inaction has an effect on the subjective diagnosticity of the information received (feedback), the threshold of acceptance or integration of the information could be different. One may imagine that this threshold is lower if the information has been actively sought rather than passively received. Another issue concerns the difference between active decision and active search for information. In several of our experiments, participants were active at both levels: they first decided which information they wanted to know and then actively sought that particular information. Clearly, the present studies could not differentiate between the two types of activity. Although we have some data that seem to favor the idea that active decision could be the crucial factor (Dardenne, 1999), further investigations are needed. Still another issue concerns the idea of ego depletion, that is, the idea that the active self has limited resources (Baumeister et al., 1998). If these resources are used in a first task that requires self-control (i.e., active choice of information), they may turn out to be absent in a subsequent and even unrelated second task. This could lead active perceivers to display an even more extreme pattern of results than passive perceivers in a second task (i.e., even less stereotype change or more resistance to latter disconfirmation). We are currently testing these and related ideas. At any rate, the present chapter makes clear that the predominant mode of presentation of the evidence used in current stereotyping research may fail to capture the rich variety of perceivers' responses to social information. It is our hope that our efforts on this front will encourage other researchers to think of more versatile ways of providing information to their participants, thereby enabling us to better capture the factors that promote or counteract stereotype maintenance.

☐ References

Allison, J. R., & Messick, D. M. (1988). The feature-positive effect, attitude strength, and degree of perceived consensus. *Personality and Social Psychology Bulletin, 14,* 231–241.

Averill, J. R. (1973). Personal control over aversive stimuli and its relationship to stress. *Psychological Bulletin, 80,* 236–303.

Banaji, M. R., & Greenwald, A. G. (1995). Implicit gender stereotyping in judgments of blame. *Journal of Personality and Social Psychology, 68,* 181–198.

Bandura, A. (1986). *Social foundations of thought and action.* Englewood Cliffs, NJ: Prentice-Hall.

Barbetta, P. M., Heron, T. E., & Heward, W. L. (1993). Effects of active student response during error correction on the acquisition, maintenance, and generalization of sight words by students with developmental disabilities. *Journal of Applied Behavior Analysis, 26*, 111–119.

Baumeister, R. F., Bratslavsky, E., Muraven, M, & Tice, D. (1998). Ego depletion: Is the active self a limited resources? *Journal of Personality and Social Psychology, 74*, 1252–1265.

Bodenhausen, G. V., & Macrae, C. N. (1998). Stereotype activation and inhibition. In R. S. Wyer (Ed.), *Advances in social cognition*. Mahwah, NJ: Erlbaum.

Brewer, M. B. (1988). A dual process of impression formation. In T. K. Srull & R. S. Wyer (Eds.), *Advances in social cognition* (pp. 1–36). Hillsdale, NJ: Erlbaum.

Brewer, M. B., & Miller, N. (1984). Beyond the contact hypothesis: Theoretical perspectives on desegregation. In N. Miller & M. B. Brewer (Eds.), *Groups in contact: The psychology of desegregation* (pp. 281–302). Orlando, FL: Academic Press.

Burger, J. M. (1989). Negative reactions to increases in perceived personal control. *Journal of Personality and Social Psychology, 56*, 246–256.

Cioffi, D., & Garner, R. (1996). On doing the decision: The effects of active versus passive choice on commitment and self-perception. *Personality and Social Psychology Bulletin, 22*, 133–147.

Cioffi, D., & Garner, R. (1998). The effects of response options on decisions and subsequent behavior: Sometimes inaction is better. *Personality and Social Psychology Bulletin, 24*, 463–472.

Connally, T., Ordóñez, L. D., & Coughlan, R. C. (1997). Regret and responsibility in the evaluation of decision outcomes. *Organizational Behavior and Human Decision Processes, 70*, 73–85.

Dardenne, B. (1999). *Action/inaction effects on stereotype change: Some implications for stereotype change models*. Unpublished data, University of Liège.

Dardenne, B., & Leyens, J.-P. (1995). Confirmation bias in social skill. *Personality and Social Psychology Bulletin, 21*, 1229–1239.

Dardenne, B., & Yzerbyt, V. Y. (1996). *Implicit theories in judgment construction*. Paper presented at the 11th General Meeting of the European Association for Experimental Social Psychology, 13–18 July, Gmunden, Austria.

Dardenne, B., & Yzerbyt, V. Y. (1997). *Implicit theory of judgment construction*. Unpublished manuscript, Catholic University of Louvain.

Dardenne, B., & Yzerbyt, V. Y. (1998). *Action/inaction effects on stereotyping*. Unpublished manuscript, University of Liège.

Dardenne, B., & Yzerbyt, V. Y. (1999). Théories naïves du jugement social: La recherche active de l'information. In J.-L. Beauvois, R.-V. Joule, & J.-M. Monteil (Eds.), *Perspectives cognitives et conduites sociales VI* (pp. 31–51). Lausanne, Switzerland: Delachaux et Niestlé.

Darley, J. M., & Gross, P. H. (1983). A hypothesis-confirming bias in labeling effects. *Journal of Personality and Social Psychology, 44*, 20–33.

Deci, E. L., & Ryan, R. M. (1987). The supports of autonomy and the control of behavior. *Journal of Personality and Social Psychology, 53*, 1024–1037.

Devine, P. G. (1989). Stereotypes and prejudice: Their automatic and controlled components. *Journal of Personality and Social Psychology, 56*, 5–18.

Devine, P. G., & Vasquez, K. A. (1998). The rocky road to positive intergroup relations. In J. L. Eberhardt & S. T. Fiske (Eds.), *Confronting racism: The problem and the response* (pp. 234–262). London: Sage.

Dolinski, D. (1998). To control or not to control. In M. Kofta, G. Weary, & G. Sedek (Eds.), *Personal control in action* (pp. 319–340). New York: Plenum Press.

Dovidio, J. F., & Gardner, S. L. (1998). On the nature of contemporary prejudice: The causes, consequences, and challenges of aversive racism. In J. L. Eberhardt & S. T. Fiske (Eds.), *Confronting racism: The problem and the response* (pp. 3–32). London: Sage.

Duckitt, J. (1992). *The social psychology of prejudice*. New York: Praeger.

Eberhardt, J. L., & Fiske, S. T. (1998). *Confronting racism: The problem and the response*. London: Sage.

Fazio, R. H. (1987). Self-perception theory: A current perspective. In M. P. Zanna, J. M. Olson, & C. P. Herman (Eds.), *Ontario Symposium on Personality and Social Psychology* (pp. 129–150). Hillsdale, NJ: Erlbaum.

Fazio, R. H., Sherman, S. J., & Herr, P. M. (1982). The feature-positive effect in the self-perception process: Does not doing matter as much as doing? *Journal of Personality and Social Psychology, 42*, 404–411.

Fiske, S. T. (1992). Thinking is for doing: Portraits of social cognition from daguerreotype to laserphoto. *Journal of Personality and Social Psychology, 63*, 877–899.

Fiske, S. T. (1998). Stereotyping, prejudice, and discrimination. In D. T. Gilbert, S. T. Fiske, & G. Lindzey (Eds), *The handbook of social psychology* (4th ed., pp. 357–411). New York: McGraw-Hill.

Fiske, S. T., & Taylor, S. E. (1991). *Social cognition*. New York: McGraw-Hill.

Gilovitch, T., & Medvec, V. H. (1994). The temporal pattern to the experience of regret. *Journal of Personality and Social Psychology, 67*, 357–365.

Gilovitch, T., & Medvec, V. H. (1995). The experience of regret: What, when, and why. *Psychological Review, 102*, 379–395.

Heckhausen, J., & Schulz, R. (1995). A life-span theory of control. *Pychological Review, 102*, 284–304.

Hewstone, M. (1996). Contact and categorization: Social psychological interventions to change intergroup relations. In C. M. Macrae, C. Stangor, & M. Hewstone (Eds.), *Stereotypes and stereotyping* (pp. 323–368). New York: Guilford Press.

Johnston, L. C. (1996). Resisting change: Information-seeking and stereotype change. *European Journal of Social Psychology, 26*, 799–826.

Johnston, L. C., & Macrae, C. N. (1994). Changing social stereotypes: The case of the information seeker. *European Journal of Social Psychology, 24*, 581–592.

Jones, J. M. (1997). *Prejudice and racism* (2nd ed.). Washington, DC: McGraw-Hill.

Jost, J. T., Kruglanski, A. W., & Nelson, T. O. (1998). Social metacognition: An expansionist review. *Personality and Social Psychology Review, 2*, 137–154.

Kahneman, D., & Miller, D. T. (1986). Norm theory: Comparing reality to its alternatives. *Psychological Review, 93*, 136–153.

Kahneman, D., Slovic, P., & Tversky, A. (1982). *Judgment under uncertainty: Heuristics and biaises*. New York: Cambridge University Press.

Kahneman, D., & Tversky, A. (1982). The simulation heuristics. In D. Kahneman, P. Slovic & A. Tversky (Eds.), *Judgments under uncertainty: Heuristics and biaised* (pp. 201–208). New York: Cambridge University Press.

Langer, E. J. (1975). The illusion of control. *Journal of Personality and Social Psychology, 32*, 311–328.

Langer, E. J., & Rodin, J. (1976). The effects of choice and enhanced personal responsibility for the aged: A field experiment in an institutional setting. *Journal of Personality and Social Psychology, 34*, 191–198.

Langer, E. J., & Roth, J. (1975). Heads I win, tails it's chance: The illusion of control as a function of the sequence of outcome in a purely chance task. *Journal of Personality and Social Psychology, 32*, 951–955.

Leyens, J.-P., Yzerbyt, V. Y., & Schadron, G. (1994). *Stereotypes and social cognition*. London: Sage.

Lories, G., Dardenne, B., & Yzerbyt, V. Y. (1998). From social cognition to metacognition. In V. Y. Yzerbyt, G. Lories, & B. Dardenne (Eds), *Metacognition: Cognition and social dimensions* (pp.1–15). London: Sage.

Lydon, J. E., & Zanna, M. P. (1990). Commitment in the face of adversity: A value-affirmation approach. *Journal of Personality and Social Psychology, 58,* 1040–1047.

Macrae, C. M., Stangor, C., & Hewstone, M. (1996). *Stereotypes and stereotyping.* New York: Guilford Press.

McComas, J., Dulberg, C., & Latter, J. (1997). Children's memory for locations visited: Importance of movement and choice. *Journal of Motor Behavior, 29,* 223–229.

Metcalfe, J., & Shimamura, A. P. (1994). *Metacognition.* Cambridge, MA: MIT Press.

Nelson, T. O. (1992). *Metacognition: Core readings.* Boston: Allyn & Bacon.

Nelson, T. O., Kruglanski, A. W., & Jost, J. T. (1998). Knowing thyself and others: Progress in metacognitive social psychology. In V. Yzerbyt, G. Lories. & B. Dardenne (Eds.), *Metacognition: Cognitive and social dimensions* (pp. 39–89). London: Sage.

Peeters, G., & Czapinski, J. (1990). Positive-negative asymmetry in evaluations: The distinction between affective and informational negativity effects. In W. Stroebe & M. Hewstone (Eds.), *European Review of Social Psychology* (pp. 33–60). Chichester, UK : Wiley.

Rodin, J. (1986). Aging and health: Effects of the sense of control. *Science, 233,* 1271-1276.

Rodin, J., & Langer, E. (1977). Long-term effect of a control-relevant intervention. *Journal of Personality and Social Psychology, 35,* 897–902.

Ross, L., Greene, D., & House, P. (1977). The "false consensus effect": An egocentric bias in social perception and attribution processes. *Journal of Experimental Social Psychology, 13,* 279–301.

Rothbaum, F., Weisz, J. R., & Snyder, S. S. (1982). Changing the world and changing the self: A two-process model of perceived control. *Journal of Personality and Social Psychology, 42,* 5–37.

Schlenker, B. R., Dlugolecki, D. W., & Doherty, K. (1993). The impact of self-presentations on self-appraisals and behavior: The power of public commitment. *Personality and Social Psychology Bulletin, 20,* 20–33.

Schulz, R. (1976). Effects of control and predicability on the physical and psychological well-being of the institutionalized ages. *Journal of Personality and Social Psychology, 33,* 563–573.

Schulz, R., & Hanusa, B. H. (1978). Long-term effects of control and predictability-enhancing interventions: Findings and ethical issues. *Journal of Personality and Social Psychology, 36,* 1194–1201.

Spranca, M., Minsk, E., & Baron, J. (1991). Omission and commission in judgments and choice. *Journal of Experimental Social Psychology, 21,* 76-105.

Swim, J. K., & Stangor, C. (1998). *Prejudice: The target's perspective.* San Diego, CA: Academic Press.

Tajfel, H. (1969). Cognitive aspects of prejudice. *Journal of Social Issues, 25,* 79–97.

Taylor, S. E. (1989). *Positive illusions: Creative self-deception and the healthy mind.* New York: Basic Books.

Taylor, S. E., Lichtman, R. R., & Wood, J. V. (1984). Attributions, beliefs about control, and adjustment to breast cancer. *Journal of Personality and Social Psychology, 46,* 489–502.

Thompson, S. C., Nanni, C., & Levine, A. (1994). Primary versus secondary and central versus consequence-related control in HIV-positive men. *Journal of Personality and Social Psychology, 67,* 540–547.

Thompson, S. C., Sobolew-Shubin, A., Galbraith, M. E., Schwankovsky, L., & Cruzen, D. (1993). Maintaining perception of control: Finding perceived control in low-control circumstances. *Journal of Personality and Social Psychology, 64,* 293–304.

Vanbeselaere, N. (1991). The different effects of simple and crossed categorizations: A result of the category differentiation process or of differential category salience? In W.

Stroebe & M. Hewstone (Eds.), *European review of social psychology* (pp. 247–278). Chichester, England: Wiley.

Webster, D. M. (1993). Motivated augmentation and reduction of the overattribution bias. *Journal of Personality and Social Psychology, 65,* 261–271.

Yzerbyt, V. Y., Dardenne, B., & Leyens, J.-P. (1998). Social judgeability concerns in impression formation. In V. Y. Yzerbyt, G. Lories, & B. Dardenne (Eds.), *Metacognition: Cognitive and social dimensions* (pp. 126–156). London: Sage.

Yzerbyt, V. Y., & Leyens, J.-P. (1991). Requesting information to form an impression: The influence of valence and confirmatory status. *European Journal of Social Psychology, 27,* 337–356.

Yzerbyt, V. Y., Lories, G., & Dardenne, B. (1998). *Metacognition: Cognitive and social dimensions.* London: Sage.

Yzerbyt, V. Y., Rocher, S., & Schadron, G. (1997). Stereotypes as explanations: A subjective essentialistic view of group perception. In R. Spears, P. J. Oakes, N. Ellemers, & S. A. Haslam (Eds.), *The social psychology of stereotyping and group life* (pp. 20–50). Cambridge, MA: Blackwell.

Zimbardo, P. G. (1969). *The cognitive control of motivation: The consequences of choice and dissonance.* Glenview, IL: Scott, Foresman.

18

CHAPTER

Andrea E. Abele

The Experience of a Positive Mood and Its Impact on Intergroup Differentiation and Stereotyping

☐ Mood as Subjective Experience

Thinking and acting are always accompanied by subjective experience. We do not only do something, but we always also experience it in a certain manner. We experience emotions like joy, pride, or anger while pursuing a goal; we experience problems while performing a task; we experience—wanted or unwanted—metacognitions during enacting a behavior; we experience ourselves as "objects" from an outside observer perspective in some situations. Sometimes our subjective experience lies in the focus of our attention, for instance, when we reflect on it. Sometimes it may be a background phenomenon and its possible influence is largely unnoticed. Sometimes we may consciously use our subjective experience as information; sometimes we may implicitly use it without being aware of this process.

Recent social psychological research has addressed the impact of subjective experience on judgment and behavior in a number of studies. Experiencing it as easy to recall a number of childhood memories, for

Address correspondence to Andrea E. Abele-Brehm, Lehrstuhl Sozialpsychologie, Universität Erlangen-Nürnberg, Bismarckstr. 6, D 91054 Erlangen, Germany. E-mail: abele@phil.uni-erlangen.de

instance, leads to the assessment that one's memory is quite good, although the easy recall was perhaps only due to the easy task (Belli, Winkielman, Read, Schwarz, & Lynn, 1998). Experiencing a happy mood leads to the conclusion that the person one is talking to is very "charming," although the positive mood was, for instance, induced by the sunny weather or a prior success (Forgas & Bower, 1987). Having just watched a romantic movie and experienced the respective emotions can lead to the conclusion that one's own relationship could be better, even though one was quite content with it before having watched the movie (Abele & Gendolla, 1999).

One especially important aspect of subjective experience is "mood," that is, the more or less positive or negative present affective state of a person. Mood is a subjective experience that—in contrast to concrete emotions elicited by significant events—usually does not attract much attention and is not consciously monitored. It is rather a background phenomenon, that tunes all other experiences as a "frame of mind" (Morris, 1989). Generally speaking, negative moods signal "noise." Something in the person's inner or outer world is unfavorable and not all right. The subjective experience of a negative mood should therefore lead to more defensiveness and/or negativity in social judgments and behavior. Positive mood, in contrast, signals "no noise." The world is a pleasant and safe place and there is no necessity to change anything. In a positive mood, the person does not have to change something, but he or she is rather "free" to do and think whatever he or she wants. In recent years, a number of theories concerned with the impact of mood on various cognitive and behavioral measures have been developed, and profound influences of mood on thinking, social judgments, and behavior have been demonstrated (for overviews, see Abele, 1995; Aspinwall, 1998; Fiedler, 1988; Forgas, 1995; Martin, Ward, Achee, & Wyer, 1993; Schwarz, 1990).

In the present paper, I will focus on one specific aspect of mood influences on social judgments. I will be concerned with positive mood states and their impact on stereotyping and intergroup differentiation. Intergroup differentiation and stereotyping are related phenomena. In both cases, the group a person belongs to has a significant influence on how he or she is evaluated. Usually outgroup members and members of stereotyped groups are less positively evaluated than ingroup members and persons without a stereotype label (cf. Diehl, 1990; Turner, 1991).

☐ Positive Mood, Intergroup Differentiation, and Stereotyping

Theories about affective influences on the differentiation of groups and on stereotyping have a long history. The scapegoat theory of prejudice, for instance, assumes that one means of reducing negative affective states is to discriminate against other persons or groups in the sense of a scapegoat (cf. Allport, 1954). The theory of downward comparison processes similarly states that downward comparisons help to improve one's negative feelings (Wills, 1981). A mood repair motive may also play a role in intergroup differentiation (Isen, 1987; see also Baird & Duck, 1999). These approaches stress the functional aspect of stereotyping as a means of negative state relief. More negative evaluations of stereotyped groups and outgroup members by persons experiencing a negative mood might reflect both their actual "frame of mind" and their attempt to repair their mood by a downward comparison.

From a functional perspective, the experience of a positive mood should not increase stereotyping or outgroup discrimination, since there is no need for negative state relief. Additionally, in a positive mood, the "frame of mind" is positive, too. This frame should also not lead to increased stereotyping.

Recent empirical research, however, suggests that positive affective states can have an impact on stereotyping and intergroup differentiation (e.g., Abele, Gendolla, & Petzold, 1998; Baird & Duck, 1999; Bodenhausen, Kramer, & Süsser, 1994; Bless, Schwarz, & Wieland, 1996a; Dovidio, Gaertner, Isen, & Lowrance, 1995; Forgas & Fiedler, 1996; Forgas & Moylan, 1991; Haddock, Zanna, & Esses, 1994; Lambert, Khan, Lickel, & Fricke, 1997; Stepper & Strack, 1993). Some findings suggest that stereotyping is reduced in a positive mood; others suggest that it is enhanced. I will now first present these studies and will group them according to whether they resulted in reduced or in enhanced stereotyping and intergroup differentiation. In a second step, I will discuss them with respect to theoretical conclusions. Finally, I will try to integrate the present state of knowledge on this specific question into a more general understanding of the impact of the subjective experience of a positive mood on thinking and acting.

Positive Mood and the Reduction of Stereotyping and/or Intergroup Differentiation

As has been demonstrated in several content areas of social judgments, positive moods tend to produce more positive judgments and negative moods tend to produce more negative judgments, known as *mood congruency* (e.g., Abele & Petzold, 1994; Bower, 1991; Forgas & Bower, 1987; Isen, 1987; Mayer, Gaschke, Braverman, & Evans, 1992). Some studies on stereotyping and intergroup differentiation found similar effects. A study by Forgas and Moylan (1991), for instance, showed that a positive mood led to more positive evaluations of targets presented in pictures than an average mood, and that this effect occurred both with respect to Caucasian- and Asian-looking targets. Similarly, correlational evidence by Haddock et al. (1994) suggests mood congruency effects in attitudes toward a stereotyped group for participants high in affect intensity.

Dovidio et al. (1995) let their participants work in groups, induced them into a positive or a neutral mood, and then presented them with a 5-minute video excerpt of another group working on a similar problem. Dependent variables were the extent of inclusive group representations and the evaluations of the ingroup (the participants' own group) and the outgroup (the group seen on the video excerpt). Groups in a positive mood, in contrast to those in a neutral mood, formed more inclusive group representations and evaluated both the outgroup and the ingroup more positively. Path-analyses revealed that the positive mood effect on inter-group evaluation was mediated by the superordinate group representa-tion. These findings, then, also demonstrate mood congruency effects. They further show that positive affective states can have another effect, namely, a more inclusive representation of groups. More inclusive group representations, in turn, predict more positive outgroup evaluations and lower levels of intergroup bias.

Positive Mood and the Enhancement of Stereotyping and/or Intergroup Differentiation

Other studies found no mood congruency, but rather the opposite effect of more stereotyping and intergroup differentiation in a positive mood. Bodenhausen et al. (1994) showed that persons induced into a positive mood in contrast to an average mood control condition assigned more guilt to a defendant who was a member of a negatively stereotyped group than to a defendant from a nonstereotyped group (see also Stepper & Strack, 1993). However, if the person was made accountable for his or her judgment, there was an opposite tendency of less stereotyping in posi-tive mood. Positive mood, then, led to a stronger reliance on stereotypes unless the participants were motivated to correct for them.

Bless et al. (1996a) induced their participants into happy, neutral, or sad mood and then let them listen to a 3-minute tape-recorded descrip-tion of a target and assess it on a number of dimensions. The target was either presented as a member of a positively evaluated occupation (Greenpeace representative) or as a member of a negatively evaluated occupation (manager in a big chemical company). The participants fur-ther received individuating information about these targets that was either mainly positive (six positive, two negative behaviors) or mainly negative (two positive, six negative behaviors). Average mood participants used both types of information in an additive manner. The evaluation was more positive for the Greenpeace representative than for the chemical company manager, and more positive for targets with mainly positive individuating information than for targets with mainly negative individuating information. The evaluations of participants induced into a positive mood, in contrast, reflected an interaction between the two types of information. There were extreme ratings of members belonging to the positive category (very positive in case of positive individuating information; very negative in case of negative individuating information) and more moderate ratings of members belonging to the negative category (slightly negative in case of negative individuating information and slightly positive in case of positive individuating information). The authors interpreted these findings as an indication of more generative processes in a positive mood. They assumed that participants induced into a positive mood reflected more on the implications of a category. If the individuating information was consistent with the categorical expectation, then reliance on the category was strong. If, in contrast, the individuating information was inconsistent with the stereotype expectation, then reliance on the individuating information became weaker.

Lambert et al. (1997) were mainly interested in stereotype correction processes in a negative mood. In their first experiment, however, they also analyzed the impact of a positive mood. A positive mood only led to more stereotyping than the control condition if negative stereotypes—but not positive stereotypes—were activated and when stereotype consistent negative traits—but not positive traits—had to be assessed.

Forgas and Fiedler (1996) analyzed resource allocation decisions to one's ingroup versus the outgroup in a minimal group design (cf. Tajfel, Flament, Billig, & Bundy, 1971), where the participants had been randomly assigned to the groups of "overestimators" or "underestimators," presumably on the basis of an initial dot estimation task. They found that a positive mood led to more intergroup differentiation and—in their third study—to shorter response latencies if the relevance of the group membership was low. In the case of high group membership relevance, in contrast, there was no stronger ingroup-outgroup differentiation in a positive mood and no difference in response latencies compared to an average mood condition. The theoretical account relies on the Affect Infusion Model (AIM; Forgas, 1995) which posits "affect infusion" on social judgments and behavior depending on the processing strategies chosen. Low relevance of the task accompanied by a positive mood should lead to heuristic processing with strong reliance on the group label and more intergroup differentiation, whereas high task relevance accompanied by a positive mood leads to substantive processing with a consideration of all accessible information and hence reduced intergroup differentiation.

In contrast to the results by Forgas and Fiedler (1996), a recent study by Baird and Duck (1999) that also applied a minimal group design and also used resource allocation decisions as the dependent variable did not reveal a stronger intergroup differentiation in a positive mood compared to the control condition. Also in contrast to Forgas and Fiedler (1996), Baird and Duck (1999) reported longer response latencies in their positive mood condition than in the control condition.

A study by Abele et al. (1998) compared ingroup-outgroup differentiation in a minimal group design (dot estimation task-random assignment to "overestimator" or "underestimator") between participants induced into a positive mood or an average mood. The dependent variables were likability ratings and the respective response latencies. Several targets presented as either ingroup members or outgroup members with either positive trait information or negative trait information had to be assessed. All targets were also presented without group label. In neither experiment did we find any mood induced differences in response latencies. The likability ratings, however, were strongly influenced by the participants' mood. Figure 18.1 shows the results of the first of these experiments.

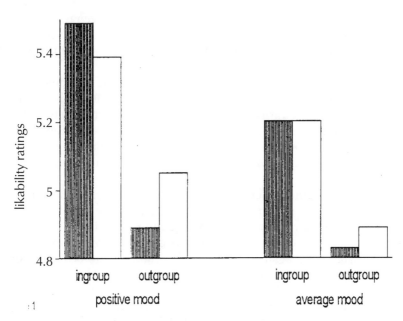

FIGURE 18.1. Ingroup-outgroup target likability ratings in the two mood conditions (Abele et al., 1998, Experiment 1).

The likability ratings of targets without group label resulted in a significant mood congruency effect, with more positive ratings in the positive mood condition than in the average mood condition. With a group label, however, the targets were rated more extremely in the positive mood condition than in the average mood condition. Ingroup members were rated more positively than the respective targets without a group label, and outgroup members were rated less positively than the respective targets without a group label. In contrast to the findings by Bless et al. (1996a), we did not find an interaction between mood, group label, and valence of the individuating information. Targets with an ingroup label were always rated more positively than targets with an outgroup label in the positive mood condition.

A comparison of targets with positive trait information versus targets with negative trait information further showed that the impact of the trait information was the same in both mood conditions if targets without a group label had been rated (positive mood mean difference $M = 4.19$; average mood mean difference $M = 4.23$). With the group label, however, the difference of targets with positive trait information versus targets with negative trait information was smaller in the positive mood condition than in the average mood condition (positive mood mean difference $M = 3.39$; neutral mood mean difference $M = 3.92$). We interpret this finding such that the weight of the individuating information is the same in both mood conditions (see targets without the group label). Even though individuating information has the same weight, its impact is smaller for targets with a group label in a positive mood, since the weight of the group label is higher under this condition.

In the second experiment, we increased the amount of individuating information and presented our participants with targets described by three traits. Additionally, we varied the consistency versus inconsistency of the individuating information (four conditions: three positive traits; three negative traits; one positive and two negative traits; one negative and two positive traits). The findings were very similar to the first study (see Figure 18.2).

There was a marginally significant mood congruency effect for the ratings of targets without a group label. Targets with a group label were again rated more extremely in the positive mood condition than in the average mood condition. Ingroup members compared with targets without group label were again rated more favorably in the positive mood condition than in the average mood. In contrast, outgroup members compared with the targets without a group label were rated less favorably in the positive mood condition. We also found that the differentiation of targets with positive versus negative individuating information was the same between both mood conditions if targets were not presented with a

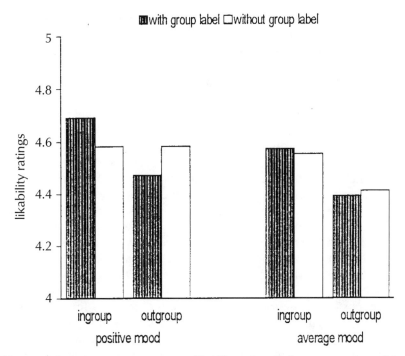

■with group label **□**without group label

FIGURE 18.2. Ingroup-outgroup target likability ratings in the two mood conditions (Abele et al., 1998, Experiment 2).

group label, but was smaller in the positive mood condition for targets with a group label. With respect to the individuating information's consistency versus inconsistency, there was no differential mood impact. We rather found for both mood conditions that the impact of the group label increased for targets with inconsistent trait information. The response latencies were longer for targets with a group label compared to targets without a group label and were longer for targets with inconsistent trait information than for targets with consistent trait information. Mood had no impact at all.

Our interpretation of these effects relies on a twofold impact of positive affective states. First, the mood congruency effect can be interpreted as an informational impact of mood. Mood is integrated into the judgment together with other accessible information, and its impact is greater when less additional information has to be considered (Abele & Gendolla, 1999; Abele & Petzold, 1994; Abele et al., 1998). This means more mood congruency for targets without a group label than for targets with a group label, and more mood congruency if only one piece of individuating information is presented than if three pieces are given. Second, the finding that positive mood induced more extreme judgments of targets belonging to the ingroup versus the outgroup can be interpreted as due to the larger weight of the group membership information. Since the weight of the individuating information is the same in both mood conditions if no group label is presented, we further conclude that individuating information is processed in the same way in a positive or neutral mood.

A recent experiment (Abele, 1999) applied a very similar methodology as Abele et al. (1998), but used stereotypes instead of ingroup-outgroup labels. The main question was whether a positive mood induction has similar effects on the evaluation—and the respective response latencies—of targets belonging to stereotyped groups as on the evaluation of ingroup members versus outgroup members created by a minimal group design. Following the above theoretical reasoning, it was posited that a positive mood leads to a stronger reliance on the group label than an average mood. It was further tested how the consistency vs. inconsistency between the group label expectation and the individuating information—positive category with positive trait, negative category with negative trait as more consistent information; positive trait, negative category or negative trait, positive category as more inconsistent information—affects the participants' judgments. The Abele et al. (1998) findings suggest main effects of group label and individuating information. The data from Bless et al. (1996a) suggest an interaction between the two types of information in a positive mood.

The participants were induced into a positive mood or were in an average mood, and then had to rate the likability of a number of targets presented by a positive trait or a negative trait and—in two thirds of the cases—also by their occupation. In half of the cases, the occupation is positively connoted ("nurse"), and in the other half, it is more negatively connoted ("stockbroker") (see Abele & Petzold, 1998). Figure 18.3 shows the results for the likability ratings.

There was no mood main effect. The main effects of trait valence—more positive ratings of targets with positive traits—and of the group label—more negative ratings of the stockbroker targets than of the no-label and nurse targets—were qualified by two interactions. One was the interaction between group label and mood condition. There was no difference between the mood conditions in the ratings of targets without a group label. In accord with the prediction, however, targets with a group label were rated more extremely in the positive than in the average mood condition. The nurse targets were rated more positively and the stockbroker targets were rated more negatively in a positive mood. The interaction between group label and trait valence means that the effects were more pronounced with respect to positive traits than with respect to negative traits.

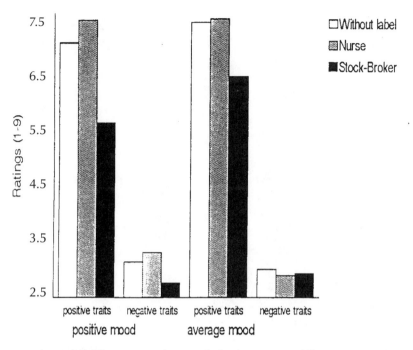

FIGURE 18.3. Likability ratings of targets belonging to two different occupations in the two mood conditions (Abele, 1999).

Replicating our previous findings (Abele et al., 1998), response latencies were shorter for targets without a group label than for targets with group label, and there was no main effect of mood. However, there was a two way interaction between mood and consistency/inconsistency of target information (see Figure 18.4).

Participants in a positive mood had the longest response latencies if they rated stockbrokers with positive traits or nurses with negative traits (that is, stereotype-inconsistent individuating information) and shorter ones for targets with stereotype-consistent traits. Average mood participants did not show this difference.

To sum up, in contrast to our previous study (Abele et al., 1998), this study did not find mood congruency effects on the likability ratings of targets without an occupation label. Two interpretations for these divergent findings are possible. First, Abele et al. (1998) applied a within participants design, and the present experiment applied a between participants design where the error variance attributable to individual differences is larger. Second, the present stereotype effects were much stronger than the previous ingroup-outgroup differentiation effects. It may well be that the strong impact of the occupation in cases of targets with a label has

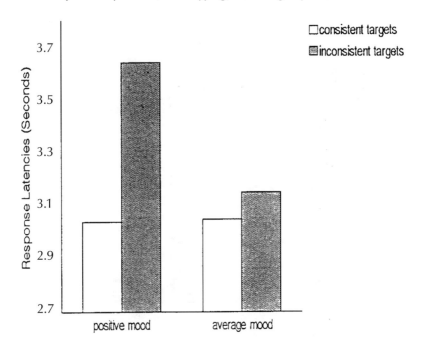

FIGURE 18.4. Response latencies in the two mood conditions (Abele, 1999).

also spread to the ratings of targets without a label, thus weakening a possible mood congruency effect.

The general hypothesis that a positive mood increases the relative weight of the occupation label but does not reduce the weight of the individuating information was supported. Participants induced into a positive mood did not differ from the average mood participants if targets without a group label had to be assessed, showing that they used the individuating information in the same way. Participants in the positive mood condition, however, differentiated more between targets with different occupations than participants in an average mood. They rated the nurse targets more positively and the stockbroker targets more negatively than the average mood participants. This effect was independent of the valence of the individuating information. These findings fit very well our previous data on mood and intergroup differentiation. They suggest that the mechanism underlying both kinds of judgments—at least when the methodology and concrete operationalization are kept constant—is the same.

Also replicating our previous findings, there was no mood main effect on the response latencies, only a main effect of the presence versus absence of the occupation label. In contrast to the previous findings, however, there was an interaction between mood and evaluative consistency versus inconsistency of the target information on the response latencies. This is a strong hint that participants in the positive mood condition elaborated more on the meaning of the occupation label and its relation to the presented trait information. In the case of evaluative consistency, they reacted as fast as the average mood group. In the case of inconsistency, they took longer to reach their judgment. I can only speculate about why we did not find such an interaction in our previous study. The most appealing post hoc interpretation seems to be that the connotative meaning and thus the impact of the labels "nurse" and especially "stockbroker" were higher than the meaning and the impact of the label "overestimator" or "underestimator."

☐ Theoretical Conclusions

Even though these findings are complex, some trends and theoretical interpretations may be drawn from them. First, the impact of positive mood seems to be higher if the motivation for the task or the task importance is low. Second, mood congruency can also exist with respect to intergroup judgments. And third, that the positive mood increased the impact of group labels and stereotypes may be due to two mechanisms: more heuristic processing and/or elaboration, and the higher weight of the group label.

The Impact of a Positive Mood Is Higher in Case of Low Task Importance

The above findings suggest that high motivation for the task, either because the person is made accountable for his or her judgment (Bodenhausen et al., 1994) or because the group assignment is subjectively very important (Forgas & Fiedler, 1996), leads to a reduction of the mood effect. This finding is in line with the AIM (Forgas, 1995), and it parallels results in other research areas of subjective experience (cf. Schwarz, Bless, Strack, & Klumpp, 1991). Subjective experience seems to receive greater weight as the accessible content becomes more equivocal.

Mood Congruency in Stereotype and Intergroup Judgments

The data show that mood congruency can—under certain conditions—also emerge in judgments of stereotyped groups and in intergroup judgments. However, this effect is relatively weak (Abele et al., 1998; Haddock et al., 1994) and may sometimes be mediated by another effect of positive mood, namely, broader categorization (Dovidio et al., 1995) or a more unusual arrangement of target couples and thus a need for more "constructive" processing (Forgas & Moylan, 1991).

Stronger Reliance on Group Labels and Stereotypes as Indicative of Heuristic Processing and/or More Creative Elaboration of the Group Label in a Positive Mood

The stronger reliance on stereotypes and on group labels in a positive mood compared to the control condition (observed in the studies by Bodenhausen et al., 1994; Forgas & Fiedler, 1996; Lambert et al., 1997), as well as the relatively stronger reliance on categorical information compared to individuating information in a positive mood (observed in the studies by Abele, 1999; Abele et al. 1998; Bless et al., 1996a) is open to two interpretations. It could be indicative of more heuristic processing or it could be indicative of more creative elaboration of the group label. Both mechanisms, heuristic processing and more creative elaboration of categories, would lead to a stronger effect of the stereotype or group label in a positive mood. The posited underlying process, however, is different.

The stronger reliance on stereotypes in a positive mood could be due to more heuristic processing (Bodenhausen et al., 1994; Chaiken, Liberman & Eagly, 1989), where a judgment is mainly based on peripheral cues such as stereotypes or group labels. Positive mood could lead to more heuristic processing due to reduced motivation for effortful processing,[1] because positive mood can serve as a signal that there are no pressing problems to be solved in the environment and that everything is all right (Schwarz, 1990; Schwarz & Clore, 1983, 1988).

Another mechanism that might underlie the observed effects is an increase in creative elaboration of the group label. As has been shown in previous research, a positive mood leads to more creative elaboration of stimulus material (Abele, 1992, 1995; Abele & Rank, 1993; Fiedler, 1988; Isen, Daubman, & Nowicki, 1987; Murray, Sujan, Hirt, & Sujan, 1990), to broader categorizations (Isen & Daubman, 1984), and to more generative processes (Bless, Clore, Schwarz, Golisano, Rabe, & Wölk, 1996b; Bless et al., 1996a). Accordingly, if targets with group label have to be assessed, persons in a positive mood might think more about the implications of the group label and might elaborate more on it. For instance, they might integrate the expectations generated by the group label with the actual information presented, and therefore the group label receives a higher weight than the individuating information (Abele, 1999; Abele et al., 1998). They might compare the stereotype expectations with the individuating information, and depending on the consistency or inconsistency of this comparison might rate the target differently (cf. Bless et al., 1996a). Or they might form larger group categories and might therefore differentiate less between them (Dovidio et al., 1995).

Is heuristic processing the mechanism underlying the positive mood effect if task importance is low rather than high, as suggested by Bodenhausen et al. (1994) and Forgas and Fiedler (1996)? A close inspection of the studies shows that this can't be the whole story. For instance, Lambert et al. (1997) did not vary task relevance, and they only found stronger stereotyping in a positive mood if stereotype and individuating information were negative and consistent (see also Bless et al., 1996a). Since Bodenhausen et al. (1994) only presented targets with stereotype consistent information (member of a stereotyped group accused of an offense consistent with the stereotype), this study could not test whether stronger stereotyping in a positive mood would still exist if stereotype inconsistent information is presented. Further, the study by Baird and Duck (1999) varied group status—which should be a relevance manipulation, too—and found no interaction between this manipulation and the positive mood induction. In addition, that, the studies by Dovidio et al. (1995), Bless et al. (1996a), Abele et al. (1998), and Abele (1999) did not instruct the participants to be especially careful or to treat the task as especially important, and their findings are more compatible with the elaborative processes assumption. Finally, one could also argue that the response latencies should be shorter in a positive mood if the stronger reliance on the group label is indicative of heuristic processing. As the above studies show, however, only Forgas and Fiedler (1996) found shorter response latencies in a positive mood, whereas Abele et al. (1998) found no differences, Baird and Duck (1999) found longer response latencies, and Abele (1999) found an interaction between evaluative consistency of the target information and mood with respect to response latencies.

Is "creative elaboration" then the mechanism underlying the positive mood effects on stereotyping and intergroup differentiation? The above findings from Dovidio et al. (1995), Bless et al. (1996a), Abele et al. (1998), and Abele (1999) suggest this possibility, the findings from Lambert et al. (1997) and Baird and Duck (1999) also fit such an interpretation, and results from Bodenhausen et al. (1994) do not contradict it. As previous research has shown, a positive mood enhances creative elaboration of material and leads to broader categorizations (Abele, 1992, 1995; Bless et al., 1996a, 1996b; Isen & Daubman, 1984; Isen et al., 1987; Murray et al., 1990). Such an enhanced creative elaboration of the stereotype information or the group label means that the person thinks more about the expectations generated by the label and/or the implications combined with it. As the present review shows, however, this general tendency can lead to somewhat different effects: it can lead to a shift in perceived group boundaries such that they become larger (cf. Dovidio et al., 1995) and group conceptualizations become more inclusive; it can lead to a different reliance on the individuating information depending on its consistency versus inconsistency with the expectation generated by the group label (Bless et al., 1996a); and it can lead to a stronger weight of the group label due to the additionally generated material in the creative elaboration process (Abele, 1999; Abele et al., 1998), which is—among others—also evident in longer response latencies when there is inconsistency between the evaluative meaning of the label and of the individuating information (Abele, 1999).

More research is needed to specify the exact preconditions of these partly different effects of creative elaboration. It may be that—among others—the specific operationalization chosen also has some impact. In the Dovidio et al. (1995) research, for instance, the ingroup was physically present and the outgroup was represented by a 5-minute video. Bless et al. (1996a) used a 3-minute audiotape of a person described by an occupation and eight behaviors. Abele et al. (1998) and Abele (1999) presented very short target descriptions on the computer screen and let their participants rate a large number of such targets.[2] As a general conclusion, it can be stated that the impact of positive affective states on intergroup judgments is multifaceted and is mediated by a number of additional variables, such as task importance and amount or kind of available information (cf. Abele, 1995; Aspinwall, 1998; Bless et al., 1996b; Fiedler, 1988; Forgas, 1995; Martin et al., 1993).

The Subjective Experience of a Positive Mood and Intergroup Judgments: General Conclusions

As was suggested above, a positive mood is a subjective experience signaling that there are no pressing problems to be solved and that everything is all right. The person is free to do and think whatever he or she wants to. Stated differently, the experience of a positive mood can facilitate creative thinking, unusual associations, and deeper processing, because there are no other urgent things to be done. Thus confronted with connotatively rich material like stereotypes or group membership information, a person in a positive mood might feel free to "gamble" with this information, to consider it from divergent perspectives, and therefore to process it more deeply. The consequence would be a stronger elaboration of the category's implications and a stronger weighting of this type of information in forming the judgment compared to connotatively less rich information. This deeper processing of the category information would then lead to greater differences in judgments of stereotyped groups in a positive mood compared to a more neutral mood. However, the experience of a positive mood does not necessarily lead to a stronger elaboration of connotatively rich material, because in a positive mood, the person can also think and do something else. Another general process, the informational impact of the experience of a positive mood as a *positive frame of mind*, seems also to exist with respect to stereotype judgments. It is, however, weaker than its impact on the elaboration of the category.

☐ Notes

[1]The other possibility—positive mood leads to more heuristic processing due to a reduced cognitive capacity—was rejected by findings from Bodenhausen et al. (1994).

[2]It is unclear how these different operationalizations of the targets, as well as the different measures—multiple measures of one target versus single measures of multiple targets—might have influenced the findings. The high similarity of the findings from Abele et al. (1998) and Abele (1999), however, suggest that the specific methodology is an important factor to consider in the analysis of positive mood effects on stereotyping and intergroup judgments.

☐ References

Abele, A. (1992). Positive and negative mood influences on creativity. Evidence for asymmetrical effects. *Polish Psychological Bulletin, 23*, 203–221.

Abele, A. (1995). *Stimmung und Leistung* [Mood and performance]. Göttingen, Germany: Hogrefe.

Abele, A. (1999). *Positive affective states and stereotyping.* Unpublished manuscript, University of Erlangen.

Abele, A., & Gendolla, G. (1999). Satisfaction judgments in positive and negative moods: Effects of concurrent assimilation and contrast producing processes. *Personality and Social Psychology Bulletin, 25*(7), 833–895.

Abele, A., Gendolla, G., & Petzold, P. (1998). Positive mood and in-group/out-group differentiation in a minimal group setting. *Personality and Social Psychology Bulletin, 24*(12), 1343–1357.

Abele, A., & Petzold, P. (1994). How does mood operate in an impression formation task? An information integration approach. *European Journal of Social Psychology, 24*, 189–206.

Abele, A., & Petzold, P. (1998). Pragmatical use of categorical information in impression formation. *Journal of Personality and Social Psychology, 75*(2), 347–358.

Abele, A., & Rank, S. (1993). Zur Stimmungkontingenz der Verarbeitung persuasiver Kommunikationen [Mood contingency in the processing of persuasive communication]. *Zeitschrift für Sozialpsychologie, 24*, 117–128.

Allport, G. W. (1954). *The nature of prejudice.* Cambridge, MA: Addison-Wesley.

Aspinwall, L. G. (1998). Rethinking the role of positive affect in self-regulation. *Motivation and Emotion, 22*(1), 1–32.

Baird, L. & Duck, J.M. (1999). *Mood and relative mood status as determinants of intergroup discrimination.* Manuscript in preparation.

Belli, R., Winkielman, P., Read, J., Schwarz, N., & Lynn, S. (1998). Recalling more childhood events leads to judgment of poorer memory: Implications for the recovered/false memory debate. *Psychonomic Bulletin and Review, 5,* 318–323.

Bless, H., Clore, G., Schwarz, N., Golisano, V., Rabe, C., & Wölk, M. (1996b). Mood and the use of scripts: Does a happy mood really lead to mindlessness? *Journal of Personality and Social Psychology, 71,* 665–679.

Bless, H., Schwarz, N., & Wieland, R. (1996a). Mood and the impact of category membership and individuating information. *European Journal of Social Psychology, 26,* 935–959.

Bodenhausen, G. V., Kramer, G. P., & Süsser, K. (1994). Happiness and stereotypic thinking in social judgment. *Journal of Personality and Social Psychology, 66,* 621–632.

Bower, G. H. (1991) Mood congruity of social judgments. In J. P. Forgas (Ed.), *Emotion and social judgment* (pp. 31–53). Oxford, England: Pergamon.

Chaiken, S., Liberman, A., & Eagly, A. H. (1989). Heuristic and systematic information processing within and beyond the persuasion context. In J. S. Uleman & J. A. Bargh (Eds.), *Unintended thought* (pp. 212–252). New York: Guilford Press.

Diehl, M. (1990). The minimal group paradigm: Theoretical explanations and empirical findings. In W. Stroebe & M. Hewstone (Eds.), *European review of social psychology* (Vol. 1, pp. 263–289). Chichester, England: Wiley.

Dovidio, J. F., Gaertner, S. L., Isen, A. M., & Lowrance, R. (1995). Group representations and intergroup bias: Positive affect, similarity, and group size. *Personality and Social Psychology Bulletin, 21,* 856–865.

Fiedler, K. (1988). Emotional mood, cognitive style, and behavior regulation. In K. Fiedler & J. P. Forgas (Eds.), *Affect, cognition, and social behavior* (pp. 100–119). Toronto, Canada: Hogrefe.

Forgas, J. P. (1995). Mood and judgment: The Affect Infusion Model (AIM). *Psychological Bulletin, 117,* 39–66.

Forgas, J. P., & Bower, G. H. (1987). Mood effects on person perception judgments. *Journal of Personality and Social Psychology, 53,* 53–60.

Forgas, J. P., & Fiedler, K. (1996). Us and them: Mood effects on intergroup discrimination. *Journal of Personality and Social Psychology, 70(1),* 28–40.

Forgas, P., & Moylan, S. J. (1991). Affective influences on stereotype judgments. *Cognition and Emotion, 5(5/6),* 379–395.

Haddock, G., Zanna, M. P., & Esses, V. M. (1994). Mood and the expression of intergroup attitudes: The moderating role of affect intensity. *European Journal of Social Psychology, 24,* 189–205.

Isen, A. M. (1987). Positive affect, cognitive processes, and social behavior. In L. Berkowitz (Ed.), *Advances in experimental social psychology* (Vol. 20, pp. 203–253). New York: Academic Press.

Isen, A. M., & Daubmann, K. (1984). The influence of affect on categorization. *Journal of Personality and Social Psychology, 47,* 1206-1217.

Isen, A. M., Daubmann, K., & Nowicki, G. (1987). Positive affect facilitates creative problem solving. *Journal of Personality and Social Psychology, 52,* 1122–1131.

Lambert A. J., Khan, S. R., Lickel, B. A., & Fricke, K. (1997). Mood and the correction of positive versus negative stereotypes. *Journal of Personality and Social Psychology, 27(5),* 1002–1016.

Martin, L. L., Ward, D. W., Achee, J. W., & Wyer, R. S. (1993). Mood as input: People have to interpret the motivational implications of their moods. *Journal of Personality and Social Psychology, 64,* 317–326.

Mayer, J. D., Gaschke, Y., Braverman, D., & Evans, T. (1992). Mood congruent judgment is a general effect. *Journal of Personality and Social Psychology, 63,* 119–132.

Morris, W. N. (1989). *Mood, the frame of mind.* New York: Springer.

Murray, N., Sujan, H., Hirt, E. R., & Sujan, M. (1990). The influence of mood on categorization. *Journal of Personality and Social Psychology, 59,* 411–425.

Schwarz, N. (1990). Feelings as information: Informational and motivational functions of affective states. In R. Sorrentino & E. T. Higgins (Eds.), *Handbook of motivation and cognition: Foundations of social behavior* (Vol. 2, pp. 527–561). New York: Guilford Press.

Schwarz, N., Bless, H., Strack, F., & Klumpp, G. (1991). Ease of retrieval as information: Another look at the availability heuristic. *Journal of Personality and Social Psychology, 61*(2), 195–202.

Schwarz, N., & Clore, G. (1983). Mood, misattribution, and judgments of well-being: Informative but directive functions of affective states. *Journal of Personality and Social Psychology, 45,* 513–523.

Schwarz, N., & Clore, G. (1988). How do I feel about it? The informative function of affective states. In K. Fiedler & J. P. Forgas (Eds.), *Affect, cognition, and social behavior* (pp. 44–62). Göttingen, Germany: Hogrefe.

Stepper, S., & Strack, F. (1993). Stereotype Beurteilung von Ost- und Westdeutschen: Der Einfluß der Stimmung (Stereotypical assessments of East and West Germans. The impact of mood). *Zeitschrift für Sozialpsychologie, 24,* 218–225.

Tajfel, H., Flament, C., Billig, M. G., & Bundy, R. P. (1971). Social categorization and intergroup behavior. *European Journal of Social Psychology, 1,* 149–178.

Turner, J. (1991). *Social influence.* Buckingham, England: Open University Press.

Wills, T. A. (1981). Downward comparison principles in social psychology. *Psychological Bulletin, 90,* 245–271.

John F. Dovidio
Samuel L. Gaertner
Stephenie Loux

CHAPTER 19

Subjective Experiences and Intergroup Relations: The Role of Positive Affect

For the past half-century, the Contact Hypothesis (Allport, 1954; Cook, 1985) has been a guiding framework for strategies designed to reduce intergroup bias and conflict. This hypothesis proposes that simple contact between groups is not sufficient to improve intergroup relations. Rather, to reduce bias, certain conditions within the contact situation, such as equal status, personal interaction, cooperative interdependence, and supportive norms (see Pettigrew, 1998) must be met.

Beyond identifying *what* characteristics of intergroup contact are critical for reducing bias, recent approaches have investigated *how* these factors operate to improve intergroup relations (e.g., Brewer & Miller, 1984; Gaertner, Dovidio, Anastasio, Bachman, & Rust, 1993; Stephan & Stephan, 1984, 1985). These perspectives typically consider the subjective experiences of people involved in contact and their perceptions and cognitive representations of the individuals and groups. Thus, how people subjectively conceive of group boundaries, rather than the functional relations

Research presented in this chapter and preparation of the manuscript were supported by NIMH Grant MH 48721. The authors are also grateful to the editors for their helpful comments on earlier versions of the work.

Address correspondence to John F. Dovidio, Department of Psychology, Colgate University, Hamilton, NY 13346. E-mail: jdovidio@mail.colgate.edu

between groups per se, is a critical determinant of intergroup attitudes. Moreover, subjective experiences, such as affect that precedes intergroup contact and arises from unrelated sources, can influence how groups are conceived. The impact of affect may be indirect, influencing what information is attended to and how it is processed, or it may be direct, influencing how others are valued. The present chapter explores how these subjective experiences shape intergroup attitudes and relations.

Consistent with the hypothesized role of the cognitive representations of the groups, factors specified by the Contact Hypothesis may reduce bias through the process of weakening the salience of the intergroup boundaries, that is, through *decategorization*. According to this perspective, under the conditions specified by the Contact Hypothesis, intergroup interaction can individuate members of the outgroup by revealing within-group differences in their opinions (Wilder, 1978), or it can produce personalizing interactions with the exchange of intimate information (Brewer & Miller, 1984; Miller, Brewer, & Edwards, 1985).

The Common Ingroup Identity Model (Gaertner, Dovidio, Anastasio, Bachman, & Rust, 1993), an alternative approach, also proposes that intergroup bias and conflict can be reduced by influencing the ways in which group members subjectively conceive of group boundaries, but this is accomplished through *recategorization* rather than decategorization. Recategorization involves using an alternative, superordinate social category to think about both the ingroup and the outgroup. This chapter, which describes a series of studies derived from the Common Ingroup Identity Model, examines the role of subjective processes and experiences—in particular, how group memberships are conceived and cognitively represented and how incidental positive affect can influence these representations and the outcomes of intergroup contact. Understanding how cognitive and affective processes can mediate and moderate the consequences of intergroup contact can help guide interventions to improve intergroup relations.

☐ The Common Ingroup Identity Model

The Common Ingroup Identity Model recognizes the central role of social cognition, specifically social categorization, in ameliorating as well as in creating intergroup bias. In particular, the model proposes that *re*categorization, in contrast to *de*categorization, may also provide an effective strategy for reducing intergroup bias. Specifically, we hypothesize that if members of different groups are induced to conceive of themselves as a single group rather than as two separate groups, attitudes toward former outgroup members will become more positive through processes involving pro-ingroup bias (Brewer, 1979; Mullen, Brown, & Smith, 1992; Tajfel & Turner, 1979).

This pro-ingroup bias has many facets. Categorization of a person as an ingroup member rather than as an outgroup member produces more positive evaluations (Brewer, 1979; Messick & Mackie, 1989; Tajfel, 1969) and perceptions of greater belief similarity (Brown, 1984; Brown & Abrams, 1986; Hogg & Turner, 1985; Stein, Hardyck, & Smith, 1965; Wilder, 1984). It also improves memory for positive information about others (Howard & Rothbart, 1980) and reduces attributions of personal responsibility for negative outcomes (Hewstone, 1990). Thus, by redefining original outgroup members as ingroup members, the cognitive and motivational processes that initially contributed to intergroup bias and conflict may be redirected toward establishing more harmonious intergroup relations.

The Common Ingroup Identity Model is summarized schematically in Figure 19.1. On the left are contextual factors and interventions. These include intergroup interdependence (e.g., cooperation), intergroup differentiation (e.g., related to physical similarity/dissimilarity), environmen-

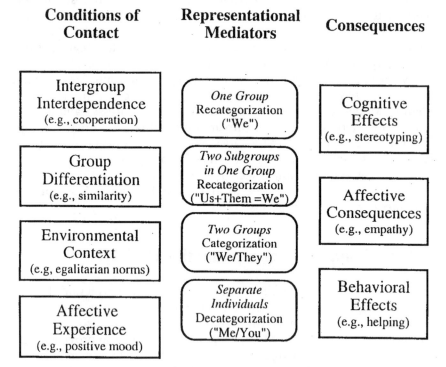

FIGURE 19.1. The Common Ingroup Identity Model: Effects of conditions of contact on the cognitive, affective, and behavioral outcomes of intergroup contact are mediated by group representations.

tal supports (e.g., egalitarian norms), and precontact experience (e.g., incidental affect). These contextual factors are hypothesized to influence cognitive representations of the memberships (center) as one group (recategorization), as two subgroups in one group (a dual identity form of recategorization), as two groups (categorization), or as separate individuals (decategorization). Within the model, intergroup cognition involved in social categorization is the critical mediator of subsequent intergroup attitudes and behavior. These resulting cognitive representations (i.e., one group, two group, two subgroups in one, or separate individuals) are then proposed to produce specific cognitive, affective, and behavioral consequences.

Although forming a single, inclusive (one group) representation is a primary form of recategorization, the development of a superordinate identity does not always require people to abandon their previous group identities. People may possess a dual identity, conceiving relations as two subgroups within another, more inclusive group. In the model, we also recognize that decategorization (seeing people as separate individuals) can reduce bias. In contrast, perceptions of the groups as separate entities (we/they) maintains and reinforces bias. In previous research, we have found evidence that aspects of intergroup contact, which have been identified by the Contact Hypothesis as key elements, decrease intergroup bias in part through changing these cognitive representations of the groups (see Dovidio et al., 1997; Gaertner et al., 1994, 1999a, 1999b, 1999c). As indicated in Figure 19.1, we propose that affective experience is a critical determinant of these cognitive representations. In the present chapter, we report five studies that investigated how affect, specifically *positive* affect, can influence these representations and thereby shape intergroup representations and relations.

☐ Affect and Social Categorization

Affect can significantly and systematically influence social categorization. Positive affect and its influence on *non*social categorization was initially investigated by Isen and Daubman (1984). In their study, participants were given the name of objects (e.g., belt) and were asked to rate how well these objects fit into categories (e.g., clothing). They found that people experiencing positive affect (but not those experiencing negative affect) demonstrated broader, more inclusive categorization of objects than did people in a neutral affect control condition. In particular, compared to those in the neutral affect group, people experiencing positive affect were more likely to include nontypical exemplars (e.g., elevator) as members of associated categories (e.g., vehicle). Regardless of the affect condition, people identified typical exemplars as members of the categories (e.g., car for vehicles), presumably because their membership was already well-defined. Isen and Daubman (1984) proposed that positive affect promotes the use of more information particularly positive material, and more diverse information through elaborative processing, thereby establishing a larger cognitive context in which more connections between nontypical exemplars and the categories can be identified (see also Abele, 1992). Similarly, positive affect produces more elaboration of information related to social stimuli (Bless, Clore, Schwarz, Golisano, Rabe, & Wölk, 1996; Bless, Schwarz, & Kemmelmeier, 1996; Bless, Schwarz, & Wieland, 1996; Fiedler, 1988).

Theoretically, these findings are consistent with Isen's (1987, pp. 234–235) hypothesis that positive affect influences the organization of cognitive material by encouraging elaborative processing. This perspective contrasts other approaches that hypothesize that positive affect leads instead to heuristic, more simplified forms of cognitive processing (Bodenhausen, 1993; Bodenhausen, Kramer, & Susser, 1994; Mackie & Worth, 1989). According to Isen, positive affect increases the accessibility of diverse ideas and produces a more complex associative context than normally occurs (Isen, Johnson, Mertz, & Robinson, 1985). As Tversky and Gati (1978) found, when people have more information and ideas about concepts, they are more likely to report similarities when they are motivated to perceive similarities and to report differences when they are motivated to perceive dissimilarities. Thus, when framed appropriately, positive affect can increase categorization breadth for neutral as well as positive stimuli (see also Murray, Sujan, Hirt, & Sujan, 1990).

Isen, Niedenthal, and Cantor (1992) extended these findings to social categorization. They hypothesized that positive affect would facilitate broader social categorization by leading people to associate what is usually seen as a neutral target with a positive category. Because positive affect primes positive material in memory, it facilitates a connection between the target and the positive category. As a consequence, people experiencing positive affect would be more likely to include nontypical exemplars into socially desirable categories. For instance, a grandmother and a bartender could both be considered examples of "nurturant people," but a bartender would be considered a nontypical exemplar, whereas a grandmother would be a typical exemplar. The results supported the predictions and the proposed mechanism. Positive affect increased the extent to which a nontypical exemplar was associated with a positive category. Also as predicted, positive affect did not increase the extent to which nontypical exemplars were associated with negative categories (i.e., emotionally unstable people and pretentious people), presumably because positive affect does not activate negative material and connections.

In general, the research on positive affect suggests that its influence on category breadth is moderated by the valence (positive or negative) of the category and by the valence and the strength (nontypical or typical) of the exemplars being considered. Isen (1993), for example, posited that positive affect has its effect by activating positive connections that exist between the category and the target being considered. As a consequence, with respect to the valence of the category, greater inclusiveness in categorization may be more likely to occur for more favorable social categories for which more positive connections exist. In contrast, positive affect would not be expected to increase the inclusiveness of categorization for negative categories for which positive connections are rare or nonexistent (Isen et al., 1992).

With respect to the qualities of the target, the effect of positive affect has been found to facilitate the inclusion of nontypical but plausible examples into a positive social categories more than typical examples (Isen et al., 1992). Typical exemplars are already highly associated with the social category. However, this effect occurs only for positive or neutral targets for which potential positive connections exist, but not for negative targets for which associations are fundamentally unfavorable (Isen et al., 1992; Murray et al., 1990). Thus, when one has information about positively or even generally neutrally valenced others, positive affect may facilitate more inclusive, superordinate categorization because, as Isen et al. (1992) explain, "people who are feeling good may recognize aspects of ideas (especially neutral or ambiguous ones) that they do not normally think of, and these features will tend to be more positive than usual, as well" (p. 67).

With respect to intergroup relations, attitudes toward outgroup members may be generally neutral for temporary laboratory groups with no current or past conflict; thus positive affect may be effective at producing the broader, more inclusive social categorizations that are hypothesized in the Common Ingroup Identity Model to be critical in reducing bias. In contrast, positive affect would not be expected to facilitate superordinate representations or to reduce intergroup bias between groups whose relations are generally negative (for which positive connections are unlikely to exist or to be activated), unless there are some other features of that context (e.g., cooperative intergroup interaction) that can establish positive connections.

The present series of studies that we present had three main objectives. One objective was to understand how incidental positive affect—affect aroused by a source external and unrelated to the behavior of outgroup members (Bodenhausen, 1993) but which could realistically be introduced into contact situations—influences intergroup attitudes. Study 1 examined this issue for laboratory groups not in conflict. Study 2 explored these effects for laboratory groups in the context of explicit intergroup cooperation and competition. Study 3 extends these findings to "real" groups with a history of competition and conflict.

The second objective, related directly to the Common Ingroup Identity Model, was to examine the mediating role of superordinate group representations for more favorable attitudes toward outgroup members and for the reduction of intergroup bias. Across the studies presented, the degree to which the manipulations influenced the extent to which the aggregate was expected to feel like one group or two separate groups was assessed, and, in turn, the relationship between these representations and intergroup attitudes was tested.

Because positive affect can both increase and decrease intergroup biases and the inclusiveness of group representations, the third objective was to understand how positive affect influences the processing of information in intergroup contact situations. Some models, such as Isen's (1987, outlined earlier; see also Abele, Gendolla, & Petzold, 1998; and chapter 18 by Abele in this volume), propose that positive affect promotes elaborative processing and the integration of diverse information, whereas other approaches suggest that it generally leads to heuristic, simplified processing and reduced attention to available information. To pursue this objective, we explored how positive affect influences memory for the behaviors of outgroup members and also how it affects the degree to which people attend to or discount information that is inconsistent with group-based expectations (see also Bless et al., 1996; Bless, Schwarz, & Kemmelmeier, 1996). In particular, Study 4 tested the accuracy of incidental recall and within-group confusions of statements made by members of outgroups in competition or cooperation with one's own group. Study 5 explored the extent to which people process expectancy-consistent and expectancy-inconsistent information as a function of affect and outcome dependency.

These studies used, with some variation, the same general paradigm. Participants were initially categorized into groups on the basis of preliminary tasks (i.e., laboratory groups), assigned randomly to a group category but ostensibly on the basis of a pretest indicating the participant's orientation (e.g., as an overestimator or underestimator), or assigned on the basis of identification with an existing, "real" entity (e.g., liberals or conservatives). The next intervention involved variations in the anticipated intergroup contact: to simply meet one another, to cooperate, to compete, or to interact with independent outcomes. Affect was then manipulated across these studies in three ways: an unexpected gift of candy (vs. no gift), a comedy videotape (vs. a travelogue), or a Velten-type procedure (Siebert & Ellis, 1991; Velten, 1968) involving making positive (vs. neutral) statements. Participants next viewed a videotape of the group with which they were going to perform a problem-solving task related to the anticipated group task (e.g., the Winter Survival Problem). The main dependent measures, besides manipulation checks for affect (e.g., happy) and intergroup relations (e.g., cooperative), included superordinate group representations (the more the group would feel like one group, on a 1 *not at all* to 7 *very much* scale, and the less like two groups, also on a 1 to 7 scale) and intergroup attitudes (evaluations on similar 1 to 7 scales in terms of, e.g., how likable and friendly the other group was). In studies that also involved prior interaction with ingroup members, a measure of bias was also computed as the difference in the evaluations of ingroup and outgroup members. The first study we present examined the role of positive affect on relations between laboratory groups without conflict.

Study 1: Positive Affect and Laboratory Groups

This experiment examined not only whether positive affect influences intergroup perceptions and evaluations among members of laboratory groups, but also how it may do so through processes outlined by the Common Ingroup Identity Model. Although the design was more complicated, we focus here on the results associated with the affect manipulation. Full details of this work are available elsewhere (Dovidio, Gaertner, Isen, & Lowrance, 1995).

The Common Ingroup Identity Model describes how different cognitive representations, reflecting the salience of common ingroup or different group boundaries, mediate the benefits of intergroup contact. We hypothesize that positive affect can systematically influence these representations and thereby influence intergroup attraction. Positive affect can facilitate the recategorization from two groups to one for at least two reasons. First, positive affect increases cognitive flexibility in approaching categorization tasks (Murray et al., 1990). Thus, people experiencing positive affect may be more open to revising their two-group representations as a function of intergroup contact than those not feeling so positively. Second, positive affect tends to promote more inclusive category representations, in particular. As we discussed earlier, Isen and her colleagues (Isen, 1987; Isen & Daubman, 1984; Isen et al., 1992) have found that positive feelings promote elaborative processing that can facilitate broader positive categorization and reduce intergroup distinctions (see also Stroessner, Hamilton, & Mackie, 1992). Thus, people in positive feeling states are likely to develop a more inclusive, superordinate group representation during intergroup contact than those in more neutral affective states. As a consequence of enhanced flexibility and a tendency toward more inclusive, positive categorization, we hypothesized in this study that people induced to experience positive affect would have lower levels of intergroup bias and more positive evaluations of members of the other group, and that these effects would occur through the recategorization of the memberships from two groups to one superordinate group.

The first phase of this experiment involved the formation of laboratory groups. Participants formed a group by working together on a problem-solving task. Next, the affect manipulation was introduced. After the small group interaction, participants in the condition designed to produce positive affect were given a gift of candy, as has been done in previous research (e.g., Isen & Daubman, 1984); in the control condition, no mention of candy bars was made. Then, participants were informed that they would be interacting with another group on a different problem-solving task. In preparation for this intergroup interaction, they saw a videotape, ostensibly of the other group (actually three confederates) performing a similar problem-solving task. Supposedly to provide baseline measures, participants were then asked their impressions about whether the groups would interact as different entities or as one group and to evaluate each of the members of the other group and their own group. The measure of this superordinate representation reflected stronger ratings of the extent to which the total aggregate would feel like one group and weaker ratings of the extent to which it would feel like two groups in later interaction. These evaluative ratings were averaged to form ingroup and outgroup evaluation scores, and a bias measure was created as the difference between the two (see Dovidio et al., 1995, for details). Participants also rated their current feeling states.

We considered how positive affect could influence intergroup evaluations through both interpersonal and intergroup routes. At the interpersonal level, an experience of a positive event or elevated mood can become associated with other people who are present at the time, which can enhance attraction (Veitch & Griffitt, 1976) through social conditioning (Byrne & Clore, 1970; Lott & Lott, 1974). Across a range of studies, people experiencing positive affect have been demonstrated to make more favorable judgments than people experiencing negative or those in neutral affective states (Abele & Petzold, 1994; Bower, 1991; Forgas & Bower, 1987). In intergroup situations, rewards associated with pleasant, cooperative interaction or success may similarly directly create more positive impressions of outgroup members (Worchel, Andreoli, & Folger, 1977). Positive affect has also been found to increase helping strangers, which suggests a generally more favorable orientation to others (Isen, 1970; Isen & Levin, 1972). Thus, positive affect might improve outgroup attitudes and reduce bias directly.

More directly related to the processes described by the Common Ingroup Identity Model, we hypothesized that positive affect can also influence intergroup attraction *indirectly* by affecting the salience of group boundaries, facilitating broader and more inclusive categorization, and reducing intergroup distinctions (Stroessner et al., 1992). From this perspective, we predicted that participants experiencing positive affect would be more likely to develop a more inclusive, superordinate representation of the aggregate than would participants in the affect control condition. Furthermore, we hypothesized that more inclusive representations of the aggregate would, in turn, predict more favorable outgroup evaluations and, as a consequence, lower levels of intergroup bias.

The results supported the predictions. As expected, positive affect increased the extent to which participants formed inclusive group representations, anticipating that the members of two groups would feel more like one superordinate group and less like two separate groups. Moreover, as hypothesized, stronger superordinate group representations further predicted more positive outgroup evaluations ($M = 5.54$ vs. 4.97, on the 1–7 scales) and lower levels of intergroup bias ($M = 0.54$ vs. 0.67). Path analysis revealed a significant indirect path from the manipulation of positive affect through more inclusive representations of the groups, to more positive evaluations and, in a separate analysis, to lower levels of bias. The direct path from the affect manipulation to outgroup evaluations (and to bias) was nonsignificant. In addition, the reduction of bias occurred in the way proposed by the Common Ingroup Identity Model: bias was reduced primarily by the more favorable ratings of the outgroup, produced as a consequence of being recategorized from members of the outgroup to members of a common, superordinate ingroup.

Overall, these results provide support for the hypothesis that positive affect can shape the outcomes of intergroup contact, as well as for the mechanisms and mediating processes proposed within the Common Ingroup Identity Model. Nevertheless, it is important to consider how generalizable these effects might be. In particular, the intergroup situation in this experiment involved laboratory groups with an intergroup relationship that was not clearly defined. That is, the groups were not in either explicit cooperation or competition with one another, factors that can have a profound impact on intergroup dynamics and ultimately on intergroup bias (Sherif et al., 1954). The nature of intergroup bias may be quite different for laboratory groups than for ecologically meaningful social entities (Mullen et al., 1992). Bias tends to be stronger and more intransigent for naturalistic groups with enduring or meaningful boundaries or with current or past conflicts. Moreover, Hewstone (1996) questions, "Can the recategorization process and the creation of a superordinate group identity overcome powerful ethnic and racial categorizations on more than a temporary basis?" (p. 351). The results of this first study, by themselves, cannot answer that question.

Conceptually, the manner in which affect influences cognitive processes may also vary as a function of the context of decision making (Isen, 1993). That is, if, as Isen (1987, 1993) suggests, positive affect facilitates elaborative processing, then the nature of information available can moderate the influence of positive affect on attitudes and behavior. If the intergroup context is one that promotes more inclusive group representations and favorable interactions, such as through cooperative activities (Gaertner et al., 1994), positive affect could facilitate more positive intergroup attitudes. In contrast, if the situation is one that reinforces separate group identities and negative interactions, such as with competitive tasks, positive affect may produce greater levels of intergroup bias compared to neutral affect. Thus, the effects we obtained for the manipulation of affect in this experiment may not necessarily generalize to situations involving explicit competitive relations between groups or to groups with histories of competition, conflict, and biases that have produced strong and meaningful intergroup boundaries. The next two experiments, therefore, investigated the influence of positive affect on bias as a function of the relationship between laboratory groups (Study 2) and in the context of relations between meaningful entities historically in competition (Study 3).

Study 2: Cooperative Versus Competitive Interdependence

There is considerable theoretical debate about the manner in which positive affect influences cognitive processing. Two alternative positions emphasize the distinction between heuristic and elaborative processing. Mackie and her colleagues have proposed that positive affect may reduce the capacity for deliberative information processing and thereby increase reliance on *heuristic cues* (Mackie et al., 1989; Worth & Mackie, 1987; Mackie & Worth, 1989). Other researchers have also proposed that positive affect may increase people's use of heuristic cues, but due to reduced *motivation* to process information systematically (Bodenhausen, 1993; Schwarz, Bless, & Bohner, 1991). With respect to intergroup relations, either of these views suggests that positive affect might increase reliance on general contextual cues in intergroup categorization and judgments. Framing potential intergroup contact in terms of cooperation or competition may provide one such contextual cue. To the extent that intergroup competition defines the relationship between two groups, positive affect could strengthen the two-group representations of these groups and thereby *increase* bias. However, when group interactions involve cooperative, friendly, or even neutral relations (as in the previous experiment), positive affect may increase the inclusiveness of one's group boundaries and consequently reduce bias. This reasoning suggests that the impact of positive affect on intergroup bias would be moderated by the competitive or cooperative nature of the intergroup contact and its effects substantially mediated by the salience of intergroup boundaries.

Alternatively, it is possible that positive affect by facilitating *elaborative* processes—that is, increased processing rather than decreased (Isen, Daubman, & Nowicki, 1987; Isen et al., 1985)—could increase bias between members of competing groups. When interpersonal dissimilarity, intergroup differences, or potentially conflictual relationships exist, more systematic thinking can increase negative biases by strengthening the salience of these interpersonal and intergroup differences and increasing the weight given to realistic or symbolic conflicts in framing relations. Because positive affect promotes elaboration and flexibility in thinking, it could increase the perception of difference between groups when people are motivated to look for distinctions (e.g., Isen, 1987, p. 234; Murray et al., 1990). For instance, Abele et al. (1998) found that positive affect increased bias in evaluations when information about ingroup-outgroup membership was provided even within the context of a minimal intergroup paradigm. Abele et al. (see also chapter 18 by Abele in this volume) propose that these results are the consequence of "creative elaboration" influencing "the weight assigned to categorizing information" (p. 1355). More systematic and elaborative thinking directed toward category information increases its impact in subsequent evaluations and judgments. Forgas and Fiedler (1996), in work derived from Forgas's (1995) Affect Infusion Model (AIM; see also chapter 11 by Forgas and colleagues in this volume), also found in a similar minimal intergroup situation that positive affect increased ingroup-outgroup differentiation on a reward allocation task.

As demonstrated in Abele et al.'s (1998) findings, these elaborative processes produce not only more positive evaluations of people identified as ingroup members, but also more negative evaluations of those described as outgroup members compared to conditions in which no group identifying information was offered. Thus, when groups have competitive or antagonistic relations, positive mood could increase sensitivity to threat and risk (Isen & Geva, 1987; Isen, Nygren, & Ashby, 1988; Isen & Patrick, 1983) and increase perceptions of difference and distrust, thereby enhancing bias. However, when group interactions involve cooperative, friendly, or even neutral relations (as in the previous experiment), positive affect may increase the inclusiveness of one's group boundaries and consequently reduce bias. Thus, both the Mackie et al. and Isen et al. research suggest that the influence of positive affect on bias may be moderated by the nature of the context and that positive affect may exacerbate intergroup bias between directly competing groups or meaningful entities with traditionally competing vested interests. However, Isen's view suggests that, although increases in group biases may be mediated in part by group representations, these increases may occur substantially in other ways as well (e.g., increasing sensitivity to threat, independent of the recognition of separate group identities).

The second study that we report utilized laboratory groups (participants randomly informed that they were over- and underestimators), and we explicitly varied the cooperative or competitive relationship between these groups. Participants ($n = 85$) who were identified randomly but ostensibly on the basis of a pretest as overestimators or underestimators viewed videotapes designed to produce positive affect (a comedy tape) or maintain neutral affect (a demonstration of wine corking). Then they individually viewed a videotape of a group reflecting the alternative orientation (underestimators or overestimators) and were led to believe that they would later be cooperating with or competing against this group for a monetary prize. The dependent measures included representations of the entities as two groups or one group and evaluations of the outgroup.

On the basis of the research suggesting that people experiencing positive affect would be more sensitive to the structure of the intergroup context than would neutral affect control participants (Isen, 1993; Mackie et al., 1989; Schwarz et al., 1991), we predicted an interaction between affect and the cooperative-competitive task structure on outgroup evaluations. Specifically, on the cooperative task, we expected positive affect participants to evaluate the other group more favorably than would neutral affect participants; however, on the competitive tasks, we anticipated that positive affect participants would evaluate the other group less favorably. Furthermore, based on our previous work on the Common Ingroup Identity Model (Gaertner et al., 1993) and on affect and intergroup bias (Dovidio et al., 1995), we hypothesized that these evaluative responses would be mediated by representations of the entities as one group or two.

Preliminary analyses revealed that the manipulations of the competitive versus cooperative intergroup relations and of affect were successful. In addition, as expected, outgroup attitudes were more favorable when the groups were cooperatively rather than competitively interdependent ($M = 5.43$ vs. 5.04, $p < .044$). Moreover, the predicted Context (Cooperative vs. Competitive) × Affect (Positive vs. Neutral) interaction was obtained ($p < .014$; see Figure 19.2). When cooperation was anticipated, positive affect participants had more positive attitudes toward the other group then did neutral affect participants ($M = 5.67$ vs. 5.19); when competition was anticipated, positive affect participants had *less* positive attitudes toward the other group then did neutral affect participants ($M = 4.80$ vs. 5.28).

Analyses of the group representations indicated, as anticipated, that

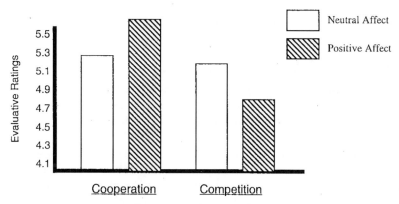

FIGURE 19.2. Intergroup evaluations as a function of affect and intergroup cooperation or competition—Study 2.

superordinate group ratings were generally correlated with outgroup ratings, $r(83) = .40$, $p < .01$, and were higher ($p < .05$) when participants anticipated intergroup cooperation than when they expected intergroup competition. The Context × Affect interaction involving those representations, however, was not significant. Nevertheless, as expected, when participants anticipated cooperation, those reporting higher levels of positive affect had higher superordinate group ratings, $r(36) = .36$, $p < .05$. In contrast, when participants anticipated competition, higher levels of positive affect tended to be negatively correlated with superordinate group ratings, $r(45) = -.11$. These correlations were significantly different from one another ($p < .05$). Moreover, supportive of the Common Ingroup Identity Model, superordinate group ratings were correlated significantly with outgroup evaluations separately and comparably within the cooperative ($r = .32$) and competitive ($r = .40$) intergroup contexts.

Overall, the findings from the present experiment extend the results of our previous laboratory work on the influence of positive affect on intergroup relations. Also, the potential mediating role of perceptions of the memberships as an inclusive, superordinate group is consistent with the propositions of the Common Ingroup Identity Model. Furthermore, these results suggest that the findings of Dovidio et al. (1995) concerning the relationship between positive affect and the reduction of intergroup bias between members of laboratory groups may not necessarily generalize to some types of meaningful entities. In particular, enduring groups and meaningful social entities, particularly those for which intergroup relations is a problem, often have histories of conflict and competition. As a consequence, positive affect may increase, rather than decrease, bias between members of these types of groups.

However, it is further possible that positive affect could increase perceptions of similarity and common fate when a common group identity is made salient (Gaertner et al., 1999b), and consequently reduce bias even between traditionally competitive groups. Isen et al. (1992) found that positive affect increased the extent to which exemplars, particularly nontypical exemplars (e.g., bartender), were perceived to be representative of positive superordinate categories (e.g., nurturant). In addition, positive affect has been found to increase the association of both the self and others to the same positive categories (Rust, 1995). In a similar fashion, positive affect may enhance the effectiveness of interventions designed to create a positive superordinate identity (e.g., through superordinate goals), even while maintaining some degree of separate group identities (e.g., African Americans, White Americans). The next experiment in this series thus examined the hypothesis that positive affect would increase bias between meaningful entities with generally conflicting interests and explored the role that emphasizing a common ingroup identity could have in reducing this bias.

Study 3: Positive Affect and Meaningful Social Entities

This experiment (see Dovidio, Gaertner, Isen, Rust, & Guerra, 1998, for more details) partially replicated the procedures of Dovidio et al. (1995; see Study 1), except that it involved social categories of some importance to participants' identity (liberals, conservatives; pro-fraternity, anti-fraternity). We note that the development of a common ingroup identity does not require groups to forsake their original identities entirely. Threats to important personal identities or the "positive distinctiveness" of one's group can in fact exacerbate intergroup prejudices (Dovidio, Gaertner, & Validzic, 1998). The development of a dual identity (two subgroups within one group), in which original and superordinate group memberships are simultaneously salient, is explicitly considered in the Common Ingroup Identity Model (see Figure 19.1). For instance, even when racial or ethnic identity is strong, a salient superordinate connection enhances interracial trust and acceptance (Huo, Smith, Tyler, & Lind, 1996). Study 3 directly examined the effects of making participants' separate and superordinate identities simultaneously salient.

As in the two studies described previously in this chapter, participants ($n = 180$) first interacted in three-person groups on problem-solving task. Then, in preparation for a combined-group interaction, they saw a videotape of another group (three confederates) performing a similar problem-solving task. This group was described as representing a historically competitive group (e.g., liberals, if participants were conservatives). Affect and the salience of group membership were independently manipulated, producing a 2 (Affect: Positive vs. Neutral) × 2 (Context: Two Groups vs. Dual Identity) design. After the small group interaction and before viewing the videotape of the other group, participants in the conditions designed to produce positive affect were either given candy bars or viewed a comedy videotaped segment; in the control conditions, either no mention of candy bars was made or participants viewed a "neutral" videotape. The salience of group membership was varied by the labels participants used to refer to the two groups and themselves throughout the experiment. In a condition designed to reinforce existing group boundaries (the Two Groups condition), participants referred to others in terms of their separate group memberships (e.g., liberals or conservatives). In a condition that emphasized the superordinate connection between the groups (the Dual Identity condition) and their interconnection, the participants' common identity as a student of the university prefaced the references to their group membership (e.g., *Colgate* liberals, *Colgate* conservatives). This condition in which subgroup and superordinate identities were salient simultaneously was found in an earlier field study to relate to reduced levels of intergroup bias in a multiethnic high school (Gaertner, Rust, Dovidio, Bachman, & Anastasio, 1994). The primary dependent measures were cognitive representations of the aggregate and group evaluations.

The results were supportive of the hypotheses. Analyses of outgroup evaluations (see Figure 19.3) and intergroup evaluative bias (i.e., favoring the ingroup over the outgroup in evaluations) demonstrated the predicted interactions ($p < .01$). As expected, in the Two Groups context, participants in the positive affect condition, compared to those in the neutral affect condition, exhibited less favorable outgroup attitudes ($M = 4.53$ vs. 5.14, $p < .05$) and higher levels of bias ($M = 1.04$ vs. 0.51, $p < .05$).

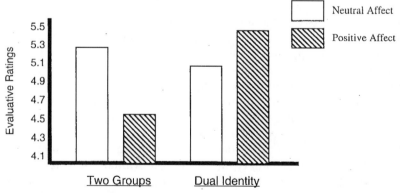

FIGURE 19.3. Intergroup evaluations as a function of affect and the salience of separate group and common group identities—Study 3.

However, in the Dual Identity condition, positive affect participants showed more positive outgroup attitudes ($M = 5.19$ vs. 4.96, $p < .05$) and lower levels of bias ($M = 0.48$ vs. 0.86, $p < .05$) than did neutral affect participants. This pattern is consistent with the hypothesized influence of positive affect on intergroup relations. As with our earlier work, ingroup evaluations did not vary as a function of the manipulations; the reduction of the bias is primarily attributable to more favorable outgroup evaluations. Also as in the previous studies, stronger superordinate group ratings were substantially correlated overall with lower levels of bias ($r = -.55$, $p < .001$) and more favorable evaluations of the outgroup ($r = .55$, $p < .001$). Consistent with our earlier work, superordinate group ratings were not significantly correlated with ingroup evaluations ($r = .12$, $p > .35$).

To evaluate the hypothesized processes contributing to increased bias in the Two Groups condition and reduced bias in the Dual Identity condition, path analyses were computed separately for each condition (see Dovidio et al., 1998). With respect to the Two Groups condition, it was hypothesized that for groups with meaningful social boundaries under conditions in which differences are salient, positive affect would lead to less inclusive group representations and therefore greater levels of bias. Consistent with this prediction, (a) the affect manipulation significantly influenced self-reported affect ($\beta = +.47$); (b) more positive affect tended to produce *weaker* superordinate group representations (i.e., stronger two-group relative to one-group representations; $\beta = -.19$), and (c) superordinate group representations, in turn, predicted lower levels of bias ($\beta = -.38$). The effect of positive feeling states on representations, and consequently on bias, was substantially different in the Dual Identity condition, as predicted. The affect manipulation influenced self-reported affect ($\beta = .37$), as in the Two Groups condition. In contrast and as hypothesized, when a common, positive, Colgate identity was made salient along with the subgroup identity in the Dual Identity condition, more positive self-reported affect predicted *stronger* superordinate group representations ($\beta = .38$). Directly supportive of the differential impact of positive affect, comparison of the paths between the two models revealed a significant difference (.38 vs. −.19, $p < .05$) between the paths from self-reported affect to superordinate group representations between the Two Groups and Dual Identity conditions. As in the Two Groups conditions and consistent with previous work, stronger superordinate representations predicted lower levels of bias ($\beta = -.56$).

Overall, the results of this experiment demonstrated not only the predicted effect for positive affect on intergroup evaluations, but also provided support for the hypothesized intervening mechanisms and processes. When group boundaries are distinct and meaningful, positive affect may increase intergroup bias. Nevertheless, when a positive superordinate identity is made salient, even while separate group identities are maintained, positive affect can help reduce intergroup bias. Furthermore, the results are consistent with propositions of the Common Ingroup Identity Model and supportive of the hypothesized processes by which positive affect influence cognitive processing (Isen et al., 1992). For meaningful social entities, affect may influence the salience of features of the social context or the existing relationship that are involved in the analysis of the situation and in shaping one's reactions. For example, Isen proposes that through enhanced deliberative processing, positive affect may increase *sensitivity* to threat. As a result, positive affect may tend to produce more *exclusive* group representations (i.e., representations of the aggregate as two groups rather than as one group) and may make the potential *consequences* of that intergroup relation more salient (relating to the direct paths, independent of superordinate representations, from manipulated affect and self-reported affect to bias). The next study was designed to examine the cognitive processes more directly.

Study 4: Intergroup Relations and Memory

This study ($n = 87$) was designed to provide a conceptual replication of the joint influence of affect and intergroup cooperation/competition we obtained earlier with laboratory groups (Study 2)—with four main differences. First, positive affect was manipulated in two ways, by videotapes and a modified Velten procedure. Second, instead of laboratory-formed groups, we used "real" social identities (pro-life/pro-choice). Participants were led to believe that the people on videotape were members of the other group. Third, in addition to cooperation and competition, we included an independent outcome condition. Fourth, to track the occurrence of more elaborative or diminished processing, we also included memory measures in this experiment. People recall fewer details about others classified as an outgroup member than as an ingroup member (Park & Rothbart, 1982), and categorization of others as an outgroup may increase intracategory errors in memory, such as confusions about which person in a group makes a specific comment (Taylor, Fiske, Etcoff, & Ruderman, 1978). Thus, we also investigated the accuracy of recognition of the assignment of statements to specific individuals on the videotape and the number of intracategory confusions in these attributions. Participants were presented with a list of comments (half actual, half new) and asked to identify whether the comment was made by a member of the other group and, if so, by whom. We assumed that to the extent that positive affect produces more deliberative processing, positive affect would both increase accuracy of statement assignment and decrease intracategory confusions; to the extent to which it promotes more heuristic processing, the opposite would be expected to occur.

The affect manipulation was successful and comparably so for the videotape and Velten procedure. The 3 (Context: Cooperative, Competitive, Independent) × 2 (Affect) analysis revealed a main effect for Context ($p <$ .007). In general, attitudes toward the outgroup were most positive in the cooperation condition ($M = 5.69$), intermediately positive in the independent condition ($M = 5.42$), and least positive in the competition condition ($M = 5.03$). Furthermore, as predicted, the Context × Affect interaction for outgroup evaluations was significant (see Figure 19.4). Consistent with the previous studies, positive affect participants, compared to those in the neutral affect control group, had more positive attitudes in the cooperation condition ($M = 5.95$ vs. 5.43) and less favorable attitudes in the competition ($M = 4.71$ vs. 5.29) and independent (real groups, $M = 5.14$ vs. 5.75) conditions.

Also consistent with the previous work, Context influenced superordinate identities ($p < .01$). Superordinate group ratings were highest in the cooperation condition, intermediate in the independent condition, and lowest in the competition condition. The Context × Affect interaction, although reflecting a pattern similar to outgroup attitudes, only approached significance ($p < .17$). Overall, however, superordinate group ratings were significantly correlated with favorable outgroup attitudes ($r = .27$, $p < .05$).

The analyses of the identification of the statements made by members of the videotaped group members indicate that participants in positive moods did not differ from participants in the neutral affect control condition in their overall accuracy for statements recalled ($F < 1$, $M = 14.05$ vs.

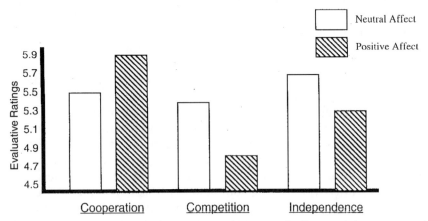

FIGURE 19.4. Intergroup evaluations as a function of affect and the context of intergroup contact—Study 4.

13.73; see also Bless et al., 1996a; Forgas, 1998). This finding was inconsistent with our assumption that positive affect would either increase accuracy by promoting elaborative processing or decrease accuracy due to more heuristic processing. The nature of intergroup interdependence, however, did influence overall accuracy in terms of the number of statements correctly identified as being said or not said. The main effect for Context was obtained ($p < .035$). Participants were most accurate in the cooperative condition, moderately accurate in the independent condition, and least accurate in the competitive condition ($M = 15.07$ vs. 14.31 vs. 12.55). This pattern is consistent with Park and Rothbart's (1982) conclusion that people recall fewer details about others classified as an outgroup member than as an ingroup member. The Affect × Context interaction did not approach significance.

Although positive affect participants did not differ in overall accuracy, they did make errors in a particular way—correctly identifying a statement but misattributing it to another outgroup member—that suggests that they were relying on category information (group-based knowledge structures) rather than on individualized processing (see Fiske & Neuberg, 1990). Specifically, positive affect participants made more intracategory errors (within-group confusions) than did neutral affect participants ($M = 5.37$ vs. 4.27, $p < .028$). The effect of Context on intracategory errors was nonsignificant ($p < .17$), but participants in the competition condition tended to have the highest level of within-group confusions, participants in the independent condition an intermediate level, and those in the cooperation condition the lowest level ($M = 5.27$ vs 4.92 vs. 4.18). The interaction between Affect and Context was also nonsignificant.

Overall, these findings for outgroup evaluations provide convergent evidence for the effects of positive affect on intergroup attitudes. People experiencing positive affect, compared to those in neutral moods, show more favorable attitudes toward outgroup members in a context of intergroup cooperation and more negative attitudes in a situation of intergroup competition. These effects are related, at least in part, by the inclusiveness of intergroup representations.

This study, however, was also designed to further illuminate some of the cognitive processes involved. The results for the memory measures, though, were not entirely consistent with expectations and do not definitively identify the operation of more elaborative or heuristic processing as a function of experiencing positive affect. The statement accuracy measure demonstrates that positive affect participants are not necessarily less able (i.e., because of limited capacity) or less motivated to process information about members of the other group. The intracategory error measure, however, indicates that they may be relying more on group-based than individuated impression processes. These findings are compatible with Bless et al.'s (1996a) conclusion that happy moods do not "decrease either cognitive capacity or processing motivation, in general" but they do "increase . . . reliance on general knowledge structures" (p. 665).

One important implication of the work of Bless et al. (1996a) is that although positive affect people may typically rely on general knowledge structures, which often allow for efficient and parsimonious processing, their cognitive resources are flexible. Bless et al. (1996a) propose: "If a situation is characterized as benign, individuals may rely on general knowledge structures, which usually serve them well. In contrast, if a situation is characterize as problematic, relying on one's usual routine is maladaptive, and attention to the specifics of the situation is called for" (p. 666). Isen's work (e.g., Isen, 1993) on positive affect and deliberative processing and findings related to positive affect and sensitivity to risk and threat indicate that positive affect participants may process "problematic" information in an even more detailed fashion than people not in positive moods. The next study examined this possibility.

Study 5: Positive Affect and Expectancy— Consistent and Inconsistent Information

This study was designed to replicate our previous studies on the effect of positive affect evaluations of outgroup members and intergroup representations. In particular, affect (positive vs. neutral) and the nature of intergroup contact (independent outcomes vs competition) were varied. However, the primary focus of the work, representing its main potential novel contribution, was to delineate more clearly the operation of deliberative or heuristic processing produced by positive affect. The data on this issue from Study 4 were equivocal. Positive affect did not reduce overall accuracy in memory for the behaviors of outgroup members, as a limited capacity (Mackie & Worth, 1989) or decreased motivation (Schwarz et al., 1991) model of heuristic processing might suggest. The higher level of within-group confusions in attributions of statements made by different outgroup members could be interpreted as consistent with either an elaborative or heuristic processing perspective (Bless et al., 1996a). Thus, Study 5 adopted an alternative strategy for examining how positive affect influences cognitive processing.

The work of Fiske and her colleagues (e.g., Ruscher & Fiske, 1990) reveals that people are more likely to process information in a bottom-up, individuated fashion than in a top-down, category-based way (see Fiske & Neuberg, 1990) when they are interdependent than when their outcomes are independent. For example, Ruscher and Fiske (1990) conducted a study in which participants, who expected to compete or not compete with another person, commented into a tape-recorder about a person's attributes, some inconsistent and some consistent with expectations. Supportive of their hypothesis, Ruscher and Fiske found that competitors increased their attention to inconsistencies (measured as the amount of time subjects attended to attribute information) compared to noncompetitors. We adapted this procedure to examine the potential parallel effects of positive affect.

Whereas heuristic (e.g., Bodenhausen et al., 1994) and elaborative (Abele et al., 1998; Isen, 1993) processing perspectives suggest that people experiencing positive affect will rely more on category-based and stereotype-consistent information than those in neutral moods, Bless, Schwarz, and Wieland (1996) propose that responses to individuating information that is inconsistent with stereotypes and other category-based expectations can help to distinguish which of these processes is promoted by positive affect. They reason: "If happy individuals use the target's category membership as a 'peripheral cue' that simplifies the judgmental task . . . any inconsistencies may either not be detected to begin with, or, if detected, may simply be ignored by happy individuals due to their reduced processing capacity or motivation" (p. 938). In contrast, if positive affect facilitates elaborative processing, Bless, Schwarz, and Wieland (1996) propose, "as it is assumed that happy individuals are sufficiently motivated and have sufficient capacity, they should be able, and willing, to elaborate on the individuating information . . . elaborating on the inconsistent information requires additional processing attention" (pp. 938–939).

Consistent with this reasoning, Bless, Schwarz, and Wieland (1996) found in a series of experiments that participants experiencing positive affect responded differently than naive neutral mood participants but like neutral mood participants were instructed to focus on individuating information. Participants experiencing positive affect and neutral mood participants were instructed to attend to individuating information, like naive neutral mood participants were influenced by category membership information as long as individuating information was not inconsistent; when individuating information was inconsistent, however, participants experiencing positive affect and neutral mood participants instructed to attend to individuating information were significantly more influenced by the individuating information than the naive neutral mood participants. This pattern of findings supports the notion that positive affect promotes elaborative rather than heuristic cognitive processing. Our Study 5 further explored this issue by directly investigating the attention paid to category-consistent and -inconsistent individuating information.

Participants ($n = 93$) who were randomly selected were informed that they had been selected on the basis of their personality to be part of a group of advertisers or accountants, along with another person "like them" in a group problem-solving task. They were told that they would be interacting with two other people who, based on the type of people they were, were members of the other group. Participants were then asked, as in Fiske and Ruscher (1990), to write a self-descriptive statement reflecting their standing on a range of attributes specified on eight separate index cards. These attributes were pretested to be positive and negative stereotypic characteristics of advertisers (outgoing, manipulative, cunning, creative) and accountants (unimaginative, intelligent, uptight, hardworking).

The manipulation of competition versus independence was the same as that used by Fiske and Ruscher (1990). Participants were informed that the experimenter was investigating how the presence of others influences performance. They were told that the task involved identifying as many different ways as possible that wind-up toys could be used to identify concepts. For example, a wind-up toy hopping away from a group of other toys might be used to convey the concept of subtraction. In the competition condition, participants were led to believe that $50 would be given to the group that best outperformed the other group ostensibly in their session. In the independent condition, participants were told that any two-person group who performed better than the 50th percentile would be eligible to win a $50 prize in a raffle; each two-person group in a session would enter a separate raffle.

Next, as in Fiske and Ruscher (1990), before the interaction was to take place, the experimenter informed participants that they would each be exchanging information on the index cards and recording their initial reactions into a tape-recorder. The experimenter then presented the participant with an unexpected gift of candy (as in Dovidio et al., 1995, Study 1) as she prepared the equipment. Each participant was then escorted into a separate cubicle. Participants then received one of four sets of index cards, ostensibly representing the responses of a member of the other group. Half of the responses were consistent with the "advertiser stereotype"; half were consistent with the "accountant stereotype." The experimenter asked participants to read each piece of information aloud and to comment on it. The main dependent measure for this study was the amount of time participants spent commenting on expectancy-consistent and -inconsistent information. If positive affect facilitates deliberative processing of "problematic," inconsistent information, positive affect (vs. neutral affect) would be expected to have parallel effects to competition (vs. independent outcomes)—both would be expected to produce longer times for thinking about expectancy-inconsistent information in particular.

Manipulation checks indicated that regardless of the group to which they were assigned, participants reported that they were more like that group (e.g., advertisers) whereas the other people had personalities more like the other group (e.g., accountants). They also supported the manipulation of competition versus independent outcomes and of positive affect.

Of central interest in this study were the effects of task (competitive vs. independent) and affect (positive vs. neutral). Replicating the work of Ruscher and Fiske (1990), participants in the competitive situation tended to spend more time attending to expectancy-inconsistent information than did those in the independent task situation, $M = 14.28$ vs. 10.40 sec, $p < .072$. A parallel main effect for affect was also obtained, $p < .03$. Participants in the positive affect condition spent more time attending to expectancy-inconsistent information than did those in the neutral affect condition, $M = 14.78$ vs. 9.90 sec. Neither main effect approached significance for expectancy-consistent information ($p > .25$). Furthermore, in an analysis of variance for expectancy-inconsistent traits, controlling for each respondent's time on consistent traits also demonstrated main effects for task ($p < .001$) and affect ($p < .015$).

Participants in this study subsequently watched members of the outgroup on videotaped interaction. Replicating the previous studies, a Context × Affect interaction was obtained ($p < .028$) for outgroup evaluations. Similar to our previous findings for groups without a history of previous conflict, on the competitive task, participants in the positive affect condition had less favorable evaluations of the outgroup than did those in the neutral affect condition ($M = 4.49$ vs. 4.93); on the independent task, they had a more favorable attitude ($M = 4.72$ vs. 4.38). As in previous studies, analyses of the group representations revealed that superordinate group ratings were generally correlated with outgroup ratings, $r(91) = .28$, $p < .01$, and were higher ($p < .04$) when participants believed that their outcomes were independent than when they expected competition. As in Study 2, however, the Context × Affect interaction was not significant.

In general, these results support our previous research on the outcomes of positive affect on intergroup attitudes within competitive and noncompetitive situations. Moreover, they help to illuminate the psychological processes involved. Consistent with the theorizing of Isen (1993) and of Bless and his colleagues (Bless et al., 1996a, 1996b, 1996c), when presented with expectancy-inconsistent information, people experiencing positive affect are both able and willing to process information in a more elaborate, detailed, and individualized fashion.

☐ Summary and Conclusions

The present series of studies addressed three main objectives: (a) to understand how incidental positive affect influences intergroup attitudes,

(b) to examine the mediating role of superordinate group representations for more favorable attitudes toward outgroup members and for the reduction of intergroup bias, and (c) to understand how positive affect influences elaborative and heuristic processing in intergroup relations.

With respect to the first objective, we found that incidental positive affect does influence intergroup attitudes, and that the effect is systematically moderated by the nature of intergroup contact. When groups have no previous history of conflict and when the immediate contact is nonthreatening (Study 1 and the Independent Outcome condition of Study 5), a "mood-congruency" effect occurs. Participants in a positive affect condition have more favorable attitudes and lower levels of bias than do those in a neutral affect condition. However, when groups are in immediate competition (Studies 2, 4, and 5) or have histories of conflict and competition (Studies 2 and 4), participants in positive affect conditions have less favorable outgroup attitudes and higher levels of bias. This bias can be mitigated by making a common, positively valued identity salient (Study 2).

This pattern of findings is consistent with the affective framework that guided the work. Specifically, Isen (1987, 1993) hypothesized that positive affect increases the accessibility of diverse ideas and produces a more complex associative context than what normally occurs. As a consequence, people experiencing positive affect are more likely to report similarities when they are motivated to perceive similarities and to report differences when they are motivated to perceive dissimilarities.

It is also possible that positive affect may relate to other, motivational processes. Trope (1998), for instance, reported that positive affect produces a mood congruency effect in terms of greater interest in positive than negative feedback when feedback is unimportant or nondiagnostic. In contrast, when the feedback is important and diagnostic, people feeling good are more likely to seek negative feedback that can assist them more in improving and achieving their goals than positive feedback. Within the present series of studies, positive affect produced more positive outgroup attitudes when group identities were temporary and laboratory-based and group outcomes were not dependent on the intergroup interaction—presumably when the situation was relatively unimportant. When motivations were aroused by the structure of the intergroup contact (e.g., competition) or by previous intergroup experience, positive affect led to more task-relevant responses, such as more positive attitudes toward outgroup members for cooperative interdependence and more negative attitudes for competitive interdependence. Nevertheless, this line of reasoning and our pattern of findings are inconsistent with other work. Forgas and Fiedler (1996), in particular, found that positive affect increased discrimination when personal relevance of the intergroup contact situation was low, but had less impact when personal relevance was high. The reason for these divergent results is unclear at the present time, but it suggests the need for continued empirical research and further theorizing about factors that moderate the influence of positive affect on intergroup attitudes.

With regard to our second objective, to understand how group representations mediate outgroup evaluations and intergroup bias, we found considerable evidence that is consistent with the central assumptions of the Common Ingroup Identity Model. Across all of the studies, more inclusive, superordinate representations predicted more positive attitudes toward the outgroup and lower levels of bias. In addition, the nature of the intergroup context influenced the inclusiveness of representations. Across the studies, expectations of cooperation produced stronger superordinate group representations, and expectations of competition created weaker superordinate group representations (i.e., feeling less like one group and more like two groups).

Superordinate group representations, however, did not entirely mediate the effects of positive versus neutral affect. Whereas higher levels of positive affect (generally) significantly predicted more inclusive representations when group interaction was neutral (independent) or favorable (cooperative), the relationship tended to be negative when the relations were currently or historically competitive. Although the differences between these correlations were significant, in none of the studies was the negative correlation itself significant. Thus, when intergroup relations are relatively negative, positive affect has its influence in ways primarily independent of superordinate group representations. As Isen's work suggests, it may increase *sensitivity* to risk or threat, but not necessarily the perceived degree of threat or difference between the groups.

The third objective was to explore how positive affect influences heuristic and elaborative cognitive processing. Our findings are consistent with those of Bless and his colleagues (Bless et al., 1996a, 1996b, 1996c) who found that although positive affect can increase reliance on general knowledge structures ("top-down" processing such as the category-based processing in Study 4), it does not exclusively produce inflexible and heuristic processing. When expectancy-inconsistent information was encountered in Study 5, participants in positive affect conditions compared to those in neutral affect conditions, like those in outcome-dependent relative to outcome-independent conditions, showed fuller, more deliberative processing. This "bottom-up" type of processing may help account for the greater impact of stereotype-inconsistent information on the impressions of people experiencing positive relative to neutral affect (Bless, Schwarz, & Wieland, 1996).

The overall pattern of results, including evaluations of outgroup members, intergroup representations, and attention and memory measures, is also consistent with the framework outlined by Abele et al. (1998; see also chapter 18 by Abele in this volume) for the role of incidental positive affect in intergroup relations. Abele et al. (1998) hypothesized that positive affect promotes elaborative processing and further proposed that "positive mood enhances the weight of categorizing information because this type of information is rich in meaning and can be easily elaborated" (p. 1355). Thus, to the extent that the nature of intergroup contact promotes more inclusive categorization (e.g., through cooperation) or separate group representations (e.g., through competition), positive affect would be expected either to decrease or increase intergroup bias—the general pattern we found across our studies. However, because positive affect leads to more elaborative processing, when information that is inconsistent with category-based expectancies is presented, people experiencing more positive affect will attend more to this material (see Bless et al., 1996a, 1996b, 1996c).

The present chapter focused exclusively on a particular type of subjective experience, positive affect, on intergroup relations. But what about negative affect? As with positive affect, negative affect has been hypothesized to influence how people process information in a number of ways. Lambert, Khan, Lickel, and Fricke (1997) outline four models of the influence of negative affect: (a) diminished cognitive capacity, in which both positive and negative affect produce "labor-saving," heuristic processing; (b) mood-as-information, in which positive affect signals that there are no pressing problems and produces heuristic processing, whereas negative affect indicates a potential problem and leads to more systematic processing (see also Bless et al., 1996a); (c) mood maintenance, in which people are motivated to relieve negative states or maintain positive ones; and (d) hedonic contingency, in which, like mood maintenance, people experiencing positive affect process information to maintain their mood, but unlike mood maintenance, people experiencing negative affect and neutral mood do not differ in their processing strategies. These models have different implications for intergroup stereotyping and attitudes (see Lambert et al., 1997). For instance, the cognitive capacity position suggests that negative affect would increase reliance on stereotypes (a heuristic type of processing), whereas the mood-as-information perspective proposes that due to more systematic processing, negative affect would decrease the influence of stereotyping.

We speculate that there may be some similarities as well as differences between the influence of positive and negative affect on the types of intergroup relations that we studied. Consistent with the mood-as-information approach (see also Bless et al., 1996a), to the extent that negative affect leads to increased systematic processing, people experiencing negative affect would be expected to be more responsive to contextual information than those in neutral moods. Thus, in terms of intergroup perceptions, when given information only about group membership, people experiencing negative affect may stereotype outgroup members more strongly than those in neutral moods (Esses & Zanna, 1995), but when given individuating information along with group membership information, they may show a weaker influence of the stereotype (Lambert et al., 1997). These effects would parallel, in both process and outcome, some of the results we demonstrated for positive affect. However, negative and positive affect may show divergent effect under other conditions. In contrast to positive affect, which increases the inclusiveness of categorization, because negative affect signals potential problems and heightens vigilance, it may facilitate "we/they" thinking and thereby strengthen intergroup boundaries and increase discrimination when the nature of intergroup is ill-defined but personally relevant (see Forgas & Fiedler, 1996). Clearly these speculations go beyond the data we have presented in this chapter, but considering how positive and negative affect operate both similarly and differently, they may help to identify productive avenues for future inquiry.

In conclusion, the five studies we describe in this chapter indicate the importance of subjective, *personal* experiences—in this case, incidental positive affect—on *intergroup* relations. Despite the obviously irrelevant source, incidental positive affect systematically influences how people think about intergroup interaction and how they respond to anticipated intergroup relations. Understanding how incidental affect shapes perceptions, cognitive processes, and impressions can also provide insight into the role of integral intergroup affect. To the extent that intergroup cooperation increases the likelihood of achieving valued goals, it is likely to produce consequent positive affect that should enhance inclusive representations and further reduce bias. Finally, this line of research may also contribute to the development of more general, models of the social impact of affect (such as the AIM Model, Forgas, 1995; see also chapter 11 by Forgas and colleagues in this volume), which consider both moderating factors (e.g., context difficulty) and mediating mechanisms (e.g., cognitive processing), and promise to integrate the diverse effects of positive and negative affect in a range of interpersonal situations.

☐ References

Abele, A. (1992). Positive and negative mood influences on creativity: Evidence for asymmetrical effects. *Polish Psychological Bulletin, 23,* 203–221.

Abele, A., Gendolla, G. H. E., & Petzold, P. (1998). Positive mood and ingroup-outgroup differentiation in a minimal intergroup situation. *Personality and Social Psychology Bulletin*, 24, 1343–1357.

Abele, A., & Petzold, P. (1994). How does mood operate in an impression formation task? An information integration approach. *European Journal of Social Psychology*, 24, 219–231.

Allport, G. W. (1954). *The nature of prejudice*. Cambridge, MA: Addison-Wesley.

Bless, H., Clore, G. L., Schwarz, N., Golisano, V., Rabe, C., & Wölk, M. (1996a). Mood and the use of scripts: Does a happy mood really lead to mindlessness? *Journal of Personality and Social Psychology*, 71, 665–679.

Bless, H., Schwarz, N., & Kemmelmeier, M. (1996b). Mood and stereotyping: Affective states and the use of general knowledge structures. In W. Stroebe & M. Hewstone (Eds.), *European review of social psychology* (Vol. 7, pp. 63–93). London: Wiley.

Bless, H., Schwarz, N., & Wieland, R. (1996c). Mood and the impact of category membership and individuating information. *European Journal of Social Psychology*, 26, 935–959.

Bodenhausen, G. V. (1993). Emotions, arousal, and stereotypic judgments: A heuristic model of affect and stereotyping. In D. M. Mackie & D. L. Hamilton (Eds.), *Affect, cognition, and stereotyping: Interactive processes in group perception* (pp. 13–37). San Diego, CA: Academic Press.

Bodenhausen, G. V., Kramer, G. P., & Susser, K. (1994). Happiness and stereotypic thinking in social judgment. *Journal of Personality and Social Psychology*, 66, 621–632.

Bower, G. H. (1991). Mood congruity for social judgments. In J. P. Forgas (Ed.), *Emotion and social judgment* (pp. 31–53). Oxford, England: Pergamon.

Brewer, M. B. (1979). Ingroup bias in the minimal intergroup situation: A cognitive-motivational analysis. *Psychological Bulletin*, 86, 307–324.

Brewer, M. B., & Miller, N. (1984). Beyond the contact hypothesis: Theoretical perspectives on desegregation. In N. Miller & M. B. Brewer (Eds.), *Groups in contact: The psychology of desegregation* (pp. 281–302). Orlando, FL: Academic Press.

Brown, R. J. (1984). The effects of intergroup similarity and cooperative vs. competitive orientation on intergroup discrimination. *British Journal of Social Psychology*, 21, 21–33.

Brown, R. J., & Abrams, D. (1986). The effects of intergroup similarity and goal interdependence on intergroup attitudes and task performance. *Journal of Experimental Social Psychology*, 22, 78–92.

Byrne, D., & Clore, G. L. (1970) A reinforcement model of evaluative responses. *Personality*, 1, 103–128.

Cook, S. W. (1985). Experimenting on social issues: The case of school desegregation. *American Psychologist*, 40, 452–460.

Dovidio, J. F., Gaertner, S. L., Isen, A. M., & Lowrance, R. (1995). Group representations and intergroup bias: Positive affect, similarity, and group size. *Personality and Social Psychology Bulletin*, 8, 856–865.

Dovidio, J. F., Gaertner, S. L., Isen, A. M., Rust, M., & Guerra, P. (1998). Positive affect, cognition, and the reduction of intergroup bias. In C. Sedikides, J. Schopler, & C. Insko (Eds.), *Intergroup cognition and intergroup behavior* (pp. 337–366). Hillsdale, NJ: Erlbaum.

Dovidio, J. F., Gaertner, S. L., & Validzic, A. (1998). Intergroup bias: Status, differentiation, and a common ingroup identity. *Journal of Personality and Social Psychology*, 75, 109–120.

Dovidio, J. F., Gaertner, S. L., Validzic, A., Matoka, A., Johnson, B., & Frazier, S. (1997). Extending the benefits of recategorization: Evaluations, self-disclosure, and helping. *Journal of Experimental Social Psychology*, 33, 401–420.

Esses, V. M., & Zanna, M. P. (1995). Mood and the expression of ethnic stereotypes. *Journal of Personality and Social Psychology*, 69, 1052–1068.

Fiedler, K. (1988). Emotional mood, cognitive style, and behavior regulation. In K. Fiedler & J. P. Forgas (Eds.), *Affect, cognition, and behavior* (pp. 100–119). Toronto, Canada: Hogrefe.

Fiske, S. T., & Neuberg, S. L. (1990). A continuum of impression formation, from category-based to individuating processes: Influences of information and motivation on attention and interpretation. In M. Zanna (Ed.), *Advances in experimental social psychology* (Vol. 23, pp. 1–74). Orlando, FL: Academic Press.

Forgas, J. P. (1995). Mood and judgment: The Affect Infusion Model (AIM). *Psychological Bulletin, 117,* 39–66.

Forgas, J. P. (1998). Mood effects on the fundamental attribution error: On being happy and mistaken. *Journal of Personality and Social Psychology, 75,* 318–331.

Forgas, J. P., & Bower, G. H. (1987). Mood effects on person perception judgments. *Journal of Personality and Social Psychology, 53,* 53–60.

Forgas, J. P., & Fiedler, K. (1996). Us and them: Mood effects on intergroup discrimination. *Journal of Personality and Social Psychology, 70,* 28–40.

Gaertner, S. L., Dovidio, J. F., Anastasio, P. A., Bachman, B. A., & Rust, M. C. (1993). The Common Ingroup Identity Model: Recategorization and the reduction of intergroup bias. In W. Stroebe & M. Hewstone (Eds.), *European review of social psychology* (Vol. 4, pp. 1–26). London: Wiley.

Gaertner, S. L., Dovidio, J. F., Nier, J., Banker, B., Ward, C., Houlette, M., & Loux, S. (1999a). The Common Ingroup Identity Model for reducing intergroup bias: Progress and challenges. In R. Brown & D. Capozza (Eds.), *Social identity processes: Trends in theory and research.* London: Sage.

Gaertner, S. L., Dovidio, J. F., Nier, J., Ward, C., & Banker, B. (1999c). Across cultural divides: The value of a superordinate identity. In D. Prentice & D. Miller (Eds.), *Cultural divides: Understanding and overcoming group conflict* (pp. 173–212). New York: Sage.

Gaertner, S. L., Dovidio, J. F., Rust, M. C., Nier, J., Banker, B., Ward, C. M., Mottola, G. R., & Houlette, M. (1999b). Reducing intergroup bias: Elements of intergroup cooperation. *Journal of Personality and Social Psychology, 76,* 388–402.

Gaertner, S. L., Rust, M. C., Dovidio, J. F., Bachman, B. A., & Anastasio, P. A. (1994). The Contact Hypothesis: The role of a common ingroup identity in reducing intergroup bias. *Small Group Research, 25,* 224–249.

Hewstone, M. (1990). The "ultimate attribution error"? A review of the literature on intergroup attributions. *European Journal of Social Psychology, 20,* 311–335.

Hewstone, M. (1996). Contact and categorization: Social psychological interventions to change intergroup relations. In C. N. Macrae, C. Stangor, & M. Hewstone (Eds.), *Stereotypes and stereotyping* (pp. 323–368). New York: Guilford Press.

Hogg, M. A., & Turner, J. C. (1985). Interpersonal attraction, social identification and psychological group formation. *European Journal of Social Psychology, 15,* 51–66.

Howard, J. M., & Rothbart, M. (1980). Social categorization for in-group and out-group behavior. *Journal of Personality and Social Psychology, 38,* 301–310.

Huo, Y. J., Smith, H. H., Tyler, T. R., & Lind, A. E. (1996). Superordinate identification, subgroup identification, and justice concerns: Is assimilation the answer? *Psychological Science, 7,* 40–45.

Isen, A. M. (1970). Success, failure, attention, and reaction to others: The warm glow of success. *Journal of Personality and Social Psychology, 15,* 294–301.

Isen, A. M. (1987). Positive affect, cognitive processes, and social behavior. In L. Berkowitz (Ed.), *Advances in experimental social psychology* (Vol. 20, pp. 203–253). Orlando, FL: Academic Press.

Isen, A. M. (1993). Positive affect and decision making. In M. Lewis & J. M. Haviland (Eds.), *Handbook of emotion* (pp. 261–277). New York: Guilford Press.

Isen, A. M., & Daubman, K. A. (1984). The influence of affect on categorization. *Journal of Personality and Social Psychology, 47,* 1206–1217.

Isen, A. M., Daubman, K. A., & Nowicki, G. P. (1987). Positive affect facilitates creative problem solving. *Journal of Personality and Social Psychology, 52,* 1122–1131.

Isen, A. M., & Geva, N. (1987). The influence of positive affect on acceptable level of risk: The person with a large canoe has a large worry. *Organizational Behavior and Human Decision Processes, 39,* 145–154.

Isen, A. M., Johnson, M. M. S., Mertz, E., & Robinson, G. F. (1985). The influence of positive affect on the unusualness of word associations. *Journal of Personality and Social Psychology, 48,* 1413–1426.

Isen, A. M., & Levin, P. F. (1972). Effect of feeling good on helping: Cookies and kindness. *Journal of Personality and Social Psychology, 21,* 384–388.

Isen, A. M., Niedenthal, P. M., & Cantor, N. (1992). An influence of positive affect on social categorization. *Motivation and Emotion, 16,* 65–78.

Isen, A. M., Nygren, T. E., & Ashby, F. G. (1988). The influence of positive affect on the subjective utility of gains and losses: It is just not worth the risk. *Journal of Personality and Social Psychology, 55,* 710–717.

Isen, A. M., & Patrick, R. (1983). The effect of positive feelings on risk-taking: When the chips are down. *Organizational Behavior and Human Performance, 31,* 194-202.

Lambert, A. J., Khan, S. R., Lickel, B. A., & Fricke, K. (1997). Mood and the correction of positive versus negative stereotypes. *Journal of Personality and Social Psychology, 72,* 1002–1016.

Lott, A. J., & Lott, B. E. (1974). The role of reward in the formation of positive interpersonal attitudes. In T. Huston (Ed.), *Foundations of interpersonal attraction* (pp. 171–189). New York: Academic Press.

Mackie, D. M., Hamilton, D. L., Schroth, H. A., Carlisle, C. J., Gersho, B. F., Meneses, L. M., Nedler, B. F., & Reichel, L. D. (1989). The effects of induced mood on expectancy-based illusory correlations. *Journal of Experimental Social Psychology, 25,* 524–544.

Mackie, D. M., & Worth, L. T. (1989). Processing deficits and the mediation of positive affect in persuasion. *Journal of Personality and Social Psychology, 57,* 27–40.

Messick, D. M., & Mackie, D. M. (1989). Intergroup relations. *Annual Review of Psychology, 40,* 45–81.

Miller, N., Brewer, M. B., & Edwards, K. (1985). Cooperative interaction in desegregated settings: A laboratory analog. *Journal of Social Issues, 41,* 63–75.

Mullen, B., Brown, R., & Smith, C. (1992). Ingroup bias as a function of salience, relevance, and status: An integration. *European Journal of Social Psychology, 22,* 103–122.

Murray, N., Sujan, H., Hirt, E. R., & Sujan, M. (1990). The influence of mood on categorization: A cognitive flexibility interpretation. *Journal of Personality and Social Psychology, 59,* 411–425.

Park, B., & Rothbart, M. (1982). Perception of out-group homogeneity and levels of social categorization: Memory for subordinate attributes of in-group and out-group members. *Journal of Personality and Social Psychology, 42,* 1051–1068.

Pettigrew, T. F. (1998). Intergroup contact theory. *Annual Review of Psychology, 49,* 65–85.

Ruscher, J. B., & Fiske, S. T. (1990). Interpersonal competition can cause individuating processes. *Journal of Personality and Social Psychology, 58,* 832–843.

Rust, M. C. (1995). *Effects of mood on categorization.* Unpublished masters thesis, Department of Psychology, University of Delaware, Newark.

Schwarz, N., Bless, H., & Bohner, G. (1991). Mood and persuasion: Affective states influence the processing of persuasive communications. In M. P. Zanna (Ed.), *Advances in experimental social psychology* (Vol. 24, pp. 161–199). Orlando, FL: Academic Press.

Sherif, M., Harvey, O. J., White, B. J., Hood, W. R., & Sherif, C. (1954). *Experimental study of positive and negative intergroup attitudes between experimentally produced groups. Robbers Cave experiment.* Norman: University of Oklahoma.

Siebert, P. S., & Ellis, H. C. (1991). A convenient self-referencing mood induction procedure. *Bulletin of the Psychonomic Society, 29,* 121–124.

Stein, D. D., Hardyck, J. A., & Smith, M. B. (1965). Race and belief: An open and shut case. *Journal of Personality and Social Psychology, 1,* 281–289.

Stephan, W. G., & Stephan, C. W. (1984). The role of ignorance in intergroup relations. In N. Miller & M. B. Brewer (Eds.), *Groups in contact: The psychology of desegregation* (pp. 229–257). Orlando, FL: Academic Press.

Stephan, W. G., & Stephan, C. W. (1985). Intergroup anxiety. *Journal of Social Issues, 41,* 157–175.

Stroessner, S. J., Hamilton, D. L., & Mackie, D. M. (1992). Affect and stereotyping: The effect of induced mood on distinctiveness-based illusory correlations. *Journal of Personality and Social Psychology, 62,* 564–576.

Tajfel, H. (1969). Cognitive aspects of prejudice. *Journal of Social Issues, 25*(4), 79–97.

Tajfel, H., & Turner, J. C. (1979). An integrative theory of intergroup conflict. In W. G. Austin & S. Worchel (Eds.), *The social psychology of intergroup relations* (pp. 33–47). Monterey, CA: Brooks/Cole.

Taylor, S. E., Fiske, S. T., Etcoff, N. L., & Ruderman, A. J. (1978). Categorical bases of person memory and stereotyping. *Journal of Personality and Social Psychology, 36,* 778–793.

Trope, Y. (1998, July). *Mood as a resource in overcoming defensive self-evaluations.* Paper presented at the European Association of Experimental Social Psychology Small Group Meeting on Subjective Experiences, Grasellenbach, Germany.

Tversky, A., & Gati, I. (1978). Studies of similarity. In E. Rosch & B. B. Lloyd (Eds.), *Cognition and categorization* (pp. 79–98). Hillsdale, NJ: Erlbaum.

Veitch, R., & Griffitt, W. (1976). Good news—bad news: Affective and interpersonal effects. *Journal of Applied Social Psychology, 6,* 69–75.

Velten, E. (1968). A laboratory task for induction of mood states. *Behavioral Research and Therapy, 6,* 473–482.

Wilder, D. A. (1978). Reducing intergroup discrimination through individuation of the outgroup. *Journal of Personality and Social Psychology, 36,* 1361–1374.

Wilder, D. A. (1984). Predictions of belief homogeneity and similarity following social categorization. *British Journal of Social Psychology, 23,* 323–333.

Worchel, S., Andreoli, V. A., & Folger, R. (1977). Intergroup cooperation and intergroup attraction: The effect of previous interaction and outcome of combined effort. *Journal of Experimental Social Psychology, 13,* 131–140.

Worth, L. T., & Mackie, D. M. (1987). Cognitive mediation of positive affect on persuasion. *Social Cognition, 5,* 76–94.

20
CHAPTER

Herbert Bless
Joseph P. Forgas

The Message Within:
Toward a Social Psychology
of Subjective Experiences

What does it feel like to be a person? How can we understand the subjective life worlds of other individuals? To what extent are the methods and
theories of empirical social psychology applicable to understanding the
subjective experiences of others? What are the key mechanisms that explain how and why subjective experiences influence our thinking and
behaviors? We started this book by posing several ambitious questions
like this. It is now time to take stock, and to review how much we were
able to achieve and what remains to be done.

As we go through our daily lives, only a small fraction of the things we
see, think, or do is dealt with at an overtly conscious, explicit level. Much
of the business of daily living is transacted at the implicit level of subjective experiences. The searchlight of consciousness can only ever illumi-

The authors are listed in alphabetical order. The preparation of this chapter was facilitated
by support from Grant DFG 289/5-2 to Herbert Bless, and from the Australian Research
Council (Special Investigator Award) and the Alexander von Humboldt Foundation (Research Prize) to Joseph P. Forgas.

Address all correspondence to either of the authors: Herbert Bless, Mikrosoziologie und
Sozialpsychologie, University of Mannheim, D-68131 Mannheim, Germany, E-mail:
hbless@sowi.uni-mannheim.de; or Joseph P. Forgas, School of Psychology, University of
New South Wales, Sydney 2052, Australia, E-mail: JP.Forgas@unsw.edu.au, Internet: http:
//www.psy.unsw.edu.au/staff/jforgas.htm

nate a tiny circle of the phenomenological field. In the background, there is always a continuous ebb and flow of feelings, associations, somatic cues, implicit memories, and dispositions—subjective experiences—that seem to play a key role in guiding us through social situations and help us to understand and respond to the many challenges of social life. The contributions to this volume provide a rich variety of empirical illustrations of how such subjective experiences impact on our social judgments and actions in the shape of feelings, memories, dispositions, or habits. Our first objective with this book was to provide an overview of recent developments in the study of how various forms of subjective experiences influence social phenomena such as person perception, stereotyping, attitude change, or memory processes. More importantly, our aim was to identify integrative links between of the different theories and mechanisms so far proposed to account for different kinds of subjective experiences.

Traditionally, subjective experiences such as affect, mood, feeling-of-knowing, surprise, or ease-of-retrieval phenomena have been discussed rather independently of each other. As a result, there has been little recognition that the same kinds of processes and mechanisms may be involved in a number of these experiences. In this final chapter, we want to take another look at the construct of "subjective experiences" and assess how far our original aims of seeking integration across previously isolated research areas we were able to achieve. What have we learned and what new questions emerged from this enterprise? Is the empirical study of subjective experiences indeed likely to emerge as a central issue in contemporary psychology, as foreshadowed in Wegner and Gilbert's stimulating introductory chapter to this volume? What have we accomplished so far, and what are the most promising directions for future research in this area? After a brief historical introduction, we want to structure this final overview along three guiding questions. First, we want to address the nature of subjective experiences; what do they have in common, and how we can distinguish between different kinds of subjective experiences? Second, we will take a look at the consequences of subjective experience on social information processing. Third, and finally, we will discuss some of the obstacles as well as some of the most promising avenues for future research.

☐ The Roots of a Social Psychology of Subjective Experience

The introductory chapter by Wegner and Gilbert suggested that placing subjective experiences into the focus of social psychological research is rather a radical idea that conflicts with our traditional notions about our discipline. Many of our readers may also have felt somewhat sceptical about such a major redefinition of our field. In fact, however, a plausible case could be made that social psychology has always been first and foremost about subjective experiences, just as Wegner and Gilbert proposed. Some of the most powerful and illuminating ideas in the discipline have long been derived from theorizing that was first and foremost about phenomenology—the subjective experiences of social actors.

For example, the symbolic interactionist tradition and George Herbert Mead's "social behaviorism" in particular represent a sophisticated attempt to construct a theory of social behavior that is based on the phenomenology and subjective experience of the social actor, yet recognizes the need to study such experiences using reliable empirical methods. Symbolic interactionism sought to correct "many of the crudities of . . . behaviourist psychology [by including] the neglected introspective phenomena" in its analysis (Desmonde, 1970, p. 57). Mead sought a reconciliation of behaviorism and phenomenology, and in constructing his theory, he was equally critical of Watson's unbridled behaviourism and Wundt's blinkered introspectionism.

The symbolic interactionist perspective focuses on the subjective, symbolic, and cognitive nature of human social life, and emphasizes the importance of an individual's subjective symbolic representations about the world as the key to understanding what people perceive, think, and do. This is precisely what most contemporary social cognitive theories also seek to achieve, and many of the chapters included in this book share the same objectives. Just like William James, Mead also clearly distinguished between the subjective, private experience of the individual—the "I," and the externally determined, socialized aspects of the self, the "me." For Mead, as for James, it was the subjective experiences of the "I" that were the source of all creative, independent, and autonomous action. In contrast, the thoroughly socialized "me" was seen as merely a follower and reactor to preexisting external expectations and norms. Understanding the subjective world of the individual—the irreducible "I" of James and Mead—is precisely what Wegner and Gilbert also proposed as the key objective for social psychology in their introductory chapter.

Mead's theories had a powerful influence on early social psychological research. For example, in their classic studies of the social psychology of situated action, W. I. Thomas, F. Znaniecki, and others devised ingenuous empirical methods to explore and represent the subjective, phenomenological experiences of individuals, such as groups of Polish migrants as they gradually adapted to their new environment in America. Unfortunately, with the passage of time and with the emergence of ever-tighter disciplinary boundaries, Mead's symbolic interactionist ideas had a far greater impact on phenomenologically oriented sociologists than on empirical social psychologists. This is rather unfortunate, as a social psychology concerned with subjective experience could find much that is of interest in symbolic interactionist theories. Given recent advances in our experimental techniques, social psychology is now also in a much better position to empirically explore symbolic interactionist theories than at any time in the past.

Symbolic interactionism is not the only historical antecedent for our enterprise, however. The study of subjective experience—that is, the phenomenological perspective in social science theorizing—produced some of our most stimulating and enduring ideas and research paradigms in experimental social psychology. Fritz Heider's now classic theorizing about what social actors need to think and do in order to effectively function in society is essentially a prolonged phenomenological treatise about the nature of subjective experiences. Heider's speculations about the nature and functions of subjective experiences have given rise to some of most productive ideas and empirical research paradigms in social psychology. His speculative explorations of subjective experience came to define the future scope of such key areas of research as person perception, attribution theory, balance and dissonance theories, and research on attitudes and attitude change, to mention but a few. Without Heider's earnest devotion to taking the study of subjective experiences seriously as the key to all social psychology, our discipline would look unrecognizably impoverished today.

Kurt Lewin was another key figure for whom the study of subjective experiences was at the very heart of social psychological research. His field theory in particular represents an explicit affirmation of the principle that the way people subjectively see and experience social situations must be the key research question guiding our discipline. Lewin's focus on subjective experiences, and the work of his students and followers, have left an indelible mark on our field. Lewinian thinking eventually gave us such dramatically successful research paradigms as research on cognitive dissonance.

The past several decades in social psychology have been characterized by the ascendancy of the social cognitive paradigm, a framework that clearly accepts that the subjective memories, feelings, and representations of actors have a critical influence on social judgments and behavior. This approach owes much to the theoretical framework of Gestalt theory, and the pioneering work of Solomon Asch, Jerome Bruner, and George Kelly, in particular. Given the obvious fact that so many of our most influential theories have their roots in phenomenological thinking, there can be little doubt that there has been a long-standing preoccupation with the nature of subjective experiences in social psychology. It is all the more surprising, then, that subjective experiences have been rarely emphasized explicitly as the key concern of our discipline. One of the objectives of this book was to try to rectify this imbalance, and in particular, to advocate the study of subjective experiences as a central integrative concept in social psychology. Of course, this is by no means a simple enterprise; even the definition of the concept is fraught with difficulties, as the next section will argue.

☐ What Are Subjective Experiences?

Research in social cognition has been strongly influenced by applying the computer metaphor to human information processing. However, humans are not computers, and conversely, computers can never fully simulate the subtle dynamics of social perception, judgments, and behavior—at least, not up to the present time. One could argue that the focal theme of this book, emphasizing the key role of subjective experiences in understanding social behavior, is precisely what differentiates human thinking from computerized information processing.

Unlike computers, human information processing is usually accompanied by individuals' multilayered and hard-to-define subjective experiences, and the results of their thinking and actions are strongly influenced by these amorphous and hard-to-pin-down experiences. At a first glance, the chapters in this book highlight the fact that the term "subjective experiences" may capture an extremely wide spectrum of different experiential phenomena. Given the variety of specific fields within which subjective experiences have been studied, it seems important to identify the shared properties of these phenomena. On the other hand, it is also desirable to clarify how different subjective experience phenomena can be distinguished from each other. In other words, we need to think about developing a classificatory taxonomy of the domain of subjective experiences that can influence social cognition and behavior.

Several such attempts have been made in recent years. One possible classification of different subjective experiences distinguishes between affective feelings, nonaffective "cognitive" feelings, and bodily feelings (Clore, 1992; Schwarz & Clore, 1996). Affective feelings are perhaps most easily and traditionally associated with subjective experiences, and several of the chapters here discuss the antecedents and consequences of affective states for social behavior. Theorists such as Damasio and his colleagues (Adolphs & Damasio, in press) specifically suggest a neurophysiological link between somatic experiences, affective states, and high-level cognitive information processing.

At an even more specific level, affective states can encompass a large variety of distinct feelings that differ in valence, intensity, duration, and the like. On the one hand, these affective feelings include unspecific, general experiences, such as moods, that are usually rather low in intensity, long in duration, and that can at best be described in terms of a simple positive/negative dimension. While most research in social cognition has focused on these diffuse affective feelings (for overviews, see Bless, in press-a; Clore, Schwarz, & Conway, 1994; Forgas, 1995, in press), affective experiences may also include far more specific and sometimes more intense emotions, such as threat, anger, or surprise. Recent research on these different forms of experiences is discussed here in a number of chapters (see, e.g., chapter 18 by Abele, chapter 16 by Bodenhausen & Moreno, chapter 13 by Bohner & Weinerth, chapter 19 by Dovidio & colleagues, chapter 11 by Forgas & colleagues, chapter 14 by Garcia-Marques & Mackie, chapter 15 by Reisenzein, chapter 12 by Sedikides & Green).

Given that research in social cognition has focused a lot on the subjective experience of affect, it is not surprising that these concerns provide one of the recurring themes in many chapters in this book. Even a brief look at this research reveals that social thinking, judgments, and behavior can all be strongly influenced even by weak, subconscious, and lingering moods and affective states. It seems that even minor and subtle changes of individuals' affective states have a pronounced impact on how they construct their social reality. The research presented here makes it very evident that ignoring affective feelings would strongly impair our understanding of individuals' social behavior. Indeed, one of the main outcomes from recent research on affect is that social thinking and behavior is almost never completely cold and rational. Subjective affective states accompany almost everything people think and do. Recent neuropsychological evidence confirms that affect far from being a source of disruption and bias, provides a key input into adaptive behaviour and decisions (Adolphs & Damasio, in press). People who suffer neural damage that impairs their ability to respond affectively to social situations tend to make disastrous social decisions and choices, even if their intelligence and cognitive abilities remain perfect.

While there seems to be quite strong consensus on the nature of affective feelings, nonaffective feelings seem more diverse and more difficult to capture. Not only the chapters included in this book, but other authors as well (cf. Clore, 1992) use this term to describe a variety of different feelings, such as experienced ease of retrieval, feelings of familiarity, feelings of knowing, or feelings of control. Perhaps one of the common themes underlying many of these terms is the shared emphasis on the subjectively experienced "fluency of information processing."

Feelings about the fluency of information processing, be it simply feelings accompanying recognition processes or the feelings associated with the generation of arguments in favor of a specific position, have a pronounced impact on the outcome of the information processing itself. Sev-

eral of the chapters here report groundbreaking work on how such subjective "cognitive" feelings as the experienced ease of retrieval (see chapter 8 by Haddock; chapter 6 by Martin & Whitaker; chapter 10 by Skurnik
et al.; and chapter 9 by Wänke & Bless), ease of simulation (chapter 5 by
Brendl), or the subjective feeling of familiarity (chapter 2 by Fiedler; chapter 14 by Garcia-Marques & Mackie; and chapter 7 by Smith) can all have
an enormous impact on an individuals' perception and responses to a
situation. Subjective experiences of "cognitive fluency" may also comprise other cognitive feelings, such as feelings of control (chapter 17 by
Dardenne et al.) and subjective awareness of information activation (chapter 3 by Dijksterhuis).

In sum, the empirical findings and theories reviewed here converge in
suggesting that it is not only the focal content of the processed information that determines social judgments and reactions. Rather, the subjectively experienced fluency of how the information processing *feels* to the
person also has a determining, if far less clearly understood influence.
One may argue about whether the term "cognitive feelings" appropriately captures the essence of these kinds of phenomena, or whether some
other label would be more suitable. For example, cognitive feelings could
also be summarized as metacognitions, thus excluding the "feeling" label
that seems to be primarily associated with affective states rather than
cognition. We will have more to say about this issue when discussing
future research directions.

Finally, subjective experiences may also encompass a third class of phenomena associated with many kinds of bodily feelings. Just like other
feelings, bodily feelings have been demonstrated to have a strong impact
on social information processing and behavior (see chapter 4 by Neumann
& Strack). The groundbreaking work of Damasio and his colleagues (see
Adolphs & Damasio, in press) specifically emphasizes that somatic feedback mechanisms frequently play a key role in regulating affective and
cognitive reactions to social situations. The available research suggests
that the study of the role of subjective bodily feelings on social behavior
deserves far more attention than has been devoted to it in the past.

Having briefly discussed some possible links and distinctions between
different forms of subjective experiences, we now want to consider what
all these phenomena might have in common. Various theoretical frame-
works have been proposed in attempting to account for the unity of subjective experiences (for examples, see Clore, 1992; Koriat & Levy-Sadot,
1999; Schwarz, in press; Strack, 1992). For example, Koriat and Levy-
Sadot argue that a specific stimulus or situation activates particular mental representations. The content of these representations will then influence individuals' subsequent processing and judgments. Importantly, and
in line with social cognition research, individuals may or may not be sub-

jectively aware of the activation of these representations (cf. Bargh, 1997; see also chapter 3 by Dijksterhuis et al.). One the one hand, the activation of the representations increases the likelihood that their content will be used in further processing. On the other hand, the activation of the representations may lead to the incidental creation of a subjective feeling.

For example, we may feel happy or sad as a result of information that is activated in a specific situation (such as hearing that we won the lottery, or learning that our dog died). Similarly, we may feel that it is easy to recall something or we may feel that something sounds familiar—without necessarily becoming consciously aware as to where these subjective feelings have come from. Because these subjective experiences or feelings are based on the specific propositional information that is activated in a particular situation, they function as if they provided some sort of a metasummary of the information itself—even if the information as such is sometimes not directly accessible. In contrast to the propositional content, the subjective experience it generates may become detached and may be accessible and used even when the original eliciting information is no longer remembered.

This ability for subjective feelings to become detached from and survive the original eliciting source may be the first shared aspect of the various forms of subjective experiences we are concerned with here. A good example of such a mechanism is when people retain a positive preference for a person or an object that they have encountered previously, even though they can no longer actually remember having seen that target at all (for a detailed discussion of such familiarity or prior exposure effects, see Zajonc, in press). In such a case, recognition memory for the person or object indicates no memory trace at all, but preference judgments, presumably based on the positive subjective experiences generated by prior exposure, reliably produce greater liking for a previously encountered target. This raises the interesting possibility, also considered by Koriat and Levy-Sadot, that subjective experiences could also provide an important link between the unconscious (inaccessible) and the conscious (accessible) aspects of social information processing (see also chapter 3 by Dijksterhuis et al. and chapter 1 by Wegner & Gilbert).

Another shared aspect of the subjective experiences considered here is their "truth" value. We may be right or wrong when we estimate the length of a river or when we predict the trustworthiness of a politician—and other people may argue with us about these judgments. However, we can hardly be wrong when we state "I feel happy," "it feels easy," or "it feels familiar." Thus, subjective experiences possess a unique epistemological status of a certain indeterminacy and of not being open to external inspection or challenge. This feature has also been recognized in classic social psychological theories. For example, both William James and

George Herbert Mead assigned special status to the subjective "I" as the source of all creative and authentic reactions that are by definition indeterminate and not entirely predictable in terms of external variables. In a similar vein, Kurt Lewin's field theory also explicitly emphasized that in order to understand social behavior, we must focus not on the social situation as it objectively is, but on the social situation as it is subjectively experienced and represented by the individual.

Depending on the situation, other people might perhaps be surprised by the subjective perceptions and experiences we have and question the appropriateness of our feelings, but they will not be in a position to question the truth or the correctness of our subjective experiences. Perhaps it is this unchallengeable "truth" value of our subjective experiences that renders them to be such a powerful influence on further information processing. As many of the chapters in this volume have demonstrated, individuals make robust use of their subjective experiences to guide their responses in a wide variety of cognitive and behavioral tasks.

While subjective experiences themselves may not be true or false, there is, of course, much scope for individuals to falsely attribute them to an origin unrelated to their actual cause. This is all the more likely as the eliciting circumstances for a subjective experience may be long forgotten when the subjective experience itself still continues to influence us (see, e.g., Zajonc's, in press, work on familiarity effects). Again, this aspect seems to apply to most of the various forms of subjective experiences discussed here. For example, individuals may incorrectly attribute their enduring affect to some contemporaneously experienced person or group—even though the original affective state resulted from some prior and completely unrelated affective experience (Byrne & Clore, 1970). Similarly, individuals may incorrectly attribute the subjectively experienced ease of retrieval to the fact that many instances are stored in memory—although the experience is due to the nature of the task that requires the retrieval of only very few instances. To make effective use of subjective experiences, individuals need to see a clear relationship between their subjective experience and the specific cognitive, judgmental, or behavioral task they are facing (see chapter 6 by Martin & Whitaker).

How are such links between subjective experiences and a particular cognitive task established? How do we know what a subjective experience refers to? To avoid the need to assume a homunculus that makes such decisions, we may assume that as a rule, subjective experiences are routinely attributed to the currently activated object of attention as a default strategy (see chapter 6 by Martin & Whitaker). Attributions to other causes, which are of course possible and plausible, require additional and further processing. Attribution manipulations have been applied to quite a number of the subjective experiences investigated in the chapters here. The results of these studies converge toward the conclusion that the impact of subjective states on cognition and behavior is usually eliminated if individuals are led to attribute their subjective experience to a different cause unrelated to the current task. For example, consistent research demonstrated that subjective experiences of positive and negative moods will no longer influence judgments when judges associate their mood with an object other than the judgmental target (Schwarz & Clore, 1983, 1996).

To summarize, then, it appears that subjective experiences may capture a wide spectrum of affective, nonaffective, and bodily feelings that typically accompany information processing and social behavior. These subjective experiences share important characteristics, such as their enduring character, their ability to become detached from the original eliciting conditions, the fact that they have no externally assessable truth value, and the fact that they can be readily associated with (and attributed to) otherwise unrelated objects. These characteristics render subjective experiences to be a potentially very important source of influence on social cognition and behavior, as we will see in the next section.

☐ The Consequences of Subjective Experience on Social Information Processing

The most obvious consequences of subjective experiences are on the qualitative outcome of information processing. For example, several of the chapters included here provide strong support for the conclusion that almost any social judgment can be influenced by individuals' subjective experiences. At the one extreme of the information processing spectrum, even the most simple and least constructive cognitive task, such as the mere recognition of previously presented information, can be strongly influenced by the person's prevailing subjective experiences (see, for example, the chapter 2 by Fiedler and chapter 4 by Neumann & Strack). At the other extreme of the processing continuum, more complex and elaborate social judgments, such as an individual's evaluation and reactions to a complex persuasive communication (chapter 16 by Bohner & Weinerth), show an equally clear propensity to be influenced by subjective experiences.

Several of the chapters here report empirical evidence that a wide variety of social judgments about persons or groups are influenced by subjective experiences (see, for example, chapter 18 by Abele, chapter 16 by Bodenhausen & Moreno, and chapter 19 by Dovidio et al. in this volume). Importantly, affective feelings are by no means the only kinds of subjective experiences that have a powerful effect on social judgments. Subjective experiences associated with cognitive feelings, such as the fluency of information processing, can also influence the outcome of person-perception judgments (chapter 8 by Haddock, chapter 10 by Skurnik et al.), including reactions to persuasive messages (chapter 9 by Wänke &

Bless), probability judgments (chapter 5 by Brendl), or judgments of similarity (chapter 6 by Martin & Whitaker).

In addition to influencing the outcome of social cognition, subjective experiences can also enter into and modify the cognitive strategies people use and the nature of their thought processes. Existing theories and the available empirical evidence suggest a number of possible mechanisms for mediating the effects of affective and nonaffective subjective experiences on cognitive strategies.

Subjective Experience as a Shortcut

Frequently, the function of subjective experiences appears to be a simple shortcut to elaborate information processing by providing a direct basis for producing certain social judgments. For example, individuals may base evaluative judgments directly on their affective state by employing a "How-do-I-feel-about-it?" heuristic (Schwarz & Clore, 1983, 1996). Similarly, the ease with which information can be retrieved from memory can short-circuit more extensive memory search strategies and be used as a direct indicator for the amount of the stored information available. Such "ease of retrieval" may in turn influence subsequent attitude judgments (chapter 8 by Haddock, Schwarz et al., 1991, Wänke, Schwarz, & Bless, 1995).

In a similar way, subjective experiences about bodily states, such as facial expressions or other somatic experiences, can also serve as a shortcut for producing evaluative judgments (e.g. Strack, Martin, & Stepper, 1988). In all of these cases, the substantive, detailed processing of social information is short-circuited by a direct reliance on subjective experiences as the most important informational cues. Such "experiential" shortcuts will frequently result in faster, more efficient, and often equally effective judgmental outcomes and decisions. However, using such experiential heuristic shortcuts may also be fraught with difficulty, as the subjective states people rely on may often by due to a source that is in fact completely unrelated to the task at hand (Schwarz & Clore, 1983). Also, the cognitive and judgmental consequences of a subjective experience may be highly volatile and easily subverted by contextual effects. Chapter 6 by Martin and Whitaker here presents a range of evidence demonstrating how the meaning and consequences of subjective experiences are readily influenced by various configural effects associated with specific contexts.

Subjective Experience Interacts with Other Information

Of course, subjective experiences are not the only foundation for constructing a response. In particular, when the task is important or personally relevant, subjective experiences are unlikely to provide the sole basis for judgments. In addition to relying on their subjective experience, individuals will additionally rely on other information that is accessible and will then need to integrate these different forms of informational bases. We only now begin to understand how subjective experiences and other information are likely to be weighted up, combined, and integrated in social cognition, although models of information integration have a rich history in social psychology (see chapter 18 by Abele; Abele & Petzold, 1998). In the simplest case, subjective experience may merely be added to and combined with other information as one among many possible sources of input. In more complex cases, subjective experiences may also interact with and alter the weight and the valence of other information that is used as the basis for a judgmental task. This may occur, for example, when people give greater weight to information and consider it more favorably simply because it comes to mind more easily, as the work reviewed by Wänke and Bless here indicates.

Subjective Experience Influences Processing Strategies

The evidence also suggests that subjective experiences may not only serve as a direct or indirect source of information entering into the judgmental processes, but can also directly influence the type of information processing adopted. For example, affective states have been found to either facilitate an analytic, piecemeal type of processing (in negative mood) or trigger information processes that are more likely to be based on prior knowledge and heuristics (in positive mood; see Bless, in press-a; Clore et al., 1994; Schwarz, 1990). Several chapters of this volume elaborate on the links between affect and information processing (for example, see chapter 13 by Bohner & Weinerth; chapter 19 by Dovidio et al.; chapter 11 by Forgas et al.).

A number of different conceptualizations have been proposed to account for the impact of subjective states on processing style. For example, some theories suggest that individuals may use their subjective experiences as a quick and usually good shorthand indicator for the kind of processing strategy required to produce an adequate response (see Schwarz, 1990). Other accounts also highlight the functional, evolutionary importance of subjective experiences in determining how we deal with social situations. For example, positive subjective states may indicate that a person may safely rely on existing internalized schematic structures and the use of top-down processes in dealing with a situation. In contrast, aversive, negative subjective states and moods may trigger a more bottom-up, situationally focussed processing style (Bless, in press-b; Fiedler, in press).

The style of information processing triggered by subjective states may differ not only with respect to bottom-up or top-down processing, but also whether or not individuals are motivated to reach a particular outcome (see Kunda, 1990). The research evidence suggests that subjective experiences such as positive or negative affect can determine the kind and extent of motivational processing used in social thinking. Different processing strategies in turn can play a critical role in increasing or reducing the intensity of an existing mood state (chapter 11 by Forgas et al.). Thus, negative subjective states may trigger a processing strategy and outcomes that are specifically guided by the motivational goal of eliminating an aversive state. For example, people experiencing negative affect and making a personally relevant decision were found as a consequence to engage in highly selected and targeted information search strategies designed to produce a personally rewarding outcome (Forgas, 1991).

Associative Consequences of Subjective Experiences

While subjective experiences can frequently result from the incidental activation of information, the reverse mechanism is equally likely to occur. In other words, the experience of affective or nonaffective feelings can trigger specific mental representations and memories. Experiencing a particular feeling activates associated concepts and makes it more likely that these concepts and memories will be recalled, used, and elaborated on in subsequent information processing. This idea has been most extensively developed in the study of affective influences on social memory, associations, learning, and judgments (Bower, 1981; Bower & Forgas, in press; Forgas, 1995). The notion of mood-congruent effects on memory and judgments is basically an extension of well-established associative network models of memory to also include subjective states as units in a representational networks. Research evidence now strongly indicates that associative network accounts of how subjective states can activate and prime memory contents can account for a wide variety of cognitive and behavioral phenomena. However, recent theories also suggest that these associative memory effects are highly dependent on the kind of information processing strategy judges adopt in a given setting (Bower & Forgas, in press; Forgas, 1995).

Thus, associative effects are most likely to occur when a task requires a degree of open and constructive processing and the active use of stored memory structures. When the task can be solved in a more direct and motivated way that precludes open memory search, associative effects tend to disappear. This principle has been most extensively studied in the context of mood effects on social memory and judgments, where it was found that the extent of mood congruence in judgments seems to be directly related to the degree of open, constructive processing required to perform a task (Forgas, 1992, 1994). As we have seen, then, subjective experiences do have a variety of consequences for social thinking, memory, and behavior. They may serve as direct input into judgments and decisions, they may interact and be combined with external stimulus information, they may influence the kinds of strategies people adopt when solving a social task, and they may indirectly prime and facilitate the use of associated information in memory.

☐ Open Issues and Directions for Future Research

In this section, we will briefly consider some of the problems and some of the potential research questions that are only now becoming apparent in the emerging literature on subjective experiences. One such issue is how we can separate the direct effects of a subjective experience on cognition and behavior from their "secondary" effects, that is, the effects that arise due to the selective priming and activation of other information. We shall also look at some of the limiting conditions that restrict the effects of subjective experiences, consider the nature and varieties of nonaffective experiences so far explored, and, finally, discuss the need for developing more complete, integrated explanations for the operation of subjective experiences in social life.

Primary and Secondary Effects

One recurrent issue suggested by the available research has to do with the difficulty of distinguishing the direct, primary effects of a subjective experience on cognition from its indirect, secondary effects, due for example to the selective priming of associated information. In many cases, these two sources of influence will have very similar consequences. For example, when studying the effects of subjectively experienced affect, the experience of positive or negative mood may sometimes be used directly to inform a judgment. However, the same mood state is also likely to increase the accessibility of positively or negatively valenced memories and concepts, and individuals may base their judgment on these concepts. The resulting judgments will be affectively congruent in either case (see Forgas, 1995; Forgas & Bower, 1987). It is not always easy to decide, however, whether such mood congruence was caused by the indirect use of affectively primed associations in constructing a response or the subjects' direct reliance on their moods to infer a judgment (Schwarz & Clore,

1983, 1996). These two mechanisms produce identical outcomes but depend on very different mediating mechanisms for their operation.

Theorists such as Forgas (1995) suggest that the empirical separation of these two mediating mechanisms requires the careful measurement and analysis of the information processing strategies used. Thus, when affective experiences directly inform a judgment, this should be a relatively fast and effortless process, characterized by fast response latencies and relatively poor recall memory for stimulus details. In contrast, when mood congruence is due to the use of memory contents selectively primed by an affective state, this should require more extensive and lengthy processing and better recall later on. It seems then that in research on subjective experiences, it would be important to empirically distinguish between such alternative direct and indirect effects, and the measurement of processing variables such as latency and recall offers one promising strategy to achieve this.

Similarly, in many situations, "cognitive fluency" experiences such as the ease with which information comes to mind (a direct, primary subjective experience) and the content and associated details of that activated information (a secondary, indirect effect) can have very similar consequences (see Schwarz et al., 1991, for a discussion of this issue). In the case of moods, the direct effect may be due to individuals simply attributing their subjective feeling as informative about a judgment. According to the underlying logic, these effects can be eliminated when the subjective state is already attributed to a previous cause (Schwarz & Clore, 1983; Schwarz et al., 1991; Wänke, Bless, & Biller, 1996). However, the attribution manipulation should not affect the indirectly activated contents, suggesting that this method might help to distinguish between direct and indirect effects. However, calling attention to a person's subjective state, as the attribution manipulation requires, may also trigger motivated processing to correct a subjective effect, however caused. In this case, the primary effect is discounted, and the secondary associative effects can also be reversed. Thus, the attribution manipulation may reverse the effects of subjective mood states, whether it was initially caused by indirect associative mood effects, or by direct, heuristic mood effects.

Another empirical paradigm involves the direct manipulation and measurement of the amount of processing involved in a task. According to the underlying logic, the secondary effects of subjective experiences that are due to the cognitive contents indirectly primed by the experience should increase with individuals' amount of processing (Forgas, 1995). Measuring processing latency can thus be an index of such secondary priming effects (Forgas, 1992, 1994). Both of the empirical approaches to separate the direct and indirect effects of subjective states—the attribution manipulation and the processing latency approach—have some strengths and some weaknesses. As we have seen above, one might argue that the (mis-)attribution manipulation can override both the direct and the indirect effects of subjective experiences such as moods, and thus may not be informative about the original mechanism that produced mood congruence.

On the other hand, experimentally obtained measures of processing latency may not control for the possibility that direct influences due to a subjective state may occur simultaneously with indirect, associative effects. Such suggestions have been made in the recent literature on persuasive communication, arguing that systematic and heuristic processing strategies may sometimes co-occur (see Chaiken & Trope, 1999). Moreover, measuring or manipulating the amount of processing required to perform a given task may often be rather difficult, as the subjective experience itself can confound levels of processing (Bless, Bohner, Schwarz, & Strack, 1990; Mackie & Worth, 1989; Schwarz, 1990; Wegener, Petty, & Smith, 1995).

It is clear that more research is needed to try to disentangle the direct and indirect, primary and secondary processes that are responsible for mediating the effects of subjective states on social cognition and behavior. This task would be greatly helped if we had a better understanding of the similarities between different kinds of subjective experiences and their effects on our thinking and actions. Most of the existing work has been concerned with subjective experiences of affect and mood. Relatively less work has been done on how the direct and indirect effects of "cognitive fluency" and somatic experiences are mediated (see chapter 9 by Wänke & Bless), and this is where the most promising future directions may lie.

The Limits of Relying on Subjective Experiences

A further issue is concerned with the reasons why individuals can but will not always use their subjective experiences as a basis for their judgments and behaviors. What are the situational or dispositional constraints that promote or inhibit the reliance on subjective experiences? For example, does increased processing motivation decrease or increase the reliance on subjective experiences of ease of retrieval? Different theorists offer opposing positions on this issue (see Rothman & Schwarz, 1998; chapter 9 by Wänke & Bless; chapter 8 by Haddock). The literature on mood effects on cognition, perhaps the most extensively researched subjective experience, suggests that there are clear boundary conditions for these effects.

Some of these boundary conditions have been explicitly incorporated in integrative theories such as the Affect Infusion Model (Forgas, 1995).

According to this model, subjectively experienced moods may inform judgments and behaviors only when no prior response can be directly accessed, there are no strong motivational objectives to determine reactions, and the task is sufficiently novel or unfamiliar to require a constructive response. Presumably, similar kinds of boundary conditions also apply to people's use of other subjective experiences to guide their actions. Understanding when and why subjective experiences may be ignored is just as important a research question as understanding when and why they are used.

The Assessment and Nature of Subjective Experiences

One key task for future research is to develop a better understanding of the nature and characteristics of subjective experiences. First, and perhaps most obviously, additional and more sophisticated measures are needed to empirically assess the features of subjective experiences, the dimensions on which they differ, and the mediating mechanisms responsible for their effects. In addition to the usual self-report measures ("how do you feel at the moment?" "how easy/difficult was it to list the six arguments in favor of . . . ?"), one may try to assess additional measures. For example, when investigating the ease of retrieval, it might be helpful to measure the latency for the recall task. While such more direct process measures have been employed in some studies concerned with ease of retrieval effects (e.g., MacLeod & Campbell, 1992), it has rarely been applied in studies that seek to separate the effects of ease of retrieval and the activated content.

Second, there is an obvious need for more sophisticated theoretical analyses of the nature of subjective experiences. While there are various theories that seek to explicitly codify and classify affective experiences (see Forgas, in press), surprisingly little work has been done on the classification of other kinds of subjective experiences. In particular, we need further evidence relevant to the question of whether cognitive feelings indeed operate like feelings, or whether they should be more properly considered as metacognitions. This is not merely a semantic or a definitional question, but it is likely to have important conceptual implications for the development of the field.

It is important to remember that the early decades of experimental psychology have already provided us with extensive evidence relevant to this question, when the investigation of experimentally manipulated phenomenological experiences using introspective methods was the dominant research paradigm. The work of psychologists such as Wundt, Titchener, and others, although rarely studied nowadays, could give us very valuable pointers about the nature, characteristics, and dimensions of various phenomenological subjective experiences. We believe that research in this direction could contribute a lot to a better understanding of subjective experiences.

The Relationship Between Subjective Experiences

Finally, the evidence contained in this volume also suggests that it is not only important to investigate the nature and processes underlying subjective experiences, but we also need to take a closer look at how different subjective experiences relate to each other. For example, in chapter 14, Garcia-Marques and Mackie have proposed that a close link may exist between experiences of familiarity and affective states. The work of Zajonc (in press) also suggests that experiences of familiarity are often associated with enduring feelings of positive evaluation, even when no direct memory trace of prior exposure to a stimulus remains. We believe that investigations of how different kinds of subjective experiences are linked and interact with each other should provide a rich domain for future research. Such attempts to study multiple, combined subjective experiences should eventually also result in a more integrated theoretical approach to subjective experiences.

☐ Conclusion

Our objective in this volume was to survey recent knowledge about the role of subjective experiences in social cognition and behavior, and to propose that subjective experiences may provide a much-needed unifying theme and focus across various domains of social psychological research. We also argued that this enterprise, although it may appear novel and even challenging in some respects (see the introduction, chapter 1, by Wegner & Gilbert), is in fact quite consistent with the dominant traditions and paradigms of our discipline. Understanding how people feel, think, and behave in social situations has always been the core objective of social psychology. Understanding the phenomenology of social actors was the key motivation of such leading theorists as Lewin, Heider, Festinger, Asch, and Kelly. It is our hope that the development of social cognitive research during the past two decades has established firm foundations on which a genuine, experimental social psychology of subjective experience can be built.

Of course, the current status of research on subjective experiences seems rather modest compared to these objectives. We believe, however, that the different subjective experience phenomena discussed in this volume share quite substantial overlaps and similarities. Investigating the spectrum of subjective experiences not separately, but in relation to each other should be a fruitful enterprise—even if it turns out that not all of the phenomena discussed here will eventually be able to be integrated within a single, overarching conceptualization of subjective experiences. There can be little doubt that the study of subjective experiences will continue to be a key theme for future research. If this volume has succeeded to stimulate increased interest and greater efforts at integration in this exciting domain, it has achieved its objective.

☐ References

Abele, A. E., & Petzold, P. (1998). Pragmatic use of categorical information in impression formation. *Journal of Personality and Social Psychology, 75,* 347–358.

Adolphs, R., & Damasio, A. (in press). The interaction of affect and cognition: A neurobiological perspective. In J. P. Forgas (Ed.), *The handbook of affect and social cognition.* Mahwah, NJ: Erlbaum.

Berkowitz, L., Jaffee, S., Jo, F., & Troccoli, B. T. (in press). On the correction of feeling-induced judgmental biases. In J. P. Forgas (Ed.), *Feeling and thinking: The role of affect in social cognition.* New York: Cambridge University Press.

Bless, H. (in press). The consequences of mood on the processing of social information. In A. Tesser & N. Schwarz (Eds.), *Blackwell handbook in social psychology.* Oxford, England: Blackwell.

Bless, H. (in press). The relation between mood and the use of general knowledge structures. In L. L. Martin & G. L. Clore (Eds.), *Mood and social cognition: Contrasting theories.* Mahwah, NJ: Erlbaum.

Bless, H., Bohner, G., Schwarz, N., & Strack, F. (1990). Mood and persuasion: A cognitive response analysis. *Personality and Social Psychology Bulletin, 16,* 331–345.

Bower, G. (1981). Mood and memory. *American Psychologist, 36,* 129–148.

Bower, G. H., & Forgas, J. P. (in press). Mood and social memory. In J. P. Forgas (Ed.) *The handbook of affect and social cognition.* Mahwah, NJ: Erlbaum.

Byrne, D., & Clore, G. L. (1970). A reinforcement model of evaluation responses. *Personality, 1,* 103–128.

Chaiken, S., & Trope, Y. (1999). *Dual-process theories in social psychology.* New York: Guilford Press.

Clore, G. L. (1992). Cognitive phenomenology: Feelings and the construction of judgment. In L. L. Martin & A. Tesser (Eds.), *The construction of social judgment* (pp. 133–64). Hillsdale, NJ: Erlbaum.

Clore, G. L., Schwarz, N. & Conway, M. (1994). Cognitive causes and consequence of emotion. In R. S. Wyer & T. K. Srull (Eds.), *Handbook of social cognition* (2nd ed., pp. 221–259). Hillsdale, NJ: Erlbaum.

Desmonde, W. H. (1970). The position of George Herbert Mead. In G. P. Stone & H. E. Farberman (Eds), *Social psychology through symbolic interaction.* London: Ginn-Blaisdell.

Fiedler, K. (in press). Toward an integrative account of affect and cognition phenomena using the BIAS computer algorithm. In J. P.Forgas (Ed.), *Feeling and thinking: The role of affect in social cognition.* New York: Cambridge University Press.

Forgas, J. P. (1991). Mood effects on partner choice: Role of affect in social decisions. *Journal of Personality and Social Psychology*, 61, 708–720.

Forgas, J. P. (1992). On bad mood and peculiar people: Affect and person typicality in impression formation. *Journal of Personality and Social Psychology, 62,* 863–875.

Forgas, J. P. (1994). Sad and guilty? Affective influences on the explanation of conflict episodes. *Journal of Personality and Social Psychology, 66,* 56–68.

Forgas, J. P. (1995). Mood and judgment: The Affect Infusion Model (AIM). *Psychological Bulletin, 117*(1), 39–66.

Forgas, J. P. (in press). *Feeling and thinking: The role of affect in social cognition.* New York: Cambridge University Press.

Forgas, J. P., & Bower, G. H. (1987). Mood effects on person perception judgements. *Journal of Personality and Social Psychology, 53,* 53–60.

Koriat, A., & Levy-Sadot, R. (1999). Processes underlying metacognitive judgments. Information-based and experienced-based monitoring of one's own knowledge. In S. Chaiken & Y. Trope (Hrsg.), *Dual-process theories in social psychology* (pp. 483–502). New York: Guilford Press.

Kunda, Z. (1990). The case for motivated reasoning. *Psychological Bulletin,* 108, 331–350.

Mackie, D. M., & Worth, L. T. (1989). Cognitive deficits and the mediation of positive affect in persuasion. *Journal of Personality and Social Psychology, 57,* 27–40.

MacLeod, C., & Campbell, L. (1992). Memory accessibility and probability judgments: An experimental evaluation of the availability heuristic. *Journal of Personality and Social Psychology, 63,* 890–902.

Rothman, J. A., & Schwarz, N. (1998). Constructing perceptions of vulnerability: Personal relevance and the use of experiential information in health judgments. *Personality and Social Psychology, 24,* 1053–1064.

Schwarz, N. (1990). Feelings as information: Informational and motivational functions of affective states. In R. M. Sorrentino & E. T. Higgins (Eds.), *Handbook of motivation and cognition: Foundations of social behavior, 2* (pp. 527–561). New York: Guilford Press.

Schwarz, N. (in press). Feelings as information: Implications for affective influences on information processing. In L. L. Martin & G. L. Clore (Eds.), *Mood and social cognition: Contrasting theories.* Mahwah, NJ: Lawrence Erlbaum Associates.

Schwarz, N., Bless, H., Strack, F., Klumpp, G., Rittenauer-Schatka, H., & Simons, A. (1991). Ease of retrieval as information: Another look at the availability heuristic. *Journal of Personality and Social Psychology, 61,* 195–202.

Schwarz, N., & Clore, G. L. (1983). Mood, misattribution, and judgment of well-being: Informative and directive functions of affective states. *Journal of Personality and Social Psychology, 45,* 513–523.

Schwarz, N., & Clore, G. L. (1996). Feelings and phenomenal experiences. In E. T. Higgins & A. W. Kruglanski (Eds.), *Social psychology handbook of basic principles* (pp. 433–465). New York: Guilford Press.

Strack, F. (1992). The different routes to social judgments: Experiments versus informational strategies. In L. L. Martin & A. Tesser et al. (Eds.), *The construction of social judgments* (pp. 249–275). Hillsdale, NJ: Erlbaum.

Strack, F., Martin, L. L., & Stepper, S. (1988). Inhibiting and facilitating conditions of the human smile: A nonobtrusive test of the facial feedback hypothesis. *Journal of Personality and Social Psychology, 54,* 768–777.

Wänke, M., Bless, H., & Biller, B. (1996). Subjective experiences versus content of information in the construction of attitude judgments. *Personality and Social Psychology Bulletin, 22,* 1105–1113.

Wänke, M., Schwarz, N., & Bless, H. (1995). The availability heuristic revisited: Experienced ease of retrieval in mundane frequency estimates. *Acta Psychologica, 89,* 83–90.

Wegener, D. T., Petty, R. E., & Smith, S. M. (1995). Positive mood can increase or decrease message scrutiny: The hedonic contingency view of mood and message processing. *Journal of Personality and Social Psychology, 69,* 5–15.

Zajonc, R. B. (in press). Feeling and thinking: Closing the debate over the independence of affect. In J. P. Forgas (Ed.), *Feeling and thinking: The role of affect in social cognition.* New York: Cambridge University Press.

AUTHOR INDEX

Abele, A., 286, 299, 323, 324, 327, 329, 330, 331, 332, 333, 334, 335, 336, 337, 344, 346, 348, 351, 361, 366, 367, 368, 377, 381, 383, 390
Abelson, R. P., 128, 138, 140
Adelman, P. K., 54, 65, 66, 255, 272, 276
Adler, 308
Adolphs, R. 181, 182, 198, 376, 377, 378, 390
Allison, J. R., 307, 317
Allport, F. H., 167, 172
Allport, G., 129, 140, 143, 160
Allport, G. W., 324, 337, 340, 368
Alvarez. P., 115, 121
Anderson, S. A., 103, 104
Arkes, H. R., 14, 34, 110, 121, 148, 160, 167, 172, 244, 255
Asch, S. E., 183, 198
Aspinwall, L. G., 323, 336, 337
Asuncion, A. G., 241, 255
Averill, J. R., 305, 317

Baars, B. J., 274, 276
Bacon, F. T., 247, 255
Baird, L., 324, 327, 335, 337
Banaji, M. R., 311, 317
Bandura, A., 308, 309, 317
Banks, W. P., 76, 85
Barbetta, P. M., 308, 318
Bargh, J. A., 39, 40, 41, 42, 43, 44, 49, 50, 57, 66, 244, 255, 288, 299, 378
Barlow, D. H., 290, 299
Baron, R., 186, 198, 234, 238
Barton, S. B., 244, 256
Bass, E., 166, 172
Bassili, J. N., 130, 136, 138, 140
Baumeister, R. F., 41, 42, 44, 50, 310, 317, 318

Becher, E., 267, 270, 276
Begg, I. M., 29, 34, 148, 160, 167, 168, 172, 247, 248, 256
Belli, R., 323, 338
Belli, R. F., 166, 172
Bem, D. J., 146, 160, 271, 276, 284, 299
Berkowitz, L., 55, 66, 89, 90, 104, 189, 190, 199, 204, 210, 212, 390
Bettelheim, B., 298, 299
Biller, B., 150, 160
Bless, H., 84, 89, 95, 104, 119, 120, 122, 143, 157, 160, 170, 172, 186, 199, 217, 218, 222, 223, 228, 234, 238, 240, 241, 242, 246, 253, 254, 255, 256, 286, 299, 324, 325, 328, 330, 334, 335, 336, 338, 344, 346, 359, 360, 361, 363, 365, 366, 368, 377, 383, 387, 390
Block, N., 274, 275, 276
Blurton Jones, N. G., 273, 276
Bodenhausen, G. V., 55, 65, 66, 127, 140, 221, 238, 240, 241, 255, 256, 285, 286, 289, 292, 295, 298, 299, 299, 311, 318, 324, 325, 333, 335, 337, 338, 343, 344, 345, 350, 361, 368, 381
Bohner, G., 217, 221, 228, 238, 377, 381, 383
Boninger, D. S., 128, 140
Bornstein, R. F., 109, 122, 246, 256
Bower, G. H., 53, 66, 183, 184, 185, 199, 324, 338, 348, 368, 384, 390
Bradburn, N. M., 164, 173
Brehm, J. W., 102, 104, 296, 300
Brendl, D. M., 78, 85, 308, 378, 382
Brewer, M. B., 254, 255, 256, 311, 318, 340, 341, 342, 368
Brown, A. S., 167, 173
Brown, R. J., 23, 34, 342, 368
Bruner, 308

Buck, R., 53, 54, 66
Burger, J. M., 182, 199, 308, 318
Byrne, D., 348, 368, 380, 390

Cacioppo, J. T., 55, 56, 57, 58, 62, 66, 98, 104, 255, 256, 300, 296
Campbell, D. T., 287, 300
Cannon, W. B., 62, 67
Carpenter, G. A., 111, 112, 122
Carpenter, W. B., 38, 50
Carr, S. J., 207, 213
Carver, C. S., 39, 41, 42, 43, 44, 46, 50, 203, 204, 213
Chaiken, S., 96, 104, 130, 140, 147, 152, 156, 160, 219, 238, 249, 254, 256, 334, 338, 387, 390
Chalmers, D. J., 274, 275, 276
Charlesworth, W. R., 262, 268, 276
Chartrand, T. L., 39, 43, 50
Chase, W. G., 245, 256
Chein, I., 298, 300
Chen, M., 57, 67
Chen, S., 39, 50, 159, 160
Churchland, P. S., 114, 122
Cialdini, R. B., 219, 235, 237, 238
Ciarrochi, H., 180, 196, 198, 199
Cioffi, D., 307, 309, 310, 318
Clark, M. S., 89, 90, 104, 183, 186, 186, 191, 199
Clore, G. L., 54, 67, 159, 160, 164, 173, 184, 189, 199, 210, 213, 274, 276, 285, 300, 376, 377, 378, 383, 390
Conally, T., 307, 318
Cook, S. W., 340, 368
Courtois, C. A., 166, 173
Croyle, R. T., 186, 199
Cunningham, M. R., 208, 213

Damasio, A. R., 182, 199, 284, 285, 300
Dardenne, B., 311, 312, 313, 314, 315, 316, 317, 318, 378
Darley, J. M., 308, 310, 318
Darwin, C., 54, 65, 67, 262, 266, 267, 276
Daubman, 343, 368
Davidson, R. J., 56, 67
Davies, M. F., 275, 276, 213, 204
Davitz, J. R., 210, 213
Deci, E. L., 308, 318
Denes-Raj, V., 69, 71, 74, 75, 84, 85, 86
Desai, M. M., 268, 277
Desmonde. W. H., 374, 390

Devine, P. G., 39, 50, 254, 256, 288, 289, 296, 300, 311, 318
Diehl, M., 323, 338
Diener, E., 204, 213
Dijker, A. J., 286, 287, 300
Dijksterhuis, A., 39, 40, 41, 44, 45, 50, 136, 140, 378
Dolinski, D., 308, 318
Dovidio, J. F., 311, 319, 324, 325, 334, 335, 336, 338, 343, 347, 348, 352, 353, 354, 356, 362, 368, 377, 381, 383
Downing, J. W., 128, 140
Duckitt, J., 311, 319
Duclos, S. E., 272, 277
Dutton, D. G., 289, 292, 300
Duval, S., 41, 42, 45, 50, 203, 213

Eagly, A. H., 129, 130, 140, 251, 256, 287, 300
Eberhardt, J. L., 311, 319
Edwards, D. J., 166, 173
Egan, D. E., 245, 256
Eich, J. M., 243, 256
Eichenbaum, H., 120, 122
Eidelberg, L., 39, 50
Einhorn, H. J., 80, 86
Ekman, P., 54, 63, 67, 204, 213, 262, 266, 272, 277
Ellis, H. C., 185, 199, 254, 256
Ellsworth, P. C., 210, 213
Epstein, S., 254, 257
Erber, M. W., 186, 189, 199
Erickson, T. D., 244, 257
Esses, V. M., 367, 368
Estrada, C. A., 90, 104
Exner, J. E., 204, 213

Fazio, R. H., 130, 138, 140, 146, 244, 254, 257, 307, 309, 319
Fenigstein, A., 205, 213
Festinger, L., 128, 140, 308
Fiedler, K., 21, 23, 26, 27, 29, 30, 34, 89, 104, 119, 122, 183, 184, 186, 197, 199, 205, 213, 240, 257, 323, 334, 336, 338, 344, 368, 378, 381, 383, 390
Fischhoff, B., 16, 34
Fiske, S. T., 243, 244, 254, 257, 283, 300, 305, 311, 318, 359, 360, 362, 368
Foa, E. B., 291, 300
Forgas, J. P., 89, 96, 104, 143, 157, 160, 170, 173, 179, 180, 182, 183, 184, 185,

186, 187, 188, 189, 190, 191, 192, 194,
195, 196, 197, 198, 199, 200, 205, 213,
240, 241, 257, 285, 286, 300, 323, 324,
326, 327, 333, 334, 335, 336, 338, 348,
351, 359, 364, 367, 369, 377, 383, 384,
385, 386, 387, 388, 391
Förster, J., 55, 56, 58, 66, 67, 118, 122
Frijda, N. H., 164, 173, 185, 200, 204, 208,
210, 213, 217, 238, 273, 277

Gadenne, V., 276, 277
Gaertner, S. L., 286, 288, 293, 300, 340,
341, 343, 350, 352, 354, 355, 369
Galambos, R., 118, 122
Garcia-Marques, T., 120, 122, 377, 378, 389
Gardiner, H. M., 117, 122
Gasche o. Gaschke, 89
Geers, A. L., 286, 300
Gerard, 308
Gibbons, F. X., 42, 46, 50, 203, 204, 213
Gigerenzer, G., 14, 29, 34
Gilbert, D. T., 14, 18, 26, 34, 39, 40, 49,
50, 167, 173, 254, 257, 373, 374
Gillund, G., 243, 257
Gilovitch, T., 308, 319
Gleicher, F., 234, 236, 238
Goleman, D., 290, 300
Gollwitzer, P. M., 79, 86
Graesser, A. C., 118, 122, 244, 257
Gray, J. A., 119, 122
Green, J. D., 208, 209, 210, 211, 213
Green, R. T., 117, 122, 207
Greenberg, J., 204, 213
Grice, H. P., 163, 169, 173
Grossberg, S., 111, 122

Haddock, G., 70, 84, 89, 95, 125, 127, 128,
129, 130, 131, 132, 133, 134, 135, 136,
137, 138, 139, 140, 141, 145, 147, 149,
158, 287, 300, 324, 325, 333, 338, 378,
381, 382, 387
Hamilton, D. L., 164, 173
Hansen, C. H., 290, 300
Harris, P. L., 274, 277
Hasher, L., 14, 34, 148, 160, 167, 173
Hass, R. G., 219, 235, 237, 238
Hastie, R., 118, 122, 244, 257
Hawkins, S. A., 16, 34, 148, 160
Heckhausen, J., 306, 319
Hefferline, R. F., 41, 42, 51
Heider, F., 18, 34, 183, 200

Helson, 53
Hertwig, R., 16, 35
Hewstone, M., 311, 319, 342, 349, 369
Higgins, E. T., 46, 51, 103, 105, 119, 120,
121, 122, 144, 162, 163, 164, 171, 173,
243, 244, 257, 258
Hilgard, E. R., 181, 200
Hilton, D. J., 80, 86, 169, 173
Hintzman, D. L., 243, 258
Hirt, E. R., 90, 92, 105, 220, 238
Hodges, S. D., 130, 136, 137, 138, 140, 141
Hogg, M. A., 342, 369
Holyoak K. J., 76, 86
Horowitz, E. L., 287, 301
Howard, J. M., 342, 369
Huffman, C., 79, 86
Hull, J. G., 204, 213, 214
Humphreys, M. S., 243, 258
Huo, Y. J., 354, 369

Ickes, W., 289, 301
Indow, T., 76, 86
Ingram, R. E., 204, 214
Irons, D., 263, 267, 270, 277
Isbell, L. M., 292, 301
Isen, A. M., 119, 123, 184, 185, 200, 218,
238, 241, 254, 258, 324, 334, 335, 338,
343, 344, 345, 346, 347, 348, 350, 351,
352, 354, 357, 360, 361, 363, 364, 369,
370
Ito, T., 181, 201
Izard, C. E., 208, 214, 262, 267, 268, 277

Jackson, J. E., 17, 35
Jackson, L. A., 287, 301
Jacoby, L. L., 14, 35, 71, 86, 103, 105, 110,
123, 168, 173, 243, 244, 245, 246, 254,
258
James, W., 38, 43, 51, 54, 62, 65, 67, 118,
120, 123, 272, 277, 284, 301
Jastrow, J., 38, 51
Jepson, C., 236, 238
Johnson, E., 242, 258
Johnson, M. K., 20, 35, 53, 67
Johnson-Laird, P. N., 25, 35
Johnston, L. C., 312, 319
Johnston, W. A., 243, 244, 258
Jones, E. E., 203, 214
Jones, J. M., 298, 301, 308, 311, 319
Jost, J. T., 309, 319
Jussim, L., 17, 18, 35, 287, 301

Kahneman, D., 70, 71, 72, 80, 86, 307, 308, 309, 319
Katz, I., 288, 301
Kaufman, E. L., 85, 86
Kelley, C. M., 148, 160, 167, 173, 254, 255, 258, 308
Kelman, H. C., 295, 301
Keltner, D., 162, 170, 173, 212, 214, 298, 301
Kimble, G., 41, 51
Kinder, D. R., 138, 141
Kirkpatrick, L. A., 69, 71, 73, 74, 75, 84, 86
Klayman, J., 28, 35
Klinger, E., 290, 301
Klinger, M. R., 85, 86
Koehler, K. J., 16, 35
Koestler, A., 41, 51
Koriat, A., 54, 67, 391
Koriat, A., 378, 391
Krosnick, J. A., 128, 138, 141
Krueger, L. E., 76, 85, 86
Kruglanski, A. W., 197, 201
Kunda, Z., 384, 391
Kuykendall, D., 248, 258

Laird, J. D., 54, 67, 255, 258, 271, 272, 277
Lambert, A. J., 296, 301, 324, 326, 334, 335, 338, 366, 367, 370
Lang, P. J., 56, 61, 67
Langer, E., 41, 51, 304, 306, 308, 309, 319
Larsen, R. J., 55, 67, 204, 214, 272, 277
Lashley, K. S., 42, 51
Latane, 308
Lavine, H., 130, 136, 137, 138, 141
Law, S., 148, 160
Lazarus, R. S., 54, 67, 208, 210, 214
Le Bon, G., 38, 51
Lerner, J. S., 296, 301
Levenson, R. W., 54, 63, 67
Levin, 347, 370
Leyens, J-Ph., 311, 319
Linville, P. W., 207, 214
Locke, K. D., 189, 201
Loftus, E. F., 15, 35
Logan, G. D., 254, 255, 258
Lombardi, W. J., 164, 173
Lories, G., 305, 309, 320
Lott, A. J., 348, 370
Lydon, J. E., 309, 320

Mac Leod, C., 388, 391
Mackie, D. M., 89, 90, 105, 205, 214, 240, 241, 258, 259, 344, 350, 351, 352, 360, 370, 387, 391
Macrae, C. N., 39, 40, 41, 42, 51, 283, 295, 297, 301, 311, 320
Mady, L. A., 148, 160
Mandler, G., 110, 123, 168, 174, 254, 255, 259, 267, 277
Manstead, A. S. R., 272, 277
Markman, A. B., 79, 86
Martens, R., 41, 51
Martin, L. L., 55, 67, 88, 94, 96, 105, 163, 164, 170, 172, 173, 189, 201, 217, 220, 234, 238, 292, 297, 301, 323, 336, 338, 378, 380, 382
Maslow, A., 4, 9
Matlin, M., 218, 238
Mayer, J. D., 89, 90, 105, 180, 182, 185, 195, 201, 324, 338
McClelland, J. L., 30, 35, 114, 115, 116, 123
McComas, J., 308, 320
McConahay, J. B., 288, 301
McDougall, W., 270, 273, 277
McGlone, M. S., 174
Mead, G. H., 374
Mees, U., 268, 277
Melton, R. J., 241, 259
Merten, J., 223, 238
Messick, D. M., 342, 370
Metcalfe, J., 113, 123, 309, 320
Meyer, W.-U., 262, 263, 264, 266, 268, 269, 274, 277
Mikulincer, M., 204, 214
Miller, D. T., 69, 70, 71, 72, 73, 74, 82, 86
Miller, G. A., 291, 301
Miller, N. E., 56, 67, 341, 370
Milner, P., 115, 123
Miner, A. C., 54, 67
Minturn, A. L., 85, 86
Monteith, M. J., 289, 295, 297, 302
Moreland, R. L., 109, 123
Moreno, K. M., 293, 302
Morris, C., 148, 161
Morris, W. N., 246, 253, 259
Morris, W. N., 323, 338
Moskovitz, G. B., 164, 174
Moylan, S., 196, 201
Mullen, B., 204, 214, 342, 349, 370
Murdock, B. B., 244, 259
Murphy, S. T., 64, 67
Murray, N., 334, 335, 338, 344, 345, 347, 351, 370

Murre, J., 115, 123
Müsseler, J., 38, 51
Myrdal, G., 287, 302

Nagel, T., 4, 9, 262, 277
Neisser, U., 182, 201
Nelson, T. O., 274, 277, 309, 320
Neuberg, S. L., 244, 254, 259
Neumann, R., 58, 67, 378
Nhouyvanisvong, A., 243, 259
Niepel, M., 269, 277
Nolen-Hoeksema, S., 183, 195, 201
Norman, D. A., 42, 43, 44, 51

Oatley, K., 266, 267, 277
Öhman, A., 290, 302
Ortony, A., 205, 214, 267, 268, 277, 284, 302
Osgood, C. E., 209, 214
Ottati, V. C., 297, 302

Palfai, T. P., 241, 259
Park, B., 357, 359, 370
Parrot, W. G., 194, 201
Peeters, G., 313, 320
Pelham, B. W., 69, 74, 75, 76, 84, 86
Pettigrew, T. F., 340, 370
Petty, R. E., 90, 128, 130, 136, 138, 141, 147, 150, 152, 161,182, 197, 201, 217, 229, 239, 249, 254, 255, 259
Pitcher, T. J., 38, 51
Pittman, T. S., 182, 201, 245, 259
Plant, E. A., 289, 294, 302
Plutchik, R., 208, 211, 214, 262, 277
Posner, M. I., 43, 51
Powers, W. T., 42, 44, 51
Priester, J. R., 55, 68
Prinz, W., 38, 51, 60, 68
Pyszczynski, T., 204, 214

Queller, S., 248, 259

Raghubir, P., 70, 86, 95, 105, 145, 161
Ratcliff, R., 115, 123
Rather, 267
Read, S. J., 92, 101, 105
Reber, R., 162, 168, 174, 216, 239
Reder, L. M., 243, 259
Reisenzein, R., 263, 264, 266, 267, 267, 268, 269, 270, 271, 272, 273, 274, 275, 276, 277, 278
Rhodewalt, F., 195, 201

Ribot, T. A., 262, 263, 267, 270, 278
Rodin, J., 304, 306, 308, 320
Roemer, L., 183, 201
Roese, N. J., 71, 86
Rojahn, D., 244, 260
Roseman, I. J., 54, 68, 204, 208, 214, 268, 276, 278
Rosenberg, M. J., 216, 239
Rosenthal, D. M., 262, 278
Rosenthal, R., 17, 35
Ross, C. A., 165, 174
Ross, L., 19, 35, 307, 320
Rothbaum, F., 305, 320
Rothman, A. J., 70, 71, 80, 86, 95, 96, 98, 100, 101, 105, 130, 133, 136, 137, 141, 145, 147, 149, 158, 161, 387, 391
Ruffman, T., 268, 278
Ruscher, J. B., 360, 361, 363, 370
Rust, M. C., 354, 370
Rusting, C., 198, 201

Salovey, P., 186, 195, 198, 201, 202, 207, 208, 211, 214, 290, 302
Sanna, C. J., 92, 106
Savitsky, K., 170, 174
Schachter, S., 78, 87, 172, 174
Schacter, D. L., 115, 123
Schank, R. L., 244, 260
Scherer, K. R., 209, 210, 214
Schlenker, B. R., 309, 320
Schmidt, H. G., 245, 260
Schooler, L., 163, 174
Schulman, A. I., 118, 123
Schulz, R., 306, 320
Schuman, H., 288, 302
Schunn, C. D., 243, 260
Schützwohl, A., 269, 271, 278, 279
Schwarz, N., 64, 68, 70, 71, 78, 80, 84, 85, 87, 89, 90, 92, 95, 106, 119, 123, 125, 126, 127, 130, 132, 133, 136, 137, 138, 139, 141, 143, 145, 147, 149, 157, 158, 161, 162, 163, 164, 169, 170, 171, 174, 183, 184, 186, 202, 205, 214, 216, 217, 219, 220, 221, 229, 234, 239, 240, 241, 242, 246, 260, 273, 275, 279, 285, 286, 302, 323, 333, 334, 338, 350, 352, 360, 370, 376, 378, 381, 382, 383, 385, 386, 387, 391
Sedikides, C., 184, 185, 186, 188, 191, 194, 196, 202, 203, 204, 206, 207, 211, 212, 214, 215, 246, 260, 309, 377
Seligman, 308

Semin, G. R., 15, 17, 35
Shallice, T., 44, 51, 61, 68
Shand, A. F., 262, 263, 266, 267, 268, 270, 279
Shavitt, S., 29, 35
Sherif, M., 349, 370
Sherman, S. J., 148, 161, 243, 244, 260
Siebert, P. S., 346, 370
Siemer, M., 170, 174
Sinclair, R. C., 217, 218, 219, 222, 224, 228, 234, 239, 254, 260
Skurnik, I., 163, 168, 169, 174, 175, 378
Sloman, S. A., 254, 255, 260
Smedslund, J., 268, 279
Smith, A., 262, 270, 279
Smith, C. A., 193, 194, 195, 196, 202, 204, 210, 215
Smith, E. R., 109, 116, 123, 243, 244, 254, 260, 302
Snyder, M., 17, 35
Solarz, A. K., 57, 68
Sperber, I., 163, 175
Spranca, M., 307, 320
Srull, T. K., 45, 51, 118, 123, 185, 202, 244, 261
Stangor, C., 244, 261, 287, 302
Stanley, H. M., 262, 263, 279
Stapel, D. A., 139, 141, 293, 302
Stein, D. D., 342, 371
Stephan, W. G., 286, 298, 302, 340, 371
Stephenson, B., 204, 215
Stepper, S., 55, 65, 66, 68, 98, 106, 145, 161, 255, 261, 324, 325, 338
Stiensmeier-Pelster, J., 263, 266, 268, 269, 274, 276, 279
Strack, F., 53, 54, 55, 68, 162, 163, 164, 171, 175, 255, 261, 272, 279, 291, 292, 302, 303, 378, 382, 391
Stroessner, S. J., 185, 202, 240, 261, 286, 303, 347, 349, 371
Swann, W. B., 17, 25, 35
Swim, J. K., 289, 298, 303, 311, 320

Tajfel, H., 311, 320, 326, 338, 342, 371
Tarde, G., 38, 51
Taylor, S. E., 306, 320, 357, 371
Tesser, A., 15, 35, 103, 106
Thayer, R. E., 290, 303
Thompson, S. C., 306, 307, 320
Thomsen, C. J., 130, 131, 142
Tice, D. M., 290, 303
Tomkins, S. S., 262, 267, 279

Trommsdorff, G., 204, 215
Trope, Y., 32, 35, 364, 371
Turner, J., 323, 338
Tversky, A., 26, 35, 70, 72, 76, 87, 95, 96, 106, 126, 135, 142, 144, 146, 161, 164, 165, 175, 344, 371

Vallacher, R. R., 42, 51
van Gelder, T., 111, 124
Vanbeselaere, N., 311, 320
Veitch, R., 348, 371
Velten, E., 346, 371
Verkuyten, M., 287, 303
von Hippel, W., 244, 261

Walther, E., 27, 36
Wänke, M., 70, 71, 72, 84, 87, 89, 95, 101, 106, 125, 133, 136, 137, 142, 144, 145, 148, 151, 161, 216, 239, 378, 382, 383, 386, 387, 391
Watkins, O. C., 117, 124
Weary, G., 189, 190, 191, 202
Webster, D. M., 315, 321
Wegener, D. T., 90, 106, 164, 167, 175, 195, 202, 205, 215, 218, 239, 241, 242, 248, 261, 291, 292, 303, 387, 392
Wegner, D. M., 19, 36, 143, 182, 188, 190, 194, 202, 205, 207, 215, 254, 263, 290, 291, 292, 295, 296, 297, 303, 373, 374, 389
Weinerth, T., 219, 235, 235, 239
Wells, G. L., 16, 36, 55, 56, 57, 66, 68
White, 308
Whittlesea, B. W. A., 168, 175
Wieland, 359, 371
Wilder, D. A., 341, 342, 371
Wiles, J., 116, 124
Wills, T. A., 324, 338
Wilson, T. D.. 43, 51, 102, 106, 130, 137, 142, 144, 161, 284, 291, 292, 303
Wing, H., 76, 87
Winkielmann, P., 64, 68, 165, 166, 172, 175
Winter, L., 39, 51, 347
Wood, J. V., 205, 206, 207, 208, 211, 212, 215
Worchel, S., 348, 371
Worth, L. T., 119, 124, 218, 239, 241, 261, 350, 371
Wright, J., 205, 215
Wundt, W., 263, 270, 279
Wyer, R., 144, 162, 175

Yonelinas, A. P., 110, 124, 244, 250, 261
Yzerbyt, V. Y., 309, 311, 312, 313, 321

Zajonc, R. B., 54, 58, 60, 65, 68, 109, 118,
    121, 124, 246, 261, 284, 303, 380, 389,
    392

Zanna, M. P., 299, 303
Zillman, D., 162, 175
Zimbardo, P. G., 306, 321
Zuckerman, 17, 36

SUBJECT INDEX

"aboutness" principle, 163
accuracy motivation, 152–159
action/inaction effects, 313–316
activation, of stereotypes, 39
activation, trait concepts, 39
active information search, 304–317
affect, see also mood and emotion
  affect and capacity, 185
  affect and motivation, 185, 186
  affect and persuasion, 216–237
  affect and social categorization, 343–367
  affect-as-information, 184, 217–218, 284–286,
  affect control, 180–198
  affect infusion, 183–198, 326, 351, 387
  affect orientation, 209
  affect-interpretation hypothesis, 217–221
  affect-priming, 184
affective processing, 57
aggregation, 28
aggression, 90
analytic mode of processing, 243
approach-avoidance, 56, 58, 60 61
acquiescence, 17
ART Model, 111–113, 117
attention, 41, 42, 43,
  attention, self-focused, 204–212
  attentional focus, 203–212
  attentional resources, 296–297
attitude, 128–135, 146–160
  attitudes, political, 138
attitude polarization, 103
attitude strength, 128–132, 138
attractor, 114, 115
automaticity, 37–49

availabilty as input, 88–104
availabilty heuristic, 70, 89, 95–97, 126, 144–146, 165
awareness, 267, 293–294
awareness of priming episode, 164

behavior selection, 43
biased ratio perception, 74–77

catastrophic inference, 115
categorization, 58, 60, 322–337, 341
CHARM model, 113–114, 117
childhood memories, 165–167
cognitive dissonance, 102, 103
cognitive effort, experience of, 88–104
cognitive-evolutionary, 264–266
  model of surprise
common ingroup identity model, 341–343
competitive interdependence, 350–354
confirmation bias, 16
connectionist memory, 109–121
constructive memory, 15
constructive processing, 334
contact hypothesis, 340, 341
control and subjective experience, 309–310
cooperative interdependence, 350–354
correction processes, 290–297
counterfactuals, 71, 72
creative processing, 335–336, 351

decategorization, 341
diagnosticity, of feelings, 78, 80, 81, 132
diagnosticity, of input, 164
distributive memory, 29–33
dual identity, 354–356

ease of processing, 242, 243
ease of retrieval, 95–101, 125–139, 144–160
ease of retrieval and, 148–160
  quality of information
elaborative processes, 351, 360
emotion, see also affect and mood
  emotion, definition of, 182
  emotion, suppression of, 290
  emotional amplification, 308
  emotional correction, 290
  emotional self-regulation, 291
event analysis, 264
event evaluation, 264
expectedness, 268–270
experience, see also feeling and subjective
    experience
  experience as input, 92–104
  experience of cognitive effort, 88–104
  experience, of surprise, 262–275
  experienced control, 305–317
  experienced ease of retrieval, 145–160
  experienced ease of retrieval, 148
 and confidence
experiential representations, 53
experiential information, 164
exteroceptive cues, 60

facial feedback, 52, 272
factuals, 71, 72
familiarity, 148
familiarity, and truth, 148, 167–170
familiarity, effects of, 116–118
familiarity, feeling of , 110–121, 168–170,
    240–254
familiarity, feeling of, 247
 and validity
familiarity, subjective experience of, 109–121
familiarity–information–processing effect,
    251
  FIPE
fear, 229–230
feeling, see also experience and subjective
    experience
  feeling of choice, 308
  feeling of familiarity, see familiarity
  feeling of knowing, 243
  feelings, diagnosticity of, 163
  informational value of feelings, 64
fluency, 243

fluency of information processing, 167–170
focal attention, 41

"hard interface" approach, 58
heuristic processing, 334–336, 344, 350,
    360
heuristic vs. substantive processing, 184–198
heuristic vs. systematic processing, 151–160, 222, 249
hypothesis testing, 16, 17

illusion of truth, 167–170
imitation, 38
impression formation, 310–313
inference theory, 270
informational value of feelings, 64
informative function of feelings, 162–172
ingroup bias, 342
ingroup/outgroup differentiation, 327–333
integral vs. incidental affect, 285
intergroup, see also stereotyping
  intergroup affect, 286–288
  intergroup competition, 346–363
  intergroup cooperation, 346–363
  intergroup differentiation, 322–337
  intergroup perception, 283–298
  intergroup relations, 340–367
  intergroup relations, and memory, 357–360
inuendo effects, 19
involvement, 129, 130, 150–160

judgmental correction, 291

likelihood judgments, 69–84
linguistic categories, 15

memory, episodic, 113–114
memory, fast-learning, 116
memory, slow-learning, 116
mental models, 25
mental simulation, 70, 71, 72, 78–85
mere considering, 13
mere exposure effect, 109
minimal group, 326–327
misattribution, 78, 81, 132
mismatch theory, 243

monitoring process, 115
mood, see also affect and emotion
  mood and capacity, 241
  mood and category breadth, 343–345
  mood and judgment, 170, 171
  mood and motivation, 241, 242
  mood and persuasion, 250–252
  mood and processing strategies, 179–198
  mood as familiarity, 245–253
  mood as input, 88
  mood congruent recall, 189
  mood information processing effect, 241
    MIPE
  mood management, 180–198
    spontaneous mood management, 191–195
    individual differences, 195–196
  mood regulation, 179–198
  mood, and feeling of familiarity, 240–254
  mood, and self-focused attention, 204–212
  mood, definitions of, 182
  mood-congruent judgments, 90
  mood-congruity, 184
motivated processing, 183, 184, 188, 189
motivation to correct, 294–296
motor cues, 60
motor influences, 52–66

noetic representations, 53
non-analytic mode of processing, 243
norm theory, 70, 71
novelty, effects of, 116–118
numerosity heuristic, 76

perception-behavior link, 38, 44–46
personal relevance, 148
persuasion, 216–237
phenomenal experience, 53
phenomenal representation, 65
positive testing, 28
posture, 55
primary control, 306
priming, awareness of, 46–49
processing capacity, 360
promotion/prevention, 119
  model of motivation

proprioceptive cues, 60
prototype, 112

reason analysis effect, 102
recategorization, 341, 347
recurrent attractor, 114–116
  autoassociative networks
reflective affective states, 210
regret, 307, 308
role fulfillment, 97–101

sample size, 69–85
secondary control, 307
self-focus, 44–46
self-fulfilling prophecy, 17
self-generation of information, 158
self-judgments, 126–128
social affective states, 210
sociality, 3
somatic-marker hypothesis, 285
source confusion, 20–24
source monitoring, 20
stability-plasticity dilemma, 110–111
stereotyping, see also intergroup, 45–49, 283–298, 304–317, 322–337
stereotype change, 310–313
subjective experiences, 383–384
  and processing strategies
  see also experience and feeling
subjective experiences, attribution of, 380
subjective experiences, truth value of, 379–380
subjective feelings, unwanted, 290
suppression of emotion, 290
surprise, 262–275
surprise, 264–266
  cognitive-evolutionary model of
symbolic interactionism, 374, 375

task importance, 333–336
trait anxiety, 196
truth monitoring, 13
truth, and repetition, 14
truth, feeling of, 14
truth, imagination, 16
type A, type B personality, 196

visual cues, 60